Ezra Pound

A BIBLIOGRAPHY

by

DONALD GALLUP

PUBLISHED FOR THE BIBLIOGRAPHICAL
SOCIETY OF THE UNIVERSITY OF VIRGINIA
AND ST. PAUL'S BIBLIOGRAPHIES BY
THE UNIVERSITY PRESS OF VIRGINIA
CHARLOTTESVILLE

THE UNIVERSITY PRESS OF VIRGINIA

Copyright © 1983 by Donald Gallup

Unpublished material by Ezra Pound copyright © 1983 by the Trustees of the
Ezra Pound Literary Property Trust

First published 1983

Library of Congress Cataloging in Publication Data

Gallup, Donald Clifford, 1913–
  Ezra Pound, a bibliography.

  Rev. ed. of: a bibliography of Ezra Pound. 1963.
  Includes index.
  1. Pound, Ezra, 1885–1972—Bibliography. I. Title.
Z8709.3.G3 1983   PS3531.082 016.811′52 82–15995
ISBN 0–8139–0976–7

Printed in the United States of America

This volume is no. 7 in the St. Paul's Bibliographies series
UK ISBN: 0–906795–07–9

St. Paul's Bibliographies
Foxbury Meadow, Godalming
Surrey GU84AE, England

The portrait of Pound on the half title page is a
drawing by Gaudier-Brzeska (Donald Gallup Collection).

Jacket and frontispiece photographs by Boris de Rachewiltz

CONTENTS

INTRODUCTORY NOTE

The present work is a completely revised and updated edition of my *A Bibliography of Ezra Pound* (London: Rupert Hart-Davis, 1963). Its plan is the same as that of the earlier book, and, with only a few exceptions, the first edition's entry numbers have been carried over without change. First editions of Ezra Pound's own books, pamphlets, and broadsides, both English and American (and occasionally published in other countries) are dealt with in detail, but books and pamphlets containing merely contributions by Pound are normally represented only by the actual first edition, with notes concerning publication elsewhere. Later impressions and editions are usually either ignored or noted very briefly, except where they have some particular significance or may be mistaken for first impressions.

The descriptive method is based upon that adopted by the American Library Association and used in the cards printed and distributed in the United States by the Library of Congress. I have modified the system, which ignores blanks and leaves containing only advertisements, in order to account for all leaves, although blank pages are not mentioned. End-papers are noted when they are present.

The general rule is that when the unnumbered printed preliminary leaves count up (as pages) to the first numbered page of the book, these leaves are not specified in the collation. When they do *not* count up, they *are* specified: *e.g.* 1 blank leaf, 3 leaves, 9–29 pp., because here the *printed* preliminary material counts up to only six pages. When the first numbered page is the verso of a leaf unnumbered on the recto, the number of the recto is supplied in square brackets: *e.g.* 1 blank leaf, 3 leaves, [9]–29 pp., thus indicating that 10 is the first page numbered. The collation "29 pp." alone indicates that the preliminary material counts up to the first numbered page and that the text ends on a page numbered 29 (page [30], being blank, is not specified). The collation "29, [1] pp.", on the other hand, indicates either that the text ends on the unnumbered page [30], or that a colophon, an index, or some other printed material appears on that page. "29 pp., 1 leaf" indicates that the text ends on page 29, page [30] is blank, and additional material not a continuation of the text appears on a final unnumbered leaf, either recto or verso or both being printed. Because the collation accounts for all leaves present in a complete copy of each book, half-title-leaves have not been noted except where the wording of the half-title-page differs significantly from that of the title-page.

Descriptions are based upon multiple copies of the books themselves, with notes drawn from information supplied by publishers and from other sources. Some items of trivial significance have been omitted, including most interviews (unless it could be established that the words reported were substantially Pound's own) and most brief fragments of letters quoted in books and articles. No attempt has been made to include in Section B the many booksellers' and auction catalogues which have printed or reproduced letters, inscriptions, and parts of manuscripts. Some omissions are due to my failure to locate files of periodicals and newspapers, and some bibliographical data are occasionally lacking for contributions which I have seen only as clippings. Translations about which I have definite information have been listed in Section D, but others certainly exist. I shall be grateful to anyone who will take the trouble to let me know of omissions and errors here or anywhere else in the bibliography.

Some general observations follow concerning specific details, first with reference to the entire book, then to particular sections. *Anonymous and pseudonymous works.* Most of the anonymous and pseudonymous works listed were acknowledged as his by Ezra Pound during his lifetime. A few items that are unsigned or signed with what I take to be pseudonyms have been attributed on stylistic evidence alone, but with indication that the authorship is uncertain.

Dates. Some of the books described are dated according to the Italian Fascist calendar, with the year reckoned from Mussolini's march on Rome in October 1922. I have supplied the normal equivalent in square brackets when it is not present on the title-page.

Edges. In book descriptions it may be assumed that all edges are trimmed and plain unless otherwise noted.

Proof copies. Although they exist for many of Pound's books, advance proof copies have been ignored. These are a normal part of the pre-publication phase of contemporary books in England

INTRODUCTORY NOTE

(and, in slightly different form, in the United States), and I have chosen to regard them as lying outside the proper scope of this work.

Special copies. Special copies (*i.e.* signed, on special paper, etc.) in Sections A and B have been described in separate entries when they have separate notes of limitation. (In referring to such notes, throughout, I have used the term *colophon*, even when the note does not come at the end of the volume and does not include printing information.)

Titles. Later titles of poems and essays have been incorporated in contents notes within square brackets following the original title. (In Sections A and B, prior *periodical* publication of contents of books has not normally been indicated, and the reader is referred for this information to the index, where the first C reference under a title will normally be to its first appearance in a periodical.) Poems of Cavalcanti and Arnaut Daniel have been identified by the numbers given to them in Pound's editions of Cavalcanti and *The Translations*—A66.

Section B. In Section B, I have labeled as "First edition," etc., books with the entirety of which Pound was concerned. This identification has been omitted for books that contain merely contributions by him, except when such books are described in more than a single edition or issue.

Section C. In Section C the arrangement is chronological, with periodicals. covering longer periods preceding those covering shorter ones and with those of exactly the same date listed alphabetically by title. (Definite articles in English titles of periodicals have generally been omitted.)

As a rule, only first periodical appearances have been listed of contributions not already printed in books; but first American periodical appearances of poems or essays already printed in England in books, and first English periodical appearances of contributions already printed in books in the United States, have been noted, as have reprints in periodicals of complete books, and a few periodical reprintings which had some particular significance. Later first periodical publication in the United States of a contribution first printed in an English periodical, and vice versa, has normally been noted only under the first entry. Complete poems quoted in the course of book reviews, with one or two very early exceptions, have not been listed.

INTRODUCTORY NOTE

The language in which a contribution is written has generally been specified when it is not that of the title. It has not been possible always to collate essays in Italian with possibly equivalent English texts, or to establish that some of the earlier Italian contributions were not, in fact, translated editorially from Pound's English. (See, in this connexion, the note to C976.)

The *Dial* Clip-sheets have been described from the copies that exist as part of the *Dial* archives deposited in the Collection of American Literature of the Beinecke Rare Book and Manuscript Library at Yale University. That set is not complete, but it seemed best to note the issues seen, particularly because most of the titles of the excerpts in these broadsides do not appear elsewhere. For attributions of some anonymous contributions to the *Dial*, I am endebted to Nicholas Joost and Alvin Sullivan, *The "Dial": Two Author Indexes* (Edwardsville, Ill.: Southern Illinois University, 1971).

Sections D and E. For Section D, the descriptive method of Sections A and B has been very much simplified: punctuation marks have been supplied and the entries standardised in order to give the essential information in the briefest possible form. In Section E the simplification has been not quite so drastic in view of the importance of some of the items.

This bibliography was submitted for publication early in 1982 and includes items published through December 1981 of which copies had been received by the end of February 1982.

ACKNOWLEDGMENTS

This bibliography has profited greatly from the contributions of others. First, I am endebted to *A Preliminary Checklist of the Writings of Ezra Pound*, compiled by John Edwards and published in New Haven by Kirgo-Books in 1953. I owe my knowledge of the existence of several items, especially in Section C, to Mr. Edwards's pioneering work. I have also examined Ian B. Angus's "A List with Descriptions of the Books of Ezra Pound for the Beginning of a Bibliography of Some Length," submitted to the School of Librarianship and Archives, University of London, for the Diploma in Librarianship (Part III), in 1952. At an early stage in the planning of the first edition, Mr. Angus had agreed to join me in the compilation of the present work, but eventually was unable to do so. I am grateful to him for advice and help. The late Hubert Creekmore kindly allowed me to consult a checklist of Pound's work that he had prepared, and gave me detailed information about his own copies of some of the books. I found useful Myles Slatin's "More by Ezra Pound," printed in the *Yale University Library Gazette* for October 1955, and have gleaned information from many other articles on Pound, especially those printed in *Paideuma*. I have profited especially from the biographies of Pound published by Charles Norman and Noel Stock, and from many other books about Pound which have appeared over the past twenty years. Since the publication of the first edition of this bibliography in 1963, many individuals have sent me corrections and suggestions for which I am most grateful. In Section D, in my listing of Greek, Japanese, Polish, and Romanian translations, I am very much endebted to Kimon Friar, the late Katue Kitasono, Sanehide Kodama, Takeshi Onodera, Leszek Engelking, Jerzy Niemojowski, and Peter Schneeman.

The typed copies of Ezra Pound's letters made by D. D. Paige for *The Letters* (1950)—A64—especially those to his father and mother, and the originals of Pound's letters to his parents, all now at Yale (the latter the gift of Princess de Rachewiltz), have been indispensable. I gratefully repeat my earlier acknowledgment to Ezra and Dorothy Pound and to A. V. Moore (their legal representative) for permission given during their lifetimes to use and quote from published and unpublished materials, and for their kindness in giving me information and in making items available for my use. For permission to quote from published and unpublished materials in this new edition, I am endebted to the Trustees of the Ezra Pound Literary Property Trust, to the New Directions Publishing Corporation, New York, and to Faber and Faber Limited, London. For unpublished materials I am endebted also to the following libraries: Cornell University Library; the Houghton Library, Harvard University; the Lilly Library, Indiana University; Humanities Research Center, University of Texas at Austin; and Yale University Library.

Although copies of a majority of the books and many of the periodicals described are in my own library, I have drawn very heavily upon other collections, particularly those originally belonging to Ezra Pound's own archives. I

ACKNOWLEDGMENTS

first had access to part of these in 1957 through the kindness of Miss Olga Rudge, with whom they were then stored at Sant' Ambrogio di Rapallo; then in 1961, at Brunnenburg, through the kindness of Mr. and Mrs. Pound and of Prince and Princess de Rachewiltz; and most recently, in 1981, again at Brunnenburg through the kindness of Princess de Rachewiltz, and in Venice thanks to Miss Rudge. The major portion of the Pound Archive is now in the Collection of American Literature of the Beinecke Rare Book and Manuscript Library at Yale; housed in the Lilly Library at Indiana University are roughly half of another portion that had been stored by Pound in 1924 with William Bird in Paris (the other half is at Yale), and the bulk of the archival materials preserved by Dorothy Pound during the St. Elizabeths period; to these two libraries I am particularly endebted. James Laughlin IV (New Directions), Pound's principal American publisher; Peter du Sautoy, Matthew Evans, and Mavis E. Pindard, on behalf of Faber and Faber Limited, his principal English publishers; and Vanni Scheiwiller, his principal Italian publisher, have very kindly allowed me to examine copies of Pound's books in their files. I have also been privileged to examine copies of books formerly or now in the possession of Bromwell Ault, Jr., Alan Clodd, John Drummond, the late A. V. Moore, the late Norman Holmes Pearson, Omar S. Pound, the late Harriet Shaw Weaver, and the late Donald G. Wing; I am grateful to all these individuals.

I am endebted also to the following libraries and individual members of their staffs: Biblioteca Berio, Genoa; Biblioteca Comunale, Milan; Biblioteca Marziana, Venice; Biblioteca Nazionale, Rome; Biblioteca dell'Istituto per gli Studi di Politica Internazionale, Milan; Biblioteca della Società Economica di Chiavari, Chiavari; Bibliothèque Nationale, Paris; Bodleian Library, Oxford; British Library, London and Colindale; Brown University Library, Providence, R.I. (David A. Jonah, Roger E. Stoddard, and the Harris Collection); Cambridge University Library, Cambridge; University of Chicago Library, Chicago, Ill. (Robert Rosenthal and the Harriet Monroe Collection); Columbia University Library, New York, N.Y. (Kenneth A. Lohf); Library of Congress, Washington, D.C.; Cornell University Library, Ithaca, N.Y. (George H. Healey, Michael Jasenas); Hamilton College Library, Clinton, N.Y. (C. Evelyn Buckley, Adelheid G. Ladewig, Walter Pilkington); the Houghton Library, Harvard University, Cambridge, Mass. (William H. Bond, William A. Jackson, Carolyn Jakeman, Roger E. Stoddard); the Lilly Library, Indiana University, Bloomington, Ind. (William R. Cagle, the late David A. Randall); the Public Library of Newark, N.J.; the Library, Museum of New Mexico (Mrs. J. K. Shishkin); New York Public Library, New York, N.Y. (Lewis Stark; the Berg Collection, the late John D. Gordan, Harvey Simmonds, Lola Szladits; the Manuscript Division); State University of New York at Buffalo, N.Y. (Robert Bertholf, David Posner, Anna Russell, Oscar A. Silverman); University of Pennsylvania Library, Philadelphia, Pa. (Neda M. Westlake); St. Louis Public Library, St. Louis, Mo.; Humanities Research Center, University of Texas at Austin (Ann Bowden, Kathy DeMoll, F. Warren Roberts); Trinity College Library, Hartford, Ct. (Marian Clarke, Donald Engley, the Watkinson Library); University of Virginia Library, Charlottesville, Va. (William H. Runge and the Clifton Waller Barrett Collection); the Chapin Library, Williams College, Williamstown, Mass. (the late H.

ACKNOWLEDGMENTS

Richard Archer); Yale University Library, New Haven, Ct. (the late James T. Babb, Matthew T. Blake, Dorothy Bridgwater, Peter Bunnell, Phyllis S. Cohen, Margaret N. Coons, Barbara Farrell, Eileen Grady, Edward Jajko, Hideo Kaneko, Herman W. Liebert, the late Frederic G. Ludwig, Louis L. Martz, John Musgrave, Leon Nemoy, Stephen Parks, Elizabeth L. Patterson, Barbara Paulson, Aleksis Rannit, Tatiana Rannit, Rutherford D. Rogers, Suzanne Rutter, David E. Schoonover, Reva Schwartz, Louis H. Silverstein, the late Barbara Simison, Warren Tsuneishi, Constance Tyson, Anne S. Whelpley, Marjorie Gray Wynne, and the Beinecke Library).

I am grateful to the following individuals and firms who have given me information, supplied copies of books, or very kindly helped me in other ways (and apologise to those whose names I may have omitted): Stephen J. Adams; Addison-Wesley Publishing Company; the late Richard Aldington; Anacapa Books (David S. Wirshup); the late Margaret Anderson; Massimo Bacigalupo; Joseph Bard; Clifton Waller Barrett; Beacon Press; Lady Beecham; the late William Bird; Blackwell's; the late Jacob Blanck; B. C. Bloomfield; Chas. H. Bohn & Co.; Boosey & Hawkes; Buddhadeva Bose; Erica Brausen; Cleanth Brooks; Butler and Tanner Ltd; Herbert Cahoon; University of California Press; Carcanet New Press Limited; the late John Carter; Bo Cavefors; *Chicago Tribune* (London Office); Lawrence W. Chisolm; Chiswick Press; Marshall Clements; the late Alvin Langdon Coburn; William Cookson; Copper Canyon Press; Timothy d'Arch Smith; Prafulla Chandra Das; J. M. Dent & Sons Ltd.; Leonard Doob; Doubleday & Company, Inc.; the late Philip C. Duschnes; Peter Dzwonkoski; John Ecklund; J. M. Edelstein; the late T. S. Eliot; Valerie Eliot; Richard Ellmann; John Espey; Eyre and Spottiswoode; Giangiacomo Feltrinelli Editore; Fontana Paperbacks; the late Jeanne Robert Foster; Foyles; Funk & Wagnalls (Harper & Row Publishers, Inc.); the late Jaime García Terrés; David Gordon; Gotham Book Mart, Inc. (Kay Steele, Frances Steloff, Andreas Brown, Philip Lyman); Greenwood Press Inc.; Eric Hamburger; Harcourt Brace Jovanovich, Inc.; Harrap Ltd.; James D. Hart; Harvard University Press (Mark Carroll); Hawthorn Books (E. P. Dutton); the late Allen T. Hazen; Heffers; William Heinemann Ltd.; Archie Henderson; Eva Hesse; the late Frederick W. Hilles; Susan Morse Hilles; Frank Hollings Bookseller (A. Miller); House of Books Ltd. (Mrs. Louis H. Cohn); the late Langston Hughes; University of Illinois Press; Indiana University Press; Richard Colles Johnson; Nicholas Joost; Michael Joseph Ltd.; László Kemenes Gefin; Hugh Kenner; Ben D. Kimpel; George Kirgo; B. J. Kirkpatrick; Alfred A. Knopf Inc. (Alfred A. Knopf, William A. Koshland); Eaghor G. Kostetsky; Michel Leiris; Mrs. Michel Licht; Brita Lindberg-Seyersted; Little, Brown & Co.; Liveright; Longmans, Green & Co., Limited; the Macmillan Company, New York; Luigi Majno; Elkin Mathews Ltd.; Ralph Maud; the late Harry M. Meacham; Edward Mendelson; University of Missouri Press; Murray Printing Company; the late N. Christophe de Nagy; Neill & Co. Ltd.; New Directions Publishing Corporation (Else Albrecht-Carrié, James Laughlin IV, Robert M. MacGregor, Griselda Ohannessian, Rhoda Rissin); S. D. Newberry; Anthony Newnham; *New York Herald Tribune* (Paris office; New York office); Charles Norman; University of North Carolina Press; Simon Nowell-Smith; Orient Longmans Ltd.; Peter Owen; D. D. Paige; Parkers; Deba P. Pat-

ACKNOWLEDGMENTS

naik; Pennsylvania State University Press; University of Pennsylvania Press; Pharos Books (Matthew Jennett); Phoenix Book Shop (Robert Wilson); the late William Pieper; Max Putzel; the late Forrest Read; William Reese; Henry Regnery; Rizzoli International Publications, Inc.; J. Albert Robbins; the late W. K. Rose; Bertram Rota Ltd. (Gabrielle Jones, Pamela Robinson, Anthony Rota, the late Bertram Rota, Arthur Uphill); Routledge & Kegan Paul Ltd.; Dominique de Roux; Peter Russell; Roberto Sanesi; Murray Schafer; Peter Schneeman; Herbert Schneidau; Schulte's Book Store (W. Pesky); Jacob Schwartz; Serendipity Book Shop (Peter Howard); the late Tibor Serly; Luigi Serravalli; Seven Gables Bookshop (the late John S. Van E. Kohn); Brooks Shepard; D. P. Singh; John J. Slocum; Neville Spearman Limited; Stanford University Press; Eric Stevens; C. A. Stonehill Inc. (Robert Barry, Sr., Robert Barry, Jr.); Edizioni di Storia e Letteratura; Tomiichi Takata; Taylor Garnett Evans & Co. Ltd.; Carroll F. Terrell; The Times Bookshop; The Times Publishing Company, Limited; Twayne Publishers (G. K. Hall & Co.); the late Carl Van Vechten; Giambattista Vicari; Viking Press (Viking Penguin, Inc.); Charlotte Ward; René Wellek; Henry W. Wenning; Wigmore Hall (H. T. C. Brickell); Isabel Wilder; the late Thornton Wilder; the H. W. Wilson Company; the late Mrs. Derwent Wood; the late Lawrence C. Wroth; Yale Co-op (Roysce Smith, Ted Wilentz); Yale University Press (James W. Boyden, Roberta Yerkes); Gerhard D. Zeller.

I am especially endebted to Noel Stock for information concerning Pound's contributions to the *New Times*, Melbourne, and to *Edge*, and for other help; to William McNaughton for identifying Pound's contributions to *Strike*; to Peter du Sautoy and to Mavis E. Pindard for information concerning books published by Faber and Faber Limited and for helpful suggestions; to James Laughlin IV for encouragement and assistance, and especially to him and Griselda Ohannessian for information concerning books published by the New Directions Publishing Corporation; to the late Agnes Bedford for help with Pound's music and related publications; to Vanni Scheiwiller for assistance with his own and other Italian publications and for reading proof on the first edition; to the late John Hayward for encouragement and for suggestions; to Rupert Hart-Davis and Nicolas Barker for patient cooperation; and, finally, to Princess de Rachewiltz, primarily responsible for the preservation of many of her father's books and papers, Curator of the Pound Archive in the Beinecke Library at Yale, who, ever since our first meeting a quarter of a century ago, has been unfailingly helpful in locating material, answering questions, and offering advice, copies of books and periodicals, hospitality, and encouragement.

The substantial assistance of a John Simon Guggenheim Memorial Foundation Fellowship in 1961 enabled me to take a six-month leave from my duties at Yale and thus made possible the completion of the first edition of this work. Without the instigation of the late Norman Holmes Pearson I should have given up many years ago the whole idea of attempting to compile a Pound bibliography, and without the urging of Robert Cross and the later support of Walker Cowen I should certainly not have revised and updated it.

A. BOOKS AND PAMPHLETS

A. BOOKS AND PAMPHLETS BY OR TRANSLATED BY EZRA POUND

INCLUDING TRANSLATIONS INTO ENGLISH OF HIS WRITINGS IN ITALIAN

Note. For syllabuses, leaflets, and broadsides, see Section E. For translations accompanied by original texts except for the de luxe edition of *Homage to Sextus Properitus* ([1976])—A38b—and when printed as part of a larger work (*e.g. The Translations* ([1953])—A66a), see Section B.

A. BOOKS AND PAMPHLETS

A1   A LUME SPENTO   [1908]

First edition:

A | LUME | SPENTO | EZRA POUND. [Venice, Printed for the author by A. Antonini]

2 leaves, 72 pp. 21·2 × 16 cm. (wrappers); 20·5 × 15·5 cm. (leaves). Green paper wrappers printed in black on page [i]; edges untrimmed. (The first 20 copies bound were trimmed in error and 15 of them were sent by Ezra Pound on 20 July 1908 to his father in Philadelphia for use as review copies. These trimmed copies measure 19·5 × 13·5 cm.)

Published about 20 July 1908 at L. 5 ($1.00); 150 copies printed. *On verso of title-leaf:* Published A. Antonini Cannaregio, 923—Venice (Italy) . . . In the City of Aldus MCMVIII.

Dedication on recto of second leaf: This Book was La Fraisne (The Ash Tree) dedicated to such as love this same beauty that I love, somewhat after mine own fashion. But sith one of them has gone out very quickly from amongst us it [is] given A Lume Spento (With Tapers Quenched) in memoriam eius mihi caritate primus William Brooke Smith Painter, Dreamer of dreams.

All examined copies have the word "is" omitted in the dedication and misprints in the note on page 10, "manuscnipt" for "manuscript," and in the last line on page 24, "immortalily" for "immortality." (In most copies the omitted word in the dedication has been supplied and the second "l" of "immortalily" crossed in manuscript by the author.)

Contents: Grace before Song—Note Precedent to "La Fraisne"—La Fraisne—Cino—In epitaphium eius—Na Audiart—Villonaud for This Yule—A Villonaud: Ballad of the Gibbet. Or the Song of the Sixth Companion—Mesmerism—Fifine Answers—Anima sola—In tempore senectus [*sic*]—Famam librosque cano—The Cry of the Eyes ["The Eyes"]—Scriptor ignotus. To K[atherine]. R. H[eyman]. Ferrara 1715—Donzella beata [with Latin "Song" ("Era mea") as epigraph]—Vana ["Praise of Ysolt," lines 1–18]—Li bel Chasteus—That Pass between the False Dawn and the True—In morte de—Threnos—Comraderie ["Camaraderie," formerly "Era Venuta"]—Ballad Rosalind—Malrin—Masks—On His Own Face in a Glass—The Tree—Invern—Plotinus—Prometheus—Aegupton ["De Aegypto," with two additional couplets]—Ballad for Gloom—For E[ugene]. Mc C[artney]. That Was My Counter-blade under Leonardo Terrone, Master of Fence—Salve O Pontifex! To Swinburne; an Hemichaunt—To the Dawn: Defiance["Defiance"]—The Decadence—Redivivus—FISTULAE: "To make her madrigal"—Song ("Love thou thy dream")—Motif ["Search"]—La Regina Avrillouse—A Rouse—Nicotine: A Hymn to the Dope—In tempore senectus [*sic*]: (An Anti-stave for Dowson)—Oltre la torre: Rolando—Make Strong Old Dreams Lest This Our World Lose Heart

3

A. BOOKS AND PAMPHLETS

Notes: The manuscript of *A Lume Spento* (the title is from the "Purgatorio," Canto III, line 132) had been almost completed when Pound left the United States for Europe early in 1908, and he had already tried unsuccessfully to interest at least one American publisher (Thomas Bird Mosher) in publishing it. Although the verso of the title-leaf describes the book as "Published [by] A. Antonini," it was in fact printed for Pound at his own expense, and it is doubtful that Antonini can have sold more than perhaps a few copies as the author's agent. Pound wrote to his parents from Venice while *A Lume Spento* was being printed: "The American reprint has got to be worked by kicking up such a hell of a row with genuine and faked reviews that Scribner or somebody can be brought to see the sense of making a reprint. I shall write a few myself and get someone to sign 'em." No signed or unsigned review located bears evidence of Pound's authorship, and there was no American edition of the book. Although in the autobibliography that he supplied for T. S. Eliot's *Ezra Pound His Metric and Poetry*—B17—Ezra Pound gives the date of publication of *A Lume Spento* as June and the number of copies printed as 100, correctly bound copies were not available until after 20 July, and, in an undated letter to his father probably of 3 August, he wrote that the "Edition was 150 copies but keep it dark . . . " Pound left Venice very soon after the printing was completed, having sent copies to his father in Philadelphia and to various friends, taking the remaining copies with him to England for distribution from there. On 3 January 1909 he wrote to his father from London: ". . . if you have copies of A Lume Spento left, hang on to 'em and mail me two. (I sent you 40 at first, I think??) Not quite that either, I guess."

Poems from *A Lume Spento* were included in *Personae* (1909)—A3, *Exultations* (1909)—A4, *Provença* (1910)—A6, and other later collections, but the book was not reprinted separately. To commemorate the fiftieth anniversary of its publication, in 1958, Vanni Scheiwiller issued in Milan a volume entitled . . . *A Lume Spento, 1908–1958*—B64—but the author allowed only seven poems from the original edition to be included. He did authorise the reprinting of both *A Lume Spento* and *A Quinzaine for This Yule* ([1908]), along with poems from the "San Trovaso" notebook, as *A Lume Spento and Other Early Poems* ([1965])—A83, but, in a special "Foreword (1964)," characterised the book as "A collection of stale creampuffs." All the poems in *A Lume Spento* were again reprinted in *Collected Early Poems* ([1976])—A98.

A2   A QUINZAINE FOR THIS YULE   [1908]

a. First edition, first issue:

[*Within thick-rule border, in 2 thick-rule rectangles separated by a floral ornament, all in black; in upper rectangle, in red:*] A QUINZAINE FOR | THIS YULE | [*in lower rectangle, in black:*] Being selected from a | Venetian sketch-book | —"San Trovaso"— | [*short rule*] BY [*short*

A. BOOKS AND PAMPHLETS

rule] | EZRA POUND [London, Pollock & Co. *On either side of the lower rectangle is a narrow thick-rule rectangle of the same height.*]

1 leaf, 1 blank leaf, [5]–27, [1] pp., 2 blank leaves. 22·5 × 14·5 cm. Sewn with red cord. (The first two leaves—the second blank—and the last two blank leaves—originally unopened at the side—serve in place of wrappers.) Edges untrimmed.

Published early December 1908 at 1*s.* 6*d.*; 100 copies printed. *Imprint on page* [28]: December, 1908. Printed and Published by Pollock & Co., 81 Mortimer Street, London, W.

Dedication on page [5]: To The Aube of the West Dawn [*i.e.* Katherine Ruth Heyman?].

All examined copies have misprints in line 5 on page 17 and line 3 up on page 18, "earth-hoard's" for "earth-horde's"; and in line 6 on page 21, "WESTON ST. LLEWMY" for "WESTON ST. LLEWMYS."

Contents: [Prose passage attributed to Weston St. Llewmys, *i.e.* Ezra Weston Loomis Pound]—Prelude. Over the Ognisanti—Night Litany—Purveyors General—Aube of the West Dawn. Venetian June—To La Contessa Bianzafior (cent. xiv.). (Defense at Parting)—Partenza di Venezia—Lucifer Caditurus—Sandalphon—Note on Sandalphon—Fortunatus—[Prose passage attributed to Weston St. Llewmys, *i.e.* Ezra Weston Loomis Pound]—Beddoesque—Greek Epigram—Christophori Columbi tumulus. (From the Latin of Hipolytus Capilupus, Early cent. MDC)—To T[homas]. H[ood]. The Amphora—Histrion—Nel Biancheggiar [formerly "For Katherine Ruth Heyman. (After One of Her Venetian Concerts.)"]

b. *Second issue:*

Title-page, pagination, size, and binding as in the first issue.

Published late December 1908 at 1*s.* 6*d.*; 100 copies printed. *Imprint on page* [28]: Printed for Elkin Mathews, Vigo Street, London, W., by Pollock & Co., Mortimer St., W., Dec. 1908.

In this issue, the misprints have been corrected, although certain typographical irregularities (*e.g.* the inverted "f" in line 3 up on page 27) are common to both issues.

Notes: During the latter part of his stay in Venice in 1908, Ezra Pound lived in the San Trovaso section of the city. His manuscript of "Night Litany" (originally "Venetian Night Litany"), and the manuscript of an unpublished poem from the "San Trovaso" notebook, "Piaza [*sic*] San Marco June," are reproduced in *Iconografia italiana di Ezra Pound* ([1955])—D61—plates 2–4 and 5. For photographs of the San Trovaso section of Venice see *A Lume Spento, 1908–1958* ([1958])—B64, which also reproduces the manuscript of "Night Litany."

The text of *A Quinzaine for This Yule* was reprinted, with poems from the "San Trovaso" notebook (and reproductions of its front cover and the manuscript of

A. BOOKS AND PAMPHLETS

"Sonnet of the August Calm") in *A Lume Spento and Other Early Poems* ([1965])—A83, and again, with most of the contents of the notebook (manuscript now at Yale), and reproduction of the manuscript of "Roundel. After Joachim du Bellay," in *Collected Early Poems* ([1976])—A98.

An (unauthorised) American reprint of this book was produced by offset in 1973 in New York by Gordon Press.

A3   PERSONAE   1909

a. *First edition:*

[*In black:*] PERSONAE | OF | EZRA POUND | [*in red: device*] | [*in black:*] LONDON | ELKIN MATHEWS, VIGO STREET | MCMIX

viii, 9–59, [1] pp., 2 blank leaves. 17·7 × 11·5 cm. Drab or (later) light brown paper boards lettered in gold on front cover: Personae | Ezra Pound, and on spine (in later copies, the five lines of title stamping on the spine measure approximately 1·5 cm. from top to bottom as against 2 cm. in earlier copies); end-papers; fore and bottom edges untrimmed.

Published 16 April 1909 at 2*s.* 6*d.*; 1000 sets of sheets printed (of which an undetermined number—not more than 500—were issued as part of *Personae & Exultations* (*1913*)). *On verso of title-leaf:* First published in April, 1909 *Imprint on page* [60]*:* [*Device*] Chiswick Press: Charles Whittingham and Co. Tooks Court, Chancery Lane, London

Dedication on page [*v*]*:* . . . This book is for Mary Moore of Trenton, if she wants it

Contents: Grace before Song—La Fraisne—Cino—Na Audiart—Villonaud for This Yule—A Villonaud: Ballad of the Gibbet. Or the Song of the Sixth Companion—Mesmerism—Fifine Answers—In tempore senectutis—Famam librosque cano—Scriptor ignotus, Ferrara 1715. To K. R. H.—Praise of Ysolt [incorporates "Vana"]—Camaraderie [formerly "Comraderie"]—Masks—Tally-O—Ballad for Gloom—For E[ugene]. Mc C[artney].—At the Heart o' Me, A.D. 751—Xenia ("And | Unto thine eyes my heart")—Occidit—Search [formerly "Motif"]—An Idyl for Glaucus—In Durance—Guillaume de Lorris Belated, A Vision of Italy—In the Old Age of the Soul—Alba Belingalis [formerly "Belangal Alba"]—From Syria. The Song of Peire Bremon "Lo Tort" . . . —From the Saddle, D'Aubigne to Diane—Marvoil—Revolt, against the Crepuscular Spirit in Modern Poetry—And Thus in Nineveh—The White Stag—Piccadilly—Notes [to the poems, including Marco Londonio's Italian version of "Nel Biancheggiar"]

Notes: An advertisement leaf of two pages, measuring 16·3 × 10·4 cm., describing the book as "Just out.—A new note in verse The season's sensation in poetry" and quoting from "Some early reviews," was distributed shortly after publication and was loosely laid in some copies. Another leaf of two pages, measuring 17·3 × 10·8 cm., describing *Exultations* as "Now ready," and quoting the same reviews of *Personae*, was printed in October 1909. This was loosely laid in some of the later copies and inserted following page [60] in others.

All the poems in *Personae* were reprinted in *Collected Early Poems* ([1976])—A98.

b. *Re-issue, with Exultations* (1913):

[*In black:*] PERSONAE | & | EXULTATIONS | OF | EZRA POUND | [*in red: device*] | [*in black:*] LONDON | ELKIN MATHEWS, CORK STREET | MCMXIII

4 leaves, vii–viii, 9–59, [1] pp., 2 blank leaves, 2 leaves, vii–viii, 9–51, [1], [10] pp., 1 blank leaf. 17·7 × 11·5 cm. Drab paper boards lettered in gold on front cover and on spine; end-papers; fore and bottom edges untrimmed. (Available with *Canzoni & Ripostes* as Ezra Pound's Poems, Volumes 1 and 2, at 3*s*. 6*d*. each.)

Published May 1913 at 3*s*. 6*d*.; not more than 500 copies issued. This volume consists of first-edition sheets of the two books with their original title-leaves excised—the conjugate leaves (pages 13–14, in each case) being pasted on to page 12—and new half-title and title-leaf for the volume (with title-page as above) inserted at the front. Of this new preliminary matter, 500 copies were printed by the Chiswick Press. The rare occurrence of the composite volume in comparison with its separate components indicates that fewer than the intended number were actually issued.

A4   EXULTATIONS   1909

a. *First edition:*

[*In black:*] EXULTATIONS | OF | EZRA POUND | [*in red: device*] | [*in black:*] LONDON | ELKIN MATHEWS, VIGO STREET | M CM IX

viii, 9–51, [1], [10] pp., 1 blank leaf. 17·8 × 11·4 cm. Dark red paper boards lettered in gold on front cover (either: Exultations | of | Ezra Pound or, probably later: Exultations | Ezra Pound) and on spine; end-papers; fore and bottom edges untrimmed.

Published 25 October 1909 at 2*s*. 6*d*.; 1000 sets of sheets printed (of which an undetermined number—not more than 500—were issued as part of *Personae & Exultations* (1913)). *Imprint on page* [52]: [*Device*] Chiswick Press: Charles Whittingham and Co. Tooks Court, Chancery Lane, London

Dedication on page [v]: To Carlos Tracy Chester "amicitiae longaevitate"

Contents: Guido Invites You Thus—Night Litany—Sandalphon—Sestina: Altaforte—Piere Vidal Old—Ballad of the Goodly Fere—Hymn III, from the Latin of Marc Antony Flaminius—Sestina for Ysolt—Portrait, from "La mère inconnue" [formerly "Un retrato"]—"Fair Helena" by Rackham—Laudantes decem pulchritudinis Johannae Templi—Aux belles de Londres—Francesca—Greek Epigram—Christophori Columbi tumulus, from the Latin of Hipolytus Capilupus—Plotinus—On His Own Face in a Glass—Histrion—The Eyes—Defiance [formerly "To the Dawn: Defiance"]—Song ("Love thou thy dream")—Nel Biancheggiar—Nils Lykke—A Song of the Virgin Mother, in the Play "Los Pastores de Belen." From the Spanish of Lope de Vega—Planh for the Young English King . . . From the Provençal of Bertrans de Born—Alba innominata. From the Provençal—Planh. It Is of the White Thoughts That He Saw in the Forest

Publisher's advertisements, [10] pages following page [52], are an integral part of the volume.

Notes: All the poems in *Exultations* were reprinted in *Collected Early Poems* ([1976])—A98.

An (unauthorised) American reprint of this book, clothbound, was produced by offset in 1973 in New York by Haskell House Publishers Ltd.

b. *Re-issue, with Personae* (1913):

For description see above under *Personae* (1909)—A3b.

A5   THE SPIRIT OF ROMANCE   [1910]

a. *First edition:*

[*In black:*] THE | [*in red:*] SPIRIT OF ROMANCE | [*in black:*] AN ATTEMPT TO DEFINE SOMEWHAT THE | CHARM OF THE PRE-RENAISSANCE | LITERATURE OF LATIN EUROPE | BY | EZRA POUND, M. A. | AUTHOR OF "PERSONÆ" AND "EXULTA-TIONS" | [*device*] | LONDON | [*in red:*] J. M. DENT & SONS, LTD | [*in black:*] 29 AND 30 BEDFORD STREET, W. C.

1 blank leaf, x, 251, [1] pp. 21·2 × 14·7 cm. Olive brown (or, later, olive green) cloth boards stamped in blind with ruled border and device on front cover and in gold on spine, with at base: J·M·DENT·&·SONS·LD; laid or (later) wove end-papers; top edges gilt or (later) stained blue-green, others untrimmed or (later) trimmed. Grey dust-jacket printed in green.

Published 20 June 1910 at 6s.; 1250 sets of sheets printed (of which 300 were used for the American issue). *Imprint on page* [252]: Printed by Turnbull and Spears, Edinburgh

Contents: Praefatio ad lectorem electum—Chapter I. The Phantom Dawn—Chapter II. Il miglior fabbro [*i.e.* Arnaut Daniel, including verse-and-prose

A. BOOKS AND PAMPHLETS

translations of the first four stanzas and the envoi of the canzone "Sols sui qui sai lo sobrafan quem sortz," pp. 18–20; and the canzon "L'aura amara," pp. 21–23; prose translations of the canzon "Sim fos amors de joi donar tant larga," pp. 24–26, and five stanzas of "Doutz brais e critz," pp. 26–28]—Chapter III. Proença [including verse-and-prose translations of Bernart of Ventadorn's "Quant ieu vey la' lauzeta mover" and of a song by Jaufré Rudel, Prince of Blaia, "Lan quand li iorn son lonc en mai," pp. 35–38, parts of "A Perigord pres del muralh," "Quan vey pels vergiers desplegar," and a song ["A War Song"] of Bertrans de Born, pp. 40–43, and Peire Vidal's "Song of Breath," pp. 44–45; verse translations of an Alba ["Compleynt of a Gentleman Who Has Been Waiting outside for Some Time"] attributed to Giraut de Bornelh [Bornello], pp. 47–48; three stanzas in praise of the Countess of Beziers by Arnaut of Marvoil, p. 53; a *sirvente* of Sordello, pp. 54–56; Pierre de Corbiac's "Queen of the Angels," p. 57, and a Pastorella of Marcabrun, pp. 59–60]—Chapter IV. Geste and Romance—Chapter V. La dolce lingua Toscana [with verse translations of "Cantico del sole" of St Francis of Assisi, pp. 88–89, Guido Guinicelli's sonnet "Vedut ho la lucente stella Diana," pp. 91–92, Guido Orlando's sonnet to Guido Cavalcanti, pp. 99–100, and Dante's "Canzone prima" from "Il Convito," pp. 102–3]—Chapter VI. Il Maestro [*i.e.* Dante]—Table of Dates—Chapter VII. Montcorbier, *alias* Villon [including parody of Walt Whitman, "Lo, behold, I eat water melons," p. 179]—Chapter VIII. The Quality of Lope de Vega [with summaries, including verse translations of excerpts, of "Los novios de Hornachuelos," pp. 198–203, and "El desprecio agradecido," pp. 209–14; verse translation of Fernando de Herrera's sonnet to Christobal Mosquera de Figueira, pp. 222–3, and prose translation of an excerpt from *Voyage d'Espagne . . . fait en l'année 1665* [*i.e. 1655*], published anonymously but given to Antoine de Brunel, pp. 224–5]—Chapter IX. Camoens—Chapter X. Poeti Latini [including verse translations of Andrea Navagero's "Inscriptio fontis," p. 236, "Prayer for Idmon," p. 237, "The Image of Pythagoras," p. 237; Camillo Capilupi's "Ad noctem," pp. 242–3; Giovanni Battista Amalteo's "Corydon," pp. 243–6; fragments from Castiglione's "Alcon," pp. 246–7; Hieronymus Angerianus' "Ad rosam (from the Erotopægnion)," p. 248, and John Carga's prayer "To the Virgin Mother, Whose Shrine Is at Lauretus," p. 250]

b. *American issue:*

[*In black:*] THE | [*in red:*] SPIRIT OF ROMANCE | [*in black:*] AN ATTEMPT TO DEFINE SOMEWHAT THE | CHARM OF THE PRE-RENAISSANCE | LITERATURE OF LATIN EUROPE | BY | EZRA POUND, M. A | AUTHOR OF "PERSONÆ" AND "EXULTATIONS" | [*device*] | LONDON | [*in red:*] J. M. DENT & SONS, LTD. | [*in black:*] NEW YORK | [*in red:*] E. P. DUTTON & CO.

21·2 × 14·7 cm. Olive cloth boards stamped in blind (with ruled border but without device) on front cover and in gold on spine, with at base: E. P. DUTTON & CO; laid end-papers; top edges gilt, others untrimmed.

A. BOOKS AND PAMPHLETS

Published July 1910 at $2·50; 300 sets of the first edition sheets issued with cancel title-leaf (with title-page as above).

c. *New edition (Part I only), with How to Read* (1932):

For description see below under *How to Read* (1931)—A33b.

d. *New edition* ([1952, *i.e.* 1953]):

EZRA POUND | [*thick-thin rule*] | THE SPIRIT | OF | ROMANCE | [*thin-thick rule*] | PETER OWEN LIMITED | London

248 pp. 21·6 × 14·5 cm. Olive cloth boards stamped in blue and gold on spine; end-papers. Tan dust-jacket printed in blue.

Published January 1953 at 16s.; number of copies unknown. *On verso of title-leaf:* ... First published 1910 Completely revised edition 1952 [*sic*] Made and printed in the Republic of Ireland by Cahill & Co., Ltd., Parkgate Printing Works, Dublin MCMLII

Contents: Praefatio ad lectorem electum (1910)—Postscript (1929)—I. The Phantom Dawn—II. Il miglior fabbro—III. Proença—IV. Geste and Romance—V. Psychology and Troubadours—VI. Lingua Toscana—VII. Dante—Table of Dates—VIII. Montcorbier, *alias* Villon—IX. The Quality of Lope de Vega—X. Camoens—XI. Poeti Latini—Index

Notes: Revisions, made in 1929 and 1932, first for the series of *Prolegomena*, of which only the first two volumes were published—A33b—and then in preparation for the abortive edition of Ezra Pound's collected prose, are for the most part confined to minor changes in phrasing and the addition of "parentheses" and footnotes, dated 1929 and 1932. The prefatory matter and the first five chapters are reprinted with a few deliberate changes from the edition of 1932.

e. *New edition, American issue, hardbound* ([1953]):

EZRA POUND | [*thick-thin rule*] | THE SPIRIT | OF | ROMANCE | [*thin-thick rule*] | A NEW DIRECTIONS BOOK [Norfolk, Conn., James Laughlin]

248 pp. 21·6 × 14·5 cm. Dark blue cloth boards stamped in silver down the spine; end-papers. Tan dust-jacket printed in blue.

Published January 1953 at $4.00; 2391 sets of sheets printed by Peter Owen for New Directions, of which 500 were bound and jacketed in the United States in 1952, and 1890 were cut down and issued in paper wrappers in 1968—A5f. *On verso of title-leaf:* ... New Directions Books are published by James Laughlin at Norfolk, Connecticut New York Office—333 Sixth Avenue, New York 14 Printed in the Republic of Ireland

f. *New edition, American issue, paperbound* ([1968]):

Title-page and pagination as in A5e.

A. BOOKS AND PAMPHLETS

20·3 × 13·8 cm. Heavy white paper wrappers printed in cream and black on pages [i] and [iv], and in black down the spine.

Published 31 October 1968 at $2.45 as New Directions Paperbook 266; 1890 sets of sheets originally supplied by Peter Owen in 1952 cut down and issued in wrappers. Verso of title-leaf as in A5e.

g. *New American edition* ([1968]):

EZRA POUND | THE SPIRIT | OF | ROMANCE | A NEW DIRECTIONS BOOK [Norfolk, Conn., James Laughlin]

6 leaves, 11–248, [2] pp., 2 blank leaves. 20·4 × 13·7 cm. Heavy white paper wrappers printed in cream and black on pages [i] and [iv], and in black down the spine.

Published December 1968 at $2.45 as New Directions Paperbook 266; 4000 copies printed. *On verso of title-leaf:* ... First published by New Directions in 1952 [*sic*]. First published as New Directions Paperbook 266 in 1968. Manufactured in the United States of America. New Directions Books are published for James Laughlin by New Directions Publishing Corporation, 333 Sixth Avenue, New York 10014.

Dedication on recto of sixth leaf: to "Smith" with thanks.

Contents as in A5d, e, and f, except for addition, on recto of sixth leaf, of "Post-Postscript," by Ezra Pound, dated: Venice, May, 1968.

A6   PROVENÇA   [1910]

a. *First edition, first impression:*

PROVENÇA | POEMS | SELECTED FROM PERSONAE, EXULTATIONS, AND | CANZONIERE | OF | EZRA POUND | [*device*] | BOSTON | SMALL, MAYNARD AND COMPANY | PUBLISHERS

1 blank leaf, vi, 84 pp., 2 blank leaves. 17·7 × 11·5 cm. Tan paper boards stamped in dark brown on front cover and up the spine (with title measuring 9 cm.); end-papers; edges untrimmed. Tan dust-jacket printed in dark brown and green (with price "$1.00 net; postage, 8 cents" on back). Copies measure 1·5 cm. across the top (including covers).

Published 22 November 1910 at $1.00; probably 200 copies printed. *On verso of title-leaf:* ... The University Press, Cambridge, U.S.A.

"*Provença* is the first American Edition of his work, and contains the best of the two volumes, *Personae* and *Exultations* ... with new poems which are to be issued in England separately under the title of *Canzoniere*." (*Dust-jacket*) The title of the projected book became *Canzoni* when it was published in 1911—A7a.

A. BOOKS AND PAMPHLETS

Dedications, page [3]: To Mary Moore; *page* [35]: To Carlos Tracy Chester; *page* [61]: To Olivia and Dorothy Shakespear

Contents: PERSONAE: La Fraisne—Cino—Na Audiart—Villonaud for This Yule—A Villonaud: Ballad of the Gibbet—Mesmerism—Famam librosque cano—In tempore senectutis—Camaraderie—For E[ugene]. McC[artney].—Ballad for Gloom—At the Heart o' Me—The Tree—An Idyl for Glaucus—Marvoil—In the Old Age of the Soul—Revolt against the Crepuscular Spirit in Modern Poetry—And Thus in Nineveh—The White Stag—Piccadilly—EXULTATIONS: Night Litany—Sestina: Altaforte—Ballad of the Goodly Fere—Portrait, from "La mère inconnue"—The Eyes—Nils Lykke—"Fair Helena" by Rackham—Greek Epigram—Histrion—Paracelsus in excelsis—A Song of the Virgin Mother—Song ("Love thou thy dream")—Planh for the Young English King—Alba innominata—Laudantes [formerly "Laudantes decem pulchritudinis Johannae Templi"]—Planh. It Is of the White Thoughts That He Saw in the Forest—CANZONIERE, STUDIES IN FORM: Octave—Sonnet in Tenzone—Sonnet ("If on the tally-board of wasted days")—Canzon: The Yearly Slain (Written in reply to Manning's "Korè." [With "Korè" by Frederic Manning])—Canzon: The Spear—Canzon, To Be Sung beneath a Window—Canzon: Of Incense—Canzone: Of Angels—Sonnet: Chi è questa?—Of Grace ["Ballata, Fragment," II]—Canzon: The Vision—To Our Lady of Vicarious Atonement (Ballata)—Epilogue: To Guido Cavalcanti—Notes [to the poems]

b. *Second impression* ([1917?]):

Title-page, collation, and size as in first impression. Tan paper boards stamped in green on front cover and up the spine (with title measuring 8·9 cm.); endpapers; edges untrimmed. Tan dust-jacket printed in green (with price "$1.00 net" on back). Copies measure 1·4 cm. across the top (including covers).

Published probably early in 1917 (a letter from the publishers to John Quinn, 4 Apr. 1917 (NYPL), states that "we have just reprinted PROVENÇA . . . "); number of copies unknown. Not only is the paper in these copies thinner, but there are several distinct signs of type-wear (*e.g.* "Laudante" and "Laudante." for "Laudantes" in the section title on pages 53 and 55 respectively). Besides the difference indicated above in size of stamping on the spine there are slight variations in some of the letters.

Note: All the poems in *Provença* were reprinted in *Collected Early Poems* ([1976])—A98.

A7   CANZONI   1911

a. *First edition:*

[*In black:*] CANZONI | OF | EZRA POUND | [*in red: device*] | [*in black:*] LONDON | ELKIN MATHEWS, VIGO STREET | MCMXI

A. BOOKS AND PAMPHLETS

viii, 51, [1], [4] pp. 19·3 × 13·3 cm. Streaky grey cloth boards lettered in gold at top of front cover, and, on spine: CAN | ZONI | OF | EZRA | POUND | ELKIN | MATHEWS , or (later) brown paper boards lettered in gold at centre of front cover, and, on spine: CAN | ZONI | ELKIN | MATHEWS ; end-papers; fore and bottom edges untrimmed.

Published July 1911 at 3s. 6d.; 1000 sets of sheets printed (of which an undetermined number—not more than 500—were issued as part of *Canzoni & Ripostes* (1913)). *Imprint at foot of page* [52]: Chiswick Press: Printed by Charles Whittingham and Co. Tooks Court, Chancery Lane, London.

Dedication on page [v]: To Olivia and Dorothy Shakespear

Contents: Canzon: The Yearly Slain (written in reply to Manning's "Korè")—Canzon: The Spear—Canzon: To Be Sung beneath a Window—Canzon: Of Incense—Canzone: of Angels—To Our Lady of Vicarious Atonement (Ballata)—To Guido Cavalcanti [formerly "Epilogue: To Guido Cavalcanti"]—Sonnet in Tenzone—Sonnet: Chi è questa?—Ballata, Fragment II (formerly "Of Grace"]—Canzon: The Vision—Octave—Sonnet ("If on the tally-board of wasted days")—Ballatetta—Madrigale—Era mea [Latin & English]—Threnos—The Tree—Paracelsus in excelsis—De Aegypto [formerly "Aegupton"]—Li bel Chasteus—Prayer for His Lady's Life, from Propertius—Speech for Psyche in the Golden Book of Apuleius ["Psyche of Eros"]—"Blandula, tenulla, vagula"—Erat hora—Epigrams. I, II (The Sea of Glass)—La Nuvoletta: Dante to an Unknown Lady . . . —Rosa sempiterna—The Golden Sestina, from the Italian of Pico della Mirandola—Rome, from the French of Joachim du Bellay—Her Monument, the Image Cut Thereon, from the Italian of Leopardi—Victorian Eclogues. I. Excuses; II. Satiemus; III. Abelard—A Prologue [formerly "Christmas Prologue"]—Maestro di tocar (W[alter Morse]. R[ummel].)—Aria—L'Art—Song in the Manner of Housman ["Mr. Housman's Message"]—Translations from Heine, I–VII—Und Drang, I–XII

Publisher's advertisements, [4] pages following page [52], are an integral part of the volume.

Notes: Ezra Pound had originally intended to include in *Canzoni* three additional sonnets, two additional longer poems, and some notes. This material was set up by the printers and is present in page-proofs sent to the author between 13 and 22 May 1911. In these proofs (now in the Humanities Research Center of the University of Texas at Austin), "L'Art" is the third of a group of four sonnets headed "Leviora," the others being "I. Against Form," "II. Hic jacet," and "IV. To My Very Dear Friend—Remonstrating for his Essay 'Mighty Mouths.'" This group is followed in the page-proof by the poem there entitled "To Hulme (T. E.) and Fitzgerald (a Certain [*i.e.* Desmond])." The next, "Song in the Manner of Housman," retained in the book as printed, is followed in the proof by a poem of 114 lines with printed title "Redondillas, or Something of that Sort," retitled in manuscript: "Locksley Hall fourty [*sic*] years further." In the proof the book ends with "Notes"—on the canzoni, on the proper names in the "Redondillas," and on "The Golden Sestina."

All the poems in *Canzoni*, plus those cancelled in proof in 1911, were reprinted

13

in *Collected Early Poems* ([1976])—A98. (*Redondillas* was also published separately in 1968—A90.)

b. *Re-issue, with Riposates* (1913):

[*In black:*] CANZONI | & | RIPOSTES | OF | EZRA POUND | WHERETO ARE APPENDED THE | COMPLETE POETICAL WORKS OF | T. E. HULME | [*in red: device*] | [*in black:*] LONDON | ELKIN MATHEWS, CORK STREET | M CM XIII

4 leaves, vii–viii, 51, [1] pp., 2 leaves, 7–63, [1], [4] pp. 19·3 × 13·7 cm. Brown paper boards lettered in gold on front cover and on spine; end-papers; fore and bottom edges untrimmed.

Published May 1913 at 3s. 6d.; not more than 500 copies issued. (Available with *Personae & Exultations* as Ezra Pound's Poems, Volumes 1 and 2, at 3s. 6d. each.) This volume consists of first-edition sheets of the two books (with the changes mentioned below) with new half-title and title-leaf for the volume (the latter with title-page as above) inserted at the front. The *Canzoni* sheets have the original title-leaf excised and the dedication leaf (pages [v–vi]) with which it had been conjugate is consequently pasted in. The two leaves of advertisements, which formed pages [53–56] in the first issue, have been excised and are inserted at the end of the volume, following *Riposates*; the leaves with which they had been conjugate (pages 49–[52]) are consequently pasted in. The *Riposates* sheets have the original half-title and title-leaf excised and a new half-title-leaf pasted in, with, on its verso, in lieu of the original list of Ezra Pound's books, the motto from the verso of the original title-leaf. Pages 13–16, with which the two excised leaves had been conjugate, are consequently pasted in. (The separate final 32-page gathering of Swift and Co. advertisements does not appear.) Of the matter actually reprinted, 500 copies were prepared by the Chiswick Press. The rare occurrence of the composite volume in comparison with its separate components indicates that fewer than the intended number were issued.

A8 RIPOSTES 1912

a. *First edition, first issue:*

RIPOSTES | OF | EZRA POUND | WHERETO ARE APPENDED | THE COMPLETE POETICAL | WORKS OF | T. E. HULME | WITH PREFATORY NOTE | [*device*] | MCMXII | STEPHEN SWIFT AND CO., LTD. | 16 KING STREET, COVENT GARDEN | LONDON

63, [1], 31, [1] pp. 19·8 × 13·4 cm. Streaky grey cloth boards stamped in gold on front cover, end-papers; edges untrimmed. Grey-blue dust-jacket printed in dark blue.

A. BOOKS AND PAMPHLETS

Published October 1912 at 3s. 6d.; an unknown number of sets of sheets printed (of which an undetermined quantity—not more than 500—were issued by Elkin Mathews as part of *Canzoni & Ripostes* (1913)—A7b; an unknown number were used for the American issue in 1913; and 400 were issued by Elkin Mathews in 1915). *Imprint on page* [64]: Printed by Neill and Co., Ltd., Edinburgh.

Dedication on page [5]: To William Carlos Williams

All examined copies have the misprint in the list of Ezra Pound's books on page [2], "PERSONAL" for "PERSONAE," which was not corrected in the later issues of the sheets.

Contents: Silet—In exitum cuiusdam—Apparuit—The Tomb at Akr Çaar—Portrait d'une femme—N[ew]. Y[ork].—A Girl—"Phasellus ille"—An Object—Quies—The Seafarer (from the early Anglo-Saxon Text)—Echoes I, II—An Immorality—Dieu! Qu'il la fait, from Charles D'Orleans—Salve Pontifex (A. C. S.)—Δώρια—The Needle—Sub mare—Plunge—A Virginal—Pan Is Dead—The Picture—Of Jacopo del Sellaio—The Return—Effects of Music upon a Company of People: I. Deux Movements [*sic*]; II. From a Thing by Schumann—The Complete Poetical Works of T. E. Hulme ("Prefatory Note," signed: E. P.; "Autumn"; "Mana Aboda"; "Above the Dock"; "The Embankment"; "Conversion")

Publisher's advertisements, "Books That Compel," 31, [1] pages following page [64], are inserted. (These have been cut out in some presentation copies, distributed after the failure of the publisher.)

Notes: Stephen Swift and Co. Ltd. had agreed to publish Ezra Pound's future books, giving him £100 per year advance royalties for a period of ten years. The first book to appear under this agreement was the English edition of the *Sonnets and Ballate of Guido Cavalcanti*—B4b—in May 1912, and the second was *Ripostes* in October. But *Ripostes* had been out only a few weeks when Ezra Pound wrote to his parents on 5 November 1912: "'Swift' is busted. They caught the *manager* in Tangier with *some* of the goods." On 29 November he was able to report to his mother that he was "getting satisfactory terms out of Swift's liquidator." Elkin Mathews agreed to take over all bound copies and sheets of *Ripostes* (subsequently re-issuing the sheets as indicated below). He sold bound copies of the Swift edition of *Sonnets and Ballate of Guido Cavalcanti*, apparently as agent for the translator, during 1913, 1914, and 1915; then a fire, presumably at the binders, where the sheets were being held, effectively settled the problem of their disposition.

All the poems in *Ripostes* were reprinted in *Collected Early Poems* ([1976])—A98.

b. *Second issue, with Canzoni* (1913):

For description see above under *Canzoni* (1911)—A7b.

c. *Third (American) issue* (1913):

RIPOSTES | OF | EZRA POUND | WHERETO ARE APPENDED | THE COMPLETE POETICAL | WORKS OF | T. E. HULME | WITH

A. BOOKS AND PAMPHLETS

PREFATORY NOTE | [*device*] | BOSTON | SMALL, MAYNARD AND
COMPANY | PUBLISHERS | 1913

63, [1] pp. 19·4 × 13·3 cm. Red paper boards lettered in black on front cover
and up the spine; end-papers; fore and bottom edges untrimmed.

Published July 1913 at $1.00; number of copies unknown. These are the first-
edition sheets with the original title-leaf excised and a cancel title-leaf—on
thinner paper—(with title-page as above) pasted to its stub.

d. *Fourth issue* (1915):

RIPOSTES | OF | EZRA POUND | WHERETO ARE APPENDED
THE | COMPLETE POETICAL WORKS OF | T. E. HULME | WITH
PREFATORY NOTE | [*device*] | LONDON | ELKIN MATHEWS, CORK
STREET | MCMXV

63, [1] pp., 1 leaf. 19·1 × 13·3 cm. Heavy off-white paper wrappers, printed in
black on page [i] with cubist design (by Dorothy Shakespear Pound), and on
page [iv] with imprint, folded over end-papers; fore and bottom edges untrimmed.

Published April 1915 at 1*s*.; 400 copies issued. These are the first-edition sheets
with the original title-leaf excised and a cancel title-leaf (with title-page as
above) pasted to its stub.

Publisher's advertisement headed: "Ezra Pound's New Book [*i.e. Cathay*]," 1 leaf
following page [64], is inserted.

Note: The wrappers, the cancel title-leaf, and the advertisement leaf were printed
by the Chiswick Press.

A9   CATHAY   1915
First edition:

CATHAY | TRANSLATIONS BY | EZRA POUND | FOR THE MOST
PART FROM THE CHINESE | OF RIHAKU, FROM THE NOTES
OF THE | LATE ERNEST FENOLLOSA, AND | THE DECIPHER-
INGS OF THE | PROFESSORS MORI | AND ARIGA | [*ornament*] |
LONDON | ELKIN MATHEWS, CORK STREET | MCMXV

31, [1] pp. 19·3 × 13·3 cm. Heavy tan paper wrappers, printed in black on
pages [i] and [iv], folded over end-papers; fore and bottom edges untrimmed.

Published 6 April 1915 at 1*s*.; 1000 copies printed. *Imprint at foot of page* [32]:
Chiswick Press: Printed by Charles Whittingham and Co. Tooks Court, Chancery Lane, London.

A. BOOKS AND PAMPHLETS

Contents: Song of the Bowmen of Shu. By Kutsugen [*i.e.* Bunno]—The Beautiful Toilet. By Mei Sheng—The River Song. By Rihaku—The River-Merchant's Wife: A Letter. By Rihaku—The Jewel Stairs' Grievance. By Rihaku [with "Note"]—Poem by the Bridge at Ten-Shin. By Rihaku—Lament of the Frontier Guard. By Rihaku—Exile's Letter. By Rihaku—The Seafarer (from the Early Anglo-Saxon Text)—From Rihaku: Four Poems of Departure [with epigraph beginning "Light rain is on the light dust"]: ("Separation on the River Kiang"; "Taking Leave of a Friend"; "Leave-taking near Shoku"; "The City of Choan")—South-Folk in Cold Country—[Note]

"I have not come to the end of Ernest Fenollosa's notes by a long way, nor is it entirely perplexity that causes me to cease from translation. . . . But if I give [the poems] . . . with the necessary breaks for explanation, and a tedium of notes, it is quite certain that the personal hatred in which I am held by many, and the *invidia* which is directed against me because I have dared openly to declare my belief in certain young artists, will be brought to bear first on the flaws of such translation, and will then be merged into depreciation of the whole book of translations. Therefore I give only these unquestionable poems." (*Note, signed:* E. P., *p.* [32])

An advertisement leaf headed "Ezra Pound's New Book [*i.e. Cathay*]" was loosely laid in some copies and inserted following page [32] in others.

Note: All the poems in *Cathay* were reprinted, with four additional poems from the Fenollosa notebooks, in *Lustra* ([1916])—A11, in *Personae* (1926)—A27, in *Selected Poems* ([1928])—A30, in *Collected Shorter Poems* ([1952])—A27d, in *The Translations* ([1953])—A66, in *Selected Poems 1908–1959* ([1975])—A97, and in *Collected Early Poems* ([1976])—A98.

A10   GAUDIER-BRZESKA   1916

a. *First edition:*

[*In red:*] GAUDIER = BRZESKA | [*in black:*] A MEMOIR BY EZRA POUND | INCLUDING THE PUBLISHED WRITINGS OF THE | SCULPTOR, AND A SELECTION FROM HIS LETTERS | WITH THIRTY-EIGHT ILLUSTRATIONS, CONSISTING OF PHOTO- | GRAPHS OF HIS SCULPTURE, AND FOUR PORTRAITS BY WAL- | TER | BENINGTON, AND NUMEROUS REPRODUCTIONS OF DRAWINGS | LONDON: JOHN LANE. THE BODLEY HEAD | NEW YORK: JOHN LANE COMPANY. MCMXVI

x pp., 1 leaf, 168 pp. XXXVIII numbered plates, incl. front., ports. 26·1 × 19·7 cm. Grey-green cloth boards embossed in blind with reproduction of a green stone charm by Gaudier-Brzeska on front cover (later—*circa* 1927–28—without design) and lettered in gold on front cover and on spine, with, at base of spine: THE BODLEY HEAD; end-papers; top edges stained grey-green, others untrimmed. White dust-jacket printed in black (with reproduction of plate IV on front).

Published 14 April 1916 at 12s. 6d.; 1000 sets of sheets printed (of which about 200 were used for the American issue, 100 were bound up in 1927–28, and 250 were re-issued by Laidlaw and Laidlaw in 1939). *On verso of title-leaf:* William Clowes and Sons, Limited, London and Beccles

Chapter XI reprints the article "Vorticism" from the *Fortnightly Review* for 1 September 1914—C158. Chapter XII incorporates most of "Affirmations . . . III. Jacob Epstein" from the *New Age* for 21 January 1915—C172, and reprints "Affirmations. . . . V. Gaudier-Brzeska" from *New Age* for 4 February 1915— C176, and "Affirmations . . . VI. Analysis of This Decade" from *New Age* for 11 February 1915—C179.

In September 1927 Ezra Pound reported to Jeanne Robert Foster that "There are 350 sheets of the GAUDIER BRZESKA Lane held up by cost of original binding . . . Only 16 bound copies left." It was eventually determined that only 100 sets of the sheets were complete with the full number of plates, and these were bound up for John Lane, in late 1927 or early 1928, in less expensive style without the design on the front cover.

b. *American issue:*

Olive green cloth boards stamped in blind with design on front cover and lettered in gold on spine, with, at base of spine: JOHN LANE | COMPANY ; end-papers; top edges gilt, others untrimmed. White dust-jacket printed in black.

Published June 1916 at $3.50; about 200 sets of first-edition sheets specially bound for sale in the United States by the John Lane Company, New York.

c. *English re-issue* ([1939]):

GAUDIER-BRZESKA | A MEMOIR BY EZRA POUND | INCLUD-ING THE PUBLISHED WRITINGS OF THE | SCULPTOR AND A SELECTION FROM HIS LETTERS | WITH THIRTY ILLUSTRA-TIONS, CONSISTING OF PHOTOGRAPHS | OF HIS SCULPTURE, AND FOUR PORTRAITS BY WALTER BENINGTON, | AND NU-MEROUS REPRODUCTIONS OF DRAWINGS | LAIDLAW & LAIDLAW LTD. | 32 ALFRED PLACE, LONDON, W.C.1

x pp., 1 leaf, 168 pp. 30 plates, incl. front., ports. 25·9 × 19·7 cm. Green cloth boards lettered in gold on spine; end-papers; top edges partly stained, others untrimmed. White dust-jacket printed in red and green.

Published February 1939 at 12s. 6d.; 250 copies issued. *On verso of title-leaf:* William Clowes and Sons, Limited, London and Beccles

On 28 July 1934, after the rights in the book had reverted to the author from John Lane, 250 sets of unbound sheets, together with 250 each of 30 (out of 38) of the plates, were sent to Mrs Pound in England. These sheets were sup-

A. BOOKS AND PAMPHLETS

plied with a cancel title-leaf (with title-page as above) and a cancel "List of Illustrations" leaf (with pages [ix]–x reprinted to omit pagination and plates XVII–XXIV) and issued by Laidlaw and Laidlaw in London. In this re-issue, the plates are grouped differently from those in the first issues, and on each plate the number has been obliterated by black cancellation.

d. *New edition* ([1960]):

[*In black:*] GAUDIER-BRZESKA | A Memoir | EZRA POUND | [*in red: reproduction of artist's monogram*] | [*in black:*] THE MARVELL PRESS [Hessle, East Yorkshire]

1 blank leaf, 7 leaves, 17–147, xxx pp., 1 blank leaf. front. (port.), illus., incl. facsim. 22 × 14·8 cm. Brown cloth boards stamped in gold on front cover and lettered in gold down the spine: GAUDIER-BRZESKA EZRA POUND THE MARVELL PRESS ; end-papers. Tan dust-jacket printed in red and dark brown.

Published September 1960 at 35s.; number of copies unknown. *On verso of title-leaf:* First published 1916 This edition first published in 1960 by The Marvell Press at 253 Hull Road Hessle East Yorkshire ... Made and printed in Great Britain at the Press of Villiers Publications, Ingestre Road, London

The frontispiece, pages x–xxx (at end), and the final blank leaf are on coated paper.

"This enlarged edition ... includes 30 pages of illustrations (sculpture and drawings) as well as the pieces on Gaudier which Pound wrote after the publication of the 1916 edition." (*Dust-jacket*) Reprints, pp. 17–135, the original text, omitting the "Præfatio" and adding "Preface to the Memorial Exhibition 1918," pp. 136–9, "Gaudier: A Postscript 1934," pp. 140–5, and "Peregrinations, 1960," pp. 146–7, the latter dated: Brunnenburg, Tirolo, 1960, and written for this new edition.

Note: A special dust-jacket with the imprint of Vanni Scheiwiller was prepared for the 30 copies exported for distribution by him in Milan, Italy.

e. *New edition, American issue* ([1961]):

[*In black:*] GAUDIER-BRZESKA | A Memoir | EZRA POUND | [*in red: artist's monogram*] | [*in black:*] A NEW DIRECTIONS BOOK [New York, James Laughlin]

Collation, size, and binding as in English issue, except that the binding is lettered in gold down the spine: GAUDIER-BRZESKA EZRA POUND NEW DIRECTIONS . Tan dust-jacket printed in red and dark brown.

Published 28 February 1961 at $8.25; 494 copies were printed, bound, and jacketed by The Marvell Press for New Directions. *On verso of title-leaf:* First published in 1916 This edition first published in 1960 [*sic*] by New Directions ... New Directions Books are published by James Laughlin, New York office,

A. BOOKS AND PAMPHLETS

333 Sixth Avenue, 14 Made and printed in Great Britain at the Press of Villiers Publications, Ingestre Road, London

f. *New edition* ([1970]):

GAUDIER-BRZESKA | A Memoir | EZRA POUND | [*artist's mono-gram*] | A NEW DIRECTIONS BOOK [New York, James Laughlin]

7 leaves, 17–147, xxx pp., incl. front. (port.), illus., facsim. 20·8 × 14·3 cm. Grey cloth boards lettered in gold down the spine; end-papers. White dust-jacket printed in black.

Published 30 March 1970 at $7.50; 1000 copies printed. *On verso of title-leaf:* ... Manufactured in the United States of America ... New Directions Books are published for James Laughlin by New Directions Publishing Corporation, 333 Sixth Avenue, New York 10014.

Contains brief "Foreword to This Edition," signed: E. P., *recto of third leaf.* The book is otherwise a reprint by offset of the 1960 edition.

Note: The book was published paperbound also by New Directions in New York 24 October 1974 at $3.25 as their Paperbook 372, in a first printing of 3090 copies.

A11   LUSTRA   [1916]

a. *First edition, first impression (unabridged text):*

LUSTRA | OF | EZRA POUND | [*quotation in 4 lines*] | 200 copies privately printed, of which this is No. ... [*number written in by the author*] | [*circular stamp (designed by Edmund Dulac) in orange-red with the author's initials in intaglio.* London, Elkin Mathews]

124 pp. front. (port.) 20·6 × 14·5 cm. Tan cloth boards lettered in dark blue on front cover and up the spine; end-papers; fore and bottom edges untrimmed.

Issued September 1916 at 5s.; 200 copies printed.

The frontispiece is a reproduction of a photograph of Ezra Pound by Alvin Langdon Coburn. It has an unprinted protective tissue.

Dedication on page [5]: V[ail de]. L[encour]. Cui dono lepidum novum libellum. [Vail de Lencour was a *nom de plume* chosen by Ezra Pound for Brigit Patmore.]

Contents: Tenzone—The Condolence—The Garret—The Garden—Ortus—Salutation—Salutation the Second—The Spring—Albâtre—Causa—Commission—A Pact—Surgit fama—Preference—Dance Figure, for the Marriage in Cana of Galilee—April—Gentildonna—The Rest—Les Millwin—Further Instructions—A Song of the Degrees—Ité—Dum capitolium scandet—*To Καλòν*—The Study in Aesthetics—The Bellaires—The New Cake of Soap—Salvationists—Epitaph—Arides—The Bath Tub—Amitiés—Meditatio—To Dives—Ladies

20

A. BOOKS AND PAMPHLETS

("Agathas"; "Young Lady"; "Lesbia illa"; "Passing")—Phyllidula—The Patterns—Coda—The Seeing Eye—Ancora—A Translation from the Provençal of En Bertrans de Born: "Dompna pois de me no'us cal"—The Coming of War: Actaeon—After Ch'u Yuan—Liu Ch'e—Fan-piece, for Her Imperial Lord—Ts'ai Chih—In a Station of the Metro—Alba—Heather—The Faun—Coitus—The Encounter—Tempora—Black Slippers: Bellotti—Society—Image from D'Orleans—Papyrus—"Ione, Dead the Long Year"—'Ιμέρρω—Shop Girl—To Formianus' Young Lady Friend, after Valerius Catullus—Tame Cat—L'Art, 1910—Simulacra—Women before a Shop—Epilogue—The Social Order—The Tea Shop—Epitaphs ("Fu I"; "Li Po")—Our Contemporaries—Ancient Wisdom, Rather Cosmic—The Three Poets—The Gipsy—The Game of Chess. Dogmatic Statement concerning the Game of Chess—Provincia deserta—*Cathay* [omitting "The Seafarer" and adding "Sennin Poem by Kakuhaku," "A Ballad of the Mulberry Road," "Old Idea of Choan by Rosoriu," and "To-Em-Mei's 'The Unmoving Cloud.' By T'ao Yuan Ming"]—Near Perigord—Villanelle: The Psychological Hour—Dans un omnibus de Londres—To a Friend Writing on Cabaret Dancers—Homage to Quintus Septimius Florentis Christianus—Fish and the Shadow

Notes: The manuscript as submitted had been set in type (by William Clowes and Sons, Ltd., London) and Ezra Pound had received page-proof, when printer and publisher (apparently frightened by the suppression in the previous year of D. H. Lawrence's *The Rainbow*) refused, on grounds of the indecorum of certain poems, to continue with the book as set. It was eventually agreed that 200 copies would be printed "almost unabridged" (*i.e.* omitting only "The Temperaments," "Ancient Music," "The Lake Isle," and "Pagani's, November 8"). These copies, although technically not published, were in fact sold by Elkin Mathews to those who requested the unabridged text when ordering the book. For the second impression, nine additional poems were omitted and one title altered, as indicated below.

b. *Second impression (abridged text):*

LUSTRA | OF | EZRA POUND | [*quotation in 4 lines*] | LONDON | ELKIN MATHEWS, CORK STREET | M CM XVI

115, [1] pp. front. (port.) 20·6 × 14·5 cm. Tan cloth boards lettered in blue on front cover and up the spine and stamped in blue (remainder copies—*circa* 1935—in blind) on back cover; end-papers; fore and bottom edges untrimmed. (Later copies have plain glassine dust-jacket.)

Published October 1916 at 5s.; about 800 copies printed. *Imprint at foot of page* [116]: London: Printed by William Clowes and Sons, Limited.

The contents are identical with those of the first impression except for the omission of nine poems ("Salutation the Second," "Commission," "The New Cake of Soap," "Epitaph," "Meditatio," "Phyllidula," "The Patterns," "The Seeing Eye," "'Ιμέρρω") and the change of title of the poem "Coitus" to "Pervigilium."

A. BOOKS AND PAMPHLETS

c. *First American edition, first impression* (1917):

LUSTRA | of Ezra Pound | with Earlier Poems | For Private Circulation | Sixty Copies Printed. New York, October 1917. | This is Number——[*number written in*]

1 blank leaf, 202 pp., 2 blank leaves. front. (port.) 19·7 × 13·6 cm. Blue cloth boards with white paper label on spine printed in black; end-papers; top edges stained blue, others untrimmed.

Distributed gratis beginning 19 September 1917, chiefly by John Quinn; 60 copies printed. *On verso of title-leaf:* ... Published October, 1917 Printed in the United States of America

The frontispiece is a reproduction of the drawing of Ezra Pound by Henri Gaudier-Brzeska (which was used also as the frontispiece for T. S. Eliot's anonymous *Ezra Pound His Metric and Poetry*—B17—published by Alfred Knopf in January 1918). It has an unprinted protective tissue. The book is printed on laid paper watermarked: Utopian . The half-title-leaf with advertisement on verso (pp. [1–2]) was excised in most copies, leaving a stub.

Dedication on page [5]: Vail de Lencour ...

Contents: [Identical with the first impression of the first (English) edition, but adding after "The Tea Shop": "Ancient Music" and "The Lake Isle"; after "Dans un omnibus de Londres": "Pagani's, November 8"; and at the end the following: Impressions of François-Marie Arouet (de Voltaire)—The Temperaments—POEMS PUBLISHED BEFORE 1911: In Durance—Piere Vidal Old—CANZONI, FIRST PUBLISHED 1911: Prayer for His Lady's Life—"Blandula, tenulla, vagula"—Erat hora—The Sea of Glass—Rome—Her Monument, the Image Cut Thereon—[Mr] Housman's Message to Mankind—Translations from Heine [I–VIII]—Und Drang [I–XII]—RIPOSTES, FIRST PUBLISHED 1912: [Silet]—In exitum cuiusdam—Apparuit—The Tomb at Akr Çaar—Portrait d'une femme—New York—A Girl—"Phasellus ille"—An Object—Quies—The Seafarer—[Echoes, II:] The Cloak—An Immorality—"Dieu! Qu'il la fait"—Salve Pontifex (A. C. S.)—Δώρια—The Needle—Sub mare—Plunge—A Virginal—Pan Is Dead—The Picture—Of Jacopo del Sellaio—The Return—THREE CANTOS OF A POEM OF SOME LENGTH: [Cantos II, III, and I, in that order, all three differing radically from the eventual final texts]

d. *Second impression:*

LUSTRA | of Ezra Pound | with Earlier Poems | New York . Alfred A. Knopf . Mcmxvii

1 blank leaf, 202 pp., 2 blank leaves. 19·7 × 13·7 cm. Yellow paper boards stamped in blue on both covers and on spine; end-papers; top edges stained blue, others roughly trimmed. Salmon dust-jacket printed in dark blue.

Published 16 October 1917 at $1.50; number of copies unknown. *On verso of title-leaf:* ... Published October, 1917 Printed in the United States of America

A. BOOKS AND PAMPHLETS

[Printed on wove paper watermarked: OLDE STYLE] (40 special copies were bound for John Quinn in the style of the first impression, with its frontispiece—not included in ordinary copies. A "Note" by John Quinn on the various editions and impressions of the book, dated 24 October 1917, printed on a folder of two leaves measuring 17·8 × 12·1 cm., was laid into some of these special copies and into later copies of the first impression.)

The contents are identical with those of the first impression except for the omission of one poem, "The Temperaments."

Note: Three copies have been located of unnumbered sheets for the first impression bound in tan paper boards similar to those of the second impression. Two of these—one at Brunnenburg in 1981—contain the half-title-leaf, which was excised from most copies of the first impression. The exact status of these copies has not been determined.

A12   CERTAIN NOBLE PLAYS   1916
OF JAPAN

First edition:

CERTAIN NOBLE PLAYS OF JAPAN: | FROM THE MANU-SCRIPTS OF ERNEST | FENOLLOSA, CHOSEN AND FINISHED | BY EZRA POUND, WITH AN INTRODUC- | TION BY WILLIAM BUTLER YEATS. | [*Device*] | THE CUALA PRESS | CHURCHTOWN | DUNDRUM | MCMXVI

2 blank leaves, 2 leaves, 1 blank leaf, xviii, [1] pp., 1 leaf, 48, [2] pp., 1 leaf, 2 blank leaves. 21·4 × 14·8 cm. Grey paper boards printed in black on front cover, with tan linen back; grey end-papers; edges untrimmed.

Published 16 September 1916 at 11s. *Colophon (verso of first leaf):* Three hundred and fifty copies of this book have been printed. This copy is No. [*number written in*] *Colophon (page* [51]): Here ends 'Certain Noble Plays of Japan:' ... Printed and published by Elizabeth Corbet Yeats at the Cuala Press, Churchtown, Dundrum, in the County of Dublin, Ireland. Finished on the twentieth day of July, in the year of the Sinn Fein rising, nineteen hundred and sixteen. [Both colophons and the four half-title-leaves are printed in red, the rest of the book in black.]

Contents: Introduction, by W. B. Yeats—Nishikigi [by Motokiyo]—Hagoromo—Kumasaka [by Ujinobu]—Kagekiyo [by Motokiyo]—Notes [to Kagekiyo, and acknowledgment, signed: Ezra Pound]

Note: These plays, without the introduction by W. B. Yeats, were reprinted in '*Noh' or Accomplishment*—A13, which was itself reprinted with the Yeats introduction in 1959 by New Directions in New York as *The Classic Noh Theatre of Japan, by Ezra Pound and Ernest Fenollosa* (New Directions Paperbook P.79).

A. BOOKS AND PAMPHLETS

A13   'NOH' OR ACCOMPLISHMENT   1916
[*i.e.* 1917]

a. *First edition:*

'NOH' | OR | ACCOMPLISHMENT | A STUDY OF | THE CLAS-
SICAL STAGE OF JAPAN | BY | ERNEST FENOLLOSA | AND |
EZRA POUND | MACMILLAN AND CO., LIMITED | ST. MAR-
TIN'S STREET, LONDON | 1916 [*i.e.* 1917]

viii, 267, [1] pp. front. (port.), music. 22·8 × 15·5 cm. Blue cloth boards stamped
in black on front cover and in gold on spine (with, at base: MACMILLAN & CO
or, later?: MACMILLAN | & CO); laid (or, later? wove) end-papers; top and fore
edges untrimmed. Yellow dust-jacket printed in red. (The frontispiece has an
unprinted protective tissue, in most copies.)

Published 12 January 1917 at 7s. 6d.; 1250 sets of sheets printed (of which an
unknown number were used for the American issue). *Imprint at foot of page*
[268]: Printed by R. & R. Clark, Limited, Edinburgh.

Contents: PART I: Introduction [by Ezra Pound]—Sotoba Komachi [by Kiyot-
sugu]—Technical Terms in Noh—Kayoi Komachi [by a Minoru]—Suma Genji
[by Manzaburo]—[Excerpts from Fenollosa's records of his conversations with
Umewaka Minoru]—PART II: Introduction to Kumasaka—Kumasaka, by Ujinobu—Shojo—Tamura—Foreword to Tsunemasa—Tsunemasa—PART III:
Fenollosa on the Noh (? about 1906)—Nishikigi, by Motokiyo—Kunuta—Hagoromo—Kagekiyo, by Motokiyo—PART IV: Awoi No Uye, by Ujinobu—Kak-
itsubata, by Motokiyo—Chorio, by Nobumitsu—Genjo, by Kongo—Appendices

Notes: "The vision and the plan are Fenollosa's. In the prose I have had but the
part of literary executor; in the plays my work has been that of translator who
has found all the heavy work done for him and who has had but the pleasure
of arranging beauty into the words." ("Note," by Ezra Pound, p. v)

The four plays "Kumasaka," "Nishikigi," "Hagoromo," and "Kagekiyo" are
here reprinted from *Certain Noble Plays of Japan* (1916)—A12. Parts I and II had
appeared, in somewhat abridged and altered form, in *Drama*, Chicago (May
1915) pp. 199–247, as "The Classical Stage of Japan: Ernest Fenollosa's Work
on the Japanese 'Noh,' Edited by Ezra Pound"—C188. Part III, with "Nishikigi" summarised and "Kagekiyo" omitted, was printed, also abridged, in *Quarterly Review*, London (October 1914), pp. 450–77, as "The Classical Drama of
Japan [Edited from Fenollosa's Manuscripts by Ezra Pound]"—C160. (Earlier
periodical publication of individual plays may be determined by reference to
the Index.)

b. *American issue* (1917):

'NOH' | OR | ACCOMPLISHMENT | A Study of the Classical Stage
of Japan | BY | ERNEST FENOLLOSA | AND | EZRA POUND |
[*device*] | NEW YORK – ALFRED A. KNOPF – MCMXVII

viii, 267, [1] pp. front. (port.), music. 23·1 × 15·5 cm. Blue cloth boards, with white paper label printed in black on spine; end-papers; edges untrimmed. Probably issued in dust-jacket.

Published June 1917 at $2.75 (later raised to $3.00); probably 350 sets of the English sheets issued with the first gathering (pp. [i]–viii) reprinted on whiter, smoother paper, with title-page as above. *On verso of title-leaf:* Published June, 1917

Notes: The play "Hagoromo" was reprinted separately as *Japanese Noh Drama Given for the First Time outside of Japan, Staged by Michio Itow for Thursday Evening Club [New York?], January Eighteenth, Nineteen Hundred Twenty Three.* "The Story of Hagoromo Translated by Ernest Fenollosa and Ezra Pound" appears on leaves 6–15 of this pamphlet, the collation of which is as follows: 2 blank leaves, [3]–15 numbered leaves, 1 blank leaf. 17 × 10·5 cm. (The leaves are unopened at right-hand edge and printed on one side only in Japanese style.) *'Noh' or Accomplishment* was reprinted, omitting "Appendix IV," in *The Translations of Ezra Pound* ([1953])—A66—pp. 213–360. In 1959, New Directions published in New York a new edition of the book with title, *The Classic Noh Theatre of Japan, by Ezra Pound and Ernest Fenollosa,* as "New Directions Paperbook P.79." This reprints the text of the first edition, adding W. B. Yeats's introduction from *Certain Noble Plays of Japan* (1916)—A12.

A14   DIALOGUES OF FONTENELLE   1917

a. *First edition, first issue:*

DIALOGUES OF | FONTENELLE | TRANSLATED BY EZRA POUND | LONDON: THE EGOIST LTD. | OAKLEY HOUSE, BLOOMS-BURY ST. | 1917

1 blank leaf, v, 9–54 pp., 1 leaf. 18·4 × 12·3 cm. Heavy gold paper wrappers printed in black on page [i].

Published October 1917 at 1s. 3d.; 500 copies printed. *Imprint on verso of title-leaf and on page* [55]: Printed at the Complete Press West Norwood, London

Contents: I. Alexander and Phriné—II. Dido and Stratonice—III. Anacreon and Aristotle—IV. Homer and Æsop—V. Socrates and Montaigne—VI. Charles V and Erasmus—VII. Agnes Sorel and Roxelane—VIII. Brutus and Faustina—IX. Helen and Fulvia—X. Seneca and Scarron—XI. Strato and Raphael of Urbino—XII. Bombastes Paracelsus and Molière

b. *Second issue* (1939):

Unsold copies of the first edition were re-issued in February 1939 by Laidlaw and Laidlaw in a red dust-jacket printed in black on front: EZRA POUND | DIA-

A. BOOKS AND PAMPHLETS

LOGUES OF | FONTENELLE | A Translation | LAIDLAW & LAIDLAW LTD. | 32, ALFRED PLACE, W.C.I ; and on front flap: RE-ISSUED | FEBRUARY | 1939 | 2/6 | NETT

Note: Ezra Pound's translation of dialogues from the *Nouveaux dialogues des morts* (Paris, 1683) of Bernard de Fontenelle appeared in the *Egoist*, London, in 12 instalments from 1 May 1916 to June 1917. The text was reprinted in *Pavannes and Divisions* (1918)—A15—pp. 49–92, and in *Pavannes and Divagations*—A74, pp. 109–42.

A15   PAVANNES AND DIVISIONS   1918

First edition:

PAVANNES AND DIVISIONS | EZRA POUND | [*device*] | NEW YORK · ALFRED A. KNOPF · MCMXVIII

5 leaves, 262 pp. front. (port.) 21 × 14·5 cm. Blue cloth boards stamped in blind on both covers (with unframed Borzoi device on back cover) and in gold on spine (with publisher's name at base in small capitals, or in capital and lower-case letters); end-papers; top edges stained blue or (later) slate, others roughly trimmed. Grey dust-jacket printed in dark blue. (Still later bindings of grey cloth boards stamped in black, or blue cloth boards stamped in green have framed device on back cover incorporating the words: BORZOI | BOOKS . Grey-cloth copies examined have publisher's name at base of spine in small capitals; blue-cloth copies have the name in capital and lower-case letters. Both these later bindings have all edges trimmed, with top edges unstained.

Published 29 June 1918 at $2.50; number of copies unknown. *On verso of title-leaf:* ... Published June 1918 Printed in the United States of America.

The frontispiece is a reproduction of a photograph of Ezra Pound by E. O. Hoppé.

Dedication on recto of third leaf: To John Quinn

Contents: PAVANNES: Jodindranath Mawhwor's Occupation—An Anachronism at Chinon—Religio, or The Child's Guide to Knowledge—Aux étuves de Wiesbaden—L'Homme moyen sensuel [poem, with note]—Pierrots [poem]—Stark Realism. This Little Pig Went to Market—Twelve Dialogues of Fontenelle—DIVISIONS: A Retrospect [including "A Few Don'ts" and "Prolegomena"]—Remy de Gourmont [I–II]—Mr. Hueffer and the Prose Tradition in Verse—The Rev. G. Crabbe, LL.B.—Arnold Dolmetsch [(1915)]—Vers libre and Arnold Dolmetsch—"Dubliners" and Mr. James Joyce—Meditations [formerly "Meditatio"]—Troubadours: Their Sorts and Conditions—Notes on Elizabethan Classicists [formerly "Elizabethan Classicists"]—APPENDICES: I. The Serious Artist—II. Extract from a Letter to "The Dial"—III. Ezra Pound Files Exceptions—IV. Vortographs—V. Arnold Dolmetsch [(1917)]

A16   THE FOURTH CANTO   1919

a. *First edition, first (proof) state:*

THE FOURTH CANTO | by | EZRA POUND | Forty | Copies of this poem, numbered 1–40 | on Japanese Vellum set up and printed by John | Rodker at his press. Completed Oct: 4 1919 | This is No. [*number written in*] | [*device*] | THE OVID PRESS [London]

1 leaf, 2–4 numbered leaves. 31 × 23 cm. (approx.) Unsewn; untrimmed.

Distributed gratis October 1919. Printed on the outside of a single sheet folded twice. An unknown number of copies had already been printed when Ezra Pound requested that the corrections described below should be made. A copy marked by Pound "proof not in series," plus copies numbered 1, 2, and 27 (the last marked "Proof" by John Rodker) have been located. The imposition was faulty for at least two of these early copies, with the result that leaves [1] and 4 are noticeably shorter than leaves 2 and 3. (In copy number 2, leaves [1] and 4 are 26·6 cm. long, and leaves 2 and 3 are 35 cm.)

b. *Second state:*

THE FOURTH CANTO | by | EZRA POUND | Forty | Copies of this poem, numbered 1–40 | on Japanese Vellum set up and privately printed | by John Rodker. Completed | Oct: 4 1919 | This is No. [*number written in*] | [*device*] | THE OVID PRESS [London]

Pagination and size as in A16a.

Besides the indicated alteration in the wording of the colophon, four minor changes in spacing and three in punctuation were made in the text, plus these corrections: leaf 3, line 9 ("Ivory dipping in silver,") added; line 8 up, "glare" for "flare"; line 3 up, "blanch-white" for "beach-white"; leaf 4, line 10 up, "Salve REGinà." for "Salve regina." Copy numbered 3 (Yale), apparently prepared especially for the author, is printed not on a single sheet but on four separate leaves of white wove paper, unwatermarked, measuring 34·7 × 24·7 cm.

Notes: On a rough proof of the text sent to the *Dial*, New York, Ezra Pound wrote: "forty copies *privately* printed, for author's convenience, NOT published." The text is reprinted in *Dial*, New York (June 1920) pp. [689]–692—C579, in *Poems 1918–21* ([1921])—A21—pp. 73–77, in *A Draft of XVI. Cantos* (1925)—A26—pp. [13]–16, and in later volumes of the Cantos.

A17   QUIA PAUPER AMAVI   [1919]

a. *First edition, ordinary copies:*

QUIA PAUPER | AMAVI | EZRA POUND | LONDON: THE EGO-IST LTD. | 23 ADELPHI TERRACE HOUSE, W.C.2

A. BOOKS AND PAMPHLETS

51, [1] pp. 25·4 × 15·9 cm. Olive-green paper boards, green cloth black, with buff paper label printed in black up the spine; end-papers; top and fore edges untrimmed. (Printed on wove paper, unwatermarked.)

Published October 1919 at 6s.; 500 copies printed. *Imprint on page* [52]: The De La More Press Ltd. 32 George Street Hanover Square London W I

Dedication (?) on page [4]: Orfeo

All examined copies have the misprint in line 11 up on page 34, "Wherefore" for "Wherefrom"; the error was corrected in manuscript by the author in most copies.

Contents: Langue d'Oc ("Alba"; "I. Compleynt of a gentleman who has been waiting outside for some time (Girart Bornello)"; "II. Avril. (Guilhem de Peitieu)"; "III. Descant on a Theme by Cerclamon"; "IV. Vergier"; "V. Canzon ('I only, and who elrische pain support') Arnaut Daniel")—Moeurs contemporaines ("I. Mr. Styrax"; "II. Clara"; "III. Soirée"; "IV. Sketch 48 b 11"; "V. 'Nodier raconte . . . '"; "VI. Stele"; "VII. I vecchii"; "VIII. Ritratto")—Three Cantos [Cantos II, III, and I, all three differing radically from the eventual final texts]—Homage to Sextus Propertius, I–XII

b. *Special copies:*

25·4 × 16·6 cm. Grey paper boards, tan cloth back, with buff paper label printed in black up the spine; end-papers; edges untrimmed. (Printed on hand-made paper, watermarked: CANSELL)

Published October 1919, simultaneously with the ordinary copies, at 10s. 6d.; 110 copies printed. *Colophon (page* [2]): The edition on Handmade Paper is limited to one hundred copies, of which this is No. [*number written in by Ezra Pound, with signature either below or on title-page opposite*] (There were 10 extra copies for presentation numbered I to X, some of them marked by Pound "out of series.") In all the special copies, the first two leaves (half-title and title) are of a different paper (watermarked: MONCK . . . | KEN . . .) from that used for the text. In most of these copies the misprint on page 34 has been corrected in manuscript by the author.

A18   INSTIGATIONS   [1920]

First edition:

INSTIGATIONS | OF | EZRA POUND | TOGETHER WITH | AN ESSAY | ON THE | CHINESE | WRITTEN | CHARACTER | BY | ERNEST FENOLLOSA | BONI AND LIVERIGHT | PUBLISHERS NEW YORK

viii, 388 pp., 2 blank leaves. 21 × 15 cm. Blue cloth boards stamped in blind on front cover and in gold on spine, with top edges stained blue, or (later?)

purple cloth stamped in blind on front cover and in yellow-green on spine, with top edges stained slate; other edges (both bindings) roughly trimmed; front end-paper (final blank leaf pasted down as back end-paper). White dust-jacket printed in black and yellow, with design by H. Brodzky on the front.

Published 25 April 1920 at $3.00; 800 copies printed. *On verso of title-leaf:* ... Printed in the United States of America

Dedication on page [v]: To My Father Homer L. Pound

Contents: I. A Study in French Poets [incorporating, at end, "Unanimisme," "De Bosschère's Study of Elskamp," and "Albert Mockel and 'La Wallonie'"]—II. Henry James (["In Explanation"], "A Shake Down," "The Middle Years," "The Notes to 'The Ivory Tower'")—III. Remy de Gourmont, a Distinction, Followed by Notes—IV. In the Vortex ("T. S. Eliot"; "Joyce" [incorporating a note on "Ulysses" and adding "De Goncourt"—C373]; "Wyndham Lewis"; "An Historical Essayist: Lytton Strachey"; "A List of Books"; "The New Poetry"; "A Distinction"; "The Classics 'Escape'" [incorporating, at end, "Cantico del sole," a poem])—V. Our Tetrarchal Précieuse (A Divagation from Jules Laforgue)—VI. Genesis, or The First Book in the Bible—VII. Arnaut Daniel [incorporating in Part II as illustrations original Provençal texts and verse translations of poems III, IV, V (one strophe only), VI (third strophe only), VIII, IX, XI (strophe one, two, four, and conclusion), XII, "Er vei vermeils, vertz, blaus, blancx, gruocs" (one strophe only), XV, XVI, and XVII]—VIII. Translators of Greek: ("Early Translators of Homer. I. Hughes Salel"; "II. Andreas Divus"; "Translation of Aeschylus")—IX. The Chinese Written Character as a Medium for Poetry, by Ernest Fenollosa [edited, with notes, by Ezra Pound]

Notes: Apparently several lots of paper of slightly varying quality were used indiscriminately. In some copies (of both bindings), the final gathering (pp. 377–[392]) is printed on paper which has remained noticeably whiter than that used in the rest of the volume.

Three lines from the note on Joyce's "Ulysses" are reprinted in a broadside, *Ulysses by James Joyce. Extracts from advance Press Notices* ... (Paris, Shakespeare & Co. [1921]), advertising the novel as "To be published in the Autumn of 1921 [*sic*]".

A19   HUGH SELWYN MAUBERLEY   1920

First edition:

[*In black:*] Hugh Selwyn | Mauberley | BY | E. P. | [*in blue: device*] | [*in black:*] THE OVID PRESS | 1920 [London, John Rodker]

1 blank leaf, 3 leaves, 9–28 pp., 1 leaf, 1 blank leaf. 25·6 × 16 cm. Brown paper boards, tan (or green) cloth back, with white paper label printed in black inlaid on front cover; initial and final blank leaf pasted down as front and back end-paper respectively; edges untrimmed. (Printed on hand-made paper water-

A. BOOKS AND PAMPHLETS

marked: HANDMADE J WHATMAN 1917 [–1918] ENGLAND [or] HANDMADE J WHAT-
MAN TURKEY MILL, 1917 ENGLAND)

Fly-title: H. S. Mauberley (Life and Contacts)

Published June 1920 at 15s. *Colophon (page* [29]): This edition of 200 copies is
the third book of the Ovid Press: was printed by John Rodker: and completed
April 23rd. 1920 Of this edition:—15 Copies on Japan Vellum numbered 1–15
& not for sale. 20 Signed copies numbered 16–35 165 Unsigned copies numbered 36–200 The initials & colophon by E. Wadsworth. . . . *On page* [8]: This
is Number [*number written in upon a background of short printed lines*]

The 20 signed copies, published simultaneously with the unsigned copies at
25s., have Ezra Pound's signature on page [8] and are bound in brown cloth
boards with tan cloth back, but are otherwise identical. The 15 copies on Japan
vellum collate as follows: 2 blank leaves, 3 leaves, 1 blank leaf, 2 leaves, 9–28
numbered leaves, 1 leaf, 3 blank leaves. They measure 20·4 × 14·2 cm., and
are bound in white parchment with red leather label lettered in gold inlaid on
front cover, with plain end-papers and edges untrimmed. The sheets for these
copies, numbered and signed on recto of leaf [8], were printed on one side only,
a sheet from the outer and one from the inner forme being placed back to back
and folded for each gathering, with the result that odd-numbered printed leaves
face to the left, even-numbered ones to the right. Copies were issued unopened,
with printed pages protected by leaves of tissue laid in, and with a natural silk
ribbon marker. (Although these copies on Japanese vellum were theoretically
not for sale, Pound wrote to his mother on 20 August 1920: "Signed copies of
Mauberley all gone, save 2 or 3 vellum copies, bound in full parchment at £3/
3." Will Ransom, in his *Private Presses and Their Books* (New York, 1929), p. 373,
states that ". . . fewer than the given number of copies were actually issued." A
number of "out of series" copies were bound in brown paper boards with green
cloth back, and some sets of sheets were not bound up.)

Contents: PART I: [I] E. P. Ode pour l'élection de son sépulchre—II. "The age
demanded an image"—III. "The tea-rose tea-gown, etc."—IV. "These fought,
in any case,"—V. "There died a myriad,"—[VI] Yeux glauques—[VII] Siena mi
fe', disfecemi Maremma—[VIII] Brennbaum—[IX] Mr. Nixon—X. "Beneath
the sagging roof"—XI. "'Conservatrix of Milésien'"—XII. "'Daphne with her
thighs in bark'"—Envoi (1919)—PART II: 1920 (Mauberley): I. "Turned from
the 'eau-forte | Par Jaquemart'"—II. "For three years diabolus in the scale"—
[III] "The age demanded"—IV. "Scattered Moluccas"—[V] Medallion

Notes: A few notes on the poem, sent by Pound to one of the editors in June
1947, are incorporated in the notes to "Hugh Selwyn Mauberley," in *Modern
Poetry, American and British, Edited by Kimon Friar and John Malcolm Brinnin* (New
York, [1951]), pp. 527–31.

The full text of the poem, incorporating four slight changes sanctioned by Pound
and with a detailed analysis, is included in John J. Espey's *Ezra Pound's Mauberley, a Study in Composition* (London [1955]) and (Berkeley and Los Angeles,
Calif., 1955). The text is also reprinted in *Poems 1918–21* ([1921])—A20—pp.
49–69, in *Personae* (1926)—A27—pp. [185]—204, in *Selected Poems* ([1928])—

A. BOOKS AND PAMPHLETS

A30—pp. [155]—172, and in other later volumes. In 1958 it was printed with "Homage to Sextus Propertius" in a single volume as *Diptych Rome-London*—A75.

A20   UMBRA   1920

a. *First edition, ordinary copies:*

UMBRA | THE EARLY POEMS OF | EZRA POUND | All that he now wishes to keep in circulation from | "Personae," "Exultations," "Ripostes," etc. With | translations from Guido Cavalcanti and | Arnaut Daniel and poems by | the late T. E. HULME | LONDON | ELKIN MATHEWS, CORK STREET | MCMXX

128 pp. 19·7 × 14·3 cm. Grey paper boards with canvas back lettered in blue on front cover and on spine; end-papers; fore and bottom edges roughly trimmed. Grey-blue dust-jacket printed in black.

Published June 1920 at 8s.; 1000 copies printed. *Imprint on verso of title-leaf:* The Riverside Press Limited, Edinburgh

On page [5]: Dedication from "Personae" This Book is for Mary Moore of Trenton, if She Wants It Other volumes from which this is collected were dedicated to Wm. Brooke Smith (in memoriam); to Carlos T. Chester; to Wm. Carlos Williams, and the intended "Arnaut Daniel" to Wm. Pierce Shepard.

Contents: PERSONAE: Grace before Song—La Fraisne—Cino—Na Audiart—Villonaud for This Yule—A Villonaud: Ballad of the Gibbet—Mesmerism—Famam librosque cano—Praise of Ysolt—For E[ugene]. McC[artney]—At the Heart o' Me—The White Stag—In Durance—Marvoil—And Thus in Nineveh—EXULTATIONS: Guido Invites You Thus—Night Litany—Sestina: Altaforte—Piere Vidal Old—Ballad of the Goodly Fere—Laudantes decem pulchritudinis Johannae Templi—Aux belles de Londres—Francesca—Prayer [formerly "Greek Epigram"]—The Tree—On His Own Face in a Glass—The Eyes—Nils Lykke—Planh for the Young English King—Alba [innominata]—Planh. Of White Thoughts He Saw in a Forest—FROM "CANZONI": Au jardin [formerly "Und Drang," XII]—FROM "POETRY AND DRAMA" FOR FEBRUARY 1912: Oboes I. For a Beery Voice—II. After Heine ["Translations from Heine, VIII"]—RIPOSTES: Silet—In exitum cuiusdam—The Tomb at Akr Çaar—Portrait d'une femme—N[ew]. Y[ork].—A Girl—"Phasellus ille"—An Object—Quies—The Seafarer—[Echoes, II:] The Cloak—Δώρια—Apparuit—The Needle—Sub mare—Plunge—A Virginal—Pan Is Dead—An Immorality—Dieu! Qu'il la fait—The Picture—Of Jacopo del Sellaio—The Return—Effects of Music upon a Company of People: I. Deux mouvements; II. From a Thing by Schumann—Phanopoeia, I., II., and III.—The Alchemist, unpublished 1912—Cantus planus—TRANSLATIONS: From the Sonnets of Guido Cavalcanti: [I–III, V–VIII, XV, XXVI,

A. BOOKS AND PAMPHLETS

XXXIII, XXXV, Madrigal, Ballata I]—From the Ballate of Guido Cavalcanti: [II–III, V–VII, XI–XIV]—Five Canzoni of Arnaut Daniel: [IX, VIII, XII, IV, XVI]—THE COMPLETE POETICAL WORKS OF T. E. HULME [with "Poem, Abbreviated [by E. P.] from the Conversation of Mr T. E. H."]—NOTES: 1. Note to "La Fraisne"—2. Personae and Portraits—Bibliography

b. *Special copies:*

19·9 × 14·8 cm. Grey paper boards with white parchment back lettered in gold; grey end-papers; top edges gilt, fore edges untrimmed, bottom edges roughly trimmed. Natural silk ribbon marker.

Published June 1920, simultaneously with the ordinary copies, at 25*s.* Imprint on verso of title-leaf as in ordinary copies.

Colophon (page [6]): One hundred copies of this Edition have been printed on English hand-made paper, for England and America, numbered and signed by the Author, of which this is No. [*number written in on a row of printed dots and signed by Ezra Pound, in some copies with year*] (There were at least four extra copies for presentation lettered A to D. Of these copy A has binding identical with that of copies 1–100, but is marked by Pound "out of series" and is signed with initials only; copy D is bound in white cloth without lettering or stamping and with marbled end-papers; it is also marked by Pound "out of series" and is signed with initials and year.)

A21   POEMS 1918–21   [1921]

First edition:

POEMS 1918–21 | INCLUDING | THREE PORTRAITS | AND | FOUR CANTOS | BY | EZRA POUND | BONI AND LIVERIGHT | PUBLISHERS NEW YORK

1 blank leaf, 4 leaves, 11–90 pp., 3 blank leaves. 24·2 × 16·6 cm. Blue paper boards with white imitation-vellum back stamped in gold on spine: Poems | [*ornament*] | EZRA | POUND | BONI & | LIVERIGHT ; end-papers; fore and bottom edges untrimmed. Grey dust-jacket printed in two shades of blue.

Published 8 December 1921 at $2.50; number of copies unknown. *On verso of title-leaf:* . . . Printed in the United States of America

Contents: PORTRAITS: 1. Homage to Sextus Propertius—2. Langue d'Oc ("Alba," I–V)—Moeurs contemporaines—3. Hugh Selwyn Mauberley—CANTOS: The Fourth Canto—The Fifth Canto—The Sixth Canto—The Seventh Canto [the first three in early versions, the seventh differing very slightly from its final form]

Note: The brief bibliography on the verso of the half-title-leaf, headed: "Ezra Pound's work is now contained in the following volumes:", lists "Physique de l'amour by Remy de Gourmont"—A22—under "Translations," with date 1921, although the book did not actually appear until August 1922.

A22 THE NATURAL PHILOSOPHY [1922] OF LOVE

a. *First edition:*

[*Within thick-thin rule border:*] THE | NATURAL PHILOSOPHY | OF LOVE | [*rule*] | BY | REMY DE GOURMONT | Translated with a Postscript By | EZRA POUND | [*rule*] | [*device: plain BL monogram in intaglio, within oval frame*] | [*rule*] | BONI AND LIVERIGHT | Publishers New York

ix, 11–222 pp., 1 blank leaf. 20·8 × 14·2 cm. Green cloth boards with tan paper label printed in brown (with 14-unit—or, later, 6-unit—ornament at top and bottom, and with "Gourmont" measuring 1·9 cm.) on spine; end-papers; top edges stained green. Blue dust-jacket printed in blue.

Published 10 August 1922 at $5.00; number of copies unknown. *On verso of title-leaf:* ... Printed in the United States of America. [Later printings, not so identified, have variant B&L monogram, unframed, on the title-page. These have label with 6-unit ornaments. Some copies, with B&L monogram stamped in blind on front cover, have label with "Gourmont" measuring 1·9 cm.; other copies, on slightly thicker paper, are unstamped and have label with "Gourmont" measuring 2·2 cm. In these copies the staining of the top edges varies. One such copy located has dust-jacket imprinted "3rd Edition ... 1925".]

A translation of Remy de Gourmont's *Physique de l'amour; essai sur l'instinct sexuel* (first published in Paris in 1903). "Translator's Postscript": pp. 206–19, dated: 21 June 1921. "Bibliography: Principal Works Consulted": pp. 220–2.

Note: Tipped in at the front in some copies is a slip: "Important Notice This work is supplied to the Bookseller on condition that all discretion shall be used in its sale or distribution. . . ." (The slip measures 8·1 × 12·5 cm., and has been noted only in copies of the first printing. A similar statement appears on the dust-jacket of later copies.)

b. *First English edition* (1926):

[*In blue:*] THE NATURAL | PHILOSOPHY | OF LOVE | [*in black:*] BY | [*in blue:*] REMY DE GOURMONT | [*in black:*] TRANSLATED WITH A POSTSCRIPT | BY | EZRA POUND | LONDON | [*in blue:*] THE CASANOVA SOCIETY | [*in black:*] 1926

1 blank leaf, x, 182, [1] pp. 26·4 × 19·7 cm. Grey paper boards, with blue cloth back, stamped in gold on spine (with "LONDON" at the foot in either italic letters

approximately 4 cm. or Roman approximately 3 cm. high), paper and cloth varying slightly in shade and texture); end-papers; edges untrimmed. White dust-jacket printed in lavender.

Published September 1926 at 21*s.*; 1500 copies printed. *On verso of title-leaf:* Printed in Great Britain by William Brendon and Son, Ltd., Plymouth *Colophon (on slip tipped in before first blank leaf):* This edition is limited to 1,500 copies on deckle-edged laid paper watermarked ANTIQUE DE LUXE of which 1,430 are for sale in England and the United States. This copy is number [*number written in on a row of printed dots*]

A23   INDISCRETIONS   1923

First edition:

INDISCRETIONS; | OR, | UNE REVUE DE DEUX MONDES. | BY | EZRA POUND. | [*Device*] | PARIS | THREE MOUNTAINS PRESS | 1923

1 blank leaf, 3 leaves, 9–62 pp., 1 leaf. 26·7 × 17·3 cm. Grey paper boards stamped in red and black on front cover, with yellow cloth back; end-papers; edges untrimmed.

Published March 1923 at 45 francs (later identified as "The Inquest, Edited by Ezra Pound, I"). *Colophon (verso of half-title-leaf):* Three hundred copies of this book were printed on Rives hand-made paper and the type distributed. This copy is Number [*number written in*] ... *Colophon (page* [63]): Hand-printed at Paris, in the Isle Saint Louis, by William Bird, amateur printer, with the collaboration of Roger Dévigne. Caslon Old-Face set by Philip Beaugié. Press-work by Robert Dill. January, 1923.

Dedication on page [7]: To A. R. Orage at whose request this fragment was first hitched together.

Notes: Although this book is not actually identified as part of "The Inquest," the author's "Postscript" (p. 62) refers to "the whole series, to which my fragment is ... a sort of foreword. They [*i.e.* the succeeding authors] have set out from five very different points to tell the truth about *mœurs contemporaines*, without fake, melodrama, conventional ending. The other MSS. are considerably more interesting than is this one of mine, which couldn't have come anywhere else in the series, and which, yet, may have some sort of relation to the series, and even a function, if only as a foil to Bill Williams' *The Great American Novel.*" The other volumes in the series, of similar format, were: II. *Women & Men* (1923) by Ford Madox Ford; III. *Elimus* (1923) by B. C. Windeler, with designs by Dorothy Shakespear [Pound]; IV. *The Great American Novel* (1923) by William Carlos Williams; V. *England* (1923) by B. M. G.-Adams, and VI. *In Our Time* (1924) by Ernest Hemingway, with portrait frontispiece by Henry Strater. The first four titles were limited to 300 copies, the fifth to 150, and the sixth to

170. Only the last one is identified (in its colophon) as part of the series. Ezra Pound's "editorial direction" was limited to his selecting and securing the manuscripts for inclusion. A broadside announcing the series, drafted by Pound, was issued by the Three Mountains Press in 1922—E2g. Another broadside concerning the series entitled "Printer's Notice," drafted by William Bird, measuring 23·8 × 14·8 cm., was loosely laid in some copies.

In a letter to Laurence Pollinger on 7 June 1936, Pound wrote concerning the series: "The little books were spaced too far apart to have the effect I meant. I mean Bill Bird took too long getting 'em out. I have always wanted 'em pubd/ as a single volume. . . . To these one shd/ add something of R[obert] McAlmon's . . ." (Pound had suggested in a letter to Bird in 1924 that a few of the then remaining copies of the series should be bound up together as *The Inquest* and possibly sold at $7.50, but his suggestion was not carried out.)

Indiscretions is a thinly disguised autobiographical fragment concerned chiefly with Pound's father. It first appeared in the *New Age*, London, in 12 instalments from 27 May to 12 August 1920, and was reprinted in *Pavannes and Divagations*—A74—pp. 3–51.

A24　　　THE CALL OF THE ROAD　　　[1923]

First edition:

THE | CALL OF THE ROAD | BY | EDOUARD ESTAUNIÉ | Translated from the French | [*device*] | BONI AND LIVERIGHT | PUBLISHERS NEW YORK

346 pp., 3 blank leaves. 19·7 × 13·3 cm. Black cloth boards stamped in grey on front cover and on spine; decorated end-papers; top edges stained yellow, fore edges roughly trimmed, bottom edges untrimmed. White dust-jacket printed in khaki and silver.

Published 9 November 1923 at $2.00; number of copies unknown. *On verso of title-leaf:* . . . Printed in the United States of America

"Translation by Hiram Janus [*i.e.* Ezra Pound]." (*Dust-jacket*)

After completing his translation of Remy de Gourmont's *Physique de l'amour*—A22, Pound on 4 January 1922 signed an agreement with Horace Liveright under the terms of which he would translate from French into English "to the best of his ability and with reasonable promptitude," such books as Mr Liveright chose, and would be paid a minimum of $500 during the two-year period covered by the contract. It was agreed that Pound would not be required to sign his own name to the translation of any work that he considered "a disgrace to humanity or too imbecile to be borne." (For the text of the agreement— obviously drafted by Pound himself—see Charles Norman's *Ezra Pound* (1960)— B69—p. 253.) Although the translation of Estaunié's *L'Appel de la route* (first published in Paris in 1922) was issued anonymously so far as the volume itself was concerned, and attributed to the pseudonymous "Hiram Janus" on its dust-jacket, Boni and Liveright's *Fall Catalogue for 1923* revealed the identity of the translator and somewhat misrepresented his opinion of the novel: "Ezra Pound, who is responsible for its exquisite English translation calls it one of the most thrilling stories of adventurous mystery that he has ever read."

A25   ANTHEIL AND THE TREATISE   1924
ON HARMONY

a. *First edition, ordinary copies:*

ANTHEIL | AND | THE TREATISE ON HARMONY | BY | EZRA POUND | PARIS | THREE MOUNTAINS PRESS | 29, QUAI D'AN-JOU, 29 | — | 1924

4 leaves, 106 pp., 1 leaf, 2 blank leaves. 18·8 × 12·3 cm. Heavy red paper wrappers printed in black on pages [i] and [iv] (with price on page [i]), and up the spine; edges untrimmed.

Published October 1924 at 10 francs; 400 copies printed. *Imprint on page* [107]: Printed at Dijon by Maurice Darantière M.CM.XXIV *Colophon (verso of half-title-leaf):* Forty copies were printed on Arches paper and numbered from 1 to 40. [Ordinary copies are printed on unwatermarked paper.]

Contents: The Treatise on Harmony [including "Prolegomena"]—George Antheil (Retrospect) [with "Postscript. July 1924."—[Notes for Performers by] William Atheling [with Marginalia Emitted by George Antheil. Memoranda from *The New Age* Selected by Agnes Bedford]—Varia

b. *Special copies:*

Title-page, pagination, and size as in ordinary copies. Heavy red paper wrappers printed in black on pages [i] and [iv] (without price on page [i]) and up the spine; edges untrimmed. Issued in a sealed glassine outer wrapper.

Published October 1924 at 40 francs; 40 copies printed. Imprint on page [107] as in ordinary copies. *Colophon (verso of half-title-leaf):* Forty copies were printed on Arches paper and numbered from 1 to 40. [*Short rule, followed by number stamped in.* Printed on Arches paper so watermarked.]

Notes: The special copies at 40 francs were sold unsigned. Some were subsequently signed by George Antheil, some by Ezra Pound, and some by both. (In 1930 Pound had in his possession 15 copies signed by Antheil only.)

Unsold copies (on both papers) were later issued with a buff paper label pasted over the imprint on the title-page: [*Within ornamental type border:*] CONTACT EDITIONS | 29, QUAI D'ANJOU, PARIS . 100 copies on ordinary paper were imported for sale in the United States by A. and C. Boni, New York. The Pound-Bird correspondence indicates that this book was actually published by Pound himself and Three Mountains Press—and, later, Contact Editions—acted merely as its distributors.

c. *First American edition* (1927):

[*Within ruled border:*] ANTHEIL | AND THE | TREATISE ON HAR-MONY | WITH | SUPPLEMENTARY NOTES | BY | EZRA POUND | CHICAGO | PASCAL COVICI, Publisher, INC. | MCMXXVII

2 blank leaves, 150 pp., 3 blank leaves. 19·6 × 13·5 cm. Brown cloth boards stamped in black on front cover and down the spine; end-papers; top edges stained brown. White dust-jacket printed in black and green.

Published 14 September 1927 at $2.00, number of copies unknown. *On verso of title-leaf:* ... Printed in the U.S.A.

The contents are identical with those of the Paris edition save for the addition of two notes on Antheil headed, respectively, "New Masses, March, 1927" ["Workshop Orchestration"]—C690—pp. 137–41, and "The New Criterion, August [*i.e.* October], 1926" ["Antheil, 1924–1926"]—C686—pp. 142–50.

Note: "The Treatise on Harmony" was first published in England in 1962 in *Patria Mia and The Treatise on Harmony* (London, Peter Owen Limited)—A63b—pp. [75]–95.

A26   A DRAFT OF XVI. CANTOS   1925

First edition:

A DRAFT OF | XVI. | CANTOS OF EZRA POUND | for the Beginning of a Poem | of some Length | now first made into a Book | with Initials by | HENRY STRATER | [*device*] | PARIS | THREE MOUNTAINS PRESS | M. CM. XXV.

65 pp., 1 leaf. 39·2 × 26·2 cm. Three-quarter white vellum and decorated paper boards (of varying colours and design) (or, later—*circa* September 1928—full red vellum boards) lettered in gold on upper-left front cover: XVI. CANTOS | OF [*or:* of] | EZRA POUND; end-papers; edges untrimmed.

Published late January 1925 at 400 francs. Printed on laid paper watermarked with a six-pointed star and the words: EZRA POUND CANTOS [*followed by the device of the Three Mountains Press*] Each Canto has caption and ornamental initial printed in red with illustrative design in background in black or in red and black. *Imprint on page* [67]: Printed [by William Bird] at the Three Mountains Press Île Saint-Louis, Paris May–December, 1924 *Colophon* (*page* [2]): The Edition of Ninety Copies consists of Five on Imperial Japan paper autographed by the author lettered A to E Fifteen on Whatman paper numbered I to XV and Seventy on Roma paper specially watermarked numbered 1 to 70 [*number printed in*]

A. BOOKS AND PAMPHLETS

The five copies on Imperial Japan paper were announced in the prospectus (see below) as to be bound in full Royal blue morocco and for sale at 1600 francs, but only three of these may actually have been bound in 1925, all sent to the binder after the copies on Roma paper described above; copy B was still in the original sheets unbound in 1981; copy D was bound in full blue morocco stamped in gold at corners with tree design modified from tail-pieces for Cantos XII and XIV, on centre front cover with reduced version of wheel design used as tail-piece for Canto VII, and on spine: XVI. | CANTOS | OF | EZRA POUND; all edges gilt; copy E was received from the binder, A.-J. Gonon in Paris, in July 1932 (it is bound in full red morocco, stamped in gold as in copy D. It has inside covers lined with red watered silk, edged with blue morocco inlay, and extra marbled-paper end-leaves, and is signed: A.-J. GONON REL. It has three fly-leaves of Japanese vellum at front and back); these three copies (B and E—both now at Trinity College Library, Hartford, Connecticut; D listed in Catalogue 31 of Black Sun Books, New York, 1975) have the author's signature below the colophon on page [2]. Copies on Whatman paper (watermarked: HANDMADE J WHATMAN 1924 [and other years as early as 1912] ENGLAND), published simultaneously, are bound in white vellum boards with turned edges and are lettered in gold on the upper centre of the front cover: XVI. CANTOS of EZRA POUND [or] XVI. CANTOS | OF | EZRA POUND; these were for sale at 800 francs. In addition to the above, a special lot of at least six other unnumbered copies was assembled from extra and proof sheets and bound in paper wrappers; these copies bear in place of a number on the colophon page the printed words: AUTHOR'S PROOF . At least two of these have pages [1]–6 and [11]–12 and end-papers printed on Roma paper, with the rest of the text on unwatermarked paper of poor quality; one has pages [1]–60 on Japan vellum, with pages 61–[68] on proofing paper. The author's own "proof" copy had apparently been received at Rapallo on 28 January 1925; others were sent at Ezra Pound's request, in June, to Agnes Bedford, Ford Madox Ford, Homer L. Pound, and Mrs B. M. [G.-Adams] Scratton. (Some unbound out-of-series copies were sent to the author. At least one on Roma paper—now at Cornell—bound by the publisher's daughter in 1933, has printed designation as author's proof.) Some extra sheets were sent to the author or were retained by the publisher and still exist—at Brunnenburg, the Lilly Library, and in the possession of OSP and DG. One of these on Japan vellum containing the first four pages of Canto IX ([31]–34) was included in the exhibition of Ezra Pound's writings at Merano in 1958 and is listed in the catalogue (*Mostra delle edizioni Poundiane 1908–1958*) as a separately published item, "The Ninth Canto (senza luogo e data).")

A few misprints (*e.g.* "theit" for "their" in line 15 on page 48, "head" for "heads" in line 10 on page 58) and the repetition at the top of page 52 of the last three lines on page 51 remained uncorrected. (Two of these three lines are again repeated in *A Draft of XXX Cantos* (1930)—A31a, b, and in the American edition of the same book—A31c, but the passage is correctly printed in the English edition—A31d.)

Note: A prospectus, including page [13] (opening of the Fourth Canto) as a specimen, was printed and distributed beginning in April 1924. (Pound ob-

38

jected to certain details of the decorative initial for the Fourth Canto and at one time requested that 20 copies of the book be printed with that initial altered or omitted—see *The Letters*—A64—p. 188—but the changes were not made and such special copies were not prepared.) A four-page folder was issued in November 1924 as an invitation to an exhibition of specimen pages of the edition, held from the 22nd to the 29th of that month at Shakespeare and Company, Paris; it contains a description of the edition on pages [2–3], and a subscription form on page [4]. A subscriber making the request when ordering his copy could have his name printed at the end of the colophon on page [22]. It is certain that some copies remained unbound because unsubscribed for; these were bound as distributed over a period of years, with the result that major and minor binding variants exist. The copies on Roma paper bound in red vellum boards were in fact issued by John Rodker in London in 1928 with similarly bound copies of *A Draft of the Cantos 17–27*—A29.

A27   PERSONAE   1926

a. *First edition:*

PERSONÆ | THE COLLECTED POEMS OF | EZRA POUND | Including | RIPOSTES | LUSTRA | HOMAGE TO SEXTUS PROPERTIUS | H. S. MAUBERLEY | [*device*] | NEW YORK | BONI & LIVERIGHT | 1926

7 leaves, 231 pp., 1 blank leaf. front. (port.), 3 plates. 23·2 × 14·5 cm. Dark blue cloth boards stamped in gold on front cover and on spine; end-papers; edges untrimmed. Brown dust-jacket printed in black.

Published 22 December 1926 at $3.50; number of copies unknown. *On verso of title-leaf:* ... Printed in the United States

Dedications, recto of third leaf: This book is for Mary Moore of Trenton, if she wants it; *page* [57]: To William Carlos Williams ... ; *page* [79]: Vail de Lencour ...

The frontispiece is a reproduction of a drawing of Ezra Pound by Henri Gaudier-Brzeska. The first plate, inserted after page [58], reproduces Dorothy Shakespear Pound's design for the cover of *Ripostes* (1915)—A8d. The two remaining plates, placed after page 60 and page 72, respectively, are reproductions of drawings by Gaudier-Brzeska in a copy of *Ripostes* (at Brunnenburg in 1981).

"Edition [*i.e.* selection] to date of all Ezra Pound's poems except the unfinished 'Cantos.'" (*Recto of fourth leaf*)

Contents: PERSONÆ OF EZRA POUND (1908, 1909, 1910): The Tree—Threnos—La Fraisne—Cino—Na Audiart—Villonaud for This Yule—A Villonaud: Ballad of the Gibbet—Mesmerism—Famam librosque cano—Praise of Ysolt—De Aegypto—For E[ugene]. McC[artney]—In Durance—Marvoil—And Thus in Nineveh—The White Stag—Guido Invites You Thus—Night Litany—Sestina:

A. BOOKS AND PAMPHLETS

Altaforte—Piere Vidal Old—Paracelsus in excelsis—Ballad of the Goodly Fere—On His Own Face in a Glass—The Eyes—Francesca—Planh for the Young English King—Ballatteta—Prayer for His Lady's Life—Speech for Psyche in the Golden Book of Apuleius—"Blandula, tenulla, vagula"—Erat hora—Rome—Her Monument, the Image Cut Thereon—Satiemus [formerly "Victorian Eclogues," II]—Mr Housman's Message—Translations and Adaptations from Heine [I–VIII]—The House of Splendour [formerly "Und Drang, VII"]—The Flame [formerly "Und Drang, VIII"]—Horae beatae inscriptio [formerly "Und Drang, IX"]—The Altar [formerly "Und Drang, X"]—Au salon [formerly "Und Drang, XI"]—Au jardin [formerly "Und Drang, XII"]—RIPOSTES (1912) [omitting "Echoes, I," "An Immorality," "Salve Pontifex (A. C. S.)," "Effects of Music upon a Company of People, I–II," and "The Complete Poetical Works of T. E. Hulme," and adding "The Alchemist" from *Umbra*]—LUSTRA [contents of first impression (A11a) through "Provincia deserta," omitting "Preference," and adding "Ancient Music" and "The Lake Isle"]—CATHAY [omitting "The Seafarer" (already included above) and adding "Sennin Poem by Kakuhaku," "A Ballad of the Mulberry Road," "Old Idea of Choan by Rosoriu," and "To-Em-Mei's 'The Unmoving Cloud'"]—POEMS FROM BLAST (1914): Salutation the Third—Monumentum aere, etc.—Come My Cantilations—Before Sleep—Post mortem conspectu [formerly "His Vision of a Certain Lady Post Mortem"]—Fratres minores—POEMS FROM LUSTRA (1915): Near Perigord—Villanelle: The Psychological Hour—Dans un omnibus de Londres—Pagani's, November 8—To a Friend Writing on Cabaret Dancers—Homage to Quintus Septimius Florentis Christianus—Fish and the Shadow—Impressions of François-Marie Arouet (de Voltaire)—[MISCELLANEOUS POEMS:] Phanopoeia [I–III]—Langue d'Oc ["Alba," I–IV]—Moeurs contemporaines [I–VIII]—Cantico del sole (from "Instigations")—HUGH SELWYN MAUBERLEY (LIFE AND CONTACTS, 1920)—HOMAGE TO SEXTUS PROPERTIUS (1917)—Cantus planus

Notes: Boni and Liveright published a second impression of this book in February 1927. A third impression was released in January 1930, and a fourth impression in May 1932, by Horace Liveright. A fifth impression, in November 1938, and a sixth impression, *circa* 1944?, were published by the Liveright Publishing Corporation. All six impressions are from the same plates, and the second through the fifth are identified (as "printings") on the verso of the title-leaf. The date—1926—remains unchanged on the title-page through the first four impressions and is removed only in the fifth and sixth impressions. 465 bound copies and 525 sets of sheets of the sixth impression were taken over by New Directions late in 1946, and the sheets, with a cancel title-leaf, were bound up in red or blue cloth boards with a new dust-jacket. (These copies are not identified as part of the sixth impression.) In 1949 New Directions published a new offset edition, with additional poems (described below).

The text of the 1926 edition is used for a so-called "limited" edition of this book in combination with *A Draft of XXX Cantos* issued in 1980 for subscribers to a series, "The Greatest Books of the Twentieth Century," by the Franklin Library, Franklin Center, Pa. The title-page reads: *Ezra Pound Personae [and] A Draft of XXX Cantos. A Limited Edition.* The volume collates: 2 blank leaves, 9

A. BOOKS AND PAMPHLETS

leaves, 351 pp., 1 blank leaf, incl. front. (port.) It measures 23·5 × 16·5 cm., and is bound in full red leather boards stamped in gold on both covers and on spine, with red-silk end-papers, all edges gilt, and with red-silk ribbon marker.

b. *New (offset) edition* ([1949]):

PERSONÆ | THE COLLECTED POEMS OF | EZRA POUND | [*device*] | A NEW DIRECTIONS BOOK [New York, James Laughlin]

7 leaves, 273 pp. front. (port.), 3 plates. 22·1 × 15 cm. Blue cloth boards stamped in gold on front cover and on spine; end-papers. Tan dust-jacket printed in light blue (with advertisement for "Books by Ezra Pound" on back flap, including *The Translations* "To be published in 1950" and "*Selected Essays* [*sic*]. To be published in 1951").

Published in May 1949 at $3.50; 3200 copies printed. *On verso of title leaf:* ... Manufactured in the United States of America New Directions Books are published by James Laughlin New York Office: 333 Sixth Avenue

"For this new printing of Personae Mr. Pound has added a number of poems from magazines and early volumes which he now considers deserving of permanent collection." (*Dust-jacket*)

A reprint by offset of *Personae* (1926), with the addition of two appendices: I. EARLY POEMS, NOT PREVIOUSLY COLLECTED, AND NOW ADDED TO THIS COLLECTION IN 1949, INCLUDING THE POEMS OF T. E. HULME: To Whistler, American (*Poetry*, 1912)—Middle-Aged (*Poetry*, 1912)—Abu Salammamm, a Song of Empire (*Poetry*, 1914)—L'Homme moyen sensuel (*Little Review*, 1917)—Pierrots, from the French of Jules Laforgue (Scène courte mais typique) (*Little Review*, 1917)—Donna mi prega (*Make It New*, 1935)—The Complete Poetical Works of T. E. Hulme (*Ripostes*, 1912)—II. VERSE OF THE THIRTIES, FIRST PRINTED IN THE NEW ENGLISH WEEKLY, AND ADDED TO THIS COLLECTION IN 1949. (PROSE BY A. R. ORAGE.): Poems of Alfred Venison, the Poet of Titchfield Street—M. Pom-Pom (*Townsman*, 1938)

Note: A second impression (3340 copies) of this offset edition—not so identified—was issued in June 1956, in a grey dust-jacket printed in dark blue, with advertisement for *Section: Rock-Drill* ([1956])—A70b—on back flap. Although copies of this later impression vary slightly in paper and binding from those of the first impression, the only significant difference is in the advertisements on the dust-jacket. Still later printings add an "Index of Titles and First Lines," pp. 275–81.

c. *First English edition* ([1952]):

PERSONÆ | COLLECTED | SHORTER POEMS | OF | EZRA POUND | FABER AND FABER | 24 Russell Square | London

1 blank leaf, 2 leaves, 7–287 pp. 20·9 × 14 cm. Rose cloth boards stamped in gold on spine; end-papers. Yellow dust-jacket printed in black and green.

A. BOOKS AND PAMPHLETS

Published 16 May 1952 at 21s.; 3000 copies printed. *On verso of title-leaf:* First published in mcmlii . . . Printed in Great Britain by R. MacLehose and Company Limited The University Press Glasgow . . .

The contents are identical with those of early printings of the American edition save for the addition of an "Index of Titles and First Lines," pp. 283–7.

d. *Second English edition* ([1968]):

COLLECTED | SHORTER POEMS | by | EZRA POUND | FABER AND FABER | 24 Russell Square | London

7 leaves, 17–297 pp. 20·7 × 13·5 cm. Purple cloth boards lettered in gold on spine; end-papers. Blue dust-jacket printed in black and red.

Published 1 July 1968 at 30s.; 6950 copies printed. *On verso of title-leaf:* First published in mcmlii . . . Second edition mcmlxviii Printed in Great Britain by Lowe & Brydone (Printers) Ltd. London, N. W. 10 . . . This is a slightly enlarged edition of the volume previously entitled *Personae*.

This new edition adds a selection of "Poems from the Classic Anthology Defined by Confucius (1954)," "An Immorality," "The Rapture," "Reflection and Advice" [*i.e.* "Pax Saturni"], "Our Respectful Homages to M. Laurent Tailhade," and "Epilogue, to my five books containing medieval studies, experiments and translations," and omits "M. Pom-Pom," and "Our Contemporaries" (although both continue to be listed, erroneously, in the index).

A28   TA HIO   1928

a. *First edition:*

[*Within ornamental-rule border:*] TA HIO | The Great Learning | NEWLY RENDERED INTO | THE AMERICAN LANGUAGE | By | EZRA POUND | [*device*] | 1928 | UNIVERSITY OF WASHINGTON BOOK STORE | Seattle

1 blank leaf, 4 leaves, [7]–35 pp., 1 leaf, 1 blank leaf. 18·6 × 12·9 cm. Black paper wrappers printed in gold on page [i], folded over stiff tan blanks; edges untrimmed. Glassine envelope printed in black on front: FIRST EDITION, with flap sealed with sticker bearing the publisher's device.

Published 10 April 1928 at 65¢ as "University of Washington Chap-books, Edited by Glenn Hughes, 14"; 575 copies printed. *On verso of title-leaf:* . . . Printed in the United States of America

"The Confucian Classics are customarily divided into the Five Ching and the Four Shu. The first of the Four Shu (or Books) is the Ta Hio, a work of which the first chapter is ascribed to Confucius, and the remainder to one of his disciples, Thseng-tseu (Tsang Tzu)." ("Note," p. [6])

A. BOOKS AND PAMPHLETS

Contents: Ta Hio, the Great Learning—The Explanation of Thseng-tseu (Or, as we should say, the "Annotations")

b. *First English edition* ([1936]):

Ta Hio | THE GREAT LEARNING | Newly rendered into the | American Language | BY | EZRA POUND | [*ideogram*] | LONDON | Stanley Nott | Fitzroy Square

32 pp. 20·2 × 13·6 cm. Yellow paper boards printed in black on front cover; end-papers. Yellow dust-jacket printed in black.

Published May 1936 at 2*s.* as "Ideogramic Series, Edited by Ezra Pound, II"; 3000 sets of sheets printed (of which 196 were used for the American issue in 1938 and 331 were bombed during the Second World War). *On verso of title-leaf:* Printed in Great Britain at The Kynoch Press for Stanley Nott Ltd., 69 Grafton Street, Fitzroy Square, London, W I 1936

Of this edition 196 sets of sheets were imported by New Directions and issued in New York in November 1938, with cancel title-leaf and excised half-title (series) leaf, as No. 4 in the "New Directions Pamphlet Series." 648 copies of the Nott 1936 edition were taken over in October 1937 by Faber and Faber; of these, 317 were sold and 331 destroyed by bombing (as noted above).

For the "Ideogramic Series, Edited by Ezra Pound," see note to No. 1 of the series, *The Chinese Written Character as a Medium for Poetry* (1936)—B36a.

Notes: A new edition (1000 copies), issued by New Directions in New York in August 1939, although announced to contain new notes and revisions by Ezra Pound, is merely a reprint.

For Ezra Pound's later English version of this text see "The Great Digest" in *Confucius. The Unwobbling Pivot & The Great Digest* (1947)—A58—and *Confucius. The Great Digest & Unwobbling Pivot* ([1951])—B53. Ezra Pound's Italian version is *Confucio. Ta S'eu. Dai Gaku. Studio integrale* (1942)—B46—and *Testamento di Confucio* (1944)—A54.

A29   A DRAFT OF THE CANTOS   1928
17–27

First edition:

[*In black:*] A DRAFT OF | THE CANTOS | 17 [*ornament*] 27 OF EZRA | POUND: [*in red:*] Initials | by Gladys Hynes | [*in black:*] JOHN RODKER [*ornament*] LONDON [*ornament*] 1928

1 blank leaf, 56 pp., 1 blank leaf. 39·1 × 25·9 cm. Red vellum boards stamped in gold on front cover: CANTOS | EP ; end-papers; edges untrimmed.

Published September 1928 at 5 guineas. Printed on the same laid paper used

A. BOOKS AND PAMPHLETS

for *A Draft of XVI. Cantos*—A26, watermarked with a six-pointed star and the words: EZRA POUND CANTOS [*followed by device of the Three Mountains Press*] Each Canto has caption and ornamental initial printed in red with illustrative design in background in black or in red and black. *On verso of title-leaf:* Printed and made in England by J. Curwen & Sons Ltd. Plaistow *Colophon (page* [5]): The Edition of One Hundred and One Copies, of which Ninety-Four are For Sale, Consists of Four on Vellum, Signed by the Author and Artist and Lettered A to D Five on Imperial Japan Paper, Signed by the Author and Lettered E to I Fifteen on Whatman Paper Numbered I to XV and Seventy on Roma Paper Specially Watermarked Numbered 1 to 70 Six copies have been sent to various Libraries under the Copyright Act, and one copy for review This Copy is Numbered [*number printed in*]

The four copies on vellum were announced as to be bound in "full Niger," but at least two were in fact bound in white vellum boards, one (A) stamped in gold, the other (D) unstamped, with vellum end-papers; the four copies were signed by author and artist on page [5], and three of them were theoretically for sale at 50 guineas each. Of the five sets of Imperial Japan sheets, copies E and F were bound in full blue morocco stamped in gold, with Imperial Japan end-papers; three sets lettered G, H, and I, although signed by the author on page [5], were still unbound at Brunnenburg in 1981; bound copies were for sale at 20 guineas each. The 15 copies on Whatman paper (watermarked: HAND MADE J WHATMAN 1927 [–1928] ENGLAND), published simultaneously, were bound in green vellum boards stamped in gold, with end-papers of Roma paper watermarked as above; these copies were for sale at 10 guineas each. (For the lettered copies the colophon reads: . . . This Copy is Lettered [*letter printed in*])

Notes: A four-page prospectus, reproducing on pages [2–3] pages [24] (opening of the 21st Canto) and [41] (opening of the 25th Canto), was printed and distributed in December 1927. A subscriber making the request when ordering his copy could have his name printed at the end of the colophon on page [5].

At least one unnumbered copy on Roma paper, at Brunnenburg in 1981, is bound in the green vellum boards used for the 15 copies on Whatman paper.

A30   SELECTED POEMS   [1928]

a. *First edition, ordinary copies:*

EZRA POUND | [*swelled rule*] | SELECTED POEMS | EDITED WITH AN INTRODUCTION | BY | T. S. ELIOT | * | THIS SELECTION INCLUDES | PERSONÆ OF EZRA POUND | RIPOSTES | LUSTRA | CATHAY | H. S. MAUBERLEY | AND SOME EARLY POEMS | REJECTED BY THE AUTHOR | AND OMITTED FROM | HIS COLLECTED EDITION | * | LONDON | FABER & GWYER

1 blank leaf, 2 leaves, vii–xxxii, 184 pp. 19·3 × 13·5 cm. Green cloth boards stamped in gold on spine, with, at base: FABER & GWYER (or, later, FABER &

A. BOOKS AND PAMPHLETS

FABER); laid end-papers; top edges stained blue-green; other edges untrimmed. Tan dust-jacket printed in black.

Published 23 November 1928 at 7s. 6d.; 1000 copies printed. *On verso of title-leaf:* First published in MCMXXVIII ... Printed in Great Britain by Butler & Tanner Limited Frome and London ...

The contents and categories are identical with those of *Personae* (1926)—A27a— except for the omission of "Ballad of the Goodly Fere," "Mr. Housman's Message," "Translations and Adaptations from Heine," "Au salon," "Au jardin," "Silet," "In exitum cuiusdam," "Les Millwin," "The Bellaires," "The New Cake of Soap," "To Formianus' Young Lady Friend," "Our Contemporaries," "Poems from *Blast* (1914)," "Cantico del sole," "Homage to Sextus Propertius," "Cantus planus," and the addition at the end of "Early Poems Rejected by the Author and Omitted from His Collected Edition" ("In tempore senectutis," "Camaraderie," "An Idyl for Glaucus," "Canzon: The Yearly Slain" [with Manning's "Korè"], "Canzon: Of Incense").

b. *Signed copies:*

xxxii, 184 pp. 20·2 × 14·3 cm. Grey paper boards with white vellum back stamped in gold; wove end-papers; top edges gilt; other edges untrimmed. Plain glassine dust-jacket.

Published 10 December 1928 at 25s. *Colophon (page* [ii]): This edition printed on English hand-made paper is limited to one hundred numbered copies. This is number ... [*number written in, signed:* E. Pound]

Note: This book has been reprinted at frequent intervals, with impressions identified on verso of title-leaf. A new edition (2300 copies) was published, also by Faber and Faber, 25 March 1949; its contents are identical with those of the first edition save for the addition of a brief "Postscript: 1948" to T. S. Eliot's introduction, and the alteration in title of one poem from "Dieu! Qu'il la fait" to "Dieu qui l'a faicte." This edition has itself been reprinted, with impressions identified on verso of title-leaf; it was issued at 6s. in the series "Faber paper covered Editions" in 1959.

A31   A DRAFT OF XXX CANTOS   1930

a. *First edition, unsigned copies:*

A DRAFT OF | XXX CANTOS | BY | EZRA POUND | HOURS PRESS | 15 rue Guénégaud | Paris 1930

1 blank leaf, 2 leaves, 7–141, [1] pp., 1 leaf, 2 blank leaves. 21·2 × 14·8 cm. Coarse natural linen boards lettered in red on front cover and up the spine; first and last blank leaves pasted down as end-papers; edges untrimmed.

Published August 1930 at 40s. *Colophon (verso of first leaf):* Justification 2 Copies real vellum marked A.—B. not for sale 10 Copies on Texas Mountain Paper signed and numbered I–X 200 copies on Canson-Mongolfier Soleil velin M. R. V. Paper 1–200 [*number written in*] *Imprint on page* [143]: Imprimé pour The Hours Press par Maître Imprimeur François Bernouard 1930 Initiales par D[orothy]. S[hakespear Pound].

b. *Signed copies:*

1 blank leaf, 2 leaves, 7–141, [1] pp., 2 leaves, 1 blank leaf. 21·3 × 15 cm. Red-orange leather boards lettered in gold on front cover and up the spine; first and last blank leaves pasted down as end-papers; edges untrimmed.

Published August 1930, simultaneously with the unsigned copies, at 5 guineas. Colophon on verso of first leaf and imprint on page [143] as in unsigned copies. *Colophon* (*page* [145]): This edition consists of 10 copies signed by the author. This is no [*number written in, signed:* Ezra Pound] (The two copies on real vellum, measuring 20 × 15 cm., are bound like the ten copies on Texas Mountain paper.)

Notes: In all examined copies, unsigned and signed, Canto VI is misnumbered "IV" on page 23.

The Hours Press was owned and operated by Nancy Cunard, who purchased from William Bird the printing press used for books published by his Three Mountains Press.

c. *First American edition* ([1933]):

A DRAFT OF | XXX | CANTOS | BY EZRA POUND | [*device*] | FARRAR & RINEHART | INCORPORATED | NEW YORK

1 blank leaf, 3 leaves, 3–149 pp., 2 blank leaves. 22·7 × 15·8 cm. Black cloth boards lettered in silver down the spine; end-papers. Yellow dust-jacket printed in brown and black.

Published 15 March 1933 at $2.50; 1000 copies printed. *On verso of title-leaf:* [*Publisher's monogram*] Printed in the United States of America by J.J. Little and Ives Co., New York Designed by Robert S. Josephy . . .

With three exceptions (copies owned by University of Virginia, Yale, and DG), all examined copies have pages 61–62 printed on a cancel leaf with line 11 up on page 62 reading: "black beetles, burrowing into the sh-t,". As originally printed, the offending word has been spelled out. (The misprints in the list of books "by Ezra Pound" on the verso of the half-title leaf, "PROVENÇ" for "PROVENÇA," and "FONTANELLE" for "FONTENELLE," are uncorrected throughout both Farrar and Rinehart impressions.)

Notes: An unbound, stapled pamphlet, *The Cantos of Ezra Pound: Some Testimonies by Ernest Hemingway, Ford Madox Ford, T. S. Eliot, Hugh Walpole, Archibald MacLeish, James Joyce, and Others* (New York, Farrar & Rinehart, Inc. [1933]), 22 [2] pp., measuring 19·6 × 13 cm., was issued in connexion with the publication of the book.

A. BOOKS AND PAMPHLETS

Farrar and Rinehart published a second impression, with the cancel leaf (pp. 61–62) and its conjugate (pp. 71–72) reprinted as an integral part of the book. These copies omit the publisher's monogram on the verso of the title-leaf, and the dust-jacket bears a notation at the top of the inside front flap: "Second Printing." 164 copies of this second impression were taken over by New Directions in 1940 and issued with a cancel title-leaf (with New Directions imprint on title-page); the binding and dust-jacket of the Farrar and Rinehart second impression were retained without alteration.

d. First English edition ([1933]):

A DRAFT OF | XXX CANTOS | BY | EZRA POUND | LONDON | FABER & FABER LIMITED | 24 RUSSELL SQUARE

1 blank leaf, 153, [1] pp., 2 blank leaves. 21·1 × 15 cm. Black cloth boards stamped in gold down the spine; end-papers; top edges stained yellow; other edges untrimmed. Orange-red dust-jacket printed in blue.

Published 14 September 1933 at 7s. 6d.; 1500 copies printed. *On verso of title-leaf:* First published in September MCMXXXIII . . . Printed in Great Britain by R. MacLehose and Company Limited The University Press Glasgow. . . .

"The present edition . . . contains Mr. Pound's latest corrections . . . " (*Dust-jacket*)

The misprints on page [2], "FONTANELLE" for "FONTENELLE," and on the front flap of the dust-jacket, "Westcott" for "Wescott," remain uncorrected throughout the first impression.

Notes: Pound's most recent corrections are incorporated in the English text printed opposite the Italian translation in *I Cantos . . . Volume primo: I primi trenta Cantos* ([1961])—D81. In the Italian translation, by Mary de Rachewiltz, partly in collaboration with the author, names of persons referred to have been substituted for fictitious names in Canto XVI.

This text is used for a so-called "limited" edition of this title in combination with *Personae*, issued in 1980 for subscribers to a series, "The Greatest Books of the Twentieth Century," by the Franklin Library, Franklin Center, Pa. The title-page reads: *Ezra Pound Personae* [*and*] *A Draft of XXX Cantos. A Limited Edition.* It collates: 2 blank leaves, 9 leaves, 351 pp., 1 blank leaf, incl. front. (port.) It measures 23·5 × 16·5 cm. and is bound in full red leather boards stamped in gold on both covers and on spine, with red-silk end-papers, all edges gilt, and with red-silk ribbon marker.

A32   IMAGINARY LETTERS   1930

First edition:

[*In red:*] Imaginary Letters | [*in black:*] by | [*in red:*] Ezra Pound |

A. BOOKS AND PAMPHLETS

[*in black:*] THE BLACK SUN PRESS | RUE CARDINALE | PARIS | [*in red:*] MCMXXX

2 blank leaves, 2 leaves, 56 pp., 2 leaves, 2 blank leaves. 21·2 × 16·4 cm. Heavy white paper wrappers, printed in red and black on pages [i] and [iv], folded over first and last blank leaves; edges untrimmed. Plain outer glassine wrapper also folded over blank leaves. Plain tan paper-covered box, measuring 21·8 × 16·5 cm.

Published October 1930 at $5.00. *Colophon* (*page* [59]): This First Edition of Imaginary Letters by Ezra Pound printed at The Black Sun Press, Paris (Maître-Imprimeur Lescaret) under the supervision of and for Caresse Crosby, September 1930, is strictly limited to 50 copies on Japanese Vellum numbered 1 to 50 and signed by the Author together with 300 copies on Navarre Paper numbered 51 to 350, and 25 copies hors-commerce. This edition to be sold at the Bookshop of Harry F. Marks 21 West 47 Street New York City and at the Black Sun Press, Paris. [*Number stamped in*] (The signed copies, which were sold at $10.00, are identical with the unsigned, except for the paper, the signature of the author on the half-title, and the box, which is covered with patterned tan paper of slightly variant, mottled texture, measuring 22 × 16·7 cm.)

In the text, the titles for Letters I–V and for the final essay are printed in red, the rest in black.

Contents: I–III. Walter Villerant to Mrs Bland Burn—IV. W. Villerant to the ex-Mrs Burn—V. Mr Villerant's morning outburst—VI. No, my dear Caroline—VII. Hepsibah!—VIII. My dear Imogene—Stark Realism: This Little Pig Went to Market, a Search for the National Type

Notes: The series of "Imaginary Letters" was begun in the *Little Review* by Wyndham Lewis with three instalments (each containing two letters of William Bland Burn to his wife) printed from May to July 1917. Ezra Pound wrote to Wyndham Lewis in the summer of 1917: "Mr Villerant has written some letters for Sept. Oct. and Nov. to keep the 'reader' in mind of the existence of the Burn family. This literary rape and adultery is most underhanded and scandalous. But Mr V. has unexpectedly come to life, that is by the time he gets to his second epistle. He will perhaps annoy the 'public' and provide B. with Aunt Sallys. He is not controversing with B. but discussing matters other, and of interest to his effete and over civilized organism." Pound's continuation of the series, printed in the *Little Review* between September 1917 and November 1918, "Imaginary Letters. IV–VI, X," and "Mr Villerant's Morning Outburst. (Four Letters [XI–XIV])," was interrupted by two additional contributions, "Imaginary Letters, VIII [*i.e.* VII]–IX," by Wyndham Lewis, printed in the *Little Review* for March and April 1918.

Ezra Pound's "Imaginary Letters, I–VIII" were reprinted in *Pavannes and Divagations*—A74—pp. 55–76. The essay "Stark Realism" had been included in 1918 in *Pavannes and Divisions*—A15—pp. 45–46; it was also reprinted in *Pavannes and Divagations*—A74—pp. 103–5.

A. BOOKS AND PAMPHLETS

a. *First edition:*

HOW TO READ | By | EZRA POUND | DESMOND HARMSWORTH | 44 Great Russell Street | LONDON

55 pp. 19·4 × 13·2 cm. Red cloth boards of rough finish stamped in silver (or, later, of smooth finish stamped in black) up the spine; end-papers; fore and bottom edges untrimmed. Grey dust-jacket printed in red.

Published 2 December 1931 at 2*s.*; number of copies unknown. *On verso of title-leaf:* ... first published in MCMXXXI ... made and printed in Great Britain by Morrison & Gibb Ltd. in the city of Edinburgh

Note: An (unauthorised) American reprint of this book, clothbound, was produced by offset in 1971 in New York by Haskell House Publishers Ltd.

b. *New edition, with The Spirit of Romance, Part I* ([1932]):

PROLEGOMENA I [–2] | EZRA POUND | HOW | TO READ | FOL-LOWED BY | THE SPIRIT OF ROMANCE | PART I | TO | Publishers | Le Beausset (Var) France

159, [1] pp. 21·7 × 13·7 cm. Heavy blue-grey paper wrappers printed in black on page [i], and up the spine: [*ornament*] POUND-PROLEGOMENA-VOL. I [*sic. Ornament*]

Published June 1932 at $1.00; number of copies unknown. *Imprint at foot of page* [160]: Printed in France Toulon Imprimerie F. Cabasson Editeur 2, rue de l'Ordonnance 1932

Contents: Prolegomena 1. How to Read—Prolegomena 2. Spirit of Romance, Part One [Chapters I–IV (with a new short prefatory note and new footnotes dated 1929 and 1932) and a new Chapter V: "Psychology and Troubadours: A Divagation from Questions of Technique," reprinted from the *Quest*, London, "about 1916," *i.e.* October 1912—C55].

Notes: Copies of this edition were imported for sale in the United States by Bruce Humphries, Boston, Mass. These copies have a grey paper label pasted over the imprint on the title-page: BRUCE HUMPHRIES, INC. | PUBLISHERS [*device*] BOSTON, U. S. A.

Later volumes of *Prolegomena* were planned to include the second part of *The Spirit of Romance* and other prose work of Ezra Pound, but the publishers went out of business before the plans could be realised. *How to Read* first appeared with title "How to Read, or Why" in three instalments in *New York Herald Tribune Books* from 13 to 27 January 1929. It was reprinted in *Polite Essays*—A42—pp. 155–92, and in *Literary Essays* ([1954])—A67—pp. 15–40.

A. BOOKS AND PAMPHLETS

a. *First edition:*

ABC | of | ECONOMICS | by | EZRA POUND | LONDON | FABER
AND FABER | 24 RUSSELL SQUARE

1 blank leaf, 2 leaves, 7–127, [1] pp. 19·2 × 13 cm. Purple cloth boards lettered
in red on spine; end-papers. Yellow dust-jacket printed in red and black.

Published 6 April 1933 at 3*s.* 6*d.*; 2031 sets of sheets printed (of which 300 were
used for the American issue and 720 were bombed during the Second World
War). *On verso of title-leaf:* First published in April MCMXXXIII . . . Printed in Great
Britain by R. MacLehose and Company Limited The University Press Glasgow
. . .

"The aim of this brochure is to express the fundamentals of economics so simply and clearly that even people of different economic schools and factions will
be able to understand each other when they discuss them." (*Prefatory note, p.* 7)

"Mr Ezra Pound was asked to deliver ten lectures in an Italian university—on
economics, not on the mummified muses. This is his necessary evisceration and
clarification of the subject; a concise introduction to 'volitionist economics.'"
(*Dust-jacket*) The lectures referred to, announced as "An Historic Background
for Economics," were given at the Università Commerciale Luigi Bocconi, Milan,
21–31 March 1933—see E1d.

Note: Extensive quotations from pages 14–25 of *A B C of Economics* were used
almost verbatim, with Ezra Pound's approval but without acknowledgment of
their source, in a novel by Graham Seton (pseudonym of Graham Seton Hutchinson) entitled *Blood Money,* first published in 1934 in London by Hutchinson
and Co. The passages occur towards the end of the novel, particularly on pages
280–3 of the first edition.

b. *American issue* ([1940]):

Ezra Pound | ABC OF ECONOMICS | NEW DIRECTIONS | Nor-
folk, Conn. [James Laughlin]

19 × 12·5 cm. Blue cloth boards, with white paper label printed in black down
the spine; end-papers. Light blue dust-jacket printed in dark blue and black.

Published 9 March 1940 at $2.00; 300 sets of the first-edition sheets, with a
cancel title-leaf (with title-page as above), were imported by New Directions
and bound and jacketed for sale in the United States. *On verso of title-leaf:* . . .
Printed in England

c. *Second edition* ([1953]):

[*In red:*] ABC | OF | ECONOMICS | [*in black:*] by | EZRA POUND
| PETER RUSSELL | THE POUND PRESS [Tunbridge Wells]

A. BOOKS AND PAMPHLETS

1 blank leaf, 2 leaves, 7–74 pp., 1 blank leaf. 21·5 × 14·3 cm. Blue cloth boards stamped in black (one copy in gold) up the spine; end-papers. Cream dust-jacket printed in black. (Later copies are bound in heavy cream paper wrappers printed in black.)

Published May 1953 at 10s. 6d.; 2000 sets of sheets were printed (of which the first 250 were bound in cloth and later lots in paper wrappers; a later impression—*circa* 1959?—has publisher's advertisements on pages [75–76], which are blank in the first impression). *On verso of title-leaf:* First edition published in 1933. This second edition is printed and published by the Pound Press, Tunbridge Wells, England, in May 1953.

A reprint save for the "Editor's notes for New Edition," p. 74. The publisher states that these notes were supplied by Ezra Pound.

A35   ABC OF READING   1934

a. *First edition:*

ABC | of | READING | by | EZRA POUND | [*device*] | LONDON | GEORGE ROUTLEDGE & SONS, LTD. | BROADWAY HOUSE: 68–74 CARTER LANE, E.C. | 1934

xii, 197 pp., 1 blank leaf. 18·9 × 12·7 cm. Rough (or, later, smooth) red cloth boards lettered in gold (or, later, black) on spine; end-papers. Cream dust-jacket printed in red.

Published 24 May 1934 at 4s. 6d.; 2000 copies printed. *On verso of title-leaf:* Printed in Great Britain by Butler & Tanner Ltd., Frome and London

"The present book is intended to meet the need for fuller and simpler explanation of the method outlined in 'How to Read' [A33]. 'How to Read' may be considered as a controversial pamphlet summarizing the more active or spiky parts of the author's earlier critical skirmishing, and taking count of an enemy. The present pages should be impersonal enough to serve as a text-book. The author hopes to follow the tradition of Gaston Paris and S. Reinach, that is, to produce a text-book that can also be read 'for pleasure as well as profit' by those no longer in school; by those who have not been to school; or by those who in their college days suffered those things which most of my own generation suffered." ("How to Study Poetry," p. ix)

b. *First American edition:*

ABC | OF READING | BY EZRA POUND | NEW HAVEN | YALE UNIVERSITY PRESS | 1934

1 blank leaf, xii, 197 pp. 21 × 13·7 cm. Green cloth boards stamped in black on spine; end-papers. Green dust-jacket printed in red and black.

Published 18 September 1934 at $2.00; 1016 copies printed. *On verso of title-leaf:* ... Printed in the United States of America ...

Note: A new edition of *A B C of Reading* was published by Faber and Faber in London on 22 March 1951 in a first impression of 2670 copies. Faber and Faber printed also 3500 sets of sheets for New Directions, who issued them, also in March 1951, as No. 30 in their "New Classics Series." This book is an exact reprint and contains no new material. In April 1960 it was issued by New Directions at $1.35 as "New Directions Paperbook 89" (9897 copies), and on 13 October 1961 by Faber and Faber at 6s. in their series of "Faber paper covered Editions" (10,000 copies).

A36   MAKE IT NEW   [1934]

a. *First edition:*

MAKE IT NEW | ESSAYS BY | EZRA POUND | [*ideograms in 4 lines*] | LONDON | FABER AND FABER LIMITED | 24 RUSSELL SQUARE

1 blank leaf, 3 leaves, 407, [1] pp. 22·6 × 15·3 cm. Fine- (later coarse-) grain green cloth boards lettered in gold on spine (publishers' name at foot in letters at first approximately 3·5 mm.—later approximately 4 mm.—high, with the "N" in "AND" at first approximately 4 mm.—later approximately 3 mm.—wide); end-papers (at first thick, later thin); top edges stained purple-brown; other edges untrimmed. Green dust-jacket printed in black and red (later with old price clipped from lower front flap and new price printed in).

Published 27 September 1934 at 12s. 6d. (later raised to 15s.); 1600 copies printed. *On verso of title-leaf:* First published in September MCMXXXIV ... Printed in Great Britain at the University Press Cambridge ... *Imprint on page* [408]: Cambridge: Printed by W. Lewis, M.A., at the University Press

Contents: Date Line—I. Troubadours: Their Sorts and Conditions (about 1912 [*i.e.* published October 1913])–II. Arnaut Daniel ([1911/]1920)—III. Notes on Elizabethan Classicists (before 1918 [*i.e.* 1917/1918])—IV. Translators of Greek (before 1918 [*i.e.* 1918/1919])—V. French Poets (["A Study in French Poets"] February [–October] 1918) [with "Postscript (anno XII [*i.e.* 1934])]—VI. Henry James and Remy de Gourmont (August 1918 and February 1919 [*i.e.* I. Henry James ("In Explanation," "A Shake Down," "'The Middle Years'" "The Notes to 'The Ivory Tower'"—1918). II. Remy de Gourmont, a Distinction. Followed by Notes (February/March 1919)])—A Stray Document ["A Retrospect," with prefatory note (1912/1913)]—VII. Cavalcanti ["Mediaevalism," "Donna mi prega," "Partial Explanation," "The Canzone," "The Other Dimension," "Hendecasyllables," "The Vocabulary," "The Canzone: Further Notes," "Guido's Relations"] (1910/1931)

b. *First American (offset) edition* (1935):

MAKE IT NEW | ESSAYS BY EZRA POUND | [*ideograms in 4 lines*] | 1935 | NEW HAVEN · YALE UNIVERSITY PRESS

1 blank leaf, 3 leaves, 407 pp. 22·3 × 15 cm. Tan cloth boards stamped in green on both covers and on spine; end-papers. Green dust-jacket printed in black.

Published 12 March 1935 at $3.75; 1000 copies printed. *On verso of title-leaf:* . . . Printed in the United States of America . . . [by offset from the first edition]

On recto of first leaf: Published on the Mary Cady Tew Memorial Fund

A37   ELEVEN NEW CANTOS   [1934]
                       XXXI–XLI

a. *First edition, first issue:*

ELEVEN | NEW | CANTOS | XXXI–XLI | BY EZRA POUND | [*device*] | FARRAR & RINEHART | INCORPORATED | PUBLISHERS NEW YORK

2 leaves, 56 pp., 2 blank leaves. 22·4 × 15·8 cm. Black cloth boards lettered in silver down the spine; end-papers. Blue dust-jacket printed in blue and black.

Published 8 October 1934 at $1.50; 1500 copies printed (of which 500 copies were used for the second issue in 1940). *On verso of title-leaf:* [*Publisher's monogram*] . . . Printed in the United States of America by J. J. Little and Ives Company, New York . . .

The misprint in the list of books "by Ezra Pound" facing the title-page, "FON-TANELLE" for "FONTENELLE," was not corrected.

Note: The first 84 lines of Canto XXXVI are Pound's revised English version of Cavalcanti's canzone "Donna mi prega."

b. *Second issue* ([1940]):

ELEVEN | NEW | CANTOS | XXXI–XLI | By Ezra Pound | [*device*] | New Directions | Norfolk Connecticut [James Laughlin]

Collation, size, binding, and dust-jacket as in first issue.

Issued Summer 1940 at $1.50; 500 copies of the first issue, purchased from Farrar and Rinehart and issued by New Directions with a cancel title-leaf (with title-page as above).

c. *First English edition* ([1935]):

A DRAFT OF | CANTOS | XXXI–XLI | BY | EZRA POUND | LON-DON | FABER & FABER LTD | 24 RUSSELL SQUARE

62 pp., 1 blank leaf. 21·1 × 15 cm. Black cloth boards lettered in gold down the spine; end-papers; fore and bottom edges roughly trimmed. Mauve dust-jacket printed in red.

A. BOOKS AND PAMPHLETS

Published 14 March 1935 at 6s.; 1500 copies printed (of which 300 were bombed during the Second World War). *On verso of title-leaf:* First published in March MCMXXXV ... Printed in Great Britain by R. MacLehose and Company Limited The University Press Glasgow ...

A38   HOMAGE TO   [1934]
               SEXTUS PROPERTIUS

a. *First separate edition:*

HOMAGE TO | SEXTUS PROPERTIUS | BY | EZRA POUND | 'QUIA PAUPER AMAVI' | LONDON | FABER & FABER LTD

1 blank leaf, 3 leaves, 9–35 pp. 22·3 × 14·4 cm. Light or dark blue boards lettered in purple down the spine; end-papers; bottom edges untrimmed. Rose dust-jacket printed in blue.

Published 8 November 1934 at 2s. 6d.; 1000 copies printed. *On verso of title-leaf:* First published in November MCMXXXIV ... Printed in Great Britain by R. MacLehose and Company Limited The University Press Glasgow ...

Notes: Reprinted from *Quia Pauper Amavi* (1919)—A17—pp. 32–51. (In the United States the poem had been included in *Poems 1918–21* ([1921])—A21—pp. 11–34, and in *Personae* (1926)—A27—pp. [205]–230.) In 1958 it was printed with "Hugh Selwyn Mauberley" in a single volume as *Diptych Rome–London*—A75.

The poem was reprinted, with "a number of minor changes authorized by Pound himself, ... a collation of all four editions of the complete poem plus the sections which were printed in *Poetry* and *The New Age* [and] ... the Latin text of Propertius' work which Pound used for his translation," in J. P. Sullivan's *Ezra Pound and Sextus Propertius, a Study in Creative Translation* (Austin, University of Texas Press [1964]), pp. [107]–171.

b. *De luxe edition* ([1976]):

[*In black:*] EZRA POUND | HOMAGE TO SEXTUS PROPERTIUS | Sette acqueforti | di | FAUSTO MELOTTI | "The Venetian Grave" | di | Archibald MacLeish | [*in red: device*] | [*in black:*] M'ARTE EDIZIONI [Milano]

2 blank leaves, 5 leaves, 1 blank leaf, 5 leaves, 1 blank leaf, 2 leaves, 2–5 numbered leaves, 1 leaf, 1 blank leaf, 9 leaves, 1 blank leaf, 5 leaves, 1 blank leaf, 5 leaves, 1 blank leaf, 7 leaves, 1 blank leaf, 2 leaves, 2 blank leaves, incl. 7 mounted col. facsims., 1 mounted port. 7 plates (each with blank guard tissue). 38 × 28·5 cm. (leaves). Sheets issued unbound in plain paper wrappers, 39 × 29 cm., stamped in blind on front, folded over first and last blank leaves. Blue cloth board portfolio, 39·5 × 29·7 cm., lettered in white down the spine. Blue cloth board case, 40·2 × 30 cm., stamped in white on side.

A. BOOKS AND PAMPHLETS

Published September 1976 in the series "Immagini e testi Serie seconda, I, a cura di Luigi Majno"; 177 copies printed. *Colophon* (*recto of final leaf*) Questa edizione ... stampata dalla Tipografia Stefanoni di Lecco ... è costituita da centosettantasette esemplari così suddivisi: un esemplare segnato con la lettera A contenente il manoscritto originale del poeta, cinque esemplari segnati con le lettere B, C, D, E, F contenenti un altro manoscritto originale del poeta, ciuque [*sic*] esemplari segnati con le lettere G, H, L, M, N contenenti un disegno originale dell' artista, trenta esemplari numerati da 1 a 30 accompagnati da un'altra prova delle sette acqueforti tirate su carta Giappone..., centosei esemplari numerati da 31 a 136 e trenta esemplari fuori commercio numerati da I a XXX riservati ai collaboratori. La riproduzione del manoscritto originale contenuta negli esemplari da A a N, da 1 a 136 e da I a X è firmata da Ezra Pound. Il testo di Archibald MacLeish è firmato dall'autore. Le acqueforti di Fausto Melotti tirate nel laboratorio di Franco Sciardelli di Milano sono numerate e sono firmate dall'artista. La fotografia di Ezra Pound è di Henri Cartier-Bresson. Le quadricromie degli antichi manoscritti properziani sono state stampate dall'Istituto Grafico Bertieri di Milano ... Milano, maggio 1976. Esemplare [*lettered or numbered in pencil*] Questo esemplare è stato stampato per ... [*name printed in. Ezra Pound's signature in pencil appears on the recto of the fifth leaf of the third count, and Archibald MacLeish's on the verso of the second leaf of the seventh count.*]

Dedication on recto of third leaf of the first count: Alla cara memoria di Ezra Loomis Pound ...

Contents: "Piú che una premessa," by Luigi Majno—"Introduzione a 'Homage to Sextus Propertius' di Ezra Pound" ["Sexti Properti Carmina Codex Neapolitanus nunc Guelferbytanus Gudianus 224 circa annum 1200 scriptus" (color facsimiles of seven pages)]—"Homage to Sextus Propertius" [VIII: facsimile reproduction of Ezra Pound's fair copy, dated Venice 1970, on five numbered leaves]—"Homage to Sextus Propertius, 'an Interpretation,'" VII–X [with Latin texts of Elegies XV, XXVIII A, B & C and XXIX A & B from Book II opposite, followed by the same elegies translated into Italian verse by Roberto Sanesi, into French prose by Don Sauveur Paganelli, and into German prose by Georg Luck]—"The Venetian Grave," by Archibald MacLeish—[Photograph of] "Ezra Pound di Henri Cartier-Bresson, Venezia, 1971" [with reproduction of Ezra Pound's fair copy of "Erat Hora," dated Venice, 9 November 1971]—"Ezra Pound: A Note on His Life and Works," by Donald Gallup.

A39   ALFRED VENISON'S POEMS   [1935]

First edition:

ALFRED VENISON'S | POEMS | SOCIAL CREDIT | THEMES | By | The Poet of Titchfield Street | STANLEY NOTT | 69 GRAFTON STREET FITZROY SQUARE | LONDON

32 pp. 19·7 × 13·5 cm. Heavy tan paper wrappers printed in red on pages [i–iv]; wire-stitched.

Published April 1935 at 6d. as "Pamphlets on the New Economics, No. 9"; 2000 copies printed. *On verso of title-leaf:* ... This edition first published in 1935 Made and printed in Great Britain by Western Printing Services Ltd., Bristol ... [A second impression, also of 2000 copies, has on verso of title-leaf: ... First impression, March [*sic*] 1935 Second impression, April 1935 ...]

Dedication on page [2]: To S[tanley]. C[harles]. N[ott].

"These poems, which are published by permission, were edited by A. R. Orage [who wrote the prose letter preceding each poem] and appeared [pseudony-mously] in The New English Weekly between February and November 1934." (*Note, p.* [2])

Contents: The Charge of the Bread Brigade—Alf's Second Bit ["The Neo-Com-mune"]—Alf's Third Bit ["Dole the Bell! Bell the Dole!"]—Alf's Fourth Bit—Alf's Fifth Bit—Alf's Sixth Bit—Alf's Seventh Bit—Alf's Eighth Bit—Alf's Ninth Bit—Alf's Tenth Bit ["Wind"]—Alf's Eleventh Bit ["Sir Launcelot Has a Newspaper Now"]—Alf's Twelfth Bit ["Ballad for the 'Times' Special Silver Number"]—Another Bit—And an Offer ["Alf's Last—And an Offer"]—Safe and Sound—Song of Six Hundred M.P.'s—Ole Kate—The Baby—National Song (E. C.)

Note: The poems were included as part of Appendix II in the new offset edition of *Personae* published by New Directions in 1949—A27b, and in the edition published by Faber and Faber in 1952—A27c. The final poems in the series, "Episcopal Fervour," printed in the *New English Weekly* for 21 March 1935—C1169, and "Peace Racket, War Racket," in the same periodical for 31 Decem-ber 1936—C1386, have not been collected.

A40   SOCIAL CREDIT   [1935]

a. *First edition:*

SOCIAL CREDIT: | AN IMPACT | By | EZRA POUND | STANLEY NOTT | 69 Grafton Street Fitzroy Square | LONDON

31 pp. front. (with blank conjugate leaf). 19·7 × 13·4 cm. Heavy tan paper wrappers printed in red on pages [i–iv]; wire-stitched. (The frontispiece is a reproduction, with printed caption, of paper money issued by the Union Lum-bering Co., Chippewa Falls, Wisconsin, signed: A. E. POUND, Secretary.)

Published May 1935 at 6d. as "Pamphlets on the New Economics, No. 8"; 4000 copies printed (of which 500 were issued as part of *The Social Credit Pamphleteer* in October 1935). *On verso of title-leaf:* This edition first published in 1935 Printed in Great Britain by Western Publishing Services Ltd., Bristol ...

Dedication on page [3]: To the Green Shirts of England.

A. BOOKS AND PAMPHLETS

b. *Re-issue, in The Social Credit Pamphleteer:*

The | Social | Credit | Pamphleteer | by | Various Hands | being | Numbers 1, 4, 5, 6, 8, 11, 12, 13, 14 and 17 of the | List noted Opposite | Stanley Nott Ltd | 69 Grafton Street | Fitzroy Square | W.I

4 leaves, plus the 10 pamphlets bound together. 19·7 × 14 cm. Brown cloth boards lettered in white on front cover and on spine; end-papers. Tan dust-jacket printed in red.

Published October 1935 at 3s. 6d.; 500 copies of the first edition of *Social Credit: An Impact*, bound up, without wrappers and with the conjugate leaf of the frontispiece excised, with the nine other pamphlets. *On verso of title-leaf:* ... This collection first published by Messrs. Stanley Nott Ltd. October 1935

"The idea of the pamphlets arose out of a conversation with A. R. Orage and ourselves and the editorial staff of the *New English Weekly*. The idea was that pamphleteering ought to be revived, but that it should be based on a need; and the need was the interest of the average man in the present economic situation. The series comprises the opinions of all sorts of thinking men and women. The pamphlets are being bought and read by all sorts and conditions of people in every part of the world.

"The Pamphlets first appeared in September 1934 and continued to be published at intervals until August 1935." (*Note on verso of title-leaf*)

A list of the "Pamphlets on the New Economics" from which this volume was selected appears on the verso of the half-title-leaf; it extends to 17 numbers (numbers 18–19 were published in 1936).

Contents: The Use of Money, by C. H. Douglas (No. 1)—Poverty amidst Plenty, by The Earl of Tankerville (No. 4)—The B.B.C. Speech and the Fear of Leisure, by A. R. Orage (No. 5)—Social Credit and the War on Poverty, by the Very Rev. Hewlett Johnson, D.D. (No. 6)—Social Credit: An Impact, by Ezra Pound (No. 8)—The Sanity of Social Credit, by Maurice Colbourne (No. 11)—Essential Communism, by Herbert Read (No. 12)—The Soul of Man in the Age of Leisure, by Storm Jameson (No. 13)—An Open Letter to a Professional Man, by Bonamy Dobrée (No. 14)—What Is This Social Credit?, by A. L. Gibson, F.C.A. (No. 17).

Note: Social Credit: An Impact was reprinted in 1951 as No. 5 of "Money Pamphlets by £" (London, Peter Russell), and, with excisions, as "An Impact," in *Impact* (1960)—A78—pp. 142–56.

A41   JEFFERSON AND/OR   [1935]
MUSSOLINI

a. *First edition, signed copies:*

JEFFERSON | AND/OR | MUSSOLINI | L'IDEA STATALE | FAS-

A. BOOKS AND PAMPHLETS

CISM AS I HAVE SEEN IT | BY | EZRA POUND | Volitionist Economics | STANLEY NOTT | 69 Grafton Street, Fitzroy Square | LONDON

4 leaves, 7–128 pp. 22·3 × 15·2 cm. Orange cloth boards lettered in black on front cover and on spine; end-papers; fore edges untrimmed, bottom edges roughly trimmed. Probably issued in orange dust-jacket printed in black.

Published July 1935 at 21s.; 30 copies printed. *On verso of title-leaf:* ... First published by Stanley Nott Ltd. 1935 Printed in Great Britain by Western Printing Services Ltd., Bristol *Colophon* (*verso of special half-title-leaf tipped in to precede regular half-title-leaf*): Of this edition there are XXX copies numbered and signed by the author of which XXV are for sale. This copy is number [*number written in, signed:* Ezra Pound]

"The body of this ms. was written and left my hands in February 1933. 40 publishers have refused it. No typescript of mine has been read by so many people or brought me a more interesting correspondence. It is here printed verbatim, unaltered. I had not seen the ms. from the time it left Rapallo till it returned here with the galley proof. It is printed as record of what I saw in February 1933. ..." (*Foreword*, April 1935, *on verso of title-leaf*)

b. *Unsigned copies:*

128 pp. Size and binding as for signed copies. Orange dust-jacket printed in black.

Published 30 August 1935 at 6s.; number of copies unknown. Identical with signed copies save that special half-title-leaf is not present.

c. *First American edition* ([1936]):

JEFFERSON | AND/OR | MUSSOLINI | L'IDEA STATALE | FASCISM AS I HAVE SEEN IT | BY | EZRA POUND | Volitionist Economics | NEW YORK: LIVERIGHT PUBLISHING CORP. | LONDON: STANLEY NOTT

3 leaves, v–xi, 11–128 pp. 22·4 × 15·3 cm. Orange cloth boards lettered in dark blue down the spine; end-papers; top edges stained dark blue, fore edges untrimmed. White dust-jacket printed in blue and black.

Published 24 January 1936 at $2.00; number of copies unknown. *On verso of title-leaf:* ... First published by Stanley Nott Ltd. 1935 ... Manufactured in the United States of America [pages 11–128 printed by offset from the first edition]

Contains "Letter sent Autumn, 1934, by Ezra Pound to Editor of the Criterion, London [*i.e.* T. S. Eliot]," pp. v–ix, not included in the English edition. (Reprinted from the *Criterion* for January 1935—C1130, where it was titled "1934 in the Autumn.")

Notes: This book was published paperbound in New York in 1970 by Liveright as their Liveright Paperbound Edition L-13 at $1.95; of the edition 507 copies were actually bound in cloth.

Pound's Italian version of this book is *Jefferson e Mussolini* (1944)—A56.

A42 POLITE ESSAYS [1937]

a. *First edition:*

POLITE ESSAYS | by | EZRA POUND | FABER AND FABER LTD | 24 Russell Square | London

1 blank leaf, 3 leaves, 207 pp. 19·3 × 13 cm. Red cloth boards stamped in gold on spine; end-papers; top edges stained yellow-green. Lavender dust-jacket printed in black and red.

Published 11 February 1937 at 7s. 6d.; 2000 copies printed. *On verso of title-leaf:* First published in February Mcmxxxvii . . . Printed in Great Britain at the University Press Cambridge . . .

Contents: 1. Harold Monro—Mr Housman at Little Bethel—Hell—2. 'We Have Had No Battles but We Have All Joined In and Made Roads'—The Prose Tradition in Verse ["Mr Hueffer and the Prose Tradition in Verse"]—Dr Williams' Position—James Joyce et Pécuchet [in French]—Mr Eliot's Solid Merit—'Abject and Utter Farce'—The Teacher's Mission—A Letter from Dr Rouse to E. P.—Retrospect: Interlude—3. Prefatio aut cimicium tumulus [from *Active Anthology* (1933)—B32]—'Active Anthology' (Retrospect Twenty Months Later)—How to Read [A33]—Civilization—Note on Dante [from Chapter VI of *The Spirit of Romance* (1910)—A5]

b. *American issue* ([1940]):

EZRA POUND | POLITE ESSAYS | NEW DIRECTIONS | Norfolk, Conn. [James Laughlin]

1 blank leaf, 3 leaves, 207 pp. 19 × 12·6 cm. Red cloth boards, with white paper label printed in black on spine; end-papers. White dust-jacket printed in grey and red.

Published January 1940 at $2.50; 700 sets of sheets with reprinted title-leaf and its conjugate were imported by New Directions and specially bound and jacketed for sale in the United States. *On verso of title-leaf:* . . . Printed in England

A43 THE FIFTH DECAD [1937]
OF CANTOS

a. *First edition:*

EZRA POUND | THE FIFTH DECAD OF | CANTOS | [*ideograms*] | FABER & FABER | LONDON

1 blank leaf, 2 leaves, 7–53 pp., 1 blank leaf. 20·9 × 15·2 cm. Black cloth boards lettered in gold down the spine; end-papers; fore edges roughly trimmed, bottom edges untrimmed. Rose dust-jacket printed in black and blue.

Published 3 June 1937 at 6s.; 1012 copies printed. *On verso of title-leaf:* First published in June MCMXXXVII . . . Printed in Great Britain by R. MacLehose and Company Limited The University Press Glasgow . . .

Contents: Cantos XLII–LI

b. *First American edition, first issue:*

EZRA POUND | THE FIFTH | DECAD OF | CANTOS | [*ornament*] | FARRAR & RINEHART | INCORPORATED | NEW YORK · TORONTO

2 leaves, 46 pp., 3 blank leaves. 22·5 × 15·6 cm. Black cloth boards stamped in silver on spine; end-papers. Tan dust-jacket printed in blue and black.

Published 29 November 1937 at $1.50; 750 copies printed (of which 419 were used for the second issue in 1940). *On verso of title-leaf:* [*Publisher's monogram*] . . . Printed in the United States of America by J. J. Little and Ives Company, New York . . .

The misprint "FONTANELLE" for "FONTENELLE" in the list of books "by Ezra Pound" on the recto of the half-title-leaf was not corrected.

c. *Second issue* ([1940]):

EZRA POUND | THE FIFTH | DECAD OF | CANTOS | [*device*] | NEW DIRECTIONS | Norfolk Connecticut [James Laughlin]

Collation, size, binding, and dust-jacket as in the first issue.

Issued Summer 1940 at $1.50; 419 copies of the first issue, purchased from Farrar and Rinehart and issued by New Directions with a cancel title-leaf (with title-page as above).

A44   CONFUCIUS   [1937]
        DIGEST OF THE ANALECTS

First edition:

CONFUCIUS | DIGEST | OF THE | ANALECTS | MILAN [Giovanni Scheiwiller] | XV [*i.e.* 1937]

2 blank leaves, 10 leaves, 1 blank leaf, 1 leaf, 2 blank leaves. 9·8 × 7·8 cm. Yellow paper wrappers, printed in black on page [i]: KUNG FU TSEU | [*ideograms*], folded over stiff white blanks and first and last blank leaves.

A. BOOKS AND PAMPHLETS

Half-title: Digest of the Analects that is, of the Philosophic Conversations.

Published June 1937 at L. 10; 245 copies printed. *Colophon (recto of final leaf):* "all'Insegna del Pesce d'Oro" Di questo volumetto nella versione di Ezra Pound, a cura di Giovanni Scheiwiller si sono stampati dalle Industrie Grafiche Pietro Vera di Milano il 15–6–1937–XV, 220 esemplari numerati su carta uso mano e 25 esemplari su carta "Japon" numerati da I a XXV per gli amici del libro Esemplare N. . . . [*number stamped in*] (The copies on "Japon" are bound in stiff vellum wrappers.)

Notes: The text was reprinted, with the omission of two short sentences, as Chapter 1, Section 1, Part I of *Guide to Kulchur* (1938)—A45—pp. 15–21.

For Ezra Pound's later translation of the complete text see *Confucian Analects* ([1951])—A65.

A45   GUIDE TO KULCHUR   [1938]

a. *First edition:*

EZRA POUND | GUIDE | TO | KULCHUR | [*row of 4 heavy dots*] | FABER & FABER LIMITED | 24 RUSSELL SQUARE | LONDON

1 blank leaf, 3 leaves, 5–359 pp. front. 20·9 × 14·2 cm. Green cloth boards lettered in gold on spine; end-papers. Cream dust-jacket printed in grey, red, and green (later copies with yellow paper sticker pasted on front flap altering price to 12*s.* 6*d.*).

Published 21 July 1938 at 10*s.* 6*d.* (later raised to 12*s.* 6*d.*); 1487 sets of sheets printed (of which 520 were used for the American issue and 230 were bombed during the Second World War). *On verso of title-leaf:* First published in June [*sic*] Mcmxxxviii . . . Printed in Great Britain by R. MacLehose and Company Limited The University Press Glasgow . . .

Dedication on page [3]*:* To Louis Zukofsky and Basil Bunting strugglers in the desert

"For valued help in proof correcting and in making this index, my sincere thanks to John Drummond.—E. P. 6 April anno XVI." (*Note at foot of page 359*)

Copies of the book were already bound when the publishers decided that certain passages were libellous and must be deleted. Ezra Pound was allowed to have five unexpurgated copies for his personal use (one of them he presented to John Drummond on 10 June 1938), and the publishers retained one copy for their files. Publication of the book was delayed from June until July while at least 15 leaves were reprinted, the original leaves excised from copies already bound, and the new leaves pasted on to the resulting stubs. For the unbound sheets the offending leaves with their conjugates were reprinted. Three copies have been located of this third state of the first edition; all other copies examined (except the six unexpurgated ones) have the following cancel leaves: pages

A. BOOKS AND PAMPHLETS

93–4, 119–20, 131–2, 157–8, 163–6, 189–90, 195–6, 241–4, 285–6, 289–90, 343–4, 351–[360].

Alterations were made as follows: page 93: "unspeakable" omitted in line 13; "Gbt" substituted for "Gib" in line 15; page 119: footnote to lines 1 and 2 omitted; page 131: "no cheating or substitution had occurred." replaced by "..." in line 3; "This shark (Peck or Peek I think his name was)" replaced by "This dogfish was probably unconscious" in line 8; "their mendacity. | This kind of thing is hired." replaced by period in line 18; page 157: "zur" replaced by "durch" in line 6 up; page 158: "Among the signal shirkers I think we may list Sr Madáriaga." omitted after "'save Spain'." in line 16; page 163: "Runciman" replaced by "......." in line 22; page 164: *The Times*" replaced by "numerous" in last line; page 165: "N.M. Butler" replaced by "some University Presidents" in line 2; page 190: "of punks, pimps and cheap dudes" omitted after "gang" in line 21; page 195: "privately: Cosmo is probably the wickedest man who ever sat in the seat of St. Augustine." replaced by "privately in such a manner that I can't print what he says without danger of libel." in lines 3 and 4; page 196: "Times, | Telegraph or any other paper" deleted and "any paper" left in lines 13–14; page 241: last line deleted; page 242: initials changed and names omitted in line 1; page 244: last 4 lines originally read: "One of the messiest characters of British public life (or filth) in our time passed many laws so ambiguous in wording that lawyers knew not how to interpret them. The same blot on humanity put through a law which led"; page 286: 8-line passage concerning Thomas Hardy's sisters omitted after line 12; page 290: lines 7–10 originally read: "Only Kipling, who had a gross and most British mind regarding women, put up some sort of episcopal frontage, because he was despicably cowardly when it came to matters of thought, outside his given limits,"; page 344: "Prof." omitted after "like" in line 20; pages 351–60: alterations in Index made necessary by cancels in text, *e.g.* "Murray, Gbt" for "Murray, Gib" on page 356.

Notes: Chapter 1, pp. 15–21, is a "Digest of the Analects, that is, of the Philosophic Conversations" of Confucius. Chapter 34, "On Arriving and Not Arriving," pp. 209–10, includes "The Lioness Warns Her Cubs," Pound's verse translation of the German text of a song of the Haussa tribe of the Sudan, collected by R. Prietze. Chapter 35, "Praise Song of the Buck-Hare," pp. 211–13, is Pound's verse translation of a folk-song of Teleuten, Siberia, collected by Wilhelm Radloff. Chapter 36, "Time-Lag," pp. 214–16, includes Pound's (partial) literal and free translations, based on Père Lacharme's Latin text, of the ode printed in *The Classic Anthology Defined by Confucius* (1954)—A69—p. 51 as Poem No. 108, "Encroachment."

A note by the publisher on the dust-jacket of the new edition published by New Directions in 1952 (see below) states that the original title for this book was *"Kulch," or Eʒ' Guide to Kulchur* and that it was so specified in the contract for the first edition.

A. BOOKS AND PAMPHLETS

b. *American issue* (1938):

EZRA POUND | CULTURE | NEW DIRECTIONS [James Laughlin] | NORFOLK–CONNECTICUT | 1938

1 blank leaf, 3 leaves, 5–359 pp. front. 20·6 × 14·2 cm. Blue cloth boards lettered in gold on spine; end-papers. White dust-jacket printed in grey and red.

Published 11 November 1938 at $2.50; 519 copies issued. These are the English sheets with the first gathering (including half-title and title-page) and all cancels with their conjugates reprinted as integral parts of the book. *On verso of title-leaf:* ... Printed in England Published in London under the title "Guide to Kulchur"

Note: After these 519 copies had been sold, New Directions imported and sold copies of the English edition at $3.00.

c. *New edition* ([1952]):

EZRA POUND | GUIDE | TO | KULCHUR | [*row of 4 heavy dots*] | A NEW DIRECTIONS BOOK [Norfolk, Conn., James Laughlin]

1 blank leaf, 379 pp., 1 blank leaf, incl. front., facsims. (music). 21·1 × 14·2 cm. Black cloth boards lettered in silver down the spine: KULCHUR by EZRA POUND; end-papers. White dust-jacket printed in blue and black.

Published 29 August 1952 at $4.00; 3500 copies printed. *On verso of title-leaf:* ... Printed in the United States of America New Directions Books are published by James Laughlin at Norfolk, Connecticut New York Office 333 Sixth Avenue

Contents: [photographic reprint of the text of the first edition through page 349, with:] ADDENDA: 1952: Aristotle's "Magna moralia"—As Sextant—Introductory Text Book [with reproduction of title-page]—[*Ideograms representing title*] Or One Word Will Ruin It All—Distinguish—Chronology for School Use—Diseases—"Heaulmière" from the Opera Villon [facsimile of manuscript in the hand of Olga Rudge]—Villon and Comment—Condensare [Although they precede the index, these additions are not included in it (it is a photographic reprint, with page numbers altered, of the index of the first edition)]—Index

Notes: The long "blurb" printed on the back of the dust-jacket for this book was written anonymously by Pound (see Noel Stock, *The Life of Ezra Pound* ([1970]), p. 432, where most of it is quoted).

Reissued paperbound in 1968 by New Directions as their Paperbook 257 at $2.35.

d. *New edition, English issue* ([1952]):

EZRA POUND | GUIDE | TO | KULCHUR | [*row of 4 heavy dots*] | PETER OWEN LIMITED · LONDON

1 blank leaf, 379 pp., 1 blank leaf, incl. front., facsims. (music). 21·2 × 14·2 cm. Blue cloth boards stamped in yellow on spine; end-papers. Yellow dust-jacket printed in black and blue.

Published 15 October 1952 at 25s.; 500 sets of sheets printed by New Directions for Peter Owen, bound and jacketed in England. *On verso of title-leaf:* . . . Printed in the U.S.A. MCMLII.

A46   WHAT IS MONEY FOR   [1939]

First edition:

[*Within ornamental-rule border: at top left:*] ? [*at top right, in type one-tenth as large:*] TWOPENCE | [*short rule*] | [*in center, with 4 thin vertical rules at the left of the first 4 lines:*] WHAT | IS | MONEY | FOR. | BY EZRA POUND | [*short rule.* London, Greater Britain Publications]

12 pp. 21·6 × 13·9 cm. Wire-stitched.

Published April 1939 at 2d.; number of copies unknown. *Imprint at foot of page 12:* Published by Greater Britain Publications, 16, Gt. Smith Street, Westminster, S. W. 1. . . . Printed by W. J. Hasted & Son, Ltd. (T. U.), 306, Mile End Road, London, E. 1.

Note: The text was reprinted in 1951, with *Introductory Text Book,* as No. 3 of "Money Pamphlets by £" (London, Peter Russell), and in *Selected Prose 1909–1965* ([1973])—A93a—pp. 260–72 (290–302 in A93b). A much condensed version appears with title "Integrity of the Word" in *Impact* (1960)—A78—pp. 91–97.

A47   CANTOS LII–LXXI   [1940]

a. *First edition:*

EZRA POUND | CANTOS | LII–LXXI | [*ideograms*] | FABER & FA-BER | LONDON

1 blank leaf, 2 leaves, 7–186, [1] pp., 2 blank leaves. 20·7 × 14·9 cm. Black cloth boards lettered in gold down the spine: Ezra Pound—A Draft of Cantos LII–LXXI (or, later: Ezra Pound—Cantos LII–LXXI F & F); end-papers; top edges stained yellow, fore edges roughly trimmed. Cream dust-jacket printed in red and black (later with old price clipped from front flap and new price stamped in).

Published 25 January 1940 at 10s. 6d. (later reduced to 8s. 6d.); 1000 copies printed. *On verso of title-leaf:* First published in February [*sic*] MCMXL . . . Printed

A. BOOKS AND PAMPHLETS

in Great Britain by R. MacLehose and Company Limited The University Press Glasgow . . .

A note by the author about this section of the poem is printed on the front flap of the dust-jacket.

b. *First American edition:*

EZRA POUND | CANTOS | LII–LXXI | [*ideograms*] | NEW DIREC-
TIONS | NORFOLK CONNECTICUT [James Laughlin]

4 leaves, 167 pp. 22·5 × 15·7 cm. Black cloth boards lettered in silver down the spine; end-papers. Cream dust-jacket printed in purple and red.

Published 17 September 1940 at $2.50; 1000 copies printed. *On verso of title-leaf:* . . . Manufactured in the United States of America

The first 500 copies have an envelope pasted to the inside back cover containing a pamphlet, *Notes on Ezra Pound's Cantos: Structure & Metric* (Norfolk, Conn., New Directions [1940]), 15, [1] pp., incl. illus. (port.). 16·5 × 11·5 cm. This consists of two essays, "Notes on the Cantos," by H. H. [*i.e.* James Laughlin], pp. 5–12, and "Notes on the Versification of the Cantos," by S. D. [*i.e.* Delmore Schwartz], pp. 13–15. The second 500 copies were issued without the envelope and pamphlet.

A48   A SELECTION OF POEMS   [1940]

First edition:

A SELECTION | OF POEMS | by | EZRA POUND | Faber and Faber | 24 Russell Square | London

80 pp. 19·2 × 12·9 cm. Blue-grey paper boards printed in orange-yellow on front cover and down the spine; end-papers. Orange dust-jacket printed in blue. (Also—later—in stiff blue-grey paper wrappers printed in blue.)

Published 5 December 1940 at 2s. 6d. in the series "Sesame Books"; 7100 copies printed. *On verso of title-leaf:* First published in November [*sic*] MCMXL . . . Printed in Great Britain by Western Printing Services Ltd., Bristol . . .

A misprint in the "Select Bibliography," p. 7, "*Tattio*" for "*Ta Hio*," was not corrected.

Contents: FROM SELECTED POEMS: Marvoil—Sestina: Altaforte—Ballatetta—Portrait d'une femme—A Girl—The Picture—Of Jacopo del Sellaio—The Return—The Alchemist—The Condolence—The Garden—Commission—The Temperaments—The Faun—Phyllidula—Society—Epitaphs—Song of the Bowmen of Shu—The River-Merchant's Wife: A Letter—Exile's Letter—Near Perigord—[From *Hugh Selwyn Mauberley*, Part 1, I:] E.P. Ode pour l'élection de son sépulchre—[Part 2, I:] Mauberley [(1920), II and III:]

A. BOOKS AND PAMPHLETS

'The Age Demanded'—FROM HOMAGE TO SEXTUS PROPERTIUS: [I:] Shades of Cal-
limachus—[IV:] Difference of Opinion with Lygdamus—[and IX:] The twisted
rhombs ceased their clamour of accompaniment—FROM A DRAFT OF XXX CANTOS:
Canto I—Canto II—FROM THE FIFTH DECAD OF CANTOS: Canto XLV.

Note: Nothing is printed here for the first time.

A49   ITALY'S POLICY OF SOCIAL   [1941]
           ECONOMICS 1930/1940
           BY ODON POR

First edition:

ITALY'S POLICY | of | SOCIAL ECONOMICS | 1939/1940 | by |
ODON POR | translated by | EZRA POUND | ISTITUTO ITALIANO
D'ARTI GRAFICHE | BERGAMO, MILANO, ROMA (ITALY)

204 pp., 2 leaves. 18·9 × 12·5 cm. (wrappers); 18·5 × 12·1 cm. (leaves). Heavy
white paper wrappers printed in two shades of blue on pages [i] and [iv] and
on spine.

Published September 1941; number of copies unknown. *On verso of title-leaf:* . . .
Printed in Italy by the Istituto Italiano d'Arti Grafiche Bergamo—September
1941–XIX

A translation of Odon Por's . . . *Politica economico-sociale in Italia anno XVII–
XVIII* (first published in Florence in 1940). Several of the footnotes in the translation, and the Appendix (leaf following page 204) do not appear in the Italian
original.

A50   CARTA DA VISITA   1942

a. *First edition:*

CARTA DA VISITA | DI | EZRA POUND | [*ideogram*] | 1942–XXI
| [Roma] EDIZIONI DI LETTERE D'OGGI [Giambattista Vicari]

62 pp., 1 blank leaf, incl. illus. 17·6 × 12·6 cm. Heavy white paper wrappers,
printed in pink, black, and green on page [i], on spine and on back flap, and in
pink and black on front flap and on page [iv]; edges untrimmed. (A later state
of the wrappers has the price on page [iv]: SEDICI LIRE).

Published December 1942 at L. 8 (later raised to L. 16) as "Biblioteca minima
tempus, 3"; 1150 copies printed. *Colophon (page* [2])*:* Questo libro . . . è stato

A. BOOKS AND PAMPHLETS

stampato in Roma il I. dicembre 1942–XXI presso L'Istituto Grafico Tiberino ... Di questo volume vengono stampate 1000 copie in tiratura ordinaria più 150 copie in tiratura speciale numerate da I a 150 [None of the special copies has been located.]

Note: A new edition (2000 numbered copies) of this pamphlet was published in Milan in July 1974 by Vanni Scheiwiller, "All'Insegna del Pesce d'Oro," as "Il Passato Presente, 4." It collates: 1 blank leaf, 3 leaves, 9–57 pp., 5 leaves, incl. front. (port.) and measures 21·2 × 15 cm.

b. *First (unpublished) edition in English* (1952):

A | VISITING CARD | 1st English Edition | By | EZRA POUND | [*ideogram*] | PETER RUSSELL | 114b Queen's Gate, London, S. W.7 | 1952

36 [*i.e.* 38] pp., 1 leaf. 1 plate. 21·5 × 13·5 cm. Stiff cream paper wrappers printed in black and red on page [i] and in black on pages [ii–iv]; wire-stitched.

Not published (but originally intended for sale at 2s. 6d. as "Money Pamphlets by £, No. 4"). *On verso of title-leaf:* Title of original work: Carta da Visita first published in Rome in 1942 The present translation is by John Drummond *Imprint at foot of page* [iv] *of wrapper:* Printed by Clements & Son (T. W.), Ltd., Tunbridge Wells, Kent.

Before any copies were distributed or sold, a fire at the publisher's destroyed all but five copies, which were badly charred. In this edition the bibliography on page [2] ends with 1951; in the fifth line up on page 18, the word "grain" is correctly spelled; and page 38 is misnumbered 36.

c. *First (published) edition in English* (1952):

Title-page as in the unpublished edition.

38 pp., 1 leaf. 1 plate. Size, binding, and series as in the unpublished edition.

Published early in 1952 at 2s. 6d.; 1000 copies printed. Verso of title-leaf and imprint at foot of page [iv] of wrapper as in the unpublished edition.

For this edition, which took the place of the burned one, the type was reset line for line. There are numerous variations in the arrangement and text of the preliminary and terminal advertisements; two titles of 1952 are added to the bibliography on page [2]; footnotes on pages 7, 15, and 18 vary; in the fifth line up on page 18, the word "grain" appears as "gain" (corrected in manuscript in some copies), and page 38 is correctly numbered.

Note: This English translation by John Drummond was reprinted, with some revisions, in *Impact* (1960)—A78—pp. 44–74, and, without those revisions, in *Selected Prose 1909–1965* ([1973])—A93a—pp. 276–305 (306–35 in A93b).

A. BOOKS AND PAMPHLETS

A51   L'AMERICA, ROOSEVELT E LE   1944
CAUSE DELLA GUERRA
PRESENTE

a. *First edition:*

[*Within border of single rule within double rule: in black:*] BIBLIOTECA
DI CULTURA POLITICA | [*rule*] | EZRA POUND | [*short rule*] | [*in
red:*] L'AMERICA, ROOSEVELT | E LE CAUSE | DELLA GUERRA
PRESENTE | [*in black:*] VENEZIA | CASA EDITRICE DELLA ED-
IZIONI POPOLARI | 1944–XXII

cover-title, 32 pp. 19·4 × 12·2 cm. Heavy buff paper wrappers printed in black
and red (as above) on page [i] and in black (with price) on page [iv]; wire-
stitched.

Published early in 1944 at L. 2 as "Biblioteca di Cultura Politica, [1]"; number
of copies unknown.

In all examined copies the tenth line up on page 16 has, pasted over it, a typed
slip of paper, correcting the line to read: "quanto egli sapesse io ero il primo a
mettere in-"; according to John Drummond, these slips were typed out by Ezra
Pound himself. Most copies have the following corrections in pencil: page 8,
line 12 up, "bene" corrected to "bono"; page 17, line 3, date "(1776)" cancelled; page 19, line 3 up, "Sir" deleted; page 22, line 13, "richiede" corrected
to "risiede"; and, in some copies, page 23, line 2 up, "sco-" corrected to "co-."

Note: Reprinted, with *Oro e lavoro*—A52a—and *Introduzione alla natura economica
degli S. U. A.*—A53a—as . . . *Lavoro ed usura: tre saggi* ([1954])—A68.

b. *First edition in English* (1951):

AMERICA, ROOSEVELT | AND THE CAUSES OF | THE PRESENT
WAR | By | EZRA POUND | PETER RUSSELL | 114b Queen's Gate,
London, S. W.7 | 1951

17, [1] pp., 1 leaf. 21·5 × 13·8 cm. Stiff cream paper wrappers printed in black
and red on page [1] and in black on pages [ii–iv]; wire-stitched.

Published late in 1951 at 2s. 6d. as "Money Pamphlets by £, No. 6"; 1000
copies printed. *On verso of title-leaf:* Title of original work: L'America, Roosevelt
e le cause della guerra presente First published at Venice in 1944 First English
edition Translated by John Drummond . . . *Imprint at foot of page* [*iv*] *of wrapper:*
Printed by Clements & Son (T. W.), Ltd., Tunbridge Wells, Kent.

Note: This English translation by John Drummond was reprinted, with excisions, as "America and the Second World War," in *Impact* (1960)—A78—pp.
184–96.

A. BOOKS AND PAMPHLETS

ORO E LAVORO [1944]

a. *First edition:*

ORO E LAVORO | alla memoria | di | AURELIO BAISI | RAPALLO | [*short rule*] | EZRA POUND [Rapallo, Tip. Moderna (Canessa)]

22, [2] pp. 23·9 × 16·9 cm. Wire-stitched.

Published Spring 1944 at L. 1; number of copies unknown. *Imprint on page* [24]: Rapallo Tip. Moderna (Canessa) 1944–XXII . . . *On verso of title-leaf:* . . . Sumptibus G. Danè

Note: Reprinted, with *L'America, Roosevelt e le cause della guerra presente*—A51a— and *Introduzione alla natura economica degli S. U. A.*—A53a—as . . . *Lavoro ed usura: tre saggi* ([1954])—A68.

b. *First edition in English, first (suppressed) impression* (1951 [*i.e.* 1952]):

GOLD AND LABOUR | 1st English Edition | by | EZRA POUND | PETER RUSSELL | 114b Queens Gate, London, S. W.7 | 1951 [*i.e.* 1952]

16 pp. 21·2 × 13·7 cm. Stiff cream paper wrappers printed in red and black on page [i] and in black on pages [ii–iv]; wire-stitched. (*Title on page* [*i*] *of wrapper:* GOLD AND WORK)

Published 13 January 1952 at 2s. 6d. as "Money Pamphlets by £, No. 2"; 1000 copies printed (most of which were destroyed by the printers). *On verso of title-leaf:* Title of original work: Oro e lavoro . . . first published at Rapallo in 1944 The present translation is by John Drummond . . . *Imprint at foot of page* [*iv*] *of wrapper:* Printed at the Ditchling Press, Sussex

After the text but not the wrappers had been printed, the publisher received a letter from the author insisting that "Work" and not "Labour" was the correct and unambiguous translation of "lavoro." The title was therefore printed on the front cover in accordance with Ezra Pound's emendation.

On 14 January 1952, the day after the delivery of the first impression to the publisher, the printers asked to take back and destroy all copies because they feared that two phrases in the text as printed might be considered libellous. (These were a reference to Churchill, Roosevelt, and Baruch in lines 40–41 of page 11, and an uncomplimentary description of Philip Gibbs in line 6 on page 14.) Some copies had already been distributed (the publisher thinks "about 20," but the actual number—most of them sent apparently to the United States— would appear to have been considerably larger); the rest were destroyed and a new impression was made from the same setting of type, but with the offending passages omitted.

A. BOOKS AND PAMPHLETS

c. *First edition in English, second impression* (1951 [*i.e.* 1952]):

GOLD AND WORK | 1st English edition | by | EZRA POUND |
PETER RUSSELL | 114b Queens Gate, London, S. W.7 | 1951 [*i.e.*
1952]

16 pp. 20·5 × 13·8 cm. Binding and series as in the first impression.

Published late January 1952 at 2*s.* 6*d.*; 1000 copies printed from the same setting
of type as the first impression and identical with it except that half of line 40
and all of line 41 on page 11, and the beginning of line 6 on page 14 have been
omitted, resulting in obvious (and unexplained) gaps in the lines cited.

Note: This English translation by John Drummond was reprinted, with revisions, as "The Enemy Is Ignorance," in *Impact* (1960)—A78—pp. 98–117, and,
without those revisions, as "Gold and Work" in *Selected Prose 1909–1965*
([1973])—A93a—pp. 306–21 (336–51 in A93b).

A53   INTRODUZIONE ALLA   1944
NATURA ECONOMICA DEGLI
S.U.A.

a. *First edition:*

[*Within border of single rule within double rule:*] BIBLIOTECA DI
CULTURA POLITICA | [*rule*] | EZRA POUND | [*short rule*] | Intro-
duzione alla natura | economica degli S. U. A. | [*short double rule*] |
VENEZIA | CASA EDITRICE DELLE EDIZIONI POPOLARI | 1944–
XXII

35, [1] pp. 19·3 × 12·2 cm. Heavy white paper wrappers printed in black and
red on page [i] and in black on page [iv]; wire-stitched. (The paper used for
both wrappers and text varies in weight and quality.)

Published June 1944 at L. 5 as "Biblioteca di Cultura Politica, [6]"; number of
copies unknown. *Colophon (foot of page* [36]): Finito di stampare il 18 Giugno
1944–XXII

Note: Reprinted, with *Oro e lavoro*—A52a—and *L'America, Roosevelt e le cause
della guerra presente*—A51a—as . . . *Lavoro ed usura: tre saggi* ([1954])—A68.

b. *First edition in English* ([1950]):

MONEY PAMPHLETS BY £ | number one | [*rule*] | An Introduction
| to the Economic Nature | of the | UNITED STATES | [*rule*] |
translated from the original Italian | by Carmine Amore [London,
Peter Russell]

A. BOOKS AND PAMPHLETS

22 pp., 1 blank leaf. 21·5 × 14 cm. Stiff cream paper wrappers printed in black and red on page [i] and in black on page [iv]; wire-stitched.

Published Spring 1950 at 2s. 6d. as "Money Pamphlets by £, No. 1"; 1000 copies printed (of which 250 were burned). *Imprint at foot of page [iv] of wrapper:* Printed by Hague Gill & Davey Ltd at Pigotts near High Wycombe

"The object of this series of reprinted pamphlets is to present to the public at a reasonable price the evidence in the much discussed case of Ezra Pound. This material has never been readily accessible to the English reader, and without it no possible opinion about Pound can be valid. Not only does the series serve as an indispensable introduction to the economic and political thought of Ezra Pound, it is an essential to the full understanding of his major poetical work, *The Cantos*." ("Publisher's Note," p. [3])

Note: This English translation by Carmine Armore was reprinted, with revisions, in *Impact* (1960)—A78—pp. 15–39, and, without those revisions, in *Selected Prose 1909–1965* ([1973])—A93a—pp. 137–55 (167–85 in A93b).

A54   TESTAMENTO DI CONFUCIO   1944

First separate edition of the Italian translation (1944):

TESTAMENTO | DI | CONFUCIO | Versione italiana di Ezra Pound | e di Alberto Luchini | * | CASA EDITRICE | DELLE EDIZIONI POPOLARI | VENEZIA 1944–XXII

1 blank leaf, 1 leaf, 5–37 pp., 1 leaf. 16·7 × 11·8 cm. Stiff white paper wrappers printed in brown on pages [i] and [iv]; wire-stitched.

Published July 1944 at L. 5; number of copies unknown. *Colophon (page [39]):* Finito di stampare il 20 Luglio 1944

Notes: For the first edition of the Italian translation (with the Chinese text) see *Confucio. Ta S'eu. Dai Gaku. Studio integrale* (1942)—B46.

For Ezra Pound's English translation of this text, see "The Great Digest" in *Confucius. The Unwobbling Pivot & The Great Digest* (1947)—A58. Ezra Pound's earlier English version is *Ta Hio, the Great Learning* (1928)—A28.

A55   ORIENTAMENTI   1944

a. *First edition:*

EZRA POUND | ORIENTAMENTI | * | VENEZIA | CASA EDITRICE DELLE EDIZIONI POPOLARI | 1944–XXII

1 blank leaf, 2 leaves, 7–132, [1] pp., 1 leaf, incl. 4 illus. 23·9 × 16·4 cm. Heavy buff paper wrappers printed in brown, red, and black on page [i], and in black on page [iv], and up the spine.

A. BOOKS AND PAMPHLETS

Printed September 1944 (not published, but originally intended for sale at L. 15); number of copies unknown. *Colophon* (*page* [136]): Finito di stampare il 30 Settembre 1944–XXII

Although the printing of the book was completed, according to the colophon, at the end of September, the distribution of copies was held up for several weeks. One copy had been sent to the author, and a number of review copies had apparently also been distributed, when it was decided to destroy the entire edition of the book because of its political and economic nature. Only a small number of copies escaped destruction: although efforts were made at the time to secure additional author's copies, none was forthcoming. (Ezra Pound did not see proofs for the book, and in his copy—at Brunnenburg in 1961—he has marked numerous misprints.)

"La portata di questo libro, o almeno l'intenzione che mi mosse a scriverlo fu già dichiarata sul *Giornale di Genova* il 13 aprile, anno XVII, 1940, e non credo di poterla riassumere in breve. Ciò che mi scusa di presentare qui una raccolta di scritti piuttosto che una trattazione organica, è che io ho tentato a più riprese di riassumerne la materia, ed ogni volta son dovuto tornare agli originali primitivi, per dettagli necessari alla comprensione dei lettori. *Carta da Visita, Oro e Lavoro, America, Roosevelt e le cause della Guerra presente* rinforzano spero, e giustificano il mio atteggiamento." (*Prefatory note*, p. [5]) Except for the first article, the contents of this book are reprinted from *Meridiano di Roma*, Rome, dates as indicated below.

Contents: Carta di identità di Ezra Pound: Nego (*Giornale di Genova*, 13 April 1940); Ezra Pound [by Ubaldo degli Uberti] (4 December 1938); Ezra Pound [selections from an interview written in 1931 and originally printed in *Broletto* by Francesco Monotti] (19 April 1942)—La contemporaneità nei Canti di Ezra Pound [selections compiled by Olga Rudge] (7 July 1940)—Condutture avvelenate (14 May 1939)—Un modo di comunicare (24 September 1939)—Ancora pericolo (7 January 1940)—Gli Ebrei e questa guerra (24 March 1940)—Antifascisti (14 April 1940)—Da far capire agli Americani (30 June 1940)—Valuta, lavoro e decadenze (7 July 1940)—Il sistema dei vampiri (4 August 1940)—Nebbie ["Perchè certe nebbie esistono ancora"] (21 July 1940)—Opinioni da rivedere (18 August 1940)—Di una nuova economia (13 October 1940)—Libero scambio (20 October 1940)—Usura e società anonime (24 November 1940)—La moneta (9 February 1941)—Libertà e dovere (23 February 1941)—Verso l'ortologia (22 June 1941)—Interesse al cento per cento (6 July 1941)—Il problema delle tasse (31 August 1941)—L'Ebreo, patologia incarnata (12 October 1941)—Bolscevismo e usura (12 October 1941)—Sul discorso di Hitler (30 November 1941)—Mondiale (18 January 1942)—La guerra degli usurai (3 May 1942)—Forze "naturali" e lo sforzo umano nell'economia (3 May 1942)—Usura contro umanità (3 May 1942)—Ob pecuniae scarsitatem (7 June 1942)—Moneta prescrittibile (5 July 1942)—Risparmio ["Problemi economici . . . "] (4 April 1943)—Wallace (22 February 1942)—Anglo-Israele (12 January 1941)—La cambiale (2 August 1942)—Credito sociale (27 September 1942)—Distinguiamo (27 September 1942)—Di un sistema economico (1 December 1940)

A. BOOKS AND PAMPHLETS

b. *Second edition (unauthorised,* [1978]):

Ezra Pound | ORIENTAMENTI [Vibo Valentia, Le officine della Grafica Meridionale SpA.]

1 leaf, 1 blank leaf, 1 leaf, 7–137 pp., 1 leaf. 17 × 11·8 cm. Heavy cream paper wrappers printed in maroon and black on page [i], and in black on page [iv] and up the spine.

Published without authorisation July 1978 at L.2,500; number of copies unknown. *Colophon (page* [140]*):* Questa edizione è stata eseguita presso le officine della Grafica Meridionale SpA in Vibo Valentia nel mese di luglio 1978

A56   JEFFERSON E MUSSOLINI   1944

First edition:

STUDI POLITICI ED ECONOMICI | [*short double rule*] 2 [*short double rule*] | EZRA POUND | JEFFERSON e MUSSOLINI | VENEZIA | CASA EDITRICE DELLE EDIZIONI POPOLARI – 1944–XXIII | CASELLA POSTALE 486

1 blank leaf, 2 leaves, [7]–110 pp., 1 leaf. 21·5 × 15 cm. Heavy buff paper wrappers printed in black and red on page [i] and up the spine, and in black on pages [iii–iv].

Printed December 1944 (not published but originally intended for sale at L. 15 as "Studi Politici ed Economici, 2"); number of copies unknown. *Colophon (page* [111]*):* Finito di stampare il giorno 6 dicembre dell'anno 1944 XXIII

The printing had hardly been completed when it was decided that because of the political and economic nature of the book the entire edition should be destroyed. Only a few copies escaped: one copy had been sent to Mussolini, although none had been sent to the author, and a few other copies had apparently been distributed for review (it is listed in the *Bollettino delle Pubblicazioni Italiane* for 1945).

A rewriting by Ezra Pound in Italian of his *Jefferson and/or Mussolini* (1935)— A41.

A57   CHIUNG IUNG   1945
        L'ASSE CHE NON VACILLA

First edition:

CHIUNG IUNG | L'ASSE CHE NON VACILLA | SECONDO DEI LIBRI CONFUCIANI | VERSIONE ITALIANA | di EZRA POUND |

A. BOOKS AND PAMPHLETS

[*ideograms*] | VENEZIA | CASA EDITRICE DELLE EDIZIONI PO-
POLARI | 1945–XXIII

47, [1] pp. 18 × 12·4 cm. (wrappers); 17 × 12 cm. (sheets). Heavy buff paper
wrappers printed in black and red on page [i] and in black on page [iv].

Published February 1945 at L. 5; number of copies unknown. *Colophon* (*at foot
of page* [48])*:* Finito di stampare il 1 febbraio 1945–XXIII nella Stamperia già
Zanetti Venezia

Although the pamphlet was published and copies were sold, the bulk of the
edition was burned immediately after the Liberation because ("asse" being the
Italian word for "axis") the text was condemned, unread, as propaganda in
favor of the Berlin–Rome–Tokyo Axis.

For Ezra Pound's English translation of this text, see "The Unwobbling Pivot"
in *Confucius. The Unwobbling Pivot & The Great Digest* (1947)—A58—and *Confucius. The Great Digest & Unwobbling Pivot* ([1951])—B53.

A58   CONFUCIUS.   1947
            THE UNWOBBLING PIVOT &
                THE GREAT DIGEST

a. *First edition:*

Confucius | The Unwobbling Pivot & | The Great Digest | trans-
lated by Ezra Pound | With notes and commentary on the text
and the ideograms, | together with Ciu Hsi's "Preface" to the
Chung Yung and | Tseng's commentary on the Testament | Pharos
[New Directions, Norfolk, Conn.] | Winter, 1947

52, [1], [11] pp. 23·5 × 16·2 cm. (wrappers); 22·8 × 15·4 cm. (sheets). Heavy
rose paper wrappers printed in black on page [i].

Published 18 March 1947 at $1.00 as "Pharos, No. 4"; 929 copies printed. *Im-
print at foot of page* [64]*:* Printer, Dudley Kimball Parsippany, New Jersey

Advertisements, [11] pages following page [53], are an integral part of the volume.

Notes: "The Unwobbling Pivot" is an English version of *Ciung Iung. L'asse che
non vacilla* (1945)—A57. "The Great Digest" is an English version of *Confucio.
Ta S'eu. Dai Gaku. Studio integrale* (1942)—B46—and of *Testamento di Confucio*
(1944)—A54; it is a revision of *Ta Hio, the Great Learning* (1928)—A28.

For a new edition, with the Chinese text, see *Confucius. The Great Digest & Unwobbling Pivot* ([1951])—B53.

A. BOOKS AND PAMPHLETS

b. *Indian edition* ([1949]):

CONFUCIUS | The Unwobbling Pivot & | The Great Digest | Translated by | EZRA POUND | With notes and commentary on the text and the ideograms | together with Ciu Hsi's "Preface" to the Chung Yung | and Tseng's commentary on the Testament | Published for | KAVITABHAVAN | by | ORIENT LONGMANS LTD. | BOMBAY :: CALCUTTA :: MADRAS

4 leaves, 44 pp. 21·1 × 13·7 cm. Heavy cream paper wrappers printed in brown on pages [i] and [iv] and down the spine; end-papers.

Published May 1949 at 2 rupees, 8 annas; 1100 copies printed. *On verso of title-leaf:* ... First Published in India 1949 Printed in India By B. K. Sen at the Modern India Press, 7 Wellington Square, Calcutta.

Contains "Dedication to Amiya Chakravarty," by Ezra Pound, recto of third leaf, not in the first edition (of which the text is an exact reprint).

Note: This book was itself reprinted, by offset, and issued 14 July 1951, in a single volume with a reduced offset reprinting of *The Chinese Written Character as a Medium for Poetry*—B36a—as *Ernest Fenollosa. The Chinese Written Character as a Medium for Poetry. With Offset of the Calcutta Edition of Pivot* ([Washington, D. C.] Square $ Series [1951]), where it appears as pages [3]–49 (pages [1]–47 in later editions).

A59   "IF THIS BE TREASON......"   [1948]

First edition:

"IF THIS BE TREASON......" | e. e. cummings/examind [*sic*] | James Joyce: to his memory | A french accent | "Canto 45" | Blast [Siena, Italy, Printed for Olga Rudge by Tip. Nuova]

1 blank leaf, 33, [1] pp. 21·3 × 15·6 cm. Stiff green paper wrappers printed in black on page [i]; wire-stitched.

Tentatively released in January and distributed gratis more generally beginning in February 1948; probably 300 copies printed. *Imprint on page* [34]: Printed for Olga Rudge by Tip. Nuova Siena, Italy. January 1948 *On verso of title-leaf:* ... Limited edition. Copy n.° [*number written in.* (Most copies were left unnumbered.)]

"These [Rome radio broadcast] 'talks' are printed from the original rough drafts. No cuts, corrections or changes have been made. I have not been able to consult the author about this or other matters. I trust he will not feel that I have taken him too 'au pied de la lettre'. Olga Rudge" (*Note*, p. [2])

Contents: E. E. Cummings—E. E. Cummings/examind [21 May 1942]—James

A. BOOKS AND PAMPHLETS

Joyce: to his memory—A French Accent [11 May 1942]—Canto 45 [Ezra Pound's introductory remarks to his reading of this Canto]—Blast [*i.e.* Wyndham Lewis's periodical of that title; 26 Apr. 1942].

A60   THE PISAN CANTOS   [1948]

a. *First edition:*

EZRA POUND | THE PISAN | CANTOS | A NEW DIRECTIONS BOOK [New York, James Laughlin]

1 blank leaf, 2 leaves, 118 pp., 2 blank leaves, incl. music. 22·1 × 14·2 cm. Black cloth boards lettered in silver down the spine; end-papers. Grey dustjacket printed in green.

Published 30 July 1943 at $2.75; 1525 copies printed. *On verso of title-leaf:* . . . Manufactured in the United States by the Vail-Ballou Press New Directions Books are published by James Laughlin New York Office—500 Fifth Avenue—18

"These ten [*i.e.* eleven] Cantos, called 'The Pisan Cantos' because they were composed when the poet was incarcerated in a prison camp near Pisa, are the most recent additions to the monumental epic poem on which Pound has been at work for more than twenty [*i.e.* thirty] years." (*Dust-jacket*)

Contents: [Cantos] LXXIV–LXXXIV

Notes: Cantos LXXII and LXXIII, omitted from the sequence, were withheld by the author. Of these two Cantos, written in Italian, 26 lines of Canto LXXII were printed as "Presenza di F. T. Marinetti" in *Marina Repubblicana*, Venice, for 15 January 1945—C1697b, and the complete Canto LXXIII appeared in the same paper for 1 February 1945—C1699a. A copyright edition of both Cantos was printed by the Ezra Pound Estate in June 1973—A94—but they still (1981) have not been released for general circulation. (The 42 lines printed as "Canto Proceeding (72 circa)" in *Vice Versa*, New York, for January 1942—C1625— were reprinted with some changes in *Drafts & Fragments of Cantos CX–CXVII* ([1969])—A91—as a fragment unassigned.)

Canto LXXV consists of seven lines followed by Janequin's motet "Les Oiseaux," reproduced (in an arrangement by Gerhart Münch for violin) in facsimile of the manuscript (in the hand of Olga Rudge).

The first page of a corrected typescript (at Yale) of *The Pisan Cantos* was transcribed, with illustration opposite, on page 170 of volume 2 of P. J. Croft's *Autograph Poetry in the English Language: Facsimiles of Original Manuscripts from the Fourteenth to the Twentieth Century* (2 volumes, London, Cassell, 1973, and New York [etc.], McGraw-Hill Book Company [1973]).

A. BOOKS AND PAMPHLETS

b. *First English edition* ([1949]):

EZRA POUND | [*rule*] | THE | PISAN | CANTOS | FABER AND FABER | LONDON

1 blank leaf, 2 leaves, 7–132 pp. 20·8 × 14·7 cm. Black cloth boards lettered in gold down the spine; end-papers. Buff dust-jacket printed in red and black.

Published 22 July 1949 at 12s. 6d.; 1976 copies printed. *On verso of title-leaf:* First published in mcmxlix . . . Printed in Great Britain by R. MacLehose and Company Limited The University Press Glasgow . . .

In the first impression, pages 104 and 105 occur in the wrong order, which should be, as numbered: 103, 105, 104, 106. The error was corrected in later impressions, which are identified on the verso of the title-leaf.

Notes: In this English edition a number of omissions and expurgations were introduced in the text. Three words referring to King David (printed as line 17 on page 7 of the American edition) were omitted after the third line up on page 11; two words referring to Winston Churchill (printed in line 3 up on page 18 of the American edition) were omitted in line 16 on page 24; an 8-line passage referring to the Prince of Wales (printed as lines 15–22 on page 22 of the American edition) was omitted after line 9 on page 28; the word "buggering" (printed in line 15 on page 46 of the American edition) was replaced by "b . . . ." in line 3 up on page 53; the name "Maritain" (printed in line 9 up on page 50 and in line 12 on page 83 of the American edition) was replaced by "M . . . . . ." in line 13 up on page 58 and in line 13 on page 95; and a reference to Léon Blum (printed as line 12 up on page 72 in the American edition) was omitted after line 8 up on page 83. (The omitted words were restored in the edition of *The Cantos* published in 1976 by Faber and Faber—A61g.)

This book was reissued paperbound in 1973 by Faber and Faber in their series of Faber paper covered Editions at 80 *p*.

A61   THE CANTOS   [1948]

a. *First collected edition:*

THE CANTOS | OF | EZRA POUND | A NEW DIRECTIONS BOOK [New York, James Laughlin]

2 leaves, 149, 56, 46 pp., 1 leaf, 167, 118 pp. front.(port.) 21·7 × 14·5 cm. Black cloth boards lettered in silver down the spine; end-papers. Green dust-jacket printed in purple.

Published 30 July 1948 at $5.00; 2897 copies printed. *On verso of title-leaf:* . . . Manufactured in the United States by the Vail-Ballou Press [Printed from the plates of the original editions] New Directions Books are published by James Laughlin New York Office—500 Fifth Avenue—18

A. BOOKS AND PAMPHLETS

The frontispiece is a reproduction of a photograph of Ezra Pound by Arnold Genthe.

"The present volume brings together all the Cantos which have been completed to date. "—(*Dust-jacket*). Contents: *A Draft of XXX Cantos* [A31c]—*Eleven New Cantos XXXI–XLI* [A37b]—*The Fifth Decad of Cantos* [XLII–LI; A43c]—*Cantos LII–LXXI* [A47b]—*The Pisan Cantos* [LXXIV–LXXXIV; A60a].

Notes: A second impression of 2228 sets of sheets, identified on the verso of the title-leaf, was prepared and about 1000 copies were bound up in January 1951. The remaining sheets of this impression were bound up in December 1952 with a number of corrections supplied by cancel leaves. Subsequent impressions, with all cancels reprinted, are identified on the verso of the title-leaf. The fifth and later impressions contain "Author's Errata" facing page 3.

Some notes to Cantos XIV, XVI, XX, XXI, XXIX, and XLV, sent by Ezra Pound to one of the editors in June 1947, are incorporated in the notes to these Cantos in *Modern Poetry, American and British, Edited by Kimon Friar and John Malcolm Brinnin* (New York, [1951]), pp. 525–7 and 561.

b. *First English collected (offset) edition* ([1950]):

EZRA POUND | SEVENTY | CANTOS | FABER & FABER | LONDON

447 pp. 20·8 × 15 cm. Black cloth boards lettered in gold on spine; end-papers. White dust-jacket printed in red and black (with title on front: LXXI [*sic*] SEVENTY CANTOS . . .)

Published 1 September 1950 at 25s.; 1633 copies printed. *On verso of title-leaf:* First published in MCML . . . Printed in Great Britain by Sir Isaac Pitman and Sons Limited . . . [by offset from original editions]

"These cantos have previously appeared, under our imprint, in four separate volumes issued from time to time as the author released his work for publication. During the war we were unable to keep all four instalments in print; rather than reprint those which we cannot supply, we have thought that the time had come to collect them all into one volume." (*Dust-jacket*)

Contents: A Draft of XXX Cantos—A Draft of Cantos XXXI–XLI—The Fifth Decad of Cantos [XLII–LI]—*Cantos LII–LXXI*

Note: The book actually contains 71 cantos. The textual differences between this and the earlier separate editions are easily detected because emendations and corrections in this photographic reprint are in slightly lighter type than the original texts.

c. *Second English collected (offset) edition* ([1954]):

THE CANTOS | OF EZRA POUND | FABER & FABER | LONDON

576 pp. 20·8 × 14·7 cm. Black cloth boards lettered in gold on spine; end-papers. Yellow dust-jacket printed in black and red.

A. BOOKS AND PAMPHLETS

Published 18 June 1954 at 25s.; 2000 copies printed. *On verso of title-leaf:* First published in MCMLIV . . . Printed in Great Britain [by offset] by Sir Isaac Pitman and Sons Limited . . .

An "Errata" slip, listing 11 items in 12 lines, is tipped in after page 576.

Contents: A Draft of XXX Cantos—A Draft of Cantos XXXI–XLI—The Fifth Decad of Cantos [XLII–LI]—Cantos LII–LXXI—The Pisan Cantos [LXXIV–LXXXIV]. (For textual differences between this and the American collected edition—A61a— see Guy Davenport's "A Collation of Two Texts of the Cantos" in *Pound Newsletter*, 6 (April 1955) pp. 5–13.)

d. *Third English collected (offset) edition* ([1964]):
Title-page as in A61c.

798 pp., 1 blank leaf. 20·6 × 14·7 cm. Black cloth boards lettered in gold on spine; end-papers. White dust-jacket printed in black.

Published 29 October 1964 at 50 s.; 7686 copies printed. *On verso of title-leaf:* . . . New Collected edition (cantos 1–109) published in mcmlxiv . . . Printed in Great Britain [by offset] by Sir Isaac Pitman and Son Limited . . .

Contents: A Draft of XXX Cantos—A Draft of Cantos XXXI–XLI—The Fifth Decad of Cantos [XLII–LI]—Cantos LII–LXXI—The Pisan Cantos [LXXIV–LXXXIV]— Section: Rock-Drill [LXXXV–XCV]—Thrones [XCVI–CIX].

e. *Second American collected edition* ([1965]):

THE CANTOS | (1–95) | EZRA POUND | A NEW DIRECTIONS BOOK [New York, James Laughlin]

2 leaves, 149, 56, 46 pp., 1 leaf, 167, 118, 107 pp., 2 blank leaves. front.(port.) 21·7 × 14·7 cm. Black cloth boards lettered in silver on spine; end-papers. White dust-jacket printed in black.

Published 30 October 1965 at $7.50; 3000 copies printed. *On verso of title-leaf:* . . . First printing Manufactured in the United States New Directions books are published for James Laughlin by New Directions Publishing Corporation, 333 Sixth Avenue, New York 10014.

The frontispiece is a reproduction of a photograph of Ezra Pound by Arnold Genthe.

Contents: A Draft of XXX Cantos (with 20-line "Author's Errata" for Cantos XI– LXXXII added on page [2])—*Eleven New Cantos XXXI–XLI—The Fifth Decad of Cantos [XLII–LI]—Cantos LII–LXXI—The Pisan Cantos [LXXIV–LXXXIV]— Section: Rock-Drill 85–95 de Los Cantares.*

f. *Third American collected edition* ([1970]):

THE CANTOS | OF | EZRA POUND | A NEW DIRECTIONS BOOK [New York, James Laughlin]

3 leaves, 802 pp., 4 blank leaves, incl. front.(port.) 20·8 × 14·3 cm. Buff cloth boards lettered in black on spine; end-papers. Orange dust-jacket printed in black.

Published 11 November 1970 at $12.00; 3000 copies printed. *On verso of title-leaf:* . . . Frontispiece photograph by Arnold Genthe. Manufactured in the United States of America. . . . First printing of *Cantos 1–117* in one volume, 1970 New Directions Books are published for James Laughlin by New Directions Publishing Corporation, 333 Sixth Avenue, New York 10014.

Contents: A Draft of XXX Cantos—Eleven New Cantos XXXI–XLI—The Fifth Decad of Cantos XLII–LI—Cantos LII–LXXI—The Pisan Cantos LXXIV–LXXXIV—Section: Rock-Drill de Los Cantares LXXXV–XCV—Thrones de Los Cantares XCVI–CIX—Drafts and Fragments of Cantos CX–CXVII. (The third printing—of 1900 copies—so identified, issued in 1972 at $12.50, and described on the jacket as "Revised," has corrections and adds "Canto CXX" on page 803. It collates: 3 leaves, 803 pp., 3 blank leaves, incl. front.(port.) Size, binding, and (reprinted) jacket as for first printing.)

g. *Fourth English collected edition* ([1976]), *hardbound copies:*

THE CANTOS | OF | EZRA POUND | FABER AND FABER · LONDON

3 leaves, 802 pp., 4 blank leaves. 21·9 × 14 cm. Red cloth boards lettered in gold on spine; end-papers. White dust-jacket printed all-over in red.

Published 17 May 1976 at £8.50; 1000 copies printed. *On verso of title-leaf:* . . . Revised Collected edition (Cantos 1–117) published in 1975 [*sic*] . . . Printed in the United States of America . . .

The sheets of the third American collected edition, but without "Canto CXX." ". . . where certain names were omitted from our edition (for example, Churchill and Pétain [see A60b *note*] in deference to the libel laws, these are now restored." (*Dust-jacket*)

h. *Paperbound copies:*

Title-page and pagination as in hardbound copies. 21·2 × 13·6 cm. Heavy white paper wrappers printed all-over in red on page [i] and spine, in red and in black on page [iv], and in black on pages [ii-iii].

Published 17 May 1976 at £4.95 in the series of Faber Paperbacks; 6000 copies printed. Verso of title-leaf and contents as in hardbound copies.

A62   SELECTED POEMS   [1949]

a. *First edition:*

EZRA POUND | SELECTED POEMS | The New Classics Series [New York, New Directions, James Laughlin] viii, 184 pp. front. (port.) 18·3 × 12·5 cm. Red cloth boards lettered in black down the spine; end-papers. White dust-jacket printed in black, grey, red, and mauve.

Published 7 October 1949 at $1.50 as "The New Classics Series, 22"; 3400 copies printed. *On verso of title-leaf:* . . . Manufactured in the United States by the Vail-Ballou Press New Directions Books are published by James Laughlin New York Office—333 Sixth Avenue [A second impression (4500 copies), not so identified, was issued in December 1950.]

The frontispiece is a reproduction of a drawing of Ezra Pound by Wyndham Lewis.

"This volume has been assembled to give the student the best of Pound's verse in compact form and to provide an effective introduction for the general reader who is not familiar with the work of this great modern poet." (*Dust-jacket*)

Contents: Autobiography—Cino—Na Audiart—Villonaud for This Yule—The Tree—The White Stag—Sestina: Altaforte—Ballad of the Goodly Fere—Planh for the Young English King—"Blandula, tenulla, vagula"—Erat hora—The House of Splendour—The Tomb at Akr Çaar—Portrait d'une femme—An Object—The Seafarer—Δῶρια—Apparuit—A Virginal—Of Jacopo del Sellaio—The Return—Tenzone—The Garret—The Garden—Salutation—The Spring—A Pact—Dance Figure—April—The Rest—Les Millwin—A Song of the Degrees—Ité—Salvationists—Arides—Amitiés—Meditatio—Coda—The Coming of War: Actaeon—In a Station of the Metro—Alba—Coitus—The Encounter—Ἱμέρρω—Tame Cat—The Tea Shop—Ancient Music—The Lake Isle—Epitaphs ("Fu I"; "Li Po")—Villanelle: The Psychological Hour—Pagani's, November 8—Alba from "Langue d'Oc"—Near Perigord—Song of the Bowmen of Shu—The Beautiful Toilet—The River Song—The River-Merchant's Wife: A Letter—Poem by the Bridge at Ten-Shin—The Jewel Stairs' Grievance—Lament of the Frontier Guard—Exile's Letter—Taking Leave of a Friend—A Ballad of the Mulberry Road—Hugh Selwyn Mauberley—from Homage to Sextus Propertius, I, III–VII, IX–X, XII—Cantos [I–III, from IV, IX, XIII, from XIV, XV, from XVI, XVII, from XX, from XXV, from XXX, from XXXVI, XXXVIII, XLV, XLVII, XLIX, from LIII, from LXII, from LXXIV, from LXXVI, from LXXIX, from LXXX, from LXXXI, from LXXXIII]

Note: The "Autobiography," p. viii, is printed here for the first time; the poems are all reprinted from earlier books by Pound.

b. *New edition* ([1957]):

EZRA POUND | SELECTED POEMS | A NEW EDITION | A New Directions Paperbook [New York, James Laughlin]

viii, 184 pp. 18 × 10·8 cm. Stiff white paper wrappers printed in black on pages [i] and [iv].

Published 21 August 1957 at $1.15 as "New Directions Paperbook ND66"; 9993 copies printed. *On verso of title-leaf:* . . . The publishers are grateful to Hugh

Kenner and Hayden Carruth for suggestions in regard to the texts in this new edition. First Published as New Directions Paperbook No. 66, 1957 Manufactured in the United States by the Vail-Ballou Press New Directions Books are published by James Laughlin New York Office—333 Sixth Avenue

Contents identical, save for minor editorial changes, with those of the first edition, except for the addition on pages 179–84 of the following: from Canto XCI—from XCIII—[Note defining usury]—from Women of Trachis

Notes: In this edition the "Autobiography" is retitled, "Biography."

A second impression (10,006 copies), not identified, was issued in January 1959, and a third impression (about 10,000 copies), identified on verso of title-leaf, in October 1960.

A63   PATRIA MIA   [1950]

a. *First edition:*

PATRIA MIA | by [*3 ornamental rules*] | EZRA POUND | [*3 ornamental rules, followed by device*] | RALPH FLETCHER SEYMOUR Publisher CHICAGO | [*ornamental rule*]

3 blank leaves, 3 leaves, 15–97 pp., 4 blank leaves. 21·5 × 15·8 cm. Brown cloth boards stamped in dark brown on both covers and down the spine; first and last blank leaves pasted down as end-papers. White dust-jacket printed in blue and black.

Published 24 May 1950 at $2.75; number of copies unknown.

This book is a reworking of "Patria mia," printed in the *New Age*, London (sections I–V, VIII–XI, VI–VII, in that order) between 5 September and 14 November 1912—C49–51, 56, 59–60, 62, 57–58—and "America: Chances and Remedies," also printed in the *New Age* in six instalments between 1 May and 5 June 1913—C79–83, 85. The revised manuscript was sent in 1913 for publication to Seymour, Daughaday and Company (publishers of the magazine *Poetry*) in Chicago. Arrangements for publication were interrupted in 1915 by the dissolution of the publishers' partnership with consequent "adjustments of assets," during which the manuscript disappeared. It came to light again in 1950. The publisher explains these circumstances in a preface (pp. 15–16).

b. *First English edition* ([1962]):

PATRIA MIA | AND | THE TREATISE | ON HARMONY | Ezra Pound | PETER OWEN LIMITED : LONDON

95 pp. 22·1 × 14·1 cm. Dark green cloth boards stamped in gold on spine; end-papers. Green dust-jacket printed in red.

A. BOOKS AND PAMPHLETS

Published April 1962 at 21s.; 1500 copies printed.

Contents: Patria Mia (pp. [7]–73)—The Treatise on Harmony (pp. [75]–95)

Notes: "The Treatise on Harmony" is reprinted from *Antheil and The Treatise on Harmony*—A25a—pp. 1–24.

"Patria Mia" was reprinted in *Selected Prose 1909–1965* ([1973])—A93b—pp. [99]–141 (not included in A93a). "The Treatise on Harmony" was reprinted in *Selected Prose 1909–1965*—A93a—pp. [75]–86 (not included in A93b), and in *Ezra Pound and Music* ([1977])—A99—pp. 293–306.

A64   THE LETTERS   [1950]

a. First edition:

THE LETTERS OF | EZRA POUND | 1907–1941 | EDITED BY D. D. PAIGE | [*quotation in 1 line*] | HARCOURT, BRACE AND COMPANY : NEW YORK

xxv, 358 pp. 24·3 × 16·5 cm. Brown cloth boards stamped in blind on front cover and in gold on spine; end-papers; top edges stained yellow. Yellow dust-jacket printed in red and brown.

Published 26 October 1950 at $5.00; 4000 copies printed. *On verso of title-leaf:* ... first edition Printed in the United States of America

Contains a "Preface," by Mark Van Doren, pp. [c]–ix. The running heads give place and year of writing. Included in the letters or as footnotes to them are: four lines omitted from "Reflection and Advice" [later, "Pax Saturni"] and four from "Commission" when those poems were printed in *Poetry* (to Harriet Monroe, 30 Mar. 1913), p. 17, footnote 1; "Sage homme," a 27-line "squib" on *The Waste Land* (to T. S. Eliot, 24 Saturnus ⟨Dec. 1921⟩, *i.e.* Jan. 1922), p. 170; text of *Bel Esprit* ([1922])—E2e (to Kate Buss, ⟨?23⟩ Mar. 1922), pp. 174–5, footnote 1; "Ballade of the most gallant Mulligan, Senator in ordinary and the frivolous milkwench of Hogan ... " (to James Joyce, 16 Jan. 1923), pp. 184–5; "Program 1929" (to Charles Henri Ford, 1 Feb. 1929), p. 223, footnote 1; six-line "Epitaph [on Harriet Monroe]" (to T. C. Wilson, ⟨?Feb.⟩ 1934), p. 253; "To —— —— on England," four lines of doggerel (to E. E. Cummings, 25 Jan. 1935), p. 265; "Song fer the Muses' Garden," six lines of doggerel (to T. S. Eliot, 28 Mar. 1935), p. 272; four lines of doggerel beginning "There onct wuzza lady named Djuna [Barnes]" (to T. S. Eliot, Jan. 1937), p. 286; four lines of doggerel beginning "A[t] contract time the Hippol's [*sic*] eye" (to Laurence Pollinger, Feb. 1937), p. 289; four lines of doggerel beginning "Sez the Maltese dawg to the Siam cat" (to T. S. Eliot, 16 Apr. 1938), p. 307; nine lines of doggerel, on the death of the *Criterion*, beginning "Who killed Cock Possum?" (to Ronald Duncan, 10 Jan. 1939), p. 320; eight-line text of the song "Buck Flea"—E4ko (to Tibor and Alice Serly, Oct. 1939), p. 326, footnote 1; ten "Lines to go into

Canto 72 or somewhere," beginning "Now sun rises in Ram sign" (to Katue Kitasono, 12 Mar. 1941), p. 348.

Notes: An advertising leaflet entitled *A Sampler from the New Book . . . The Letters of Ezra Pound 1907–1941* . . . , 14, [2] pp., wire-stitched, was issued in an edition of 15,000 copies by the publishers.

A new (offset) edition (8000 copies) was issued in paper binding by Harcourt, Brace & World, Inc. in New York on 31 October 1962 at $2.25 as "Harvest Book HB 54."

The two letters to T. E. Lawrence printed (apparently from retained carbon copies) on pages 152–3 and 154–5 are reprinted (from the originals) with slight variations in *Letters to T. E. Lawrence, Edited by A. W. Lawrence* (London [1962]), pp. 149–51.

This book was published paperbound by New Directions in New York 24 March 1971 at $2.95 with title *The Selected Letters of Ezra Pound 1907–1941* as their Paperbook 317, in a first printing of 4470 copies.

b. *First English edition* ([1951]):

THE LETTERS OF | EZRA POUND | 1907–1941 | edited by | D. D. PAIGE | [*quotation in 2 lines*] | FABER AND FABER | 24 Russell Square | London

1 blank leaf, 2 leaves, 7–464 pp. 22·5 × 15 cm. Red cloth boards lettered in gold on spine; end-papers; top edges stained yellow (or, later—1958, blue). Orange dust-jacket printed in red and black (or, later—1958, green dust-jacket printed in green and red).

Published 22 March 1951 at 25*s.* (raised to 30*s.* in 1958); 2990 sets of sheets printed (of which 971 were issued 3 December 1958 at 30*s.*).

On verso of title-leaf: First published in mcmli . . . Printed in Great Britain by Western Printing Services Limited, Bristol . . .

This edition does not contain the preface by Mark Van Doren. The running heads give place and Pound's age at time of writing.

c. *Second English edition* ([1971]):

THE SELECTED LETTERS OF | EZRA POUND | 1907–1941 | EDITED BY D. D. PAIGE | FABER AND FABER | LONDON

xxv, 358 pp. 22·3 × 14 cm. Green cloth boards stamped in gold' on spine; end-papers. Cream dust-jacket printed in yellow, black, and green.

Published 11 October 1971 at £3.50; 750 copies printed. *On verso of title-leaf:* . . . This edition published in the U. K. by Faber and Faber Limited 3 Queen Square London W. C. I . . . This book was originally published in 1950 as *The Letters of Ezra Pound, 1907–1941.*

A. BOOKS AND PAMPHLETS

"This reissue is a copy of the original American edition, which differs slightly from the original British edition." (*Dust-jacket*)

Contents as in A64a, from which the text was reproduced by offset.

A65   CONFUCIAN ANALECTS   [1951]

a. *First edition:*

CONFUCIAN | ANALECTS | Reprinted by permission of the | HUDSON REVIEW | 439 West Street | NEW YORK 14, N. Y. | SQUARE $ SERIES | P. O. Box 552 G. P. O. | New York 1, N. Y.

98 pp., 1 leaf. 21·6 × 14 cm. Stiff grey paper wrappers (with, in some copies, white paper wrap-around printed in red) printed in black on pages [i] and [iv], on flaps, and down the spine; stapled.

Published Autumn 1951 at $1.00; number of copies unknown. (Reprinted from the *Hudson Review* for Spring and Summer 1950—C1720 & 1725.) *On verso of title-leaf:* ... 1951 [Two copies have been noted with verso of title-leaf blank. They have untrimmed wrappers measuring 22·7 × 14·4 cm.]

Publisher's advertisement, 1 leaf following page 98, is inserted.

Notes: For Ezra Pound's earlier summary of the text see *Confucius. Digest of the Analects* ([1937])—A44—which was reprinted with minor omissions as the first chapter of Section I, Part I, of *Guide to Kulchur* (1938)—A45—pp. 15–21.

This book was reprinted by offset, along with the Stone Classics edition of *The Great Digest and The Unwobbling Pivot*, in September 1969 in New York by New Directions as their Paperbook 285 at $2.45 (but available also in cloth at $6.50). Some copies were printed and bound with pages 280 and 281 transposed; the error was corrected in 4000 bound copies by a four-page tip-in. This reprint contains "Procedure" and "Brief Concordance," both by Pound, pp. 191–2.

b. *First English edition* ([1956]):

CONFUCIAN | ANALECTS | [*thick-thin rule*] | translated and | introduced by | EZRA POUND | [*thin-thick rule*] | PETER OWEN LIMITED | London

135, [1] pp. 22 × 14·3 cm. Gold cloth boards lettered in purple down the spine; end-papers. (Bound up at various times in slightly variant cloths; in a late binding of *circa* 1961, the cloth is light brown and is lettered in gold.) Yellow dust-jacket printed in purple.

Published 15 February 1956 at 16s.; about 1500 copies printed. *On verso of title-leaf:* ... Printed in Great Britain by Boscombe Printing Co. (1933) Ltd., 1 Haviland Road, Bournemouth MCMLVI

Contains "Procedure," pp. 7–8, and "Brief Concordance," p. [136], not in the first American edition. (Peter Owen reprinted these by offset, presumably in 1956, as a 2-page leaflet, 27·8 × 21·4 cm., headed on page [1]: CONFUCIAN ANALECTS. "Procedure" appears on page [1] and "Brief Concordance" on page [2] with, at the foot of that page, a statement by Kasper & Horton that "The new London edition of ANALECTS, published by Peter Owen ... price 16 shillings, U.S.A. $2.25, contains this extra page. We have no objection to the import and sale of that edition, at that price.")

A66   THE TRANSLATIONS   [1953]

a. *First edition:*

The | TRANSLATIONS OF | EZRA POUND | With an Introduction by | HUGH KENNER | FABER AND FABER | 24 Russell Square | London

1 blank leaf, 2 leaves, 7–408 pp. 22·7 × 14·7 cm. Blue cloth boards stamped in gold on spine; end-papers; top edges stained yellow. Orange dust-jacket printed in black and red.

Published 31 July 1953 at 30s.; 1398 copies printed. *On verso of title-leaf:* First published in mcmliii ... Printed in Great Britain by R. MacLehose and Company Limited The University Press Glasgow ... [Verso of half-title-leaf lists eight titles "by the same author".]

Contents: Introduction by Hugh Kenner—Cavalcanti Poems (Introduction dated 15 November 1910) (1912; revised 1920, 1931)—Arnaut Daniel Poems (*Umbra* and *Instigations* 1920)—Cathay (1915)—The Seafarer (*Ripostes*, 1912; also reprinted with *Cathay* 1915)—Noh Plays (1916)—Dust for Sparrows by Remy de Gourmont ([*Dial*] 1920)—MISCELLANEOUS POEMS: To Formianus' Young Lady Friend; after Valerius Catullus (*Lustra*, 1916 [*i.e. Quia Pauper Amavi*, 1919])—Her Monument, the Image Cut Thereon; from the Italian by Leopardi ([*Canzoni*] 1911)—Rome; from the French of Joachim du Bellay ([*Canzoni*] 1911)—Dieu! Qu'il la fait; from Charles D'Orleans (*Ripostes*, 1912)—Pierrots: from the French of Jules Laforgue (*The Little Review*, 1917 [and *Pavannes & Divisions*, 1918])

Note: The selection of the contents was made by Ezra Pound.

b. *American issue, hardbound* ([1953]):

The | TRANSLATIONS OF | EZRA POUND | With an Introduction by | HUGH KENNER | NEW DIRECTIONS [New York, James Laughlin]

1 blank leaf, 2 leaves, 7–408 pp. 22·2 × 14·5 cm. Black cloth boards lettered in silver down the spine; end-papers. White dust-jacket printed in green and black.

Published 31 August 1953 at $6.00; 4863 sets of sheets printed by Faber and

A. BOOKS AND PAMPHLETS

Faber for New Directions, of which 2000 were bound and jacketed in the United States. (Of these sheets, 750 sets were bought back by Faber and Faber for use—with cancel title-leaf—in their re-issue of the book, announced for Autumn 1962 but postponed until 8 February 1963—A66c; 1820 sets were issued in the United States in paper binding by New Directions 20 March 1963—A66d.) *On verso of title-leaf:* Printed in England New Directions Books are published by James Laughlin New York Office: 333 Sixth Avenue, New York City . . . [Verso of half-title-leaf lists nine titles "by the same author" and two titles "about the author."]

Contents as in A66a.

c. *English re-issue of the American issue* ([1963]):

Title-page and pagination as in A66a. 22·3 × 14·7 cm. Blue cloth boards stamped in gold on spine; end-papers; top edges stained yellow. Blue dust-jacket printed in black and red.

Published 8 February 1963 at 42 *s.*; 750 sets of sheets (originally printed for New Directions but bought back by Faber and Faber) issued with a cancel title-leaf. *On verso of title-leaf:* . . . Reissued mcmlxiii Printed in Great Britain by R. MacLehose and Company Limited The University Press Glasgow . . .

d. *American re-issue* ([1963]):

Title-page and pagination as in A66b. 20·4 × 13·7 cm. Heavy white paper wrappers printed in black on page [i] (with photograph of Ezra Pound by Boris de Rachewiltz), on page [iv], and on spine.

Published 20 March 1963 as New Directions Paperbook 130 at $2.25; 1820 sets of sheets (originally printed for New Directions by Faber and Faber in 1953) cut down and issued in wrappers. (Versos of title-leaf and half-title-leaf as in A66b.)

e. *Enlarged edition* ([1964]):

EZRA POUND | TRANSLATIONS | With an Introduction by | HUGH KENNER | NEW DIRECTIONS [Norfolk, Conn., James Laughlin]

1 blank leaf, 2 leaves, 7–448 pp. 20·4 × 13·6 cm. Heavy white paper wrappers printed in black on page [i] (with photograph of Ezra Pound by Boris de Rachewiltz), on page [iv], and on spine.

Published 18 February 1964 as New Directions Paperbook 145 at $2.25; 10,000 copies printed. *On verso of title-leaf:* . . . Enlarged edition, ND Paperbook 145, 1963 [*sic*] . . . Manufactured in the United States New Directions Books are published by James Laughlin at Norfolk, Connecticut. New York Office: 333

A. BOOKS AND PAMPHLETS

Sixth Avenue, New York City 14. ... [Verso of half-title-leaf lists 14 titles of "Other Books (in print) by Ezra Pound".]

Pages 9–397 are a reprint by offset of these pages in the earlier editions; the section "Miscellaneous Poems," pp. [399]–408 in A66a–d, has been expanded to occupy pages [399]–448, with these contents: Egyptian: Conversations in Courtship (1960)—Horace: "Ask not ungainly" (*Odes*, I, 11—1963); "By the flat cup" (*Odes*, I, 31—1964); "This monument will outlast" (*Odes*, III, 30—1964)—Catullus: To Formianus' Young Lady Friend (*Lustra*, 1916); XXVI (1957); LXXXV (1963)—Rutilius: Roma (1963)—Navagero: Inscriptio fontis (*The Spirit of Romance*, 1910)—Kabir: Certain Poems (*Modern Review*, 1913)—[Arnaut] Daniel: Chansson doil (*New Age*, 1911); Rica conquesta (*New Age*, 1912); For Right of Audience (*New Age*, 1911); Canzon: Of the Trades and Love (*New Age*, 1912); Le ferm voler (*Hesternae Rosae*, 1913)—Bertrand de Born: A War Song (*The Spirit of Romance*, 1910)—Ventadorn: "Quant l'herba fresq el fuell apar" (*Hesternae Rosae*, 1913); The Lark (*The Spirit of Romance*, 1910)—Folquet de Romans: Las grans beautatz (*Hesternae Rosae*, 1913)—Cercalmon: Descant on a Theme (*Quia Pauper Amavi*, 1919)—Li Viniers: Mère au Sauveour (*Hesternae Rosae*, 1913)—D'Orléans: "Dieu! qu'il la fait" (*Ripostes*, 1912)—du Bellay: Rome (*Canzoni*, 1911)—de Boufflers: Air: Sentir avec ardeur (1963)—Rimbaud: Cabaret vert (*Rimbaud*, 1957); Comedy in Three Caresses (1957); Anadyomene (1957); Lice-Hunters (1957)—Tailhade: Rus (*Rimbaud*, 1957)—Laforgue: Pierrots (*Pavannes & Divisions*, 1918)—Lubicz-Milosz: Strophes (*Dial*, 1921)—Guinicelli: "Vedut ho la lucente stella Diana" (*The Spirit of Romance*, 1910)—Orlandi: Sonnet to Guido Cavalcanti (*Dial*, 1929)—St. Francis: Cantico del Sole (*The Spirit of Romance*, 1910)—Leopardi: Her Monument (*Canzoni*, 1911)—Montanari: Autunno (*Imagi*, 1951); Stagione di fiori (1951); Pomeriggio di Luglio (1951); Notte dietro le Persiane (1951); L'ultima ora (1963).

f. *English issue* ([1971]):

The | TRANSLATIONS OF | EZRA POUND | With an Introduction by | HUGH KENNER | FABER AND FABER | London

Pagination as in A66e. 19·9 × 13·3 cm. Heavy white paper wrappers printed in pink, black, and green on pages [i] and [iv], in pink and black on spine, and in black on pages [ii] and [iii].

Published 8 February 1971 in the series of Faber paper covered Editions at £ 1.25; 6000 copies printed. *On verso of title-leaf:* ... First published in this (enlarged) edition 1970 [*sic*] Printed in Great Britain by Latimer Trend and Co. Ltd., Whitstable ... [Verso of half-title-leaf lists ten titles "by Ezra Pound".]

Contents as in A66e.

A67   LITERARY ESSAYS   [1954]

a. *First edition:*

LITERARY ESSAYS | OF | EZRA POUND | Edited with an Intro-

A. BOOKS AND PAMPHLETS

duction | by | T. S. ELIOT | FABER AND FABER LIMITED | 24
Russell Square | London

1 blank leaf, 2 leaves, vii–xv, 464 pp. 22·3 × 14·8 cm. Grey cloth boards lettered in gold on spine; end-papers; top edges stained blue-grey. Yellow dust-
jacket printed in red and black.

Published 22 January 1954 at 30s.; 1745 copies printed. *On verso of title-leaf:* First
published in mcmliv ... Printed in Great Britain by R. MacLehose and Company Limited The University Press Glasgow ...

Contents: Introduction by T. S. Eliot—PART ONE: THE ART OF POETRY: A Retrospect—How to Read—The Serious Artist—The Teacher's Mission—The Constant Preaching to the Mob—Mr Housman at Little Bethel—Date Line—PART
TWO: THE TRADITION: The Tradition—Troubadours–Their Sorts and Conditions—Arnaut Daniel—Cavalcanti—Hell—The Renaissance—Notes on Elizabethan Classicists—Translators of Greek: Early Translators of Homer [includ-
ing "Translation of Aeschylus"]—The Rev. G. Crabbe, LL.B.—Irony, Laforgue,
and Some Satire—The Hard and Soft in French Poetry—Swinburne versus His
Biographers—Henry James—Remy de Gourmont—PART THREE: CONTEMPORA-
RIES: Lionel Johnson ["Preface" to *Poetical Works of Lionel Johnson* (1915)—B9]—
The Prose Tradition in Verse ["Mr. Hueffer and the Prose Tradition in Verse"]—
The Later Yeats—Robert Frost (Two Reviews) [excerpt from "In Metre," *New
Freewoman*, 1 September 1913, and "Modern Georgics," *Poetry*, December 1914]—
D. H. Lawrence [review of *Love Poems and Others, Poetry*, July 1913]—Dr Wil-
liams' Position—Dubliners and Mr James Joyce—Ulysses ["Paris Letter, May,
1922. Ulysses," *Dial*, New York, June 1922]—Joyce—T. S. Eliot—Wyndham
Lewis—Arnold Dolmetsch—Vers libre and Arnold Dolmetsch—Brancusi—In-
dex

Note: A new (offset) edition (7500 copies), issued 10 February 1961 at 12s. 6d.
in the series "Faber paper covered Editions," is identified on verso of title-leaf
as a lithographic reprint.

b. *American issue* ([1954]):

LITERARY ESSAYS | OF | EZRA POUND | Edited with an Intro-
duction | by | T. S. ELIOT | A NEW DIRECTIONS BOOK [Norfolk,
Conn., James Laughlin]

1 blank leaf, 2 leaves, vii–xv, 464 pp. 22·3 × 15 cm. Black cloth boards lettered
in silver down the spine; end-papers. White dust-jacket printed in red and black.

Published 26 February 1954 at $6.00; 5000 sets of sheets printed by Faber and
Faber for New Directions. These were bound and jacketed in the United States,
2000 in 1954, 1000 in 1956, 1000 in 1961, and the remainder, making 748 copies, in 1966. *On verso of title-leaf:* First published in mcmliv New Directions
Norfolk, Conn. ... Printed in Great Britain by R. MacLehose and Company
Limited The University Press Glasgow ... New Directions books are published by James Laughlin

A. BOOKS AND PAMPHLETS

Note: An edition paperbound was issued by New Directions 31 March 1968 at $3.25 as their Paperbook 250 in a first printing of 5030 copies.

A68 LAVORO ED USURA [1954]

First collected edition:

EZRA POUND | LAVORO ED USURA | Tre Saggi | [*quotation in 3 lines*] | [*device*] | ALL'INSEGNA DEL PESCE D'ORO | MILANO [Vanni Scheiwiller]

99, [2] pp., 1 leaf. 18·4 × 12·6 cm. (wrappers); 17·8 × 12·2 cm. (leaves). Blue paper wrappers, printed in black on page [i] and up the spine, folded over stiff cream blanks. White paper wrap-around printed in black with Ezra Pound's definition in English of usury. (This appears also on the verso of the title-leaf, where it is followed by the Italian translation.)

Published February 1954 at L. 700 in the series "Scritti Italiani di Ezra Pound contro l'Usura"; 1000 copies printed. *Colophon (page* [103])*:* Questa edizione curata da Vanni Scheiwiller è stata impressa dalla Stamperia Valdonega di Verona in mille esemplari numerati da I a 1000 · Febbraio MCMLIV Esemplare [*number written in*]

"Sono qui riuniti per la prima volta, e integralmente ristampati, i tre introvabili opuscoli che Ezra Pound scrisse e pubblicò in italiano a Rapallo e a Venezia nel 1944 e che la guerra disperse." ("Nota dell'editore," p. 99)

Contents: Oro e lavoro—A52a—L'America, Roosevelt e le cause della guerra presente—A51a—Introduzione alla natura economica degli S. U. A.—A53a—Postscriptum ai tre saggi [by Ezra Pound]—Appunto bibliografico—Nota dell'editore—Indice

Note: This is a reprint of the texts of the three pamphlets, correcting misprints and adding Ezra Pound's footnote to *Oro e lavoro*, p. 7, and his "Postscriptum ai tre saggi," p. 97.

A69 THE CLASSIC ANTHOLOGY 1954
DEFINED BY CONFUCIUS

a. *First edition:*

[*In right half of title-page:*] THE CLASSIC | ANTHOLOGY | DE-FINED BY | CONFUCIUS | EZRA | POUND | [*in left half of title-page: a vertical thick-rule rectangle containing, at top: Shih (Odes) ideo-gram representing the Chinese title of the book, and at bottom:*] HAR-VARD | UNIVERSITY | PRESS | CAMBRIDGE | MCMLIV

A. BOOKS AND PAMPHLETS

1 blank leaf, 3 leaves, [ix]–xv, [1], 223, [1] pp. 22·7 × 16·2 cm. Grey-green paper boards with decorative design of wavy black and grey vertical lines, with white paper label printed in black on spine; end-papers. White dust-jacket printed in black and red with, on back, a reproduction of Wyndham Lewis's portrait of Ezra Pound.

Published 10 September 1954 at $5.00; 4000 sets of sheets printed (of which 785 were used for the English issue in 1955). *On verso of title-leaf:* ... Printed in the United States of America

Contents: Key to Pronunciation—Introduction, by Achilles Fang—Part I. Folk Songs (Kuo Feng)—Part II. Elegantiae, or Smaller Odes (Siao Ya)—Part III. The Greater Odes (Ta Ya)—Part IV. Odes of the Temple and Altar (Sung)

b. *English issue* ([1955]):

[*Title-page as in first issue, except at bottom:*] FABER AND FABER | 24 RUSSELL SQUARE | LONDON

Pagination and size as in A69a. Blue cloth boards stamped in gold on spine; end-papers. Yellow dust-jacket printed in red and black.

Published 25 February 1955 at 30s.; 785 sets of first-edition sheets, with a cancel title-leaf (with title-page as indicated), were imported by Faber and Faber and bound and jacketed for sale in England. (In the copy sent to the Cambridge University Library the American title-leaf was not cancelled, in error.) *On verso of title-leaf:* First published in England mcmlv—Printed in the United States of America ... [on paper without watermark.]

Notes: A second impression of 1506 copies was prepared by the Harvard University Press in June 1955. Of this impression 756 copies, with title-leaf as in the English issue of the first impression but integral, were imported by Faber and Faber and bound and jacketed for sale in England, at 30s., beginning 25 September 1955. These copies have a misprint "AIRS OF PIE" for "AIRS OF PEI" in the running-title at the foot of page 19. The paper is watermarked "WARREN'S OLDE STYLE", and the (reprinted) jacket has two errors on the back: "by GEORGE BAKER" for "by GEORGE BARKER" and "by EDWIN MOORE" for "by EDWIN MUIR". (The 750 sets of sheets prepared simultaneously by the Harvard University Press with their own imprint have the date MCMLV on the title-page, are identified on the verso of the title-leaf as "Second Printing", and have the misprint on page 19. These sheets were not issued and in November 1963 were destroyed by the publisher, although at least one set survives (DG).)

The book was published with the original title, paperbound, in July 1974 by Faber & Faber in their series of Faber paper covered Editions at £ 1.25. It was published paperbound also by New Directions in New York in September 1959 at $1.45 as their Paperbook 81, with title: *The Confucian Odes: The Classic Anthology Defined by Confucius. Ezra Pound*, in a first printing of about 10,000 copies (reprinted by offset from the Harvard edition). In 1976, a third printing, so identified, was issued paperbound by the Harvard University Press in Cam-

A. BOOKS AND PAMPHLETS

bridge, Mass., at $2.95 as a Harvard Paperback, with title: ... *Shih-ching: The Classic Anthology Defined by Confucius. Ezra Pound.*

Poem No. 108, "Encroachment," (page 51) is a complete translation of the ode of which Ezra Pound's partial literal and free translations (based on Père Lacharme's Latin text) were printed in Chapter 36 of *Guide to Kulchur* ([1938])—A45—pp. 214–16. Poem No. 167 (pages 86–87) is a new translation of the ode of which Ernest Fenollosa's version was edited and printed by Pound as "Song of the Bowmen of Shu."

A70   SECTION: ROCK-DRILL   1955

a. *First edition:*

[*In black:*] EZRA POUND | [*in red:*] SECTION: ROCK-DRILL | [*in black:*] 85–95 | de los cantares | [*device*] | ALL'INSEGNA DEL PESCE D'ORO | MILANO · MCMLV [Vanni Scheiwiller]

1 blank leaf, 3 leaves, 107, [1] pp., 1 leaf, 1 blank leaf. 20·6 × 12·6 cm. Grey paper boards printed in brown and black on front cover and in black up the spine; end-papers. Plain cellophane dust-jacket.

Half-title: Cantos 85–95 of Ezra Pound

Published September 1955 at L. 2000; 506 copies printed. *Colophon (page* [109]): Questa edizione originale dei Cantos 85–95 di Ezra Pound curata da Vanni Scheiwiller è stata impressa dalla Stamperia Valdonega di Verona in cinquecento esemplari numerati e in tre esemplari su carta japon "ad personam" per il 12 settembre 1955. Esemplare [*number written in*] (The three de luxe copies and one proof copy were bound in beige silk stamped in red on the front cover and up the spine: they measure 21·3 × 13 cm. and were issued in a tan paper-covered box measuring 21·8 × 13·3 cm. They have at the end of the colophon in place of the word "Esemplare," "Questo esemplare è stato stampato per ... [*name of recipient printed in*]." Two extra sets of sheets for de luxe copies were bound in 1965, one for the publisher himself (to replace his original copy stolen), the other for DG.

"This volume has been printed in conformity with the typographical instructions given by the author." (*Note*, p. [108])

Note: This section of the Cantos derives its name from the title of a review by Wyndham Lewis of *The Letters of Ezra Pound*—A64b—in the *New Statesman and Nation* for 7 April 1951: "The Rock Drill," itself a reference to Jacob Epstein's sculpture of that title of 1915–1916.

b. *First American (offset) edition* ([1956]):

[*In black:*] EZRA POUND | [*in grey:*] SECTION: ROCK-DRILL | [*in black:*] 85–95 | de los cantares | A NEW DIRECTIONS BOOK [New York, James Laughlin]

A. BOOKS AND PAMPHLETS

1 blank leaf, 3 leaves, 107, [1] pp., 2 blank leaves. 20·6 × 13 cm. Black cloth boards lettered in silver down the spine; end-papers. Grey dust-jacket printed in red-brown.

Published 30 March 1956 at $3.00; 2081 copies printed. *On verso of title-leaf:* ... First Printing Manufactured in the United States [Printed by offset from the first edition] New Directions Books are published by James Laughlin New York Office—333 Sixth Avenue—14

c. *First English (offset) edition* ([1957]):

[*In black:*] EZRA POUND | [*in red:*] SECTION: ROCK-DRILL | [*in black:*] 85–95 | de los cantares | FABER AND FABER | 24 Russell Square | London

2 leaves, 107, [1] pp. 20·8 × 13·6 cm. Black cloth boards stamped in gold down the spine; end-papers. Yellow dust-jacket printed in red-brown.

Published 15 February 1957 at 12s. 6d.; 2000 copies printed. *On verso of title-leaf:* First published in England in mcmlvii ... Printed in Great Britain by Bradford & Dickens London WCI ... Reproduced, by permission, from the original edition published by Vanni Scheiwiller, All'Insegna del Pesce d'Oro, Milan, 1955 ...

A71   ENRICO PEA. MOSCARDINO   1956

First edition:

ENRICO PEA | MOSCARDINO | translated by | EZRA POUND | [*device*] | ALL'INSEGNA DEL PESCE D'ORO | MILANO · MCMLVI [Vanni Scheiwiller]

1 blank leaf, 81, [1] pp., 1 leaf, 1 blank leaf. 18·2 × 12·5 cm. (wrappers); 17·8 × 12·2 cm. (sheets). Grey paper wrappers, folded over stiff white blanks, printed in black on page [i] and up the spine.

Published February 1956 at L. 1000; 1000 copies printed. *On verso of title-leaf:* ... This edition is published by arrangement with New Directions, New York Printed in Italy *Colophon (page* [84]): Questa edizione curata da Vanni Scheiwiller ... è stata impressa dalla Stamperia Valdonega di Verona in 1000 esemplari numerati l'8 Febbraio MCMLVI [*device*] Esemplare N. [*number written in*]

Reprinted from *New Directions*, New York, 15 ([1955]) pp. 86–131—C1742. This is Ezra Pound's translation, made in June and July 1941, of the first volume, *Moscardino* (first published in Milan in 1922), of Enrico Pea's four-volume novel, *Il romanzo di Moscardino*. It contains an introductory note by Enrico Pea, pp. 3–6, and a list of "Books by Enrico Pea," pp. 81–[82].

A. BOOKS AND PAMPHLETS

A72   SOPHOKLES   [1956]
WOMEN OF TRACHIS

a. *First edition:*

SOPHOKLES | Women of | Trachis | A version by | EZRA POUND | London | Neville Spearman

1 blank leaf, xxiii, 66 pp., 2 blank leaves. front. (port.) 18·9 × 12·8 cm. Red cloth boards lettered in gold down the spine; end-papers (first and/or final blank leaf pasted down as end-paper in some copies, and underneath end-paper in others). Grey dust-jacket printed in red and blue.

Published 30 November 1956 at 10s. 6d.; 1000 copies printed. *On label pasted on page* [iv]: First published in 1956 . . . Owing to the format of this edition, it has not been possible to set a number of the longer lines of the verse at full length as originally intended; the layout has been adapted in consultation with the author. *Imprint at foot of page* [iv]: Printed in Great Britain by The Alcuin Press Welwyn Garden City, Herts.

The frontispiece is a reproduction of a portrait of Ezra Pound made in 1954 by Sheri Martinelli.

Dedication on page [3]: A version for Kitasono Katue, hoping he will use it on my dear old friend Miscio Ito, or take it to the Minoru if they can be persuaded to add to their repertoire.

Contents: Foreword [by Denis Goacher]—Ezra Pound's Translation of Sophokles [by S. V. Jankowski]—Women of Trachis—Editorial Declaration [by Denis Goacher and Peter Whigham]—Why Pound Liked Italy [by Ricardo M. degli Uberti, originally published in Italian in *Corriere della Liguria* (14 April 1956) and in English translation in *Academia Bulletin*, Washington, D.C., [1] (1956)]

Note: This work was taken over by Faber and Faber and issued 27 January 1969 in their series of Faber paper covered Editions at 7s.

b. *First American (offset) edition* ([1957]):

SOPHOKLES | Women of | Trachis | A version by | EZRA POUND | New York | New Directions [James Laughlin]

1 blank leaf, xxiii, 66 pp., 2 blank leaves, incl. front. (port.) 22·2 × 14·2 cm. Black cloth boards lettered in silver down the spine; end-papers. (Some copies have the second blank leaf at the end pasted down underneath the back end-paper.) White dust-jacket printed in black and red.

Published 27 March 1957 at $3.00; 3000 copies printed. *On verso of title-leaf:* . . . New Directions Books are published by James Laughlin. New York office: 333 Sixth Avenue, New York (14).

This edition was printed in November 1956 by the Murray Printing Company, Forge Village, Mass., from reproduction proofs supplied by Neville Spearman. Because of an error in trimming the negative, the final two lines on page 24 were omitted in all 3000 copies. When the publisher discovered the error in the first lot of copies received from the binder, Chas. H. Bohn & Co., Inc., New York, in February 1957, the printer prepared and sent to the binder 3000 copies of a four-page cancel fold (pp. 23–24 and 37–38). Apparently eleven bound copies with the error were set aside, but for the remaining 999 copies already bound, a cancel leaf (pp. 23–24, cut from the fold) was inserted and the defective leaf excised. (There is a noticeable variation among copies in the expertness with which the operation was performed.) In October 1957 an additional 1008 sets of sheets were bound up. Before these copies were sewn, the four pages 23–24 and 37–38 were replaced with the cancel fold. The final lot of approximately 980 sets of sheets was handled in the same way when it was bound in 1970.

A73   GAUDIER-BRZESKA   [1957]

First edition:

EZRA POUND | GAUDIER-BRZESKA | with a | VORTEX MANI- FESTO | [*device*] | ALL'INSEGNA DEL PESCE D'ORO | MILANO [Vanni Scheiwiller]

27, [1] pp., 1 leaf, 28 pp., 6 leaves, 1 blank leaf, incl. front. (port.), illus. 10 × 7·4 cm. Stiff plain white paper wrappers. Cream dust-jacket printed in red and black.

Published July 1957 at L. 600 as "Serie Illustrata, 58"; 500 copies printed. *Colophon (recto of sixth leaf following page 28):* . . . Questo volumetto a cura di Vanni Scheiwiller è stato stampato dalle Off. Grafiche "Esperia" di Milano, in mille copie numerate da 1 a 500 per l'edizione in lingua inglese e da 501 a 1000 per l'edizione in lingua italiana, in occasione della XI Triennale di Milano, il 9 luglio 1957. Copia N. [*number stamped in*]

A misprint, "Episten" for "Epstein," in line 14 on page 27 (first count), was corrected in manuscript by the publisher in many copies.

Contents: Henri Gaudier-Brzeska [by Ezra Pound], pp. 5–[18] (first count)— Vortex [by] Gaudier-Brzeska, pp. 19–[28] (first count)—illustrations, pp. 1–28 (second count)—Biographical Note—Bibliography—[List of] Illustrations

Notes: "Henri Gaudier-Brzeska" is reprinted from *A Memorial Exhibition of the Work of Henri Gaudier-Brzeska* (1918)—B18—pp. 3–[8]. "Vortex [by] Gaudier-Brzeska" is reprinted from *Blast,* London, 1 (20 June 1914), pp. 155–8, and from *Gaudier-Brzeska* (1916)—A10—pp. 9–13.

For the Italian translation, which continues the numbering of copies of the edition in English, see D66.

A. BOOKS AND PAMPHLETS

A74 PAVANNES AND DIVAGATIONS [1958]

a. *First edition:*

EZRA POUND | PAVANNES | AND | DIVAGATIONS | A NEW
DIRECTIONS BOOK [Norfolk, Conn., James Laughlin]

xi, 243 pp. 1 illus. (facsim.), 1 plate (port.) 21·8 × 14·7 cm. Brown cloth boards lettered in white down the spine; end-papers. White dust-jacket printed in black and yellow.

Published 10 July 1958 at $4.75; 4000 copies printed. *On verso of title-leaf:* ...
New Directions Books are published by James Laughlin at Norfolk, Connecticut. New York office at 333 Sixth Avenue (14). CK design. Printed in the United States of America. ...

"Many of Ezra Pound's contributions to modern literature appeared originally in little magazines, in pamphlets, and in books which went quickly out of print. The present collection has been made in order to bring before the public today works which have been difficult to obtain for many years. Some pieces in this book are published here for the first time, most have been taken from a variety of out-of-the-way sources, and a very few, reprinted from Mr. Pound's other well known collections, have been included because they seem in keeping with the spirit of the rest." ("Publisher's note," p. [i])

Contents: Epitaph by Rex Lampman—Indiscretions, or Une revue de deux mondes—Imaginary Letters—PAVANNES: Jodindranath Mawhwor's Occupation—An Anachronism at Chinon—Religio or, The Child's Guide to Knowledge—Aux étuves de Wiesbaden—Stark Realism—Twelve Dialogues of Fontenelle—Chronicles from *Blast:* 1. "Lest the Future Age . . . "; 2. On the Rage or Peevishness which Greeted the First Number of *Blast*; 3. Lawrence [*sic*] Binyon—Madox Ford at Rapallo—A Matter of Modesty—Genesis or, The First Book in the Bible—Our Tetrarchal Précieuse—Postscript to *The Natural Philosophy of Love* by Remy de Gourmont—Musicians: God Help 'Em—FRIVOLITIES: The Sneeze—Mr. Housman's Message—The New Cake of Soap—Ancient Music—Our Contemporaries—M. Pom-Pom—Abu Salammamm–A Song of Empire—"In 1914 There Was Mertons"—Words for Roundel in Double Canon—"Neath Ben Bulben's Buttoks Lies"—APHORISMS: Definition—Mencken—The Value—The Fable—APPENDIX: POEMS BY 5 FRIENDS: Cat by Maurice Craig—Neothomist Poem by Ernest Hemingway—Home-Thoughts, from an Old Lag by Barry Domville—4 Poems by Saturno Montanari with EP's "Guides" to Them—Poem and Drawing by Jaime de Angulo [with "De Angulo's Poem Translated," by E. P.]

Note: New Directions also published an edition of this book paperbound in New York 16 April 1975 at $3.45 as their Paperbook 397, in a first printing of 4000 copies. (The verso of the title-leaf gives the date incorrectly as 1974.)

b. *First English (offset) edition* ([1960]):

EZRA POUND | PAVANNES | AND | DIVAGATIONS | PETER OWEN
LIMITED [London]

A. BOOKS AND PAMPHLETS

xi, 243 pp., incl. illus. (facsim.) 22·2 × 14·1 cm. Blue cloth boards stamped in gold on spine; end-papers. Yellow dust-jacket printed in lavender.

Published 29 April 1960 at 25s.; 1000 copies printed. *On verso of title-leaf:* ... Made and Printed in Great Britain by Lowe and Brydone (Printers) Ltd. London, N. W. 10 First Published in the British Commonwealth 1960 ... [Printed by offset from the first edition, but omitting the plate.]

A75   DIPTYCH ROME-LONDON   [1958]

a. *First edition in this form, copies for sale in the United States:*

[*In red:*] DIPTYCH | ROME-LONDON | [*in black:*] HOMAGE | TO SEXTUS PROPERTIUS | & | HUGH SELWYN MAUBERLEY | CONTACTS AND LIFE | BY | [*in red:*] EZRA POUND | [*in black:*] NEW DIRECTIONS [James Laughlin, New York]

1 blank leaf, 76, [1] pp., 1 leaf, 1 blank leaf. 29·4 × 20·5 cm. Brown paper boards stamped in gold on front cover and down the spine; end-papers; top edges gilt, others untrimmed. Brown cardboard box (measuring 29·8 × 20·9 cm.) with brown cloth back, top and bottom, with tan paper label printed in black on side: EZRA POUND | DIPTYCH ROME–LONDON | Homage to Sextus Propertius | & | Hugh Selwyn Mauberley | Contacts and Life | A NEW DIRECTIONS BOOK

Published 24 October 1958, simultaneously with copies for sale in Great Britain and in Italy, at $30.00. *Colophon* (*page* [79]): This edition of Ezra Pound's Diptych was printed in Bembo type by Hans Mardersteig on the hand-press of the Officina Bodoni, Verona, for James Laughlin, Faber and Faber Limited, and Vanni Scheiwiller. The edition consists of 200 numbered copies on Pescia paper, of which Numbers 1 to 125 are for sale in the United States, Numbers 126 to 175 in Great Britain, and Numbers 176 to 200 in Italy, all signed by the author. December MCMLVII [*device in red*] This copy is Number [*number printed in, with Pound's signature below device, in blue, green or red ink*]

Note: A reprint, under this new title, of *Homage to Sextus Propertius* (printed in *Quia Pauper Amavi* (1919)—A17—and separately published in 1934—A38) and *Hugh Selwyn Mauberley* (1920)—A19.

b. *Copies for sale in Great Britain:*

Identical with copies for sale in the United States save for publisher's name (FABER & FABER) on title-page and label. Published at 10 guineas.

c. *Copies for sale in Italy:*

Identical with copies for sale in the United States save for publisher's name and place (VANNI SCHEIWILLER | MILANO) on title-page and publisher's name on label. Published at L. 18,000.

A. BOOKS AND PAMPHLETS

A76   VERSI PROSAICI   [1959]

First edition:

EZRA POUND | VERSI PROSAICI | BIBLIOTECA MINIMA [Caltanissetta, Roma, Salvatore Sciascia Editore]

58 pp., 3 leaves. 6·4 × 11·4 cm. (wrappers); 6·1 × 11 cm. (leaves). Heavy cream paper wrappers, folded over stiff white blanks, printed in black up the spine and stamped in blind on page [i], with cream paper label printed in black on page [i].

Half-title: Pound

Published June 1959 at L. 1000 in the series "Biblioteca minima"; 250 copies printed. *Colophon (page* [61])*:* Raccolta originale dei Versi Prosaici di Ezra Pound Tiratura limitata di 250 copie di cui le prime 30 riservate all'Autore Nelle copie dal N. 25 al N. 90 è inclusa un'acquaforte firmata di Giancarlo Scorza Copia N. [*number written in*] *Colophon (page* [63])*:* Questo volumetto della Biblioteca Minima diretta da Giambattista Vicari è stato stampato nel giugno 1959 *Imprint on page* [64]*:* Salvatore Sciascia Editore Caltanissetta . . . Roma . . . Tipografia Ferraiolo, Roma

The special copies numbered 25 to 90 (and for sale at L. 3000) have, inserted after the title-leaf, an eau-forte, signed at lower left: G. Scorza 59, and (in most copies) numbered at lower right, but are otherwise identical with copies numbered 1 to 24 and 91 to 250. Some of the ordinary copies were specially bound in dark green or red leather (or fabrikoid), stamped in blind on pages [i] and [iv], and in gold on page [i]: POUND | [*ornament*], and with decorated end-papers. These copies measure 6·7 × 11·7 cm. (binding).

In the entire edition the ideogram on page 36 is printed upside down.

"Questi Versi Prosaici non appartengono ai Cantos (a Los Cantares) ma forse ne rischiareranno alcuni ritornelli a qualche lettore benevolo." (*Note by Ezra Pound,* p. [59])

A77   THRONES   1959

a. *First edition (Italian):*

[*In black:*] EZRA POUND | [*in red:*] THRONES | [*in black:*] 96–109 | de los cantares | [*in red: 3 ideograms within border*] | [*in black:*] ALL'INSEGNA DEL PESCE D'ORO | MILANO · MCMLIX [Vanni Scheiwiller]

1 blank leaf, 3 leaves, 126 pp., 2 leaves, 1 blank leaf. 20·6 × 12·6 cm. Tan paper boards printed in red and black on front cover, and in black on back cover and up the spine; end-papers. Plain cellophane dust-jacket.

A. BOOKS AND PAMPHLETS

Half-title: Cantos 96–109 of Ezra Pound

Published 7 December 1959 at L. 3000; 300 copies printed. *Colophon (recto of second leaf following page* 126)*:* Questa edizione originale ... curata da Vanni Scheiwiller è stata impressa dalla Stamperia Valdonega di Verona in trecento esemplari numerati il 12 settembre 1959. [*Device*] Esemplare [*number stamped in*]

"This volume has been printed in conformity with the typographical instructions given by the author." (*Note, p.* [128])

Some of the copies have a misprint in line 9, page 85, "no war" for "One war," with "no" cancelled in manuscript by the publisher.

b. *First American (offset) edition* ([1959])*:*

EZRA POUND | THRONES | 96–109 | de los cantares | [*3 ideograms within border*] | A NEW DIRECTIONS BOOK [New York, James Laughlin]

3 leaves, 126 pp., 1 leaf, 1 blank leaf. 20·8 × 12·8 cm. Black cloth boards lettered in silver down the spine; end-papers. Grey dust-jacket printed in dark blue.

Published 7 December 1959 at $3.50; 3000 copies printed. *On verso of title-leaf:* ... Manufactured in the United States [Printed by offset from the Italian first edition] New Directions Books are published by James Laughlin New York Office · 333 Sixth Avenue 14

In later copies, an "erratum" slip, correcting the misprint in line 9, page 85 ("no war" for "One war"), is tipped in at the foot of the third leaf.

c. *First English (offset) edition* ([1960])*:*

[*In black:*] EZRA POUND | [*in red:*] THRONES | [*in black:*] 96–109 | de los cantares | [*in red: 3 ideograms within border*] | [*in black:*] FABER AND FABER | 24 RUSSELL SQUARE | LONDON

3 leaves, 126 pp., 1 leaf, 1 blank leaf. 20·7 × 13·7 cm. Red cloth boards stamped in gold down the spine; end-papers. Green dust-jacket printed in red and dark grey.

Published 4 March 1960 at 18*s.*; 2290 copies printed. *On verso of title-leaf:* First published in England in mcmlx ... Printed lithographically in Great Britain at the University Press, Oxford from type set at the Stamperia Valdonega in Verona. ...

In this edition, lines 8 and 9 on page 85 are omitted.

A78   IMPACT   1960

First edition:

IMPACT | Essays on Ignorance and the Decline | of American

A. BOOKS AND PAMPHLETS

Civilization | by | EZRA POUND | Edited with an introduction by
NOEL STOCK | CHICAGO | HENRY REGNERY COMPANY | 1960

xviii, 285 pp. 21·6 × 14·5 cm. Grey cloth boards stamped in red on front cover
and on spine; end-papers. White dust-jacket printed in black and red.

Published 13 June 1960 at $5.00; 5000 copies printed. *On verso of title-leaf:* ...
Manufactured in the United States of America ...

" ... in the sort of work collected in this volume ... [Ezra Pound] spent many
years feeling his way through an unmapped land, gathering facts long out of
print or available only in rare pamphlets or the archives of learned societies etc.
For this reason I have discarded a large quantity of material and, generally
speaking, have attempted to present his mature view as it was, say, in 1940."
("Introduction," by Noel Stock, p. xviii) Most of the extracts printed in Section
II and some of the letters in Section III are at least slightly condensed.

Contents: Of Misprision of Treason [from Coke's "Institutes"]—Introduction,
by Noel Stock—I. ESSAYS ON IGNORANCE AND THE DECLINE OF AMERICAN CIVILI-
ZATION: National Culture, a Manifesto (1938)—Destruction by Taxation (1938)
[incorporating "The Dismantled Manor House (1939)," and "Feasible Justice
(1959)"]—An Introduction to the Economic Nature of the United States [Car-
mine Amore's translation of *Introduzione alla natura economica della S. U. A.*—
A53a—with corrections] (1944)—Bureaucracy the Flail of Jehovah [con-
densed] (1928)—A Visiting Card [John Drummond's translation of *Carta da
visita*—A50a—condensed and revised] (1942)—Possibilities of Civilization: What
the Small Town Can Do [condensed] (1936)—Murder by Capital [condensed]
(1933)—Integrity of the Word [a much condensed revision of *What Is Money
For?*—A46] (1939)—The Enemy is Ignorance [John Drummond's translation of
Oro e lavoro—A52a—condensed] (1944)—Mang Tsze: The Ethics of Mencius
[corrected] (1938)—[Social Credit,] An Impact [A40, condensed and revised]
(1935)—In the Wounds: Memoriam A. R. Orage [condensed] (1935)—The Jefferson–Adams Letters as a Shrine and a Monument ["The Jefferson-Adams
Correspondence," complete, with a new footnote by Ezra Pound, dated: 1959,
p. 175] (1937)—America and the Second World War [John Drummond's translation of *L'America, Roosevelt e le cause della guerra presente*—A51a—condensed]
(1944)—Immediate Need of Confucius [slightly revised, with a new footnote
by Ezra Pound, dated: 1959, p. 200] (1937)—II. GISTS—SHORTER PIECES AND
EXTRACTS FROM UNCOLLECTED ESSAYS: Our Contemporaries—Pastiche: The Regional, II, VII–IX, XV—The Revolt of Intelligence, V—Credit and the Fine
Arts—Definitions—The Public Convenience [from C689]—Summary of the
Situation [from C689]—Prolegomena—The Arts [from C707]—Desideria—
Drive Back the Government [paragraph from the end of "Bureaucracy the Flail
of Jehovah"]—Peace—Open Letter to Tretyakow—Hunger Fighters—Peace
Pathology—To the Historical Society of America—Private Worlds—[An
American] So-called "Writers" Congress—[John Buchan's] Cromwell—To-
wards Orthology—History and Ignorance—The Movement of Literature—The
Individual in His Milieu—The Acid Test—Without a Distorting Lens [from
C1330]—Race—Sincerity [from C1359]—On Theorists—On Military Vir-

A. BOOKS AND PAMPHLETS

tue—Our Own Form of Government—W. E. Woodward, Historian—When Will School Books . . . ?—Reorganize Your Dead Universities—A Dull Subject [from C1461]—Marx [from C1459]—Emergency (Letter to Basil Bunting, 24 November 1938)—Text Books—Social Credit ([from] *What Is Money For?*—A46 [with footnote from page 136 of Pound's translation of Odon Por's *Italy's Policy of Social Economics*—A49])—The American System, Why Not Revive It?—III. LETTERS TO AMERICA: To Senator S. S. Brookhart, 18 March 1931—To W. E. Woodward, 7 February 1934(?)—To Henry Morgenthau Jr., 7 August 1934—To Upton Sinclair, 30 January 1935—To T. C. Wilson, 28 November 1936—To William Langer, December 1936—To Senator H. T. Bone, 1936 (?)—To Henry Seidel Canby 14 February 1938 (?)—To Claude Bowers, 16 April 1938—To Van Wyck Brooks, 16 April 1938—To Dr. Joseph Brewer, 11 September 1939—To Ernest Minor Patterson, 6 February 1940, & 12 March 1940—To Editor of the Annals, American Academy of Social & Political Science, 3 June 1940—To D. MacPherson, 16 November 1940—To the Committee of Progress, National Institute of Art[s] & Letters, 1941 (?)—To National Institute of Art[s] and Letters, 15 May 1941—APPENDIX: Letter to Nicholas Murr[a]y Butler . . . Carnegie Endowment for Peace, 18 June 1928, signed by Albert Mensdorff, but drafted jointly by Ezra Pound and Count Mensdorff, with reply and covering letter to Ezra Pound—SELECT BIBLIOGRAPHY

A79   NUOVA ECONOMIA   1962
                  EDITORIALE

First separate edition:

EZRA POUND | NUOVA ECONOMIA | EDITORIALE | MILANO [Vanni Scheiwiller] – MCMLXII

1 blank leaf, 7 leaves. 7·2 × 5·7 cm. Cream paper wrappers, folded over stiff white blanks, printed in black on page [i].

Distributed gratis October–November 1962; 200 copies printed. *Colophon (verso of final leaf):* "all'Insegna della Baita van Gogh" fuori serie Questo volumetto a cura di Vanni Scheiwiller è stato stampato a Milano dalla Tipografia U. Allegretti di Campi in duecento copie non venali numerate da I a 200 in occasione del 77° compleanno di Ezra Pound e del 73° compleanno di Giovanni Scheiwiller Milano 30 ottobre–8 novembre 1962 Copia N. [*number written in on a row of printed dots*]

Reprinted from *Scritti e disegni dedicati a Scheiwiller* (Milan, 1937)—B39—pp. 72–73.

Note: This tribute was again reprinted by Vanni Scheiwiller, with the same title, as the foreword to *Edizioni Giovanni e Vanni Scheiwiller 1925–1965* . . . (Milano [1965])—of which there were 5,000 ordinary and 300 special, signed copies—pp. 5–6; in *Edizioni di Giovanni e Vanni Scheiwiller 1925–1968* . . . (Milano [1968]), pp. 5–6, and, also in 1968, in the 4-page catalogue of an exhibition at the

A. BOOKS AND PAMPHLETS

Libreria Galleria G. Greco in Mantua, . . . *Mostra delle edizioni Scheiwiller 1925–1968*, pp. [1–2].

A80   LOVE POEMS OF   [1962]
                     ANCIENT EGYPT

First edition:

[*Across facing pages, in black:*] LOVE POEMS OF ANCIENT EGYPT | A New Directions Book Translated by Ezra Pound and Noel Stock | [*reproduction of an Egyptian painting in black on a lavender background.* Norfolk, Conn., James Laughlin]

3 leaves, 33 pp. col. illus. 17·6 × 12 cm. Stiff plain white paper wrappers. White dust-jacket printed in black and lavender on page [i] and in black on page [iv].

Published 28 November 1962 at $1.50; 5049 copies printed. *On verso of title-leaf:* ... Manufactured in the United States of America New Directions Books are published by James Laughlin at Norfolk, Connecticut. New York Office: 333 Sixth Avenue (14).

"These versions are based on literal renderings of the hieroglyphic texts into Italian by Boris de Rachewiltz, which first appeared in the volume *Liriche Amorose degli Antichi Egiziani*, published by Vanni Scheiwiller, Milan, in 1957. Most of the original Egyptian texts have survived only in incomplete form, but, for the purpose of modern adaptation, it has seemed desirable to present each poem as complete. The sources for the poetry are: the Turin (Maspero) Papyrus, the Harris 500 and Chester Beatty I & II Papyri in the British Museum, and the Ostrakon No. 25218 pottery in the Cairo Museum—all dating between 1567 and 1085 B.C. . . . " ("Note," *verso of title-leaf*)

"Ezra Pound's incomparable gifts as a translator delight us anew in *Conversations in Courtship* . . .

"Illness having prevented Mr. Pound from continuing the work, the remaining poems . . . have been translated by the poet Noel Stock." (*Dust-jacket*)

Contents: Conversations in Courtship [translated by Ezra Pound]—Love Lyrics—More Love Lyrics—Pleasant Songs of the Sweetheart Who Meets You in the Fields—Pleasant Songs—Garden Songs—Sweet Phrases—Haste [all translated by Noel Stock]

Notes: A second printing, identified only on the back flap of the wrapper, was issued in December 1963 (5200 copies).

A hardbound edition with title *Come Swiftly to Your Love: Love Poems of Ancient Egypt*, illustrated by Tom di Grazia, was published in Kansas City, Mo., by Hallmark Editions in 1971 at $2.50.

A. BOOKS AND PAMPHLETS

A81   EP TO LU   1963

First edition:

EP to LU | NINE LETTERS WRITTEN | TO LOUIS UNTERMEYER BY | [*in facsimile of signature:*] Ezra Pound | EDITED BY J. A. ROBBINS | [*short rule*] | Indiana University Press / 1963 | Bloomington

48 pp., incl. facsims. 21 × 13·6 cm. Brown paper boards stamped in blue on both covers and down the spine; end-papers. Plain acetate dust-jacket.

Published 29 July 1963 at $6.00; 1539 copies printed. *On verso of title-leaf:* ... Manufactured in the United States of America

Notes: Letter V is an autobiographical summary communicated to Louis Untermeyer in 1930. On page [16] is reproduced the first page of Ezra Pound's original typescript, titled and (incorrectly) dated in Louis Untermeyer's hand: "Ezra Pound to LU—a statement 'in order to put the facts straight.' Rapallo. 1932." It was printed, with the incorrect date (and with the title erroneously identified as being "in Pound's hand"), in *Paris Review* for Summer/Fall 1962—C1888— as "An Autobiographical Outline (Written for Louis Untermeyer)." For separate edition see A103.

Letter VI, 1 March [1930], incorporates Pound's translation of Heine's "Diese Damen," in three 4–line stanzas.

A82   THE SEAFARER   [1965]

First separate edition:

EZRA POUND | THE SEAFARER | From the Anglo-Saxon | With a Portrait of the Poet by | OSKAR KOKOSCHKA | [*device*] | Verlag Ars librorum · Gotthard de Beauclair | Frankfurt am Main

1 blank leaf, 2 leaves, [vii]–xiii, [1] pp., 1 blank leaf, incl. plate (port.) Unbound sheets, 51·3 × 40 cm., issued in brown paper board portfolio, 51·5 × 40·5 cm., with yellow paper label printed in black on front cover, and yellow paper label printed in black up the spine.

Published mid-July 1965 at DM 260 ($65.00); 200 copies printed. *Colophon (page [xiv]):* XI. Ars librorum Druck ›The Seafarer‹ is taken from ›Personae‹ of Ezra Pound ... The printing of Oskar Kokoschka's lithograph was undertaken by Emil Matthieu of Zürich, and that of the poem in Monotype Bell by Hans Christians of Hamburg. The paper used for this edition is Vélin d'Arches. The impression is limited to 195 numbered copies, signed by both poet and artist; 25 additional copies A–Z are reserved for the publisher and are not for sale. Printed in Germany 1965 This is Copy No. ›[*number written in in pencil*]‹ [The portrait—recto of second leaf—dated "xii. 64," is signed in pencil by the artist, and numbered, at lower-left; Ezra Pound's signature in pencil appears below the fly-title on page [vii].]

Note: A three-page prospectus, mailed August 1965, offered 165 copies at DM 260, plus 30 [*sic*] copies with an additional signed print of the lithograph on royal Japan at DM 460 ($115.00). The prospectus reproduces the portrait at approximately half-size and contains a photograph of the artist at work on the lithograph.

| A83 | A LUME SPENTO AND OTHER EARLY POEMS | [1965] |

a. *First edition:*

EZRA POUND | A LUME SPENTO | AND OTHER EARLY POEMS | NEW DIRECTIONS [New York, James Laughlin]

128 pp., incl. facsims. front. (port.) 22·3 × 14·5 cm. Decorated paper boards, with blue cloth back, stamped in gold on front cover and on spine, with black-and-white reproduction of a photograph of the San Trovaso section of Venice set into front cover and, in the earliest copies only, descriptive label printed in black set into back cover; end-papers. Plain acetate dust-jacket.

Published 30 October 1965 at $5.00; 6500 copies printed. *On verso of title-leaf:* . . . First printing . . . Manufactured in the United States of America New Directions books are published for James Laughlin by New Directions Publishing Corporation, 333 Sixth Avenue, New York 14.

Contents: Foreword (1964) signed: E. P.—*A Lume Spento* (1908), with facsimile of title-page and dedication page—*A Quinzaine for This Yule* (1909 [*i.e.* 1908]), with facsimile of title-page—Some Poems from the "San Trovaso" Notebook ("The 'San Trovaso' Notebook," by Mary de Rachewiltz; "San Vio," "Roundel for Arms," "Roundel after Joachim du Bellay," "Sonnet of the August Calm," "To Ysolt, for Pardon," "Piazza San Marco," "Some comfort 'tis to catch Will Shaxpeer stealing," "XCVIII (After Shakespeare's sonnet)," "Alma Sol Veneziae," "Ballad of Wine Skins"), with facsimile of front cover of the "San Trovaso" notebook and manuscript of "Sonnet of the August Calm")—Bibliographical Note—Index of Titles and First Lines.

b. *English issue* ([1966]):

EZRA POUND | A LUME SPENTO | AND OTHER EARLY POEMS | FABER AND FABER | 24 Russell Square London

128 pp., incl. facsims. front. (port.) 22·3 × 14·3 cm. Blue cloth boards stamped in gold on spine; end-papers. Yellow dust-jacket printed in black, red, and green.

A. BOOKS AND PAMPHLETS

Published 6 January 1966 at 25 *s.*; 1115 copies printed. *On verso of title-leaf:* First published in England in mcmlxv [*sic*] . . . Printed in U. S. A. . . .

Contents as in A83a.

A84 ÊTRE CITOYEN ROMAIN . . . [1965]

First edition:

EZRA POUND | Être Citoyen Romain | était un privilège | Être Citoyen Moderne | est un calamité | [*device*] | Editions Dynamo | Pierre Aelberts, éditeur | LIÈGE

1 blank leaf, 1 leaf, 7–13 pp., 1 leaf, 2 blank leaves. front. (port.) 19 × 14 cm. Heavy buff paper wrappers printed in black on page [i]; sewn. Outer plain glassine wrapper.

Published 30 October 1965; 51 copies printed. *Colophon (page* [16])*:* . . . Édition originale ornée d'un portrait d'auteur et tirée à 40 exemplaires vélin blanc et 11 exemplaires hollande impérial Van Gelder, avec deux portraits . . . et numerotés 1 à 51 par l'éditeur. Achevé d'imprimer le 30 octobre 1965 par L'Imprimerie Nationale de Liège. [*Description of paper and number written in and initialed by publisher*] Brimborions n° 142 bis . . . [*No copy on Van Gelder has been seen.*]

A reprint of "Le major C–H Douglas et le situation en Angleterre" from *Les Écrits Nouveaux*, Paris, for August and September 1921—C624—pp. [143]–149.

A85 CANTO CX [1965]

First edition:

[*In red:*] EZRA POUND | [*swelled rule*] | CANTO | CX [Cambridge, Mass., As Sextant Press]

1 blank leaf, 4 leaves, 2 blank leaves. mounted front. (port.) 30 × 20 cm. (wrappers); 29·5 × 19·5 cm. (leaves). Heavy orange paper wrappers printed in black on page [i]; sewn; edges untrimmed.

Privately printed by Laurence Scott and Guy Davenport for the author's 80th birthday 30 October 1965; 118 copies printed. *Colophon (verso of fourth leaf):* This is Number [*number written in*] of an edition limited to eighty copies [plus 26 copies lettered A to Z for the printers, and 12 copies marked *hors série*] printed as a present for Ezra Pound on his eightieth birthday October 30, 1965 Cambridge, Massachusetts, U. S. A. As Sextant Press: Guy Davenport/Laurence Scott

Note: The frontispiece portrait of Ezra Pound is by Laurence Scott and is signed and dated in pencil below the mounted reproduction of the engraving.

A. BOOKS AND PAMPHLETS

a. *First edition in this form; copies for sale in the United States:*

[*In black:*] EZRA POUND'S | [*in red:*] CAVALCANTI | POEMS | [*device, with border in black*] | [*in black:*] A NEW DIRECTIONS BOOK [New York, James Laughlin]

1 blank leaf, 105, [1] pp., 1 leaf, 1 blank leaf. 29·3 × 19·2 cm. Yellow paper boards, with white parchment back, lettered in gold on front cover and up the spine; end-papers; top edges gilt, others untrimmed. Plain acetate dust-jacket. Heavy grey paper box with cream paper label printed in black on side.

Published November 1966 at $40.00; 115 copies printed. *On verso of title-leaf:* . . . Printed in Italy *Colophon (page* [108])*:* This edition . . . was printed in Dante type on the hand-press of the Officina Bodoni, Verona, for James Laughlin, Faber and Faber, Vanni Scheiwiller and Giovanni Mardersteig. The edition consists of 190 copies on Pescia paper of which Numbers 1 to 115 are for sale in the United States, Numbers 116 to 165 in Great Britain and Numbers 166 to 190 in Italy; ten copies on Japanese paper are marked with the Letters A to J. All copies are signed by the author. May MDCCCLXVI [*device in red. Signed in blue ink by Ezra Pound*] This is Number [*number printed in*]

Contents: Foreword [by Ezra Pound, dated:] Venezia, 1965—Sonnet I–XXV—Madrigal—Ballata I–XIV—Canzone 'Donna mi prega' ⟨Early Version⟩—Canzone 'Donna mi prega' ⟨As in Canto XXXVI⟩—Notes [by Pound]—Sonnets and Ballate: Introduction to Edition of 1912—Mediaevalism—The Other Dimension

b. *Copies for sale in Great Britain* ([1967])*:*

Identical with copies for sale in the United States save for imprint on title-page: FABER AND FABER | TWENTY FOUR RUSSELL SQUARE | LONDON and box without label.

Published January 1967 at 12 guineas; 50 copies printed. Colophon and contents as in copies for sale in the United States.

c. *Copies for sale in Italy* ([1966])*:*

Identical with copies for sale in the United States save for imprint: VANNI SCHEIWILLER · MILANO and box without label.

Published September 1966 at L. 24,000; 25 copies printed. Colophon and contents as in copies for sale in the United States.

d. *Copies on Japanese paper* ([1966])*:*

[*In black:*] EZRA POUND'S | [*in red:*] CAVALCANTI | POEMS | [*device, with border in black*] | [*in black:*] VERONA · MDCCCLXVI

A. BOOKS AND PAMPHLETS

Pagination as in copies on Pescia paper for sale in the United States. 29·3 × 19·5 cm. Dark grey paper boards, with red morocco back, lettered in gold on front cover and up the spine; end-papers; top edges gilt; other edges untrimmed. Plain acetate dust-jacket. Dark grey cardboard box (without label).

Published September 1966; not for sale; 10 copies printed. Verso of title-leaf, colophon, and contents as in copies on Pescia paper for sale in the United States, the colophon ending: This is copy [*letter printed in*]

A87   CANTOS 110–116   1967

CANTOS 110–116 | Ezra Pound | printed & published | by the FUCK YOU/press | at a secret location | in the lower east side | New York City | USA | 1967 | Cover by Joe Brainard | The FUCK YOU/press | [*device*]

14 leaves. 27·9 × 21·6 cm. Heavy white paper wrappers printed in black on page [i] with design incorporating title: THE CANTOS OF EZRA POUND CX–CXVI; wire-stitched.

Published without authorisation in November 1967; 300 copies printed. *Colophon (recto of final leaf):* Limited edition of 300 copies of which this is No. . . . [*number written in*] [Text reproduced from typewritten copy.]

Contents: [Canto] CX—[Notes for Canto] CXI [omitting lines 1–2]—[From Canto] CXII [with additional final line]—[Canto] CXIII [first 74 lines, omitting five and adding one, then 20 unidentified lines, then "For the blue flash and the moments" from "Notes for Canto CXVII et seq."]—Canto 114 [lines 1–11, 58–62, 64–69, then one unidentified line, then variant of line nine of "For the blue flash and the moments," then lines 11–14 of "From Canto CXV"]—[Canto] 115 [repeating lines 11–14 already printed as part of Canto 114].

A88   POUND/JOYCE   [1967]

a. *First edition:*

POUND [*diagonal extending from right to left across two lines*] JOYCE | The Letters of Ezra Pound to James Joyce, | with Pound's Essays on Joyce | Edited and with Commentary by Forrest Read | A NEW DIRECTIONS BOOK [New York, James Laughlin]

vi, 314 pp. 24 × 16·3 cm. Brown cloth boards stamped in gold on spine; end-papers. Yellow dust-jacket printed in brown and black.

Published 15 November 1967 at $10.00; 2900 copies printed. *On verso of title-leaf:* . . . Manufactured in the United States of America. New Directions Books are published for James Laughlin by New Directions Publishing Corporation, 333 Sixth Avenue, New York 10014. First Printing

Contains letters from Ezra Pound to James Joyce (twelve of them reprinted from *The Letters of Ezra Pound* ([1950])—A64) and these essays: "A Curious History"; "*Dubliners* and Mr James Joyce"; from "The Non-Existence of Ireland"; "Mr. James Joyce and the Modern Stage"; "Meditatio"; "James Joyce: At Last the Novel Appears"; "James Joyce and His Critics: Some Classified Comments"; "Joyce"; "*Ulysses*"; "A Serious Play"; "Paris Letter: Ulysses"; "James Joyce et Pécuchet"; "Le Prix Nobel"; from "After Election"; "Past History"; "Monumental" [from *Guide to Kulchur*]; "James Joyce: To His Memory." Appendix A prints "Letters on Lustra, to Elkin Mathews, 1916"; Appendix C, "Pound's deletions from *Ulysses*, 'Calypso' episode, 1918."

Note: The book was published also by New Directions in New York 30 March 1970 at $2.75 as their Paperbook 296, in a first printing of 5050 copies.

b. *English issue* [(1969)]:

POUND | [*diagonal extending from right to left across two lines*] JOYCE | The Letters of Ezra Pound to James Joyce, | with Pound's Essays on Joyce | Edited and with Commentary by Forrest Read | FABER AND FABER | 24 Russell Square · London

vi, 314 pp. 22·3 × 14·5 cm. Blue cloth boards printed in gold on spine; endpapers. White dust-jacket printed in cream, black, red, and green.

Published 10 February 1969 at 70 *s.*; 2000 copies printed. *On verso of title-leaf:* First published in England in mcmlxviii [*sic*] ... Printed in Great Britain by John Dickens & Co Ltd Northampton ...

Contents as in A88a.

A89   SELECTED CANTOS   [1967]

a. *First edition of this selection:*

SELECTED CANTOS | OF EZRA POUND | FABER & FABER | LONDON

121 pp., 3 blank leaves. 19·8 × 13 cm. Heavy white paper wrappers printed in green, red, and black on page [i] and down the spine, and in black on pages [ii–iv].

Published 7 December 1967 at 7s. 6d. in the series "Faber paper covered Editions"; 36,000 copies printed. *On verso of title-leaf:* This selection first published in mcmlxvii ... Printed in Great Britain by Latimer Trend & Co Ltd Whitstable ...

Dedication on page [5]: To Olga Rudge "Tempus loquendi"

A. BOOKS AND PAMPHLETS

Contains "Foreword" by Ezra Pound, dated 20 October 1966, p. 9, and Cantos I, IV, IX, XIII, XIV, XVI, XXXI, from XXXVIII, XLII (omitting first eight lines), from XLIII, XLIV, XLV, from LII, LIII, from LXII, LXXXI, LXXXIV, from LXXXV, from LXXXVIII, XCV, from XCIX, from CV, from CVIII, and from CIX. *On page [ii] of wrapper:* "This selection . . . was made by Ezra Pound himself in September 1965 [*i.e.* 1966]. It contains those complete Cantos (and short passages from a few others) that he himself considers to provide the best introduction to the whole work for those coming to it for the first time. . . ." ("Publisher's Note," page [6], gives date of selection correctly as September 1966.)

b. *American issue* ([1970]):

SELECTED CANTOS | OF EZRA POUND | A NEW DIRECTIONS BOOK [New York, James Laughlin]

4 leaves, 119 pp. 20·3 × 13·6 cm. Heavy white paper wrappers printed in grey and black on page [i] (with photograph of the author, about 1938, by James Angleton), and in black on page [iv] and down the spine.

Published 21 October 1970 at $1.95 as New Directions Paperbook 304; 7000 copies printed. *On verso of title-leaf:* . . . Typographic design by Giovanni Mardersteig Manufactured in the United States of America New Directions Books are published for James Laughlin by New Directions Publishing Corporation, 333 Sixth Avenue, New York 10014

Contents as in A89a, with additions. "The basic selection for this book was made by Ezra Pound in September, 1966 . . . In this American edition . . . in the style of the Mardersteig first printings of *The Pisan Cantos, Section Rock-Drill* and *Thrones,* the more compressed setting making a few extra pages available, the following passages were added by the publisher: 1. *Canto LII.* The section based on Lü Shih's *Spring and Autumn* was completed by the addition of 78 lines, to the end of the Canto. 2. The first 107 lines of *Canto LXXXIII.* 3. The fragment of *Canto CXV* and *Canto CXVI* from *Drafts & Fragments of Cantos CX–CXVII* which were first published in book form in 1969." ("Publisher's Note," signed J[ames]. L[aughlin]., p. 2.) Pound's "Foreword" is on page 1.

A90   REDONDILLAS   [1968]

First edition:

[*In red:*] REDONDILLAS, | [*in black:*] OR SOMETHING OF THAT SORT | BY EZRA POUND | A NEW DIRECTIONS BOOK [New York, James Laughlin]

1 blank leaf, 11 leaves. 28·5 × 23 cm. Half grey paper boards with linen back, with white paper label on spine printed upward in black and red; end-papers; edges untrimmed. Plain off-white dust-jacket.

A. BOOKS AND PAMPHLETS

Published mid-March 1968 at $60.00; 110 copies printed. *On verso of title-leaf:*
... Printed in the United States of America *Colophon (recto of final leaf):* [*in red:*]
One hundred and ten copies of Redondillas, signed by the author, of which one
hundred are for sale, were printed by Robert Grabhorn & Andrew Hoyem, San
Francisco, California, mcmlxvii. [*Signed in purple ink:*] Ezra Pound

An "Erratum" slip, 4·3 × 19 cm., is tipped in before the final leaf.

Contents: A Note on Pound's Redondillas, by Noel Stock—Redondillas—Notes
[by Pound] on the Proper Names in the Redondillas. (The poem and Pound's
notes on it are reprinted from a set of page-proofs for *Canzoni* (1911) at the
Humanities Research Center of the University of Texas at Austin—see A7a.)

A91   DRAFTS & FRAGMENTS OF   [1969]
                 CANTOS CX-CXVII

a. *First edition:*

EZRA POUND | DRAFTS & FRAGMENTS | OF CANTOS CX—CXVII
| A NEW DIRECTIONS BOOK [New York, James Laughlin]

32 pp. 20·8 × 14 cm. Black cloth boards stamped in blind on front cover and
in silver down the spine; end-papers. White dust-jacket printed all-over in buff,
and in blue.

Published 26 April 1969 at $3.95; 3000 copies printed. *On verso of title-leaf:* ...
Manufactured in the United States of America ... New Directions Books are
published for James Laughlin by New Directions Publishing Corporation, 333
Sixth Avenue, New York 10014 ...

Dedication on page [1]: To Olga Rudge

Contents: Canto CX—Notes for Canto CXI—From Canto CXII—Canto CXIII—
Canto CXIV—From Canto CXV—Canto CXVI—Fragments of Cantos ("Addendum for Canto C, 'The Evil is Usury'" [formerly "Canto Proceeding (LXXII
circa)"]; "Now sun rises in Ram sign"; "Notes for Canto CXVII et seq.: 'For
the blue flash and the moments', 'M'amour, m'amour,' 'La faillite de François
Bernouard'")

b. *English issue* ([1970]):

EZRA POUND | DRAFTS & FRAGMENTS | OF CANTOS CX—CXVII
| FABER AND FABER | LONDON

32 pp. 22·3 × 14·1 cm. Black cloth boards stamped in gold down the spine;
off-white end-papers. Buff dust-jacket printed in black, red, and grey.

Published 23 February 1970 at 20 s.; 2000 copies printed. *On verso of title-leaf:*
First published in England in 1970 ... Printed in Great Britain by Latimer
Trend & Co. Ltd Whitstable ...

Contents as in A91a.

A. BOOKS AND PAMPHLETS

c. *Limited edition, copies for sale in the United States:*

[*In black:*] EZRA POUND | [*in red:*] DRAFTS & FRAGMENTS OF
CANTOS | CX–CXVII | [*in black:*] New Directions [New York,
James Laughlin] & The Stone Wall Press [Iowa City, Iowa, K. K.
Merker]

5 blank leaves, 5 leaves, 9–40 pp., 1 leaf, 3 blank leaves. 32·2 × 22·5 cm. Red
cloth boards with white paper label on spine printed in black; first and final
blank leaves pasted down as end-papers; edges untrimmed. Dark grey cardboard box with paper label printed in black on side.

Published 30 October 1969 at $100.00; 210 copies printed. *On verso of title-leaf:*
New Directions Books are published for James Laughlin by New Directions
Publishing Corporation, 333 Sixth Avenue, New York 10014 . . . *Colophon (recto
of leaf following page 40):* This edition . . . was printed on the hand-press by K. K.
Merker, The Stone Wall Press, Iowa City, in Romanée type on Umbria paper.
The edition consists of 310 copies: Numbers 1 to 200 for New Directions, New
York; Numbers 201 to 300 for Faber and Faber Ltd, London; Numbers 301 to
310 for The Stone Wall Press. All copies are signed by the author. December
MDCCCCLXVIII [*signed in blue ink by Ezra Pound and numbered in ink, followed by
device printed in red*]

Contents as in the first edition. A slip, 11·1 × 15.2 cm., listing "Errata" in 8
lines, is laid in.

d. *Copies for sale in England* ([1970]):

Identical with the American copies save for imprint (Faber &
Faber : 24 Russell Square : London | The Stone Wall Press : Iowa
City) and verso of title-leaf.

Published February 1970 at £ 42.00; 100 copies printed.

A92　　　　　　　AN ANGLE　　　　　　[1972]

a. *De luxe edition:*

EZRA POUND | [*in facsimile of Ezra Pound's handwriting:*] An Angle
| MIT SIEBEN ORIGINALLITHOGRAPHIEN | VON GIUSEPPE
SANTOMASO | ERKER-PRESSE ST. GALLEN

1 blank leaf, 12 leaves, 1 blank leaf, 9 leaves, 1 blank leaf, incl. 7 col. plates.
Unbound sheets, 45·8 × 37 cm., issued in white paper wrappers folded over
first and final blank leaves, printed in black on page [i]. Grey cloth board port-

folio, with white cloth back printed in black up the spine. Grey cloth board box with white cloth top and bottom, 48 × 38 cm.

Published Spring 1972; 200 copies printed. *Colophon (recto of final leaf):* "An Angle" erschien im Frühjahr 1972 in der Erker-Presse, Franz Larese und Jürg Janett, Gallusstrasse 32, St. Gallen. Der Band enthält den Canto XVII (aus "A Draft of XXX Cantos") und Fragmente des Canto LXXVI (aus den Pisaner Cantos) von Ezra Pound sowie sieben Originallithographien von Giuseppe Santomaso. Der Text wurde in der Handschrift des Künstlers lithographiert. Das Buch, auf Vélin-de-Rives-Bütten in einer einmaligen Auflage von 200 Exemplaren gedruckt, erschien in drei Ausgaben: Nummern 1 bis 30: *Vorzugsausgabe*. Den Exemplaren dieser Ausgabe ist je eine Mappe mit der vollständigen Suite der Originallithographien von Giuseppe Santomaso beigegeben. Alle Blätter der Suiten wie auch die in diesen Büchern enthaltenen Lithographien sind signiert und numeriert. Nummern 31 bis 80: *Ausgabe ad personam*. Diese Exemplare tragen eine persönliche Widmung. Der Erlös aus ihrem Verkauf geht als Geschenk des Dichters und des Künstlers an das "Consultative Committee for the *Unesco International Campaign for Venice*". Die Spende ist bestimmt für die Restaurierung des Kapitelsaals der Basilica dei Frari in Venedig ... Nummern 81 bis 200: *Normalausgabe*. Alle Bücher sind im Impressum numeriert und von Ezra Pound und Giuseppe Santomaso signiert. Jedem Band wird eine Schallplatte beigegeben, auf welcher der Dichter die im Buch enthaltenen Texte liest. Dieses Exemplar trägt die Nummer [*number written in in ink over a short printed line, followed by signatures of artist and author*]

Contents: Canto XVII [*in facsimile of Ezra Pound's handwriting, copied out especially for this edition, signed and dated at end:* Venezia, 6 aprile 1971]—from Canto LXXVI (Pisan's) [*the final 89 lines*]. (The recording is placed in a triangular sleeve pasted at the bottom right of the inside back cover of the portfolio. See E51.)

Note: To commemorate the first "Erker-Treffen"—a meeting at Schloss Hagenwil on 2 December 1972 of artists, authors, and friends of the Erker-Galerie, the Erker-Verlag, and the Erker-Presse—200 copies of a portfolio of prints and lithographic facsimiles of manuscripts was issued, *Erker-Treffen 1* [*names of contributors in eight lines*] Erker-Presse [St. Gallen, 1973?] Ezra Pound's contribution consists of a reproduction of the following in his handwriting: Avec mes homages | Ezra Pound | pour prendre congé .

b. *Reduced facsimile edition* ([1975?]):

Title-page as in A92a.

12 leaves, 1 blank leaf, 10 leaves, 1 blank leaf, incl. col. illus., facsims. 16 × 12·2 cm. Heavy plain white paper wrappers. Heavy white paper dust-jacket printed in black on front.

Published probably in October 1975; number of copies unknown. *Colophon (recto of final leaf):* Von dieser Publikation erschien eine Sonderausgabe von 100 Exemplaren, denen je eine von Giuseppe Santomaso geschaffene Original-Radierung beigelegt ist. Die Exemplare dieser Ausgabe wie die Radierungen selbst sind

A. BOOKS AND PAMPHLETS

signiert und numeriert. Dieses Exemplar trägt die Nummer [*no numbered copy seen*]

A93   SELECTED PROSE 1909–1965   [1973]

a. *First edition:*

Selected Prose | 1909–1965 | EZRA POUND | Edited, with an Introduction by William Cookson | FABER AND FABER | LONDON

1 blank leaf, 2 leaves, 3–444 pp. 22·4 × 14·5 cm. Black cloth boards stamped in blue and gold on spine; end-papers. White dust-jacket printed in black, tan, and blue.

Published 29 January 1973 at £ 6.00; 2500 copies printed. *On verso of title-leaf:* First published in 1973 ... Printed in Great Britain by Western Printing Services Ltd, Bristol ...

Contents: Foreword, by Ezra Pound, dated Venice, 4 July 1972—Introduction [by William Cookson]—PART ONE: I GATHER THE LIMBS OF OSIRIS [C26, 28, 32, 35, 41, and 42, omitting translations available in *The Translations of Ezra Pound*]—PART TWO: RELIGIO: Religio or The Child's Guide to Knowledge—Axiomata—Credo—Terra Italica—Ecclesiastical History—On the Degrees of Honesty in Various Occidental Religions—Religio—Statues of Gods—Deus est amor—Quotations from Richard of St. Victor [from B68]—PART THREE: The Treatise on Harmony—PART FOUR: CONFUCIUS AND MENCIUS: Immediate Need of Confucius—Mang Tsze—PART FIVE: AMERICA: What I Feel about Walt Whitman—The Jefferson-Adams Letters as a Shrine, and a Monument—*Introductory Text-Book*—National Culture, A Manifesto 1938—*An Introduction to the Economic Nature of the United States*—PART SIX: CIVILISATION, MONEY AND HISTORY: Provincialism the Enemy—Kublai Khan and His Currency—Probari ratio—Economic Democracy—Definitions [Etc.—C675]—The State [from C689]—Prolegomena [C693]—Bureaucracy the Flail of Jehovah [complete]—Peace—The City—Murder by Capital—*ABC of Economics*—John Buchan's *Cromwell* ... —History and Ignorance—Banks [from *Social Credit*]—The Individual in His Milieu—Values [from "Demarcations"—C1387]—For a New Paideuma—*What Is Money For?*—Freedom de facto—*A Visiting Card*—*Gold and Work*—Sovereignty—Del Mar—Feasible Justice [from "Destruction by Taxation" in *Impact*]—Gists [from *Impact*]—PART SEVEN: THE ART OF POETRY: The Wisdom of Poetry—The Approach to Paris [from IV and V]—Affirmations [IV]: As for Imagisme—Beddoes and Chronology—Landor—Prefatio aut cimicium tumulus—PART EIGHT: CONTEMPORARIES: The Divine Mystery—Allen Upward Serious—Remy de Gourmont [I–II]—Marianne Moore and Mina Loy—Wyndham Lewis at the Goupil—Hudson: Poet Strayed into Science—Jean Cocteau Sociologist—Obituary: A. R. Orage ["He Pulled His Weight"]—In the Wounds: (Memoriam A. R. Orage)—D'Artagnan Twenty Years After—Ford Madox (Hueffer) Ford; Obit—For T. S. E[liot].

A. BOOKS AND PAMPHLETS

Note: The book was also published by Faber and Faber in London 2 May 1978 at £ 3.50 in their series of Faber Paperbacks, in a first impression of 8000 copies.

b. *First American edition* ([1973]):

Selected Prose | 1909–1965 | EZRA POUND | Edited, with an Introduction by William Cookson | A NEW DIRECTIONS BOOK [New York, James Laughlin]

4 leaves, 7–475 pp., 1 blank leaf. 21 × 14·5 cm. Yellow cloth boards stamped in black on spine; end-papers. White dust-jacket printed in black.

Published 13 June 1973 at $15.00; 250 copies printed. *On verso of title-leaf:* . . . Manufactured in the United States of America First published clothbound . . . in 1973 . . . New Directions Books are published for James Laughlin by New Directions Publishing Corporation, 333 Sixth Avenue, New York 10014

Contents as in A93a, except for the omission of "Statues of Gods" (from Part Two) and "The Treatise on Harmony" (Part Three), and the addition of "Patria Mia" (as Part Four). A leaf of errata (reproduced from type-written copy) is laid in.

Note: This book was also published by New Directions in New York 28 April 1975 at $4.75 as their Paperbook 396, in a first printing of 3990 copies.

A94   CANTOS LXXII & LXXIII   1973

First (copyright) edition:

Ezra Pound | CANTOS LXXII & LXXIII | Washington, D. C. | 1973

1 leaf, 15 pp., 1 leaf. 21·6 × 14 cm. Heavy green paper wrappers printed in black on page [i]; wire-stitched.

Published June 1973; 25 copies printed. *On verso of title-leaf:* . . . Published simultaneously in Canada by McClelland [*inserted in manuscript:* and] Stewart, Ltd. Manufactured in the United States of America [*contents reproduced from typewritten copy*] *Colophon* (*page* [18]): . . . 25 copies of this first printing . . . were published in June, 1973 by The Estate of Ezra Pound. This is copy number [*number written in*]

In Italian. *Contents:* Canto LXXII (Presenza)—Canto LXXIII (Cavalcanti—Correspondenza Repubblicana)

Note: Only two copies were sold in June 1973, one in the United States (now privately owned), the other in Canada (brought out in cooperation with the McClelland and Stewart Publishing Company and now located in the North York Public Library, Toronto), and two copies deposited with the Copyright

Office. The distribution of the remaining 21 copies was not made until after the settlement of the Ezra Pound Estate in July 1978.

A95   DK / SOME LETTERS   [1975]

First edition:

Dk / | Some Letters of Ezra Pound | Edited with Notes by Louis Dudek | D C Books [Montreal, Canada]

1 blank leaf, 4 leaves, 11–145 pp., 1 blank leaf, incl. facsims. 22·3 × 15·7 cm. Heavy tan paper wrappers printed in dark brown on page [i] (with facsimile of the letter of 19 March '67 in light brown as background), and down the spine.

Published 15 January 1975 at $6.00; 2,000 copies printed. *On verso of title-leaf:* ... Published by DC Books, 5 Ingleside Avenue, Montréal, Canada ... [The entire book is printed in brown.]

Letters to Louis Dudek, dating from 1949 to 1967, reproduced in facsimile, with annotations by Dudek.

A96   CERTAIN RADIO SPEECHES   1975

First edition:

[*Within thick-thin-rule border:*] certain | RADIO | SPEECHES | of | Ezra Pound | FROM THE RECORDINGS AND TRANSCRIPTIONS | OF HIS WARTIME BROADCASTS | ROME, 1941–1943 | ED- ITED | BY | William Levy | MCMLXXV | [*rule*] | COLD TURKEY PRESS | [*rule*] | ROTTERDAM | [*short rule*]

54 leaves. 29·4 × 20·3 cm. Heavy white paper wrappers, with black cloth back, printed in red and black on pages [i] and [iv].

Published without authorisation in October 1975 at Fl. 7.50 (£ 1.50; 20 NF; $4.50); 500 copies printed. *On verso of title-leaf:* ... 1975 ... First Edition 250 [*number written in in ink*] Designed, Printed and Published by Cold Turkey Press ...

Reproduced from typewritten copy. A leaf of yellow glassine precedes the title-leaf and follows the last leaf. An "Addendum" sheet, listing sound recordings of the thirteen speeches, is laid in.

Contents: Station Identification [by William Levy]—SPEECHES: Those Paren- thesis [*sic*] (7 Dec. 1941)—[The] Pattern (30 Mar. 1942)—Question of Motive (13 Apr. 1942)—Universality (4 May 1942)—To Be Late (14 May 1942)— With Phantoms (18 May 1942)—As a Beginner ["As a Beginning"] (28 May

A. BOOKS AND PAMPHLETS

1942)—The Fallen Gent[leman] (19 June 1942)—On Continuity ["Continuity"] (6 & 7 July 1942)—Darkness (13 & 14 July 1942)—Public Memory ["To the Memory of G. K. Chesterton"] (13 June 1943)—Materialism (26 June 1943)—A Few Friends ["Civilization"] (24 July 1943)—GESTURES: Access to Source [a letter to Levy from the National Archives concerning the radio speeches]—More Speeches: an Annotated Checklist—Found Objects [documents].

A97   SELECTED POEMS 1908–1959   [1975]

a. *First edition of this selection, hardbound copies:*

EZRA POUND | SELECTED POEMS | 1908–1959 | FABER & FABER | 3 QUEEN SQUARE   LONDON

1 blank leaf, 2 leaves, 7–186 pp., 3 blank leaves. 20·3 × 13·5 cm. Blue cloth boards stamped in gold on spine; front end-paper (final blank leaf pasted down as back end-paper). White dust-jacket printed in red and black.

Published 27 October 1975 at £ 3.50; 3000 copies printed. *On verso of title-leaf:* First published 1975 . . . Printed in Great Britain by Latimer Trend & Company Ltd Plymouth . . .

"This selection takes the place of T. S. Eliot's pioneer edition published in 1928 and is very largely the same as the selection that has been available for some years in the United States, though there is additional material." (*Dust-jacket*)

Contents: FROM PERSONAE (1908, 1909, 1910): Cino—Na Audiart—Villonaud for This Yule—The Tree—Sestina: Altaforte—Ballad of the Goodly Fere—Planh for the Young English King—"Blandula, Tenulla, Vagula"—Erat Hora—The House of Splendour—La Fraisne—A Villonaud: Ballad of the Gibbet—Marvoil—Piere Vidal Old—FROM RIPOSTES (1912): Portrait d'une Femme—An Object—The Seafarer—Δώρια—Apparuit—The Return—FROM LUSTRA: Tenzone—The Garret—The Garden—Salutation—Salutation the Second—The Spring—Commission—A Pact—Dance Figure—April—Gentildonna—The Rest—Les Millwin—A Song of the Degrees—Ité—The Bath Tub—Liu Ch'e—Arides—Amitiés—Meditatio—Ladies—Coda—The Coming of War: Actaeon—In a Station of the Metro—Alba—Coitus—The Encounter—'Ιμέρρω—"Ione, Dead the Long Year"—The Tea Shop—The Lake Isle—Epitaphs—Villanelle: the Psychological Hour—Alba from "Langue d'Oc"—Near Perigord—CATHAY [omitting "The Seafarer" (already included above) and adding "Sennin Poem by Kakuhaku," "A Ballad of the Mulberry Road," "Old Idea of Choan by Rosoriu," and "To-Em-Mei's 'The Unmoving Cloud'"]—HOMAGE TO SEXTUS PROPERTIUS (1917)—HUGH SELWYN MAUBERLEY [(1920)]—CANTOS: Cantos I–III—from Canto IV—Canto IX—Canto XIII—from Canto XIV—Canto XVII—from Canto XX—from Canto XXV—from Canto XXX—from Canto XXXVI—Canto XXXVIII—Canto XLV—Canto XLVII—Canto XLIX—Canto LI—from Canto LIII—from Canto LXII—from Canto LXXIV—from Canto

LXXVI—from Canto LXXIX—from Canto LXXX—from Canto LXXXI—
from Canto LXXXIII—from Canto XCI—from Canto XCIII.

b. *Paperbound copies:*

Title-page as in hardbound copies.

1 blank leaf, 2 leaves, 7–186 pp., 3 blank leaves. 19·6 × 12·6 cm. Heavy white
paper wrappers printed in red and black on pages [i] and [iv], in black on pages
[ii] and [iii], and in red on spine.

Published 27 October 1975 at £ 1.30 in the series of Faber Paperbacks; 12,000
copies printed. Verso of title-leaf as in hardbound copies save for addition of
"Conditions of Sale" in six lines.

Contents as in hardbound copies. This paperbound was reprinted in 1977 with
title *Selected Poems* and with these additions: from Canto XCVIII—from Canto
CVII—from Canto CX—from Canto CXV—from Canto CXVI. The pagina-
tion of this new impression is: 1 blank leaf, 2 leaves, 7–192 pp. Size and binding
as in A97a. The price was £ 1.50 (later raised to £ 1.95).

A98   COLLECTED EARLY POEMS   [1976]

a. *First edition:*

COLLECTED EARLY | POEMS OF | EZRA | POUND | Edited by
Michael John King, | with an introduction by Louis L. Martz | A
NEW DIRECTIONS BOOK [New York, James Laughlin]

xxii, 330 pp., incl. front. (port.), illus. (facsims.) 23·4 × 16·2 cm. Buff linen
cloth boards stamped in blue down the spine; end-papers; white dust-jacket
printed in blue (with, in the earliest copies, an error "eary" for "early" on the
spine).

Published 9 November 1976 at $22.50; 2570 copies printed. *On verso of title-leaf:*
... Manufactured in the United States of America First published clothbound
in 1976 ... New Directions Books are published for James Laughlin by New
Directions Publishing Corporation, 333 Sixth Avenue, New York 10014

"Our aim has been to collect here all the poems that Pound published, whether
in book form, in periodicals, or in miscellanies, through the year 1912. ... The
poems in his six volumes of 1908, 1909, 1911, and 1912 have here been reprinted, including translations that appeared in these volumes; we have otherwise excluded translations from this book. ... We have ... printed the poems
only once, normally following the text of their first appearance in book form.
... A special situation exists with regard to the selections from *Canzoni* which
were published seven months earlier ... in *Provença* (Boston). Here we have
chosen to follow the texts given in the complete volume *Canzoni* ...

"To these published poems we have added twenty-three hitherto unpublished

A. BOOKS AND PAMPHLETS

poems from the San Trovaso Notebook . . . [and] a selection of eleven [hitherto
unpublished] poems from . . . miscellaneous manuscripts . . . We have also added
six poems, five of them hitherto unpublished, derived from the proof sheets of
Pound's volume *Canzoni* in the Humanities Research Center of the University
of Texas . . . [and] several passages from the original typescript of 'Hilda's Book,'
the collection of early poems which Pound presented to Hilda Doolittle, probably in 1907. Finally, we have added in an appendix a small group of miscellaneous published verse dating from the years 1913–1917, which has not hitherto
been collected . . ." (*Introduction to* "Notes," *signed* M. K[ing]. *and* L. L. M[artz].,
p. 289–90.) Variant words and stanzas of poems and additional comments by
Pound are incorporated in the "Notes," pp. 293–324.

Contents: A LUME SPENTO (1908)—A QUINZAINE FOR THIS YULE (1908)—
PERSONAE (1909)—EXULTATIONS (1909)—CANZONI (1911)—RIPOSTES
(1912)—UNCOLLECTED MISCELLANEOUS POEMS (1902–1912): Ezra on the
Strike—A Dawn Song—To the Raphaelite Latinists—In epitaphium—Thersites: on the Surviving Zeus—The Fault of It—For a Beery Voice—L'Invitation—Epilogue—POEMS WITHDRAWN FROM CANZONI: Leviora, I: Against
Form; II: Hic jacet; IV: To my very dear friend, remonstrating for his essay
upon "Mighty mouths"—To Hulme (T. E.) and Fitzgerald (A Certain)—Redondillas, or Something of That Sort—THE ALCHEMIST (TWO VERSIONS)
(1912)—POEMS FROM THE SAN TROVASO NOTEBOOK: San Vio. June—Roundel
for Arms—Roundel. After Joachim du Bellay—Sonnet of the August Calm—
To Ysolt. For Pardon—For Ysolt. The Triad of Dawn—Piazza San Marco—
Lotus-bloom—For a Play. (Maeterlinck)—The Rune—Narcotic Alcohol—
Blazed—For the Triumph of the Arts—Alma Sol Veneziae—Fragment to
W[illiam]. C[arlos]. W[illiams].'s Romance—⟨Fragmenti⟩—⟨In That Coun-
try⟩—Autumnus. To Dowson (Antistave)—Fratello mio, Zephyrus [formerly
"The Banners"]—For E. McC[artney]. The Rejected Stanza—Ballad of Wine
Skins—I Wait—⟨Shalott⟩—Battle Dawn—For Italico Brass—Envoi. A mon
bien aimé—⟨Additional Poems in the San Trovaso Notebook:⟩ ("She is a thing
too frail to know | our life," "Thoughts moving | in her eyes," "I have felt
the lithe wind | blowing")—Statement of Being—Das Babenzorn—POEMS FROM
MISCELLANEOUS MANUSCRIPTS: Swinburne: A Critique—To E. B.
B[rowning].—The Summons—Ballad of the Sun's Hunting—Quia amore lan-
gueo—Capilupus Sends Greeting to Grotus—The Hills Whence—From Che-
bar—"Chommoda"—"It Is a Shame (with Apologies to the Modern Celtic
School)"—The Logical Conclusion—APPENDIX: UNCOLLECTED MISCELLANEOUS
POEMS (1913–1917): Pax Saturni—Xenia, I: The Street in Soho; II "The cool
fingers of science delight me"—The Choice—Xenia, IV "Come let us play
with our own toys"; V "She had a pig-shaped face, with beautiful coloring"—
Legend of the Chippewa Spring and Minnehaha, the Indian Maiden—Homage
to Wilfrid Scawen Blunt—Pastoral—Gnomic Verses—Our Respectful Homages to M. Laurent Tailhade—Et faim sallir les loups des boys—Love-song to
Eunoë—Another Man's Wife—Poem: Abbreviated from the Conversation of
Mr. T. E. H[ulme].—Reflection—To a City Sending Him Advertisements—NOTES

Note: The illustration on page [319] reproduces the original manuscript of
"Roundel. After Joachim du Bellay" from the "San Trovaso" notebook.

A. BOOKS AND PAMPHLETS

b. *English issue* ([1977]):

COLLECTED EARLY | POEMS OF | EZRA | POUND | Edited by
Michael John King, | with an introduction by Louis L. Martz |
FABER AND FABER · LONDON

xxii, 330 pp., incl. front. (port.), illus. (facsims.) 23·5 × 15·5 cm. Red cloth
boards lettered in gold on spine; end-papers. White dust-jacket printed in red
and black.

Published 4 April 1977 at £ 12.00; 2000 copies printed. *On verso of title-leaf:* ...
Printed in the United States of America First Published in England in 1977 ...

Contents as in A97a.

A99   EZRA POUND AND MUSIC   [1977]

a. *First edition:*

EZRA | POUND | and music | The Complete Criticism | Edited
with commentary by R. Murray Schafer | A NEW DIRECTIONS
BOOK [New York, James Laughlin]

xiii, 530 pp., incl. front. (port.), illus. (facsims.) 23·4 × 16 cm. Brown cloth
boards lettered in green on spine; end-papers. White dust-jacket printed in
green.

Published 16 November 1977 at $40.00; 1000 copies printed. *On verso of title-leaf:* ... Manufactured in the United States of America First published cloth-bound by New Directions in 1977 ... New Directions Books are published for James Laughlin by New Directions Publishing Corporation, 333 Sixth Avenue, New York 10014

Dedication on page [v]: To the memory of Agnes Bedford, friend of the poet, friend of the editor

The frontispiece is a reproduction of a photograph of a portrait of Ezra Pound "believed to have been painted *c*. 1922 by Stowitz." The illustrations include facsimiles of a page from a copybook (p. [7]); an early transcription of the text and melody of a song by Gaucelm Faidit (p. [8]); manuscript notes on programmes for recitals by Arthur Rubinstein (p. [235]) and Wladimir Cernikoff (p. [236]); and the programme for the Rudge–Antheil concert of 11 December 1923 (p. [249]; see E3g).

"The purpose of this volume is to bring forward Ezra Pound's musical theorizings and criticisms in sequence. A projected second volume will deal with his chief attempts to realize these ideas in musical compositions. ... Absent from the present collection are only interposed remarks on music from the published books and letters, though many of these will be mentioned in the editorial notes." ("Preface," p. ix)

A. BOOKS AND PAMPHLETS

Contents: Preface [by the editor]—Introduction [by the editor]: The Music in Pound's Poetry—1 ENGLAND: THE EARLY REVIEWS (1908–1917): [Editor's introductory remarks incorporate reprints of C8 and 10] I Gather the Limbs of Osiris [X]: On Music—[Affirmations, I:] Arnold Dolmetsch—Vers libre and Arnold Dolmetsch—[Review of] *The Interpretation of the Music of the XVIIth and XVIIIth Centuries,* by Arnold Dolmetsch—Arnold Dolmetsch—Gilbert and Sullivan—Russian Matinées [from "In Their Degree"—C547]—Musical Comedy—Pavlova—2 ENGLAND: THE NEW AGE MUSIC CRITIC, "WILLIAM ATHELING" (1917–1921): Le Mariage de Figaro—Some Recent Concerts—["Raymonde Collignon"]—Francesco Vigliani and Others—D'Alvarez the Indiscriminate—["Music": Letter to Editor of the *New Age*—C341]—Dämmerung of the Piano—A Programme, and the Maladministered Lyric—Music [C342]—The Gaelic—Rosing, the Magnificent—Rosing—Varia—'Cellists, Etc.—Felix Salmond, Excellent 'Cellist—Music [C368]—Stroesco Improved; Nevada; Purnell—Arthur Williams ('Cello)—Music [C384 and 387]—The Avoidable—Prom—Music [C409]—Moiseiwitsch; Rosing—Functions of Criticism—Stroesco; Violinists—Van Dieren; Tinayre; Rosing's All Russian Programme—Hebrides, Kennedy-Fraser—Miscellaneous—Music ... [C430]—Moussorgsky. Rosing; Stroesco; Haley—Mr. Rosing Experiments—Rosowsky; Rosing; Di Veroli—Lamond; Tinayre; Collignon—Music [C450]—Pot-Shots—Music [C457]—Mainly Stroesco—Music [C463 and 465]—Post-Mortems—Varia; Dolmetsch—Music [C493]—At the Ballet—Music [C507]—Marquesita—Music [C515 and 520]—The Pye-ano—Music [C530 and 536]—Cernikoff—Music [C539, 546, 552, and 564]—Mignon Nevada, et varia—Music [C600, 604, 605, 609, 610, and 613]—3 FRANCE AND ITALY (1921–1927): [Editor's introductory remarks incorporate reprints of C653 and 654] George Antheil (Retrospect)—Atheling: Notes for Performers—Varia—The Treatise on Harmony [all four from *Antheil*—A25]—The Unpublished Work of Fanelli—The Form—London Letter—Antheil, 1924–1926—Workshop Orchestration—Unindignant Denial—4 THE RAPALLO YEARS (1928–1941): Anti-Scriabin [translated into English by Schafer from Pound's Italian]—Hungarian Composers in Rapallo [tr.]—Exceptional Program of Musical Events in Rapallo [tr.]—The Pianist Münch [tr.]—The Violinist Olga Rudge [I–II, tr.]—Second Concert: Tuesday 14th November ... [tr.]—Splendid Success of the Second Concert [tr.]—Warm Reception in Genoa for the Tigullian Musicians [tr.]—"Inverno musicale" [C996, tr.]—Inverno musicale: Future Concerts [tr.]—Meaning and Importance of William Young's Music [tr.]—The Singer Lonny Mayer [tr.]—Planned Tigullian Music: Inverno Musicale [tr.]—Olga Rudge and Gerhart Münch in Florence and Chiavari [tr.]—Tibor Serly, Composer—Music and Money—Throttling Music—Money versus Music—Tigullian Studies [C1305, 1318, and 1323, all tr.]—Marconi's Violins [tr.]—Mediaeval Music and Yves Tinayre—Civilization [from *Polite Essays*—A42]—Mostly Quartets—Music and Brains—Music in Ca' Rezzonico—Ligurian View of a Venetian Festival—The Art of Luigi Franchetti [tr.]—The New Hungarian Quartet [tr.]—The Return of Gerhart Münch [tr.]—Concerts of March 29 and April 1 [tr.]—Tigullian Musical Life [tr.]—Tigullian Musical Season [tr.]—February Concerts: The Pianist Renata Borgatti [tr.]—Tigullian Musical Studies [tr.]—Tigullian Musical Season [tr.]—Janequin, Francesco da Milano—Muzik, as Mistaught—Musicians; God

A. BOOKS AND PAMPHLETS

Help 'Em—Musicians—Anita de Alba, and Possibilities for Rapallo [tr.]—Mr. Pound Replies—Mozart Concerts in March in Rapallo [tr.]—The Vivaldi Revival [tr.]—Vocal or Verbal [tr.]—A Letter from Rapallo [C1530]—Vivaldi and Siena [tr.]—5 POSTSCRIPT (1942–1972): [Editor's introductory remarks quote a typed note from Ezra Pound to the Librarian of the Library of Congress written in the summer of 1960] Appendix I: The Developing Theories of Absolute Rhythm and Great Bass—Appendix II: Glossary of Important Musical Personalities—Appendix III: Why a Poet Quit the Muses [by] George Antheil—INDEX OF PROPER NAMES

b. *English issue* ([1978]):

EZRA | POUND | and music | The Complete Criticism | Edited with commentary by R. Murray Schafer | FABER & FABER | 3 QUEEN SQUARE, LONDON

Pagination, binding, jacket, and size as in A99a save for name of publisher on binding and jacket, and price on jacket.

Published 6 March 1978 at £ 25.00; 1300 copies printed. *On verso of title-leaf:* First published in Great Britain 1978 . . . Manufactured in the United States of America . . .

Contents as in A99a.

A100   SULLA MONETA   [1977]
First edition:

Ezra Pound | SULLA MONETA | Edizioni di Ar [Padova]

17, [1] pp., 1 leaf. 19·5 × 12 cm. Heavy white paper wrappers printed in black and red on page [i] and in black on page [iv].

Published in November 1977 at L. 800 as "Quaderni del Veltro, II"; number of copies unknown. *On verso of title-leaf:* Edizioni di Ar Padova, via Patriarcato 34, 1977 *Colophon* (*recto of final leaf*): Finito di stampare dalla tm tiemme industria grafica – manduria nel mese di novembre 1977

Contents: Nota introduttiva [by the editor]—Discussioni e proposte [reprinted from the essay "Terminologia" in *Meridiano di Roma* for 16 May 1943—C1658]—Problemi economici [reprinted from *Orientamenti* (1944)—A55].

A101   "EZRA POUND SPEAKING"   [1978]
First edition:

"EZRA POUND | SPEAKING" | RADIO SPEECHES OF | WORLD

A. BOOKS AND PAMPHLETS

WAR II | Edited by Leonard W. Doob | CONTRIBUTIONS IN AMERICAN STUDIES, NUMBER 37 | GREENWOOD PRESS | WEST-PORT, CONNECTICUT · LONDON, ENGLAND [*publisher's device printed to left of preceding 2 lines*]

xv, 465 pp., 1 leaf, 2 blank leaves. 24·1 × 16·2 cm. Red cloth boards stamped in black on front cover and on spine; end-papers. (Issued without dust-jacket.)

Published 30 June 1978 at $29.95 in the series "Contributions in American Studies, 37"; 1,750 copies printed. *On verso of title-leaf:* . . . First published in 1978 . . . Printed in the United States of America . . . 1

"The present collection consists of original manuscripts Pound prepared to read on Rome radio, divided into two parts:

"Part 1 includes all of the available manuscripts (105) for the broadcasts recorded by the F[ederal] C[ommunications] C[ommission]: October 2, 1941, to December 7, 1941; January 29, 1942, to July 26, 1942; February 18, 1943, to July 25, 1943. . . . To date . . . it has been impossible to locate five of Pound's original manuscripts, hence the FCC versions in these instances, imperfect though they are, have been substituted . . . In a few instances gaps in the manuscripts themselves have been filled by sections of the FCC transcripts; these substitutions are clearly indicated.

"Part 2 includes 10 speeches written before the FCC monitoring unit had been established . . . as well as speeches either not used or not monitored. They have been selected by Mary de Rachewiltz because in her opinion they represent a fair sample of Pound's central ideas and themes.

"The anonymous and pseudonymous scripts Pound also wrote are not included . . . because they merely repeat ideas already expressed in other speeches." ("Introduction," pp. [xi]–xii)

Contents: PART I. 110 FCC-RECORDED SCRIPTS: 1 (1941 Oct. 2) Last Ditch of Democracy—2 (Oct. 26) Books and Music—3 (Nov. 4) The Golden Wedding—4 (Nov. 6) This War on Youth—on a Generation—5 (Dec. 7) Those Parentheses—6 (1942 Jan. 29) On Resuming—7 (Feb. 3) 30 Years or a Hundred—8 (Feb. 10) The Stage in America—9 (Feb. 12) Canto 46 [a reading of the Canto with introductory explanation]—10 (Feb. 17) Sale and Manufacture of War—11 (Feb. 19) Power—12 (Feb. 26) America was Intentions—13 (Mar. 2) Napoleon, Etc.—14 (Mar. 6) Why Pick on the Jew?—15 (Mar. 8) Gold: England—16 (Mar. 15) England—17 (Mar. 19) And the Time Lag—18 (Mar. 22) But How?—19 (Mar. 23) But How? Second Item—20 (Mar. 26) McArthur—21 (Mar. 30) The Pattern—22 (Apr. 6) Destruction—23 (Apr. 9) Indecision—24 (Apr. 12) Comic Relief—25 (Apr. 13) Question of Motive—26 (Apr. 16) Clarification—27 (Apr. 19) To Social Creditors—28 (Apr. 20) Aberration—29 (Apr. 23) MacLeish—30 (Apr. 26) Blast—31 (Apr. 27) Opportunity Recognized—32 (Apr. 30) Non-Jew—33 (May 4) Universality—34 (May 9) The Duration—35 (May 10) The Precarious—36 (May 11) A French Accent—37 (May 14) To be Late (Essere in Ritardo)—38 (May 17) Free Speech in Albion (alias England)—39

A. BOOKS AND PAMPHLETS

(May 18) With Phantoms—40 (May 21) E. E. Cummings Examined—41 (May 24) Brain Trust—42 (May 28) As a Beginning—43 (May 31) Brain Trust: Second Spasm—44 (June 4) As to Pathology and Psychoses—45 (June 8) The Keys of Heaven—46 (June 14) The British Imperium—47 (June 15) Violence—48 (June 19) The Fallen Gentleman (Il Signor Decaduto)—49 (June 25) That Interval of Time—50 (June 28) The Giftie—51 (July 2) Disbursement of Wisdom—52 (July 6) Continuity—53 (July 10) How Come—54 (July 12) Freedumb Forum—55 (July 13) Darkness—56 (July 17) Perfect Phrasing—57 (July 19) July 16th, an Anniversary—58 (July 20) Superstition—59 (July 26) Axis Propaganda—60 (1943 Feb 18) More Homely—61 (Feb. 19) That Illusion—62 (Feb. 21) Serviti—63 (Feb. 23) Complexity—64 (Mar. 7) Toward Veracity—65 (Mar. 9) Pots to Fracture—66 (Mar. 14) Anglophilia—67 (Mar. 16) To Explain—68 (Mar. 19) More Names—69 (Mar. 21) Pogrom—70 (Mar. 25) To Recapitulate—71 (Mar. 26) Financial Defeat: U. S.—72 (Mar. 30) Usurocracy—73 (Apr. 4) Lyric Tenors—74 (Apr. 6) Fetish—75 (Apr. 13) Valentine—76 (Apr. 17) J. G. Blaine—77 (Apr. 18) Canute—78 (Apr. 20) Zion—79 (Apr. 24) Conscience—80 (Apr. 27) On Retiring—81 (May 2) On the Nature of Treachery—82 (May 4) Romance—83 (May 8) Philosemite—84 (May 9) Lord Bleeder—85 (May 11) Sumner Welles—86 (May 15) Economic Aggression—87 (May 16) Administration—88 (May 18) Economic Oppression—89 (May 22) In the Woodshed—90 (May 23) Soberly—91 (May 24) ⟨Title unknown⟩—92 (May 25) And Back of the Woodshed—93 (May 29) Surprise—94 (June 1) Big Jew—95 (June 5) Debt—96 (June 12) ⟨Therapy⟩—97 (June 13) To the Memory [of G. K. Chesterton]—98 (June 15) ⟨Obsequies⟩—99 (June 19) War Aims—100 (June 20) ⟨On Brains or Medulla⟩—101 (June 22) Stalin—102 (June 26) Materialism—103 (June 29) Communist Millionaires—104 (July 3) Coloring—105 (July 4) ⟨Title unknown⟩—106 (July 6) Credit: Legality—107 (July 17) Audacia/Audacity—108 (July 20) Objection (Protesta)—109 (July 24) Civilization—110 (July 25) Lost or Stolen (Perduto o rubato)—PART II: 10 MISCELLANEOUS SCRIPTS: 111 (early 1941) Homesteads—112 (1941) March Arrivals—113 (1941) America was Promises—114 (1941) Aristotle and Adams—115 (1942) To Consolidate—116 (1941) To Albion—117 (1941) Two Pictures—118 (1941) Quisling—119 (1943) Philology—120 (1941) Church Peril—APPENDIX 1: The Content Analysis: Methodology—APPENDIX 2: Quantitative Analysis—APPENDIX 3: Pound's Critics—APPENDIX 4: Style and Techniques—BIBLIOGRAPHY—GLOSSARY AND INDEX TO NAMES

A102   LETTERS TO IBBOTSON   [1979]

First edition:

EZRA POUND | Letters to Ibbotson, 1935–1952 | Edited | by | Vittoria I. Mondolfo and Margaret Hurley | Introduction | by | Walter Pilkington | National Poetry Foundation | University of Maine | Orono, Maine

A. BOOKS AND PAMPHLETS

3 leaves, 145 pp., incl. illus., facsims. 23·6 × 15·9 cm. Red cloth boards stamped in gold on spine; end-papers. White dust-jacket printed in orange and black (with reproduction on front of pencil sketch of Pound, 4 August 1970, by Ilse Engel).

Published 21 May 1979 at $12.95 in the publisher's "Ezra Pound Scholarship Series [3]"; 400 copies printed. *On verso of title-leaf:* Limited Edition: 400 Printed at the University of Maine Press . . .

An "Errata" slip, 6·5 × 15·1 cm., supplying footnotes omitted on page 91, was loosely inserted.

An edition of the letters from Pound to Joseph Darling Ibbotson (1869–1952), Professor of English Literature, Anglo-Saxon, and Hebrew, and Librarian at Hamilton College, under whom Pound studied during his undergraduate years at Hamilton, in 1903–1905. The original letters are in the Hamilton College Library. The transcript of each of the 35 letters from Pound and one letter from Dorothy Pound (6 March 1937) is followed by a reproduction of the letter. Included also are reproduction of a printed announcement of Rapallo concerts for 3 March–25 April [1935] and reproduction and transcript of a printed program for the concert of 3 and 18 February [1937].

A103 AN AUTOBIOGRAPHICAL [1980]
OUTLINE

First separate edition:

AN AUTOBIOGRAPHICAL OUTLINE / EZRA POUND / NADJA [New York]

1 blank leaf, 9 leaves. 18·6 × 18·5 cm. Grey paper outer wrappers printed in black on page [i]; plain lavender inner wrappers; sewn.

Published March 1980 at $35.00; 226 copies printed. *Colophon (recto of eighth leaf):* An Autobiographical Outline was printed in March. . . . 200 numbered copies are for sale and 26 are lettered and reserved by Nadja. . . . [*Number written in.*] (At least some of the 26 lettered copies were actually for sale—at $50.00. They are otherwise identical with the numbered copies.) Printed on rectos only. Fly-title and recto of ninth leaf printed in lavender ink. The text is on Saunders paper; the wrappers are of Kizuki and Tosa papers.

This *Autobiographical Outline* was communicated to Louis Untermeyer as a letter (Letter V in *EP to LU: Nine Letters Written to Louis Untermeyer* . . . (1963)—A81, where the editor, J. A. Robbins, points out that the date 1932 assigned to the letter in a manuscript note by Untermeyer on the original typescript is an error for 1930, according to both internal evidence and "Mr. Untermeyer's reflection on the point".) It is here reprinted from the *Paris Review* for Summer/Fall 1962— C1888—retaining the incorrect dating and the erroneous identification of Untermeyer's notation as "In Pound's hand".

A. BOOKS AND PAMPHLETS

A104   LETTERE 1907–1958   [1980]

First edition:

Ezra Pound | Lettere 1907–1958 | Prefazione e cura di Aldo Tagliaferri | [*publisher's device*] | Feltrinelli Editore Milano

1 blank leaf, 2 leaves, 7–177 pp., 3 leaves. 22·2 × 14·2 cm. Heavy white paper wrappers printed in black and orange on pages [i] and [iv], and on spine.

Published April 1980 at L. 8000 as "I fatti e le idee. Saggi e Biografie, 468"; 3073 copies printed. *On verso of title-leaf:* . . . Traduzione dall'americano e dal francese di Girolamo Mancuso e Wilma Rodeghiero Prima edizione italiana: april 1980 . . . *Colophon (recto of final leaf):* Finito di stampare nel mese di aprile 1980 dalla Edigraf s.n.c. – Segrate (MI)

"La presente scelta . . . mira soprattutto ad illustrare i vari momenti dell'attività critico-letteraria e della poetica poundiana." ("Nota del curatore," p. 27)

Contains translations of letters written to various correspondents in English and in French, in part from *The Letters* ([1950])—A64, and in part from other sources, together with first publication of letters in Italian to Carlo Linati (pp. 93–98), Eugenio Montale (pp. 104–5), Manlio Dazzi (pp. 107–10), Giovanni Scheiwiller (pp. 122–4), Carlo Peroni (pp. 130–1), Giambattista Vicari (pp. 141, 145, 155–6), Vittorio Bodini (pp. 143–5), Luigi Berti (pp. 145–6, 149–55, 156–7, 162), Enrico Pea (pp. 146–8), Cornelio Di Marzio (pp. 148–9), Elio Vittorini (pp. 157–62), and Fernando Mezzasoma (pp. 162–3). This is the first publication in book form for letters (here printed in Italian translation) to Viola Baxter Jordan, ⟨24 Oct. 1907⟩, pp. 29–30; Harriet Monroe, Dec. 1913, p. 45, and 31 Jan. 1915 (in part), pp. 49–50, 51; Francis Picabia, ⟨21 Apr. 1921⟩, p. 80; E. Montale, 23 Jan ⟨1929⟩, p. 105; Sir Norman Angell, 13 Apr. ⟨1935⟩, pp. 111–12; Felix Schelling, Apr. 1934, pp. 112–13; Francesco Monotti, 30 Jan. ⟨1936⟩, pp. 118–19; A. Camerino, ⟨Dec? 1937⟩, pp. 127–8; Giovanni Scheiwiller, Dec. ⟨1938⟩, p. 133; Curzio Malaparte, 5 Feb. ⟨1940⟩, p. 137; William Carlos Williams, 22 Mar. ⟨1940⟩, p. 139; Natalie C. Barney, 17 Dec. 1952, 6 May ⟨1953⟩, 4 Jan. 1954, pp. 165–8; C. Izzo, 2 Oct. ⟨1956⟩, 10 Jan. 1958, pp. 168–71; and Josef Stummvoll, ⟨27 Apr. 1958⟩, pp. 171–2.

A105   EZRA POUND AND   [1980]
                 THE VISUAL ARTS

First edition:

EZRA | POUND | and the | visual | arts | Edited with an introduction by Harriet Zinnes | [*quotations from Canto XLV and Canto LXXIV in 9 lines*] | A NEW DIRECTIONS BOOK [New York, James Laughlin]

A. BOOKS AND PAMPHLETS

xxiv, 322 pp., incl. front. (port.) 6 illus. on 3 plates. 23·6 × 16 cm. Brown cloth boards lettered in gold on spine; end-papers. White dust-jacket printed in brown.

Published 24 November 1980 at $25.95; 1900 copies printed. *On verso of title-leaf:* ... Manufactured in the United States of America First published cloth-bound by New Directions in 1980 ... New Directions Books are published for James Laughlin by New Directions Publishing Corporation, 80 Eighth Avenue, New York 10011

The frontispiece is a reproduction of a vortograph of Ezra Pound made in 1917 by Alvin Langdon Coburn.

"This volume is composed not only of articles in various periodicals ... , but also of those materials in books and letters that relate to the subject of the visual arts. ... A decision has been made ... to include ... only more or less extended comments or comments which, though repeated elsewhere, are in one particular place expressed with special perception or concision." ("Preface," p. vii)

Contents: Preface [by the editor]—Introduction [by the editor]—1 SELECTIONS FROM THE NEW AGE: Whistler [excerpt from "Patria mia, II"—C49]—America: Chances and Remedies [V]. Proposition III: The College of the Arts—Affirmations [II]: Vorticism; [III]: Jacob Epstein; [V]: Gaudier-Brzeska—Synchromatism—Affirmations [VI]: Analysis of This Decade—Provincialism the Enemy, III [excerpt]; IV [excerpt]—Art Notes: At Heal's; The Loan Exhibition at the Grafton—Letters [*sic*] to the Editor: ... Art [C324]—Art [Notes]: The New English Art Club—Art, and Pastels—Art Notes: The National Portrait Society; Processes; Water; At the Alpine Club Gallery; Water, Still More of It; "Gaudier-Brzeska"—The Royal Academy—Art Notes: Still the Academy; The International; [Paul] Nash, Nicholson, Orpen; The Tenth London Salon of the Allied Artists Association; "Fresh Wholesome Sentiment"; Buildings, I; Building: Ornamentation!; Kinema, Kinesis, Hepworth, Etc.; Parallelograms; Super-fronts; Leicester Gallery, Etchings; Jean de Bosschère, and the Less Fortunate; Canadian War Memorial: A Commendation; Canada, and the Remnants; Navy, Mostyn, Lithography, Etc.—Wyndham Lewis at the Goupil—Art Notes [C446, 451, 452, 454, 455, and 458]—Art Notes: Rutter's Adelphi Gallery—Art Notes [C464]—Art Notes: Five Ordeals: By Water; Capt. Guy Baker's Collection at the South Kensington Museum—Art Notes [C504, 512, 518, 526, 529, and 534]—Art and Luxury—Art Notes [C43]—Art Notes: The Functions of Criticism—Credit and the Fine Arts: A Practical Application—2 VORTICIST PUBLICATIONS: *Blast* [a note written for the projected "Collected Prose"]—Vortex: Pound—"Et faim sallir le loup des boys" and "Dogmatic Statement on the Game and Play of Chess [from C194]—The Vortographs [from B13]—3 SELECTIONS FROM MISCELLANEOUS PUBLICATIONS: The Curse—Demarcations—That Audience, or The Bugaboo of the Public—Epstein, Belgion and Meaning—[Review of] *Stones of Rimini* [by Adrian Stokes]—Paris Letter, December, 1921 [C633]; December, 1922 [C650]; February, 1923 [C651]—Total War on "Contemplatio"—The New Sculpture—Exhibition at the Goupil Gallery—The Caressability of the Greeks—Wyndham Lewis [C146]—Edward Wadsworth, Vorticist—Gaudier: A Postscript 1934—The Public Convenience [from C689]—Vorticism—The Death of Vorticism—Sculpshure—Brancusi—Historical Survey—The Biennale—Ma-

chines—To Whistler, American—Ezra Pound Files Exceptions—The Sympo-
sium [review of *The Quattro Cento*, by Adrian Stokes]—The War and Diverse
Impressions—4 SELECTIONS FROM THE [UNPUBLISHED] JOHN QUINN CORRESPON-
DENCE—5 SELECTIONS FROM PUBLISHED BOOKS: Excerpts from *ABC of Reading*—
Excerpts from *Ezra Pound and Music*—Preface to the Memorial Exhibition [of
Gaudier-Brzeska] 1918 [B18]—Excerpts from *Guide to Kulchur*—Selections from
Impact—Selections from *Literary Essays*—Excerpt from *Polite Essays*—From *Ri-
postes*—From *Selected Letters*—From [*The*] *Translations*—6 SELECTIONS FROM UN-
COLLECTED MANUSCRIPTS AND PAPERS: [Letters, or excerpts from letters, to Mr.
and/or Mrs. Homer L. Pound, Harriet Monroe, Edward Wadsworth, Jeanne
Robert Foster, Henry Allen Moe [on Wyndham Lewis], and Editor, *The Listener*]—The Best in English [excerpt from an article sent to Harriet Monroe
during May 1915, presumably for *Poetry*]—Tentative Propositions or Outline
for Discussion [on machines]—Collected Prose [notes for the projected edi-
tion]—Brancusi and Human Sculpture—Albert C. Barnes—GLOSSARY—INDEX.

A106   FROM SYRIA   1981

First separate edition:

EZRA POUND | From Syria | The Worksheets, Proofs, and Text
| Edited | with an Introduction by | ROBIN SKELTON | 1981 |
COPPER CANYON PRESS [Port Townsend, Washington]

8 pp. 28 facsims. on 14 plates. 23·5 × 15·5 cm. Black cloth boards with buff
paper label printed in black down the spine. Issued without dust-jacket.

Published 1 December 1981 at $30.00; 250 copies printed. *On verso of title-leaf:*
. . . This book is published simultaneously in the pages of *The Malahat Review.*
. . . Copper Canyon Press P. O. Box 271 Port Townsend, Wa 98368

Contents: Introduction—First Draft [autograph manuscript, with title: "The Song
of Peire Bremon lo Tort that he sent unto his lady in Provence he being then
in Syria, a crusader," dated Madrid. May 1906.]—Second Draft [typescript, corrected, with title as in first draft except that "Peire" is spelled "Piere"]—Third
Draft [autograph manuscript, with title: "From Syria The Song of Peire Bremon "Lo Tort" that he made for his Lady in Provença: he being in Syria a
crusader," with variant manuscript of part of the title opposite first page]—First
Proof [for *Personae* ([1909]), 1st copy, with manuscript corrections by the au-
thor]—First Proof (2nd copy) [also with author's manuscript corrections]—
Second Proof (1st copy) [dated 19.3.09, with manuscript corrections, probably
by Elkin Mathews]—Second Proof (2nd copy) [also dated 19.3.09 and with
manuscript corrections, some of them by the author]—First Edition [*i.e. Personae*, pp. 48–[50]].

Note: The introduction and the facsimiles appeared in the *Malahat Review*, Victoria, B. C., for July 1981—C1983—of which copies were actually distributed
in early September.

B. BOOKS AND PAMPHLETS

B. BOOKS AND PAMPHLETS EDITED OR WITH CONTRIBUTIONS BY EZRA POUND

INCLUDING HIS TRANSLATIONS WHEN PUBLISHED WITH ORIGINAL TEXTS*

Note: No attempt has been made to include in this section the many booksellers' and auction catalogues which have printed or reproduced letters, inscriptions, and parts of manuscripts of Ezra Pound.

*Except for the de luxe edition of *Homage to Sextus Propertius* ([1976])—A38b—and when printed as part of a larger work (*e.g. The Translations* ([1953])—A66a).

B1   THE BOOK   1909
              OF THE POETS' CLUB

THE BOOK OF THE POETS' CLUB | [*ornament*] | [London, The
Poets' Club] CHRISTMAS, 1909

1 blank leaf, 1 leaf, [5]–55 pp., 1 blank leaf. 22·7 × 17·8 cm. (wrappers);
21·7 × 17·5 cm. (leaves). Heavy orange paper wrappers printed in black on
page [i]; edges untrimmed. The final blank leaf is inserted.

Published (not sold?) December 1909; number of copies unknown.

The heading for the first page of the table of contents and the titles in the text
are printed in red, the rest in black.

Contains "In epitaphium," p. 27; "Epigram [I]," p. 38; "Song" ("Era mea," with
English version beginning "Mistress mine, in what far land"), p. 46, and "Par-
acelsus in excelsis," p. 53, by Ezra Pound. Among the 25 other contributors are
Regina Miriam Bloch, T. E. Hulme, F. W. Tancred, and Selwyn Image.

Note: The Poets' Club had been founded in 1908 with T. E. Hulme as honorary
secretary. (For an account of its history, particularly in its relation to the activities of T. E. Hulme, see Alun R. Jones, *The Life and Opinions of T. E. Hulme*
(London, 1960), pp. [25]–37.) Ezra Pound was not represented in the first anthology by members of the group, *For Christmas MDCCCCVIII*, published in
January 1909. He was introduced by his publisher Elkin Mathews at the Poets'
Club dinner on 23 February 1909, and was elected an honorary member in
December of that year. At the meeting of the Club on the 20th of that month,
he read the second chapter ("Il miglior fabbro [Arnaut Daniel]") of his forthcoming book *The Spirit of Romance*—A5, and his own "The Ballad of the Goodly
Fere" was "declaimed" by the Irish poet Joseph Campbell. *The Second Book of
the Poets' Club* (1911) and *The Third Book of the Poets' Club* (1913) contain nothing
by Ezra Pound.

B2   MISS FLORENCE SCHMIDT . . .   [1910]
             BOOK OF WORDS

[*At upper left, within thick-thin rule rectangle:*] BECHSTEIN HALL. |
[*Rule*] | TUESDAY, MAR. 1st, at 8.15 | [*rule*] | Miss FLORENCE |
SCHMIDT | and Miss ELSIE HALL | Vocal and Pianoforte Re-
cital | [*short rule*] | Accompanist: Miss DAISY BUCKTROUT |
[*short rule*] | BECHSTEIN GRAND PIANOFORTE. | [*Double rule*] |
BOOK OF WORDS—SIXPENCE [London, Bechstein Hall]

8 pp. 25·5 × 19 cm. Wire-stitched.

Sold at the recital, 1 March 1910 at 6d.; about 300 copies printed.

Contains a group each of Italian, French, and English, and a second group of French songs, as sung by Miss Schmidt (Mrs Derwent Wood), with English versions of the Italian and French songs by Ezra Pound. (These are separated by three groups of titles of "Pianoforte Soli" performed by Miss Hall.) Except for the "Chanson Provençal" in the final group, of which only the English version is printed, texts appear in the left-hand column, with English versions at right. Only the English versions of the first two French songs have printed attribution to Pound. In a letter to his mother on 2 March 1910, Pound stated that the translations were all done in one day, with the exception of the first Verlaine, "which I had done, more or less, some time ago."

Contents: (*a*) Aria: Cantata Spirituale. Leonardo Leo; (*b*) Siciliana: "Tre giorni son che Nina." Pergolesi; (*c*) Aria: "Non so più cosa son" (*Le Nozze di Figaro*). Mozart—SONGS: (*a*) Clair de Lune [text by Paul Verlaine]. Gabriel Fauré; (*b*) Lied Maritime [text by the composer]. Vincent d'Indy; (*c*) "Ariettes Oubliées" (No. 3) [text by Verlaine]. Debussy; (*d*) "Aquarelles" (Green) [text by Verlaine]. Debussy; (*e*) "Fêtes Galantes"—Fantoches [text by Verlaine]. Debussy—SONGS: (*a*) "My Johnny was a shoemaker"; (*b*) The Lake Isle of Innisfree [text by W. B. Yeats] (*Country Lover*). Graham Peel; (*c*) "The Little Waves of Breffny" [text by Eva Gore-Booth] (*Country Lover*). Graham Peel; (*d*) "I will make you brooches" [text by R. L. Stevenson]. Graham Peel—SONGS: (*a*) "Lisette" [Old French text] (Bergerette). XVIII. Century; (*b*) Chanson Provençal; Aria; (*c*) "Manon." Massenet.

B3   SELECTION FROM   [1912]
                 COLLECTION YVETTE
                   GUILBERT

First edition:

[*Within ornamental border:*] Selection from Collection | Yvette Guilbert | English Translations | by | Ezra Pound | [*list of contents (10 songs), giving French and English titles and page numbers, in 20 lines*] | Augener Ltd. | London

30 pp., 1 leaf, incl. music. 31·4 × 23·8 cm. Greyish-tan paper boards with buff paper label (measuring 14·1 × 11·7 cm.) printed in black on page [i]; plain linen back; end-papers. (Or, much later, heavy yellow paper wrappers printed in orange and black on page [i].)

Published 19 April 1912 at 5s.; number of copies unknown. *Imprint at foot of page 2:* Stich u. Druck von B. Schott's Söhne in Mainz. [Plate no.] 29515 . . .

Later copies in the first binding have, stamped from type on the title-page

B. BOOKS AND PAMPHLETS

above the imprint: [*short rule*] | Harmonized and arranged | by | GUSTAVE FERRARI | [*short rule*]. (Much later, the secondary binding described above was supplied for remaining first-edition sheets, with title on cover incorporating the name of the composer. This late binding was still available from the publisher in 1957.)

A misprint on the title-page, "mary" for "marry" in the English title of the eighth song, and several other misprints in the text were not corrected.

A selection—two from Volume 1 (Du Moyen Âge à la Renaissance), five from Volume 3 (Chansons de tous les temps), three from Volume 4 (Chansons et rondes anciennes)—from the *Collection Yvette Guilbert . . . Chansons arrangées et harmonisées par Gustave Ferrari*, published by Augener in 1911. Each song has music for voice and piano accompaniment, with words in French and English.

Contents: 1. Suivez, beautez (de Villon). Pursue ye beauty—2. Quand je revis ce que j'ay tant aimé (de Berthaud). When I behold that which I loved so much—3. Le Roy a fait battre tambour (1599). The King's had flunkeys beat the drum—4. La belle fille et le petit bossu (XVIIième siècle). In the rue Chiffonier—5. Les cloches de Nantes (XVIIième siècle). In Nant' in prison there—6. L'inutile défense (1761). These mothers always—7. Aimez, vous avez quinze ans (1781). Love for you have fifteen years—8. Il est pourtant temps de me marier. O but it is time now to marry me—9. Les conditions impossibles. Going through a wood—10. C'est la fille d'un pauvre homme. Yes, it is a poor man's daughter.

Note: The first song, "Suivez, beautez," with words by Villon, was used by Ezra Pound in his opera "Le Testament"—E3h, one of two songs in the opera not actually composed by him.

B4   SONNETS AND BALLATE OF   [1912]
              GUIDO CAVALCANTI

a. *First edition:*

THE SONNETS AND BALLATE | OF | GUIDO CAVALCANTI | WITH TRANSLATION AND INTRODUCTION | BY | EZRA POUND | AUTHOR OF "PROVENÇA," "THE SPIRIT OF ROMANCE" | "PERSONÆ," "EXULTATIONS," "CANZONI" | [*device*] | BOSTON | SMALL, MAYNARD AND COMPANY | PUBLISHERS

xxiv, 119 pp. 20·6 × 16·5 cm. Grey paper boards with imitation vellum corners and back, stamped in gold and blind on spine; end-papers; edges untrimmed.

Published 27 April 1912 at $2.00; number of copies unknown. *On verso of title-leaf:* . . . The University Press, Cambridge, U.S.A.

Dedication on page [v]*:* As much of this book as is mine I send to my friends Violet [Hunt] and Ford Maddox [*sic*] Hueffer

Italian text and English translation on opposite pages.

B. BOOKS AND PAMPHLETS

Contents: Introduction (dated 15 November 1910)—Sonnets (I–XXXV)—Madrigal—Ballate (I–XIV)

b. *First English edition* (1912):

SONNETS AND | BALLATE OF | GUIDO | CAVALCANTI | WITH
TRANSLATIONS | OF THEM AND AN | INTRODUCTION BY |
EZRA POUND | [*device*] | MCMXII | STEPHEN SWIFT AND CO.,
LTD. | 16 KING STREET, COVENT GARDEN | LONDON

vii, [1], 135, [1], 31, [1] pp. 19·8 × 13·4 cm. Streaky grey cloth boards lettered in gold on front cover and on spine; end-papers; edges untrimmed. Grey dust-jacket printed in blue.

Published May 1912 at 3*s*. 6*d*.; number of copies unknown. (Ezra Pound states in the bibliography of his work which he supplied for T. S. Eliot's anonymous *Ezra Pound His Metric and Poetry* (1917 [*i.e.* 1918])—B17—that the bulk of this edition was destroyed by fire, presumably at the binders, where sheets were being held as late as November 1915—see note on Swift and Co. under *Ripostes*—A8.) *Imprint on page* [136]: Printed by Neill and Company, Limited, Edinburgh.

Publisher's advertisements, "Books That Compel," 31, [1] pp. following page [136], are inserted. (In several presentation copies, presented presumably after the failure of Swift and Co., these advertisements have been cut out.) The status of a copy reported bound without advertisements has not been determined.

Contents identical with the American edition, except for slight revisions in the Introduction and in some of the translations, particularly of Sonnets VII and XVI, and Ballata IV.

B5   WALTER MORSE RUMMEL . . .   [1913]
           HESTERNAE ROSAE, SERTA II.

First edition:

[*Initials in green, rest in blue:*] Walter Morse Rummel | (1912) |
[*ornament*] | [*in green:*] Hesternae Rosae | [*in blue: ornament*] | SERTA
II. | Neuf Chansons de Troubadours des XIIième et XIIIième Siècles
| pour une voix avec accompagnement | de Piano | Adaptation
française par M. D. Calvocoressi | Adaptation anglaise par Ezra
Pound | Net 3/– | [*in center:*] Augener Ltd. | 63 CONDUIT STREET
(Regent St. Corner), W. 16 NEWGATE STREET, E. C. | 57 HIGH
STREET, MARYLEBONE & 18 GREAT MARLBOROUGH STREET,
W. | LONDON | [*below, at left:*] MAX ESCHIG | PARIS | [*at right:*]
BOSTON MUSIC CO. | BOSTON

B. BOOKS AND PAMPHLETS

3 leaves, 42 pp., incl. 1 illus., music. 31·3 × 23·6 cm. Heavy grey paper wrappers printed in blue and green on page [i], in dark blue on page [iii], and in blue on page [iv].

Published 26 March 1913 at 3s.; number of copies unknown. *Imprint at foot of page 42:* [plate no.] 14557 Augener's Music Printing Office [Another edition—1929?—gives price on title-page as "6/–" and imprint on title-page as: Augener Ltd. 18 Great Marlborough Street, & 57 High Street, Marylebone, London, W. 1 The imprint at the foot of page 42 becomes: 14557 Printed in England by Augener Ltd., Acton Lane, London, W. 4. Pages [i] and [iii] of the wrappers also vary.]

"Under the collective title of Hesternæ Rosæ (Roses of Yesterday) the writer intends to gather whatever interesting and unknown material he may come across in his study of the music of the early and late past. . . .

"The first volume [*i.e.* Serta I.] (Nine French Songs of the 17th Century) is here followed by a collection of Nine Troubadour Songs of the 12th and 13th Centuries. . . . The two Daniel melodies are here published for the first time to the writer's knowledge, and he is indebted to Mr. Ezra Pound, M.A., for communicating them from the Milan Library. . . .

"The writer with the help of Mr. Ezra Pound, an ardent proclaimer of the artistic side of mediæval poetry, has given these melodies the rhythm and the ligature, the character which, from an artistic point of view, seems the most descriptive of the mediæval spirit." ("Preface," *signed:* W. M. R., *and dated:* 1912)

Each song has original text with M. D. Calvocoressi's modern French and Pound's English translation.

Contents: I. Chansson doil mot ("With words both clear and exquisite"). Arnaut Daniel—II. Lo ferm voler ("Firm desire that doth enter"). Arnaut Daniel—III. Quant l'herba fresq el fuell apar ("When grass starts green and flowers rise"). Bernart de Ventadour—IV. Las grans beautatz ("Her beauty and the fineness of her thought"). Folquet de Romans (Rotmans)—V. Tant m'abelis ("So pleaseth me joy and good love and song"). B. de Palazol—VI. Mère au Sauveour ("Maiden and Virgin loyal"). Williaume li Viniers—VII. Li granz desirs ("The great desire sheds fragrance o'er my thinking"). Li Cuens d'Angou—VIII. Mainta ien me mal razona ("Many people here miscall me"). Pierol—IX. A l'entrade ("When cometh the clear time in, eya!"). Chanson à danser

Notes: The "French words" of "VI. Mère au Sauveour" with "English Version" credited to Ezra Pound are reprinted in *Concert Given on July 1st, by Yves Tinayre & Leopold Ashton: Programme* . . . ([London? Wigmore Hall? 192–?]), p. [2].

This song was used by Pound in his opera "Le Testament"—E3h, one of two songs in the opera not actually composed by him.

A facsimile reproduction of the complete . . . *Hesternae Rosae* was incorporated as pp. 71–118 in . . . *The Music of the Troubadours Edited by Peter Whigham* . . . *Texts and Translation* (Santa Barbara, Calif., Ross-Erikson [1979]).

B. BOOKS AND PAMPHLETS

B6   CHIPPEWA COUNTY   1913
         WISCONSIN PAST AND   [*i.e.* 1914]
                   PRESENT

[*Within double-rule border:*] Chippewa County | WISCONSIN | PAST
AND PRESENT | A Record of Settlement, Organization, Progress
and | Achievement | [*short rule*] | ILLUSTRATED | [*short rule*] | VOL-
UME I [–II] | [*short rule*] | CHICAGO | THE S. J. CLARKE PUB-
LISHING COMPANY | 1913 [*i.e.* 1914]

2 volumes (vol. 1: 1 blank leaf, 1 leaf, 431 pp.; vol. 2: 1 blank leaf, 1 leaf, 5–
493 pp.). plates, incl. ports. 27 × 19·5 cm. Dark green cloth boards with brown
leather corners and back, with spine stamped in gold: HISTORY | OF | CHIPPEWA
COUNTY | WISCONSIN | VOL. I[–II] | ILLUSTRATED; green marbled end-papers.

Published early in 1914 at $18.00; number of copies unknown.

Edited by W. L. Kershaw. Preface to the first volume, signed by the publishers,
dated: November, 1913. (The second volume is devoted exclusively to biographical sketches and portraits of various individuals, families, and firms of
Chippewa County.)

Contains "Legend of the Chippewa Spring and Minnehaha, the Indian Maiden,"
pp. 80–81, vol. 1, signed: Ezra Pound. (The table of contents gives the title as
"The Legend of Hiawatha and Chippewa Spring.") The poem, in 44 lines,
imitative of Henry W. Longfellow, appears at the end of Chapter II, "The In-
dians." Chapter XXIX, "Reminiscent," pp. 409–24, vol. 1, is chiefly the remi-
niscences of Thaddeus C. Pound (1833–1914) "while on a visit, from his home
in Chicago, to his friends in Chippewa Falls in the summer of 1913 ... "

B7   DES IMAGISTES   1914

a. *First edition (book issue):*

DES IMAGISTES | AN ANTHOLOGY | [*ornament*] | NEW YORK |
ALBERT AND CHARLES BONI | 96 FIFTH AVENUE | 1914

63 pp. 19·5 × 13·4 cm. Blue cloth boards stamped in blind and in gold on
front cover and in gold on spine; wove end-papers; fore edges roughly trimmed,
bottom edges untrimmed.

Published 2 March 1914 at $1.00; number of copies unknown.

Part of the same impression as the *Glebe* for February 1914—C125, but with
binding as above in place of pale olive paper wrappers printed in green (with,
on front: DES IMAGISTES | [*thick ornamental rule*] | [*monogram:*] The Glebe | [*short
thick ornamental rule*] | VOLUME I | NUMBER 5 | [*short thick ornamental rule*] | FEBRUARY
| 1914 | [*short thick ornamental rule*] | SUBSCRIPTION | Three Dollars Yearly | THIS ISSUE
50 CENTS | [*thick ornamental rule*] | AN ANTHOLOGY) and title-page (as above) with

an ornament in place of the *Glebe* monogram. At least two lots of paper were used, apparently indiscriminately, for both periodical and book, one without watermark, the other watermarked with a capital D within a diamond above the words: Regal Antique. The periodical has, inserted at the end, a leaf of advertisements printed on yellow paper not present in the book. Later copies of both periodical and book have, tipped in at the front, a slip (measuring approximately 6·5 × 13 cm.) acknowledging permission to reprint certain poems from *Poetry*. This slip was printed and inserted at the instance of Harriet Monroe.

Edited by Ezra Pound, who sent the manuscript to Alfred Kreymborg, then one of the editors of the periodical, in the summer of 1913. Alfred Kreymborg in his autobiographical *Troubadour* (New York, 1925—see especially pages 204 and 205, where excerpts from two letters and a card to him from Pound are quoted) states that he and his co-editor Man Ray originally planned to publish the Imagist anthology as the first number of the *Glebe*, but the plans were changed by Albert and Charles Boni when they took over the financing of the periodical. (The first number when it appeared was dated September 1913.)

Contains "*Dória*," "The Return," "After Ch'u Yuan," "Liu Ch'e," "Fan-piece for Her Imperial Lord," and "Ts'ai Chi'h," by Ezra Pound, pp. 41–46. "To Hulme (T. E.) and [Desmond] Fitzgerald," also by Pound, is printed (with a note at the end: "Written for the cenacle of 1909 vide Introduction to 'The Complete Poetical Works of T. E. Hulme,' published at the end of 'Ripostes.'"), pp. 57–58, as the first of four "Documents," the last of which (p. 63) is a page of bibliographical information concerning published writings of the contributors to the volume. The other poets represented are Richard Aldington (ten poems, and one of the "Documents"), H. D. (seven poems), F. S. Flint (five), Skipwith Cannell (one), Amy Lowell (one), William Carlos Williams (one), James Joyce (one), Ford Madox Hueffer (one, and one of the "Documents"), Allen Upward (one), and John Cournos (one).

b. *English (book) issue:*

DES IMAGISTES | AN ANTHOLOGY | [*ornament*] | [*stamped in:*] LONDON: THE POETRY BOOKSHOP | 35 DEVONSHIRE STREET, | THEOBALDS RD., W.C. | [*in some copies:*] ° | [*in all copies, printed:*] NEW YORK | ALBERT AND CHARLES BONI | 96 FIFTH AVENUE | 1914

63 pp. 19 × 13 cm. Green paper boards lettered in black on front cover: IMAGISTES | THE POETRY BOOKSHOP; and up the spine: IMAGISTES; laid end-papers.

Published April 1914 at 2s. 6d.; number of copies unknown. The American (book-issue) sheets with English imprint printed below the half-title on page [1] and stamped from type (as indicated above) on the title-page, with position and quality of impression varying from copy to copy. (At least two stamps were used, one with an ornamental "o," the other without it.) The acknowledgment slip to *Poetry* was not tipped into the English issue of the book.

B. BOOKS AND PAMPHLETS

c. *Shay re-issue of the periodical issue* (1917):

DES IMAGISTES | AN ANTHOLOGY | NEW YORK | FRANK SHAY, PUBLISHER | 1917

63 pp. 19·2 × 13·3 cm. Blue paper wrappers printed in red-brown on page [i]: Des Imagistes, an anthology | [*device*] | FRANK SHAY, PUBLISHER | NEW YORK; and up the spine: DES IMAGISTES: An Anthology 1914

Published 1917; number of copies unknown.

Copies of the *Glebe* for February 1914—C125—with wrappers removed (all copies examined have offset from the front wrapper of the periodical and some have, at the joints, traces of the original olive paper of the wrappers and the yellow paper of the advertisement leaf) and with the original title-leaf excised and replaced by a cancel title-leaf (with title-page as above).

d. *Shay (?) re-issue of the periodical issue* ([*circa* 1920?]):

DES IMAGISTES | AN ANTHOLOGY | [*monogram:*] The Glebe | NEW YORK | ALBERT AND CHARLES BONI | 96 FIFTH AVENUE | 1914 [*i.e.* New York, Frank Shay? *circa* 1920?]

63 pp. 19·2 × 13·3 cm. White paper wrappers printed all-over in orange (or green) and in black on page [i]: [*ornamental rule*] | DES IMAGISTES | [*ornamental rule*] | AN ANTHOLOGY | [*ornamental rule*]

Published about 1920?; number of copies unknown.

Copies of the *Glebe* for February 1914—C125—with wrappers removed (offset and traces of paper as in 1917 re-issue) and new wrappers supplied, but with the original title-leaf for the periodical uncancelled. (The wrappers are similar to those used for other publications issued in 1920 by Frank Shay.)

†B8   WALTER MORSE RUMMEL   [1914]
TEN SONGS FOR CHILDREN
YOUNG AND OLD

WALTER MORSE RUMMEL | [*design of child with toy*] | 10 | SONGS for CHILDREN | YOUNG and OLD | [*short rule*] | [*English titles of the 10 songs in 10 lines*] | [*ornament*] | [*in center:*] AUGENER LTD. | 63 CONDUIT STREET (Regent St. Corner), W. 16 NEWGATE STREET, E. C. | 57 HIGH STREET, MARYLEBONE & 18 GREAT MARLBOROUGH STREET, W. | LONDON | [*below, at left:*] MAX ESCHIG | 13 Rue Laffitte, | PARIS | [*at right:*] BOSTON MUSIC CO. | BOSTON

29 pp. 30·1 × 23cm. (trimmed copy). Issued unbound? wire-stitched?

Published 1 May 1914; number of copies unknown. *At foot of opening page of each song:* . . . [plate no.] 14728 *Imprint at foot of page 29:* . . . Augener's Music Printing Office

Each song has music for voice and piano accompaniment, with words in English and French. The French adaptations of the English songs were made by Thérèse Chaigneau.

Contains "Slumber Song (Berceuse) From the French," with footnote to the first line of the English text: "English version by Claude Aveling [*i.e.* Ezra Pound?]," pp. 19–21. Of the other songs, the English texts of five are by H. D. [*i.e.* Hilda Doolittle Aldington], and of three are by Richard Aldington.

Ezra Pound wrote to his mother on 21 October 1911: " . . . I've done nothing useful for some weeks except correct a few proofs and translate an old French song for W[alter]. R[ummel]. Very dull song at that, only he wants to print it in both languages." It is almost certain that the "old French song" is the "Berceuse" in this collection. (Ezra Pound later signed his musical criticism in the *New Age* with the pseudonym, William Atheling.)

†*Note (1981):* Claude Aveling was the author and translator of other works of this date and later with which Ezra Pound had no connexion. The attribution of "Berceuse" to Pound must therefore be incorrect. The entry is left for the record.

B9   POETICAL WORKS OF   1915
                 LIONEL JOHNSON

POETICAL WORKS OF | LIONEL JOHNSON | [*device*] | LONDON : ELKIN MATHEWS | CORK STREET MCMXV

3 leaves, [v]–xix pp., 1 leaf, 320 pp. 3 plates, incl. front. (port.) 19·5 × 13·5 cm. Green cloth boards with bevelled edges lettered in gold on spine; end-papers; fore edges roughly trimmed, bottom edges untrimmed. (Each plate, printed on special paper, has a protective tissue with descriptive letter-press.)

Published late October 1915 at 5*s.*; 1500 sets of sheets printed (of which 900 were used for the American issue). *Imprint at foot of page 320:* Chiswick Press: Printed by Charles Whittingham and Co. Tooks Court, Chancery Lane, London.

The earliest copies released have all the following misprints: page xv, line 4, and line 2 of note, "Christiana" for "Christina"; page 144, line 5 up, "a joy" for "the joy"; line 4 up, "the glory" for "a glory"; page 148, line 1, "right" for "rite"; page 228, line 8 up, "enslave" for "unslave"; page 296, line 4, "The Castilian" for "The high Castilian." Later copies have a cancel leaf correcting the misprints on page xv, but other errata are uncorrected. Still later copies have all the misprints corrected by cancels.

B. BOOKS AND PAMPHLETS

Contains "Preface" by Ezra Pound, dated: 1914, pp. [v]–xix. In a letter to Lord Alfred Douglas on 18 May 1935, Pound stated that he "certainly did not bother about Lionel [Johnson]'s text other than to, I think, select from some inédits." A letter from Pound to Elkin Mathews indicates that Ezra Pound and Dorothy Shakespear did, however, read proofs for the Lionel Johnson text.

While the book was being printed, the Macmillan Company of New York agreed to take sheets of the English edition, but requested that Pound's preface be removed from these copies. Since in the first edition leaves of the preface are conjugate with the first leaf, the half-title-leaf, the title-leaf, and the list-of-illustrations leaf, the Chiswick Press was obliged to reimpose the preliminary matter for the American issue, at the same time altering the imprint on the title-page to read: NEW YORK | THE MACMILLAN COMPANY | LONDON: ELKIN MATHEWS | MCMXV

Initially, only 500 sets of sheets seem to have been prepared in this manner. These were exported by Elkin Mathews without the cancels for the text and were issued by Macmillan in New York (at $2.25) in late December 1915. These sheets were bound in green cloth boards with bevelled edges similar to the binding of the English copies, but with the publisher's name: MACMILLAN at the base of the spine. The Chiswick Press records indicate that a second lot of 200 sets of the preliminary matter was prepared in December 1915 and a third lot of 200 in January 1916. These were presumably exported by Elkin Mathews soon after receipt, along with two matching lots of first-edition sheets, supplied with the four cancels for the text. These sheets were bound by Macmillan in blue cloth boards, with, at the base of the spine: MACMILLAN CⱰ | NEW YORK

Although Pound's preface was initially withdrawn only from the American issue and at the request of the Macmillan Company, a "Second thousand" published in London by Elkin Mathews and in New York by Macmillan in 1917, and a later impression published by Elkin Mathews in 1926 do not contain the preface. It was withdrawn from the later English impressions apparently because it included extensive quotations from notes sent by Lionel Johnson to Katharine Tynan and printed by her after his death, in the *Dublin Review* for October 1907. In the comments quoted, Lionel Johnson dealt harshly with William Watson, Richard Le Gallienne, Arthur Symons, and Francis Thompson, all of whom had been published at one time or another by Elkin Mathews, and three of whom were alive in 1915.

Note: Ezra Pound's "Preface" was reprinted as "Lionel Johnson" in *Literary Essays* ([1954])—A67—pp. 361-70.

B10 · CATHOLIC ANTHOLOGY 1915

First edition:

CATHOLIC | ANTHOLOGY | 1914–1915 | [*device*] | LONDON | ELKIN MATHEWS, CORK STREET | 1915 vii, 99, [1] pp. 19·4 × 13·3 cm. Grey paper boards printed in black with design by D[orothy]. S[hakespear Pound].; end-papers; fore and bottom edges untrimmed.

Published November 1915 at 3*s*. 6*d*.; 500 copies printed. *Imprint on page* [100]: [Device] Chiswick Press: Charles Whittingham and Co. Tooks Court, Chancery Lane, London.

Edited by Ezra Pound. (Shortly after publication, according to Ezra Pound, protests were received by Elkin Mathews from Francis Meynell and other Catholics because of the title of the anthology; but the book was not suppressed and was still in print in the original—and only—edition, at the published price, as late as April 1936.)

Contains "Contemporania (The Garret—The Garden—Albâtre—In a Station of the Metro—Further Instructions—The Study in Aesthetics—Heather—The Gipsy—Dogmatic Statement Concerning the Game of Chess: Theme for a Series of Pictures)," by Ezra Pound, pp. 86–92. "Poem: Abbreviated [by Pound] from the Conversation of Mr. T. E. H[ulme]." appears on page 22. The other poets represented in the anthology are W. B. Yeats (one poem), T. S. Eliot (five poems, including "The Love Song of J. Alfred Prufrock"), Douglas Goldring (one), Alice Corbin [Henderson] (one), Orrick Johns (three), and Alfred Kreymborg (two), Edgar Lee Masters (ten), Harriet Monroe (one), M[axwell]. B[odenheim]. (two), Harold Monro (four), Carl Sandburg (two), Allen Upward (one), William Carlos Williams (two), and John Rodker (four).

B11   OTHERS   1916

OTHERS | AN ANTHOLOGY OF THE NEW VERSE | EDITED BY | ALFRED KREYMBORG | [*device*] | [*thick rule*] | NEW YORK [*ornament*] ALFRED A KNOPF [*ornament*] MCMXVI

4 leaves, 152 pp. 21 × 13·2 cm. Dark-brown paper boards stamped in gold on both covers and on spine, or (later) tan paper boards stamped in red on front cover and on spine and (in some copies) in blind on back cover; brown end-papers, or (later) plain end-papers; top edges stained brown, or (later) unstained. Orange dust-jacket printed in black.

Published 25 March 1916 at $1.50; number of copies unknown. *On verso of title-leaf:* ... Published March, 1916 Printed in America

Contains "The Tea Shop," "Phylidula [*sic*]," "The Patterns," "Shop Girl," "Another Man's Wife," and "Coda," by Ezra Pound, pp. 83–84, constituting the first book publication for these poems. All six are here reprinted from the periodical *Others* (also edited by Alfred Kreymborg) for November 1915—C210.

B. BOOKS AND PAMPHLETS

B12   12 OCCUPATIONS BY   1916
JEAN DE BOSSCHÈRE

a. *First edition, ordinary copies:*

12 OCCUPATIONS | BY | JEAN DE BOSSCHÈRE | FRENCH TEXT | WITH TWELVE DESIGNS BY THE AUTHOR | AND AN EN-GLISH TRANSLATION | LONDON | ELKIN MATHEWS, CORK STREET | MCMXVI

31, [1] pp., incl. 12 illus. 19·3 × 14·5 cm. (wrappers); 18·5 × 14 cm. (leaves). Heavy orange paper wrappers printed in black on pages [i–iv]; wire-stitched and sewn (into wrappers) with yellow thread.

Published September 1916 at 1s. 6d.; number of copies unknown. *Imprint at foot of page* [32]*:* Printed by Wm. Brendon and Son, Ltd., Plymouth, England.

"English [prose] translation [by Ezra Pound, anonymously]," pp. 26–[32]. The pamphlet is a selection from De Bosschère's *Les métiers divins* (first published in Paris in 1913), itself part of a work subsequently published under the title *Le bourg.* "Works by Jean de Bosschère," on page [iii] of wrappers.

b. *Special copies:*

1 leaf, 31, [1] pp., 1 leaf, incl. 12 col. illus. 19 × 14·2 cm. Orange paper boards printed in black on covers and up the spine; end-papers.

Published September 1916 at 21s.; 50 copies printed. *Colophon (verso of half-title-leaf):* Fifty copies of this work have been coloured by the Author, of which this is number [*number written in and signed with initials by the artist*]

"Works by Jean de Bosschère," on verso of leaf following page [32]. (Although the text of this list is the same, it has been reset, for the most part in smaller type than that used for it in the ordinary copies.)

B13   . . . VORTOGRAPHS AND   [1917]
PAINTINGS BY ALVIN
LANGDON COBURN

THE CAMERA CLUB | 17 JOHN STREET, ADELPHI, | STRAND, W. C. | (NEXT THE LITTLE THEATRE.) | VORTOGRAPHS AND PAINTINGS | BY | ALVIN LANGDON COBURN | [*design*] | Open until February 28th 1917 [London, The Camera Club]

7, [1] pp. 20·3 × 12·9 cm. Wire-stitched.

Distributed gratis at the exhibition, February 1917; number of copies unknown. *Imprint on page* [8]*:* Women's Printing Society, Ltd., Brick Street, Piccadilly.

B. BOOKS AND PAMPHLETS

Contains notes written anonymously by Ezra Pound, pp. 2–5, entitled on page 2, "The Vortographs," and on page 3, "The Camera Is Freed from Reality." Pound's notes are followed by a "Postscript by Alvin Langdon Coburn," on page 6, and a "Catalogue," listing the exhibits, on page 7. (The notes were reprinted, with the omission of the first paragraph, the first sentence of the second paragraph, and one other sentence, as "Vortographs" in *Pavannes and Divisions* (1918)—A15—pp. 251–5, and, complete, in *Ezra Pound and the Visual Arts* ([1980])—A105—pp. 154–7.)

B14   THE NEW POETRY   1917

THE NEW POETRY | AN ANTHOLOGY | EDITED BY | HARRIET MONROE | AND | ALICE CORBIN HENDERSON | EDITORS OF POETRY | New York | THE MACMILLAN COMPANY | 1917 | All rights reserved

xxxi pp., 1 leaf, 404 pp., 4 leaves, 1 blank leaf. 19·6 × 13·7 cm. Green cloth boards stamped in blind and in gold on front cover and in gold on spine; end-papers; top edges stained brown or (later) unstained, fore edges untrimmed, bottom edges roughly trimmed.

Published 28 February 1917 at $1.75; 4000 copies printed. *On verso of title-leaf:* . . . Set up and electrotyped. Published February, 1917. *Imprint on page 404:* . . . Printed in the United States of America.

Contains "*Dória*," "The Return," "Piccadilly," "N[ew]. Y[ork].," "The Coming of War: Actaeon," "The Garden," "Ortus," "The Choice," "The Garret," "Dance Figure," "From 'Near Perigord,'" "An Immorality," "The Study in Aesthetics," "Further Instructions," "Villanelle: The Psychological Hour," "Ballad of the Goodly Fere," "Ballad for Gloom," "La Fraisne," "The River-Merchant's Wife: A Letter," and "Exile's Letter," by Ezra Pound, pp. 257–76. This constitutes first book publication for "The Choice" and first book publication in the United States for all except "*Dória*," "The Return," "N[ew]. Y[ork].," "An Immorality," "Ballad of the Goodly Fere," "Ballad for Gloom," and "La Fraisne." Of the 20 poems, 11 had been printed in *Poetry*, Chicago, edited by Harriet Monroe and Alice Corbin Henderson.

B15   PASSAGES FROM THE LETTERS   1917
        OF JOHN BUTLER YEATS

First edition:

PASSAGES FROM THE LETTERS OF | JOHN BUTLER YEATS: SELECTED | BY EZRA POUND. | [*Device*] | THE CUALA PRESS | CHURCHTOWN | DUNDRUM | MCMXVII

2 blank leaves, 4 leaves, 60 pp., 1 leaf, 1 blank leaf. 21·4 × 14·9 cm. Blue-grey paper boards printed in black on front cover; linen back, with white paper label printed in black up the spine: LETTERS. J. B. YEATS; blue-grey end-papers; edges untrimmed.

Published May 1917 at 10s. 6d.; 400 copies printed. *Colophon* (*verso of second leaf*): Four hundred copies of this book have been printed. *Colophon* (*page* [61]): Here ends 'Passages from the Letters of John Butler Yeats,' selected by Ezra Pound. Published and printed by Elizabeth Corbet Yeats on paper made in Ireland, at the Cuala Press, Churchtown, Dundrum, in the County of Dublin, Ireland. Finished in the last week of February, nineteen hundred and seventeen.

The fly-title, both colophons, and the motto (verso of fourth leaf) are printed in red, the rest in black. An "Errata" slip, correcting a misprint, "self-deserving" for "self-deserting" in line 12 up on page 47, was loosely laid into some copies.

"Editor's Note," third leaf, dated: May 20th, 1916. Although Ezra Pound states in this note that the letters in the book were written by J. B. Yeats to (his son) W. B. Yeats between 1911 and 1916, there are selections dated in 1906, 1908, 1909, and 1910, as well.

Note: The selection for *Further Letters of John Butler Yeats* (Dundrum, Cuala Press, 1920) was made by Lennox Robinson.

B16   THE NEWARK   1917
ANNIVERSARY POEMS

THE NEWARK | ANNIVERSARY POEMS | Winners in the Poetry Competition | HELD IN CONNECTION WITH | THE 250TH ANNIVERSARY CELEBRATION | OF THE | FOUNDING OF THE CITY OF NEWARK, NEW JERSEY | MAY TO OCTOBER, 1916 | TOGETHER WITH | THE OFFICIAL NEWARK CELEBRATION ODE | AND OTHER ANNIVERSARY POEMS | —GRAVE AND GAY | Introductory Chapters and a Plan for a | National Anthology of American Poetry | By HENRY WELLINGTON WACK | Editor of the Newarker | THE COMMITTEE OF ONE HUNDRED | FRANKLIN MURPHY | Chairman | NEW YORK | LAURENCE J. GOMME | 1917

4 leaves, vii–xiii, 187 pp., 2 blank leaves. 19·8 × 13·6 cm. Green paper boards lettered in gold on front cover, with white cloth back lettered in gold on spine; end-papers; top edges gilt, others untrimmed.

Published 6 August 1917 at $1.25; number of copies unknown.

B. BOOKS AND PAMPHLETS

"Amongst other inspirational features of its anniversary program, Newark undertook an unusual literary enterprise. It offered $1,000 in prizes for poems upon the city's 250th anniversary. It invited all kinds of poems, from any part of the world, on any phase of Newark's historical, industrial, social, aesthetic or civic life. . . .

"That philosophic iconoclast, Ezra Pound, earlier exponent of the Imagist School of Poetic Palpitation, writing from London, assaulted our civic sensibilities in a poem of violence directed at the head, heart, and hands of Newark. Of his poem, one of the judges remarked that it is 'Captious, arrogant, hypercritical, but [has] some merit.' Another judge cast it into the discard. But it won a prize and fits snugly into the rationale of the present volume. Also there is food for thought in our London poet's catechistic cadences. Let us not begrudge him the high appraisal of our poetry judges." ("The Sunny Side of the Newark Poetry Competition," pp. 21, 26–27)

Contains "To a City Sending Him Advertisements," a poem (printed in 72 lines) by Ezra Pound, pp. 100–2. This was awarded one of the ten special prizes (after the first three) of fifty dollars each.

B17   EZRA POUND HIS   1917
                 METRIC AND POETRY   [*i.e.* 1918]

EZRA POUND | HIS METRIC AND POETRY | NEW YORK [*ornament*] ALFRED A. KNOPF [*ornament*] 1917

31 pp. front. (port.) 19·4 × 12·7 cm. Rose paper boards lettered in gold on front cover; end-papers. Plain buff dust-jacket.

Published January 1918 at 35¢.; 1000 copies printed.

(Issued in connexion with the publication, also by Knopf, of *Lustra* (1917)—A11d.) The book was written anonymously by T. S. Eliot, but Ezra Pound went over the manuscript, making corrections and changes before sending it on to John Quinn for publication by Knopf. (T. S. Eliot's original typescript, with title, corrections, and deletions in Ezra Pound's manuscript, is in the Houghton Library at Harvard.)

Contains "Bibliography of Books and Partial Bibliography of Notable Critical Articles by Ezra Pound," by Pound, anonymously, pp. 29–31. (The typescript, prepared by Pound, with numerous corrections and additions in his manuscript, is also at Harvard. This was sent to John Quinn on 18 April 1917 by Pound, who wrote in a covering letter: "I have compiled the bibliography. It is in a beastly mess, but let Knopf straighten it out or retype it." It was in fact printed almost verbatim from Pound's typescript.)

B. BOOKS AND PAMPHLETS

B18   A MEMORIAL EXHIBITION   1918
                   OF THE WORK OF
             HENRI GAUDIER-BRZESKA

A MEMORIAL EXHIBITION OF THE WORK | OF HENRI
GAUDIER-BRZESKA | Born 1891. Killed in Action 1915 | WITH
A PREFATORY NOTE BY | EZRA POUND | ERNEST BROWN &
PHILLIPS | THE LEICESTER GALLERIES | LEICESTER SQUARE,
LONDON | MAY-JUNE, 1918.

14, [2] pp. 4 plates. 14·6 × 11·4 cm. Blue paper wrappers printed in black on
pages [i–iv]; wire-stitched.

Published May 1918 at 6d.; number of copies unknown. *Imprint on page [iv] of
wrappers:* Miles & Co. Ltd. Wardour St. W.

"Henri Gaudier-Brzeska," by Ezra Pound, pp. 3–[8]. (This was reprinted in . . .
Gaudier-Brzeska with a Vortex Manifesto ([1957])—A73—pp. 5–[18], in *Gaudier-
Brzeska* ([1960])—A10d—& ([1961])—A10e—pp. 136–9, and in *Ezra Pound
and the Visual Arts* ([1980])—A105—as "Preface to the Memorial Exhibition
1918," pp. 249–52. "Catalogue [of the exhibits]," pp. 9–14.

B19   KORA IN HELL . . .   1920
        BY WILLIAM CARLOS WILLIAMS

KORA IN HELL:| IMPROVISATIONS | BY | WILLIAM CARLOS
WILLIAMS | [*device*] | BOSTON | THE FOUR SEAS COMPANY
| 1920

86 pp., 3 blank leaves. 24·5 × 16 cm. Grey paper boards stamped in black on
front cover and down the spine; end-papers. Orange-brown dust-jacket printed
in black.

Published October 1920 at $2.00; number of copies unknown. *On verso of title-
leaf:* . . . The Four Seas Press Boston, Mass., U.S.A.

In his "Prologue," William Carlos Williams quotes on pages 13–14 excerpts
from Ezra Pound's letter to him of 10 November 1917. The complete letter is
printed in *The Letters*—A64—pp. 123–5.

Note: This book was published paperbound in San Francisco in 1957 by City
Lights Books at $1.25 as "The Pocket Poet Series, 7."

B20   FIVE TROUBADOUR SONGS . . .   [1920]
             BY AGNES BEDFORD

First edition:

FIVE | [*ornament*] | TROUBADOUR SONGS | WITH THE ORIG-

INAL PROVENÇAL WORDS | AND | English Words adapted [by Ezra Pound] from | CHAUCER, | Arranged | BY | AGNES BEDFORD. | [*Short rule*] | PRICE 5/ = NET | [*short rule*] | BOOSEY & C° | 295, REGENT STREET, LONDON, W. | [*at left:*] 9, EAST 17TH STREET, | NEW YORK. | [*In center:*] AND | [*at right:*] 384, YONGE STREET, | TORONTO. | [*In center: short rule*] | THESE SONGS MAY BE SUNG IN PUBLIC WITHOUT FEE OR LICENSE. | THE PUBLIC PERFORMANCE OF ANY PARODIED VERSIONS, HOWEVER, IS STRICTLY PROHIBITED. | [*Short rule*] | COPYRIGHT 1920 BY BOOSEY & CO

2 leaves, 24 pp. (music) 31 × 25 cm. Heavy red paper wrappers printed in black on pages [i], [iii–iv].

Published 10 December 1920 at 5s.; 250 copies printed. *Plate number at the foot of each page of music:* H.10124.

Each song has music for voice and piano accompaniment, with words in English and Provençal.

"Two of the lyrics are pastiche; in the case of Faidit's lament for Coeur de Lion, the subject matter is definite, here I have made a condensation of the original poem, and interpolated certain data which would have been known to Faidit's audience, but of which a modern auditor may require some glose [*sic*] or reminder." ("Proem," *2nd leaf, signed:* Ezra Pound. William Atheling.)

Contents: Proem [by Ezra Pound]—Miels com no pot dir, by Pons de Capdoil. Madame, ye ben of beauté shryne (English words adapted from Chaucer)—Cant par la flor, by Ventadour. Hyde, Absalon, thy tresses clere (English words from Chaucer)—Molt era dolz mei cossir, by Miroil. Your eyen two will slay me (English words from Chaucer)—Nom allegra chan ni cric, by Faidit. Lovers high upon the wheel (English words from Chaucer)—Fort chant oiaz, by Faidit. Sad song ye hear (English words by Pound)

B21   CONTACT COLLECTION [1925]
    OF CONTEMPORARY WRITERS

CONTACT COLLECTION OF | CONTEMPORARY WRITERS | Djuna Barnes | Bryher | Mary Butts | Norman Douglas | Havelock Ellis | F. M. Ford | Wallace Gould | Ernest Hemingway | Marsden Hartley | H. D. | John Herrman | James Joyce | Mina Loy | Robert McAlmon | Ezra Pound | Dorothy Richardson | May Sinclair | Edith Sitwell | Gertrude Stein | W. C. Williams [Paris, Contact Editions]

2 blank leaves, 4 leaves, 338 pp., 1 leaf, 2 blank leaves. 19·4 × 14·3 cm. Heavy grey paper wrappers, printed in black on pages [i] and [iv] and up the spine, folded over first and last blank leaves; edges untrimmed.

Published June 1925 at $3.00; 300 copies printed. *Colophon (page* [339])*:* Printed at Dijon by Maurice Darantière M.CM.XXV

Edited by Robert McAlmon, who, with William Bird, also published the book.

Contains "A Canto" [*i.e.* the first 60 lines of Canto XX], by Ezra Pound, pp. [214]–216.

B21a BOHEMIAN LITERARY AND [1928]
SOCIAL LIFE IN PARIS...
SISLEY HUDDLESTON

a. *English edition:*

[*In black, within single-rule border (with corner decorations) in red:*] BO-HEMIAN | LITERARY AND | SOCIAL LIFE | IN PARIS | Salons | Cafés Studios | by | SISLEY HUDDLESTON | [*device*] | GEORGE G. HARRAP & CO. LTD. | LONDON BOMBAY SYDNEY

450, [1] pp., incl. illus. front. (port.), plates. 22·5 × 15·5 cm. Brown cloth boards stamped in blind on front cover and in gold on spine; end-papers; top edges stained red, other edges untrimmed. Probably issued in dust-jacket.

Published 19 October 1928 at 21*s.*; 2000 copies printed. *On verso of title-leaf:* First published 1928 ... Printed in Great Britain at The Ballantyne Press by Spottiswoode, Ballantyne & Co. Ltd. Colchester, London & Eton

Contains quotation from Ezra Pound on "the new *rôle* of music in the modern world," p. 99; passages from *Antheil,* pp. 99–101; a paragraph from his announcement of his periodical *Exile*—E2ha—p. 102; and part of a long letter to Huddleston, pp. 102–4.

b. *American edition* (1928)*:*

PARIS SALONS | CAFÉS, STUDIOS | BY SISLEY HUDDLESTON | BEING SOCIAL, ARTISTIC | AND LITERARY MEMORIES | Il-lustrated | [*device*] | J. B. LIPPINCOTT COMPANY | PHILADEL-PHIA & LONDON | 1928

366 pp., 1 blank leaf. front. (port.), plates. 24·2 × 16·5 cm. Orange cloth boards stamped in blue and green on front cover and on spine; end-papers; top edges stained orange. Probably issued in dust-jacket.

Published 19 October 1928 at $5.00; number of copies unknown. *On verso of title-leaf:* ... Printed in the United States of America

B. BOOKS AND PAMPHLETS

In this edition the quotations from Pound appear on pages 84, 85–86, 87, and 87–88.

B22   OMAGGIO A MODIGLIANI   [1930]

omaggio | a | Modigliani | 1884–1920 [Milano, Giovanni Schei-
willer]

1 blank leaf, 38 leaves, 1 blank leaf, incl. mounted front. (port.) 20·7 × 15·7
cm. Green paper wrappers, printed in black on pages [i] and [iv], and up the
spine, folded over stiff white blanks; edges untrimmed. Plain glassine outer
wrapper.

Distributed gratis February 1930; 200 copies printed. *Colophon* (*recto of leaf* [38]):
il presente volume, fuori commercio, è stato composto e stampato in soli 200
esemplari, numerati a mano, su carta mano-macchina delle cartiere miliani di
fabriano, per onorare la memoria del pittore Amadeo Modigliani, a cura e spese
di giovanni scheiwiller, nelle officini grafiche della s. a. t. e. (società anonima
tipografica editoriale) milano, via spartaco 8, il 25 gennaio 1930 esemplare
numero [*number written in*]

Contains, on verso of leaf [31], a three-line contribution headed, "ezra pound":
"premature death of Modigliani removed a definite, valuable and emotive force
from the contemporary art world." This was sent to Giovanni Scheiwiller as
part of a letter dated: 26 November 1929. (For the complete letter, see *The
Letters*—A64—p. 225.)

B23   MY THIRTY YEARS' WAR . . .   1930
          BY MARGARET ANDERSON

[*Within double-thick and double-thin rule border:*] MY THIRTY | YEARS'
WAR | an autobiography by | Margaret Anderson | NEW YORK:
COVICI, FRIEDE | PUBLISHERS: MDCCCCXXX

5 leaves, 215, [2], 216–74 pp., 1 blank leaf. front. (port.), 15 plates, 3 illus. (incl.
facsims.) 24 × 16·5 cm. Yellow cloth boards stamped in brown on front cover
and on spine; end-papers; top edges stained brown. Yellow dust-jacket printed
in red and black.

Published 20 May 1930 at $4.00; number of copies unknown. *On verso of title-
leaf:* . . . Typography by S. A. Jacobs Printed in the United States of America by
the Stratford Press, Inc., New York

Contains letters from Ezra Pound to Margaret Anderson, chiefly concerning
contributions to the *Little Review*, Chicago, New York, Paris (which she edited
with Jane Heap), pp. 159–72, 216–18.

B. BOOKS AND PAMPHLETS

Note: Sheets for an unknown number of copies were imported and published in London by Alfred A. Knopf Ltd. in October 1930 at 15*s*. These were bound up first in rough, later smooth (shiny) black cloth boards.

B24   ADOLF LOOS   1930
ZUM 60. GEBURTSTAG

ADOLF LOOS | ZUM 60. GEBURTSTAG | AM 10. DEZEMBER 1930 | [*short thick rule*] | IM VERLAG DER BUCHHANDLUNG RICHARD LANYI | WIEN 1930

67, [1] pp., 2 blank leaves. 2 plates (incl. front.) 23·2 × 15·2 cm. Stiff tan paper wrappers printed in brown on page [i].

Published 10 December 1930 at S. 4.50; 1000 copies printed. *On verso of title-leaf:* Gedruckt in einer einmaligen Auflage von 1000 Exemplaren Dieses Exemplar trägt die Nummer [*number stamped in*] Druck: Manz . Wien IX Buchbinderarbeit: F. Rollinger . Wien

Edited by Otto Loos. Contains a brief message headed, "Ezra Pound," p. 43: "NONSENSE! Adolf Loos will never be sixty years old. Er hat sein vierzehnte Jahr jetz geendet. I am sorry not to be at his party."

B25   TORCHBEARER   1931
BY HARRY CROSBY

[*In red:*] TORCHBEARER | [*in black:*] by | [*in red:*] Harry Crosby | [*in black:*] With Notes by Ezra Pound | The Black Sun Press | Rue Cardinale | Paris | [*in red:*] MCMXXXI

2 blank leaves, 5 leaves, 1 blank leaf, 44 pp., 2 leaves, viii pp., 1 blank leaf, 2 leaves, 2 blank leaves, incl. port. 23·1 × 17·8 cm. (Collected Poems of Harry Crosby, Vol. IV.) Heavy white paper wrappers, printed in red and black on page [i] and in red on spine, folded over first and last blank leaves; fore and bottom edges untrimmed. Plain glassine outer wrapper. (Foot of spine has either "1931" or (later?) author's name.) Issued with volumes I, II, and III as a set, for sale at $20.00, in a red cloth box measuring 23·5 × 18 cm. as "Collected Poems of Harry Crosby, Vol. IV."

Published November 1931 at $5.00; 500 copies printed.

Colophon (recto of first leaf following page viii): This First Edition of Torchbearer by Harry Crosby, with notes by Ezra Pound, being Volume IV of the Collected Poems of Harry Crosby, is printed in hand-set dorique type at the Black Sun Press, Paris, 1931, under the direction of and for Caresse Crosby and is strictly limited to twenty lettered copies on Japanese Vellum and fifty numbered copies on Holland Paper together with the sheets for five hundred copies on uncut Navarre [*number written in, in some copies*]

Mr Harry F. Marks, the American agent for this edition, stated that to the best of his knowledge, the sets on Japanese vellum were never printed, and the full fifty copies on Holland (announced to sell at $40.00 the set, bound) were probably not published. No copy on Holland paper has been seen. At least several of the Navarre copies were numbered, in some instances with numbers between 1 and 50 theoretically reserved for the Holland sets. In the Navarre copies the paper is watermarked: PAPETERIES LAFUMA.

"Notes," by Ezra Pound, viii pp. at end. "Books by Harry Crosby," 2nd leaf following page viii.

| B26 | READIES FOR | 1931 |
| | BOB BROWN'S MACHINE | |

READIES | for | Bob Brown's Machine | by | A. Lincoln Gillespie Jr. John A. Farrell | Alfred Kreymborg John Banting | Axton Clark Kay Boyle | B.C. Hagglund K. T. Young | Carlton Brown Laurence Vail | Charles Beadle Lloyd Stern | Clare L. Brackett Manuel Komroff | Charles Henri Ford Nancy Cunard | Daphne Carr Norman MacLeod | Donal MacKenzie Paul Bowles | Eugene Jolas Peter Neagoè | Ezra Pound Richard Johns | Filippo Tommaso Marinetti Robert McAlmon | George Kent Rose Brown | Gertrude Stein Rue Menken | Herman Spector Samuel Putnam | Hilaire Hiler Sidney Hunt | Hiler, pere [*sic*] Theodore Pratt | J. Jones Walter Lowenfels | James T. Farrell Wambly Bald | Jay du Von William Carlos Williams | Roving Eye Press | Cagnes-sur-Mer (A.-M.) | 1931

4 leaves, 5–208 pp., incl. plate. 21·7 × 13·5 cm. Heavy green paper wrappers lettered in black on page [i] and up the spine. ("Contents" and plate are on two leaves of coated paper inserted before page 5.)

Published late December 1931 at $2.00; 300 copies printed.

"The text in this book, contributed by experimental modern writers, has been expressly written to be read on the reading machine. The use of hyphens, arrows, other connectives and punctuation is solely to suggest that the reading matter is to pass in a pleasant reading size at a pleasing speed before the reader's eye on a tape unrolled by a motor." ("Preface," by Hilaire Hiler, p. 7)

Contains "Highbrow's Translation from Horace (Persicos odi)," an eight-line poem by Ezra Pound, p. 114. Except for the insertion between words of a total of six marks of equation, the poem is printed in normal fashion.

B. BOOKS AND PAMPHLETS

B27 GUIDO CAVALCANTI RIME [1932]

First edition:

GUIDO | CAVALCANTI | RIME | EDIZIONE RAPPEZZATA | FRA LE ROVINE | GENOVA | EDIZIONI MARSANO S. A. | VIA CASAREGIS, 24 | ANNO IX [*i.e.* X].

1 blank leaf, 2 leaves, 7–56, pp., 1 blank leaf. 40 numbered plates on 20 leaves. 29 × 22·5 cm. Stiff red paper wrappers printed in black on pages [i] and [iv] (with date imprint on page [i]: Anno X.) and on spine; edges untrimmed.

Published late January 1932 at L. 75; about 500 copies printed. The circumstances under which the book was printed (see below) involved the use of four different kinds of paper: the first 56 pages, the following xvi pages, and the final blank fly-leaf (which is inserted) are on wove paper of fair quality; the 40 numbered plates (following page xvi) are on wove paper of smoother finish; the final 56 pages are on wove paper of better quality, presumably of English make, or (in at least one copy now at Harvard) Japanese vellum.

Edited by Ezra Pound (whose identity is indicated only by the initials: E.P.).

Dedication on page [5] (*first count*): A Manlio Dazzi che ha mangiato "Ai Dodici Apostoli" e con me diviso le fatiche di quest' edizione. (1928–31).

"Save for a few necessary corrections, by which I mean corrections not emendations; and for a few sonnets completely recast, I have left my early translations of the Sonnets and Ballate as they were originally printed, and perforce, for I am further removed from the years 1910–12 than from the original Italian. There is simply no use my trying to mix the two periods. The work for the rest of the poems in this edition has been spent on the italian text, and shows more in the table of variants than anywhere else." (*Note, p.* 36 (*second count*))

Contents: I. Ad lectorem E. P.—Sonetti (testo stampato [with new English translations of five]—Ballate (testo stampato)—La Frottola, e suo ritmo: Carta per mostrare dove si trovano le rime manoscritte—Indice dei manoscritti nelle diverse biblioteche—Indice delle Rime—Indice delle Tavole—II. Plates (tavole fotografiche): Testo completo delle rime nei diversi manoscritti—III. Frammenti dell'edizione bilingue: Mediaevalism—Donna mi prega [English translation]—Partial Explanation—The Canzone [Italian text of "Donna mi prega"]—The Other Dimension—The Vocabulary—The Canzone: Further Notes—Sonnets & Ballate [Introduction to the edition of 1912]—[Six] Sonnets [Italian text (duplicating pages 13–15 of the first count) with English translation (from the 1912 edition) opposite for the first five]

Notes: In 1928, Ezra Pound proposed to Faber and Gwyer (as his English publishers were then styled) that they bring out a new edition of his *The Sonnets and Ballate of Guido Cavalcanti,* to which would be added Dante Gabriel Rossetti's translations, and facsimiles of the principal Cavalcanti manuscripts. The probable cost of the illustrations was a stumbling block until Faber and Gwyer discovered that they could be printed inexpensively by Ullmann in Germany. In November 1928, having been assured by Pound that an American publisher could easily be found to take 500 of the sheets, Faber and Gwyer made plans to issue an edition of 1000, all to be signed by Pound, of which 500 would be for sale in England at not more than 25s. Specimen pages were prepared by Oliver Simon at the Curwen Press (Bruce Rogers in the U. S. having declined to print the book), but it soon became evident that Pound's stipulations as to type-size and the inclusion of additional material would make the book much too expensive for Faber and Gwyer to undertake. When both Horace Liveright and Random House, the first two American publishers whom they approached, refused to agree to take sheets, Faber and Gwyer wrote Pound, on 15 Jan. 1929, that they could proceed with the book only if he would permit them to do it much more economically; otherwise they suggested that he might prefer to get some other firm to print it according to his plan.

By Spring 1929, the Aquila Press in London had agreed to take over publication of the edition. The Press announced plans for "a monumental and definitive edition of the works of Guido Cavalcanti . . . prepared by Ezra Pound[.] A full critical text of the poems will be printed . . . together with photographic reproductions of the original manuscripts, an extensive commentary and variant readings, variants of the Di Giunta editio princeps of 1527 being given in Gloze. A complete translation by Mr. Pound & the renderings of certain of the poems by Dante Gabriel Rossetti will be included. Details of the price & format of the book will be announced later together with specimen pages." A subsequent announcement gave the title as "The Complete Works of Guido Cavalcanti" and set publication for December 1929 in an edition of 470 copies (450 for sale), bound in full natural Niger at five guineas, and 50 copies on (Japanese) vellum specially bound at twenty guineas.

The printing of the edition, under the supervision of John Sibthorp, was actually begun and a sample copy (DG) was bound up in full brown leather boards stamped on front cover and up the spine: THE WORKS OF GUIDO CAVALCANTI. This contained only the first gathering (pp. [1]–8) repeated eleven times. Later, another sample copy (OSP) was bound up, containing the first four gatherings (pp. [1]–32) filled out with blank leaves. After 56 pages had been printed, the Aquila Press failed. The completed sheets (presumably about 470 sets on paper and about 50 on Japanese vellum, plus at least one set on real vellum) were sent to Ezra Pound in Rapallo.

The failure of the Aquila Press radically altered the character of the edition. To rescue the essential parts "from the ruins," Pound had the Italian texts and the scholarly apparatus printed in Genoa by the Edizioni Marsano and the reproductions printed in Germany (all at his own expense). To these he added the 56 pages of the abortive English edition because they were already printed and because they contained his commentary (pp. [11]–15) on the "Donna mi prega," with the Italian text (pp. [16]–21). The fragmentary nature of the book is most marked at its end where the six sonnets repeat texts already given in identical form at the beginning, and where the English translations break off with number five. Five new translations of later sonnets are included in the only possible position—given the fragmentary nature of the edition so far as the English versions are concerned—and appear along with the Italian texts in the first part of the book. (These are apparently the "few sonnets completely recast" to which Pound refers in the note quoted above. They are numbers 7, 13, 14, 16, and 17, and they appear on pages 16, 20, 21, 22, and 23 of the first count.) The early translations of the Ballate are omitted completely.

Three Canzoni not included in Pound's edition, "Io son la donna che volge la rota," "O povertà come tu sei un manto," and "O lento, pigro, ingrato, ignaro che fai," were printed, with facsimiles of the manuscripts and Italian texts as . . . *Tre Canzoni di Guido Cavalcanti, con i fac-simili dei manoscritti senesi* . . . (Siena, Casa Editrice Ticci, 1949), edited by Olga Rudge, as No. XIX in the series "Quaderni dell'Accademia Chigiana." The edition was of 300 numbered copies and was issued at L. 300 in June 1949.

B28   PROFILE   1932

First edition:

[*In black:*] EZRA POUND | [*in red:*] PROFILE | [*in black:*] AN AN-
THOLOGY COLLECTED IN MCMXXXI | MILAN [Giovanni Schei-
willer] MCMXXXII

1 blank leaf, 3 leaves, 9–142 pp., 3 leaves. 20·8 × 15·8 cm. (wrappers); 20·4 × 15·4 cm. (leaves). Grey-green paper wrappers, printed in black on page [i] and up the spine, folded over stiff white blanks. Plain glassine outer wrapper.

Published late May 1932 at $3.00; 250 copies printed. *On verso of title-leaf:* . . . Printed in Italy *Colophon* (*recto of third leaf following page 142*): Edition privately printed for John Scheiwiller limited to 250 numbered copies. Copy N. [*number stamped in*] Tipografia Card. Ferrari—Milano

"A collection of poems which have stuck in my memory and which may possibly define their epoch, or at least rectify current ideas of it in respect to at least one contour." (*Note by Ezra Pound, recto of first leaf*)

Contains poems by Arthur Symons (one), Ezra Pound (six), Padraic Colum (two), James Joyce (one), William Carlos Williams (four), Ford Madox Ford (three), Walter de la Mare (two), T. E. Hulme (five), H. D. (two), Richard Aldington (two), Allen Upward (three), W. B. Yeats (one), Alice Corbin Henderson (one), T. S. Eliot (three), Marianne Moore (five), Mina Loy (one), Donald Evans (two), E. E. Cummings (five), Ernest Hemingway (one), Robert McAlmon (one), R. Cheever Dunning (two), Archibald MacLeish (two), Louis Zukofsky (one), Joseph Gordon Macleod (one), Howard Weeks (one), Basil Bunting (one), Emanuel Carnevali (two), Parker Tyler (one), and two groups of poems from *New Masses*, New York. The poems are printed chronologically by date of composition and are linked by prose passages by Pound. (Pound's own contributions are "The Tree," p. 16, "The Coming of War: Actaeon," p. 45, "The Gipsy," p. 50, "Dogmatic Statement Concerning the Game of Chess,"

B. BOOKS AND PAMPHLETS

p. 51, "'Nodier raconte ... '" ["Moeurs contemporaines," V], pp. 71–72, and "'H. S. Mauberley,' Section II, Poem II," pp. 72–73, all reprinted from earlier books.)

B29   AN "OBJECTIVISTS"   1932
                  ANTHOLOGY

AN "OBJECTIVISTS" ANTHOLOGY | EDITED BY LOUIS ZU-
KOFSKY | [Le Beausset, Var, France & New York, N. Y.] TO,
PUBLISHERS MCMXXXII

1 blank leaf, 3 leaves, [9]–210 pp., 1 leaf. 22·6 × 14·1 cm. Heavy tan paper wrappers printed in black on page [i] and up the spine; edges untrimmed.

Published Summer 1932 at 10 francs; number of copies unknown. *On recto of half-title-leaf:* To, Publishers Le Beausset, Var, France New York, P O Box 3 Station F *Imprint on page* [211]: Printed by Maurice Darantière at Dijon, France M.CM.XXXII

Dedication on page [27]: ... To Ezra Pound who ... is still for the poets of our time the most important.

A collection of poems chiefly by contributors to the "Objectivists" number of *Poetry*, Chicago (February 1931), also edited by Louis Zukofsky. These include Basil Bunting, Robert McAlmon, Carl Rakosi, Kenneth Rexroth, Charles Reznikoff, William Carlos Williams, and Louis Zukofsky. Ezra Pound "gave over to young poets the space offered him" in *Poetry*, but is represented in this book along with T. S. Eliot and Mary Butts, other non-contributors to the special number of the periodical.

Contains poem ["Yittischer Charleston"] beginning "Gentle Jheezus sleek and wild," pp. [44]–45, with excerpts from a letter to the editor concerning it, p. 45, and "Words for Roundel in Double Canon," pp. 45–46, by Ezra Pound. In a letter to Ronald Duncan on 7 July 1947 Pound stated that the first line of "Yittischer Charleston" should have been printed "Jazzing Jhesus [*sic*], sleek and wild."

Note: This book was distributed in the United States by Bruce Humphries, Boston, Mass. A leaf of errata, reproduced from typewritten copy, was laid into later copies.

B30   AMERICANS ABROAD   1932
AMERICANS | ABROAD | An Anthology | edited by | PETER
NEAGOE | WITH AUTOGRAPHED PHOTOGRAPHS AND | BIO-
GRAPHIC SKETCHES OF THE AUTHORS | 1932 | THE SERVIRE
PRESS [*ornament*] THE HAGUE (HOLLAND)

xi, 475 pp., incl. illus. (ports.). 23·6 × 15·9 cm. Grey cloth boards stamped in blue on front cover and on spine; tan end-papers; top edges stained red. White dust-jacket printed in blue and red. (Also in white paper boards printed in blue and red, and in yellow paper boards lettered in brown on front cover, with grey cloth back stamped in brown; top edges stained grey.)

Published 1 December 1932 at $2.50; number of copies unknown.

" . . . this Anthology is devoted to those American artists who have been living and working, during the after-war decade, in Europe—all of that time or part of it." ("Foreword," by Peter Neagoe, p. xi)

Contains a brief note by Ezra Pound in lieu of a biography, p. [315], with an unsigned reproduction of his life mask, by Nancy Cox McCormack. "Canto XX," pp. [316]–321, is reprinted with minor alterations from *A Draft of XXX Cantos* (1930)—A31.

B31   F. FERRUCCIO CERIO   [1932]
       [LE "FIAMME NERE"?]

First edition:

[*Ornament, followed by dots, then:*] (Titolo) [*dots, followed by orna-ment*] | DI | F. Ferruccio Cerio | ADATTATO PER L'ESTERO | DA | Ezra Pound [Rapallo, Printed as manuscript for F. Ferruccio Cerio]

29 leaves, 1 blank leaf. 37·9 × 26 cm. Mulberry paper wrappers; stapled.

Printed as draft for private circulation 21 December 1932; number of copies unknown. Printed on rectos of leaves only. *At foot of leaf* [29]: In Rapallo 21–12–XI

A scenario (in Italian) for a proposed film treatment of the history of Italian fascism prepared for the decennial celebration. It is divided into three parts: Capitolo I—1918— . . . la diritta via era smarrita . . . (Quadro I–VI); Capitolo II—1919–1922— . . . nave senza nocchier in gran tempesta non donna di pro-vincie ma bordello! (Quadro I–XIII); Capitolo III . . . per l'universo penetra e risplende (Quadro I–IX). The text is printed, for the most part, in three col-umns, the first devoted to technical directions, the middle (wider column) to descriptions of scenes and dialogue, the third to notes concerning the musical accompaniment and changes to be made for foreign consumption. These latter notes, presumably by Ezra Pound, are extensive only for Quadro XII of Capi-tolo II, "Marcia su Roma." Here (leaves [20–23]) the text is printed in two columns of equal width, the left-hand column headed "Italia," the right, "Es-tero," with more than twice as much material in the right-hand column (leaves [22] and [23] have the left-hand column blank).

It is probable that the scenario was printed at the Arti Grafiche Tigullio in

Rapallo for use of the author in attempting to secure production of the film. The proposed film was not made and the scenario was never published. On one of the three copies at Brunnenburg (in 1961) is written in an unidentified hand (not Ezra Pound's): "Le 'Fiamme Nere' (??)." This copy has manuscript additions and corrections, presumably by F. Ferruccio Cerio.

B32   ACTIVE ANTHOLOGY   [1933]

First edition:

ACTIVE | ANTHOLOGY | EDITED BY | EZRA | POUND | LON- DON | FABER AND FABER LTD | 24 RUSSELL SQUARE

255 pp. 19·1 × 13·3 cm. Red-brown cloth boards stamped in blue on spine; end-papers; top edges stained blue. Yellow dust-jacket printed in black and red.

Published 12 October 1933 at 7s. 6d.; 1516 sets of sheets printed (of which 750 were bombed during the Second World War). *On verso of title-leaf:* First published in October MCMXXXIII ... Printed in Great Britain by R. MacLehose and Company Limited The University Press Glasgow ...

"My anthology *Profile* was a critical narrative, that is I attempted to show by excerpt what had occurred during the past quarter of a century. In this volume I am presenting an assortment of writers, mostly ill known in England, in whose verse a development appears or in some case [*sic*] we may say "still appears" to be taking place, in contradistinction to authors in whose work no such activity has occurred or seems likely to proceed any further." (*Note, p.* [5])

Contents: Praefatio, aut tumulus cimicium—William Carlos Williams—Basil Bunting—Louis Zukofsky—Louis Aragon, translated by E. E. Cummings— E. E. Cummings—E. Hemingway—Marianne Moore—George Oppen—D. G. Bridson—T. S. Eliot—Ezra Pound—Notes on Particular Details

Ezra Pound is represented by a group of brief selections from the Cantos made and annotated by John Drummond, with a further note by Louis Zukofsky. The preface is reprinted as "Prefatio aut cimicium tumulus" in *Polite Essays* ([1937])— A42a—pp. 135–52, and in *Selected Prose 1909–1965* ([1973])—A93a—pp. 359– 70 (389–400 in A93b).

B33   NEGRO ANTHOLOGY   1934

NEGRO | ANTHOLOGY MADE BY | NANCY CUNARD | 1931– 1933 | Published by | Nancy Cunard at Wishart & Co | 9 John Street · London · W · C · 2 | 1934

viii, 580, iii, [581]–854, [2] pp. illus. (ports., facsim., music). 1 col. fold. map. 31·5 × 26 cm. Brown linen (or, later, shiny black cloth) boards stamped in red on covers and on spine; end-papers (double at front, single at back); top edges stained brown.

Published 16 February 1934 at 42*s.*; 1150 copies printed (of which all save ten of the copies then remaining unsold were bombed in September 1940). On *verso of title-leaf:* ... Printed in England *Imprint on page* [856]*:* Printed ... at The Ballantyne Press Spottiswoode, Ballantyne & Co. Ltd. Colchester, London & Eton Blocks by Leonardson & Co., 1 Slingsby Place, W. C. 2

Pages i–iii, following page 580, (containing "The Negress in the Brothel, by René Crevel. Translated from the French by Samuel Beckett"), are printed on slightly different paper, with imprint at foot of page i: Printed at the Utopia Press, London, E. C. 2. The coloured folding map is inserted after page [582].

Contents: America—Negro Stars—Music—Poetry—West Indies and South America—Europe—Africa

Contains (in the section devoted to Africa) "Leo Frobenius, by Ezra Pound," pp. 623–4. (Pound's note incorporates two short paragraphs by Frobenius.) On page 141 appears "A Letter to Ezra Pound [from Langston Hughes]," sent to Nancy Cunard, with an unsigned note, by Pound.

B34   DISCRETE SERIES   1934
BY GEORGE OPPEN

DISCRETE | SERIES | BY | GEORGE OPPEN | WITH A PREFACE BY EZRA POUND | THE OBJECTIVIST PRESS | 10 WEST 36 STREET, NEW YORK | 1934

vi pp., 1 leaf, 7–37 pp. 19·6 × 13·3 cm. Green cloth boards, with white paper label printed in black down the spine; end-papers; fore and bottom edges untrimmed. Grey dust-jacket printed in green.

Published 13 March 1934 at $1.00; number of copies unknown. *On verso of title-leaf:* ... Printed in the United States of America by J. J. Little and Ives Company, New York

"Preface," pp. v–vi.

Note: "The Objectivist Press is an organization of writers who are publishing their own work and that of other writers whose work they think ought to be read. ... Advisory Board: Ezra Pound, William Carlos Williams, Louis Zukofsky, Sec'y" (*Dust-jacket*)

B35   MODERN THINGS   [1934]

MODERN THINGS – | [*short double rule*] | EDITED BY | PARKER TYLER | [*device*] | NEW YORK | THE GALLEON PRESS

92 pp., 2 blank leaves. 22·3 × 13·8 cm. Violet cloth boards printed in white on front cover, with white cloth back; end-papers; top edges stained red. Grey dust-jacket printed in black and violet.

Published September 1934 at $2.00; number of copies unknown. *On verso of title-leaf:* . . . Manufactured and Printed in U. S. A

". . . the intention of this anthology is to present an elect body of work, composed by those moderns who have worked successfully in literary styles for a number of years to the accompaniment of ever-growing critical and general recognition, together with those younger moderns who . . . have had successes definitely meriting critical attention. These poems have been collected with applied reference to the unity of a continuous contemporary literary impulse, operating through related and developing modes of writing." ("Introduction," p. 5)

Contains "Canto XXXIV [*i.e.* sections amounting to less than half of the complete Canto]," by Ezra Pound, pp. 18–21, with notes interpolated by the editor. (The other contributors include T. S. Eliot, E. E. Cummings, Marianne Moore, William Carlos Williams, Wallace Stevens, Gertrude Stein, Louis Zukofsky, and Parker Tyler.)

B36   THE CHINESE WRITTEN   [1936]
CHARACTER AS A MEDIUM FOR
POETRY

a. *First separate edition:*

The Chinese Written Character | as a Medium for Poetry | BY | ERNEST FENOLLOSA | [*ornament*] | AN ARS POETICA | [*ornament*] | With a Foreword and Notes | BY | EZRA POUND | [*ideogram*] | LONDON | STANLEY NOTT | FITZROY SQUARE

52 pp. 21·7 × 17·5 cm. Black cloth boards, with imitation vellum back stamped in red with rule on each side and lettered in red down the spine; end-papers; top edges stained black. Cream dust-jacket printed in red and black.

Published 3 March 1936 at 5s. as "Ideogramic Series, Edited by Ezra Pound, 1"; 2000 sets of sheets printed (of which 200 were bombed during the Second World War). The unsold stock was transferred 9 September 1937 to Faber and Faber, who sold 173 copies. *On verso of title-leaf:* Printed in Great Britain by The Kynoch Press 1936

Reprinted from *Instigations* (1920)—A18—with a few minor changes and the addition of a "Foreword," pp. 5–6, a brief "Terminal Note," p. 37, and an appendix "With Some Notes [on Chinese Written Characters] by a Very Ignorant Man," pp. [39]–52.

Notes: Of the "Ideogramic Series, Edited by Ezra Pound," only this first number and a second, *Ta Hio, the Great Learning* (1936)—A28b—were published. The third number was to have been William Carlos Williams's *In the American Grain*, but Stanley Nott ceased his publishing activities before the book could be printed. Pound's editing of the later numbers in the series was to have been confined to his selecting and securing the manuscripts for inclusion.

This book was reprinted (omitting the fly-title to the appendix), reduced, by offset and issued 14 July 1951, in a single volume with offset of the Indian (1949) edition of Pound's *Confucius. The Unwobbling Pivot & The Great Digest*, at $1.00, as *Ernest Fenollosa. The Chinese Written Character as a Medium for Poetry. With Offset of the Calcutta Edition of Pivot* ([Washington, D. C.] Square $ Series [1951]), where it appears as pp. [50]–96 (pp. [49]–96 in later impressions). Some copies have stamp in blue on title-page and above the imprint on page [iv] of the wrapper: John Kasper, Publisher | Box 552, G.P.O. N.Y.1, N.Y. An advertisement leaf—at first a broadside printed on green paper, measuring 15·3 × 7·9 cm., and later a leaf of two pages, measuring 14 × 7·3 cm., headed *The Unwobbling Pivot Pound's masterly translation of Confucius' basic work* and quoting Pound's "Note" to "The Great Digest" (from page 29), was distributed at the time of publication and was loosely laid into some copies. Page [2] of the later advertisement leaf is headed *Pound's Introductory Text-book* and reprints E2r, with a typed statement added along the lefthand margin: "Lincoln was shot for understanding what Jeff wrote to Crawford in 1816".

b. *American issue:*

The Chinese Written Character | as a Medium for Poetry | BY | ERNEST FENOLLOSA | [*ornament*] | AN ARS POETICA | [*ornament*] | With a Foreword and Notes | BY | EZRA POUND | [*ideogram*] | ARROW EDITIONS | NEW YORK

52 pp. 22 × 17 cm. Green paper boards stamped in blind with white paper label printed in black inlaid on front cover, and white paper label printed in black on spine; end-papers. Yellow dust-jacket printed in green.

Published November 1936 at $1.50 (series as for English edition); number of copies unknown. These are the English sheets with a reprinted title-leaf (with title-page as above) and its conjugate. *On verso of title-leaf:* . . . Printed in Great Britain by The Kynoch Press 1936

Note: This book was published paperbound in San Francisco in 1964 by City Lights Books at $1.25. Copies of the edition were distributed overseas by the Scorpion Press, Lowestoft.

B37   MEMORIAL   1936
                  HERMAN VANDENBURG AMES

Memorial | [*ornament*] | HERMAN | VANDENBURG | AMES | Late Professor of American | Constitutional History | University of

B. BOOKS AND PAMPHLETS

Pennsylvania | [*ornament*] | Edited by | EDWARD P. CHEYNEY | AND | ROY F. NICHOLS | University of Pennsylvania Press | PHILADELPHIA | 1936

vii, [1], 31 pp. 23·5 × 18 cm. Blue cloth boards stamped in blind on front cover and lettered in gold on front cover and down the spine; end-papers.

Distributed gratis beginning 26 June 1936; 150 copies printed. *On verso of title-leaf:* ... Manufactured in the United States of America London Humphrey Milford Oxford University Press

"On May 7, 1935, a memorial meeting was held ... at the University of Pennsylvania where many gathered to pay final tribute. The words then spoken are here recorded, accompanied by a few of the many letters and memorials written in appreciation of Dr. Ames's long life of service to education and scholarship." ("Foreword," p. v)

Contains letter from "Ezra Pound, College '05, Rapallo, Italy, April 8, 1935," pp. 20–22.

B38   ERNEST RHYS   [1936]
                  LETTERS FROM LIMBO

ERNEST RHYS | [*ornament, short thick-thin rule, ornament*] | LETTERS FROM LIMBO | With 63 Reproductions | of Letters | London | J. M. DENT AND SONS LTD.

1 blank leaf, 2 leaves, v–xvii, 289 pp., 1 leaf, incl. 63 facsims. front. (port.) 21·2 × 14 cm. Red cloth boards stamped in gold and in blind on spine; end-papers; top edges stained red. Cream dust-jacket printed in black and red.

Published October 1936 at 10s. 6d.; number of copies unknown. *On verso of title-leaf:* ... Made in Great Britain at The Temple Press Letchworth ... First Published 1936

Letters for the most part addressed to Ernest Rhys in his capacity as editor of J. M. Dent and Sons Ltd., printed with explanatory comments.

Contains excerpts from a letter to Ernest Rhys from Ezra Pound, dated: 14 [or 16?] Nov. [1932], pp. 228–31, with a facsimile of the first page (p. [229]). A short second letter, pp. 231–2, dated: 2 June anno XIII [*i.e.* 1935], gives Rhys permission to print the first.

B38a   IGOR STRAWINSKY   1936

[*In black:* | IGOR | [*in brown, across two pages:*] STRAWINSKY | [*in black:*] EDITED by MERLE ARMITAGE | Articles and critiques by

B. BOOKS AND PAMPHLETS

Eugene Goossens, | Henry Boys, Olin Downes, Merle Armitage, | Emile Vuillermoz, Louis Danz, José Rodriguez, | Manuel Komroff, Jean Cocteau, Eric Satie, | & an abridged analysis by Boris de Schloezer | G. SCHIRMER [*arranged in two lines:*] 1936 INC [*in one line:*] NEW YORK

5 leaves, v, 158 pp., 1 leaf. 16 plates (incl. ports.) 20·8 × 15·8 cm. Brown cloth boards lettered in blue on front cover and on spine; end-papers printed in brown. Probably issued in dust-jacket.

Published 1 November 1936 at $5.00; number of copies unknown. *On page* [159]: Designed by Merle Armitage Printed under the Direction of Lynton R. Kistler by Adcraft (Hand lettering on title page and cover by William Stutz) (Binding by C. Frank Fox)

Contains, as Chapter 11, [Strawinsky, by] "Boris de Schloezer [translated from the French by Ezra Pound] 1928," pp. 69–137. "An abridgment, selected from articles which appeared in the 1928–29 issue of *The Dial* [C726, 733, 738, 742–3, 745, 749]." ("Acknowledgements," p. 157)

B39   SCRITTI E DISEGNI   1937
                 DEDICATI A SCHEIWILLER

SCRITTI E DISEGNI | DEDICATI À | SCHEIWILLER | MILANO 1937–XV

1 blank leaf, 1 leaf, [5]–103 pp., 1 leaf, 1 blank leaf, incl. illus. 21·5 × 16·7 cm. (wrappers); 21 × 16·2 cm. (leaves). Grey paper wrappers, printed in black on page [i], folded over stiff white blanks; end-papers.

Distributed gratis Spring 1937; 500 copies printed. *Colophon* (*page* [4]): questo volume stampato in 500 copie numerate a iniziativa e spese di Gio Ponti, venne curato da Lamberto Vitali. esemplare N. [*number stamped in*] . . . Officina d'Arte Grafica A. Lucini & C.–Milano

Contains, under the heading "Ezra Pound," a tribute to Giovanni Scheiwiller, written in Italian by Pound, pp. 72–73. This was reprinted separately by Vanni Scheiwiller in Milan in 1962 as . . . *Nuova economia editoriale*—A79, and, with the same title, in 1965, as the foreword to *Edizioni Giovanni e Vanni Scheiwiller 1925–1965* . . . (Milano [1965])—of which there were 5000 ordinary and 300 special, signed copies—pp. 5–6; in 1968, in *Edizioni di Giovanni e Vanni Scheiwiller 1925–1968* . . . (Milano [1968]), pp. 5–6; and, also in 1968, in the four-page catalogue of an exhibition at the Libreria Galleria G. Greco in Mantua, . . . *Mostra delle edizioni Scheiwiller 1925–1968*, pp. [1–2].

B. BOOKS AND PAMPHLETS

B40   RECOGNITION OF   [1937]
                ROBERT FROST

RECOGNITION OF | ROBERT FROST | [*rule*] | Twenty-Fifth An-
niversary | Edited by | RICHARD THORNTON | [*ornament*] | NEW
YORK | HENRY HOLT AND COMPANY

xx, 312 pp., 2 blank leaves. 9 plates (incl. front., ports.) 24·2 × 16·8 cm. Green
cloth boards stamped in gold on spine; end-papers; top edges stained green,
fore edges untrimmed, bottom edges roughly trimmed. White dust-jacket printed
in green.

Published 23 November 1937 at $2.50; number of copies unknown. *On verso of
title-leaf:* . . . Printed in the United States of America

Contains, in the section "Early Recognition," "First American Notice, III, by
Ezra Pound," pp. 50–53, an article (originally entitled "Modern Georgics")
reprinted, with the omission of two paragraphs, from *Poetry*, Chicago, for December 1914—C164.

B41   AUTHORS TAKE SIDES   [1937]
              ON THE SPANISH WAR

AUTHORS TAKE SIDES | ON THE SPANISH WAR | LEFT RE-
VIEW | 2 Parton Street | London | W. C. 1

[32] pp. 24·8 × 15·7 cm. Yellow paper wrappers printed in red on pages [i–iv];
wire-stitched. Red paper wrap-around printed in black.

Published December 1937 at 6*d.*; number of copies unknown. *On verso of title-
leaf:* Made and printed in Great Britain for Left Review by Purnell and Sons,
Ltd. (T.U.) Paulton (Somerset) and London

Consists of answers to a questionnaire sent to various writers in June 1937.
Ezra Pound's reply appears under the heading "Neutral?" on page [29]. The
questionnaire is dated from Paris, June 1937, and is signed by Louis Aragon,
W. H. Auden, José Bergamin, Jean Richard Bloch, Nancy Cunard, Brian How-
ard, Heinrich Mann, Ivor Montagu, Pablo Neruda, Ramón Sender, Stephen
Spender, and Tristan Tzara. A similar questionnaire was distributed in the United
States, and the answers of American writers were published as *Writers Take
Sides: Letters about the War in Spain from 418 American Authors*, by the League of
American Writers in New York in May 1938.

Note: Ezra Pound's reply was reprinted in Appendix 3, "Excerpts Taken from
Authors Take Sides on the Spanish War," to a similar publication, *Authors Take Sides
on Vietnam . . . Edited by Cecil Woolf and John Bagguley* (London, Peter Owen
[1967]), p. 227. (Of this book, ordinary copies, sold at 37*s.* 6*d.*, were bound in
black cloth, and 300 special copies, at 50*s.*, in blue cloth boards.)

B. BOOKS AND PAMPHLETS

B42   A POET'S LIFE . . .   1938
BY HARRIET MONROE

[*Within double-thin and single-thick rule border:*] A | POET'S LIFE |
Seventy Years | in a Changing World | BY | HARRIET MONROE
| [*ornament*] | NEW YORK | THE MACMILLAN COMPANY | 1938

1 blank leaf, viii pp., 2 leaves, 488 pp., 1 blank leaf. front. (port.), 16 plates
(incl. facsims.) 24 × 16·5 cm. Green cloth boards stamped in green on front
cover and in green and blind on spine; end-papers. Tan dust-jacket printed in
black and red.

Published 8 March 1938 at $5.00; 2500 copies printed. *On verso of title-leaf:* . . .
Printed in the U. S. A. . . . Set up and printed. Published March, 1938. First
Printing

Contains letters and quotations from letters from Ezra Pound to Harriet Monroe, chiefly concerning contributions to *Poetry*, Chicago, 1912–15, pp. 259–60,
261, 262–3, 264–7, 268, 367–8; "A Few Don'ts by an Imagiste," pp. 298–301;
an excerpt from "The Audience," pp. 365–6; and a tribute to Harriet Monroe
["In Memory of Harriet Monroe"], pp. 469–70. (The book was published post-
humously.) "The italics in Mr. Pound's correspondence did not appear in the
original letters, but are here supplied, at his request, to emphasize points which
he wishes stressed in 1937." (*Note*, p. 261) On page 267 appear two footnotes
supplied by Pound in January 1937.

B43   FASCIST EUROPE   1938
EUROPA FASCISTA

FASCIST | EUROPE | EUROPA FASCISTA | AN ANGLO-ITALIAN
SYMPOSIUM EDITED BY | ERMINIO TURCOTTI AND PUB-
LISHED UNDER | THE AUSPICES OF THE NATIONAL INSTI-
TUTE | OF FASCIST CULTURE OF PAVIA | RACCOLTA DI SCRITTI
ITALO-INGLESI | EDITA DA ERMINIO TURCOTTI | E PUBBLI-
CATA SOTTO GLI AUSPICI DELLA SEZIONE PAVESE |
DELL'ISTITUTO NAZIONALE | DI CULTURA FASCISTA | Vol-
ume I | MILANO 28 OTTOBRE 1938–ANNO XVII

1 blank leaf, 1 leaf, 5–157, [1] pp., 2 leaves, 1 blank leaf, [4] pp. 24·4 × 17·5
cm. (wrappers); 24·1 × 17 cm. (leaves). Heavy buff paper wrappers printed in
black and red on pages [i] and [iv] and up the spine, and in brown on page [iii].

Published 28 October 1938 at L. 15; number of copies unknown. *On verso of
title-leaf:* . . . Salesian Printing School–Milano *On page* [*iii*] *of wrappers:* Scuola
Salesiana di Stampa . . . Milano

Contains "Ubicumque lingua Romana," by Ezra Pound, dated: January 1938

B. BOOKS AND PAMPHLETS

XVI, pp. 41–46, with Italian translation [by Erminio Turcotti?] with same title, pp. 47–52.

Advertisements, [4] pp. at end, are on paper of smoother finish than that used for the rest of the volume.

Note: Page [iv] of the wrappers carries an advertisement for a second volume, announced for "Early in Spring 1940," but this was not published. A four-page prospectus announced this work (volume one) as to be titled: "Dawn" "Fascist Europe" A Symposium . . .

B44   WE MODERNS   [1939]

[*Within white box of irregular shape set into reproduction of Carl Van Vechten's photograph of a painting by Ruth Bower:*] WE MODERNS | GOTHAM BOOK MART | 1920–1940 | [*in white rectangle at bottom:*] The Life of the Party at FINNEGANS WAKE in our Garden | on Publication Day | Painting by Ruth Bower Photograph by Carl Van Vechten [New York, Gotham Book Mart]

cover-title, 3–88, [2] pp. 20·4 × 13·8 cm. (wrappers); 19·7 × 13·3 cm. (leaves). Heavy white paper wrappers printed in black on pages [i–iv]; stapled. Printed on uncoated paper. (Also 500 copies, issued simultaneously, at $1.00, in stiff white paper wrappers identically printed, with spiral, loose-leaf binding. Printed on coated paper.)

Distributed gratis 17 December 1939; 3500 copies printed. *Imprint at foot of page* [*iv*] *of wrappers:* Printed in United States of America Schoen Printing Company, New York

A catalogue of first and other editions by contemporary authors, grouped by author, with brief introductory biographies by other writers, published to commemorate the twentieth anniversary of Frances Steloff's Gotham Book Mart. Compiled by Frances Steloff and Kay Steele. "For those desiring to keep this catalogue up to date, we have issued a limited quantity in loose-leaf binding . . . which will also provide space for several introductions expected from abroad unavoidably delayed because of war conditions." (*Note on page* [*ii*] *of wrappers* (*both bindings*))

Contains "T. S. Eliot," by Ezra Pound, a note to a listing of titles by Eliot, pp. 24–25.

B45   JACOB EPSTEIN   [1940]
         LET THERE BE SCULPTURE

a. *Ordinary copies:*

Jacob Epstein | LET THERE BE | SCULPTURE | AN AUTOBI-

B. BOOKS AND PAMPHLETS

OGRAPHY | [*device*] | MICHAEL JOSEPH LTD. | 26 BLOOMS-
BURY STREET, [LONDON] W. C. I

335 pp. front., 47 plates. 23·7 × 16·3 cm. Red cloth boards stamped in silver
on spine; end-papers. Cream dust-jacket printed in black and red.

Published 25 November 1940 at 18s.; 4000 copies printed. *On verso of title-leaf:*
First published in 1940 Set and printed in Great Britain by William Brendon &
Son, Ltd., at the Mayflower Press, Plymouth, in Walbaum type, twelve point,
leaded, on a toned antique-wove paper made by John Dickinson, and bound by
James Burn.

Contains "Ezra Pound's Estimate [of Jacob Epstein's sculpture in an exhibition
at the Goupil Gallery] from 'The Egoist,' 16th March, 1914"—C134—pp. 71–
72. This was included also in the revised and extended edition of the book
published as *Epstein an Autobiography* ([London, 1955]), pp. 57–58.

b. *Special copies:*

3 leaves, 5–335 pp. front., 47 plates. 23·3 × 15·6 cm. Natural vellum boards
stamped in gold on spine; end-papers; top edges gilt. Issued in plain white
cardboard box, measuring 24·2 × 16·8 cm.

Published, simultaneously with the ordinary copies, at 42s.; 100 copies printed.
Colophon (leaf tipped in after half-title-leaf): This edition is limited to one hundred
copies signed and numbered by the author This is Number [*number written in on
a row of dots, signed:* Jacob Epstein.]

B46   CONFUCIO ...   1942
                   STUDIO INTEGRALE

First edition:

CONFUCIO | [*short ornamental rule*] | TA S'EU | DAI GAKU | STU-
DIO | INTEGRALE | Versione italiana | di | Ezra Pound | e di |
Alberto Luchini | [*rule*] | 1942–RAPALLO–XX | Scuola Tipografica
Orfanotrofio Emiliani

29, [3] pp. 24·3 × 17·1 cm. Heavy buff paper wrappers printed in black on
pages [i] and [iv] (with price); wire-stitched. Printed on unwatermarked paper
of poor quality. (Some copies were printed on a better, thicker paper, watermarked: P. M. FABRIANO MILIAFLEX. These have heavier cream paper wrappers
without price. The cream wrappers occur (probably by mistake) on at least one
poor-paper copy (OSP).)

Published early 1942 at L. 4; number of copies unknown.

A note on the edition by Ezra Pound is printed on pages [31–30], but otherwise the text is printed, and the pamphlet paged, from back to front. Each page has Chinese text with Italian version below.

On 3 November [1941] Pound wrote to Mrs Virgil Jordan: " . . . I am . . . making a real translation of Confucius' Ta S'eu (wrongly spelled Ta Hio, by the frogs whom I followed in earlier edtns/ . . . Have just finished the Italian draft/ and a bloke, called Luchini is supposed to put it into real Italian."

Notes: For separate edition of the Italian translation without the Chinese text, see *Testamento di Confucio* (1944)—A54. For Pound's English version, see "The Great Digest" in *Confucius. The Unwobbling Pivot & The Great Digest* (1947)— A58—and *Confucius. The Great Digest & Unwobbling Pivot* ([1951])—B53. Pound's earlier English version is *Ta Hio, The Great Learning* (1928)—A28.

B47   TWENTIETH CENTURY   1942
                   AUTHORS

TWENTIETH CENTURY | AUTHORS | A Biographical Dictionary of Modern Literature | Edited by | STANLEY J. KUNITZ | and | HOWARD HAYCRAFT | COMPLETE IN ONE VOLUME WITH | 1850 BIOGRAPHIES AND | 1700 PORTRAITS | [*device*] | NEW YORK | THE H. W. WILSON COMPANY | NINETEEN HUNDRED FORTY-TWO

vii, 1577 pp., 2 blank leaves, incl. illus. (ports.). 25·7 × 18 cm. Green cloth boards stamped in gold on spine; end-papers.

Published 1 December 1942 at $8.50; number of copies unknown. *On verso of title-leaf:* . . . Set up and published at the press of The H. W. Wilson Company November 1942 Printed in the United States of America

The entry under the name of Ezra Pound consists chiefly of his letter, dated from Rapallo, 12 May 1939, incorporating the *Introductory Text-Book* ([1939])— E2r—pp. 1121–2. An editorial note states that the letter has been printed exactly as requested by Pound.

B48   SAMUEL PUTNAM   1947
        PARIS WAS OUR MISTRESS

SAMUEL PUTNAM | PARIS, | Was Our Mistress | MEMOIRS OF A LOST | & FOUND GENERATION | [*quotation in five lines*] | New York | THE VIKING PRESS | 1947

viii, 264 pp. 22 × 14·9 cm. Tan cloth boards stamped in green on front cover and on spine; end-papers; top edges stained blue-green. White dust-jacket printed in green, red, and black.

B. BOOKS AND PAMPHLETS

Published 2 May 1947 at $3.00; number of copies unknown. *On verso of title-leaf:* ... First published ... in May 1947 ... Printed in U. S. A. by Vail-Ballou Press, Inc.

Contains excerpts from "After Election,"—C797, pp. 153–4, and "Fungus, Twilight, or Dry Rot"—C833, pp. 154–5, two articles contributed by Ezra Pound to the *New Review*, Paris (edited by Samuel Putnam), for January/February and August/September/October 1931, respectively, with a brief note from Pound to Samuel Putnam on his resignation as adviser to the *New Review*, p. 157, and nine lines from "Canto 80," pp. 159–60.

B49   SPEARHEAD   [1947]

[*In lower third, at right of line drawing of spearhead extending from bottom to top:*] SPEARHEAD | 10 YEARS' EXPERIMENTAL | WRITING IN AMERICA | A NEW DIRECTIONS BOOK [New York, James Laughlin]

604 pp., incl. 8 plates on 6 leaves. 23·2 × 15·8 cm. Beige cloth boards stamped in black down the spine; end-papers. White dust-jacket printed in grey, yellow, and black.

Published 10 November 1947 at $5.00; 4975 copies (of which 999 were distributed in England by the Falcon Press). *On verso of title-leaf:* ... Printed in the United States by Dudley Kimball at his press in Parsippany, New Jersey New Directions Books are Published by James Laughlin New York Office—500 Fifth Avenue

"[The purpose of this book] ... is to commemorate, and celebrate, the first ten years' activity of New Directions by reprinting some of the best work that was published in the annual volumes *New Directions in Prose & Poetry*, many of which are no longer in print ... [and] to present an impartial historical survey of the significant *experimental* and *advance guard* writing in the United States during the past decade." ("Editorial Notes," *signed:* J[ames]. L[aughlin]., *p.* 9)

Contains "Four Cantos [by] Ezra Pound" (Cantos XLV, XLIX, LI, and the last 34 lines of Canto LXXXI), pp. 474–9, a first appearance in book-form for only the last item. (None of these selections had been printed in *New Directions in Prose & Poetry*. The first three are reprinted from *The Fifth Decad of Cantos*, first published in the United States by Farrar and Rinehart in 1937—A43b—and reissued by New Directions in 1940—A43c. The complete Canto LXXXI was included in *The Pisan Cantos*, first published by New Directions in 1948—A60.)

B50   THE CASE OF EZRA POUND   1948
             BY CHARLES NORMAN

THE CASE OF | EZRA POUND | BY | CHARLES NORMAN | THE BODLEY PRESS | NEW YORK 1948

71 pp. 17·7 × 12·7 cm. Stiff blue paper wrappers printed in black on pages [i] and [iv] and on spine; end-papers.

Published 1 October 1948 at $1.50; number of copies unknown. *On verso of title-leaf:* . . . Manufactured in the United States of America by the Kedem Press

Sub-title on page [i] of wrappers: with opinions by Conrad Aiken E. E. Cummings F. O. Matthiessen William Carlos Williams Louis Zukofsky

"The article on Pound appeared in *PM*, Sunday, November 25, 1945 [C1704]. To bring it up to date, I have added the findings of the psychiatrists appointed by the District Court of the United States, the federal jury's verdict, and a section dealing with Pound's latest *Cantos*. . . . I have . . . to thank Mr. Louis Zukofsky for permission to use his statement, which reached me too late for publication in *PM* . . . and the British Library of Information, which placed the recordings and transcripts of Pound's broadcasts at my disposal." ("Foreword," pp. 12–13)

Contains brief excerpts from Ezra Pound's broadcasts over Rome Radio, 29 January, 3 February, 16, 23 April, 10, 26, 31 May, 28 June, 20, 22 July 1942, and 4 May 1943, pp. 38–42, 43.

B51 PATERSON (BOOK THREE) . . . [1949] WILLIAM CARLOS WILLIAMS

PATERSON | (BOOK THREE) | [*following four lines within a rectangular box of five concentric rules:*] A NEW | DIREC- | TIONS | BOOK | WILLIAM CARLOS | WILLIAMS [New York, James Laughlin]

2 blank leaves, 2 leaves, [52] pp., 2 blank leaves. 24 × 16 cm. Beige cloth boards stamped in blue across both covers and back, and lettered in gold on front cover; first and last blank leaves pasted down as front and back end-papers; fore and bottom edges untrimmed. Pale green dust-jacket printed in red.

Published 7 December 1949 at $3.00; 1000 copies printed. *On verso of title-leaf:* . . . Manufactured in the United States New Directions Books are published by James Laughlin New York Office: 333 6th Ave., N. Y. C. 14 *Colophon (page [52]):* Of this first edition of Paterson: Book III, one thousand copies have been printed for New Directions by the Van Vechten Press in Metuchen, New Jersey. The types used are Original English Caslon and Linotype Caslon Old Face, and the paper is Victorian Laid. The printing was completed in September, 1949.

An unsigned letter from Ezra Pound to William Carlos Williams, dated: 13 Oct [1948?], is incorporated, without indication of authorship, in section 3, on page [44].

Note: This book was first published in London by MacGibbon and Kee as part of *Paterson, Books I–V*, 13 August 1964 at 30s.

B. BOOKS AND PAMPHLETS

B52 THE POETRY OF EZRA POUND [1951]
HUGH KENNER

The Poetry | of Ezra Pound | [*ornamental rule*] | HUGH KENNER |
FABER AND FABER | 24 Russell Square | London

1 blank leaf, 4 leaves, 11–342 pp., 1 blank leaf. 22·5 × 14·7 cm. Orange cloth
boards stamped in blind on front cover and in gold on spine; end-papers. Grey
dust-jacket printed in green.

Published 13 July 1951 at 25s.; 1900 copies printed. *On verso of title-leaf:* First
published in mcmli . . . Printed in Great Britain by R. MacLehose and Company
Limited The University Press Glasgow . . .

Contains, as Appendix 1, "This Hulme Business," by Ezra Pound, pp. 307–9.
The article is reprinted from *Townsman*, London, for January 1939—C1494.

Note: New Directions purchased sheets for 2000 copies from Faber and Faber
and published this book in New York in August 1951 at $4.00. *On verso of title-
leaf:* Printed in Great Britain.

B53 CONFUCIUS. THE GREAT [1951]
DIGEST & UNWOBBLING PIVOT

a. *First edition:*

CONFUCIUS | THE GREAT DIGEST | & | UNWOBBLING PIVOT
| A NEW DIRECTIONS BOOK [New York, James Laughlin. *On
facing page:*] Stone Text from | rubbings supplied by | WILLIAM
HAWLEY | A Note on the | Stone Editions by | ACHILLES FANG |
TRANSLATION & COMMENTARY BY | EZRA POUND

1 blank leaf, 4 leaves, 11–187 pp., 1 leaf, 1 blank leaf, incl. facsims. 24·2 × 15·7
cm. Black cloth boards stamped in gold on both covers, and down the spine:
EZRA POUND CONFUCIUS; end-papers. White dust-jacket printed in yellow and
black.

Published 19 December 1951 at $3.50; 3000 sets of sheets printed (of which
350 were used for the English issue in 1952). *On verso of title-leaf:* Printer: Blue
Ridge Mountain Press of Parsippany, New Jersey . . . New Directions Books
are published by James Laughlin New York Office—333 Sixth Avenue

Dedication on page [8]*:* An edition for Walter de Rachewiltz

The text has reproductions of rubbings at left, translations and comments at
right. "The Stone-Classics title refers to the Nineteenth Roll of the book of
Ceremonies, and divides the Great Learning into 42 sections. Notes from E.P.'s
earlier edition are left where they were." (*Note*, p. 23)

Notes: For earlier edition (without the Chinese text) see *Confucius. The Unwob-*

B. BOOKS AND PAMPHLETS

bling Pivot & The Great Digest (1947)—A58. For Pound's Italian translation (with the Chinese text) see *Confucio. Studio integrale & L'asse che non vacilla* ([1955])—B55.

The English text was reprinted by offset along with the *Analects* and issued by New Directions in New York 15 October 1969 as *Confucius. The Great Digest. The Unwobbling Pivot. The Analects.* The first printing was of 4040 sheets, 1000 clothbound at $6.50 and 3040 paperbound at $2.45, all with the statement on verso of title-leaf: "First published as New Directions Paperbook 285 in 1969." The paperbound copies had pages 279–82 incorrectly printed as 279, 281, 280, 282. All save a few of these were corrected by the insertion of a four-page cancel. (For the clothbound copies the complete gathering containing the error was reprinted before the sheets were bound.)

b. *English issue* ([1952]):

CONFUCIUS | THE GREAT DIGEST | & | UNWOBBLING PIVOT | PETER OWEN LIMITED | London | [*facing page as in first issue*]

2 blank leaves, 4 leaves, 11–187 pp., 1 leaf, 2 blank leaves, incl. facsims. 23·9 × 15·5 cm. Black cloth boards lettered in yellow down the spine: CONFUCIUS EZRA POUND; first and last blank leaves pasted down as end-papers (following blank leaf at front and preceding blank leaf at end tipped in to serve as flyleaves). American dust-jacket over-printed on lower front flap: 25/ Published by Peter Owen Ltd. 50 Old Brompton Road London S W 7, England Printed in the United States

Published 20 February 1952 at 25s.; 350 sets of first-edition sheets imported and bound with cancel title-leaf (with title-page as above). *On verso of title-leaf:* . . . Printed in the U. S. A. MCMLII [Sheets for a second impression, with integral English title-leaf, were imported, bound, jacketed, and issued beginning March 1952. These have on verso of title-leaf: A Directions Book published by Peter Owen Limited 50 Old Brompton Road London SW7 Printed by Blue Ridge Mountain Press at Parsippany, New Jersey in the United States of America

B54   THE LITTLE REVIEW   1953
ANTHOLOGY

THE LITTLE REVIEW | ANTHOLOGY | Edited by MARGARET ANDERSON | HERMITAGE HOUSE, INC. | New York, 1953

383 pp. 21·7 × 15·1 cm. Grey-green paper boards stamped in black on front cover, with grey cloth back stamped in black on spine; end-papers; top edges stained green, fore edges untrimmed. White dust-jacket printed in green and black.

Published 19 January 1953 at $3.95; number of copies unknown. *On verso of title-leaf:* . . . Manufactured in the United States of America

Contains the following material by Ezra Pound, all reprinted from the *Little Review*, edited by Margaret Anderson and Jane Heap: "Editorial"—C254, pp. 99–102; "[Review of] Certain Noble Plays of Japan [and] Noh, or Accomplishment . . . "—C270, pp. 131–3; "The Reader Critic: Advice to a Young Poet . . ."—C310, pp. 135–6; "Summary" [part of "Editorial on Solicitous Doubt"—C289], pp. 145–6; "The Reader Critic: Letters from Ezra Pound"—C290, pp. 146–8; [excerpts from] "A Study in French Poets"—C327, pp. 164–75; "Co-operation (A Note on a Volume Completed)"—C372, pp. 185–6; "Marianne Moore and Mina Loy" [part of "A List of Books"—C336], pp. 188–9; "The Chinese Written Character as a Medium for Poetry (Abridged)"—C486, 491, 503, 514, pp. 190–206; "Poems" ["Homage à la Langue d'Oc"]—C354, pp. 206–11; "In Explanation"—C380, pp. 225–9; "Phanopoiea [*sic.* I–III.]"—C416, pp. 232–3; [excerpts from] "De Gourmont: A Distinction"—C438, pp. 255–8; "Breviora"—C406, pp. 269–72; "Hudson: Poet Strayed into Science"—C574, p. 295; "Brancusi"—C627, pp. 312–16; "From Ezra [from a letter]"—C744, p. 366.

B54a GISTS FROM AGASSIZ 1953

GISTS FROM AGASSIZ | OR, | PASSAGES ON THE INTELLI-GENCE | WORKING IN NATURE | [*quotation from* Dante (Par. i.1–3) *in four lines*] | selected by | JOHN KASPER | SQUARE DOLLAR SERIES | Kasper & Horton | New York | 1953

96 pp. 21·5 × 14 cm. Heavy grey paper wrappers printed in black on pages [i–iv], on flaps, and down the spine; stapled.

Published in 1953 at $1.00; number of copies unknown. *On verso of title-leaf:* . . . Printed in United States of America

Contains an anonymous three-paragraph blurb on page [ii] of the wrapper by Ezra Pound (manuscript at Yale). The first two paragraphs concern the Square Dollar Series; the final, one-sentence paragraph concerns Agassiz.

B54b THOMAS H. BENTON. BANK OF [1954]
THE UNITED STATES

THOMAS H. | BENTON | BANK OF THE UNITED STATES | SQUARE $ SERIES [Kasper & Horton, New York]

cover-title, 2 leaves, 73, [2] pp., incl. front. (port.) 21·5 × 14 cm. Grey paper wrappers printed in black on pages [i–iv], on flaps, and down the spine; stapled.

Published in 1954 at $1.00; number of copies unknown. *On verso of title-leaf:* . . . Printed in the United States of America

B. BOOKS AND PAMPHLETS

Title-page (recto of second leaf) reproduces title of Benton's *Thirty Years' View* (New York, London, D. Appleton and Company, 1854). Above that title appear the words: "This present volume is reprinted as a mark of respect | for the centennial of" and below is printed: "SQUARE DOLLAR SERIES | Kasper & Horton | New York | 1954 (The text is offset from pages 187–205 of Volume I of the 1854 edition of *Thirty Years' View*, with each of that book's two columns enlarged to occupy a full page, and with running-title as in the cover-title given above. Pages [74–75] have running-title at top but are otherwise blank.)

Contains an anonymous three-paragraph blurb on page [ii] of wrapper by Ezra Pound, the first two paragraphs (on the Square Dollar Series) reprinted from B54a, the final, one-sentence paragraph (on Benton) printed here for the first time.

B54x   WYNDHAM LEWIS   [1954]
                        BY HUGH KENNER

a. *First issue:*

[*Device (hand holding pen), at left of first two lines*] Wyndham Lewis | BY HUGH KENNER | THE MAKERS OF MODERN LITERATURE | New Directions Books–Norfolk, Connecticut [James Laughlin]

1 blank leaf, xv, 169 pp., 2 blank leaves. front. (port.) 18·2 × 12·8 cm. Olive paper boards lettered in brown down the spine.

Published 23 August 1954 at $2.50; 4000 sets of sheets printed, of which 2000 were hardbound in 1954 and the remaining sheets, making 1924 copies, were used for the second issue in 1964. *On verso of title-leaf:* . . . New Directions Books are published by James Laughlin . . . Manufactured in the United States of America by the Vail-Ballou Press, Inc., Binghamton, N. Y.

Contains, p. xiii, a one-sentence statement by Ezra Pound about Wyndham Lewis. (It was written, about 1951, as an "introduction" for a proposed but never published chrestomathy, "A Book of Wyndham Lewis," to be edited by Kenner.)

Note: This book was published in London, 11 November 1954, by Methuen at 12s.6d.

b. *Second issue* ([1964]):

Title-page and pagination as in first issue. 17·8 × 11·6 cm. Heavy white paper wrappers printed in black on pages [i] and [iv], and on spine. Issued without frontispiece.

Published 6 April 1964 as New Directions Paperbook ND167 at $1.75; the remaining first-issue sheets paperbound to make 1924 copies. Verso of title-leaf as in first issue.

Contents as in first issue.

B55   CONFUCIO   [1955]
STUDIO INTEGRALE
& L'ASSE CHE NON VACILLA

First edition:

CONFUCIO | STUDIO INTEGRALE | & | L'ASSE CHE NON VA-
CILLA | Versione e commento di | EZRA POUND | con una nota
sui classici in pietra | di Achilles Fang | [*device*] | ALL'INSEGNA
DEL PESCE D'ORO [Vanni Schewiller] | MILANO

1 blank leaf, 195, [1] pp., 1 leaf, 1 blank leaf, incl. front., facsims. 18·3 × 12·7
cm. Cream paper wrappers, printed in black on pages [i] and [iv] and up the
spine, folded over stiff white blanks.

Published February 1955 at L. 150 in the series "Scritti Italiani di Ezra Pound";
1000 copies printed. *Colophon* (*page* [198]): Questa edizione curata da Vanni
Scheiwiller è stata impressa dalla Stamperia Valdonega di Verona in mille esemplari numerati da I a 1000 · l'8 Febbraio MCMLV Esemplare [*number written in on
a row of dots*]

Contents: Una nota sui classici in pietra di Achilles Fang [translated by Mary de
Rachewiltz]—Ta Hsio, Studio integrale. Versione italiana di Ezra Pound e Al-
berto Luchini, revisionata ed aggiornata—Chung Yung. L'asse che non vacilla,
Il secondo dei libri Confuciani. Versione italiana, revisionata ed aggiornata di
Ezra Pound—Nota personale—Appunto bibliografico: Studi e traduzioni di E. P.
dal cinese e giapponese—Nota del editore

This edition contains "Nota personale," pp. 191–2, by Ezra Pound, not included
in the edition in English—B53. (A new impression of 2000 numbered copies
was issued by the same publisher in Milan in February 1960 as Number 2 in
his "Serie Ideografica, a cura di Ezra Pound.")

Notes: "Studio integrale" is a revised version of the translation of "The Great
Digest" first published with the Chinese text as *Confucio. Ta S'eu. Dai Gaku.
Studio integrale* (1942)—B46—and reprinted separately as *Testamento di Confucio*
(1944)—A54. "L'asse che non vacilla" is a revised version of the translation of
"The Unwobbling Pivot" first published as *Ciung Iung. L'asse che non vacilla*
(1945)—A57.

B56   LA MARTINELLI   1956

LA MARTINELLI | Introduction | by | EZRA POUND | MILAN
[Vanni Scheiwiller]–MCMLVI

11, [1] pp., 12 leaves, incl. col. front., 10 col. plates. 9·9 × 7·2 cm. Stiff white
paper wrappers printed in black on page [i] and up the spine. White dust-jacket
printed in black and with coloured reproduction of one of the plates.

Published February 1956 at L. 600; 500 copies printed. *Colophon* (*recto of final*

B. BOOKS AND PAMPHLETS

leaf): This booklet limited to 500 numbered copies has been edited by Vanni Scheiwiller in february 1956. Copy N. [*number stamped in*] Color photography: Gordonprint–Washington. Color engraving: Fotoincisione Artigiana–Milano. Printing: Officine Grafiche "Esperia"–Milano. Printed in Italy

Contains introduction by Ezra Pound, pp. 5–[12]. The plates are colour photographs of the work of the American artist Sheri Martinelli, including (as the ninth plate) a portrait of Pound.

B56a   ALEXANDER DEL MAR   [1956]
            ROMAN AND MOSLEM MONEYS

Alexander | DEL MAR | ROMAN AND MOSLEM | MONEYS | Square Dollar Series | P. O. Box 6964 | Washington 20, D. C.

102, [4] pp. 21 × 14 cm. Grey paper wrappers printed in black on pages [i–iv], both flaps, and down the spine; stapled.

Published Spring? 1956 at $1.00 as "Square Dollar Series, 6"; number of copies unknown.

An offset reproduction of "Chapter V. Rome," "Chapter VI. The Sacred Character of Gold," and "Chapter IX. Moslem Moneys," pp. [60]–132 and [163]–184 from Del Mar's *History of Monetary Systems* ... (London, Effingham Wilson, 1895), with chapters renumbered I–III and paged 3–[103]. On pages [104–6] is reprinted Norman Holmes Pearson's review-article, "Square $ Series [1–5]," from *Shenandoah*, Lexington, Va., for Autumn 1955.

The wrappers contain, on page [ii], "Our Common Heritage" (chiefly on Blackstone), signed: "John Vignon" [*i.e.* Ezra Pound], reprinted from *New Times*, Melbourne, for 11 Feb. 1956—C1806a; and, on page [iii], Pound's "Note," reprinted from his translation of Confucius. *The Great Digest*, followed by: the third paragraph of his comment on Louis Agassiz, reprinted from B54a; his note on Del Mar, printed as "An Observation" in *Strike*, Washington, D. C., for Aug. 1955—C1760; and the final (one-sentence) paragraph from his note on Thomas H. Benton, reprinted from B54b.

B57   RICCARDO DA S. VITTORE   1956
            PENSIERI SULL'AMORE

First edition:

RICCARDO DA S. VITTORE | PENSIERI | SULL'AMORE | MILANO [Vanni Scheiwiller] · MCMLVI

1 blank leaf, 40, [1] pp., 1 leaf, 1 blank leaf. 7·1 × 5·4 cm. White paper wrappers, printed in brown and black on page [i] and in black on front flap and up the spine, folded over stiff white blanks.

B. BOOKS AND PAMPHLETS

Fly-title: Richardi excerpta accurante Ezra Pound

Published November 1956 at L. 200; 500 copies printed. *Colophon* (*page* [43]): "all'insegna della Baita van Gogh" Di questo volumetto a cura di Vanni Scheiwiller furono impresse dalla Stamperia Valdonega di Verona cinquecento copie numerate 30 ottobre 1956 Copia N. [*number stamped in*]

Twenty-one brief excerpts in Latin, selected by Ezra Pound and printed one to a page, pp. 7–27; "Richardi . . . vita": pp. 29–30; "Note dell'editore": pp. 31–34; "Richardi . . . opera": pp. 35–[41]. (Fourteen of the Latin excerpts, slightly revised or condensed, are reprinted with English translations in *Richard of Saint Victor: Benjamin Minor* (1960)—B68—pp. 10–11.)

B58   DE MORIBUS   1956
                BRACHMANORUM

First edition:

DE MORIBUS | BRACHMANORUM | LIBER | SANCTO AMBROSIO | FALSO ADSCRIPTUS | APO EDITIONS | Vanni Scheiwiller, Via Melzi d'Eril 6, Milano | MCMLVI

2 blank leaves, 2 leaves, 32 pp., 3 leaves, 1 blank leaf. 18·2 × 12·8 cm. Grey-green paper wrappers, printed in black on page [i] and up the spine, folded over stiff white blanks.

Published December 1956 at L. 400 as "APO Editions, [1]"; 500 copies printed. *Colophon* (*recto of third leaf following page* 32): Libellus hic compositus typisque excusus est, accurante Vanni Scheiwiller, in Officina Typographica Valdonega Veronae, die XXX mensis Novembris A. D. MCMLVI * Excusa sunt quingenti exemplaria numerata Exemplar N. [*number stamped in*]

Edited anonymously by Ezra Pound. (The publisher had planned a series of texts edited "A PO[UND].")

Note: The treatise "De moribus Brachmanorum," erroneously attributed to St Ambrose, Bishop of Milan, is a free translation of the "De gentibus Indiæ et Bragmanibus" of Palladius, successively bishop of Helenopolis and of Aspona, who died *circa* A.D. 430.

B59   DR. JOSEPH BARD . . .   1957
            EL DINAMISMO DE
            UNA NUEVA POESÍA

Dr. JOSEPH BARD, F. R. S. L. | El Dinamismo | de una nueva Poesía | INSTITUTO DE ESTUDIOS HISPANICOS | PUERTO DE LA CRUZ.—TENERIFE (CANARIAS) | –1.957–

23, [1] pp., 2 leaves, incl. 3 facsims. 21·1 × 15·3 cm. Heavy white paper wrappers printed in red and black on page [i]; wire-stitched.

Published March 1957; number of copies unknown. *On verso of title-leaf:* Joseph Bard, Editor.—Gráficas Orotava ... *Colophon (page* [24])*:* Se terminó de imprimir en La Orotava (Tenerife), el día veintitrés de marzo de mil novecientos cincuenta y siete.

"Conferencia pronunciada el día 8 de marzo de 1.957, en el Salón de Actos dei Instituto de Estudios Hispánicos del Puerto de la Cruz. (Tenerife)." (*Note, p.* [6])

"Carta de Ezra Pound a Joseph Bard.," a typewritten letter dated: Rapallo, 17 December 1932 is reproduced with printed caption on three pages following page [24]. (The reproductions are printed so that the first page is followed by the third and then the second.) Parts of three other letters from Pound to Bard are printed in Spanish translation on pages 15 and 16, the first without date (but written in December 1931), the second dated: 24 December 1931, and the third: 6 January 1932.

B60   RIMBAUD   1957

First edition:

[*In red:*] RIMBAUD | by | EZRA POUND | [*in black: device*] | ALL'INSEGNA DEL PESCE D'ORO [Vanni Scheiwiller] | MI- LANO·MCMLVII

1 blank leaf, 17 pp., 2 leaves, incl. front., illus. 18·1 × 12·5 cm. Cream paper wrappers printed in black and red on page [i], folded over stiff white blanks; sewn.

Half-title: Five French Poems

Published April 1957 at L. 400; 500 copies printed. *Colophon (recto of second leaf following page* 17)*:* This booklet edited by Vanni Scheiwiller has been printed by Stamperia Valdonega, Verona in 500 numbered copies. 9 April 1957 Copy N. [*number stamped in*]

The French text and the English translation are printed on opposite pages.

"The '*Study of French Poets*' appeared in the *Little Review* nearly 40 years ago. The student hoped that the selection would stimulate thought and that possibly one or two of the thousands of aspirants for literary glory would take up the matter. As no adequate translations have yet appeared, he now takes pity on those who haven't had time to learn French but might like to know what the French authors were writing about, and herewith *starts to provide a guide* to the meaning of the poems then given in the original only." (*Note, signed:* E. P., *p.* 5)

Contents: [Note signed: E. P.]—[Rimbaud] Comédie en trois baisers: Comedy in Three Caresses—Au cabaret-vert: Cabaret Vert—Vénus Anadyomène: Ana-

B. BOOKS AND PAMPHLETS

dyomene—Laurent Tailhade (1854–1919). Rus: Laurent Tailhade. Rus—[Rimbaud] Les chercheuses de poux: Lice-Hunters

Note: The English translation (only) of "Comedy in Three Caresses" was reprinted in *The Guinness Book of Poetry 1959/60* (London, [1961]), pp. 100–1.

B61   LATIN POETRY   [1957]
IN VERSE TRANSLATION

a. *Hardbound copies:*

LATIN POETRY | IN VERSE TRANSLATION | From the Beginnings to the Renaissance | EDITED BY | L. R. Lind | UNIVERSITY OF KANSAS | [*rule*] | HOUGHTON MIFFLIN COMPANY | BOSTON·The Riverside Press Cambridge

xxxix, 438 pp., 1 blank leaf. 21·6 × 13·6 cm. Blue cloth boards lettered in gold on front cover and on spine; end-papers.

Published 18 September 1957 at $3.25; number of copies unknown. *On verso of title-leaf:* ... The Riverside Press Cambridge, Massachusetts Printed in the U. S. A. ...

The section devoted to Catullus contains as poem No. 26 an otherwise untitled four-line translation by Ezra Pound, p. 35. This version was printed as "Catullus" in *Edge*, Melbourne, for May 1957—C1838—and as "The Draughty House (Catullus)" in the *European*, London, for January 1959—C1867. It was printed also in *Papillon: Quattuor epigrammata, 30 Ottobre 1957* ([1957])—E2v—p. [4]. An earlier version appeared as "The Draughty House" in *Furioso*, New Haven, Ct., for New Year 1940—C1528.

b. *Paperbound copies:*

Title-page as in hardbound copies.

xxxix, 438 pp., 1 leaf. 20·9 × 13·3 cm. Stiff white paper wrappers printed in red on pages [i] and [iv], and on spine.

Published 18 September 1957 at $1.45 as "Riverside Editions, C20"; number of copies unknown. Verso of title-leaf as in hardbound copies. (A list of the series appears on verso of final leaf.)

B61x   I WANTED TO WRITE A POEM   [1958]
WILLIAM CARLOS WILLIAMS

[*In red:*] I Wanted to Write a Poem | [*in black:*] William Carlos Williams | [*in red:*] The Autobiography of the Works of a Poet |

B. BOOKS AND PAMPHLETS

[*in black:*] Reported and Edited by Edith Heal | Beacon Press Beacon Hill Boston

ix pp., 1 leaf, 99 pp. 23·5 × 15·5 cm. Brown cloth boards printed in white down the spine; end-papers. White dust-jacket printed in black and red.

Published 9 April 1958 at $3.95; 3543 copies printed. *On verso of title-leaf:* ... Printed in United States of America

Contains "Introductory Note [to six of the poems from Williams's *The Tempers* (1913), as printed in the *Poetry Review* for October 1912—C54] by Ezra Pound," pp. 12–13.

Note: This book was issued in September 1967 by the same publisher at $1.95 at its Beacon Paperback 261. An English edition was published in London, also in 1967, by Jonathan Cape, clothbound at 18s., and paperbound at 7s. 6d.

B61y   FREDERIC A. BIRMINGHAM   [1958]
           THE WRITER'S CRAFT

Frederic A. Birmingham | The Writer's Craft | [*quotation in two lines*] | HAWTHORN BOOKS, INC. | PUBLISHERS, NEW YORK

351, [1] pp. 23·3 × 15·8 cm. Grey paper boards with brown cloth back stamped in silver on spine. White dust-jacket printed in black and red.

Published 25 April 1958 at $4.95; number of copies unknown. *On verso of title-leaf:* ... First Edition, April 1958

Contains, in Chapter 3, "To Be or Not To Be: A Writer," the first sixteen paragraphs, omitting the eighth, of "Hickory [*i.e.* Andrew Jackson]—Old and New," by Ezra Pound, reprinted from *Esquire* for June 1935—C1206—pp. 70–72.

Note: This book was published in London in 1959 by Arthur Barker Limited at 21s.

B62   PATERSON (BOOK FIVE) ...   [1958]
           WILLIAM CARLOS WILLIAMS

PATERSON | (BOOK FIVE) | [*following four lines within a rectangular box of five concentric rules:*] A NEW | DIREC- | TIONS | BOOK | WILLIAM CARLOS | WILLIAMS [New York James Laughlin]

1 blank leaf, 4 leaves, [33] pp., 2 blank leaves. 24 × 16·3 cm. Beige cloth boards stamped in orange across both covers and back, and lettered in gold (53 copies with "genuine gold stamping," according to the publisher) on front cover and

down the spine; end-papers; fore edges untrimmed. Cream dust-jacket printed in red and black.

Published 17 September 1958 at $3.00; 3000 copies printed. *On verso of title-leaf:* . . . Manufactured in the United States . . . New Directions Books are published by James Laughlin New York Office: 333 Sixth Avenue, New York 14

An unsigned letter from Ezra Pound to William Carlos Williams, dated: 13 N[o]v [1956], is incorporated, without indication of authorship, in section 2, on page [12]. The letter is printed complete save for the deletion of two personal names.

Note: This book was first published in London by MacGibbon and Kee as part of *Paterson, Books I–V* on 13 August 1964 at 30s.

B63   THE ARMCHAIR ESQUIRE   [1958]

THE ARMCHAIR | Esquire | Edited by ARNOLD GIN- GRICH | and L. RUST HILLS | INTRODUCTION BY Granville Hicks | [*device*] | G. P. PUTNAM'S SONS New York

354, 24 pp., 3 blank leaves. 22 × 15 cm. Black cloth boards stamped in red and silver on front cover and on spine; end-papers. White dust-jacket printed in red, silver, and black.

Published 6 October 1958 at $3.95; number of copies unknown. *On verso of title-leaf:* . . . Manufactured in the United States of America . . .

Contains "Reflexshuns on Iggurunce," by Ezra Pound, pp. 48–53, reprinted from *Esquire*, Chicago, for January 1935—C1131. An appendix, "A Check-List of Contributions of Literary Import to *Esquire*, 1933–1958," 24 pp., compiled by E. R. Hagemann and James E. Marsh, and listing on page 19 Pound's contributions to the periodical, follows page 354.

Note: This book was published in London in 1959 by Heinemann at 18s. (Early copies were bound in blue cloth boards; later copies, being remaindered in 1963, were bound in blue paper boards.) An edition was published in New York paperbound in October 1960 by Popular Library at 75¢. (In this edition the appendix is omitted.)

B64   . . . A LUME SPENTO 1908–1958   [1958]

First edition:

EZRA POUND | A Lume Spento | 1908–1958 | a cura di Vanni Scheiwiller | [*device*] | ALL'INSEGNA DEL PESCE D'ORO [Vanni Scheiwiller] | MILANO

B. BOOKS AND PAMPHLETS

1 blank leaf, 63 pp., 1 leaf, 1 blank leaf, incl. front., illus., ports, facsims. 10 × 7·4 cm. Stiff grey paper wrappers printed in black on page [i] and up the spine. Grey-green dust-jacket printed in black. (The first blank leaf and pages [3]–12 are of grey paper uncoated; the rest of the book is printed on coated paper. The illustrations, portraits, and facsimiles are numbered in sequence from I to XXX.)

Published November 1958 at L. 500 as "Serie Illustrata, N. 64"; 2000 copies printed. *On verso of title-leaf:* . . . Printed in Italy *Colophon (page* [64]): . . . Questo volumetto a cura di Vanni Scheiwiller è stato stampato dalle Off. Grafiche "Esperia" di Milano in duemila copie numerate de 1 a 2000, per ricordare il cinquantenario del primo libro di Ezra Pound, in occasione della mostra delle edizioni poundiane promossa dall'Azienda Autonoma di Soggiorno e Cura di Merano il 30 ottobre 1958 Copia N. [*number stamped in*]

Contents: A Lume Spento 1908: Piccola Antologia: [for poems translated see D71]—Documenti: [reproductions of pages [2], 3–4, 9–11, 16, 30, 42, 60–61 of *A Lume Spento* ([1908])—A1; title-page of *A Quinzaine for This Yule* ([1908])—A2; manuscript of "Venetian Night Litany" ["Night Litany"], pp. [30], [32], [34], with translation by Mary de Rachewiltz on pages 31, 33, 35; manuscript of "Statement of Being," p. [36], with English transcription marked: "(inedito, 1907)," and translation by Carlo Izzo, p. 37; manuscript of "For Italico Brass," pp. [38], [40], [42], with English transcription marked: "(inedito, 1907)," pp. 39, 41, 43; page 27 of *A Quinzaine for This Yule*; part of page 59 of *Personae* (1909)—A3; selections from "Canto LXXVI (1948)," translated by Mary de Rachewiltz, pp. 51, 53, 55; with various photographs chiefly of the San Trovaso section of Venice]—Edizioni—Bibliografia—Opere di E. P. Pubblicate in Italia—Indice dei Documenti—Indice delle Poesie

Note: "Statement of Being," p. 37, and "For Italico Brass," pp. 39, 41, 43, both written in 1907, are here printed for the first time, with reproductions of the original manuscripts of these two poems and of "Venetian Night Litany," first published, with title "Night Litany," in *A Quinzaine for This Yule* ([1908])—A2— pp. 8–9.

B65   . . . CANTO 98   [1958]

First edition:

EZRA POUND | CANTO 98 | tradotto da Mary de Rachewiltz | [*device*] | ALL'INSEGNA DEL PESCE D'ORO [Vanni Scheiwiller] | MILANO

1 blank leaf, 2 leaves, 7–30 pp., 1 leaf, incl. front. 12 × 9 cm. Plain stiff grey paper wrappers. Pale blue dust-jacket printed in brown.

Published November 1958 at L. 500 in the publisher's "Serie Letteraria"; 1000 copies printed. *On verso of title-leaf:* . . . Printed in Italy *Colophon (page* [31]): . . . Questo volumetto a cura di Vanni Scheiwiller è stato impresso dalle Officine

B. BOOKS AND PAMPHLETS

Grafiche Aldo Garzanti di Milano in mille copie numerate da I a 1000 l'8 novembre 1958 Copia N. [*number written in*]

"Il *Canto 98* di Ezra Pound è stato pubblicato in esclusiva mondiale (Exclusive Serial Rights per il testo inglese e la traduzione) da *L'Illustrazione Italiana*, Anno 85, n. 9, Milano, settembre 1958 [—C1863 & D158]. . . .

"Il disegno a lato del frontespizio è della giovane pittrice americana Sheri Martinelli, che dopo sei anni d'abbozzi, sempre scontenta dei risultati, produce il primo disegno che l'accontenta, illustrando un verso dei *Cantos* 'the sea's claw' 'the stone eyes look seaward' 'my undine'." ("Nota dell' editore," p. 27)

Contains "Servizio di comunicazioni," in Italian, signed: "Ezra Pound, Brunnenburg, 22 luglio 1958.," pp. 7–9.

B66   1889 [PER I 70 ANNI DI   1959
             GIOVANNI SCHEIWILLER]

1889 [Per i 70 anni di Giovanni Scheiwiller] | MILANO–[Vanni Scheiwiller] 8 NOVEMBRE 1959

1 blank leaf, 2 leaves, [7]–78 pp., 1 leaf, incl. 2 illus. (front., facsim.) 18·3 × 12·6 cm. Tan paper wrappers, printed in black with drawing by Giuseppe Viviani on darker tan background on page [i], and in black on spine, folded over stiff white blanks.

Half-title: Per i 70 anni di Giovanni Scheiwiller

Distributed gratis beginning 8 November 1959; 300 copies printed. *Colophon* (*page* [79]): Questa edizione fuori commercio curata da Mia Silvano e Vanni Scheiwiller è stata impressa dalla Tipografia U. Allegretti di Campi in Milano in 300 copie numerate da I a 300 per festeggiare, l'8 Novembre 1959, i 70 anni di Giovanni Scheiwiller. Copia n. . . . [*number printed in*]

Contains "Baijo's Poem in the Koshigen," by Ezra Pound, p. 58. This is edited from the unpublished manuscript notes of Ernest Fenollosa, and was printed simultaneously, with a note by Pound, in Italian translation, in Mary de Rachewiltz's translation of *Cathay: Catai* (1959)—D76—p. 43, with note p. 45.

B67   MY LIFETIME IN LETTERS   [1960]
             UPTON SINCLAIR

MY LIFETIME | IN LETTERS | Upton Sinclair | UNIVERSITY OF MISSOURI PRESS | COLUMBIA

1 blank leaf, 2 leaves, vii–xxi pp., 1 leaf, 412 pp. front. (port.) 23·5 × 16 cm. Blue cloth boards stamped in gold on front cover and on spine; end-papers; top edges stained blue. White dust-jacket printed in black and blue.

B. BOOKS AND PAMPHLETS

Published 8 February 1960 at $6.50; 4000 sets of sheets printed (of which only 2000 were bound up in 1960), the rest destroyed. *On verso of title-leaf:* . . . Printed and bound in the United States of America by Von Hoffmann Press, Inc.

Contains five letters, dating from 10 September 1934 to 26 September 1936, and two postcards from Ezra Pound to Upton Sinclair, with comments by Sinclair, pp. 368–76. An expurgated and much shortened form of the letter of 30 January 1935 (pp. 372–4) is printed in *Impact* (1960)—A78—pp. 271–2.

B68   RICHARD OF SAINT VICTOR   1960
BENJAMIN MINOR

Richard of Saint Victor | BENJAMIN MINOR | Translated from Latin | by S. V. Yankowski | [*ornament*] | [*thick rule*] | Ansbach [Privately published by Elisabeth Kottmeier and E. G. Kostetzky] 1960

97, [1] pp., 1 leaf. 1 mounted illus., facsim. 20·9 × 14·9 cm. White paper wrappers, printed in grey and black on pages [i] and [iv] and up the spine, folded over and pasted to stiff white blanks.

Published September 1960 at $1.00; 400 copies printed. *Imprint on page* [2]: . . . Printed in Western Germany Gesamtherstellung: Wiedfeld & Mehl, Ansbach [50 special copies, published, simultaneously with the ordinary copies, at $1.50, have imprint on title-page in Ukrainian characters: Ansbach, Editions on the Mountain, 1960. The collation, size, binding, and contents (except for special note on page [2]) are identical.]

Contains 14 brief "Quotations from Richard's works Selected and translated by Ezra Pound," pp. 10–11. These are selected from the 21 Latin quotations printed in *Riccardo da S. Vittore: Pensieri sull'amore* (1956)—B57—pp. 7–27, but several have been slightly revised or condensed. Additional "Quotations from Richard's works Selected and translated by St. V. Yankowski" are printed on page [99].

B69   EZRA POUND   1960
BY CHARLES NORMAN

EZRA POUND | by | CHARLES NORMAN | THE MACMILLAN COMPANY | New York 1960

xvi pp., 1 leaf, 493 pp. front. (port.), 4 plates, facsims. 21·5 × 14·5 cm. Brown cloth boards stamped in gold on front cover and in dark brown and gold on

B. BOOKS AND PAMPHLETS

spine; end-papers. White dust-jacket printed in brown and orange, with photograph of Ezra Pound by Alvin Langdon Coburn on front.

Published 31 October 1960 at $6.95; 7567 copies printed. *On verso of title-leaf:* ... First Printing ... Printed in the United States of America ...

The frontispiece is a reproduction of a photograph of Ezra Pound by Alvin Langdon Coburn.

Contains the following material by Ezra Pound here first printed in book-form: "Belangal Alba" [1905 version]—C1, p. 12: first two stanzas of "The Mourn of Life"—C677, p. 15; excerpts from "Burgos: A Dream City of Old Castile"— C4, pp. 17–18; "[Dawn Song]"—C5, p. 21; letter to the *New York Herald*, Paris— C8, p. 28; synopses of Polytechnic lectures—E1b, c—pp. 31–32, 34; excerpts from "What I Feel about Walt Whitman"—C1744, p. 33; excerpts from letters to Charles Norman, pp. 224, 464–5; "Memorandum of Agreement" with H. B. Liveright, p. 253; letter to J. H. Rogers, p. 320; paragraph from Ezra Pound's address at Hamilton College in 1939 after receiving his honorary degree, p. 370; excerpts from "European Paideuma," pp. 372–3, with sentences from a letter to Douglas Fox, pp. 373–4; letter to Mrs Lulu Cunningham—C1814, pp. 375–6; excerpt from a letter to Carlo Linati, p. 377; excerpts from the Italian broadcasts—those in B50, including eight additional paragraphs from that of 23 April 1942 ["MacLeish"], pp. 385, 391–5; letter to Francis Biddle, U. S. Attorney General, 4 Aug. 1943, pp. 389–90; excerpts from letters to Julien Cornell, p. 431; quotation from *Edge* handout, p. 439; brief excerpts from letters to Marianne Moore, p. 440, Louis Zukofsky, pp. 445–6, and Carl Dolmetsch, pp. 463–4.

B70   LEO FROBENIUS   [1961]
              IL LIUTO DI GASSIRE

a. *First edition:*

LEO FROBENIUS | IL LIUTO | DI GASSIRE | Leggenda africana con una nota | di | EZRA POUND | [*device*] | ALL'INSEGNA DEL PESCE D'ORO [Vanni Scheiwiller] | MILANO

39, [1] pp. 10 × 6 cm. White paper wrappers, printed in red and blue on pages [i] and [iv], and in black on both flaps and up the spine, folded over and pasted to stiff white blanks. White paper wrap-around printed in black.

Published April 1961 at L. 300 as "Serie Oltremare a cura di Giacomo Prampolini N. 15"; 3000 copies printed. *On verso of title-leaf:* Traduzione dal tedesco di Siegfried Walter de Rachewiltz ... Printed in Italy *Colophon (page* [40]): ... Questo volumetto a cura di Vanni Scheiwiller è stato impresso dalla Stamperia Valdonega di Verona l'8 aprile 1961

Contains "Significato di Leo Frobenius," by Ezra Pound, pp. 5–15. "*Significato di Leo Frobenius* è la ristampa dello scritto di Ezra Pound apparso sul 'Broletto,'

B. BOOKS AND PAMPHLETS

n. 28, Como, aprile 1938 [—C1446], con l'esclusione della nota finale e di una frase da me ritenuta sorpassata." ("N[ota]. d[ell']. E[ditore].," p. 39)

b. *De luxe edition* (1976):

IL LIUTO DI GASSIRE | leggenda africana di | LEO FROBENIUS | con due scritti di | EZRA POUND | illustrata da incisioni di | FRANCA GHITTI | EDIZIONI DI VANNI SCHEIWILLER | MI-LANO—MCMLXXVI

2 leaves, 9–33 pp., 2 leaves, 7 plates, 1 blank leaf, 1 leaf, 1 blank leaf. Unbound sheets, 35 × 25 cm., issued in green paper wrappers, 37·5 × 26·5 cm., folded over heavy white paper, printed in black on page [i]. Issued in wooden box, 41 × 30 cm., with leather hinges, and clasp fastening over wooden peg, with title burned on lid.

Published 15 December 1976; 55 copies printed. *On verso of title-leaf:* ... Printed in Italy *Colophon* (*page* [35]): Questa edizione a cura di Vanni Scheiwiller e Franco Maestrini è stata stampata in quaranta esemplari numerati da 1 a 40 più quindici esemplari fuori commercio: dieci numerati in numeri romani da I a X e cinque contrassegnati dalle vocali A E I O U. Le incisioni originali e firmate di Franca Ghitti sono state tirate a Milano sul torchio di Giorgio Upiglio il 30 novembre 1976 Esemplare N. [*number or letter written in in pencil*]

Contents: Significato di Leo Frobenius [by Ezra Pound, in Italian]—A Note on Leo Frobenius [by Pound, in English]—Gassires Laute [by Frobenius, in German]—Il liuto di Gassire [by Frobenius, translated into Italian by S. W. de Rachewiltz]—Nota dell'Editore: Pound & Frobenius [*signed:* V[*anni*]. S[*cheiwiller*].]

Note: Proofs of the portfolio were exhibited at Brunnenburg, 10 July 1976, on the occasion of the opening of the Agricultural Museum there (see colophon on recto of final leaf). The publication of the book on 15 December 1976 was commemorated at the Galleria dei Bibliofili, Milan. For that occasion a brochure was prepared, consisting of sheets for pages [13]–24 and one of the plates, laid into a green-paper folder, 35 × 25 cm., with white paper label on page [i] printed in brown: *Galleria dei Bibliofili . . . Roberto Sanesi e Vanni Scheiwiller presentano Il Liuto di Gassire . . . Invito.* (Milano, Galleria dei Bibliofili, 15 December 1976.)

B71   LUIGI SERRAVALLI   [1961]
                   NOSTRO ESILIO

LUIGI SERRAVALLI | Nostro esilio | (con una lettera di Ezra Pound) | REBELLATO EDITORE PADOVA

45 pp., 1 leaf, incl. facsim. 17·1 × 11·7 cm. Stiff black paper wrappers, printed in grey on pages [i] and [iv], on both flaps, and up the spine, folded over stiff white blanks.

B. BOOKS AND PAMPHLETS

Published Spring 1961 at L.700 in the series "Collana Zecchini d'Oro"; 500 copies printed. *On page* [2]: . . . I Edizione: 1961 Stampato in Italia–Printed in Italy Ed. "Biblioteca del Castello" Cittadella di Padova *Colophon* (*page* [48]): Questo volume "Nostro esilio" . . . è stato impresso su carta uso mano con caratteri Aster nelle Officine Grafiche S. T. A. di Vicenza a cura di Bino Rebellato Editore in Padova

Contains a letter in Italian (of commendation on the poems) from Ezra Pound to Luigi Serravalli, reproduced in facsimile of the autograph manuscript on page [5], with printed transcription below, dated: Roma, 13 Aprile 1961.

B72   THIS DIFFICULT INDIVIDUAL,   1961
EZRA POUND. BY EUSTACE MULLINS

This Difficult Individual, | Ezra Pound | By EUSTACE MUL-LINS | [*quotation in seven lines*] | FLEET PUBLISHING CORPORA-TION | 230 PARK AVENUE · NEW YORK 17, N. Y.

6 pp., 2 leaves, 13–388 pp., 1 blank leaf, incl. plates (ports.) 20·8 × 14·8 cm. Grey cloth boards stamped in black down the spine; end-papers. White dust-jacket printed in yellow and black, with photograph of Ezra Pound by the author on front.

Published 18 September 1961 at $5.00; number of copies unknown. *On verso of title-leaf:* . . . Printed in the United States of America . . .

Contains the following material by Ezra Pound here first printed in book-form: letters to Eustace Mullins, pp. 98–99, 133, 169, 169–70, 250, 318, 320, 321, 325, 326–8; editorials in *Exile*, pp. 163–6, 170–1; extensive excerpts from Rome radio broadcasts, 7 Dec. 1941, 29 Jan., 3 and 19 Feb., 8, 19, and 30 Mar., 9, 13, 20, 26, and 30 Apr. 1942, pp. 205–15; 18 and 31 May, 4 and 8 June 1942, pp. 217–19; 25 June, 6, 13, and 26 July 1942, 25, 26, 28, and 30 Mar., 4, 18, 20, and 27 Apr., 2, 4, 8, and 23 May, 5, 12, 19, 22, and 26 June, 4, 6, and 17 July 1943, pp. 220–33; note in *Four Pages*, Galveston, Texas, for Sept. 1950, p. 311; contribution to *Strike*, Washington, D.C., for Nov. 1955—C1778—p. 317 (other contributions to *Strike*, quoted on pp. 315, 316, and 336, as by Pound, are not by him, according to the editor of that periodical); excerpt from letter to H. R[*i.e.* M]. Meacham, p. 356.

Note: In connexion with the publication of the book, the publishers issued a window-card for distribution to booksellers, reproducing Ezra Pound's letter to Eustace Mullins, dated: 6 Ap[ril 19]59. This card measures 61 × 31 cm., is printed in black, and is titled: *Letter from Ezra Pound (April 6, 1959. Rapallo) To Eustace Mullins, Reprinted on P. 98–99 of This Difficult Individual Ezra Pound by Eustace Mullins.*

B. BOOKS AND PAMPHLETS

B72a   VAGABOND SCHOLAR . . . BY   1962
          BRUNO LIND

VAGABOND | SCHOLAR | A VENTURE | INTO THE PRIVACY |
OF GEORGE SANTAYANA | by | BRUNO LIND | [*device, incorpo-
rating publisher's name, place, and date:* Bridgehead Books: New York
| 1962]

191 pp. front. (port.) 10 illus. (incl. facsims.) on 4 plates. 22·2 × 14·5 cm. Blue
cloth (and, later? maroon, orange—and possibly other color cloth—of varying
shades and patterns) boards, lettered in gold down the spine; end-papers. White
dust-jacket printed in black and red.

Published 6 March 1962 at $5.95; number of copies unknown. *On verso of title-
leaf:* Copyright 1962 by Seven Sirens Press, Inc. . . .

Contains a letter from Ezra Pound to George Santayana, "Sometime in March,"
1951, pp. 65–66.

Note: Bruno Lind is the pseudonym of R. C. Hahnel.

B73   SPIRITUALITÀ E ATTIVISMO   1962
          NELLA LETTERATURA
          CONTEMPORANEA

BIBLIOTECA DELL'USSERO | diretta da Vittorio Vettori | [*double
rule*] | Quaderni Internazionali | I | SPIRITUALITÀ E AT-
TIVISMO | NELLA LETTERATURA | CONTEMPORANEA | [*de-
vice*] | GIARDINI EDITORE PISA | 1962

1 blank leaf, 2 leaves, 7–233 pp., 3 leaves. 19·5 × 14 cm. (wrappers); 19 × 13·5
cm. (leaves). Heavy white paper wrappers printed in blue on pages [i] and [iv],
on flaps, and on spine.

Published December 1962 at L. 2000 as "Biblioteca dell' Ussero, I"; number of
copies unknown. *Colophon (recto of final leaf):* Finito di stampare con i tipi della
Tipografia Editrice U. Giardini il dì 1° Dicembre 1962

Contains, in an appendix of "Documenti," a note in Italian "G. Bottai," by Ezra
Pound, pp. 223–4, written originally for the last number of G. Bottai's review
ABC but not published.

B74   THE LETTERS OF   [1963]
          WYNDHAM LEWIS

THE LETTERS OF | WYNDHAM LEWIS | [*short thick-thin rule*] |
EDITED BY | W. K. ROSE | METHUEN & CO LTD | 36 Essex
Street London WC2

B. BOOKS AND PAMPHLETS

xxxi, 580 pp., incl. 2 illus.(1 facsim.) col. front., 16 illus. (incl. ports., facsims.) on 12 plates. 22·3 × 14·7 cm. Red cloth boards stamped in gold on spine; end-papers; top edges stained yellow. White dust-jacket printed in red and black.

Published 4 April 1963 at 63s.; 3000 copies printed. *On verso of title-leaf:* First published 1963 . . . Printed in Great Britain by Western Printing Services Ltd, Bristol . . .

Contains excerpts from letters from Ezra Pound to Wyndham Lewis, 1916–1954, in footnotes on pages 83, 160, 394, 397, 404, 437, 441, 548, and 558.

Note: This book was published in Norfolk, Ct., 25 March 1964 by New Directions (James Laughlin) at $8.50 in a first printing of 3000 sets of sheets, for which the text was printed by offset and the frontispiece and plates were purchased from Methuen. (The first 2000 copies were bound in blue cloth boards lettered in gold on spine; the remaining sheets were bound up in 1967 to make 954 copies, these in pink cloth boards lettered in brown. Both bindings have the same buff dust-jacket printed in tan and black.) Contents as in the English edition.

B75   WRITERS AT WORK . . .   [1963]
SECOND SERIES

[*Row of type ornaments*] | Writers at Work | [*ornament*] | The Paris Review Interviews | SECOND SERIES | Introduced by Van Wyck Brooks | NEW YORK: THE VIKING PRESS [*preceding six lines flanked at each side by a single vertical rule*] | [*row of type ornaments*] | [*rule*] | [*row of type ornaments*]

6 leaves, 368 pp., 2 blank leaves, incl. illus. (ports., facsims.) 21·9 × 15 cm. Black cloth boards stamped in blue on front cover and in blue and gold on spine; end-papers; top edges stained black. White dust-jacket printed in gold, red, and black.

Published April 1963 at $6.50; 7000 copies printed. *On verso of title-leaf:* The interviews and biographical notes in this volume have been prepared for book publication by George Plimpton . . . Published in 1963 . . . Printed in the U. S. A. by The Murray Printing Co.

Contains "Ezra Pound," pp. [35]–59, an interview conducted by Donald Hall, recorded on tape, and edited by Pound (but not completely proofread by him), reprinted from the *Paris Review* for Summer/Fall 1962—C1889. (This includes as an illustration "Note to Base Censor," in facsimile of Pound's typescript, page [36].) The other interviews in the book are with Robert Frost, Marianne Moore, T. S. Eliot, Boris Pasternak, Katherine Anne Porter, Henry Miller, Al-

B. BOOKS AND PAMPHLETS

dous Huxley, Ernest Hemingway, S. J. Perelman, Lawrence Durrell, Mary McCarthy, Ralph Ellison, and Robert Lowell.

Note: This book was published in London on 11 November 1963 by Secker & Warburg at 30s. The English edition, without illustrations, omits the interviews with Perelman and Ellison, and adds an interview with Henry Green. An edition was published in New York paperbound, also by the Viking Press, in 1965 at $1.65 as its Compass Book 175.

B76   HAWKINS OF THE   1963
                       PARIS HERALD

Hawkins of | the Paris | HERALD | BY ERIC HAWKINS, managing EDITOR, | Paris Herald, for 36 years | with ROBERT N. STURDEVANT | [*publishers' device*] | SIMON AND SCHUSTER : NEW YORK : 1963

284 pp., 2 blank leaves. 23·5 × 16 cm. Black cloth boards lettered in gold on front cover and in gold and blue on spine; end-papers; top edges stained blue. White dust-jacket printed in black, blue, and pink.

Published 3 May 1963 at $5.95; number of copies unknown. *On verso of title-leaf:* ... First Printing ... Manufactured in the United States of America by H. Wolff, New York

Contains in Chapter 15, "Ezra Pound," four letters and notes from Pound addressed to but not printed in the *New York Herald*, Paris, pp. 180–1, and reprints Pound's note in lieu of biography from *Americans Abroad* (1932)—B30—p. 182.

B77   SELECTED WRITINGS BY   [1964]
                 NATALIE CLIFFORD BARNEY

selected writings by | NATALIE CLIFFORD BARNEY | edited with an introduction by | MIRON GRINDEA | ADAM Books [London]

162 pp., incl. illus. (ports., facsims.) 2 plates (incl. 1 fold.) 22·1 × 14·5 cm. Brown cloth boards with blue cloth back lettered in gold down the spine; end-papers. Blue dust-jacket printed in dark blue.

Published June 1964 at 45s. ($7.00); 100 copies printed. *On verso of title-leaf:* ... This is a limited edition of one hundred copies signed by the author [*number stamped in. Signed:* Natalie C. Barney]

A reissue of the special number of *Adam*, London, 299, dated 1962 but published early in 1963. Contains "On Writing and Writers," by Natalie C. Barney, translated from the French—*circa* 1924?—by Ezra Pound—C1893—pp. 54–57.

B78 CONFUCIUS TO CUMMINGS [1964]

a. *First edition, hardbound copies:*

Confucius to Cummings | An Anthology of Poetry | Edited by Ezra Pound & Marcella Spann | A NEW DIRECTIONS BOOK [New York, James Laughlin]

1 blank leaf, xxii, 353 pp., 3 blank leaves. 20·8 × 14·4 cm. Yellow cloth boards with black cloth back stamped in gold; end-papers. White dust-jacket printed in black, yellow, and grey.

Published 12 November 1964 at $6.75; 2300 copies printed. *On verso of title-leaf:* ... Manufactured in the United States of America. New Directions Books are published for James Laughlin by New Directions Publishing Corporation, 333 Sixth Avenue, New York, 14. ...

"This anthology is Ezra Pound's own choice of the poetry of various ages and cultures—ranging from his translations of the Confucian Odes up to E. E. Cummings—which he considers the finest of its type. ..."

"Nearly a hundred poets are represented, a number of them in Pound's own translations, with emphasis on the Greek and Latin, Chinese, Troubadour, Renaissance, and Elizabethan. ... Of particular interest are the notes on certain of the poems and poets which Pound has supplied in comment on his selections." (*Dust-jacket*) Of Pound's own translations only Godeschalk's "Sequaire," p. 75–76, and Pietro Metastasio's "'Age of Gold,'" p. 177, are printed here complete for the first time in book form. Pound's "A Note on [Thomas] Hardy and [Ford Madox] Ford" is printed as "Appendix I," pp. 325–9. "Appendix V: Selections [by Marcella Spann] from the Criticism of Ezra Pound," pp. 337–40, is chosen chiefly from the *ABC of Reading*, but includes two notes, here published for the first time, "from the Pound notebooks, 5 February 1956," p. 338.

b. *Paperbound copies:*

Title-page as in hardbound copies.

1 blank leaf, xxii, 353 pp., 2 leaves, 1 blank leaf. 20·4 × 13·7 cm. Heavy white paper wrappers printed in black and grey on page [i] and on spine, and in black on page [iv].

Published 12 November 1964 at $2.75 as New Directions Paperbook 126; 6000 copies printed. Verso of title-leaf as in hardbound copies.

Contents as in hardbound copies but with "New Directions Paperbooks," 2 leaves following page [354].

B. BOOKS AND PAMPHLETS

B79   EZRA POUND'S KENSINGTON   [1965]
       ... PATRICIA HUTCHINS

EZRA POUND'S | KENSINGTON | An Exploration | 1885–1913 | [*ornamental rule*] | PATRICIA HUTCHINS | FABER AND FABER | 24 Russell Square | London

180 pp., incl. illus., diagr., facsim. 12 illus. (incl. ports.) on 4 plates. 22·2 × 14·3 cm. Grey cloth boards stamped in blue and gold on spine; end-papers; top edges stained blue. White dust-jacket printed in yellow and black.

Published 11 February 1965 at 30s.; 4500 copies printed. *On verso of title-leaf:* First published in mcmlxv ... Printed in Great Britain by Western Printing Services Limited, Bristol ...

"Under a title insisted on by Mr Pound himself, Patricia Hutchins has brought together much hitherto unpublished material from letters, periodicals and interviews ... " (*Dust-jacket*) Contains excerpts from letters and notes from Ezra Pound to Patricia Hutchins, 1953 to 1961, pp. 18, 20, 21, 22, 23, 25, 37, 40, 44–45, 48, 55, 57, 58, 59, 68, 69–70, 71, 72, 76, 83, 84, 94, 95, 98, 103–4, 107, 124, 125, 128, 129, 130, 134–5, and 140–1. (A typed letter of 18 Aug. 1957, quoted in part, pp. 18 and 20, is reproduced in facsimile, p. 19.) A letter to Mrs. Elkin Mathews of 1922 is quoted, p. 60. Pound's printed letter to the Editor in the *New Age* for 21 Dec. 1911, "On the 'Decline of Faith,'"—C29—is reprinted, p. 84, and various brief quotations from uncollected articles appear throughout.

Note: This book was published in Chicago, Ill., in May 1965 by the Henry Regnery Company at $5.00.

B80   EZRA POUND PERSPECTIVES   [1965]

[*In grey:*] EZRA | [*in black:*] POUND | perspectives | [*single rule*] | essays in honor of his eightieth birthday | edited with an introduction by NOEL STOCK | HENRY REGNERY COMPANY | CHICAGO

xiii, 219 pp., 2 blank leaves, incl. illus., ports., facsims. front.(port.) 24·1 × 15·3 cm. Buff cloth boards stamped in brown down the spine; end-papers. White dust-jacket printed in grey, black, and red (with photograph of Ezra Pound by Marion Morehouse on back). (The statement on the back flap of the jacket that Noel Stock "is the custodian of Ezra Pound's papers" was later cancelled by black stamping.)

Published late December 1965 at $5.95; 3500 copies printed. *On verso of title-leaf:* ... Manufactured in the United States of America

Contains, as illustrations, reproductions of notes and manuscripts of Ezra Pound, including a manuscript of "The Rune (1908)," a poem from the "San Trovaso"

B. BOOKS AND PAMPHLETS

notebook, p. 23; a note to Dorothy Pound in her copy of *Provença*, p. 31; a page of the corrected typescript of "Homage to Sextus Propertius," p. 137; a notebook jotting used in Canto VI, p. [139]; the first four typed lines of Canto II, p. 164; the opening typed page of "The Music of Beowulf," p. [187]; a manuscript of the opening lines of Canto XLV, p. [188]; a page of corrected typescript of "Vou Club"—C1433—with postscript addressed to the Editor of *Globe*, p. 202; corrected typescript of " . . . a brace of axioms"—C1464—and the opening lines of "Muzik, as Mistaught"—C1462—p. 203; a page of typescript of the end of Canto LXXXI and the opening of Canto LXXXII, p. 208; and a typed page of comment on *Ezra Pound, a Collection of Essays Edited by Peter Russell* ([1950]), p. 209. The illustrations include also the following printed material: "How I Began"—C86—p. [1]; the first page of "Raphaelite Latin"—C2—p. 22; a leaf of galley proof of *The Spirit of Romance*, corrected by Homer Pound, p. 24; a leaf of page proof (for *Canzoni*, 1911) showing the first page of "Redondillas," p. [68]; a leaf of proof of the "Eighth Canto"—C640—as corrected to become part of Canto II, p. 165; a leaf of proof for Canto II, p. 166. (Hugh Kenner's essay, "Leucothea's Bikini: Mimetic Homage," incorporates two brief quotations from Pound's notebooks on De Mailla, pp. 30 and 34.)

B81   HARVARD ADVOCATE   [1966]
CENTENNIAL ANTHOLOGY

HARVARD ADVOCATE | CENTENNIAL | ANTHOLOGY | edited by Jonathan D. Culler | SCHENKMAN PUBLISHING CO., INC. | Cambridge, Massachusetts

xxxi pp., 1 leaf, 106 pp., 1 leaf, 107–264 pp., 1 leaf, 265–460 pp., incl. illus. 14 illus. (incl. ports.) on 7 plates. 24·2 × 17 cm. Red cloth boards stamped in black and gold on spine; end-papers. White dust-jacket printed in red, purple, olive, and black.

Published 17 March 1966 at $7.95; 5000 copies printed. *On verso of title-leaf:* . . . Printed in the United States of America

Contains "Canto XXXVIII"—C1012—pp. 166–71, and "A Problem of (Specifically) Style"—C1120—pp. 171–4, by Ezra Pound, the first appearance in book form for the essay.

B82   THE HOUND & HORN . . . BY   1966
LEONARD GREENBAUM

THE HOUND & HORN | THE HISTORY OF A LITERARY QUARTERLY | by | LEONARD GREENBAUM | University of Michigan

B. BOOKS AND PAMPHLETS

| [*publishers' device*] | 1966 | MOUTON & CO. | LONDON · THE HAGUE · PARIS

275 pp. front., 1 plate (port.) 21·6 × 14·3 cm. Buff cloth boards stamped in gold on spine; end-papers. White dust-jacket printed in brown and black.

Published July 1966 at 30 Dutch guilders (42 francs) as "Studies in American Literature, 6"; number of copies unknown. *On verso of title-leaf:* ... Printed in The Netherlands

Contains excerpts from letters from Ezra Pound to Lincoln Kirstein and other editors of the *Hound & Horn*, 16 March 1929 to 10 January 1930, pp. 89, 107, 109, 110, 111, 112, 113, 114, 115, 118–20, 122; from "Small Magazines"— C787—pp. 102, 104, 117; from "Our Contemporaries and Others"—C815— p. 119; and from "Murkn Magzeens"—C1079—p. 123.

B83   THE TRIAL OF EZRA POUND ... [1966]
      BY ... JULIEN CORNELL

THE TRIAL | OF EZRA POUND | A Documented Account of the Treason Case | by the Defendant's Lawyer | JULIEN CORNELL | THE JOHN DAY COMPANY | NEW YORK

4 leaves, 215, [1] pp., incl. facsims. 22 × 14·7 cm. Dark grey cloth boards stamped in gold on spine; end-papers. White dust-jacket printed in black, red, and green.

Published October 1966 at $5.00; number of copies unknown. *On verso of title-leaf:* ... Printed in the United States of America

Contains "Letter from Ezra Pound to [the law firm of] Shakespear and Parkyn," 5 Oct. 1945, pp. 7–11; seventeen autograph and typed letters from Pound to Julien Cornell, 1945–1948, reproduced in facsimile with printed comments by Cornell, pp. 70–109; and transcripts of Rome radio broadcasts, 23 April 1942 ["MacLeish"] and 15 May 1943 ["Economic Aggression"], pp. 139–44; with various other documents and letters relating to the trial, including "Lines from [Canto LXXX of] the Pisan Cantos ... Enclosed with ... Letter [from Cornell to Dr. Wendell Muncie, 6 Dec. 1945]," pp. 33–34.

Note: This book was published in London in September 1967 by Faber and Faber Ltd at 30 s. Contents as in the first edition.

B84   KABIR POESIE   [1966]

First edition:

KABIR | POESIE | a cura di | EZRA POUND | E GHANSHYAM

B. BOOKS AND PAMPHLETS

SINGH | [*publisher's device*] | ALL'INSEGNA DEL PESCE D'ORO
[Vanni Scheiwiller] | MILANO

1 blank leaf, 1 fold. leaf, 1 leaf, 5–67, [1] pp., 1 blank leaf, incl. fold. front.
(facsim.) 10 × 6 cm. Stiff white cloth wrappers printed all-over in blue, to which
are attached (at spine) and over which are folded white paper outer wrappers
printed in green and black on pages [i] and [iv], and in black on flaps and up
the spine. White paper wrap-around printed in black.

Published 30 October 1966 at L.400 as "Serie Oltremare a cura di Giacomo
Prampolini, 23"; number of copies unknown. *On verso of title-leaf:* . . . Printed in
Italy *Colophon* (*page* [68]): . . . Questo volumetto a cura di Vanni Scheiwiller è
stato impresso dalla Stamperia Valdonega di Verona il 30 ottobre 1966

Contains "Certain Poems of Kabir, Translated by Kali Mohan Ghose and Ezra
Pound," ten poems in English, with Singh's Italian translation opposite, pp.
[11]–37. Reprinted from the *Modern Review*, Calcutta for June 1913—C84. (Only
the Italian translation, by Ghanshyam Singh, is given for the remaining thirty
poems.)

B85   T. S. ELIOT THE MAN   [1966]
                          AND HIS WORK

T. S. ELIOT | THE MAN AND HIS WORK | [*rule*] | A Critical
Evaluation by Twenty-six | Distinguished Writers | EDITED BY
| Allen Tate | A Seymour Lawrence Book | DELACORTE PRESS
| NEW YORK

1 blank leaf, vi pp., 1 leaf, 400 pp., 3 blank leaves. 16 ports. on 8 plates. 21 ×
14·7 cm. Brown cloth boards stamped in gold and black on front cover and on
spine; brown end-papers: top edges stained brown. White dust-jacket printed
in blue, black, and brown.

Published November 1966 at $6.50; number of copies unknown. *On verso of
title-leaf:* . . . Printed in the United States of America First printing . . .

A reprint, with some new material, of the T. S. Eliot memorial issue of the
Sewanee Review for Winter [1965/]1966. Contains "For T. S. E.," by Ezra Pound—
C1906—p. [89].

Notes: This book was published in London in April 1967 by Chatto & Windus
at 36s. An edition paperbound was published in New York, also in April 1967,
by Dell Publishing Company, Inc., at $2.45 as their Delta Book 2263. An edi-
tion paperbound was published in London and Harmondsworth, Middlesex, in
1971, by Penguin Books in association with Chatto & Windus at 50p. as a
Pelican Book.

B. BOOKS AND PAMPHLETS

B86   LETTERS OF JAMES JOYCE   [1966]

LETTERS | OF | JAMES JOYCE | VOLUME II[–III] | edited by | RICHARD ELLMANN | FABER AND FABER | 24 Russell Square | London

2 volumes (*volume 2:* 1 blank leaf, 2 leaves, vii–lxxii, 472 pp. 15 plates (incl. ports., facsims.); *volume 3:* 2 blank leaves, 2 leaves, ix–xxxi, 584 pp. 11 plates (incl. ports., facsims.)) 24·1 × 15·5 cm. Grey cloth boards stamped in gold on spine; end-papers; top edges stained blue. Cream dust-jacket printed in black, green, and red.

Published 1 December 1966 at 12 guineas for the 2 volumes; 2000 sets printed. *On verso of title-leaf (both volumes):* First published in mcmlxvi ... Printed in Great Britain by R. MacLehose and Company Limited The University Press Glasgow ...

Contains, in volume 2, letters from Ezra Pound to James Joyce, 15 Dec. 1913, pp. 326–7; 17–19 Jan. 1914, pp. 327–8; ⟨about 7 Sept. 1915⟩, pp. 364–7; 2 Sept. 1916 (incorporating four-line limerick beginning "There was once a young writer named Joyce"), pp. 383–6; 19 Dec. 1917, pp. 413–14; and 22 Nov. 1918, pp. 423–4; to W. B. Yeats, ⟨about 22 July 1915⟩, p. 354; to A. Llewelyn Roberts, 3 Aug. 1915, pp. 358–60; to James B. Pinker, 30 Jan. 1916, pp. 372–3; to Edward Marsh, 21 Aug. 1916, pp. 381–2; to Sir Horace Rumbold, 11 Apr. 1919, pp. 437–8; to Carlo Linati, 6 June 1920, pp. 469–71; and, in volume 3, letters to Jenny Serruys [later Bradley], postmarked 20 July 1920, p. 9; and to Joyce, 21 Dec. 1931, pp. 237–8. (The letter in volume 2 to Harriet Shaw Weaver, 17 Mar. 1916, p. 375, and that in volume 3 to Joyce, 15 Nov. 1926, pp. 145–6, are reprinted from *The Letters of Ezra Pound, 1907–1941* ([1950])—A64.)

Notes: These two volumes were published in New York on 2 December 1966 by the Viking Press at $25.00 (or boxed with a reprint of the first volume at $35.00). Contents as in the English edition.

The first volume of the Joyce *Letters*—without volume designation—was edited by Stuart Gilbert and published in 1957, in London by Faber and Faber, and in New York by the Viking Press. It contains no letters from Pound.

B87   EZRA POUND: AN EXHIBITION   [1967]

· · ·

[*Reproduction of a drawing of Ezra Pound by Wyndham Lewis, within thick-rule frame*] | [*thick rule*] | Drawing by Wyndham Lewis | Ezra Pound [*in facsimile of Pound's handwriting*] | An Exhibition held in March 1967 | THE ACADEMIC CENTER AND UNDERGRADUATE LIBRARY | THE UNIVERSITY OF TEXAS [Austin]

B. BOOKS AND PAMPHLETS

62 pp., 1 leaf, incl. illus. (ports., facsims.) 25·4 × 12·5 cm. Buff paper wrappers printed in black and red on page [i], and in black on page [iv] (with reproduction of Gaudier-Brzeska drawing of Ezra Pound from his copy of *Ripostes*).

Published 31 March 1967 at $5.00; 3000 copies printed. *On verso of title-leaf:* ... Manufactured in the United States of America Published on the occasion of a Symposium entitled Make It New: Translation and Metrical Innovations, Aspects of Ezra Pound's Work. The University of Texas, March 15–17, 1967. *Colophon (verso of leaf following page 62):* This catalogue has been printed by the Printing Division of The University of Texas. The seal on the front cover was designed by Edmund Dulac ... The catalogue was compiled by David Farmer. Design and typography by Kim Taylor

Contains, as illustrations, letters from Ezra Pound to Hugh Walpole, 30 July 1920, p. 27, Samuel Putnam, 30 Oct. 1926, p. 29, and Joseph Bard, 17 Dec. 1932, p. 35; a manuscript note on page proofs for *Lustra*, p. 34; an inscription to Elkin Mathews in a copy of *Personae* (1909), p. 37; the first page of a typed manuscript of "Musicians, God Help 'Em," p. 38; and, in the text, brief excerpts from unpublished letters, pp. 9, 15, 22, 44, and 51. (Pages 25–40 are printed on buff paper.)

B88   FORD MADOX FORD AND THE   [1967]
          TRANSATLANTIC REVIEW
              BERNARD J. POLI

Ford Madox Ford | and the | TRANSATLANTIC REVIEW | [*at left of preceding three lines: thick vertical rule and circular device (of the periodical)*] | Bernard J. Poli | SYRACUSE UNIVERSITY PRESS

x pp., 1 leaf, 179 pp., incl. facsim. 23·3 × 15·7 cm. Green cloth boards stamped in gold and brown on spine; end-papers. White dust-jacket printed in buff and black.

Published 29 May 1967 at $5.50; 2149 copies printed. *On verso of title-leaf:* ... Manufactured in the United States of America First Edition 1967 ...

Reprints from the *Transatlantic Review* for June 1924—C662a—a pseudonymous letter from Ezra Pound to Ford Madox Ford, 17 May 1924, pp. 83–84.

Note: This book represents an extensive revision of an earlier edition, reproduced from typewritten copy, issued in Paris in June 1965 as a thesis for the Doctorat ès Lettres at the University of Paris. The thesis edition has title: *Université de Paris. Faculté des Lettres et Sciences Humaines. Ford Madox Ford and The Transatlantic Review, Paris 1924. Thèse complémentaire pour le Doctorat ès Lettres présentée par Bernard Poli* ... It collates: 1 blank leaf, 2 leaves, vi, 356 pp., 1 blank leaf. plates (facsims.), and is bound in buff paper wrappers, 26·2 × 20·6 cm. In that edition the Pound contribution appears on pages 343–4.

B. BOOKS AND PAMPHLETS

B89   CARLO IZZO. CIVILTÀ   1967[–1968]
        AMERICANA

[*In black:*] BIBLIOTECA DI STUDI AMERICANI | [*short rule. In red:*]
14 [–15. *In black: short rule*] | CARLO IZZO | [*in red:*] CIVILTÀ
AMERICANA | [*in black:*] VOL. I [–II] | SAGGI [–IMPRESSIONI E
NOTE] | ROMA 1967 [–1967, *i.e.* 1968] | EDIZIONI DI STORIA E
LETTERATURA

2 volumes (*volume* 1: 1 blank leaf, 3 leaves, 9–438 pp., 1 leaf; *volume* 2: 1 blank
leaf, 3 leaves, 9–300 pp., 4 leaves). 22 × 14·4 cm. Heavy cream paper wrappers
printed in red and black on page [i] and in black up the spine.

Volume 1 published 9 September 1967, volume 2, 31 January 1968, the set at
L. 7000, as "Biblioteca di Studi Americani, a cura di Agostino Lombardo, 14–
15"; 990 copies printed. *Colophon* (*volume 1, page* [439]): Giugno 1967 ABETE
Azienda Beneventana Tipografica Editoriale Roma . . . *Colophon* (*volume 2, page*
[308]): Dicembre 1967 . . .

The appendix, volume 2, pp. [247]–285, consists of "24 lettere e 9 cartoline
inedite di Ezra Pound," written 1935–1940, with explanatory text and notes (in
Italian) by Izzo. The letters are written for the most part in English; Italian
translations by Izzo are printed as footnotes, pp. 274–84. (Part of a letter to
Izzo of 2 Oct. 1956, in English, is quoted in the final footnote.)

B90   EZRA POUND: A CLOSE-UP, BY   [1967]
        MICHAEL RECK

Ezra Pound | A CLOSE-UP | [*swelled rule*] | by Michael Reck |
McGraw-Hill Book Company | New York Toronto London Syd-
ney

xi pp., 1 leaf, 205 pp., 2 blank leaves, incl. front. (facsim.) plates (port., facsims.)
21·8 × 14·7 cm. Grey paper boards with black cloth back stamped in gold on
spine and, at lower-right of back cover, with the number 51350; end-papers.
White dust-jacket printed in brown, black, and blue (with photograph of Ezra
Pound by Boris de Rachewiltz, Autumn 1958, on front).

Published 8 September 1967 at $5.95; number of copies unknown. *On verso of
title-leaf:* . . . Printed in the United States of America. . . . First Edition 51350

Contains, as frontispiece (p. [ii]), facsimile of manuscript note, written in 1955,
from Ezra Pound, introducing Reck to Juan Ramón Jiménez, and reproductions
of two typed letters to Reck, 12 Mar. 1954, on the second and third, and 17 May
1955 on the fourth pages of the plates following page 98. (The note to Jiménez
is quoted in part on page 95.)

Note: This book was published in London in March 1968 by Rupert Hart-Davis

B. BOOKS AND PAMPHLETS

Ltd. at 36s. Contents as in the American edition, except that the plates follow page 82. An edition, paperbound, was published in New York, Toronto, and Sydney by McGraw-Hill Book Company in 1973 at $2.95 in the series of McGraw-Hill Paperbacks. A Spanish translation, *Ezra Pound en primer plano*, by Maria Jose Sanchez Carrasco, was published in Barcelona by Ediciones Picazo in June 1976.

B91   THE CAGED PANTHER BY   [1967]
              HARRY M. MEACHAM

[*Across two pages:*] THE | CAGED | PANTHER | by Harry M. Meacham | Ezra Pound at | Saint Elizabeths | [*quotation in three lines from* Pisan Cantos, LXXXIII] | Twayne Publishers, Inc. | New York [*eight short vertical rules at left of these two lines*]

222 pp., 1 blank leaf, incl. illus. (ports., facsims.) 21·4 × 14·5 cm. Grey cloth boards stamped in gold on front cover and on spine; grey end-papers. White dust-jacket printed in black and red (with photograph of Ezra Pound by the *Richmond News Leader* on the front and drawing of him by Jean Cocteau on the back). (The illustrations, pp. [97–112], are printed on coated, cream paper.)

Published 15 December 1967 at $5.00; number of copies unknown. *On verso of title-leaf:* . . . Manufactured in the United States of America

Contains 54 letters and notes from Ezra Pound to Harry Meacham, 27 Mar. 1957 to 3 Nov. 1960, pp. 39–41, 45, 48–54, 57, 58, 65–66, 68–71, 72–87, 133–5, 145–52, 167–81, 185–7, 189–90, and 192–3 (nine of the letters are also reproduced in facsimile on pp. [97–102], [108], and [110]. Prints also a letter and parts of other letters from Pound to Dr. Winfred Overholser, 1950–1959, pp. 115–16; and letter to Christian Herter, U. S. Secretary of State, 14 Sept. 1958, pp. 166–7. An English translation of the Oreglia interview with Pound from the *Dagens Nyheter*, Stockholm, for 5 Nov. 1958—see C1864a—is given, pp. 34–39 (the two aphorisms—in Pound's English—p. 37).

B92   THE CASE OF EZRA POUND BY   [1968]
              CHARLES NORMAN

THE CASE OF | EZRA POUND | [*short rule*] | by Charles Norman | [*rule*] | Funk and Wagnalls, New York

x, 209 pp., 2 blank leaves. 23·5 × 16 cm. Brown cloth boards with purple cloth back stamped in gold, red, and silver on spine; buff end-papers. White dust-jacket printed in brown, orange, and black.

B. BOOKS AND PAMPHLETS

Published 6 March 1968 at $5.95; number of copies unknown. *On verso of title-leaf:* . . . Printed in the United States of America

Contains brief excerpts from Ezra Pound's Rome radio broadcasts, 3 Feb. 1942–4 May 1943 (reprinted, for the most part, from B69, but with additional excerpts from 2, 6, 14 July 1942, and 19, 26, and 30 Mar. 1943), pp. 48–55; a broadcast interview between Pound and Al Sanders, 12 May 1943, pp. 56–61; an undated note to Richard Aldington, p. 200; and various documents relating to the case.

B93   ROBERT McALMON. BEING   1968
         GENIUSES TOGETHER . . .

[*Across two pages:*] Robert McAlmon Being | Geniuses | Together | 1920–1930 | [*on left-hand page, opposite* Together:] Revised and with supplementary chapters by | Kay Boyle | [*at foot of right-hand page:*] Doubleday & Company, Inc., Garden City, New York | 1968

xiv pp., 1 leaf, 392 pp. 53 illus. (incl. ports., facsims.) on 16 plates. 24 × 16·3 cm. Brown cloth boards stamped in blind on front cover, with buff cloth back stamped in brown and gold; green end-papers. White dust-jacket printed in brown, green, and black.

Published 7 June 1968 at $6.95; 11,000 copies printed. *On verso of title-leaf:* . . . First Edition in the United States of America

Contains a note from Ezra Pound to Robert McAlmon (on a letter from T. S. Eliot to Pound), ⟨April? 1926⟩, in the footnote, p. 255; and an excerpt by Pound on McAlmon from "Crosby Continental Editions"—C921—pp. 369–70.

Note: Being Geniuses Together was first published in London by Secker & Warburg in 1938. (It contains nothing by Pound.) This revised edition was published, also in London, by Michael Joseph in 1970 at 60s. The Pound contributions appear on pages 228 and 329.

B94   THE AMERICAN LITERARY   [1968]
         ANTHOLOGY / 1

a. *Hardbound copies:*

[*Across two pages:*] the American Literary Anthology / 1 | The First Annual Collection of the | Best from the Literary Magazines | [*on left-hand page:*] Selected by John Hawkes, Walker Percy, William | Styron (fiction); John Ashbery, Robert Creeley, | James Dickey (poetry); and William Alfred, | Robert Brustein, Benjamin DeMott,

B. BOOKS AND PAMPHLETS

F. W. Dupee, | Susan Sontag, John Thompson (essays and criticism) | [*on right-hand page, opposite preceding five lines:*] Farrar, | Straus & | Giroux [*with publishers' device to left of these three lines*] | NEW YORK

xvi, 495 pp. 21·6 × 14·4 cm. Red cloth boards stamped in white and gold down the spine; gold end-papers; top edges stained yellow. White dust-jacket printed in black, red, and gold.

Published 17 June 1968 at $6.95; number of copies unknown. *On verso of title-leaf:* ... First edition, 1968 ... Printed in the United States of America ...

Contains "Canto CXVI," by Ezra Pound, pp. [247]–249, reprinted, with corrections, from the *Niagara Frontier Review* for Fall 1965/Spring 1966—C1901.

b. *Paperbound copies:*

Title-page and pagination as in hardbound copies. 21 × 14 cm. Heavy white paper wrappers printed in green and black on pages [i] and [iv], and on spine; top edges plain.

Published 17 June 1968 at $2.95; number of copies unknown. Verso of title-leaf as in hardbound copies.

Contents as in hardbound copies.

B95   THE MAN FROM NEW YORK ...   1968
B. L. REID

The Man | from | New York | JOHN QUINN AND HIS FRIENDS | B. L. REID | [*publisher's device*] | New York | OXFORD UNIVERSITY PRESS | 1968

xviii, 708 pp., 1 blank leaf, incl. illus. (facsims.) front., 33 illus. (incl. ports.) on 10 plates. 23·4 × 16 cm. Half-green, half-grey cloth boards stamped in silver on front cover and on spine; end-papers. Cream dust-jacket printed in brown and black.

Published 7 November 1968 at $12.50; 7500 copies printed (of which 1500 were for sale in England). *On verso of title-leaf:* ... Printed in the United States of America

Contains excerpts from letters from Ezra Pound chiefly to John Quinn, 1915–1922, pp. 86, 199–200, 203, 204, 205, 223, 224, 225, 242, 248, 249, 250, 252, 253, 254, 256, 272–3, 274, 275 (including two limericks on the James Joyce-Quinn-E. Byrne Hackett affair beginning "The ex-Irlandais that hight Hackett" and "In a life so lacking in condiment"), 277, 280, 282, 283, 285, 286–7, 290,

B. BOOKS AND PAMPHLETS

291, 292, 307, 320, 338, 341–2, 343, 345, 347, 348, 351–2, 389, 406, 407–8, 419, 436, 437, 439, 441, 461, 492, 493, 532, and 534.

Note: 1500 copies of this book were imported for sale in London in January 1969 also by the Oxford University Press at 7 guineas.

B96   THE BARB OF TIME . . .   1969
DANIEL D. PEARLMAN

The | Barb of Time | [*ornamental rule*] | ON THE UNITY OF | EZRA POUND'S CANTOS | [*ornamental rule*] | DANIEL D. PEARLMAN | New York · OXFORD UNIVERSITY PRESS · 1969

x, 318 pp. 8 illus. on 2 plates. 21·5 × 14·5 cm. Brown cloth boards stamped in gold on spine; end-papers. Cream dust-jacket printed in brown and blue.

Published 13 November 1969 at $8.50; number of copies unknown. *On verso of title-leaf:* . . . Printed in the United States of America . . .

"Appendix A, On the Early Cantos: From the Letters of Ezra Pound to John Quinn," pp. 299–303, prints brief quotations, most of them printed here for the first time, from letters written 31 Dec. 1916 to 11 Aug. 1923. "Appendix B, The Source of the Seven Lakes Canto," pp. 304–11, prints English translation, by Sanehide Kodama, of the Chinese and Japanese poems in the sixteenth- or seventeenth-century manuscript owned by Pound and used as the basis for Canto XLIX, along with reproductions of "representative portions" of the manuscript on the two plates following page 310.

B97   A RETURN TO PAGANY   [1969]

[*Across two pages:*] A Return to [*device*] PAGANY | [*rule*] | The History, Correspondence, and | Selections from a Little Magazine 1929–1932 | Edited by STEPHEN HALPERT | with RICHARD JOHNS | Introduction by KENNETH REXROTH | BEACON PRESS Boston

xviii pp., 1 leaf, 519 pp., 2 blank leaves, incl. facsims. 25·8 × 18·3 cm. Blue paper boards stamped in blind on front cover, with orange cloth back stamped in white down the spine; blue end-papers. White dust-jacket printed in blue and red.

Published 27 December 1969 at $12.50; number of copies unknown. *On verso of title-leaf:* . . . Beacon Press books are published under the auspices of the Unitarian Universalist Association . . . Printed in the United States of America

Contains "The First Year of 'Pagany' and the Possibility of Criteria," by Ezra

Pound—C796—pp. 232–9; facsimiles of letters from Pound to Richard Johns, [1930–32], pp. 212–13, 327–8, and 380, and to William Carlos Williams, 22 Mar. [1931], pp. 259–62.

B98   JAMES JOYCE : THE CRITICAL   [1970]
HERITAGE

JAMES JOYCE | THE CRITICAL HERITAGE | Edited by | ROBERT H. DEMING | Assistant Professor of English, Miami University | VOLUME ONE [–TWO] | 1902–1927 [–1928–1941] | [rule] | LONDON: ROUTLEDGE & KEGAN PAUL

2 volumes (*volume* 1: xiii, 385 pp.; *volume* 2: xi, 387–821 pp.) 22·1 × 14·6 cm. Blue cloth boards lettered in gold on spine; end-papers. White dust-jacket printed in gold and green (vol. 1), brown (vol. 2).

Published 5 March 1970 at 6 guineas the set, in the publishers' "The Critical Heritage Series"; number of copies unknown. *On verso of title-leaf:* Published 1970 in Great Britain . . . Printed . . . by W. & J. Mackay & Co Ltd, Chatham

Contains, in volume 1, "Pound on *A Portrait* 1917," pp. 82–84 (a reprint of "James Joyce At Last the Novel Appears"—C246); "A Pound Editorial on Joyce and Wyndham Lewis 1917," p. 119 (an extract from "Editorial" in the *Little Review* for May 1917—C254); "Pound on *Exiles* and the Modern Drama 1916," pp. 133–5 (a reprint of part of "Mr. James Joyce and the Modern Stage" from *Drama* for February 1916—C216); and, in volume 2, "Pound on *Ulysses* and Wyndham Lewis 1933," pp. 596–7 (an extract from "Past History" in the *English Journal* for May 1933—C939).

B99   THE LIFE OF EZRA POUND   [1970]
NOEL STOCK

The Life of | EZRA POUND | Noel Stock | [*publishers' device*] | London Routledge & Kegan Paul

xvii, 472 pp., 1 blank leaf. 22 illus. (incl. ports., facsims.) on 6 plates. 24·1 × 16·2 cm. Black cloth boards lettered in gold on spine; end-papers. White dust-jacket printed in black (with photograph of Ezra Pound by Ferdinando Carpanini on front).

Published 11 June 1970 at £ 3.50; number of copies unknown. *On verso of title-leaf:* First published in 1970 . . . Printed in Great Britain by Western Printing Services Ltd Bristol . . .

Contains the following material—chiefly excerpts—by Ezra Pound here first printed in book-form: "Ezra on the Strike" (two stanzas), p. 14; "The Mourn of Life" (complete), pp. 27–28; "Raphaelite Latin" and "Interesting French Publications," p. 31; letter to L. Burtron Hessler, p. 41; poem on Shakespeare (one stanza), p. 49; "Sonnet of the August Calm" (eight lines), p. 51; inscription to his father in *Exultations*, p. 76; "I Gather the Limbs of Osiris, II," p. 108; "Prolegomena (1912)," p. 109; "Status rerum [I]," pp. 128–9; letter to Tagore ⟨Dec. 1912?⟩, pp. 128–9, and 1929, p. 283; "interview" with Flint in *Poetry* for March 1913—C73a—p. 132; "An Essay in Constructive Criticism," pp. 151–2; "Allen Upward Serious," pp. 156–7; "Affirmations . . . I. Arnold Dolmetsch," pp. 170–1; letter to Milton Bronner, 21 Sept. 1915, p. 182; "The Passport Nuisance"—C697—p. 224, and C648—pp. 225–6; "Hudson: Poet Strayed into Science," pp. 230–1; typed letter (with manuscript additions) to Hugh Walpole, 30 July 1920, reproduced as illustration no. 11 on plate facing p. 238; "Possibilities of Civilization: What the Small Town Can Do," pp. 251–2; letters to W. B. Yeats, 19 June 1924, pp. 255–6, and Henry Allen Moe, 31 Mar. 1925, p. 258; invitation from the Pounds to "Le Testament," p. 263; letter to Nicholas Murray Butler (drafted with Mensdorff), 18 June 1928, p. 276; "Mr Aldington's Views on Gourmont," pp. 280–1; "Program 1929," p. 282; "Credo" (*Front*), p. 295; letters to *Chicago Tribune*, Paris, 25 June 1932—C863—p. 302, and 13 Mar. 1933—C928—p. 308; "Past History," p. 310; letters to Dorothy Sayers, pp. 318–19, President Roosevelt, 1934, p. 319, George H. Tinkham, Mar. 1935, p. 326, and A. S. Elwell Sutton, [1939?], pp. 326–7; "Alberta and the British Press," p. 334; "Twelve Years and Twelve Years. 'A Keystone of Europe,'" pp. 335, 336; "Manifesto (1936)," pp. 340–1; letters to Joseph Brewer, 6 May 1938, p. 349, Henry S. Canby, 14 Feb. 1938, p. 352, Claude G. Bowers, 13 May 1938, p. 352, and Van Wyck Brooks, 4 June 1938, p. 353; note in Dorothy Pound's copy of *Cantos LII–LXXI*, p. 375; letters to James Laughlin, Feb. 1940, pp. 375–6, Editor of *Annals* of the Academy of Political and Social Science, 1940, p. 376, A. L. Gibson, 24 Mar. 1940, p. 379, C. H. Douglas, 3 Apr. 1940, pp. 380–1, E. E. Cummings, 18 Jan. 1941, p. 385, National Institute of Arts and Letters, 15 May 1941, p. 386, and William Carlos Williams, 14 July 1941, pp. 386–7, and 23 July 1941, p. 388; Rome radio broadcast ["Continuity"], 6 & 7 July 1942, pp. 394–5; advertisement leaflet for Square $ Series, p. 430; and message in the *Chinese World*, San Francisco, 23 Sept. 1954 ("Kung is to China as water is to fishes"), p. 433. (There are many brief quotations from other letters and articles, and the text of *Volitionist Economics*—E2m—is reprinted, pp. 321–2.)

Note: This book was published in New York on 20 July 1970 by Pantheon at $10.00. Contents as in the first edition. An edition paperbound was published also in New York in December 1974 by Avon in its series of Discus Books at $2.65.

B99a   VITTORIO VETTORI   [1970]
                          TERRADILUNA . . .

Vittorio Vettori | Terradiluna e altre poesie | con un autografo di Ezra Pound | [*publisher's device*] | Giardini [Pisa]

B. BOOKS AND PAMPHLETS

1 blank leaf, 4 leaves, 11–43 pp., 1 leaf, 1 blank leaf. 21 × 15·5 cm. Heavy mulberry paper wrappers printed in black on pages [i] and [iv], and up the spine.

Published after 15 June 1970 at L. 1200 as "Biblioteca dell'Ussero, diretta da Vittorio Vettori, nuova serie LXI"; number of copies unknown. *Colophon* (*page* [46]): A cura dell'Accademia pisana dell'Arte-Sodalizio dell'Ussero Finito di stampare il 15 giugno 1970 per i tipi della Tipografia "Editrice Giardini" di Pisa

Contains postscript in Italian to a letter from Pound to Vettori, signed: Ez P, in facsimile of Pound's autograph, recto of third leaf; with "Postilla all'autografo," signed: V. V., on verso.

B100   VITTORUGO CONTINO. EZRA   [1970]
POUND IN ITALY

a. *First* (*trade*) *edition:*

[*In black:*] VITTORUGO CONTINO | EZRA POUND IN ITALY | FROM THE PISAN CANTOS | [*in grey:*] SPOTS & DOTS [Venezia, Gianfranco Ivancich Editore]

[150] pp., 1 blank leaf, incl. illus., ports., facsims. 29 × 24·2 cm. Cream paper boards printed in silver and black on front cover and in silver up the spine; end-papers. Issued without dust-jacket.

Published 30 October 1970 (distributed by Alfieri in Venice and by Wittenborn and Company in New York at $24.00); number of copies unknown. Verso of title-leaf blank. Printed on coated paper. Copies sold in the United States in 1970 have a paper label pasted on page [4]: American Distributor: Wittenborn and Company 1018 Madison Ave., New York, N. Y. 10021. *Imprint on page* [150]: Printed in Italy by Grafiche Le.Ma.–Maniago october 1970 for the 85th birthday of Ezra Pound Distributor: Alfieri, Venice

Half-title: Ezra Pound in Italy

Consists of photographs mostly of Ezra Pound and Venice by Contino, with a brief "Introduction" by Pound; passages chiefly from *The Pisan Cantos*, with notes by Olga Rudge, and answers to questions from Pier Paolo Pasolini and Vanni Ronsisvalle, all written out by Pound and reproduced both in facsimile of his manuscript and in type. (The answers, translated, were used for an Italian documentary film, "An Hour with Ezra Pound," filmed by RAI Televisione Italiana.)

b. *Limited edition:*

Title-page as in the trade edition.

1 blank leaf, [152] pp., 1 blank leaf, incl. illus., ports., facsims. 29 × 24·5 cm. Full red leather boards stamped in gold on front cover and up the spine; end-

B. BOOKS AND PAMPHLETS

papers. Grey paper cardboard box, 30 × 24·5 cm., with red-leather covered top and bottom.

Prepared for publication in October 1970 but no copies sold; 300 copies printed. Verso of title-leaf blank. Printed on uncoated paper. *Imprint on page* [152]*:* Printed in Italy by Grafiche Le.Ma.–Maniago october 1970 *On page* [2]*:* . . . for the 85th birthday of Ezra Pound *Colophon (page* [3])*:* Special edition limited to 300 of which this is n. [*number written in (in some copies) signed:* Ezra Pound]

Note: Although some copies were distributed gratis in 1970 and subsequently, the bulk of the edition is still (1981) in the hands of the publisher.

c. American edition ([1978])*:*

EZRA POUND IN ITALY | FROM THE PISAN CANTOS | Photographs by VITTORUGO CONTINO | Edited by GIAN-FRANCO IVANCICH | RIZZOLI | NEW YORK

1 blank leaf, [148] pp., 1 blank leaf, incl. illus., ports., facsims. 29·2 × 24·4 cm. Black cloth boards lettered in white on front cover and on spine; end-papers. White dust-jacket printed in black.

Published 28 October 1978 at $27.50; number of copies unknown. *On verso of title-leaf:* Published in the United States of America in 1978 . . . *Imprint on page* [148]*:* Printed in Italy by Grafiche Le.Ma. – Maniago – Pn – 1978

Half-title: Ezra Pound in Italy Spots & Dots

Text and illustrations as in B100a.

B101   DEAR MISS WEAVER . . . JANE   [1970]
LIDDERDALE & MARY
NICHOLSON

[*Rule*] | DEAR MISS WEAVER | Harriet Shaw Weaver 1876–1961 | [*rule*] | JANE LIDDERDALE | & MARY NICHOLSON | FABER AND FABER | London

1 blank leaf, 2 leaves, 7–509 pp., 1 blank leaf. 51 illus. (ports., facsims.) on 15 plates. 24·1 × 15·7 cm. Blue cloth boards stamped in red and gold on spine; green end-papers (front end-paper reproducing pages [1] and [4] of *Extracts from Press Notices of Ulysses by James Joyce* ([1922]), back end-paper reproducing pages [1] and [4] of *Extracts from Some Press Notices of A Portrait of the Artist as a Young Man. By James Joyce* ([1917]). White dust-jacket printed in black, green, and blue.

Published 9 November 1970 at 90s.; 5600 copies printed. *On verso of title-leaf:* First published in 1970 . . . Printed in Great Britain by Latimer Trend & Co Ltd Plymouth . . .

B. BOOKS AND PAMPHLETS

Contains excerpts from letters from Ezra Pound to Dora Marsden, pp. 67, 68, 70, and 77, Harriet Shaw Weaver, pp. 97, 112, 120–1, 129–30, 132, and 133–4, Jane Lidderdale, p. 108, and John Quinn, p. 115; and from uncollected articles. A reproduction of a drawing of Pound by Henri Gaudier-Brzeska appears as illustration no. 16 on the plate opposite p. 97.

Note: This book was published in New York in 1971 by the Viking Press at $15.00. Contents as in the English edition.

B102   ETRUSCAN GATE . . . DOROTHY   1971
SHAKESPEAR POUND

ETRUSCAN GATE | A NOTEBOOK WITH DRAWINGS | AND WA-TERCOLOURS BY | Dorothy Shakespear Pound | EDITED BY | Moelwyn Merchant | 1971 | THE ROUGEMONT PRESS·EXETER

4 leaves, 11, [12–36] pp., incl. front. illus. (ports., facsims.) 27·4 × 20·8 cm. Red cloth boards lettered in gold on front cover and up the spine; red end-papers. Grey dust-jacket lettered in red.

Published January 1971, the signed copies at £7.00, the unsigned at £5.00; 300 copies printed. *Colophon (page* [35])*:* This limited edition of three hundred copies was designed and printed by Eric Cleave at the Rougemont Press Exeter, and published in January 1971 ... The illustrations are reproduced by lithography with the co-operation of Omar Pound who generously lent the originals. The first hundred copies are signed by the artist and author of the 'Notebook' this copy being number [*number written in, followed in copies 1–100 by signature:* D. Shakespear Pound]

Contains "Plaint: It is of the white thoughts that he saw in the Forest," by Ezra Pound (an early, slightly variant version of "Planh: Of white thoughts he saw in a Forest"), p. 3; and reproduction of four small sketches by him of a (black) cat named Schwartz, p. [10]. The book includes also reproductions of two drawings of Pound by Wyndham Lewis, verso of fourth leaf and p. [4], an oil painting of him by Lotte Frumi, Venice, 1964, verso of third leaf, and a photograph of Dorothy and Ezra Pound, "Rapallo [*i.e.* Brunnenburg, Tirolo]," pp. [16–17].

B103   CYRIL CONNOLLY'S ONE   [1971]
HUNDRED MODERN BOOKS

a. *Hardbound copies:*

[*In black:*] Cyril Connolly's | [*in red:*] ONE HUNDRED MODERN BOOKS | [*in black:*] From England, France and America 1880–1950 | Catalog by Mary Hirth with an Introduction by Cyril Con-

B. BOOKS AND PAMPHLETS

nolly | An Exhibition: March–December 1971 | The Humanities Research Center · The University of Texas at Austin

1 leaf, 4–120 pp., 1 leaf, incl. illus. front. 19·9 × 26·1 cm. Blue cloth boards stamped in red on front cover and down the spine; red end-papers. Issued without dust-jacket.

Published 7 March 1971 at $5.95; 520 copies printed. *Colophon (verso of final leaf):* This catalog has been printed on Adena Eggshell. The type is Linotype Caledonia for the text with Sistina and Palatino for the titling. Design by William R. Holman.

Contains reproduction of a complete typed letter from Ezra Pound to Donal McKenzie, item 66E, p. 80, with an excerpt from it printed, pp. 79–80. There is also a brief quotation from a letter to Milton Bronner, 21 Sept. 1915, about the Cantos, p. 79.

b. *Paperbound copies:*

Title-page and pagination as in hardbound copies. 19·3 × 25·5 cm. Heavy white paper wrappers printed all-over in blue and red on page [i] and down the spine; red fly-leaf at front and back.

Published 7 March 1971 at $5.95; 3020 copies printed. Colophon as in hardbound copies.

Contents as in hardbound copies.

B104   ARTHUR MIZENER. THE   [1971]
                      SADDEST STORY

Arthur Mizener | THE SADDEST STORY | A | Biography | of | FORD MADOX FORD | [*ornament*] | THE WORLD PUBLISHING COMPANY | New York and Cleveland

xxiii, 616 pp. 30 illus. (incl. ports.) on 8 plates. 23·3 × 16·2 cm. Black cloth boards lettered in blind up the front cover, with red cloth back stamped in gold; black end-papers. Black cloth-covered cardboard box printed in grey.

Published 29 March 1971 at $20.00; number of copies unknown. *On verso of title-leaf:* ... First printing—1971 ... Printed in the United States of America World Publishing Times Mirror

Contains letters or excerpts of letters from Ezra Pound to Stella Bowen, p. [1]; to Brigit Patmore, p. 239; to Ford Madox Ford, pp. 216, 318, 319, 416, 445–6, 455, and 577, notes 22–23.

Note: This book was published in London by the Bodley Head in May 1972 at £ 5.00. Contents as in the American edition.

B. BOOKS AND PAMPHLETS

B105   MARY DE RACHEWILTZ   [1971]
DISCRETIONS

[*Across two pages:*] Mary de Rachewiltz DISCRETIONS [*ornament*] | [*on left-hand page:*] illustrated with photographs | An Atlantic Monthly Press Book [*to right of these two lines: publishers' device*] | Little, Brown and Company Boston Toronto | [*on right-hand page: quotation in five lines from* Ezra Pound, Canto LXXXI]

4 leaves, 312 pp. 27 illus. (incl. ports., facsim.) on 8 plates. 21·5 × 14·7 cm. Gold cloth boards stamped in gold down the spine; orange end-papers. White dust-jacket printed all-over in black, gold, and orange.

Published 30 June 1971 at $8.95; probably 5000 copies printed. *On verso of title-leaf:* ... First Edition ... Atlantic, Little, Brown books are published by Little, Brown and Company in association with the Atlantic Monthly Press ... Printed in the United States of America

Contains "Laws for Maria," by Ezra Pound, pp. 69–70; letters and excerpts of letters from him, pp. 108, 109–10, 139, and 157–8; an inscription "from the Odes of Chêng," p. 274; and explanations throughout of personal references in the Cantos.

Note: This book was published in London in November 1971 by Faber and Faber at £ 3.75. Contents as in the American edition. A paperbound edition, with title *Ezra Pound, Father and Teacher: Discretions,* was published in New York in 1975 by New Directions at $4.75 as their Paperbound Book 405. An Italian translation, by the author, *Discrezioni, storia di un' educazione,* was published in Milan in June 1973 by Rusconi Editore at L. 3500.

B106   TESTIMONIANZE A SAN   [1971]
GIORGIO

Testimonianze a san giorgio [Venezia, Fondazione Giorgio Cini, 1971]

85 pp., 1 leaf. 23 × 25 cm. Heavy plain red paper wrappers.

Published October 1971 for gratis distribution; number of copies unknown. *Colophon (page [87]):* Finito di stampare nell' ottobre 1971 dalla Stamperia di Venezia

Issued in connexion with the commemoration of the twentieth anniversary of the Giorgio Cini Foundation in Venice and the publication of *Venezia 1951– 1971: Venti anni di attività della fondazione giorgio cini* (Venezia, Fondazione Giorgio Cini [1971]). Contains various tributes to the Foundation on the occasion of the anniversary including a nine-line contribution by Ezra Pound, p. 75.

B. BOOKS AND PAMPHLETS

Note: Ezra Pound's tribute was reprinted as item 1, "To Vittorio Cini . . . for the twentieth anniversary of the Cini Foundation," on page [1] of the catalogue of an exhibition arranged by Olga Rudge at the Foundation headquarters in Venice in September 1977, *Micro mostra Poundiana alla Fondazione Giorgio Cini,* 3–24 *settembre 1977 (Venezia, Isola di San Giorgio Maggiore [1977]).* This pamphlet collates: cover-title, [8] pp. 15 × 10 cm. Wire-stitched. It also prints, as item 5, p. [1], Pound's note to Cario Linati, 10 March 1947, and, as item 6, p. [2], his "Message . . . to a Venetian friend [Guido Cadorin], 1972."

B107   T. S. ELIOT. THE WASTE LAND   [1971]
A FACSIMILE . . .

a. *First edition, trade:*

T. S. ELIOT | THE WASTE LAND | A FACSIMILE AND TRAN-
SCRIPT | OF THE ORIGINAL DRAFTS | INCLUDING THE AN-
NOTATIONS | OF EZRA POUND | EDITED BY | VALERIE ELIOT
| FABER AND FABER [London]

xxx pp., 1 leaf, 149 pp., 1 blank leaf, incl. facsims. 28·6 × 22·5 cm. Blue cloth boards stamped in gold on spine; end-papers. White dust-jacket printed in black and red.

Published 8 November 1971 at £ 5.00; 11,000 copies printed. *On verso of title-leaf:* First published in 1971 . . . Printed in Great Britain at the University Press Oxford by Vivian Ridler Printer to the University . . .

Contains "Preface" by Ezra Pound, p. [vii], dated 30 September 1969; brief excerpts from letters from Pound to John Quinn, 4 June 1920, pp. xviii–xix, and 21 Feb. 1922, p. xxii; and Pound's annotations on various drafts of *The Waste Land* (and of miscellaneous poems related to it) in facsimile, with transcripts printed opposite in red, pp. [6]–13, [22]–23, [26]–27, [30]–35, [38]–47, [50]–51, [54]–55, [62]–71, [82]–87, [98]–101, [104]–107, and [120]–121.

Note: This book was issued, also by Faber and Faber, revised, paperbound, in their series of Faber Paperbacks at £ 5.95 on 9 June 1980 in a first impression of 6000 copies.

b. *First edition, limited:*

Title-page as in the trade issue.

xxxii pp., 2 leaves, 155, [1] pp., incl. front. (port.), facsims. 28·6 × 22·2 cm. Red cloth boards stamped in gold on front cover and on spine; buff end-papers; top edges stained buff. Red cloth board box with buff paper label on side printed

B. BOOKS AND PAMPHLETS

in red: ... LIMITED EDITION (The label prints "Draft" for "Drafts" in the sub-
title.)

Published 8 November 1971 at £ 12.00; 500 copies printed. *Colophon* (*page*
[156])*:* This edition is limited to 500 numbered copies of which this is number
[*number written in in ink*]

This issue contains, besides the frontispiece photograph of T. S. Eliot, a facsimile of the mailing label addressed by Eliot to John Quinn, p. [xxxv], and facsimiles of three bills from the Albemarle Hotel, Cliftonville, Margate, pp. [149–
51], with printed caption, p. [147].

c. *American issue, trade:*

T. S. ELIOT | THE WASTE LAND | A FACSIMILE AND TRAN-
SCRIPT | OF THE ORIGINAL DRAFTS | INCLUDING THE AN-
NOTATIONS | OF EZRA POUND | EDITED BY | VALERIE ELIOT
| HARCOURT BRACE JOVANOVICH, INC. | NEW YORK

1 blank leaf, xxx pp., 1 leaf, 149 pp., incl. facsims. 28·5 × 22·4 cm. Blue cloth
boards stamped in gold on spine and on back cover; blue end-papers. White
dust-jacket printed all-over in cream, black, and red.

Published 10 November 1971 at $22.50; 4000 copies printed. *On verso of title-
leaf:* ... Printed in the United States of America ...

Contents as in the English trade issue.

Note: This book was issued, also by Harcourt Brace Jovanovich, revised, paperbound, as their Harvest [Book] Special, 270, at $7.50 in 1974. *On verso of title-
leaf:* ... Printed in the United States of America ... A

d. *American issue, limited:*

Title-page as in the trade issue.

5 leaves, ix–xxx pp., 1 leaf, 149 pp. front. (port.), 4 plates (incl. facsims.)
28·7 × 22·5 cm. Grey cloth boards stamped in gold on spine and on back
cover; grey end-papers. Grey cardboard box with cream paper label on side
printed in black and red.

Published 10 November 1971 at $50.00; 250 copies printed. *On verso of title-leaf:*
... First edition ... Printed in the United States of America ... *Colophon* (*recto
of first leaf*)*:* This first edition is limited to 250 copies for sale in the United
States of America This copy is number [*number written in in ink*]

This issue contains, besides the frontispiece photograph of T. S. Eliot, a facsimile of the mailing label addressed by Eliot to Quinn on the plate preceding page
[1], and facsimiles of three bills from the Albemarle Hotel on recto and verso
of the second, and recto of the third plate following page 146 (the first plate
bears a descriptive caption).

B. BOOKS AND PAMPHLETS

B108   THE POUND ERA, BY   1971 [*i.e.*
        HUGH KENNER   1972]

The | Pound | Era | [*drawing by Henri Gaudier-Brzeska*] | By HUGH
KENNER | UNIVERSITY OF CALIFORNIA PRESS | BERKELEY
AND LOS ANGELES 1971

1 blank leaf, xiv, 606 pp., 1 blank leaf, incl. illus., ports., facsims. 23·4 × 15·8
cm. Blue cloth boards stamped in gold on front cover and down the spine.
White dust-jacket printed in black and red.

Published 27 March 1972 at $14.95; 3500 copies printed. *On verso of title-leaf:*
. . . Printed in the United States of America Designed by Dave Comstock

Contains brief quotations from uncollected articles, and from miscellaneous
unpublished material by Ezra Pound, notably the following: manuscript notes
for "I Vecchii," p. 7; conversation, Sept. 1952 (on T. S. Eliot), p. 12; manuscript
note, 1950, on fly-leaf of the *Analects*—A65—p. 103; notes for an unpublished
essay, "L'uomo nel ideogramma," including four lines of verse beginning "Poetry speaks phallic direction," p. 104; letters to Harriet Monroe, 17 Sept. 1915
(on H.D.), p. 177, Dec. 1918 and 14 Apr. 1919, p. 286; letters to Margaret
Anderson, 17 Nov. 1917, p. 178, 22 June 1917, p. 242, 3 Apr. 1917, p. 281, 17
May 1917, p. 284, 7 July 1918, p. 296; lines from "Canto 120," pp. 266 and 379;
two brief telegrams, 20 and 22 Dec. 1915, and a letter to John Quinn, May
1916, p. 281; unused detail for Canto LXXXIV, p. 515; variant version of "Baijo's Poem in the Koshigen," p. 545; and note on fly-leaf of Morrison's Chinese
Dictionary, p. 569.

Note: This book was published in London in July 1972 by Faber and Faber at
£ 8.50. Contents as in first edition.

B109   THE LEFT BANK REVISITED   [1972]

THE LEFT BANK | REVISITED: | Selections from the | Paris Trib-
une 1917–1934 | [*rule*] | Edited with an Introduction | by Hugh
Ford | Foreword by Matthew Josephson | The Pennsylvania State
University Press | University Park and London

xxiv pp., 1 leaf, 334 pp., incl. illus. (ports.), 15 ports. on 2 plates. 23·7 × 16
cm. Yellow cloth boards stamped in black and gold on spine; yellow end-papers.
White dust-jacket printed in brown and black.

Published 23 August 1972 at $12.50; 2000 copies printed.

Contains contributions by Ezra Pound to the European edition of the *Chicago
Tribune*: "Left vs. Right"—C762—pp. 54–55; "[Mr.] Ezra Pound and Passports"—C674—p. 180; a brief excerpt, quoted under the heading "Pound Denounces Idiocy of U. S. Mail Act,"—C695a—p. 181; "Montparnasse For-

ever!"—C761—pp. 182–3; an interview by Mary Howell, 19 April 1930, quoting Pound at length, "Pound Paints Peccadilloes of Pedants in Money Murdered Marts of Learning"—C768a—pp. 183–5; "Europe Rearms"—C892a—p. 185; "Rearmament"—C926a—p. 186; and "England and America"—C927a—p. 186.

B110   FORD MADOX FORD   [1972]
MODERN JUDGEMENTS

Ford Madox Ford | MODERN JUDGEMENTS | edited by | RICH-ARD A. CASSELL | MACMILLAN [London and Basingstoke]

191 pp. 22·3 × 14·2 cm. Blue cloth boards lettered in gold on the spine; end-papers. White dust-jacket printed all-over in ivory and in black and red.

Published in November 1972 at £3.50; number of copies unknown. *On verso of title-leaf:* ... First published 1972 by The Macmillan Press Ltd London and Basingstoke Associated companies in New York Toronto Dublin Melbourne Johannesburg and Madras ... Printed in Great Britain by Hazell Watson and Viney Ltd Aylesbury, Bucks

Contains "Ford Madox Ford (1939)," by Ezra Pound, pp. [33]–36, a reprint of Pound's tribute in "Homage to Ford Madox Ford 1875–1939" from *New Directions,* 7 (1942)—C1623, in turn a reprint of "Ford Madox (Hueffer) Ford; Obit" from *Nineteenth Century and After* for August 1939—C1514.

B111   AN ALPHABET FOR POUND   1972

AN ALPHABET FOR POUND | contents | [*short rule. List of contents by letter of the alphabet in 24 lines*] | Edited by Ralph Maud in connection | with English 414 Fall [*i.e.* December] 1972 Simon | Fraser University [Burnaby 2, B. C.]

Title from page [ii] of cover, 38 pp. illus. 28 × 21·6 cm. Stapled. Heavy white paper wrappers printed in black on pages [i] (with photograph of Benin bronze) and [ii], with page 38 on page [iii].

Published December 1972 for gratis distribution; number of copies unknown. *On page 38:* ... 4 December 1972 [Reproduced from typewritten copy.]

"It will be evident that most of this *Alphabet for Pound* was put together before the poet's death on 1st of November 1972. It now stands as an attempt by some of us in Vancouver, British Columbia, to 'heap up mine arms,' as Elpenor begs us to." (*Statement by the editor,* p. 38) Reproduces on page 18 two typed notes from Ezra Pound to Denis Goacher, 22 and 27 November [1956?], and on page 20—reprinted from B82, p. 71—the first page of a letter from Pound to Julien Cornell.

B. BOOKS AND PAMPHLETS

B112   EZRA POUND   [1972]
               THE CRITICAL HERITAGE

EZRA POUND | THE CRITICAL HERITAGE | Edited by | ERIC
HOMBERGER | School of English and American Studies | Uni-
versity of East Anglia | [*rule*] | ROUTLEDGE & KEGAN PAUL :
LONDON AND BOSTON

xix, 500 pp. 22 × 14·8 cm. Blue cloth boards stamped in gold on spine; end-
papers (back end-paper with printed list of series). White dust-jacket printed
in green and brown.

Published 12 December 1972 at £ 6.50 in the publishers' "The Critical Heritage Series"; number of copies unknown. *On verso of title-leaf:* First published
1972 . . . Printed in Great Britain by W & J Mackay Limited, Chatham

Contains letters from Ezra Pound written in reply to reviews: on John Bailey's
unsigned review, "The Poems of Cavalcanti," from the *Times Literary Supplement*
for 5 Dec. 1912—C67—p. 93; on "'Homage to Propertius,'" in reply to Adrian
Collins's unsigned review, from the *New Age* for 4 Dec. 1919—C516—pp. 163–
4; on "Propertius and Mr. Pound," in reply to a review by Robert Nichols, from
the *Observer*, London, for 25 Jan. 1920—C533a—pp. 169–70, with Nichols's
reply, pp. 170–1; "A Pound of Poetry," in reply to H. B. Parkes on *Profile*, from
the *New English Weekly* for 12 Jan. 1933—C911—p. 243; and "Who or What?"
in reply to D. G. Bridson's review on the Cantos, from the same periodical for
12 Oct. 1933—C978—p. 268.

B113   WILLIAM M. CHACE. THE   1973
               POLITICAL IDENTITIES
          OF EZRA POUND & T. S. ELIOT

WILLIAM M. CHACE | The Political Identities of | EZRA POUND
& T. S. ELIOT | [*publisher's device*] | Stanford University Press |
STANFORD, CALIFORNIA | 1973

xviii, 238 pp. 22·2 × 14·5 cm. Buff cloth boards lettered in black on spine; end-
papers. Buff dust-jacket printed in black and red.

Published 27 December 1973 at $8.95; 2594 copies printed. *On verso of title-leaf:*
. . . Printed in the United States of America . . .

Contains, as Appendix B, pp. [225]–232, "Ezra Pound Speaking: A Broadcast
from Rome." This is the talk "England," broadcast 15 March 1942. (A copy of
Pound's typescript for this broadcast was filed with the U. S. Copyright Office
by the Ezra Pound Estate in 1973.)

B. BOOKS AND PAMPHLETS

B114   YONE NOGUCHI. COLLECTED   1975
        ENGLISH LETTERS

YONE NOGUCHI | COLLECTED ENGLISH LETTERS | [edited by]
IKUKO ATSUMI | with Illustrations | TOKYO | THE YONE NO-
GUCHI SOCIETY | 1975

239 pp., incl. illus. (ports., facsims.) 30 × 20·5 cm. Heavy yellow paper wrappers printed in brown on pages [i] and [iv].

Published early in 1975 at 2500 Yen; number of copies unknown. Title-leaf of
heavy yellow paper. Text reproduced from typewritten copy.

Contains "Ezra Pound to Yone Noguchi," a letter postmarked, London, 2 Sept.
1911, pp. 210–11.

B115   POUND. DONALD DAVIE   [1975]
Pound | Donald Davie | Fontana/Collins [London]

125, [3] pp. 18 × 10·8 cm. Heavy white paper wrappers printed in black and
with painting in colors on page [i], and in black on page [iv] and on spine.

Published June 1975 at 60p. in the series "Fontana Modern Masters, Editor:
Frank Kermode"; 12,500 copies printed. *On verso of title-leaf:* First published in
Fontana 1975 . . . Set by Richard Clay (The Chaucer Press), Ltd, Bungay, Suf-
folk Printed in Great Britain by William Collins Sons and Co Ltd, Glasgow . . .

Contains two letters from Ezra Pound to Thomas Hardy, Feb. 1921, pp. 46–47,
and 31 Mar. 1921, pp. 48–49, 51. (Publishers' advertisements, pp. [126–8].)

Note: This book was published, hardbound, in New York in 1976 by the Viking
Press at $7.95 in its series "Modern Masters, Edited by Frank Kermode."

B116   EZRA POUND'S PENNSYLVANIA   1976
        . . . NOEL STOCK

[*In gold:*] EZRA POUND'S PENNSYLVANIA | [*in black:*] Compiled
for the most part from | Mr. Carl Gatter's researches into | origi-
nal sources and documents | by | Noel Stock | THE FRIENDS OF
THE UNIVERSITY OF | TOLEDO LIBRARIES | [Toledo, O.] 1976

111, [1] pp., incl. illus. (ports., facsims.) 22·9 × 15·3 cm. Heavy brown paper
wrappers printed in black, with buff paper outer wrapper printed in black on
pages [i] and [iv], back flap, and down the spine, attached to and folded over
inner wrappers; grey fly-leaf at front and back.

B. BOOKS AND PAMPHLETS

Published 23 January 1976 at $10.00; 1000 copies printed. *On verso of title-leaf:* . . . First published in 1976 by the Friends of the University of Toledo Libraries Toledo, Ohio 43606 *Colophon (page* [112]): *[in gold:]* . . . Printed in December 1975 . . . by Printers Three Inc. of Toledo, Ohio and published by the Friends of the University of Toledo Libraries in January 1976 in an edition of 1000 numbered copies. This is copy number *[number written in in ink]*

Contains "Ezra on the Strike," pp. 34–35 (with reproduction of the printed poem—C o—p. 40); "Belangal Alba," p. 47; brief excerpts from poems in "Hilda's Book" (four lines from "The Lees," four lines from "Ver Novum," and three lines from "Shadow"), p. 55; excerpts from letters and two poems written to Mary Moore (of Trenton), with inscription to her from *Personae*, pp. 66–67, 73, 74; reproduction of a manuscript of "Autumnus," p. 69, and of page 4 from Mrs. Wood's program, *i.e. Miss Florence Schmidt . . . Book of Words* ([1910])—B2, p. 71; excerpts from letters to Floyd Dell, pp. 78–79; reproduction of page 12 of the *Evening Bulletin*, Philadelphia, for 20 February 1928—C704—pp. 83–84; "The Dramatist . . . 6th June 1953," a four-line poem on T. S. Eliot, pp. 91–92; letters and excerpts from letters to the Gatters, pp. 92, 102–4; and an inscription to the Heacock sisters in *Selected Poems*, p. 111.

B117   EZRA POUND: THE LAST   [1976]
                ROWER . . . BY C. DAVID
                HEYMANN

ALSO BY C. DAVID HEYMANN | The Quiet Hours (Verse) | Ezra Pound: | The | Last | Rower | [*to left of preceding three lines:*] A | Political | Profile | by | [*in center:*] C. David Heymann | A Richard Seaver Book | The Viking Press | New York

xii, 372 pp., incl. front. (port.), illus., ports. 24 × 16 cm. Green paper boards with black cloth back stamped in green and violet; end-papers. White dustjacket printed in black and green (with photograph of Ezra Pound in Venice in the 1960s by Horst Tappe on back).

Published 30 March 1976 at $12.50; 7500 copies printed. *On verso of title-leaf:* . . . First published in 1976 by The Viking Press . . . Printed in U.S.A. . . .

Contains reprints of *Volitionist Economics*—E2m—p. 70, and *Introductory Text Book*—E2r—pp. 72–73; excerpts from Rome radio broadcasts, 2 and 26 Oct., 4 and 6 Nov., and 6 Dec. 1941, pp. 103–7, and 26 Jan. 1942, pp. 113–14, with briefer quotations, in part reprinted from B92, pp. 116–21; excerpts (translated) from contributions to *Il Popolo di Alessandria*, pp. 141–2; excerpts (tr.) from letters to Fernando Mezzasoma, 1 Feb. and Nov. 1944, p. 143; excerpts (tr.) from a "service note" to Mezzasoma, 15 Jan. 1944, pp. 145–7; letters to Giorgio Almirante, 16 May 1944, (tr.) p. 151, and William Carlos Williams, Feb. 1946, p. 222; contributions to *Strike*—C1776 and 1783—pp. 225–6; excerpts from letters to Archibald MacLeish, pp. 236, 238, 266, 267, and 270; excerpt (tr.) from "Ezra

B. BOOKS AND PAMPHLETS

Pound ai falsificatori"—C1869—pp. 265–6; and quotations from interviews: with the *New York Herald Tribune*, 18 Jan. 1960—C1881a—p. 269, Allen Ginsberg's "Encounters with Ezra Pound," pp. 296–8, and Heymann's own, pp. 307–9, and 312–13. In Appendix I, "Letters to Benito Mussolini," pp. 317–27, are printed nine letters from Pound to Mussolini, 1933–1943, translated from the Italian by Robert Connolly. Appendix II, "Letters to Galeazzo Ciano," pp. 327–31, prints four letters from Pound to Ciano, 1934, the first translated by Connolly, the others written in English. Appendix III, "Letters to Fernando Mezzasoma," pp. 331–6, prints excerpts of seven letters from Pound to Mezzasoma, 1944, all translated by Connolly. A letter from Pound to President Woodrow Wilson, undated, but received 29 Mar. 1913, is printed in footnote 17, p. 347.

Note: This book was published in London 20 September 1976 by Faber and Faber at £ 5.95 in a first impression of 4000 copies. Contents as in the American edition. An edition paperbound was published in 1980 in New York by Seaver Books at $6.95.

B118   EZRA POUND: THE LONDON   1976
            YEARS

EZRA POUND | The London Years | [Sheffield] SHEFFIELD UNIVERSITY LIBRARY | 23 April–13 May 1976

[32] pp. 25·4 × 20·2 cm. Heavy grey paper wrappers printed in black on page [i] (with reproduction of a drawing of Ezra Pound by Wyndham Lewis) and page [iv]; wire-stitched.

Published 23 April 1976 at £ 1.00; 450 copies printed. *Imprint on page* [iv] *of wrappers:* Printed by W. Bishop & Sons (Sheffield) Ltd. *Colophon (page* [4]): This Catalogue printed in a Limited Edition of 450 copies

Compiled by Philip Grover. Seven postcards from Ezra Pound to his mother-in-law, Olivia Shakespear, all written in 1919 during a walking-tour of Provence, are quoted on pages [11], [12], [13], [16], [18], and [20]. (Canto IV, "Near Perigord," and "Provincia deserta," are reprinted, pp. [23–32].)

Note: The text of the catalogue is reproduced, reduced and with pages rearranged, in facsimile at the end of Philip Grover, *ed.*, *Ezra Pound: The London Years* (New York, AMS Press [1978]), and a photograph of the postcard postmarked 29 May 1919 is reproduced as an illustration.

B119   NICCOLÒ ZAPPONI. L'ITALIA   [1976]
            DI EZRA POUND

NICCOLÒ ZAPPONI | L'ITALIA DI | EZRA POUND | BULZONI EDITORE [Roma]

1 blank leaf, 2 leaves, 7–226 pp., 1 leaf. 21 × 15 cm. Heavy brown paper wrappers printed in black and green on page [i], and in black up the spine and on flaps.

Published May 1976 at L. 4000 as "Università di Roma. Facoltà di Lettere e Filosofia. Istituto di Letteratura Inglese e Americana. Studi e Ricerche, 3"; number of copies unknown. *At foot of page* [227]: Tipo-lito Domograf – 00174 Roma – cir.ne tuscolana, 38 . . .

Contains substantial extracts from Ezra Pound's Italian writings and excerpts from a number of his English articles translated into Italian, along with letters (in Italian) to Benito Mussolini, 22 Dec. 1936, p. 52; 12 Feb. 1940, p. 53; 10 May 1943, pp. 54–55, with explanatory note from Pound to Mussolini's secretary, pp. 55–56; extracts from letters (in Italian) to Alessandro Chiavolini, 28 Apr. 1932, p. 48; 23 Oct. 1936, p. 51; extract from note (in Italian) for "il Magg. Rapicavoli (?)," Oct. 1935, p. 51; and two letters to Curzio Malaparte, 1938–1939, one in English, the other in Italian, p. 138. Printed in the appendix, pp. 205–10, are: "Progetto di organizzazione internazionale ('lega o convegno dei popoli') inviato da Ezra Pound a Benito Mussolini il 15 ottobre 1935"; "Due lettere di Ezra Pound a Odon Por [12 Jan. 1937 (in English) and 3 Feb. 1941 (in Italian)]"; and "Lettera di Ezra Pound al Professor Yang Feng-chi [22 Nov. 1944 (in Italian)]."

B120   HARRIET MONROE AND THE   [1977]
POETRY RENAISSANCE . . .
ELLEN WILLIAMS

Harriet Monroe | and the | Poetry Renaissance | The First Ten Years of Poetry, 1912–22 [*ornament*] | ELLEN WILLIAMS | UNIVERSITY OF ILLINOIS PRESS | Urbana Chicago London

xiv, 312 pp., 1 blank leaf. 23·5 × 15·5 cm. Brown cloth boards stamped in gold down the spine; end-papers. White dust-jacket printed in buff, red, and black.

Published 16 March 1977 at $10.95; 2000 copies printed. *On verso of title-leaf:* . . . Manufactured in the United States of America . . .

Contains letters and excerpts from letters to *Poetry* or its editor, pp. 7, 35, 35–36, 37, 38, 39–40, 45, 47, 55, 63, 67, 72, 73, 74, 75, 76, 77–78, 80, 93, 94–95, 121, 127, 129, 132, 133, 153, 159, 164–5, [175], 179, 182, 186, 202–3, 204, 254; and these printed contributions or excerpts from them: "Poetry: A Magazine of Verse"—C142—pp. 95–96; "Drunken Helots and Mr Eliot"—C258—p. 125; "Vortex"—C149—p. 132; "The Audience"—C159—pp. 160–1; and from "Small Magazines"—pp. 283, 284. (Other excerpts from letters, articles, and poems are reprinted from published books.)

B. BOOKS AND PAMPHLETS

B121   FIRST FLOWERING   [1977]

FIRST | FLOWERING | THE BEST OF | THE | HARVARD AD-
VOCATE | [*device in center, with, at left:*] Preface, | "Our Man at
Harvard," | by | NORMAN | MAILER | [*and, at right:*] Introduction
| by | ROBERT | FITZGERALD | [*in center:*] RICHARD M. SMOLEY
| Editor | [*publishers' device*] | ADDISON-WESLEY PUBLISHING
COMPANY | Reading, Massachusetts · Menlo Park, California |
London · Amsterdam · Don Mills, Ontario · Sydney

xvi, 335, [1] pp., incl. illus., ports. 28·4 × 22 cm. White paper boards stamped
in gold on spine; orange end-papers. White dust-jacket printed all-over in orange and in cream and black, marked: FACSIMILE EDITION

Published 5 April 1977 at $15.00; 5000 copies printed. *On verso of title-leaf:* . . .
Printed in the United States of America. . . . A . . .

Contains "Ignite! Ignite!"—C995—pp. 143–5, and "A Problem of (Specifically) Style"—C1120 note—pp. 146–7. (The second essay had been reprinted
earlier in the *Harvard Advocate Centennial Anthology* ([1966])—B81.)

B122   LITERARY AMERICA 1903–1934:   [1979]
       THE MARY AUSTIN LETTERS

Literary | America | 1903–1934 | THE | MARY AUSTIN | LETTERS
| Selected and Edited by T. M. Pearce | CONTRIBUTIONS IN
WOMEN'S STUDIES, NUMBER 5 | GREENWOOD, PRESS | WEST-
PORT, CONNECTICUT · LONDON, ENGLAND [*publisher's device
at left of preceding two lines*]

xv, 296 pp., 2 leaves, 2 blank leaves, including front. (port.) 21·8 × 14·7 cm.
Green cloth boards stamped in gold on front cover and on spine; end-papers.
Issued without dust-jacket.

Published 19 April 1979 at $17.95 as "Contributions in Women's Studies, 5";
1445 copies printed. *On verso of title-leaf:* . . . First published in 1979. . . . Printed
in the United States of Amercia . . . 1

Contains a letter from Ezra Pound to Mary Austin, 13 April 1930, with particular reference to Nicholas Murray Butler and the Carnegie Endowment for
International Peace, p. 235. The editor's introductory comment appears on pages
232–4.

B123   END TO TORMENT . . . H. D.   [1979]
a. *Hardbound copies:*

end to torment | A memoir of Ezra Pound by [*to right of these two*
218

B. BOOKS AND PAMPHLETS

lines:] H. D. | Edited by Norman Holmes Pearson and Michael
King | With the poems from "Hilda's Book" by | EZRA POUND |
A NEW DIRECTIONS BOOK [New York, James Laughlin]

xii, 84 pp., incl. front. (port.) 20·9 × 14·2 cm. Green cloth boards with grey
cloth back lettered in silver down the spine; end-papers. White dust-jacket printed
in grey and black.

Published 25 June 1979 at $8.50; 1500 copies printed. *On verso of title-leaf:* ...
Manufactured in the United States of America First published clothbound and
as New Directions Paperbook 476 in 1979 ... New Directions Books are published for James Laughlin by New Directions Publishing Corporation, 80 Eighth
Avenue, New York 10011

The frontispiece is a "Photograph of H. D. by Ezra Pound".

Contains "Hilda's Book," by Ezra Pound, pp. 67–84. "The poems in 'Hilda's
Book' were composed during the first years of Pound's friendship with Hilda
Doolittle, 1905–07, the period recalled in her memoir, *End to Torment.* Four of
the poems were later published, with some changes, in Pound's early volumes:
'La Donzella Beata,' 'Li Bel Chasteus,' 'Era Venuta' (as 'Comraderie'), and 'The
Tree.' The poem entitled 'To draw back into the soul of things. Pax' is included
in another version ('Sonnet of the August Calm') in the San Trovaso Notebook
of 1908, as is 'The Banners' ('Fratello Mio Zephyrus')." (*Note by* M[*ichael*].
K[*ing*]., *pp. 67–68*)

Contents: "Child of the Grass"—"I strove a little book to make for her"—"Being
alone where the way was full of dust, I said | 'Era mea | In qua terra'"—La
Donzella Beata—The Wings—Ver Novum—To One That Journeyeth with Me—
Domina—The Lees—Per Saecula—Shadow—"One whose soul was | so full
of rose"—The Banners ["Fratello Mio Zephyrus"]—"'To draw back into the
soul of things.' Pax" ["Sonnet of the August Calm"]—Green Harping—From
another sonnet—Li Bel Chasteus—The Arches—Era Venuta ["Comraderie"]—The Tree—Thu Ides Til—L'Envoi—The Wind—Sancta Patrona Domina
Caelae—Rendez-vous

b. *Paperbound copies:*

Title-page and pagination as in hardbound copies. 20·3 × 13·2
cm. Heavy white paper wrappers printed in black and grey on
pages [i] and [iv] and down the spine.

Published 25 June 1979 at $3.95 as New Directions Paperbook 476; 3900 copies
printed. Verso of title-leaf as in hardbound copies.

Contents as in hardbound copies.

c. *English issue* ([1980]):

[*Title-page as in American issue down to imprint, then: publisher's device*]
| CARCANET NEW PRESS LIMITED [Manchester]

xii, 84 pp., incl. front. (port.) 21·4 × 13·3 cm. Heavy white paper wrappers printed all-over in blue and in black.

Published 24 January 1980 at £ 2.95; 1500 copies printed. *On verso of title-leaf:* ... First published in Great Britain in 1980 ... Printed ... by Billings, Guildford

Contents as in American issue.

B124   THE ... O'DONNELL   1979
COLLECTION OF MODERN
LITERATURE

[*In black:*] The Edward and Catherine O'Donnell | Collection of Modern Literature | [*in red: ornament*] | [*in black:*] An Exhibition | Fall 1979 | The University of Rochester Library

cover-title, 23 pp. 21·4 × 13·9 cm. Heavy cream paper wrappers printed in black and red with title-page (as above) on page [i]; wire-stitched.

Published 18 November 1979 for distribution gratis; 1000 copies printed. *Colophon (page 23):* This catalogue was compiled by Peter Dzwonkoski and printed in an edition of 1,000 copies. ... Four copies have been specially hand-bound in leather by Fred Jordan of Victor, New York. The exhibition was mounted by Mary M. Huth. ...

Contains reproduction of a typewritten "Letter from Ezra Pound to Francesco Monotti." 14 April [1940], p. [8].

B125   WILLIAM CARLOS WILLIAMS   [1980]
THE CRITICAL HERITAGE

WILLIAM | CARLOS WILLIAMS | THE CRITICAL HERITAGE | Edited by | CHARLES DOYLE | Professor of English | University of Victoria, British Columbia | [*rule*] | ROUTLEDGE & KEGAN PAUL | LONDON, BOSTON AND HENLEY

xix, 436 pp. 22·3 × 14 cm. Blue cloth boards lettered in gold on spine; end-papers (back end-paper with printed list of series). White dust-jacket printed in grey, brown, and black.

Published 6 March 1980 at £ 13.50 in the publishers' "The Critical Heritage Series"; number of copies unknown. *On verso of title-leaf:* First published in 1980 ... Printed in Great Britain by Redwood Burn Limited Trowbridge & Esher ... [Pages xv–xix, and text, pp. 1–436 reproduced from typewritten copy.]

Contains Ezra Pound's review of *The Tempers* from the *New Freewoman* for 1
Dec. 1913—C117—pp. 52–53. (Two letters from Pound to Williams are reprinted from *The Letters of Ezra Pound 1907–1941* ([1950])—A64.)

B126   '76 . . . BY FORREST READ   [1981]

a. *Hardbound copies:*

'76 | One World | and The Cantos | of Ezra Pound | by Forrest
Read | The University of North Carolina Press Chapel Hill

xii, 476 pp. illus., facsims. 23·6 × 15·7 cm. Blue cloth boards stamped in white
on spine; end-papers. White dust-jacket printed in red and black.

Published 29 May 1981 at $25.00; 1250 copies printed. *On verso of title-leaf:* . . .
Manufactured in the United States of America . . .

Contains "The Little Review Calendar" and "Note to Calendar"—C634 *bis*—
p. 39 (with Read's addition of "And | fifty | 2 | weeks | in | 4 | seasons" at the
left, the "Calendar" repeated, without the addition, on p. [75]); "Origo," pp.
305–6, "a mythic background for transforming prophetic revolutionary tradition formed in the mind into personal struggle carried out in the mind (and
heart)," sent to Douglas Fox in 1938 or 1939; "To R[obert]. B[rowning].," pp.
448–52, "an unpublished poem of 1907," with comments, in a text, "lightly
edited, from a letter to Viola Baxter [later Jordan], dated 1907, at Yale."; with
excerpts from letters and uncollected articles, *passim*.

b. *Paperbound copies:*

Title-page and pagination as in hardbound copies. 22·8 × 15 cm.
Heavy white paper wrappers printed in red and black on pages
[i] and [iv] and on spine.

Published 29 May 1981 at $14.00; 750 copies printed. Verso of title-leaf as in
hardbound copies.

Contents as in hardbound copies.

C. CONTRIBUTIONS TO PERIODICALS

Items are arranged chronologically. Contributions to periodicals of the same date are arranged alphabetically by periodical. Contributions to the same issue of a periodical are listed in the order of their appearance. (Contributions to a particular periodical are indexed under the periodical.) The place of publication is given after the title for newspapers and when a periodical appears in this list for the first time (or for the first time after a change in its place of publication). Titles of poems are printed in small capital letters. Letters to editors are indicated by the symbol ✉. An item not seen is marked by an asterisk.

Note: Ezra Pound took an active editorial interest (often unacknowledged on mastheads) in many of the periodicals to which he contributed. He was closely associated with the *New Freewoman* in its final days and continued to be identified with its successor the *Egoist* until its demise. He was Foreign Correspondent of *Poetry* from September 1912 to February 1919, Foreign (later, London) Editor of the *Little Review* from May 1917 to April 1919 and from Autumn 1921 to Spring 1924, and Paris Correspondent of the *Dial* from October 1921 to July 1923. He himself edited the *Exile* throughout its brief existence from Spring 1927 to Autumn 1928. He was at various times more or less closely associated in an editorial capacity with *Blast* (1914–1915), *Broletto* (1938), *Dial* (1927–1929), *Edge* (1956), *Four Pages* (1950), *Hound & Horn* (1929–1931), *L'Indice* (1930–1931), *Il Mare* (1932–1939), the *New Review* (1931–1932), *Strike* (1955–1956), *Townsman* (1938–1941), and *Voice* (1956–1957).

C. CONTRIBUTIONS TO PERIODICALS

1902

co EZRA ON THE STRIKE. *Times Chronicle*, Jenkintown, Pa. (8 Nov. 1902).
A poem of four eight-line stanzas, influenced by James Whitcomb Riley
and the Rev. William Barnes Lower; unsigned. Reprinted as by Ezra Pound
in the *Times Chronicle* for 9 Nov. 1972 in an article by Ruth Levine, "*Times
Chronicle* First Publisher: Poet Ezra Pound Treasured Childhood in 'Old
Wyncote,'" pp. [1], 4. Again reprinted in *Poetry Australia*, 46 ([Spring?]
1973) 14–15.

1905

C1 BELANGAL ALBA. *Hamilton Literary Magazine*, Clinton, N. Y., XXXIX. 9 (May
1905) 324.
Signed: E. P. Reprinted, with slight revisions, as "Alba Belingalis." "Belangal Alba" was reprinted in the *Hamilton Literary Magazine*'s *Continental:
Commemorative Edition* ([1962]) 77.

1906

C2 Raphaelite Latin. *Book News Monthly*, Philadelphia, Pa., XXV. 1 (Sept. 1906)
[31]–34.
Includes the author's verse translations of "De morte Raphaelis pictoris"
by Castiglione, "Ad noctem" by Camillo Capilupi, and "Ad rosam (from
the *Erotopaegnion*)" by Hieronymus Angerianus.

C3 Interesting French Publications. *Book News Monthly*, XXV. 1 (Sept. 1906) 54–
55.
A review of *Origine et esthétique de la tragédie* and *Le secret des troubadours*, by
M. Péladan.

C4 Burgos, a Dream City of Old Castile. *Book News Monthly*, XXV. 2 (Oct.
1906) 91–94.

C5 A DAWN SONG. *Munsey's Magazine*, New York, XXXVI. 3 (Dec. 1906) 380.

1908

C6 TO THE RAPHAELITE LATINISTS. *Book News Monthly*, XXVI. 5 (Jan. 1908)
[358].
"By Weston Llewmys [*i.e.* Ezra Weston Loomis Pound]."

C7 M. Antonius Flamininus and John Keats, a Kinship in Genius. *Book News
Monthly*, XXVI. 6 (Feb. 1908) [445]–447.

C8 ✉ The Event of the Coming Piano Season. *New York Herald*, Paris (21 June
1908) 9.

C. CONTRIBUTIONS TO PERIODICALS

Signed: E. P. On Katherine Ruth Heyman, the pianist.

C9 HISTRION. *Evening Standard and St. James's Gazette*, London (26 Oct. 1908) 3.

C10 FOR KATHERINE RUTH HEYMAN. (AFTER ONE OF HER VENETIAN CON-CERTS). *Evening Standard and St. James's Gazette*, London (8 Dec. 1908) 3. Reprinted as "Nel Biancheggiar."

C10a BALLAD FOR GLOOM . . . THRENOS . . . *American Journal Examiner*, New York (14 Dec. 1908).
Quoted complete in a review of *A Lume Spento* by Ella Wheeler Wilcox (clipping in Homer Pound's scrapbook thus identified), along with the eight-line epigraph headed "Make-strong old dreams lest this our world lose heart," and part of "La Fraisne" (the last 13 lines, followed by lines 24–36).

1909

C11 The "Brunhild" of Frederic Manning. Reviewed . . . *Book News Monthly*, XXVII. 8 (Apr. 1909) 620–1.

C12 SESTINA: ALTAFORTE. *English Review*, London, II. 3 (June 1909) 419–20.

C13 PICCADILLY. *Book News Monthly*, XXVII. 12 (Aug. 1909) 920. Reprinted from *Personae* (1909)—A3.

C14 THREE POEMS. *English Review*, III. 3 (Oct. 1909) 382–4.
Contents: Ballad of the Goodly Fere—Nils Lykke—Un retrato [*sic.* Reprinted as "Portrait from 'La mère inconnue.'"]

C15 BALLAD OF THE GOODLY FERE. *Literary Digest*, New York, XXXIX. 18 (30 Oct. 1909) 730–1.
Reprinted from the *English Review* for Oct. 1909—C14. Reprinted also in the Philadelphia *Evening Bulletin* (2 Dec. 1909), in the Alumni number of the *Hamilton Literary Magazine* (1910), and in the same publication's *Continental: Commemorative Edition* ([1962]) 78–79.

C16 AND THUS IN NINEVEH. *Literary Digest*, XXXIX. 22 (27 Nov. 1909) 958. Reprinted from *Personae* (1909)—A3.

1910

C17 THREE POEMS. *English Review*, IV. 2 (Jan. 1910) 193–7.
Contents: Canzon: The Yearly Slain ⟨Written in reply to Manning's "Persephone" [*i.e.* "Korè"]⟩—Canzon: The Spear—Canzon: To Be Sung beneath a Window.

C17a MESMERISM; BALLAD FOR GLOOM. *Literary Digest*, XL. 9 (26 Feb. 1910) 404.
Part of an article, "Current Poetry," pp. 402–4. Both poems reprinted from *A Lume Spento* ([1908])—A1—and *Personae* (1909)—A3. "Mesmerism" was

reprinted also in *Reedy's Mirror*, XIX. 50 (10 Mar. 1910) 17, and "Ballad for Gloom" in the same periodical, XIX. 56 (21 Apr. 1910) 7.

C18 TWO POEMS. *Current Literature*, New York, XLVIII. 3 (Mar. 1910) 342–3.
Contents: Ballad of the Goodly Fere—Histrion. Reprinted from *Exultations* (1909)—A4.

C19 LA REGINA AVRILLOUSE (MY QUEEN APRIL). *Philadelphia Ledger*, Philadelphia, Pa. (19 Mar. 1910).
Reprinted from *A Lume Spento* ([1908])—A1.

C20 TWO POEMS. *English Review*, V. 1 (Apr. 1910) 9–11.
Contents: Canzon: Of Incense—Thersites; on the Surviving Zeus.

C20a ✉ A Correction. *New Age*, London, VI. 26 (28 Apr. 1910) 620.
With reference to an article by E. Pugh in the issue for 21 Aug.

C21 THE VISION. *Forum*, New York, XLIV. 4 (Oct. 1910) 423–4.

C22 The Science of Poetry. *Book News Monthly*, XXIX. 4 (Dec. 1910) 282–3.
A review of *The Science of Poetry and the Philosophy of Language*, by Hudson Maxim.

C23 CHRISTMAS PROLOGUE. *Sunday School Times*, Philadelphia, Pa., LII. 49 (3 Dec. 1910) [613].
Reprinted, with an additional four lines at the end, as "A Prologue."

1911

C24 THE FAULT OF IT. *Forum*, New York, XLVI. 1 (July 1911) 107.

C25 I Gather the Limbs of Osiris ... I. (A translation from the early Anglo-Saxon text). *New Age*, London, X. 5 (30 Nov. 1911) 107.
"(Under this heading Mr. Pound will contribute expositions and translations in illustration of 'The New Method' in scholarship.—The Editor.)"
This first part of 12 is devoted to "The Seafarer," with a "Philological Note."

C26 I Gather the Limbs of Osiris [II] ... A Rather Dull Introduction. *New Age*, X. 6 (7 Dec. 1911) 130–1.

C27 I Gather the Limbs of Osiris, III. Guido Cavalcanti. *New Age*, X. 7 (14 Dec. 1911) 155–6.
Includes verse translations of Sonnets VII and XXXV, and Ballate V, VII, and IX, by Cavalcanti.

C28 I Gather the Limbs of Osiris ... IV. A Beginning. *New Age*, X. 8 (21 Dec. 1911) 178–80.

C29 ✉ On the "Decline of Faith." *New Age*, X. 8 (21 Dec. 1911) 191.
Signed: E. P.

C30 I Gather the Limbs of Osiris, V. Four Early Poems of Arnaut Daniel. *New Age*, X. 9 (28 Dec. 1911) 201–2.
Includes verse translations of "Chansson doil," "Can chai la fueilla," "Lancan son passat il giure," and "For Right of Audience."

C. CONTRIBUTIONS TO PERIODICALS

1912

C31 ECHOS. *North American Review*, New York, CXCV. 674 (Jan. 1912) 75.
Contents: I (Trecento) Guido Orlando, Singing—II Two Cloaks [reprinted as "The Cloak"].

C32 I Gather the Limbs of Osiris ... VI. On Virtue. *New Age*, X. 10 (4 Jan. 1912) 224–5.

C33 I Gather the Limbs of Osiris ... VII. Arnaut Daniel: Canzoni of His Middle Period. *New Age*, X. 11 (11 Jan. 1912) 249–51.
Includes verse translations of "Autet e bas," and "L'aura amara."

C34 I Gather the Limbs of Osiris ... VIII. CANZON: OF THE TRADES AND LOVE. *New Age*, X. 12 (18 Jan. 1912) 274–5.
Verse translation from Arnaut Daniel.

C35 I Gather the Limbs of Osiris ... IX. On Technique. *New Age*, X. 13 (25 Jan. 1912) 297–9.

C36 THE COMPLETE POETICAL WORKS OF T. E. HULME. *New Age*, X. 13 (25 Jan. 1912) 307.
Contents: Autumn—Mana Aboda—Conversion—Above the Dock—Embankment. (Probably not edited by Ezra Pound, but reprinted by him as appendix to *Ripostes* (1912)—A8.)

C37 ✉ The Art of the Novel. *New Age*, X. 13 (25 Jan. 1912) 311.

C38 Prologomena [*sic*]. *Poetry Review*, London, I. 2 (Feb. 1912) 72–76.
Includes "Credo."

C39 POETRY. *Poetry Review*, I. 2 (Feb. 1912) 77–81.
Contents: Oboes (I. For a beery voice; II. After Heine; III. An Immorality)—Sub mare—L'Invitation—Salve Pontifex—Dieu! Qu'il la fait—Δώρια.

C40 CANZONE: OF ANGELS. *Fortnightly Review*, London, XCI (N.S.). 542 (1 Feb. 1912) [277]–278.

C41 I Gather the Limbs of Osiris ... X. On Music. *New Age*, X. 15 (8 Feb. 1912) 343–4.

C42 I Gather the Limbs of Osiris ... XI. *New Age*, X 16 (15 Feb. 1912) 369–70.
Includes prose translation of "En breu brisaral temps braus," by Arnaut Daniel.

C43 I Gather the Limbs of Osiris ... XII.—THREE CANZONI OF ARNAUT DANIEL. *New Age*, X. 17 (22 Feb. 1912) 392–3.
Verse translations of "Sols sui que sai," "Rica conquesta. The Song 'Of High All-attaining,'" and "Bird-Latin" (an early version of "Glamour and Indigo").

C44 The Book of the Month. *Poetry Review*, I. 3 (Mar. 1912) 133.
A review of *High Germany*, by Ford Madox Hueffer.

C45 The Wisdom of Poetry. *Forum*, XLVII. 4 (Apr. 1912) 497–501.

C46 SILET. *Smart Set*, New York, XXXVII. 1 (May 1912) 122.

C47 TWO POEMS. *English Review*, XI. 3 (June 1912) 343–4.

C. CONTRIBUTIONS TO PERIODICALS

Contents: The Return—Apparuit.

c48 Patria mia, I. *New Age*, XI. 19 (5 Sept. 1912) 445.
The first of 11 instalments.

c49 Patria mia, II. *New Age*, XI. 20 (12 Sept. 1912) 466.

c50 Patria mia, III. *New Age*, XI. 21 (19 Sept. 1912) 491–2.

c51 Patria mia, IV. *New Age*, XI. 22 (26 Sept. 1912) 515–16.

c52 TO WHISTLER, AMERICAN. ON THE LOAN EXHIBIT OF HIS PAINTINGS
AT THE TATE GALLERY. *Poetry*, Chicago, Ill., I. 1 (Oct. 1912) 7.
The autograph manuscript of this poem, as submitted to Harriet Monroe
for publication in *Poetry*, is reproduced in facsimile in *Famous Verse Manuscripts . . . Prepared by the Editors of Poetry* ([Chicago, 1954]), pp. 20–21.

c53 MIDDLE-AGED, A STUDY IN AN EMOTION. *Poetry*, I. 1 (Oct. 1912) 8.

c54 [Introductory note to] A Selection from *The Tempers*. By William Carlos
Williams. *Poetry Review*, I. 10 (Oct. 1912) 481–2.

c55 Psychology and Troubadours. *Quest*, London, IV. 1 (Oct. 1912) 37–53.
Reprinted as Chapter V of *The Spirit of Romance* (in editions published 1932
and later)—A5c–e.

c56 Patria mia, V. *New Age*, XI. 23 (3 Oct. 1912) 539–40.

c57 Patria mia, VI. *New Age*, XI. 24 (10 Oct. 1912) 564.

c58 Patria mia, VII. *New Age*, XI. 25 (17 Oct. 1912) 587–8.

c59 Patria mia, VIII. *New Age*, XI. 26 (24 Oct. 1912) 611–12.

c60 Patria mia, IX. *New Age*, XI. 27 (31 Oct. 1912) 635–6.

c61 Bohemian Poetry. *Poetry*, I. 2 (Nov. 1912) 57–59.
A review of *An Anthology of Modern Bohemian Poetry*, translated by P. Selver.

c62 Patria mia, X. *New Age*, XII. 1 (7 Nov. 1912) 12.

c63 Patria mia, XI. *New Age*, XII. 2 (14 Nov. 1912) 33–34.

c64 ✉ The Black Crusade. *New Age*, XII. 3 (21 Nov. 1912) 69.

c65 Tagore's Poems. *Poetry*, I. 3 (Dec. 1912) 92–94.
On the six poems by Rabindranath Tagore, in his own prose translation
from Bengali into English, printed in the same issue, pp. 84–86.

c66 ✉ The Black Crusade. *New Age*, XII. 5 (5 Dec. 1912) 116.

c67 ✉ The Poems of Cavalcanti. *Times Literary Supplement*, London, 569 (5
Dec. 1912) 562.
On the review of his *Sonnets and Ballate of Guido Cavalcanti*—B4b, and of
Dante Gabriel Rossetti's *Poems and Translations* in the issue for 21 Nov.
1912.

1913

c68 Status rerum [I]. *Poetry*, I. 4 (Jan. 1913) 123–7.
(In English.)

C. CONTRIBUTIONS TO PERIODICALS

c69 Through Alien Eyes, I. *New Age*, XII. 11 (16 Jan. 1913) 252.
The first of four instalments.

c70 Through Alien Eyes, II. *New Age*, XII. 12 (23 Jan. 1913) 275–6.

c71 Through Alien Eyes, III. *New Age*, XII. 13 (30 Jan. 1913) 300–1.

c72 [A review, signed: E. P., of] *Présences*, par P. J. Jouve. *Poetry*, I. 5 (Feb. 1913) 165–6.

c73 Through Alien Eyes, IV. *New Age*, XII. 14 (6 Feb. 1913) 324.

c73a Imagisme [by F. S. Flint]. *Poetry*, I. 6 (Mar. 1913) 198–200.
Facts gleaned by Flint from "an Imagiste [*i.e.* Pound]." Actually drafted by Pound and rewritten by Flint. See C1900.

c74 A Few Don'ts by an Imagiste. *Poetry*, I. 6 (Mar. 1913) 200–6.
Substantial portions of this and the preceding article by Flint are quoted by Rebecca West in her "Imagisme," in the *New Freewoman* for 15 Aug. 1913, pp. 86–87, introducing "The Contemporania of Ezra Pound" (see note to C76).

c75 Rabindranath Tagore. *Fortnightly Review*, XCIII (N.S.). 555 (1 Mar. 1913) [571]–579.

c76 CONTEMPORANIA. *Poetry*, II. 1 (Apr. 1913) 1–12.
Contents: Tenzone—The Condolence—The Garret—The Garden—Ortus—Dance Figure. For the Marriage in Cana of Galilee—Salutation—Salutation the Second—Pax Saturni [originally "Reflection and Advice"]—Commission—A Pact—In a Station of the Metro. Reprinted, omitting "The Condolence," "Ortus," "Pax Saturni," "Commission," and "A Pact," as "The Contemporania of Ezra Pound," in *New Freewoman*, London, I. 5 (15 Aug. 1913) 87–88, where the poems are introduced by Rebecca West's essay, "Imagisme," quoting portions of C73a and 74.

c77 [A review of] *A Boy's Will*, by Robert Frost. *Poetry*, II. 2 (May 1913) 72–74.

c78 [A review of] *Helen Redeemed and Other Poems*, by Maurice Hewlett. *Poetry*, II. 2 (May 1913) 74–76.

c79 America: Chances and Remedies . . . I. *New Age*, XIII. 1 (1 May 1913) 9–10.
The first of six instalments, all six reprinted as part of *Patria Mia* ([1950])—A63.

c80 America: Chances and Remedies . . . II. *New Age*, XIII. 2 (8 May 1913) 34.

c81 America: Chances and Remedies . . . III. Proposition I—That I Would "Drive the Auto on the Seminars." *New Age*, XIII. 3 (15 May 1913) 57–58.

c82 America: Chances and Remedies . . . IV. Proposition II—That I Would Drive the Seminars on "The Press." *New Age*, XIII. 4 (22 May 1913) 83.

c83 America: Chances and Remedies . . . V. Proposition III—The College of the Arts. *New Age*, XIII. 5 (29 May 1913) 115–16.

c84 CERTAIN POEMS OF KABIR. TRANSLATED BY KALI MOHAN GHOSE AND EZRA POUND FROM THE EDITION OF MR. KSHITI MOHAN SEN. *Modern Review*, Calcutta, XIII. 6 (June 1913) 611–13.

C. CONTRIBUTIONS TO PERIODICALS

c85 America: Chances and Remedies ... VI. *New Age*, XIII. 6 (5 June 1913) 143.

c86 How I Began ... *T. P.'s Weekly*, London, XXI. 552 (6 June 1913) 707.
Includes accounts of Elkin Mathews' acceptance of *Personae* for publication, and the composition of "Ballad of the Goodly Fere," "Sestina: Altaforte," and "In a Station of the Metro" (the last poem is reprinted, but without title).

c87 [A review of] *Love Poems and Others*, by D. H. Lawrence. *Poetry*, II. 4 (July 1913) 149–51.
Reprinted as "D. H. Lawrence."

c88 [A review of] *Odes et prières*, par Jules Romains. *Poetry*, II. 5 (Aug. 1913) 187–9.

c89 [A review, signed: E. P., of] *Art and Swadeshi*, by Ananda K. Coomaraswamy. *Poetry*, II. 6 (Sept. 1913) 226–7.

c90 POEMS. *Smart Set*, XLI. 1 (Sept. 1913) 17–18.
Contents: N[ew]. Y[ork].—A Girl—An Immorality—A Virginal—Sub mare—Pan Is Dead. Reprinted from *Ripostes* (1912)—A8.

c91 In Metre. *New Freewoman*, London, I. 6 (1 Sept. 1913) 113.
A review, signed: E. P., of *Love Poems and Others*, by D. H. Lawrence; *Peacock Pie*, by Walter de la Mare; and *A Boy's Will*, by Robert Frost.

c92 The Approach to Paris ... I. *New Age*, XIII. 19 (4 Sept. 1913) 551–2.
The first of seven instalments.

c93 The Approach to Paris ... II. *New Age*, XIII. 20 (11 Sept. 1913) 577–9.
In part, on Remy de Gourmont.

c94 In Metre. *New Freewoman*, I. 7 (15 Sept. 1913) 131–2.
A review, signed: E. P., of *The Dominant City* and *Fool's Gold*, by John Gould Fletcher.

c95 The Approach to Paris ... III. ["Monsieur Romains, Unanimist"]. *New Age*, XIII. 21 (18 Sept. 1913) 607–9.
Includes prose translation of a long passage from *Puissances de Paris*, by Jules Romains.

c96 ✉ "The Approach to Paris." *New Age*, XIII. 21 (18 Sept. 1913) 615.

c97 The Approach to Paris ... IV. *New Age*, XIII. 22 (25 Sept. 1913) 631–3.
On Charles Vildrac.

c98 ✉ "The Approach to Paris." *New Age*, XIII. 22 (25 Sept. 1913) 647.

c99 Paris. *Poetry*, III. 1 (Oct. 1913) 26–30.
"I have just finished a series of critical articles on French verse (*The New Age*, Sept. 4 and following [C92, 93, 95, 97, 104, 105, and 108]). I propose to give here merely a summary of my conclusions." A few sentences from this article relating to Henri-Martin Barzun were quoted on page [5] of a seven-page prospectus for Barzun's *Panharmonie Orphique, Poème Orchestral*, issued in New York in Nov. 1924 by W. E. Rudge Inc.

C. CONTRIBUTIONS TO PERIODICALS

C100 [A review, signed: E. P., of] *Poems and Songs (Second Series)*, by Richard Middleton. *Poetry*, III. 1 (Oct. 1913) 33–34.

C101 Troubadours: Their Sorts and Conditions. *Quarterly Review*, London, CCXIX. 437 (Oct. 1913) 426–40.

C102 "PHASELLUS ILLE." *Smart Set*, XLI. 2 (Oct. 1913) 80.
(In English.) Reprinted from *Ripostes* (1912)—A8.

C103 Reviews. *New Freewoman*, I. 8 (1 Oct. 1913) 149–50.
Proposing a mock "scientific norm" for reviews. Signed: Z. Almost certainly by Ezra Pound.

C104 The Approach to Paris . . . V. *New Age*, XIII. 23 (2 Oct. 1913) 662–4.
Contents: [I.] Laurent Tailhade—II. De Regnier—III. Corbière.

C105 The Approach to Paris . . . VI. *New Age*, XIII. 24 (9 Oct. 1913) 694–6.
On Francis Jammes. A brief paragraph (with reference to Richard of St. Victor) was reprinted in *Agenda*, XVII. 3/4/XVIII. 1 (Autumn/Winter/Spring 1979/1980) 71.

C106 The Serious Artist . . . I[–II]. *New Freewoman*, I. 9 (15 Oct. 1913) [161]–163.
The first of three instalments.

C106a Religio, or The Child's Guide to Knowledge. *New Freewoman*, I. 9 (15 Oct. 1913) 173–4.
Unsigned.

C107 ✉ The Order of the Brothers Minor. *New Freewoman*, I. 9 (15 Oct. 1913) 176.

C108 The Approach to Paris . . . VII. *New Age*, XIII. 25 (16 Oct. 1913) 726–8.
On Arthur Rimbaud, Paul Fort, André Spire, Henri-Martin Barzun, and others.

C109 POEMS. *Poetry*, III. 2 (Nov. 1913) 53–60.
Contents: Ancora—Surgit fama. Fragment from an unwritable play—The Choice—April—Gentildonna—Lustra (I. [The Rest]; II. [Les Millwin]; III. Further Instructions)—Xenia (I. The Street in Soho; II. "The cool fingers of science delight me"; III–V [A Song of the Degrees, I–III]; VI [Ité]; VII. Dum capitolium scandet). ("Xenia, I–VII" reprinted in *Paideuma*, Orono, Me., X. 2 (Fall 1981) 240–1.)

C110 PORTRAIT D'UNE FEMME. *Smart Set*, XLI. 3 (Nov. 1913) 88.
(In English.) Reprinted from *Ripostes* (1912)—A8.

C111 Rabindranath Tagore. His Second Book into English. *New Freewoman*, I. 10 (1 Nov. 1913) 187–8.
A review of *The Gardener*.

C112 The Serious Artist, III.—Emotion and Poesy. *New Freewoman*, I. 10 (1 Nov. 1913) 194–5.

C113 The Divine Mystery. *New Freewoman*, I. 11 (15 Nov. 1913) 207–8.
A review of *The Divine Mystery*, by Allen Upward.

C114 The Serious Artist. IV. *New Freewoman*, I. 11 (15 Nov. 1913) 213–14.

C114a IKON. *Cerebralist*, London, I (Dec. 1913) 43.
A prose poem, signed: E. P.

C115 Peals of Iron. *Poetry*, III. 3 (Dec. 1913) 111–13.
A review, signed: E. P., of *Fire and Wine* and *The Dominant City*, by John Gould Fletcher.

C116 ZENIA [*sic*]. *Smart Set*, XLI. 4 (Dec. 1913) 47–48.
Contents: [I. To Dives]—II. [Alba]—III. (Epitaph)—IV. "Come let us play with our own toys"—V. "She had a pig-shaped face, with beautiful coloring" [The Rapture]—VI. [Causa]—VII. [The Bath Tub]—VIII. [Arides]—IX. [The Encounter]—X. Simulacra—XI. (Tame Cat).

C117 The Tempers. *New Freewoman*, I. 12 (1 Dec. 1913) 227.
A review, signed: E. P., of *The Tempers*, by William Carlos Williams.

C118 Paul Castiaux. *New Freewoman*, I. 12 (1 Dec. 1913) 227.
A review, signed: E. P., of *"Lumières du monde" poèmes*, by Castiaux.

C119 POEMS. *New Freewoman*, I. 12 (1 Dec. 1913) 228.
Contents: Further Instructions—Les Millwin—Ancora—April—Gentildonna—Surgit fama—Convictions, I–III [A Song of the Degrees, I–III]—The Choice—The Rest.

C120 Ford Madox Hueffer. *New Freewoman*, I. 13 (15 Dec. 1913) 251.
A review of *Collected Poems*.

1914

C121 The Tradition. *Poetry*, III. 4 (Jan. 1914) 137–41.

C122 Ferrex on Petulance. *Egoist*, London, I. 1 (1 Jan. 1914) 9–10.
Signed: Ferrex.

C122a Porrex on Ferrex. *Egoist*, I. 1 (1 Jan. 1914) 10.
Signed: Porrex.

C123 ✉ Mr. Hawkins on Mr. Carter. *Egoist*, I. 1 (1 Jan. 1914) 19.
In Cockney dialect, signed: Henery Hawkins; concerning Huntly Carter. Almost certainly by Ezra Pound.

C124 A Curious History. *Egoist*, I. 2 (15 Jan. 1914) 26–27.
On James Joyce and *Dubliners*. Reprinted, May 1917, as a broadside (see E2d).

C125 Des Imagistes. *Glebe*, New York, I. 5 (Feb. 1914) 1–63.
Edited by Ezra Pound. For fuller description see B7.

C126 The Bourgeois. *Egoist*, I. 3 (2 Feb. 1914) 53.
Signed: Bastien [*i.e.* Baptiste] von Helmholtz.

C127 John Synge and the Habits of Criticism. *Egoist*, I. 3 (2 Feb. 1914) 53–54.
Signed: Bastien von Helmholtz. A brief paragraph was reprinted in *Agenda*, XVII. 3/4/XVIII. 1 (Autumn/Winter/Spring 1979/1980) 71.

C128 The New Sculpture. *Egoist*, I. 4 (16 Feb. 1914) 67–68.

C. CONTRIBUTIONS TO PERIODICALS

C129 An Essay in Constructive Criticism. With Apologies to Mr F--d M-d-x H--ff-r in the "Stoutlook." *Egoist*, I. 4 (16 Feb. 1914) 76.
Signed: Herrmann Karl Georg Jesus Maria. With footnote at end signed: William Michael R-s-tti. Almost certainly by Ezra Pound.

C130 ✉ A Correction. *Egoist*, I. 4 (16 Feb. 1914) 79.
Signed: Baptiste von Helmholtz; pointing out that his note "The Bourgeois"—C126—appeared "by some slight error" over the signature of his brother, Bastien von Helmholtz. (Both names are pseudonyms of Ezra Pound.)

C131 Homage to Wilfrid Blunt. *Poetry*, III. 6 (Mar. 1914) 220–3.
This account by Ezra Pound of the presentation "in token of homage" to W. S. Blunt, on Sunday, 18 Jan., of "a reliquary carved in Pentelican marble by the brilliant young sculptor Gaudier Brzeska," reprints the "verses of homage signed by the committee" and read by Pound, who also wrote them, anonymously. The poem had been printed with title "To Wilfrid Blunt" in the *Times*, London, for 20 Jan. 1914 (p. 5), and was included also in Richard Aldington's account of the ceremony, "Presentation to Mr. W. S. Blunt," in the *Egoist* for 2 Feb. 1914 (p. 56). It was reprinted, with suggested attribution to Pound, in Harold Monro's *Some Contemporary Poets (1920)* (London, Leonard Parsons [1920]), p. 37, and appeared also in Edith Finch's *Wilfrid Scawen Blunt 1840–1922* (London, Jonathan Cape [1938]), p. 337.

C132 [EIGHT POEMS]. *Poetry and Drama*, London, II. 1 (Mar. 1914) 20–24.
Contents: Albâtre—Society—To Formianus' Young Lady Friend—Coitus—Heather—The Faun—Tempora—A Translation from the Provençal ["Dompna pois de me no'us cal"] of En Bertrans de Born.

C133 [Introductory note to the first instalment of] The Causes and Remedy of the Poverty of China. By F. T. S. *Egoist*, I. 6 (16 Mar. 1914) 105.
(The same note was repeated before the second and third instalments in the *Egoist*, I. 7 (1 Apr. 1914) 131, and I. 10 (15 May 1914) 195.)

C134 Exhibition at the Goupil Gallery. *Egoist*, I. 6 (16 Mar. 1914) 109.
Contents: I. [Sculpture]—II. [Painting]. Part I was reprinted as "Ezra Pound's Estimate" in Jacob Epstein's *Let There Be Sculpture* ([1940])—B45—pp. 71–72.

C135 ✉ The Caressability of the Greeks. *Egoist*, I. 6 (16 Mar. 1914) 117.

C136 On Certain Reforms and Pass-Times. *Egoist*, I. 7 (1 Apr. 1914) 130–31.
Signed: Herman [*sic*] Carl Georg Jesus Maria. Almost certainly by Ezra Pound.

C137 Allen Upward Serious. *New Age*, XIV. 25 (23 Apr. 1914) 779–80.

C138 NISHIKIGI [TRANSLATED FROM THE JAPANESE OF MOTOKIYO BY ERNEST FENOLLOSA]. *Poetry*, IV. 2 (May 1914) 35–48.
Edited by Ezra Pound.

C139 The Later Yeats. *Poetry*, IV. 2 (May 1914) 64–69.
A review of *Responsibilities: Poems and a Play*, by W. B. Yeats.

C. CONTRIBUTIONS TO PERIODICALS

C140 Mr. Hueffer and the Prose Tradition in Verse. *Poetry*, IV. 3 (June 1914) 111–20.
A review of *Collected Poems*, by Ford Madox Hueffer. Reprinted as "The Prose Tradition in Verse."

C141 [TWO POEMS]. *Poetry and Drama*, II. 6 (June 1914) 194.
Contents: Fan-Piece for Her Imperial Lord—Ts'ai Chi'h. Reprinted "From the Anthology des Imagistes"—B7b.

C142 Poetry: A Magazine of Verse. *Egoist*, I. 11 (1 June 1914) 215.
Signed: Bastien von Helmholtz. Under the heading: "Reviews."

C143 First Novels. *Egoist*, I. 11 (1 June 1914) 215.
Signed: Baptiste von Helmholtz. Under the heading: "Reviews."

C144 Revolutionary Maxims. *Egoist*, I. 11 (1 June 1914) 217–18.
Quotations from the *Times Literary Supplement*, London; selected, anonymously, by Ezra Pound.

C145 ✉ The Dangers of Occultism. *Egoist*, I. 11 (1 June 1914) 220.

C146 Wyndham Lewis. *Egoist*, I. 12 (15 June 1914) 233–4.

C147 Revelations [I]. *Egoist*, I. 12 (15 June 1914) 234–5.
Quotations from the *Times Literary Supplement*, London, with one short one from the *Times*, London; selected, anonymously, by Ezra Pound.

C148 POEMS. *Blast*, London, 1 (20 June 1914) 45–50.
Contents: Salutation the Third—Monumentum aere, etc.—Come My Cantilations—Before Sleep—His Vision of a Certain Lady Post Mortem [Post mortem conspectu]—Epitaphs (Fu I; Li Po)—Fratres minores [with first two and last lines cancelled in ink in most copies]—Women before a Shop—L'Art—The New Cake of Soap—Meditatio—Pastoral.

C149 Vortex. Pound. *Blast*, 1 (20 June 1914) 153–4.

C150 Suffragettes. *Egoist*, I. 13 (1 July 1914) 254–6.
Signed: Bastien von Helmholtz.

C151 Revelations [II]. *Egoist*, I. 13 (1 July 1914) 256–7.
Quotations from the *Times Literary Supplement*, London; selected, anonymously, by Ezra Pound.

C152 "Dubliners" and Mr. James Joyce. *Egoist*, I. 14 (15 July 1914) 267.
A review of *Dubliners*. (A quotation from this review, printed in seven lines, appeared on page [1] of *Extracts from Press Notices of Dubliners by James Joyce* ([Zürich? The Author? 1914?]), a two-page leaflet measuring 19·1 × 12·7 cm., issued in connexion with the publication of the book.)

C153 Northcliffe's Nice Paper Again. *Egoist*, I. 14 (15 July 1914) 278.
Quotations from the *Times Literary Supplement*, London; selected, anonymously, by Ezra Pound.

C154 POEMS. *Poetry*, IV. 5 (Aug. 1914) 169–77.
Contents: To Καλὸν—The Study in Aesthetics—The Bellaires—Salvationists, I–III—Amitiés, I–IV [the fourth in Latin]—Ladies [originally "Le donne"] (Agathas [originally "Agathas intacta"]; Young Lady; Lesbia illa;

Passing [originally "Passante"])—The Seeing Eye—Abu Salammamm–A Song of Empire.

C154a God in London. A.D. 1914. *Egoist*, I. 15 (1 Aug. 1914) 286.
Suggested mottoes for London, extracted from the *Times*, London. Unsigned, but almost certainly by Ezra Pound.

C155 The Glamour of G. S. Street. *Egoist*, I. 15 (1 Aug. 1914) 294–5.

C156 Edward Wadsworth, Vorticist. An authorised appreciation. *Egoist*, I. 16 (15 Aug. 1914) 306–7.

C157 Some Rejected Mottoes. *Egoist*, I. 16 (15 Aug. 1914) 318.
"The following appropriate mottoes for London were not published in the 'Times.'" Unsigned, but almost certainly by Ezra Pound. (See C154a.)

C158 Vorticism. *Fortnightly Review*, XCVI (N.S.). 573 (1 Sept. 1914) [461]–471.
Reprinted in *Gaudier-Brzeska* (1916)—A10—pp. 94–109.

C159 The Audience. I. *Poetry*, V. 1 (Oct. 1914) 29–30.
(Part II, following, is by Harriet Monroe.)

C160 The Classical Drama of Japan [Edited from Ernest Fenollosa's manuscripts by Ezra Pound]. *Quarterly Review*, CCI. 441 (Oct. 1914) 450–77.
Includes, as examples, a Saibara, a Kagura, quotations from "Atsumori" and "Nishikigi," and two Noh plays in full, "Kinuta" and "Hagoromo." A short introductory note, signed: E.P., ends: "So far as possible, I shall print these documents as they stand." Reprinted, in expanded form, in Part III of *'Noh' or Accomplishment* (1916 [*i.e.* 1917])—A13.

C161 "On the Imbecility of the Rich." *Egoist*, I. 20 (15 Oct. 1914) 389–90.
"By Bastien von Helmholtz."

C162 Those American Publications. *Egoist*, I. 20 (15 Oct. 1914) 390.
"By Baptiste von Helmholtz."

C163 Preliminary Announcement of the College of Arts. *Egoist*, I. 21 (2 Nov. 1914) 413–14.
"This interesting prospectus [by Ezra Pound] comes to hand. Its value is such that we hasten to print it entire." With "Remarks" at the end, also by Pound. (Actually the prospectus was not printed until late November. See E2c.)

C164 Modern Georgics. *Poetry*, V. 3 (Dec. 1914) 127–30.
A review of *North of Boston*, by Robert Frost. Reprinted, with the omission of two paragraphs, as "First American Notice, III, by Ezra Pound," in *Recognition of Robert Frost . . . Edited by Richard Thornton* ([1937])—B40—pp. 50–53, in the section "Early Recognition."

C165 DEAD IŌNÈ. *Poetry and Drama*, II. 4 (Dec. 1914) 353.
Reprinted as "'Ione, Dead the Long Year.'"

C166 ✉ Another Raid on German Trade. *Egoist*, I. 23 (1 Dec. 1914) 447.
In dialect, signed: Alf Arpur. Almost certainly by Ezra Pound.

C167 The Words of Ming Mao "Least among the Disciples of Kung-Fu-Tse." *Egoist*, I. 24 (15 Dec. 1914) 456.

C. CONTRIBUTIONS TO PERIODICALS

Signed: M. M. Contributed by Ezra Pound.

1915

C168 Webster Ford [a pseudonym of Edgar Lee Masters]. *Egoist*, II. 1 (1 Jan. 1915) 11–12.

C169 Affirmations . . . I. Arnold Dolmetsch. *New Age*, XVI. 10 (7 Jan. 1915) 246–7.
The first of seven instalments.

C170 Affirmations . . . II. Vorticism. *New Age*, XVI. 11 (14 Jan. 1915) 277–8.

C171 ✉ A Blast from London. *Dial*, Chicago, Ill., LVIII. 686 (16 Jan. 1915) 40–41.
On the younger generation in America. Reprinted, in part, as "Extract from a Letter to 'The Dial.'"

C172 Affirmations . . . III. Jacob Epstein. *New Age*, XVI. 12 (21 Jan. 1915) 311–12.
Reprinted in *Gaudier-Brzeska* (1916)—A10—pp. 111–20.

C173 Affirmations . . . IV. As for Imagisme. *New Age*, XVI. 13 (28 Jan. 1915) 349–50.

C174 ✉ Vorticism. *New Age*, XVI. 13 (28 Jan. 1915) 359.

C175 The Renaissance . . . I.—The Palette. *Poetry*, V. 5 (Feb. 1915) 227–33.
The first of three instalments.

C176 Affirmations . . . V. Gaudier-Brzeska. *New Age*, XVI. 14 (4 Feb. 1915) 380–2.
Reprinted in *Gaudier-Brzeska* (1916)—A10—pp. 121–30.

C177 ✉ Synchromatism. *New Age*, XVI. 14 (4 Feb. 1915) 389–90.

C178 ✉ Vorticism. *New Age*, XVI. 14 (4 Feb. 1915) 391.

C179 Affirmations . . . VI. Analysis of This Decade. *New Age*, XVI. 15 (11 Feb. 1915) 409–11.
Reprinted in *Gaudier-Brzeska* (1916)—A10—pp. 133–41.

C180 ✉ Imagisme. *New Age*, XVI. 15 (11 Feb. 1915) 415.

C181 Imagisme and England. A Vindication and an Anthology. *T. P.'s Weekly*, XXV. 641 (20 Feb. 1915) 185.

C182 Affirmations . . . VII. The Non-existence of Ireland. *New Age*, XVI. 17 (25 Feb. 1915) 451–3.
A brief paragraph (with reference to J. M. Synge) was reprinted in *Agenda*, XVII. 3/4/XVIII. 1 (Autumn/Winter/Spring 1979/1980) 71.

C183 ✉ Affirmations. *New Age*, XVI. 17 (25 Feb. 1915) 471.

C184 POEMS. *Poetry*, V. 6 (Mar. 1915) 251–7.
Contents: Provincia deserta—Image from D'Orleans—The Spring—The Coming of War: Actaeon—The Gipsy—Dogmatic Statement Concerning the Game of Chess: Theme for a Series of Pictures.

C. CONTRIBUTIONS TO PERIODICALS

C185 EXILE'S LETTER, FROM THE CHINESE OF RIHAKU (LI PO) ... *Poetry*, V. 6 (Mar. 1915) 258–61.

"Translated by Ezra Pound from the notes of the late Ernest Fenollosa and the decipherings of the Professors Mori and Araga [*sic*]."

C186 The Renaissance. II. *Poetry*, V. 6 (Mar. 1915) 283–7.

C186a ✉ *Triad*, Wellington, N. Z., XXII. 12 (10 Mar. 1915) 178–9.

Dated 21 Dec. 1914, in reply to an attack on *Blast*, 1, the letter is printed complete (but with minor alterations) as part of an article, "Mr. Ezra Pound and Vorticism," by Frank Morton, one of the editors, pp. 178–80.

C187 [A review, signed: E. P., of] *Ernest Dowson*, by Victor Plarr. *Poetry*, VI. 1 (Apr. 1915) 43–45.

C188 The Classical Stage of Japan: Ernest Fenollosa's Work on the Japanese "Noh," Edited by Ezra Pound. *Drama*, Chicago, Ill., V. 18 (May 1915) 199–247.

Contents: Sotoba Komachi, by Kiyotsugu—Kayoi Komachi, by a Minoru—Suma Genji, by Manzaburo—Fenollosa's records of conversations with Umewaka Minoru, 15 May 1900, 6 May, 2 June—Kumasaka, by Ujinobu—Shojo—Tamura—Foreword to Tsunemasa—Tsunemasa. Reprinted, in expanded form, as Parts I and II of '*Noh' or Accomplishment* (1916 [*i.e.* 1917])—A13.

C189 The Renaissance. III. *Poetry*, VI. 2 (May 1915) 84–91.

C190 Affirmations: Edgar Lee Masters. *Reedy's Mirror*, St. Louis, Mo., XXIV. 13 (21 May 1915) 10–12.

C191 Hark to Sturge Moore. *Poetry*, VI. 3 (June 1915) 139–45.

C192 ✉ A Rejoinder. *Poetry*, VI. 3 (June 1915) 157–8.

Answering criticism by Leroy Titus Weeks.

C193 SONG OF THE BOWMEN OF SHU. *Evening Bulletin*, Philadelphia, Pa. (5 June 1915 [?]).

Reprinted from *Cathay* (1915)—A9.

C193a ✉ ... Mr. Pound's Disgust. *Reedy's Mirror*, XXIV. 18 (25 June 1915) 26.

On a review of Edgar Lee Masters' *Spoon River Anthology*.

C194 POEMS. *Blast*, 2 (July 1915) 19–22.

Contents: Dogmatic Statement on the Game and Play of Chess—The Social Order—Ancient Music—Gnomic Verses—Our Contemporaries—Our Respectful Homages to M. Laurent Tailhade—Ancient Wisdom, Rather Cosmic—Et faim sallir le loup des boys.

C195 Chronicles. *Blast*, 2 (July 1915) 85–86.

Signed: E. P. *Contents:* I. 'Lest the future age ... '—II. On the Rage or Peevishness Which Greeted the First Number of *Blast*—III. Lawrence [*sic*] Binyon.

C196 THE RIVER-MERCHANT'S WIFE. *Current Opinion*, New York, LIX. 1 (July 1915) 55.

Reprinted from *Cathay* (1915)—A9.

C. CONTRIBUTIONS TO PERIODICALS

C197 LOVE-SONG TO EUNOË. *Smart Set*, XLVI. 3 (July 1915) 395.

C198 "The Pleasing Art of Poetry." *New Age*, XVII. 10 (8 July 1915) 229–31.

C199 ✉ *Boston Evening Transcript*, Boston, Mass. (14 July 1915) 21.
On Robert Frost, and Ezra Pound's own first publication in England. Quoted
in a column by E. F. E., "Writers and Books: The Literary World Today."
Reprinted (from retained carbon copy?) with the (incorrect) supplied date
"August," in *Letters*—A64—pp. 62–63.

C199a ✉ The Vorticists. *Westminster Gazette*, London, XLVI. 6908 (30 July 1915) 3.
On J[ohn]. M[iddleton]. M[urry].'s "grave misrepresentation" of Gaudier-
Brzeska's work in the issue for 22 July, with his reply.

C200 [A review, signed: E. P., of] *Poems*, by E. Scotton Huelin; *Sounds from Another Valley*, by H. F. Sampson: *The Song of the Five*, by Cecil Garth. *Poetry*,
VI. 5 (Aug. 1915) 257–8.

C201 ALBÂTRE. *Smart Set*, XLVI. 4 (Aug. 1915) 130.
Reprinted from *Poetry and Drama* for Mar. 1914—C132.

C202 ✉ "Blast" and a Critic. *Outlook*, London, XXXVI. 914 (7 Aug. 1915) 183.
The first of two letters under this heading, the second signed: J. M.

C203 ✉ Mr. Pound, Mr. Stephens, Mr. Joyce. *Reedy's Mirror*, XXIV. 24 (6 Aug.
1915) 13.

C204 American Chaos [I]. *New Age*, XVII. 19 (9 Sept. 1915) 449.

C205 American Chaos [II]. *New Age*, XVII. 20 (16 Sept. 1915) 471.

C206 Foreword to the Choric School. *Others*, Grantwood, N. J., I. 4 (Oct. 1915)
[53–54].

C207 Robert Bridges' New Book. *Poetry*, VII. 1 (Oct. 1915) 40–44.
Signed: E.P. A review of *Poems Written in the Year MCMXIII*.

C208 HER LITTLE BLACK SLIPPERS. *Smart Set*, XLVII. 2 (Oct. 1915) 134.
Reprinted as "The Little Black Slippers" in *Hamilton Literary Magazine* for
Nov. 1915. Reprinted by the author as "Black Slippers: Bellotti."

C208a Inconsiderable Imbecilities. *Egoist*, II. 10 (1 Oct. 1915) 161.
Quotations from the *Times Literary Supplement*, London; selected, anonymously, by Ezra Pound.

C209 This Super-Neutrality. *New Age*, XVII. 25 (21 Oct. 1915) 595.

C210 [POEMS]. *Others*, I. 5 (Nov. 1915) 84–85.
Contents: The Tea Shop—Phylidula [*sic*]—The Patterns—Shop Girl—Another Man's Wife—Coda.

C211 TWO POEMS. *Poetry*, VII. 3 (Dec. 1915) 111–21.
Contents: Near Perigord—Villanelle: The Psychological Hour.

C212 On "Near Perigord." *Poetry*, VII. 3 (Dec. 1915) 143–6.
Notes, signed: E. P., including (pp. 143–5) his translation of Bertrans de
Born's canzon "Dompna pois de me no'us cal," reprinted from *Poetry and
Drama* for Mar. 1914—C132.

C213 Remy de Gourmont [Part I]. *Fortnightly Review*, XCVIII (N. S.). 588 (1
Dec. 1915) [1159]–1166.

C. CONTRIBUTIONS TO PERIODICALS

1916

C214 Remy de Gourmont [Part II]. *Poetry*, VII. 4 (Jan. 1916) 197–202.

C215 REFLECTION. *Smart Set*, XLVIII. 1 (Jan. 1916) 219.
An unsigned poem, with text: "I know that what Nietzsche said is true, |
And yet— | I saw the face of a little child in the street, | And it was
beautiful." Probably by Ezra Pound. (Reprinted in *Collected Early Poems*
([1976])—A98—p. 286.)

C216 Mr. James Joyce and the Modern Stage. A Play and Some Considerations.
Drama, Chicago, Ill., VI. 21 (Feb. 1916) 122–32.
A review of *Exiles*. (A quotation from this review, in nine lines, was printed
on page [1] of *Extracts from Press Notices of Exiles by James Joyce* ([Zürich?
The Author? 1918]), a four-page leaflet, measuring 21·2 × 13·9 cm.)

C217 Literary Prizes. *Poetry*, VII. 6 (Mar. 1916) 304–5.
Signed: E. P.

C218 ✉ *Poetry*, VII. 6 (Mar. 1916) 321–3.
An extract. On requirements for poetry.

C219 Meditatio. *Egoist*, III. 3 (1 Mar. 1916) 37–38.
On censorship. Reprinted as "Meditations."

C220 ✉ A Letter from London. *Little Review*, Chicago, Ill., III. 2 (Apr. 1916)
7–8.
On the tariff on books.

C221 ✉ *Little Review*, III. 2 (Apr. 1916) 36.
An extract. On the Jan./Feb. issue, and on the *Egoist*.

C222 Status rerum—the Second. *Poetry*, VIII. 1 (Apr. 1916) 38–43.
In continuation of C68.

C223 Dialogues of Fontenelle, Translated by Ezra Pound. I. Alexander and Phriné.
Egoist, III. 5 (1 May 1916) 67–68.
The first of 12 instalments.

C224 This Constant Preaching to the Mob. *Poetry*, VIII. 3 (June 1916) 144–5.
Reprinted as "The Constant Preaching to the Mob."

C225 AWOI NO UYE: A PLAY BY UJINOBU. *Quarterly Notebook*, Kansas City,
Mo., I. 1 (June 1916) [9]–16.
Edited by Ezra Pound from the Fenollosa manuscripts, with an introduc-
tion.

C226 Dialogues of Fontenelle, Translated by Ezra Pound. II. Dido and Stratonice. *Egoist*, III. 6 (1 June 1916) 87–88.

C227 FROM THE CHINESE. *New Age*, XIX. 8 (22 June 1916) 186–7.
"From the notes of the late Ernest Fenollosa." *Contents:* Old Idea of Choan—
A Ballad of the Mulberry Road—Sennin Poem—To-Em-Mei's "The Un-
moving Cloud."

C228 ... TO-EM-MEI's "THE UNMOVING CLOUD." *Others*, III. 1 (July 1916)
31–32.

C. CONTRIBUTIONS TO PERIODICALS

"From the Chinese; from the notes of the late Ernest Fenollosa." Reprinted from the *New Age* for 22 June 1916—C227.

c229 Dialogues of Fontenelle, Translated by Ezra Pound. III. Anacreon and Aristotle. *Egoist*, III. 7 (1 July 1916) 103.

c230 KAKITSUHATA [*i.e.* KAKITSUBATA], BY MOTOKIYO. FROM THE NOTES OF ERNEST FENOLLOSA, FINISHED BY EZRA POUND. *Drama*, VI. 23 (Aug. 1916) 428–35.

c231 Dialogues of Fontenelle, Translated by Ezra Pound. IV. Homer and Æsop. *Egoist*, III. 8 (Aug. 1916) 119.

c232 ✉ Ezra Pound Files Exceptions. *Reedy's Mirror*, XXV. 32 (18 Aug. 1916) 535–6.
On W. M. Reedy's review of *Gaudier-Brzeska*—A10b—in the issue for 14 July.

c233 Dialogues of Fontenelle, Translated by Ezra Pound. V. Socrates and Montaigne. *Egoist*, III. 9 (Sept. 1916) 133–4.

c234 POEMS OLD AND NEW. *Poetry*, VIII. 6 (Sept. 1916) 275–82.
Contents: The Fish and the Shadow—O Atthis ["Ἱμέρρω"]—The Three Poets—Pagani's—The Lake Isle—Impressions of François-Marie Arouet (de Voltaire)—Homage to Quintus Septimius Florentis Christianus—Dans un omnibus de Londres. A sentence from Ezra Pound's letter concerning "Homage to Quintus Septimius Florentis Christianus" is quoted in "Notes," p. 329.

c235 Thomas MacDonagh as Critic. *Poetry*, VIII. 6 (Sept. 1916) 309–12.
A review of *Literature in Ireland.*.

c236 Dialogues of Fontenelle, Translated by Ezra Pound. VI. Charles V and Erasmus. *Egoist*, III. 10 (Oct. 1916) 151.

c237 Dreiser Protest. *Egoist*, III. 10 (Oct. 1916) 159.
Includes reprint of "A Protest."

c238 The War and Diverse Impressions. Mr. [C. R. W.] Nevinson Thinks That the Public Is More Interested in the War than It Is in Art. *Vogue*, London, XLVIII. 7 (1 Oct. 1916) 74–75.
Unsigned.

c239 An American on America. *Times Literary Supplement*, London, 770 (19 Oct. 1916) 494.
A review, unsigned, of *The American Crisis and the War*, by William Morton Fullerton.

c240 Dialogues of Fontenelle, Translated by Ezra Pound. VII. Agnes Sorel—Roxelane. *Egoist*, III. 11 (Nov. 1916) 170.

c241 Das schone [*sic*] Papier vergeudet. *Little Review*, III. 7 (Nov. 1916) 16–17.
(In English.) On the tariff on books.

c242 Dialogues of Fontenelle, Translated by Ezra Pound. VIII. Brutus and Faustina. *Egoist*, III. 12 (Dec. 1916) 183.

c243 SWORD-DANCE AND SPEAR-DANCE: TEXTS OF THE POEMS USED WITH

C. CONTRIBUTIONS TO PERIODICALS

MICHIO ITOW'S DANCES. BY EZRA POUND, FROM NOTES OF MASIRNI UTCHIYAMA. *Future*, London, I. 2 (Dec. 1916) 54–55.
Includes "Song for a Foiled Vendetta," "The Sole Survivor," "In Enemies' Country just after War," "Honogi," and "Yamadera," with introductory notes and explanation of historical background.

C243a In the World of Letters. *Future*, I. 2 (Dec. 1916) 55–56.
Notes on T. S. Eliot, Alan Seeger, Fritz Vanderpyl, Jean de Bosschère, and Dorothy Richardson. Unsigned, but a clipping in a scrapbook at Yale is marked by Ezra Pound as his.

C244 Mr. Yeats' New Book. *Poetry*, IX. 3 (Dec. 1916) 150–1.
A review, signed: E. P., of *Responsibilities and Other Poems*, by W. B. Yeats.

1917

C245 Dialogues of Fontenelle. Translated by Ezra Pound. IX. Helen and Fulvia. *Egoist*, IV. 1 (Jan. 1917) 5.

C246 James Joyce: at Last the Novel Appears. *Egoist*, IV. 2 (Feb. 1917) 21–22.
A review of *A Portrait of the Artist as a Young Man*. (A quotation from this review, in nine lines, was printed on page [1] of *Extract from Press Notices of A Portrait of the Artist as a Young Man by James Joyce* ([Zürich? The Author? 1917?]), a four-page leaflet, measuring 19·1 × 12·4 cm., and, shortened to four lines, on page [1] of *Extracts from Some Press Notices of A Portrait of the Artist as a Young Man. By James Joyce* ([London, The Egoist, Ltd., 1917]), also a leaflet of four pages, measuring 22 × 14 cm., both issued in connexion with the publication of the novel. Pages [1] and [4] of the second leaflet were reproduced in facsimile as back end-paper in Jane Lidderdale and Mary Nicholson's *Dear Miss Weaver* ([1970])—B101.)

C247 ✉ Dreiser Protest. *Egoist*, IV. 2 (Feb. 1917) 30.

C248 The Rev. G. Crabbe, LL. B. *Future*, I. 4 (Feb. 1917) 110–11.

C249 Émile Verhaeren, May 21st, 1855–Nov. 29th, 1916. *Poetry*, IX. 5 (Feb. 1917) 256–9.

C250 Things to Be Done. *Poetry*, IX. 6 (Mar. 1917) 312–14.
Signed: E. P.

C251 Dialogues of Fontenelle. Translated by Ezra Pound. X. Seneca and Scarron. *Egoist*, IV. 3 (Apr. 1917) 38–39.

C252 A Flock from Oxford. *Poetry*, X. 1 (Apr. 1917) 41–44.
A review, signed: E. P., of *Wheels, An Anthology of Verse*.

C253 Dialogues of Fontenelle. Translated by Ezra Pound. XI. Strato, [and] Raphael of Urbino. *Egoist*, IV. 4 (May 1917) 57–58.

C254 Editorial. *Little Review*, New York, IV. 1 (May 1917) [3]–6.
Accepting the post of Foreign Editor.

C255 PIERROTS: SCENE COURTE MAIS TYPIQUE (AFTER THE "PIERROTS" OF JULES LAFORGUE). *Little Review*, IV. 1 (May 1917) 11–12.
By "John Hall."

C. CONTRIBUTIONS TO PERIODICALS

C256 Jodindranath Mawhwor's Occupation. *Little Review*, IV. 1 (May 1917) 12–18.

Reprinted in *Much Ado*, St. Louis, Mo. (1920?) as "Pavannes, by Ezra Poun [*sic*]: Jodindranath Mawhwor's Occupation."

C257 Dialogues of Fontenelle. Translated by Ezra Pound. XII. Bombastes Paracelsus and Molière. *Egoist*, IV. 5 (June 1917) 70–71.

C258 Drunken Helots and Mr. Eliot. *Egoist*, IV. 5 (June 1917) 72–74.

A review of *Prufrock and Other Observations*, by T. S. Eliot.

C258a James Joyce and His Critics: Some Classified Comments. *Egoist*, IV. 5 (June 1917) 74.

Quotations from reviews of *A Portrait of the Artist as a Young Man* compiled, according to Patricia Hutchins, by Ezra Pound, and reprinted with minor omissions in her *James Joyce's World* (London [1957]), pp. 112–13. A letter from Pound to John Quinn, 17 May [1917] (NYPL), indicates that the quotations may have been compiled by T. S. Eliot and not by Pound; however, a clipping of C258a is present among the manuscripts collected by Pound himself for his projected "Collected Prose" (Yale).

C259 An Anachronism at Chinon. *Little Review*, IV. 2 (June 1917) 14–21.

C260 THREE CANTOS. I. *Poetry*, X. 3 (June 1917) 113–21.

A letter from Ezra Pound concerning the Cantos is quoted under "Notes," p. 167. Two sections of this first Canto (which differs completely from the version eventually published in the series) were reprinted as "Passages from the Opening Address in a Long Poem" in *Future*, London, II. 3 (Feb. 1918) 63.

C261 Wax Tablets. *Poetry*, X. 3 (June 1917) 160–1.

A review, signed: E. P., of *Tablettes de cire*, by A. de Brimont.

C261a ✉ An Imagist. *Saturday Review*, London, CXXIII. 3216 (16 June 1917) 550.

On the review of *'Noh,' or Accomplishment*—A13—in the issue for 9 June.

C262 Vers libre and Arnold Dolmetsch. *Egoist*, IV. 6 (July 1917) 90–91.

A review of *The Interpretation of the Music of the XVIIth and XVIIIth Centuries*, by Arnold Dolmetsch.

C263 Aux étuves de Weisbaden [*sic*], A. D. 1451. *Little Review*, IV. 3 (July 1917) 12–16.

(In English.)

C264 THREE CANTOS. II. *Poetry*, X. 4 (July 1917) 180–8.

(Differs radically from final version.) About 80 lines were reprinted as "Images from the Second Canto of a Long Poem" in *Future*, London, II. 4 (Mar. 1918) 96.

C265 IMPRESSIONS OF FRANÇOIS-MARIE AROUET (DE VOLTAIRE). *To-day*, London, I. 5 (July 1917) 185–6.

Reprinted from *Poetry* for Sept. 1916—C234.

C266 Provincialism the Enemy. I. *New Age*, XXI. 11 (12 July 1917) 244–5.

The first of four instalments.

C. CONTRIBUTIONS TO PERIODICALS

c267 Provincialism the Enemy. II. *New Age*, XXI. 12 (19 July 1917) 268–9.

c268 Provincialism the Enemy. III. *New Age*, XXI. 13 (26 July 1917) 288–9.

c269 Arnold Dolmetsch. *Egoist*, IV. 7 (Aug. 1917) 104–5.

c270 List of Books: Comment by Ezra Pound. *Little Review*, IV. 4 (Aug. 1917) 6–11.
> *Contents:* [1] *Passages from the Letters of John Butler Yeats* [B15]—2. James Joyce's Novel [*i.e. A Portrait of the Artist as a Young Man*]—3. *Certain Noble Plays of Japan* [A12]. . . . *Noh, or Accomplishment* [A13]—4. *The Interpretation of the Music of the XVIIth and XVIIIth Centuries,* by Arnold Dolmetsch—5. *Prufrock and Other Observations,* by T. S. Eliot.

c271 Stark Realism; This Little Pig Went to Market (A Search for the National Type). *Little Review*, IV. 4 (Aug. 1917) 16–17.

c272 THREE CANTOS. III. *Poetry*, X. 5 (Aug. 1917) 248–54.
> (Differs radically from final version.) A passage, chiefly Ezra Pound's version of Andreas Divus, was reprinted as "An Interpolation Taken from Third Canto of a Long Poem" in *Future*, London, II. 5 (Apr. 1918) 121, with added footnote: "The above Passages from the Odyssey, done into an approximation of the metre of the Anglo-Saxon 'Sea-farer.'"

c273 T. S. Eliot. *Poetry*, X. 5 (Aug. 1917) 264–71.
> A review, signed: E. P., of *Prufrock and Other Observations*.

c274 Provincialism the Enemy.—IV. *New Age*, XXI. 14 (2 Aug. 1917) 308–9.

c275 Studies in Contemporary Mentality . . . I.—"The Hibbert." *New Age*, XXI. 16 (16 Aug. 1917) 348–9.
> An analysis of the British Press, the first of 20 instalments.

c276 Studies in Contemporary Mentality . . . II.—"Blackwood's." *New Age*, XXI. 17 (23 Aug. 1917) 369–70.

c277 Studies in Contemporary Mentality . . . III.—On Quarterly Publications. *New Age*, XXI. 18 (30 Aug. 1917) 384–5.

c278 Elizabethan Classicists . . . I. *Egoist*, IV. 8 (Sept. 1917) 120–2.
> The first of five instalments, all five reprinted as "Notes on Elizabethan Classicists."

c279 Beddoes (and Chronology). *Future*, I. 11 (Sept. 1917) 318–20.
> Under the heading: "Art and Life."

c280 ["Editor's Note," signed: E. P., to] Inferior Religions [by] Wyndham Lewis. *Little Review*, IV. 5 (Sept. 1917) [3].
> A further footnote is supplied by the editor on page 7.

c281 L'HOMME MOYEN SENSUEL. *Little Review*, IV. 5 (Sept. 1917) 8–16.
> (In English.) With note, signed: E. P., on page 9.

c282 Imaginary Letters. IV. (Walter Villerant to Mrs. Bland Burn). *Little Review*, IV. 5 (Sept. 1917) 20–22.
> "Imaginary Letters, I–III. (Six Letters of William Bland Burn to His Wife)," were written by Wyndham Lewis and appeared in the issues for May, June, and July 1917.

C. CONTRIBUTIONS TO PERIODICALS

c283 Studies in Contemporary Mentality . . . IV.—The "Spectator." *New Age*, XXI. 19 (6 Sept. 1917) 406–7.

c284 Studies in Contemporary Mentality . . . V.—"The Strand," or How the Thing May Be Done. *New Age*, XXI. 20 (13 Sept. 1917) 425–7.

c285 Studies in Contemporary Mentality . . . VI.—"The Sphere," and Reflections on Letter-Press. *New Age*, XXI. 21 (20 Sept. 1917) 446–7.

c286 Studies in Contemporary Mentality . . . VII. Far from the Expensive Veal Cutlet. *New Age*, XXI. 22 (27 Sept. 1917) 464–6.
In part, on the *Quiver*.

c287 Elizabethan Classicists . . . II. *Egoist*, IV. 9 (Oct. 1917) 135–6.

c288 Imaginary Letters. V. (Walter Villerant to Mrs. Bland Burn). *Little Review*, IV. 6 (Oct. 1917) 14–17.

c289 Editorial on Solicitous Doubt. *Little Review*, IV. 6 (Oct. 1917) 20–22.
Repeated in IV. 8 (Dec. 1917) 53–55. Latter half reprinted as "Summary" in *The Little Review Anthology*—B54—pp. 145–6.

c290 ✉ Letters from Ezra Pound. *Little Review*, IV. 6 (Oct. 1917) 37–39.
Under the heading: "The Reader Critic." Replying to letters.

c290a ✉ This Approaches Literature! *Little Review*, IV. 6 (Oct. 1917) 39.
Under the heading: "The Reader Critic," as from Abel Sanders; enclosing a translation of a secret German document, "taken from a German prisoner captured near Ypres," titled, "Committee for the increase of population."

c291 ✉ *Poetry*, XI. 1 (Oct. 1917) 38.
An extract, dated: 18 Aug. 1912. Quoted in Harriet Monroe's article "These Five Years," pp. 33–41. On helping *Poetry* and sending his first contributions, "an over-elaborate 'Imagiste' affair"—"Middle-Aged"—and "To Whistler, American."

c292 Studies in Contemporary Mentality . . . VIII.—The Beating Heart of the Magazine. *New Age*, XXI. 24 (11 Oct. 1917) 505–7.
More on the *Quiver*.

c293 Studies in Contemporary Mentality . . . IX.—Further Heart Throbs. *New Age*, XXI. 25 (18 Oct. 1917) 527–8.
On the *Family Herald* and *Punch*.

c294 Studies in Contemporary Mentality . . . X.—The Backbone of the Empire. *New Age*, XXI. 26 (25 Oct. 1917) 545–6.
On *Chambers's Journal*.

c295 Elizabethan Classicists . . . III. *Egoist*, IV. 10 (Nov. 1917) 154–6.

c296 Landor (1775–1864). A Note . . . *Future*, II. 1 (Nov. 1917) 10–12.
Under the heading: "Art and Life."

c297 Imaginary Letters. VI. (Walter Villerant to Mrs. Bland Burn). *Little Review*, IV. 7 (Nov. 1917) 39–40.

c298 Irony, Laforgue, and Some Satire. *Poetry*, XI. 2 (Nov. 1917) 93–98.

C. CONTRIBUTIONS TO PERIODICALS

C299 William H. Davies, Poet. *Poetry*, XI. 2 (Nov. 1917) 99–102.
A review of *Collected Poems*.

C300 Studies in Contemporary Mentality . . . XI.—The Bright and Snappy. *New Age*, XXII. 1 (1 Nov. 1917) 10–11.
On *Answers*.

C301 Studies in Contemporary Mentality . . . XI [contd.].—Hash and Rehash. *New Age*, XXII. 2 (8 Nov. 1917) 28–30.
More on *Answers*.

C302 Studies in Contemporary Mentality . . . XII.—The Emblematic. *New Age*, XXII. 3 (15 Nov. 1917) 48–49.
On "Old Moore" and the *Christian Herald*.

C303 Studies in Contemporary Mentality . . . XIII.—The Celestial. *New Age*, XXII. 4 (22 Nov. 1917) 69–70.
More on the *Christian Herald*.

C304 Art Notes. By B. H. Dias. At Heal's [and "Leicester Gallery" (on Jacob Epstein)]. *New Age*, XXII. 4 (22 Nov. 1917) 74–75.
The first of Ezra Pound's critical articles for the *New Age* signed with this pseudonym. They continue at intervals until 8 Apr. 1920.

C305 Studies in Contemporary Mentality . . . XIV.—Progress, Social and Christian. *New Age*, XXII. 5 (29 Nov. 1917) 89–90.
On the *British Weekly*.

C306 Elizabethan Classicists . . . IV. *Egoist*, IV. 11 (Dec. 1917) 168.

C307 A Letter from Remy de Gourmont. *Little Review*, IV. 8 (Dec. 1917) [5]–8.
Reprinted, in part, in "Remy de Gourmont, a Distinction."

C308 That Boston Paper Again. *Little Review*, IV. 8 (Dec. 1917) 22.
An unsigned note from the "London Office" concerning the *Atlantic Monthly*.

C309 The Reader Critic. *Little Review*, IV. 8 (Dec. 1917) 55–56.
On Henry W. Longfellow. With a two-line "News Item," signed: E. P., p. 56.

C310 Advice to a Young Poet. *Little Review*, IV. 8 (Dec. 1917) 58–59.
From a letter to Maxwell Bodenheim; unsigned. Under the heading: "The Reader Critic."

C311 Music. By William Atheling. Le mariage de Figaro. *New Age*, XXII. 6 (6 Dec. 1917) 113–15.
The first of Ezra Pound's critical articles for the *New Age* signed with this pseudonym. They continue at intervals until 6 Jan. 1921.

C312 Studies in Contemporary Mentality . . . XV.—A Nice Paper. *New Age*, XXII. 7 (13 Dec. 1917) 129–30.
On *Forget-Me-Not*.

C313 Studies in Contemporary Mentality . . . XVI.—Aphrodite popularis. *New Age*, XXII. 8 (20 Dec. 1917) 148–9.
On *Nash's Magazine*.

C314 Art Notes. By B. H. Dias. The Loan Exhibition at the Grafton [and "Serbo-

Croatians" (including Mestrovic)]. *New Age*, XXII. 8 (20 Dec. 1917) 152–3.

C315 Studies in Contemporary Mentality . . . XVII.—The Slightly Shop-Worn. *New Age*, XXII. 9 (27 Dec. 1917) 167–8.
On various periodicals, plus the *Church Times*.

1918

C316 "The Middle Years" . . . *Egoist*, V. 1 (Jan. 1918) 2–3.
A review of Henry James's *The Middle Years*. Reprinted in *Little Review*, V. 4 (Aug. 1918) 39–41, and as part of "Henry James."

C316a Elizabethan Classicists . . . V. *Egoist*, V. 1 (Jan. 1918) 8–9.

C317 America's Critic. *Little Review*, IV. 9 (Jan. 1918) 10–12.
"By Raoul Root." One of "Three Views of H. L. Mencken ('A Book of Prefaces')."

C318 Thoughts from a Country Vicarage. *Little Review*, IV. 9 (Jan. 1918) 52–53.
Signed: E. P.

C318a ✉ MR. LINDSAY. *Little Review*, IV. 9 (Jan. 1918) 54–55.
A 58–line "poem," written in four minutes thirty-one seconds in imitation of Vachel Lindsay's style, signed: Abel Sanders. Under the heading: "The Reader Critic."

C318b The Quintuple Effulgence or The Unapproachable Splendour. *Little Review*, IV. 9 (Jan. 1918) 56.
Signed: S. O. S. With reference to John Masefield. Almost certainly contributed by Ezra Pound.

C319 The Yeats Letters. *Poetry*, XI. 4 (Jan. 1918) 223–5.
A review, signed: E. P., of *Passages from the Letters of John Butler Yeats, Selected by Ezra Pound*—B15.

C320 Music. By William Atheling. Some Recent Concerts [and "Raymonde Collignon"]. *New Age*, XXII. 10 (3 Jan. 1918) 189–90.
Parts of three paragraphs from the section of this review relating to Raymonde Collignon were reprinted (in 29 lines) headed "Mr. Ezra Pound says:" in a broadside quoting Ernest Newman, the *Times*, and other periodicals. It is titled *Raymonde Collignon*, measures 25·5 × 20·3 cm., and was issued as publicity presumably in London in 1918.

C321 Studies in Contemporary Mentality . . . XVIII.—Nubians. *New Age*, XXII. 10 (3 Jan. 1918) 192–4.
Two brief paragraphs were reprinted in *Agenda*, XVII. 3/4/XVIII. 1 (Autumn/Winter/Spring 1979/1980) 71–72.

C322 Studies in Contemporary Mentality . . . XIX.—? Versus Camouflage. *New Age*, XXII. 11 (10 Jan. 1918) 208–9.

C323 ✉ Contemporary Mentality. *New Age*, XXII. 11 (10 Jan. 1918) 219.

C324 ✉ Art. *New Age*, XXII. 11 (10 Jan. 1918) 219.
Signed: B. H. Dias.

C. CONTRIBUTIONS TO PERIODICALS

C325 Art [Notes]. By B. H. Dias. The New English Art Club. *New Age*, XXII. 12 (17 Jan. 1918) 235–6.

C326 Music. By William Atheling. Francesco Vigliani and Others. *New Age*, XXII. 13 (24 Jan. 1918) 248–9.

C327 A Study in French Poets. *Little Review*, IV. 10 (Feb. 1918) [3]–61. Title on cover: A Study of French Modern Poets.

C328 The Hard and the Soft in French Poetry. *Poetry*, XI. 5 (Feb. 1918) 264–71.
Signed: E. P.

C329 Music. By William Atheling. D'Alvarez, the Indiscriminate. *New Age*, XXII. 15 (7 Feb. 1918) 292–3.

C330 Art—and Pastels. By B. H. Dias. *New Age*, XXII. 16 (14 Feb. 1918) 310.

C331 Music. By William Atheling. Dammerung of the Piano. *New Age*, XXII. 17 (21 Feb. 1918) 334–5.

C332 Art Notes. By B. H. Dias. The National Portrait Society. *New Age*, XXII. 18 (28 Feb. 1918) 356–7.

C333 The Classics "Escape." *Little Review*, IV. 11 (Mar. 1918) 32–34.
On censorship, quoting Section 211 of the U. S. penal code.

C334 CANTICO DEL SOLE. *Little Review*, IV. 11 (Mar. 1918) 35.
(In English.) Signed: Ezra I. Y. H. X. Reprinted as part of "The Classics 'Escape.'"

C335 [A review of] "Tarr," by Wyndham Lewis. *Little Review*, IV. 11 (Mar. 1918) 35.

C336 A List of Books. *Little Review*, IV. 11 (Mar. 1918) 54–58.
Contents: George S. Street—Frederick [*sic*] Manning—C. F. Keary—"*Others [Anthology for 1917]*." Part of the comment on the last item is reprinted as "Marianne Moore and Mina Loy" in *The Little Review Anthology* (1953)—B54—pp. 188–9.

C337 ✉ Astronomy. *Little Review*, IV. 11 (Mar. 1918) 59.
Quoting from the *Evening Standard*, London; signed: X [*i.e.* Ezra Pound?]

C338 Raymonde Collignon. *Little Review*, IV. 11 (Mar. 1918) 60.
A brief note, signed: E. P.

C339 Swinburne versus Biographers. *Poetry*, XI. 6 (Mar. 1918) 322–9.
A review of *The Life of Algernon Charles Swinburne*, by Edmund Gosse.

C340 Music. By William Atheling. A Programme, and the Mal-administered Lyric. *New Age*, XXII. 19 (7 Mar. 1918) 377–8.

C341 ✉ Music. *New Age*, XXII. 20 (14 Mar. 1918) 403.
Signed: William Atheling.

C342 Music. By William Atheling. *New Age*, XXII. 21 (21 Mar. 1918) 412–13.

C343 Music. By William Atheling. The Gaelic [and "Kennedy-Fraser"]. *New Age*, XXII. 22 (28 Mar. 1918) 434.

C344 Books Current, Reviewed by Ezra Pound: Henry James as Expositor. *Future*, II. 5 (Apr. 1918) 128–30.
Reviews of *The Sense of the Past* and *The Ivory Tower*; with, at the end, brief notes on *The Turkish Empire, Its Growth and Decay*, by Lord Eversley, and *India and the Future*, by William Archer.

C344a The Criterion. *Little Review*, IV. 12 (Apr. 1918) 11.
Unsigned, but almost certainly contributed by Ezra Pound.

C345 Unanimism. *Little Review*, IV. 12 (Apr. 1918) 26–32.
Reprinted as part of "A Study of French Poets."

C346 Chinese Poetry [I]. *To-day*, III. 14 (Apr. 1918) 54–57.
The first of two instalments.

C347 Art Notes. By B. H. Dias. Processes. *New Age*, XXII. 23 (4 Apr. 1918) 456–7.

C348 Art Notes. By B. H. Dias. Water. *New Age*, XXII. 24 (11 Apr. 1918) 472.

C349 Music. By William Atheling. Rosing, the Magnificent [and "Debussy"]. *New Age*, XXII. 25 (18 Apr. 1918) 486.

C350 Henry James—The Last Phase. *Newark Sunday Call*, Newark, N. J. (21 Apr. 1918) pt. III, p. 12.
In part, recast from the article in the *Future* for Apr. 1918—C344.

C351 Art Notes. By B. H. Dias. At the Alpine Club Gallery. *New Age*, XXII. 26 (25 Apr. 1918) 503–4.

C352 The Anglo-French Society and M. Davray. *Egoist*, V. 15 (May 1918) 72.

C353 Books Current. By Ezra Pound: Joyce. *Future*, II. 6 (May 1918) 161–3.
A review of *A Portrait of the Artist as a Young Man*, with, at the end, a comment on *Chamber Music* and brief notices of *The Crescent Moon*, by F. Brett Young, and *My Adventures as a German Secret Service*, by Capt. Horst von der Goltz.

C354 POEMS. *Little Review*, V. 1 (May 1918) 19–31.
Contents: Homage à la langue d'or [*i.e.* d'Oc. "Alba"; I–V]—Moeurs contemporaines, I–VIII, IX."Quis multa gracilis?" "Homage à la langue d'Oc" reprinted as "Langue d'Oc."

C355 Imaginary Letters [X]. (W. Villerant to the ex-Mrs. Burn). *Little Review*, V. 1 (May 1918) 52–55.
"Imaginary Letters" [VII-] VIII and IX were written by Wyndham Lewis and appeared in the issues for Mar. and Apr. 1918.

C355a The Criterion. *Little Review*, V. 1 (May 1918) 62.
Unsigned, but almost certainly contributed by Ezra Pound.

C356 Chinese Poetry. II. *To-day*, III. 15 (May 1918) 93–95.

C357 Music. By William Atheling. Rosing [and others, including Myra Hess]. *New Age*, XXIII. 1 (2 May 1918) 10–11.

C358 Art Notes. By B. H. Dias. Water, Still More of It. *New Age*, XXIII. 2 (9 May 1918) 29.

C. CONTRIBUTIONS TO PERIODICALS

C359 Music. By William Atheling. Varia [including Raymonde Collignon, singing the Rummel Troubadour songs]. *New Age*, XXIII. 3 (16 May 1918) 44–45.

C360 Art Notes. By B. H. Dias. "Gaudier-Brzeska." *New Age*, XXIII. 4 (23 May 1918) 58–59.

C361 Music. By William Atheling. 'Cellists, Etc. *New Age*, XXIII. 5 (30 May 1918) 72–73.

C362 Books Current, Reviewed by Ezra Pound: The New Poetry. *Future*, II. 7 (June 1918) 188–90.
Chiefly on T. S. Eliot, Marianne Moore, Mina Loy, and William Carlos Williams.

C363 ✉ Ben Hecht. *Little Review*, V. 2 (June 1918) 55.
An extract, captioned: E. P., London. Under the heading: "The Reader Critic."

C364 The Royal Academy. By B. H. Dias. *New Age*, XXIII. 6 (6 June 1918) 91.

C365 Music. By William Atheling. Felix Salmond, Excellent 'Cellist. *New Age*, XXIII. 7 (13 June 1918) 107–8.

C366 Art Notes. By B. H. Dias. Still the Academy. *New Age*, XXIII. 8 (20 June 1918) 125–6.

C367 HOMAGE À LA LANGUE D'OC ["Alba"; I–V]. *New Age*, XXIII. 9 (27 June 1918) 137–8.
Reprinted from *Little Review* for May 1918—C354. Reprinted as "Langue d'Oc."

C368 Music. By William Atheling. *New Age*, XXIII. 9 (27 June 1918) 140.
On Miss Lilias Mackinnon, Rosing, etc.

C369 Books Current, Reviewed by Ezra Pound. *Future*, II. 8 (July 1918) 209–10.
Contents: The Professorial [Sir Henry Newbolt's *A New Study of English Poetry*]—Hueffer [Ford Madox Hueffer's *On Heaven, and Other Poems*]—Students and a Scholar [brief comments on other books].

C370 Our Tetrarchal Précieuse (A Divagation from Jules Laforgue). *Little Review*, V. 3 (July 1918) [3]–12.
"By Thayer Exton."

C371 Our Contemporaries. *Little Review*, V. 3 (July 1918) 35–37.
Signed: E. P.

C372 Cooperation (A Note on the Volume Completed) [by] E. P. *Little Review*, V. 3 (July 1918) 54–56.

C373 De Goncourt. *Little Review*, V. 3 (July 1918) 56.
An introductory note to a reprinting of the preface to the first edition of *Germinie Lacerteux*. (Followed, p. 58, by an "Errata" note, signed: E. P., making a correction in C336.)

C374 From the Clergy. *Little Review*, V. 3 (July 1918) 60.
A note, signed: E. P., to a letter.

C. CONTRIBUTIONS TO PERIODICALS

c375 Art Notes. By B. H. Dias. The International. *New Age*, XXIII. 10 (4 July 1918) 155.

c375a ✉ Art Notes. *New Age*, XXIII. 10 (4 July 1918) 159.
Signed: Harold B. Harrison. Congratulating the periodical "upon having obtained the services of an art critic of the independence of mind of Señor B. H. Dias." Possibly by Ezra Pound himself.

c376 Music. By William Atheling. Stroesco Improved, Nevada, Purnell. *New Age*, XXIII. 11 (11 July 1918) 168.

c377 Art Notes. By B. H. Dias. Nash, Nicholson, Orpen [and "Tooth's Gallery, Bond Street"]. *New Age*, XXIII. 12 (18 July 1918) 189.

c378 Music. By William Atheling. Arthur Williams ('Cello) [and "Vladimir Rosing" etc.]. *New Age*, XXIII. 13 (25 July 1918) 205–6.

c379 Early Translators of Homer . . . I. Hughes Salel. *Egoist*, V. 7 (Aug. 1918) 95–97.
The first of three instalments under this general title. Three additional instalments appeared as "Hellenist Series, IV–VI"—C414, 433, and 448.

c380 In Explanation. *Little Review*, V. 4 (Aug. 1918) 5–9.
On Henry James, introducing the two following articles (the second, "'The Middle Years'" reprinted from the *Egoist* for Jan. 1918—C316) and incorporating an earlier essay entitled "Brief Note."

c381 A Shake Down. *Little Review*, V. 4 (Aug. 1918) 9–39.
Reprinted as part of "Henry James."

c382 The Notes to "The Ivory Tower" [by Henry James. I]. *Little Review*, V. 4 (Aug. 1918) 62–64.
"Recast from an article in *The Future*"—C344. Reprinted as part of "Henry James."

c383 Art Notes. By B. H. Dias. The Tenth London Salon of the Allied Artists Association [and "Grafton Gallery (No Pearls, by Request)"]. *New Age*, XXIII. 14 (1 Aug. 1918) 223–4.

c384 Music. By William Atheling. *New Age*, XXIII. 15 (8 Aug. 1918) 241–2.
In part, on Vladimir Rosing.

c385 Art Notes. By B. H. Dias. "Fresh Wholesome Sentiment" [and "New English"]. *New Age*, XXIII. 16 (15 Aug. 1918) 255–6.

c386 What America Has to Live Down . . . I. *New Age*, XXIII. 17 (22 Aug. 1918) 266–7.
The first of five instalments.

c387 Music. By William Atheling. *New Age*, XXIII. 17 (22 Aug. 1918) 271–2.

c388 What America Has to Live Down . . . II. *New Age*, XXIII. 18 (29 Aug. 1918) 281–2.

c389 Art Notes. By B. H. Dias. Buildings—I. *New Age*, XXIII. 18 (29 Aug. 1918) 287–8.

c390 Early Translators of Homer . . . II. Andreas Divus. *Egoist*, V. 8 (Sept. 1918) 106–8.

C. CONTRIBUTIONS TO PERIODICALS

Includes a slightly abbreviated early version of Canto I (here called III).

C391 Books Current, Reviewed by Ezra Pound: "Tarr," by P. Wyndham Lewis. *Future*, II. 9 (Sept. 1918) 237–9.
With brief notes on Lytton Strachey and Sacheverell Sitwell.

C392 [Note, signed: E. P., to] The Western School [by] Edgar Jepson. *Little Review*, V. 5 (Sept. 1918) 5.

C393 The Notes for "The Ivory Tower" [by Henry James. II]. *Little Review*, V. 5 (Sept. 1918) 50–53.

C394 ✉ On the American Number. *Little Review*, V. 5 (Sept. 1918) 62–64.
Captioned: E. P., London. Under the heading: "The Reader Critic."

C395 What America Has to Live Down ... III [–IV]. *New Age*, XXIII. 19 (5 Sept. 1918) 297–8.

C396 Music. By William Atheling. The Avoidable. *New Age*, XXIII. 19 (5 Sept. 1918) 302–3.

C397 What America Has to Live Down ... V. *New Age*, XXIII. 20 (12 Sept. 1918) 314–15.

C398 Art Notes. By B. H. Dias. Building: Ornamentation! *New Age*, XXIII. 20 (12 Sept. 1918) 320.

C399 What America Has to Live Down ... VI [and "Conclusions, I–IV"]. *New Age*, XXIII. 21 (19 Sept. 1918) 329.
Two brief paragraphs were reprinted in *Agenda*, XVII. 3/4/XVIII. 1 (Autumn/Winter/Spring 1979/1980) 72.

C400 Music. By William Atheling. Prom. *New Age*, XXIII. 21 (19 Sept. 1918) 335.

C401 Tariff and Copyright. *New Age*, XXIII. 22 (26 Sept. 1918) 348–9.

C402 Art Notes. By B. H. Dias. Kinema, Kinesis, Hepworth, Etc. *New Age*, XXIII. 22 (26 Sept. 1918) 352.

C403 Early Translators of Homer ... III. [Hughes Salel, contd.]. *Egoist*, V. 9 (Oct. 1918) 120–1.

C404 Books Current, Reviewed by Ezra Pound: Lytton Strachey on Left Over Celebrity. *Future*, II. 10 (Oct. 1918) 265–6.
A review of *Eminent Victorians*. Reprinted in *Instigations*—A18—as "An Historical Essayist: Lytton Strachey on Left-Over Celebrity," and in *Agenda*, XVII. 3/4/XVIII. 1 (Autumn/Winter/Spring 1979/1980) 48–53 as "Lytton Strachey on Left Over Celebrity."

C405 De Bosschère's Study of Elskamp. *Little Review*, V. 6 (Oct. 1918) 5–8.
A review of *"Max Elskamp," essai*, by Jean de Bosschère. Reprinted as part of "A Study in French Poets."

C406 Breviora. *Little Review*, V. 6 (Oct. 1918) 23–24.

C407 Albert Mockel and "La Wallonie." *Little Review*, V. 6 (Oct. 1918) 51–64.
Reprinted as part of "A Study in French Poets."

C407a The Audience. *Little Review*, V. 6 (Oct. 1918) 64.

C. CONTRIBUTIONS TO PERIODICALS

Unsigned, but almost certainly contributed by Ezra Pound (see C421a).

C408 Copyright and Tariff. *New Age*, XXIII. 23 (3 Oct. 1918) 363–4.

C409 Music. By William Atheling. *New Age*, XXIII. 23 (3 Oct. 1918) 364–5.

C410 Music. By William Atheling. Moiseiwitsch; Rosing. *New Age*, XXIII. 25 (17 Oct. 1918) 395–6.

C411 Art Notes. By B. H. Dias. Parallelograms [and "The A. B. C."] *New Age*, XXIII. 25 (17 Oct. 1918) 400–1.

C412 Art Notes. By B. H. Dias. Super-Fronts. *New Age*, XXIII. 26 (24 Oct. 1918) 414.

C413 Music. By William Atheling. Functions of Criticism [and "Rosing, and Laurel Crowns"]. *New Age*, XXIII. 27 (31 Oct. 1918) 428–9.

C414 Hellenist Series . . . IV. Sappho. *Egoist*, V. 10 (Nov./Dec. 1918) 130–1.
In continuation of "Early Translators of Homer," I–III—C379, 390, and 403.

C415 Books Current, Reviewed by Ezra Pound. *Future*, II. 11 (Nov. 1918) 286–7.
Reviews of *Oriental Encounters*, by Marmaduke Pickthall; *Studies in Literature*, by Sir Arthur Quiller-Couch; *Exiles*, by James Joyce; *The Sheepfold*, by Laurence Housman; with comments on *170 Chinese Poems*, translated by Arthur Waley, and *Purple Passion*, by Gertie de S. Wentworth-James.

C416 NINE POEMS. *Little Review*, V. 7 (Nov. 1918) [1]–6.
Contents: Cantus planus—Chanson arabe—Dawn on the Mountain (Omakitsu)—Wine (Rihaku)—Φανοποεία ["Phanopoeia"] (I. Rose white, yellow, silver; II. Saltus; III. Concava vallis)—Glamour and Indigo. A Canzon from the Provençal of "En Ar. Dan'el" [with "Foot-note"]—Upon the Harps of Judea.

C417 Mr. Villerant's Morning Outburst. (Four Letters). *Little Review*, V. 7 (Nov. 1918) 7–12.
In continuation of "Imaginary Letters." Unsigned, but the issue is described as being "Devoted chiefly to Ezra Pound." Reprinted as "Imaginary Letters, V–VIII."

C418 H.D.'s Choruses from Euripides [by] E. P. *Little Review*, V. 7 (Nov. 1918) 16–20.

C419 Tariff and Copyright. *Little Review*, V. 7 (Nov. 1918) 21–25.
A digest of the articles in the *New Age* for 26 Sept. and 3 Oct.—C401 and 408.

C420 Memorabilia. *Little Review*, V. 7 (Nov. 1918) 26–27.

C421 The Disease of "American" "Criticism." *Little Review*, V. 7 (Nov. 1918) 43–44.
Signed: E. P.

C421a The Audience. *Little Review*, V. 7 (Nov. 1918) 44.
Unsigned. Under the heading: "The Reader Critic."

C. CONTRIBUTIONS TO PERIODICALS

C422 Genesis, or, The First Book in the Bible. ("Subject to Authority"). *Little Review*, V. 7 (Nov. 1918) 50–64.
Unsigned and, according to a footnote, "translated from an eighteenth-century author [*i.e.* Voltaire]."

C422a The Highbrow—How He Looks on American Newspapers. *Pep*, Cleveland, O., III. 11 (Nov. 1918) 10–11, 18.
The editor explains in a note that Ezra Pound's title for this essay was "Stavvi Minos Orribilmente" (a quotation from Dante's Inferno).

C423 Music. By William Atheling. Stroesco; Violinists. *New Age*, XXIV. 1 (7 Nov. 1918) 11–12.

C424 Music. By William Atheling. Van Dieren; Tinayre; Rosing's All-Russian Programme. *New Age*, XXIV. 2 (14 Nov. 1918) 27–28.

C425 Art Notes. By B. H. Dias. Leicester Gallery, Etchings [and "London Group, at Heal's"]. *New Age*, XXIV. 3 (21 Nov. 1918) 44–45.

C426 Music. By William Atheling. Hebrides, Kennedy-Fraser. *New Age*, XXIV. 4 (28 Nov. 1918) 59–60.

C427 ✉ Puritanism. *New Age*, XXIV. 4 (28 Nov. 1918) 63.

C428 Books Current, Reviewed by Ezra Pound. *Future*, II. 12 (Dec. 1918) 311–12.
Contents: "Tarr" [a note on his review]—Lady Gregory and the Cuala Press [with a note on] "The Kiltartan Poetry Book."

C429 Music. By William Atheling. Miscellaneous. *New Age*, XXIV. 6 (12 Dec. 1918) 91–92.

C430 Music. By William Atheling. *New Age*, XXIV. 7 (19 Dec. 1918) 107–8.

C431 GLAMOUR AND INDIGO [WITH POEMS IX, XVII, AND XI]. *New Age*, XXIV. 8 (26 Dec. 1918) 122–4.
"(From the Provençal of En Arnaut Daniel)." The first is here reprinted from the *Little Review* for Nov. 1918—C416.

C432 Art Notes. By B. H. Dias. Jean de Bosschère, and the Less Fortunate. *New Age*, XXIV. 8 (26 Dec. 1918) 126–7.

1919

C433 Hellenist Series . . . V. Aeschylus. *Egoist*, VI. 1 (Jan./Feb. 1919) 6–9.
Reprinted with heading: "Translation of Aeschylus" as part of "Translators of Greek."

C434 Music. By William Atheling. Moussorgsky. Rosing, Stroesco, Haley. *New Age*, XXIV. 9 (2 Jan. 1919) 142–3.

C435 Music. By William Atheling. Mr. Rosing Experiments. *New Age*, XXIV. 10 (9 Jan. 1919) 159–60.

C436 Art Notes. By B. H. Dias. Canadian War Memorial: A Commendation. *New Age*, XXIV. 11 (16 Jan. 1919) 179–80.

C. CONTRIBUTIONS TO PERIODICALS

C437 Art Notes. By B. H. Dias. Canada, and the Remnants [and "Pastels"]. *New Age*, XXIV. 13 (30 Jan. 1919) 212.

C438 De Gourmont: A Distinction (Followed by Notes). *Little Review*, V. 10/11 (Feb./Mar. 1919) [1]–19.
Reprinted as "Remy de Gourmont, a Distinction, Followed by Notes."

C439 [Footnote, signed: E. P., to] M. de Gourmont and the Problem of Beauty [by] Frederic Manning. *Little Review*, V. 10/11 (Feb./Mar. 1919) 26–27.

C440 [Footnote, signed: E. P., to] Remy de Gourmont, After the Interim [by] Richard Aldington. *Little Review*, V. 10/11 (Feb./Mar. 1919) 34.

C441 The Death of Vorticism. *Little Review*, V. 10/11 (Feb./Mar. 1919) 45, 48. Unsigned.

C441a Books Current, Reviewed by Ezra Pound: Swinburne's Letters. *Future*, III. 1 (Feb. 1919) 18–19.
A review of *The Letters of Algernon Charles Swinburne*, edited by Edmund Gosse and Thomas J. Wise.

C442 Music. By William Atheling. Rosowsky, Rosing, Di Veroli. *New Age*, XXIV. 14 (6 Feb. 1919) 227–8.

C442a ... War Paintings by Wyndham Lewis. *Nation*, London, XXIV. 19 (8 Feb. 1919) 546–7.
Under the heading: "Art." Reprinted in *Agenda*, VII. 3/VIII. 1 (Autumn/ Winter 1969/1970) 85–87.

C443 Art Notes. By B. H. Dias. Navy, Mostyn, Lithography, Etc. [and "Academy," "Cinema," "Lithographs, Dilapidations, Etc."]. *New Age*, XXIV. 15 (13 Feb. 1919) 240–1.

C444 Art Notes. By B. H. Dias. Wyndham Lewis at the Goupil. *New Age*, XXIV. 16 (20 Feb. 1919) 263–4.

C445 Music. By William Atheling. Lamond, Tinayre, Collignon. *New Age*, XXIV. 17 (27 Feb. 1919) 281.

C446 ✉ Art Notes. *New Age*, XXIV. 17 (27 Feb. 1919) 283.

C447 To Discriminate. *Theatre-Craft*, London, [1] ([Spring? 1919]) 33–34.
On the need for small and simplified theatres. Under the heading: "The Allied Arts of the Theatre."

C448 Hellenist Series ... VI. *Egoist*, VI. 2 (Mar./Apr. 1919) 24–26.

C449 POEMS FROM THE PROPERTIUS SERIES, I–IV. *Poetry*, XIII. 6 (Mar. 1919) 291–9.
Contents: [Homage to Sextus Propertius] I—II—III—IV [*i.e.* VI].

C450 Music. By William Atheling. *New Age*, XXIV. 18 (6 Mar. 1919) 295–6.

C451 Art Notes [including "National Portrait Society"]. By B. H. Dias. *New Age*, XXIV. 19 (13 Mar. 1919) 310–11.

C452 ✉ Art Notes. *New Age*, XXIV. 19 (13 Mar. 1919) 315.
Signed: B. H. Dias.

C453 Music. By William Atheling. Pot-shots. *New Age*, XXIV. 20 (20 Mar. 1919) 329–30.

C. CONTRIBUTIONS TO PERIODICALS

C454 ✉ Art Notes. *New Age*, XXIV. 20 (20 Mar. 1919) 331.
Two letters, the first signed: B. H. Dias; the second: Ezra Pound.

C455 Art Notes [including "Exhibitions"]. By B. H. Dias. *New Age*, XXIV. 21 (27 Mar. 1919) 342.

C456 ✉ Concerning Certain Effusions of the "Chicago Daily News" Correspondent. *Little Review*, V. 12 (Apr. 1919) 61.
To Margaret Anderson, one of the editors, on Ben Hecht. Under the heading: "The Reader Critic."

C457 Music. By William Atheling. *New Age*, XXIV. 22 (3 Apr. 1919) 359–60.

C458 Art Notes [including "The Women's International"]. By B. H. Dias. *New Age*, XXIV. 23 (10 Apr. 1919) 378–9.

C459 Music. By William Atheling. Mainly Stroesco. *New Age*, XXIV. 24 (17 Apr. 1919) 396–7.

C460 ✉ Mohamedanism [*sic*]. *New Age*, XXIV. 24 (17 Apr. 1919) 398–9.

C461 Art Notes. By B. H. Dias. Rutter's Adelphi Gallery [and "The Fine Art Society," "W. G. Robb," "Epstein," "Sibyl Meugens," "W. Dacres Adams," "At the Leicester Gallery. The Society of Twenty-five Painters"]. *New Age*, XXIV. 25 (24 Apr. 1919) 411–12.

C462 Avis. *Little Review*, VI. 1 (May 1919) 69–70.
(In English.)

C463 Music. By William Atheling. *New Age*, XXV. 1 (1 May 1919) 12–13.
On Jehanne Chambard, Myra Hess, and Yves Tinayre.

C464 Art Notes [including "The London Group"]. By B. H. Dias. *New Age*, XXV. 2 (8 May 1919) 29–30.

C465 Music. By William Atheling. *New Age*, XXV. 4 (22 May 1919) 68–69.

C466 Art Notes. By B. H. Dias. Five Ordeals [including "By Water" and "Leicester Gallery"]. *New Age*, XXV. 5 (29 May 1919) 88–89.

C467 Durability and De Bosschère's Presentation. *Art & Letters*, London, N.S. II. 3 (Summer 1919) 125–6.

C468 Books Current, Reviewed by Ezra Pound. *Future*, III. 2 (June 1919) 57–58.
Reviews of *The Tunnel*, by Dorothy Richardson; *The Secret City*, by Hugh Walpole; *Books in General*, by Solomon Eagle [*i.e.* J. C. Squire]; *Rhyme and Revolution in Germany*, by J. G. Legge; with a single sentence on *Nous autres à Vauquois*, by André Pezard.

C469 Music. By William Atheling. Post-mortems [and "Anathema"]. *New Age*, XXV. 6 (5 June 1919) 103.

C470 Pastiche. The Regional. I. *New Age*, XXV. 7 (12 June 1919) 124.
The first of 18 instalments.

C471 HOMAGE TO SEXTUS PROPERTIUS . . . I. *New Age*, XXV. 8 (19 June 1919) 132–3.
Reprinted form *Poetry* for Mar. 1919—C449.

C. CONTRIBUTIONS TO PERIODICALS

c472 Music. By William Atheling. Varia, Dolmetsch. *New Age*, XXV. 8 (19 June 1919) 135–6.

c473 Pastiche. The Regional. II. *New Age*, XXV. 9 (26 June 1919) 156.

c474 HOMAGE TO SEXTUS PROPERTIUS ... II [*i.e.* IV]. DIFFERENCE OF OPINION. *New Age*, XXV. 10 (3 July 1919) 170.

c475 Pastiche. The Regional. III. *New Age*, XXV. 11 (10 July 1919) 188.

c476 HOMAGE TO SEXTUS PROPERTIUS ... III. *New Age*, XXV. 12 (17 July 1919) 200.
Reprinted from *Poetry* for Mar. 1919—C449.

c477 ✉ A Correction. *New Age*, XXV. 13 (24 July 1919) 219.
Signed: William Atheling.

c478 Pastiche. The Regional.—IV. *New Age*, XXV. 13 (24 July 1919) 220.

c479 HOMAGE TO SEXTUS PROPERTIUS ... IV [*i.e.* VIII]. *New Age*, XXV. 14 (31 July 1919) 231.

c479a Thoughts and Opinions: ... Ezra Pound. *Colour*, London, XI. 1 (Aug. 1919) 21.
Four paragraphs beginning "The 'difficulty' of the best art ..." The last of four contributions printed under this heading.

c480 Pastiche. The Regional. V. *New Age*, XXV. 15 (7 Aug. 1919) 252.

c481 HOMAGE TO SEXTUS PROPERTIUS ... V. *New Age*, XXV. 16 (14 Aug. 1919) 264.

c482 Pastiche. The Regional. VI. *New Age*, XXV. 16 (14 Aug. 1919) 268.

c483 Pastiche. The Regional. VIII[–IX; *i.e.* VII]. *New Age*, XXV. 17 (21 Aug. 1919) 284.
A brief paragraph was reprinted in *Agenda*, XVII. 3/4/XVIII. 1 (Autumn/Winter/Spring 1979/1980) 72.

c484 HOMAGE TO SEXTUS PROPERTIUS ... VI. *New Age*, XXV. 18 (28 Aug. 1919) 292.
Reprinted from *Poetry* for Mar. 1919—C449.

c485 Pastiche. The Regional. VIII. *New Age*, XXV. 18 (28 Aug. 1919) 300.
A sentence (on provincialism) was reprinted in *Agenda*, XVII. 3/4/XVIII. 1 (Autumn/Winter/Spring 1979/1980) 72.

c485a Thoughts and Opinions: ... Ezra Pound. That Audience, or The Bugaboo of the Public. *Colour*, XI. 2 (Sept. 1919) 42.
Six paragraphs beginning: "The curse of a large audience is not its largeness but crassness of its criteria." The second of two contributions printed under this heading.

c486 The Chinese Written Character as a Medium for Poetry, by Ernest Fenollosa and Ezra Pound [I]. *Little Review*, VI. 5 (Sept. 1919) 62–64.
With notes by Pound. (The first of four instalments.)

c487 Pastiche. The Regional. IX. *New Age*, XXV. 20 (11 Sept. 1919) 336.
Two brief passages were reprinted in *Agenda*, XVII. 3/4/XVIII. 1 (Autumn/Winter/Spring 1979/1980) 72–73.

C. CONTRIBUTIONS TO PERIODICALS

c488 Pastiche. The Regional. X. *New Age*, XXV. 21 (18 Sept. 1919) 352.

c489 Art Notes. By B. H. Dias. Capt. Guy Baker's Collection at the South Kensington Museum. *New Age*, XXV. 22 (25 Sept. 1919) 364–5.

c490 Pastiche. The Regional. XI. *New Age*, XXV. 22 (25 Sept. 1919) 368.

c491 The Chinese Written Character as a Medium for Poetry, by Ernest Fenollosa and Ezra Pound [II]. *Little Review*, VI. 6 (Oct. 1919) 57–64.

c492 Pastiche. The Regional. XII. *New Age*, XXV. 23 (2 Oct. 1919) 384.

c493 Music. By William Atheling. *New Age*, XXV. 24 (9 Oct. 1919) 396–7.

c494 Pastiche. The Regional. XIII. *New Age*, XXV. 24 (9 Oct. 1919) 400.

c495 The Drama. Daddies. *Outlook*, London, XLIV. 1132 (11 Oct. 1919) 363. Signed: M. D. Adkins.

c496 At the Ballet. By William Atheling. *New Age*, XXV. 25 (16 Oct. 1919) 412.

c497 The Drama. Gilbert and Sullivan. *Outlook*, XLIV. 1133 (18 Oct. 1919) 389–90.
Signed: M. D. Adkins.

c498 "Ésope," France and the Trade Union. *New Age*, XXV. 26 (23 Oct. 1919) 423–4.
On the Federation Society of Arts, Letters, and Sciences proposed by Banville d'Hostel in the magazine *Ésope*.

c499 Art Notes. By B. H. Dias. *New Age*, XXV. 26 (23 Oct. 1919) 427–8.
On the Russian ballet.

c500 Pastiche. The Regional. XIV. *New Age*, XXV. 26 (23 Oct. 1919) 432.

c501 Pastiche. The Regional. XV. *New Age*, XXV. 27 (30 Oct. 1919) 448.

c502 ✉ Mr. Pound and His Poetry. *Athenaeum*, London, XCIII. 4670 (31 Oct. 1919) 1132.
In answer to T. S. Eliot's review, in the issue for 24 Oct., of *Quia Pauper Amavi*—A17.

c503 The Chinese Written Character as a Medium for Poetry, by Ernest Fenollosa and Ezra Pound [III]. *Little Review*, VI. 7 (Nov. 1919) 55–60.

c504 Art Notes. By B. H. Dias. *New Age*, XXVI. 1 (6 Nov. 1919) 13–14.

c505 Pastiche: The Regional. XVI. *New Age*, XXVI. 1 (6 Nov. 1919) 16.
In part, reprinting "A Request from the Provost of the University of Pennsylvania" for "a record of . . . religious affiliations." A brief passage was reprinted in *Agenda*, XVII. 3/4/XVIII. 1 (Autumn/Winter/Spring 1979/1980) 73.

c506 The Revolt of Intelligence [I]. *New Age*, XXVI. 2 (13 Nov. 1919) 21–22.
The first of 10 instalments.

c507 Music. By William Atheling. *New Age*, XXVI. 2 (13 Nov. 1919) 28–29.

c508 ✉ Regional. *New Age*, XXVI. 2 (13 Nov. 1919) 31.
On "Pastiche. The Regional. XV"—C501.

c509 Pastiche: The Regional. XVII. *New Age*, XXVI. 2 (13 Nov. 1919) 32.

C. CONTRIBUTIONS TO PERIODICALS

C510 Music. By William Atheling. Marquesita. *New Age*, XXVI. 3 (20 Nov. 1919) 42–43.

C511 Pastiche: The Regional. XVIII. *New Age*, XXVI. 3 (20 Nov. 1919) 48.
A brief paragraph was reprinted in *Agenda*, XVII. 3/4/XVIII. 1 (Autumn/Winter/Spring 1979/1980) 73–74.

C512 Art Notes. By B. H. Dias. *New Age*, XXVI. 4 (27 Nov. 1919) 60–61.

C513 Masks and Abysmal Ignorance. *Theatre-Craft*, 3 ([Winter 1919/1920?]) 42, 45–46.

C514 The Chinese Written Character as a Medium for Poetry, IV, by Ernest Fenollosa and Ezra Pound. *Little Review*, VI. 8 (Dec. 1919) 68–72.

C515 Music. By William Atheling. *New Age*, XXVI. 5 (4 Dec. 1919) 78–79.

C516 ✉ "Homage to Propertius." *New Age*, XXVI. 5 (4 Dec. 1919) 82–83.
In reply to a review by Adrian Collins in the issue for 27 Nov.

C517 [The] Revolt of Intelligence.—II. *New Age*, XXVI. 6 (11 Dec. 1919) 90–91.

C518 Art Notes. By B. H. Dias. *New Age*, XXVI. 6 (11 Dec. 1919) 96–97.

C519 [The] Revolt of Intelligence.—III. *New Age*, XXVI. 7 (18 Dec. 1919) 106–7.

C520 Music. By William Atheling. *New Age*, XXVI. 7 (18 Dec. 1919) 112.

C521 ✉ Ezra Pound on the League of Ideas. *Much Ado*, St. Louis, Mo., X. 2 (Christmas 1919) [16–17].
To Harry Turner, the Editor, with Turner's reply.

1920

C522 The Curse. *Apple (of Beauty and Discord)*, London, I. 1 (Jan. 1920) 22, 24.
Of museums.

C523 A CANTICLE … (Special to H[arry]. T[urner]., of St. Louis). *Much Ado*, X. 3 (1 Jan. 1920) [1].
A 38-line poem, on America; not intended for publication.

C524 The Revolt of Intelligence … IV. *New Age*, XXVI. 9 (1 Jan. 1920) 139–40.
Six paragraphs, captioned "Shaw and Journalism," were reprinted in *Agenda*, XVII. 3/4/XVIII. 1 (Autumn/Winter/Spring 1979/1980) 264–5.

C525 Music. By William Atheling. *The Pye-ano. New Age*, XXVI. 9 (1 Jan. 1920) 144–5.

C526 Art Notes. By B. H. Dias. *New Age*, XXVI. 9 (1 Jan. 1920) 145–6.

C527 ✉ *New Age*, XXVI. 9 (1 Jan. 1920) 147.
Incorporating another letter sent to the Editor of "an American weekly called the 'Dial,'" on a passage in the *Dial* for 29 Nov. 1919, announcing a change of policy for the "new" *Dial*.

C528 The Revolt of Intelligence … V. *New Age*, XXVI. 10 (8 Jan. 1920) 153–4.

C529 Art Notes. By B. H. Dias. *New Age*, XXVI. 10 (8 Jan. 1920) 159–60.

C. CONTRIBUTIONS TO PERIODICALS

C530 Music. By William Atheling. *New Age*, XXVI. 11 (15 Jan. 1920) 175–6.

C531 The Revolt of Intelligence ... VI. *New Age*, XXVI. 11 (15 Jan. 1920) 176–7.
One paragraph, captioned "Divorce Reform," was reprinted in *Agenda*, XVII. 3/4/XVIII. 1 (Autumn/Winter/Spring 1979/1980) 217.

C532 The Revolt of Intelligence ... VII. *New Age*, XXVI. 12 (22 Jan. 1920) 186–7.

C533 ✉ The Flagellants. *New Age*, XXVI. 12 (22 Jan. 1920) 195.
On "Homage to Sextus Propertius."

C533a ✉ Propertius and Mr. Pound. *Observer*, London (25 Jan. 1920) 5.
In reply to a review by Robert Nichols in the issue for 11 Jan., with Nichols's answer.

C534 Art Notes. By B. H. Dias. *New Age*, XXVI. 13 (29 Jan. 1920) 205–6.
In part, on drawings by Wyndham Lewis, and on Edward Wadsworth.

C535 ✉ A Letter from London. *Much Ado*, X. 5 (2 Feb. 1920) [1–2].
To Harry Turner, the Editor, chiefly on economics, with Turner's comment, pp. [2–3].

C536 Music. By William Atheling. *New Age*, XXVI. 14 (5 Feb. 1920) 220–1.

C537 Art and Luxury. By B. H. Dias. *New Age*, XXVI. 15 (12 Feb. 1920) 238–9.
Includes letters written to the *Observer*, London, on the plumage trade, from H. J. Massingham, Willoughby Dewar, and Clementina Black.

C538 Music. By William Atheling. Cernikoff [etc.]. *New Age*, XXVI. 16 (19 Feb. 1920) 254–5.

C539 Music. By William Atheling. *New Age*, XXVI. 17 (26 Feb. 1920) 268–9.

C540 Arnaut Daniel (Razo [*i.e.* a prose preface]). *Art & Letters*, N.S. III. 2 (Spring 1920) 44–49.
Reprinted as "Arnaut Daniel," part I.

C541 Dada No. 1. [*Dada*, Paris, 7:] *Dadaphone* (Mar. 1920) [7].
Partly in French, partly in English.

C542 The Revolt of Intelligence ... VIII. *New Age*, XXVI. 18 (4 Mar. 1920) 287–8.

C543 Art Notes. By B. H. Dias. *New Age*, XXVI. 18 (4 Mar. 1920) 291–2.
In part, on Jacob Epstein.

C544 Dramedy. *Athenaeum*, XCIV. 4688 (5 Mar. 1920) 315.
A review, signed: T. J. V., of "Mumsée" by Edward Knoblock at the Little Theatre.

C545 The Revolt of Intelligence ... IX. *New Age*, XXVI. 19 (11 Mar. 1920) 301–2.

C546 Music. By William Atheling. *New Age*, XXVI. 19 (11 Mar. 1920) 309–10.

C547 In Their Degree. *Athenaeum*, XCIV. 4689 (12 Mar. 1920) 348–9.

A drama review, signed: T. J. V. *Contents:* Tagore—[R. B.] Sheridan—Russian Matinées.

c548 The Revolt of Intelligence ... X. *New Age,* XXVI. 20 (18 Mar. 1920) 318–19.

c549 ✉ Mr. Pound and the "Dial." *New Age,* XXVI. 20 (18 Mar. 1920) 327.
A letter from the Editor of the *Dial* quoting and replying to Ezra Pound's letter in the *New Age* for 1 Jan. 1920—C527; with Pound's answer.

c550 Pseudothello. *Athenaeum,* XCIV. 4690 (19 Mar. 1920) 378.
A review, signed: T. J. V., of "Carnival" at the New Theatre.

c551 Realities. *Athenaeum,* XCIV. 4690 (19 Mar. 1920) 379.
A review, signed: T. J. V., of "Grierson's Way," by H. V. Esmond, at the Ambassador's Theatre.

c552 Music. By William Atheling. *New Age,* XXVI. 21 (25 Mar. 1920) 338–9.

c553 The Culinary Vein. *Athenaeum,* XCIV. 4691 (26 Mar. 1920) 423–4.
A review, signed: T. J. V., of "Come Out of the Kitchen," by A. E. Thomas, at the Strand Theatre.

c554 The Independent Theatre. *Athenaeum,* XCIV. 4691 (26 Mar. 1920) 424.
A review, signed: T. J. V., of three one-act plays at the Lyric Theatre, Hammersmith.

c555 [A review of] *Economic Democracy* [by Major C. H. Douglas]. *Little Review,* VI. 11 (Apr. 1920) 39–42.

c556 ✉ A Letter from London. *Much Ado,* X. 9 (1 Apr. 1920) [21–22].
To Harry Turner, the Editor, signed: E. P., chiefly on economics; with Turner's reply, pp. [22–23].

c557 Masaryk. *New Age,* XXVI. 22 (1 Apr. 1920) 350–1.

c558 "Probari ratio." *Athenaeum,* XCIV. 4692 (2 Apr. 1920) 445.
A review, signed: J. L., of *Economic Democracy,* by Major C. H. Douglas.

c559 Musical Comedy. *Athenaeum,* XCIV. 4692 (2 Apr. 1920) 457.
A review, signed: T. J. V., of "Society, Ltd.," by A. Branscombe and A. Carrington, at the Scala Theatre.

c560 Vaudeville. *Athenaeum,* XCIV. 4692 (2 Apr. 1920) 457–8.
A review, signed: T. J. V., of "The Truth about the Russian Dancers," by Sir J. M. Barrie, at the Coliseum.

c561 Art Notes. By B. H. Dias. The Functions of Criticism [and "The Evidence"]. *New Age,* XXVI. 23 (8 Apr. 1920) 372.
The last of Ezra Pound's critical articles on art, signed with this pseudonym, for the *New Age.* Their place is taken, beginning 11 Nov. 1920, by a column, "Art," by R. A. Stephens.

c562 The Obvious. *Athenaeum,* XCIV. 4693 (9 Apr. 1920) 487.
A review, by T. J. V., of "From Morn to Midnight," By Georg Kaiser, translated from the German by Ashley Dukes, at the Lyric Theatre, Hammersmith; and "Uncle Ned," by Douglas Murray, at the St. James's.

c563 Frivolity Not Unpleasing. *Athenaeum,* XCIV. 4693 (9 Apr. 1920) 487–8.

C. CONTRIBUTIONS TO PERIODICALS

A review, signed: T. J. V., of "The Young Person in Pink," by Gertrude Jennings, at the Haymarket Theatre.

c564 Music. By William Atheling. *New Age*, XXVI. 24 (15 Apr. 1920) 387–8.

c565 The Drama as a Means of Education. *Athenaeum*, XCIV. 4694 (16 Apr. 1920) 520.
A review, signed: T. J. V., of "The Fold," by the Marchioness Townshend, at the Queen's Theatre.

c566 Divertissement. *Athenaeum*, XCIV. 4694 (16 Apr. 1920) 521.
A review, signed: T. J. V., of the Ballet at the Duke of York's Theatre.

c567 Hapsburgiania. *New Age*, XXVI. 25 (22 Apr. 1920) 399–400.

c568 Vulgus profanum. *Athenaeum*, XCIV. 4695 (23 Apr. 1920) 552.
A review, signed: T. J. V., of Heywood's "Fair Maid of the West," at the Lyric Theatre, Hammersmith, and "Birds of a Feather," by H. V. Esmond, at the Globe.

c569 Gogol. *Athenaeum*, XCIV. 4695 (23 Apr. 1920) 553.
A review, signed: T. J. V., of Gogol's "The Government Inspector," translated by T. H. Hall, at the Duke of York's Theatre. (In the issue for 7 May 1920, editorial regret is expressed that this review contained words "which might be construed as imputing to Miss Mary Grey want of ability in her profession of an actress.")

c570 Pavlova. *Athenaeum*, XCIV. 4695 (23 Apr. 1920) 553.
A review, signed: T. J. V., of the Ballet at the Drury Lane Theatre.

c571 That Human Touch. *Athenaeum*, XCIV. 4696 (30 Apr. 1920) 583–4.
A review, by T. J. V., of "Ned Kean of Old Drury," by Arthur Shirley, at the Kennington Theatre.

c572 Politics. *Athenaeum*, XCIV. 4696 (30 Apr. 1920) 584.
A review, by T. J. V., of "The Grain of Mustard Seed," by H. M. Harwood, at the Ambassador's Theatre.

c573 Touch. *Athenaeum*, XCIV. 4696 (30 Apr. 1920) 584.
A review, signed: T. J. V., of "Mary Rose," by Sir J. M. Barrie, at the Haymarket Theatre.

c574 Hudson: Poet Strayed into Science. *Little Review*, VII. 1 (May/June 1920) 13–17.

c575 Music. By William Atheling. Mignon Nevada, et varia. *New Age*, XXVII. 2 (13 May 1920) 28.

c576 Kublai Khan and His Currency. *New Age*, XXVII. 3 (20 May 1920) 37–38.

c577 Arthur Symons. *Athenaeum*, XCIV. 4699 (21 May 1920) 663–4.
Reprinted in *Agenda*, XVII. 3/4/XVIII. 1 (Autumn/Winter/Spring 1979/1980) 54–57.

c578 Indiscretions; or, Une revue de deux mondes . . . I. *New Age*, XXVII. 4 (27 May 1920) 56–57.
The first of 12 instalments.

c579 THE FOURTH CANTO. *Dial*, New York, LXVIII. 6 (June 1920) [689]–692.

C. CONTRIBUTIONS TO PERIODICALS

A reprint of *The Fourth Canto* (1919)—A16.

C580 Indiscretions; or, Une revue de deux mondes . . . II. *New Age*, XXVII. 5 (3 June 1920) 76–77.

C581 Indiscretions; or, Une revue de deux mondes . . . III. *New Age*, XXVII. 6 (10 June 1920) 91–92.

C582 Indiscretions; or, Une revue de deux mondes . . . IV. *New Age*, XXVII. 7 (17 June 1920) 105–6.

C583 Indiscretions; or, Une revue de deux mondes . . . V. *New Age*, XXVII. 8 (24 June 1920) 124–5.

C584 Obstructivity. *Apple (of Beauty and Discord)*, I. 3 (July/Sept. 1920) 168, 170, 172.

C585 Indiscretions; or, Une revue de deux mondes . . . VI. *New Age*, XXVII. 9 (1 July 1920) 140–1.

C586 Indiscretions; or, Une revue de deux mondes . . . VII. *New Age*, XXVII. 10 (8 July 1920) 156–7.

C586a Julien Benda. *Athenaeum*, XCV. 4706 (9 July 1920) 62.
A review, signed: B. L., of *Belphégor*, by Julien Benda.

C587 Indiscretions; or, Une revue de deux mondes . . . VIII. *New Age*, XXVII. 11 (15 July 1920) 172–3.

C588 Indiscretions; or, Une revue de deux mondes . . . IX. *New Age*, XXVII. 12 (22 July 1920) 187–8.

C588a ✉ Oh, Those Passports. *New York Herald*, Paris (22 July 1920)

C589 Indiscretions; or, Une revue de deux mondes . . . X. *New Age*, XXVII. 13 (29 July 1920) 204.

C590 El arte poético en Inglaterra contemporánea. *Hermes*, Bilbao, IV. 62 (Aug. 1920) 447–50.
"Ezra Pound . . . ha escrito expresamente para *Hermes* este sabrosísimo artículo"—*Note*, p. 450.

C591 Indiscretions; or, Une revue de deux mondes . . . XI. *New Age*, XXVII. 14 (5 Aug. 1920) 221–2.

C592 Indiscretions; or, Une revue de deux mondes . . . XII. *New Age*, XXVII. 15 (12 Aug. 1920) 236–7.

C593 ✉ *Much Ado*, XI.4 (15 Aug. 1920) [11–12].
To Harry Turner, the Editor, signed: Ezra. With postscript, "Alternate Remedies," signed: E. P. On passports.

C594 [Note, signed: E. P., to] Bibi-la-Bibiste (roman) par les Sœurs X . . . *Little Review*, VII. 3 (Sept./Dec. 1920) 24.

C594a ✉ Lettre anglaise. *Littérature*, Paris, 1. sér., 16 (Sept./Oct. 1920) 48.
Reprinted in *Modern Language Notes*, Baltimore, Md., LXXIV. 7 (Nov. 1959) 608–9, and in *Paideuma*, VII. 1/2 (Spring/Fall 1978) 140.

C595 Dust for Sparrows, by Remy de Gourmont; translated [with notes] by Ezra Pound. I. *Dial*, LXIX. 3 (Sept. 1920) [219]–224.

C. CONTRIBUTIONS TO PERIODICALS

With sub-title: "Things, Thought, Felt, Seen, Heard, and Dreamed." The first of nine instalments.

c596 H. S. MAUBERLY [*sic*]. *Dial*, LXIX. 3 (Sept. 1920) [283]–287.
A reprint of the first six poems of Part I of *Hugh Selwyn Mauberley* (1920)—A19. Preceded by a drawing of Ezra Pound by Wyndham Lewis.

c596a [SELECTIONS FROM] FEVER CHART BY PAUL MORAND. *Dial*, LXIX. 3 (Sept. 1920) [289], 291.
Contents: Nice—Sample. Translated anonymously by Ezra Pound. (With the French texts opposite.)

c597 ✉ The "Dial." *New Age*, XXVII. 18 (2 Sept. 1920) 275.
Stating that he is not "Continental Editor" for the *Dial*.

c597a ✉ The Crusades. A Reply to Mr. Chesterton. *Daily Telegraph*, London, 20,412 (17 Sept. 1920) 12.
Replying to an article, "The New Jerusalem. The Crusade. Chapter XI," by G. K. Chesterton, in the issue for 10 Sept., attacking Ezra Pound, especially for views expressed in his "Pastiche. The Regional. XVIII"—C511—six paragraphs of which are quoted in Pound's letter.

c597b Saint-Loup: A Portrait, by Marcel Proust. *Dial*, LXIX. 4 (Oct. 1920) [347]–350.
Translated anonymously by Ezra Pound?

c598 Dust for Sparrows, by Remy de Gourmont; translated [with notes] by Ezra Pound. II. *Dial*, LXIX. 4 (Oct. 1920) [368]–371.

c599 The Island of Paris: A Letter. September, 1920. *Dial*, LXIX. 4 (Oct. 1920) [406]–411.

c600 Music. By William Atheling. *New Age*, XXVII. 25 (21 Oct. 1920) 356.

c601 Dust for Sparrows, by Remy de Gourmont; translated [with notes] by Ezra Pound. III. *Dial*, LXIX. 5 (Nov. 1920) [484]–488.

c601a Case: Mallarmé, by Fernand Divoire. *Dial*, LXIX. 5 (Nov. 1920) [514].
Translated anonymously by Ezra Pound.

c602 The Island of Paris: A Letter. October, 1920. *Dial*, LXIX. 5 (Nov. 1920) [515]–518.
In part, on Maurice Vlaminck.

c603 ✉ Here's Your Chance, Washington University. *Much Ado*, XI. 9 (1 Nov. 1920) [2–3].
To Harry Turner, the Editor, dated: 15 Oct. [*i.e.* Sept.] and 30 Sept.

c604 Music. *New Age*, XXVIII. 2 (11 Nov. 1920) 21.
Signed: William Atheling.

c605 Music. *New Age*, XXVIII. 4 (25 Nov. 1920) 44.
Signed: William Atheling. In part, on Lilias Mackinnon, Roland Hayes, and Olga Rudge.

c606 Dust for Sparrows, by Remy de Gourmont; translated [with notes] by Ezra Pound. IV. *Dial*, LXIX. 6 (Dec. 1920) [615]–618.

C. CONTRIBUTIONS TO PERIODICALS

c607 The Island of Paris: A Letter. November 1920. *Dial*, LXIX. 6 (Dec. 1920) [635]–639.

c608 ✉ *Literary Review* [of the New York *Evening Post*], I. 13 (4 Dec. 1920) 26. Outlining policies for an American literary journal.

c609 Music. *New Age*, XXVIII. 6 (9 Dec. 1920) 68. Signed: William Atheling. On Arthur Rubinstein.

c610 Music. *New Age*, XXVIII. 8 (23 Dec. 1920) 92–93. Signed: William Atheling. In part, on Roland Hayes and Arthur Rubinstein.

1921

c610a ✉ "Sculpshure." *Little Review*, VII. 4 (Jan./Mar. 1921) 47. Signed: Abel Sanders. On George G. Barnard.

c611 Dust for Sparrows, by Remy de Gourmont; translated [with notes] by Ezra Pound. V. *Dial*, LXX. 1 (Jan. 1921) [24]–28.

c612 [A review, signed: E. P., of] *Poésies 1917–1920*, [by] Jean Cocteau. *Dial*, LXX. 1 (Jan. 1921) 110.

c613 Music. *New Age*, XXVIII. 10 (6 Jan. 1921) 117–18. Signed: William Atheling. The last of Ezra Pound's notes on music signed with this pseudonym for the *New Age*. Those in the issue for 21 April 1921 are signed: H. R., and are not by Pound.

c614 Axiomata. *New Age*, XXVIII. 11 (13 Jan. 1921) 125–6. Ezra Pound's "intellectual will and testament" on leaving England.

c615 Dust for Sparrows, by Remy de Gourmont; translated [with notes] by Ezra Pound. VI. *Dial*, LXX. 2 (Feb. 1921) [164]–168. Three passages from this translation, the first captioned "For Revolutionaries," the second "Five Epigrams on Prohibition," and the third "One Good Thing," appear as part of a printed three-column broadside, *Clip-sheet from The Dial* . . . ([New York, 1921]), distributed to the Press in late January as publicity for the February issue.

c616 ✉ [On passports]. *Chicago Tribune*, Paris (5 Feb. 1921) 2.

c617 Dust for Sparrows, by Remy de Gourmont; translated [with notes] by Ezra Pound. VII. *Dial*, LXX. 3 (Mar. 1921) [313]–316. A short paragraph from this translation, captioned "Patriotism," appears as part of a printed three-column broadside, *Clip-sheet from The Dial* . . . ([New York, 1921]), distributed to the Press in late February as publicity for the March issue.

c617a Paris Letter, February, 1921, by André Germain. *Dial*, LXX. 3 (Mar. 1921) [329]–331 Translated anonymously by Ezra Pound?

c618 Some Notes on Francisco de Quevedo Villegas. *Hermes*, V. 69 (Mar. 1921) 199–213.

C. CONTRIBUTIONS TO PERIODICALS

A sentence was reprinted in *Agenda*, XVII. 3/4/XVIII. 1 (Autumn/Winter/ Spring 1979/1980) 74.

c619 Thames Morasses. *Poetry*, XVII. 6 (Mar. 1921) 325–9.

c620 Dust for Sparrows, by Remy de Gourmont; translated [with notes] by Ezra Pound. VIII. *Dial*, LXX. 4 (Apr. 1921) [417]–421.

c620a [Brief comments, in French, on] Ouvrages reçues. *Action*, Paris, I. 7 (May 1921) 56.
Notes on *Credit Power and Democracy*, by C. H. Douglas; *The Sacred Wood*, by T. S. Eliot; and *Otherworld*, by F. S. Flint.

c621 Dust for Sparrows, by Remy de Gourmont; translated [with notes] by Ezra Pound. IX. *Dial*, LXX. 5 (May 1921) [559]–561.
A paragraph from this translation, captioned "Love and Music," appears as part of a printed three-column broadside, *Clip-sheet from The Dial . . .* ([New York, 1921]), distributed to the Press in late April as publicity for the May issue.

c622 [A review of] *Credit Power and Democracy*, by Maj. C. H. Douglas and A. R. Orange [*i.e.* Orage]. *Contact*, New York, [4] ([Summer 1921]) [1].

c622a Wreck, by Jean Giraudoux. *Dial*, LXXI. 1 (July 1921) [35]–42.
Translated anonymously by Ezra Pound.

c622b [A review of] *Pastorales Parisiennes*, par Guy-Charles Cros. *Dial*, LXXI. 1 (July 1921) 120.
Unsigned. Under the heading: "Briefer Mention."

c623 KONGO ROUX. [*391*, Paris, 15 (10 July 1921):] *Le Pilhaou-Thibaou*, [10].
In French, with final section headed: "Sommaire." (The complete issue was reprinted in *391: Revue publiée de 1917 à 1924 par Francis Picabia. Re-édition intégrale présentée par Michel Sanouillet . . . I.* (Paris, Le Terrain Vague [1960]), pp. 97–108.

c623a [Paris]. [*391*, Paris, 15 (10 July 1921):] *Le Pilhaou-Thibaou*, [14].
Signed: Ezra. A brief comment, in French, printed along the right-hand side of the page.

c624 Le major C.-H. Douglas et la situation en Angleterre. *Les Écrits Nouveaux*, Paris, VIII. 8/9 (Aug./Sept. 1921) [143]–149.
"Nous avons respecté les savoureux exotismes de cet article écrit directe-ment en français . . . "—*Note*, p. [143]. The principal passages of the article were extracted and printed, also in French, in *Progrès civique*, Paris, III. 108 (10 Sept. 1921) 20–21, with title: "La réforme du crédit est la clef de toutes les autres." The complete article was reprinted in 1965 as . . . *Être Citoyen Romain était un privilège Être Citoyen moderne est un calamité*—A84.

c625 THREE CANTOS. *Dial*, LXXI. 2 (Aug. 1921) [198]–208.
Contents: The Fifth Canto—The Sixth Canto [first two-thirds only]—The Seventh Canto.

c626 Parisian Literature. *Literary Review* [of the New York *Evening Post*], I. 49 (13 Aug. 1921) 7.

C. CONTRIBUTIONS TO PERIODICALS

In large part, on Francis Picabia, with notes on Marcel Proust, Paul Morand, and Francis Bernouard. Under the heading: "Literature Abroad."

c627 Brancusi. *Little Review*, VIII. 1 (Autumn 1921) 3–7.
An excerpt from this essay, printed in six lines, appeared in *Brancusi Exhibition November 17–December 15, 1926* (New York, Brummer Gallery [1926]), p. [40].

c628 Historical Survey. *Little Review*, VIII. 1 (Autumn 1921) 39–42.

c628a THE POEMS OF ABEL SANDERS. To Bill Williams and Else von Johann Wolfgang Loringhoven y Fulano. *Little Review*, VIII. 1 (Autumn 1921) 111. The first poem refers to Else von Freytag-Loringhoven's "criticism" of William Carlos Williams's *Kora in Hell*. The text of both poems was reproduced in Alan Young's *Dada and After: Extremist Modernism and English Literature* ([Manchester] Manchester University Press [1981]), p. 86.

c629 Turkish Night (To the Princess Lucien Murat), by Paul Morand. Translated from the French by Ezra Pound. *Dial*, LXXI. 3 (Sept. 1921) [281]–291.

c630 Paris Letter. September, 1921. *Dial*, LXXI. 4 (Oct. 1921) [456]–463.
In part, on Marcel Proust and Paul Morand. A paragraph from this letter, captioned "French Malice and British," appears as part of a printed three-column broadside, *Clip-sheet from The Dial . . . September 22, 1921* ([New York 1921]), distributed to the Press as publicity for the October issue.

c631 STROPHES, BY O. W. DE LUBICZ-MILOSZ; TRANSLATED BY EZRA POUND. *Dial*, LXXI. 5 (Nov. 1921) [581]–582.
A translation of his "Symphonie de Novembre."

c631a Divertimenti. *Fanfare*, London, I. 3 (1 Nov. 1921) 52.
Under this general title are printed contributions (in English) from several writers including Ezra Pound, who, in four short sentences, defines "An impressionist."

c632 ✉ For a Rhenish Republic. *Chicago Tribune*, Paris (7 Dec. 1921) 4.

1922

c633 Paris Letter. December, 1921. *Dial*, LXXII. 1 (Jan. 1922) [73]–78.
In part, on Constantin Brancusi and Alfred Jarry.

c634 Paris Letter. January, 1922. *Dial*, LXXII. 2 (Feb. 1922) [187]–192.

c634a The Little Review Calendar. *Little Review*, VII. 2 (Spring 1922) [2].
A proposed new calendar, starting "p[ost]. s[criptum]. U[lysses]." on 31 Oct. 1921; with a "Note to Calendar," p. 40, both contributed anonymously by Ezra Pound.

c634b Stop Press. *Little Review*, VIII. 2 (Spring 1922) 33.
Signed: Abel Sanders.

c634c FRENCH SCHOOL OF POETRY, SYNTHÈSE. WESTERN SCHOOL OF POETRY, SYNTHÈSE. *Little Review*, VIII. 2 (Spring 1922) 33.

Two lines of verse in French, printed below first caption, followed by three lines in English under the second caption, signed: Abel Sanders.

c635 Suppressed Passage. *Little Review*, VIII. 2 (Spring 1922) 34.
Includes lines removed from Ezra Pound's letter in the *Literary Review* of the New York *Evening Post* for 4 Dec. 1920—C608.

c635a Boll Weevil. *Little Review*, VIII. 2 (Spring 1922) 34.
Two-line comment, signed: Abel Sanders, on an article by Robert Morss Lovett in the *Dial* for Jan. 1922.

c636 ✉ Supports Bonus. *Chicago Tribune*, Paris (9 Mar. 1922) 4.

c637 The New Therapy. *New Age*, XXX. 20 (16 Mar. 1922) 259–60.
On Dr. Louis Berman and glands.

c638 Credit and the Fine Arts . . . A Practical Application. *New Age*, XXX. 22 (30 Mar. 1922) 284–5.
On Bel Esprit. (See E2e.)

c639 Paris Letter. March, 1922. *Dial*, LXXII. 4 (Apr. 1922) [401]–405.
In large part, on Flaubert.

c640 EIGHTH CANTO. *Dial*, LXXII. 5 (May 1922) [505]–509.
Reprinted, with revisions, as Canto II.

c641 ✉ Ezra Pound on Sandburg. *Double-Dealer*, New Orleans, La., III. 17 (May 1922) 277–8.

c642 Paris Letter. May, 1922. *Ulysses* [by James Joyce]. *Dial*, LXXII. 6 (June 1922) [623]–639.
Reprinted as "Ulysses."

c643 James Joyce et Pécuchet. *Mercure de France*, Paris, CLVI. 575 (1 June 1922) 307–20.
In French. (An 11-line extract from this article was printed on page [1] of a four-page leaflet headed *Extracts from Press Notices of Ulysses by James Joyce* ([London, Egoist Press, 1922]), of which a first edition of 4000 copies, printed on honey-colored paper, was published at the beginning of October. A revised edition, adding 13 new extracts for a total of 47, consisting of 1000 copies printed on pink paper, was issued early in December. Pages [1] and [4] of the first edition were reproduced in facsimile as front end-paper in Jane Lidderdale and Mary Nicholson's *Dear Miss Weaver* ([1970])—B101.) An English translation of Ezra Pound's article, by Fred Bornhauser, with title: "James Joyce and Pécuchet, " was printed in *Shenandoah*, Lexington, Va., III. 3 (Autumn 1952) [9]–20.

c644 ✉ [Answers to three questions]. *Chapbook*, London, 27 (July 1922) 17–18.
Followed by an extract from Ezra Pound's letter.

c645 On the Swings and Roundabouts: The Intellectual Somersaults of the Parisian vs. the Londoner's Efforts to Keep His Stuffed Figures Standing. *Vanity Fair*, New York, XVIII. 6 (Aug. 1922) 49.

c646 Paris Letter. August, 1922. *Dial*, LXXIII. 3 (Sept. 1922) [332]–337.
In large part, on Flaubert's *Bouvard et Pécuchet*; with a note at the end on Bel Esprit. (See E2e.)

C. CONTRIBUTIONS TO PERIODICALS

c647 Paris Letter. October, 1922. *Dial,* LXXIII. 5 (Nov. 1922) [549]–554.
In part, on Bel Esprit. (See E2e.)

c648 ✉ The Passport Nuisance. *Chicago Tribune,* Paris (20 Nov. 1922) 4.

1923

c649 On Criticism in General . . . *Criterion,* London, I. 2 (Jan. 1923) 143–56.

c650 Paris Letter. December, 1922. *Dial,* LXXIV. 1 (Jan. 1923) [85]–90.

c651 Paris Letter. February, 1923. *Dial,* LXXIV. 3 (Mar. 1923) [273]–280.

c652 MALATESTA CANTOS. (CANTOS IX TO XII OF A LONG POEM). *Criterion,*
I. 4 (July 1923) 363–84.
Reprinted, with revisions, as Cantos VIII–XI.

c653 ✉ Ezra Pound Jumps at Conclusions. *Chicago Tribune,* Paris, (14 Dec. 1923) 4.
On George Antheil's concert, pointing out that the violin sonatas were
Antheil's and not Pound's.

c654 ✉ From Mr. Pound. *Chicago Tribune,* Paris (15 Dec. 1923) 4.
On the Antheil-Pound music.

1924

c655 TWO CANTOS. *Transatlantic Review,* Paris, I. 1 (Jan. 1924) 10–14.
Contents: One Canto [Canto XIII]—Another Canto [Canto XII, first half
only].

c656 Notes for Performers, by William Atheling, with Marginalia Emitted by
George Antheil [I]. *Transatlantic Review,* I. 2 (Feb. 1924) 109–15.
Excerpts, selected by Agnes Bedford, reprinted from the *New Age.* With a
"Foreword by E. P.," pp. 109–10, and a note, "George Antheil," p. 110,
also signed: E. P. The first of three instalments.

c656a PICCADILLY. *Daily Worker,* New York, I. 329 (2 Feb. 1924), *Special Magazine Supplement,* p. [3].
Reprinted from *Personae* (1909) and *Provença.*

c657 ✉ A Passport Collector. *Chicago Tribune,* Paris (24 Feb. 1924) 4.

c658 Le prix Nobel . . . *Der Querschnitt,* Berlin, IV. 1 (Spring 1924) 41–44.
In English, "Specially Written for 'Der Querschnitt,'" with translation into
German, "Der Nobel-Preis," pp. 44–46. On the award of the Prize to W. B.
Yeats, with comments on Thomas Hardy, James Joyce, and others.

c659 Treatise on Harmony. *Transatlantic Review,* I. 3 (Mar. 1924) 77–81.

c659a NEW YORK. *Daily Worker,* I. 365 (15 Mar. 1924), *Special Magazine Supplement,* p. [1].
Reprinted from *Ripostes, Lustra* (1917), and *Umbra.*

c660 George Antheil. *Criterion,* II. 7 (Apr. 1924) 321–31.

c661 Death of Arsène Lupin. *Transatlantic Review,* I. 4 (Apr. 1924) 209.
A "communication," signed: E. P. Report of the death of Battistino Travail.

C. CONTRIBUTIONS TO PERIODICALS

c662 Notes for Performers, by William Atheling, with Marginalia Emitted by George Antheil [II]. *Transatlantic Review*, I. 5 (May 1924) 370–3.

c662a ✉ [On Numbers V and VI]. *Transatlantic Review*, I. 6 (June 1924) 480.
Signed: Old Glory. Under the heading: "Communications."

c662b [Aphorism]. *391*, Paris, 18 (July 1924) [1].
In French. On modern painting. The complete issue was reprinted in *391* ([1960]), pp. 121–6 (see note to C623).

c663 Fiddle Music. *Transatlantic Review*, II. 2 (Aug. 1924) 220–1.
A reproduction of the manuscript of the music (in Ezra Pound's hand).

c664 Notes for Performers, by William Atheling, with Marginalia Emitted by George Antheil [III]. *Transatlantic Review*, II. 2 (Aug. 1924) 222–5.

c665 ✉ A Communication. *1924: A Magazine of the Arts*, Woodstock, N. Y., 3 ([Sept./Nov.] 1924) 97–98.
On T. S. Eliot's *The Waste Land*, with particular reference to the notes.

c666 Law and the Merchant of Venice . . . *Der Querschnitt*, IV. 4 (Autumn 1924) 237–8.

c667 ✉ To the Editor . . . *Transatlantic Review*, II. 3 (Sept. 1924) 312.
Recommending Sadakichi Hartmann's *Confucius*. Under the heading: "Communications."

c668 AFTER READING CHINESE POEMS, BY NATALIE C. BARNEY. ARRANGED BY EZRA POUND. *Transatlantic Review*, II. 4 (Oct. 1924) 437.

c669 The Unpublished Work of Fanelli. *Transatlantic Review*, II. 5 (Nov. 1924) 566–7.

c670 The Form; (ou 'Je cherche un ami sérieux'). *Transatlantic Review*, II. 5 (Nov. 1924) 568.
Signed: E. P.

c671 London Letter. *Transatlantic Review*, II. 5 (Nov. 1924) 569.
Signed: E. P. Quoting "a musician resident in England [*i.e.* Agnes Bedford?]."

c672 Varia. *1924: A Magazine of the Arts*, 4 (Dec. 1924) 132–5.
"These notes are selected from a forthcoming [*sic*] book . . . *Antheil and A Treatise on Harmony* [A25a]."

c673 ✉ Thanksgiving? *Chicago Tribune*, Paris (2 Dec. 1924) 4.
Signed: E. P. On passport regulations.

c674 ✉ Mr. Ezra Pound and Passports. *Chicago Tribune*, Paris (7 Dec. 1924) 4.

1925

c674a Englischer Brief. *Europa Almanach*, Potsdam (1925) 36–37.
An English translation by Peter Schneeman, "English Letter," was printed in *Paideuma*, VII. 1/2 (Spring/Fall 1978) 315–16, following his article, "Pound's 'Englischer Brief': A Look toward Germany," pp. [309]–314.

c675 Definitions etc. *Der Querschnitt*, V. 1 (Jan. 1925) 54.

c676 ✉ Passports and [Charles] Hughes. *Chicago Tribune*, Paris (8 Feb. 1925) 6.

C. CONTRIBUTIONS TO PERIODICALS

c677 THE MOURN OF LIFE. *Times-News-Miner*, Hailey, Idaho (21 May 1925) 7.
An "infantile production," "never yet published, and kindly furnished to
The Times-News-Miner by the father of the poet." Reprinted in an interview
with Homer L. Pound by Mary Dixon Thayer in the Philadelphia *Evening
Bulletin* for 20 Feb. 1928.

c678 AMBITION. *Times-News-Miner*, Hailey, Idaho (21 May 1925) 7.
In an article entitled "Hailey Sends Literary Genius out into the World of
Letters," this six-line poem "kindly furnished . . . by the father of the poet,"
is printed for the first time.

c679 ✉ *Times-News-Miner*, Hailey, Idaho (16 July 1925)
In an article "Ezra L. Pound Is Recognized," Pound's letter concerning
(and correcting errors in) the article of 21 May 1925, is printed.

c680 CANTOS XVII-XIX. *This Quarter*, Paris, I. 2 (Autumn/Winter 1925/1926)
5–16.

c681 Mr. Dunning's Poetry. *Poetry*, XXVI. 6 (Sept. 1925) 339–45.
On Ralph Cheever Dunning's "The Four Winds," unpublished except in
Poetry and the *Transatlantic Review*. Reprinted in *Paideuma*, X. 3 (Winter
1981[/1982]) [605]–609.

c682 ✉ From Mr. Pound. *Chicago Tribune*, Paris (3 Sept. 1925) 4.
Stating that he has no editorial connexion with any current periodical and
is not a receiving station for manuscripts unaccompanied by return post-
age.

c683 ✉ Pound on Passports. *New York Herald*, Paris (15 Sept. 1925) 4.

c684 ✉ [Col. Billy] Mitchell and Passports. *Chicago Tribune*, Paris (18 Nov. 1925) 4.
Signed: E. P.

1926

c685 ✉ Not in Congress, He Says. *New York Herald*, Paris (19 Jan. 1926) 4.

c686 Antheil, 1924–1926. *New Criterion*, London, IV. 4 (Oct. 1926) 695–9.

c687 ✉ Pound Joins the Revolution! *New Masses*, New York, II. 2 (Dec. 1926) 3.

1927

c688 PART OF CANTO XX. *Exile*, Paris, 1 (Spring 1927) 1–6.
In an attempt to secure copyright in the United States for the first number
of the *Exile*, a small number of copies—but at least 25—were printed, in
Feb. 1927, of a three-column broadside containing "Part of Canto XX"
(the entire selection, with text printed as prose, but with the first letter of
each line of poetry capitalised) and the first three paragraphs and part of
the fourth paragraph of "Adolphe 1920" by John Rodker. This broadside,
printed on unwatermarked wove paper measuring 27·7 × 21·4 cm., is
headed at the top of the first column: Printed in the United States of Amer-
ica | Copyright by EZRA POUND, 1927 | THE EXILE | (a periodical) |
edited by | EZRA POUND | No. 1 primavera | 1927 | (February) | [*short
rule*]. The American copyright was not granted on the grounds that the

submitted broadside was neither a periodical nor a book, but the first number of the periodical carries a notice on page [ii] of the cover: ". . . Copyrights fully protected in all countries including the United States of America, local printings where by law required to assure copyright. E. Pound, 1927." No other "local printings" than the above have been located, and the United States copyright is the only one specifically claimed in the periodical itself for Pound's and Rodker's contributions.

c689 The Exile [I]. *Exile*, 1 (Spring 1927) [88]–92.
Editorial comment, signed: E. P., including notes later reprinted in *Impact* (1960)—A78—as "The Public Convenience" and "Summary of the Situation."

c690 Workshop Orchestration. *New Masses*, II. 5 (Mar. 1927) 21.
On George Antheil.

c690a ✉ Pound vs. Gellert. *New Masses*, II. 5 (Mar. 1927) 25.
A letter to Hugo Gellert, one of the editors; in part, on Brancusi. With Gellert's reply addressed to Pound.

c691 ✉ American Book Pirates. *New Statesman*, New York, XXIX. 729 (16 Apr. 1927) 10–11.

c692 ✉ From the Editor of "The Exile." *Poetry*, XXX. 3 (June 1927) 174–5.
On the editorial policy of the *Exile*.

c692a ✉ Ezra Pound Deplores Censorship Literature. *Publishers' Weekly*, New York, 111 (4 June 1927) 2189.

c693 Prolegomena. *Exile*, Chicago, 2 (Autumn 1927) 35.
Reprinted as the first of "Two Essays" in *Laurentian*, Canton, N. Y., LXV. 1 (Nov. 1957) 17.

c693a Modern Thought. *Exile*, 2 (Autumn 1927) 117.
Quotations from Benito Mussolini, Vl. Ulianov (Krylenko, Podvoisky, and Gorbunov), Remy de Gourmont, and "Le sieur McAlmon." Edited by Ezra Pound.

c694 The Exile [II]. *Exile*, 2 (Autumn 1927) 118–21.
Signed: E. P. Including "Note re 1st Number" and "Notice to Contributors."

c695 ✉ Mr. Pound Likes It. *New Republic*, New York, LII. 670 (5 Oct. 1927) 177a.
On *The Torrents of Spring*, by Ernest Hemingway.

c695a Ezra Pound Denounces Idiocy of U. S. Mail Act. Lauds Recent "Tribune" Editorial against Reform Law. *Chicago Tribune*, Paris (1 Nov. 1927) 2.
An interview, quoting Pound and printing "Section 211" of the U. S. penal code.

c696 ✉ The Passing of the Ang-Sax? *New Republic*, LII. 676 (16 Nov. 1927) 341.

c697 The Passport Nuisance. *Nation*, New York, CXXV. 3256 (30 Nov. 1927) 600–2.

C. CONTRIBUTIONS TO PERIODICALS

c698 Mr. Pound on Prizes. *Poetry*, XXXI. 3 (Dec. 1927) 155–9.
Six paragraphs were quoted in an article with the same title in *Literary Digest* (14 Jan. 1928) 26.

c699 ✉ Pound for President? *Nation*, CXXV. 3258 (14 Dec. 1927) 684–5.

c699a ✉ Allan [*sic*] Upward. *Saturday Review of Literature*, New York, IV. 21 (17 Dec. 1927) 462.
Under the heading: "Points of View." Reprinted in the same periodical, XXVII. 32 (5 Aug. 1944), and XLVII. 35 (29 Aug. 1964) 63.

1928

c700 PART OF CANTO XXVII. *Dial*, LXXXIV. 1 (Jan. 1928) [1]–3.
73 lines. A passage of 23 lines from this section, captioned "Part of Canto XXVII," appears as part of a printed three-column broadside, *Clip-sheet from The Dial . . . December 27, 1927* ([New York, 1927]), distributed to the Press as publicity for the January issue.

c701 ✉ *Dial*, LXXXIV. 1 (Jan. 1928) [89].
An extract, stating Ezra Pound's proviso on accepting the *Dial* Award for 1927. This brief quotation was reprinted in *Poetry*, XXXI. 5 (Feb. 1928) 293.

c702 CANTO XXII. *Dial*, LXXXIV. 2 (Feb. 1928) [113]–117.

c703 ✉ From Ezra Pound. In Reply to The Forum Debate, "Should the Negro Be Encouraged to Cultural Equality?" *Forum*, New York, LXXIX. 2 (Feb. 1928) 314.

c704 [Letter to his father]. *Evening Bulletin*, Philadelphia (20 Feb. 1928) 12.
A recent letter, quoted complete in Mary Dixon Thayer's "Ezra Pound's Father Tells How Son Went to London with a Shilling and Found Fame."

c705 PART OF CANTO XXIII. *Exile*, 3 (Spring 1928) 28–31.
"(The opening of this canto is too obscure to be printed apart from the main context of the poem)." The first 34 lines are omitted.

c706 [Ralph Cheever] Dunning. *Exile*, 3 (Spring 1928) 53–60.

c706a More Bolshevik Atrocities (With Acknowledgement to the Chicago Tribune). Text and Subtitle from Paris Edition, 1 Dec. 1927. *Exile*, 3 (Spring 1928) 97–101.
Unsigned. Quotations, with linking comments.

c707 The Exile [III]. *Exile*, 3 (Spring 1928) 102–7.
Editorial comment, signed: E. P., including a paragraph reprinted in *Impact* (1960)—A78—as "The Arts."

c708 Desideria. [By E. P.] *Exile*, 3 (Spring 1928) 108.
Reprinted in *Agenda*, XVII. 3/4/XVIII. 1 (Autumn/Winter/Spring 1979/1980) 265.

c709 Interaction. [By E.P.] *Exile*, 3 (Spring 1928) 109.

c710 Mediaevalism and Mediaevalism (Guido Cavalcanti). *Dial*, LXXXIV. 3 (Mar. 1928) [231]–237.

C. CONTRIBUTIONS TO PERIODICALS

"... the following pages are extracted from explanatory matter in a critical edition of Guido Cavalcanti ..." Reprinted as "Mediaevalism." A long paragraph from this essay, captioned "The Mediterranean Sanity," appears as part of a printed three-column broadside, *Clip-sheet from The Dial* ... *February 28, 1928* ([New York, 1928]), distributed to the Press as publicity for the March issue. The same paragraph appears also in the *Clip-sheet* ... *March 3, 1928* ([New York, 1928]), distributed as publicity for the April issue.

c711 ✉ [Letter to "The Phoenecian," *i.e.* The Phoenician—W. R. Benét]. *Saturday Review of Literature*, IV. 32 (3 Mar. 1928) 660.
On the issue of the periodical for 14 Jan. and Robert McAlmon. Quoted complete in the column "The Phoenix Nest."

c712 ✉ Ezra Pound and Will Irwin Denounce Copyright and Boston Censorship. *Chicago Tribune*, Paris (9 Mar. 1928) 2.
An article quoting a letter from Pound to the *Tribune*, which in turn quotes Irwin.

c713 Where Is American Culture? *Nation*, CXXVI. 3276 (18 Apr. 1928) [443]–444.

c714 ✉ New Cantos from Ezra Pound. *Forum*, LXXIX. 5 (May 1928) 799.

c715 ✉ From Ezra Pound. *Chicago Tribune*, Paris (26 May 1928) 4.
On Samuel Roth and the piracy of James Joyce's *Ulysses*.

c716 The Damn Fool Bureaukrats. *New Masses*, New York, IV. 1 (June 1928) 15.

c717 DONNA MI PREGA BY GUIDO CAVALCANTI WITH TRADUCTION AND COMMENTARY BY EZRA POUND: Followed by Notes and a Consideration of the Sonnet. *Dial*, LXXXV. 1 (July 1928) [1]–20.
Contents: Donna mi prega [translation]—Partial Explanation—The Canzone [text]—The Other Dimension—Hendecasyllables. (A long paragraph from the commentary, captioned "The Canzone and the Sonnet," and 15 lines from the poem, captioned "'Love, by Name ... ,'" appear as part of a printed three-column broadside, *Clip-sheet from The Dial* ... *June 22, 1928* ([New York, 1928]), distributed to the Press as publicity for the July issue.)

c718 ✉ Poundings, Continued. *Forum*, LXXX. 1 (July 1928) 156–7.

c719 Simplicities. *Exile*, New York, 4 (Autumn 1928) 1–6.

c720 Bureaucracy the Flail of Jehovah. *Exile*, 4 (Autumn 1928) 6–15.
Reprinted as the second of "Two Essays" in *Laurentian*, Canton, N. Y., LXV. 1 (Nov. 1957) 17–22, and, by itself, in the *Anagogic & Paideumic Review*, San Francisco, I. 1 (Sept. 1959) 5–8. Reprinted also in *Impact* (1960)—A78—in condensed form, and with a paragraph from the end printed separately as "Drive Back the Government."

c721 Peace. *Exile*, 4 (Autumn 1928) 15–19.

c722 Article 211 [of the U. S. penal code]. *Exile*, 4 (Autumn 1928) 20–23.

C. CONTRIBUTIONS TO PERIODICALS

Contents: Article 211—Kick—Zum Beispiel. Reprinted as "Kick" in *Morada*, Albuquerque, N.M., 1 (Autumn [1929]) 11.

c723 The City. *Exile*, 4 (Autumn 1928) 24–29.

c723a Wanted ... *Exile*, 4 (Autumn 1928) 99–100.
Three short notes by Ezra Pound are erroneously attributed in the running-title to Benjamin Peret, author of the preceding article.

c724 Data. *Exile*, 4 (Autumn 1928) 104–17.
Includes bibliographical notes, and others headed "Rudge-Krause," "Olga Rudge," and "Berlin."

c725 ✉ [On passports]. *Chicago Tribune*, Paris (12 Sept. 1928) 4.

c726 Igor Stravinsky, by Boris de Schloezer; Translated from the French by Ezra Pound. *Dial*, LXXXV. 4 (Oct. 1928) [271]–283.
The first of seven instalments. (A paragraph from this translation, captioned "When Is Music National?," appears as part of a printed three-column broadside, *Clip-sheet from The Dial ... September 27, 1928* ([New York, 1928]), distributed to the Press as publicity for the October issue.)

c727 Dr. Williams' Position. *Dial*, LXXXV. 5 (Nov. 1928) [395]–404.
Two paragraphs from this essay, one captioned "Literature and Truth," the other "Dr. Williams vs. Old Lavender," appear as part of a printed three-column broadside, *Clip-sheet from The Dial ... October 29, 1928* ([New York, 1928]), distributed to the Press as publicity for the November issue.

c728 ✉ The Irish Censorship. *Spectator*, London, CXLI. 5240 (1 Dec. 1928) 819.
On "Mr. Yeats' article on the Irish Censorship Bill (in your issue of September 29th)."

c729 ✉ Irish Censorship. *Chicago Tribune*, Paris (3 Dec. 1928) 4.
On Thomas P. Gunning, Fribourg University, and the Irish censorship law.

c730 ✉ *Chicago Tribune*, Paris (7 Dec. 1928) 4.
On the *Tribune*'s failure to measure the extent of post-war retrogression in European countries.

c731 ✉ The Irish Censorship. *Chicago Tribune*, Paris (15 Dec. 1928) 4.
On Thomas P. Gunning.

c732 ✉ Says Mr. Pound. *Chicago Tribune*, Paris (19 Dec. 1928) 4.
Replying to Thomas P. Gunning.

1929

c733 Stravinsky: His Technique, by Boris de Schloezer; Translated from the French by Ezra Pound [I]. *Dial*, LXXXVI. 1 (Jan. 1929) [9]–26.
A continuation of the translation of his *Igor Stravinsky*. (A paragraph from this translation, captioned "Orchestral Bewitchment," appears as part of a printed three-column broadside, *Clip-sheet from The Dial ... December 23,*

1928 ([New York, 1928]), distributed to the Press as publicity for the January issue.)

c734 Mr. Aldington's Views on Gourmont. *Dial*, LXXXVI. 1 (Jan. 1929) [68]–71.

A review of *Remy de Gourmont. Selections . . . Chosen and Translated by Richard Aldington.* (A paragraph from this review, captioned "A Champion of Honesty," appears as part of a printed three-column broadside, *Clip-sheet from The Dial . . . December 23, 1928* ([New York, 1928]), distributed to the Press as publicity for the January issue.)

c735 How to Read, or Why. Part I: Introduction. *New York Herald Tribune Books*, New York, V. 17 (13 Jan. 1929) [1], 6.

c736 How to Read, or Why. Part II, or What May Be an Introduction to Method. *New York Herald Tribune Books*, V. 18 (20 Jan. 1929) [1], 5–6.

c737 How to Read, or Why. Part III. Conclusions, Exceptions, Curricula. *New York Herald Tribune Books*, V. 19 (27 Jan. 1929) [1], 5–6.

c738 Stravinsky: His Technique, by Boris de Schloezer; Translated from the French by Ezra Pound [II]. *Dial*, LXXXVI. 2 (Feb. 1929) [105]–115.

Two short paragraphs from this translation, captioned "Melodie Rhythm and Negro Rhythm," appear as part of a printed three-column broadside, *Clip-sheet from The Dial . . . January 23, 1929* ([New York, 1929]), distributed to the Press as publicity for the February issue.

c739 Program 1929. *Blues*, Columbus, Miss., I. 2 (Mar. 1929) 29.

c740 Practical Suggestions. *Poetry*, XXXIII. 6 (Mar. 1929) 327–33.

c740a ✉ A Correction. *New York Herald Tribune Books*, V. 25 (10 Mar. 1929) 25.

Stating that the French translation of Confucius referred to in his article of 27 Jan.—C737—is by M. G. Pauthier not Gauthier.

c741 ✉ Spread of Bureaucracy. *Times*, London (14 Mar. 1929) 12.

c742 The Problem of Style, by Boris de Schloezer; Translated from the French by Ezra Pound [I]. *Dial*, LXXXVI. 4 (Apr. 1929) [298]–303.

A continuation of the translation of his *Igor Stravinsky*.

c743 The Problem of Style, by Boris de Schloezer; Translated from the French by Ezra Pound, II. *Dial*, LXXXVI. 5 (May 1929) [394]–403.

Two passages from this translation, the first captioned "Stravinsky Is like Bach," the other "Another Definition of Style," appear as part of a printed three-column broadside, *Clip-sheet from The Dial . . . April 26, 1929* ([New York, 1929]), distributed to the Press as publicity for the May issue.

c744 ✉ From Ezra. *Little Review*, XII. 2 (May 1929) 41.

Responding to a request for contributions to the final number, telling the editors to print what they already have of his; with Margaret Anderson's riposte.

c745 A Classic Art, by Boris de Schloezer; Translated from the French by Ezra Pound. I. *Dial*, LXXXVI. 6 (June 1929) [463]–474.

The first part of the final section of the translation of his *Igor Stravinsky*.

C. CONTRIBUTIONS TO PERIODICALS

(Two short paragraphs from this translation, captioned "Classic and Romantic," appear as part of a printed three-column broadside, *Clip-sheet from The Dial . . . May 28, 1929* ([New York, 1929]), distributed to the Press as publicity for the June issue.)

C746 St George at Silene. *Dial*, LXXXVI. 6 (June 1929) [517].
A review of *St George at Silene*, by Alvaro Guevara.

C747 ✉ A Possibly Impractical Suggestion. *Poetry*, XXXIV. 3 (June 1929) 178.
That peace "propaganda" should consider the actual state of the world.

C748 Guido's Relations. *Dial*, LXXXVI. 7 (July 1929) [559]–568.
With verse translation of the sonnet by Guido Orlando beginning "Say what is love, whence doth he start," and of Sonnet VII of Cavalcanti (in "pre-Elizabethan English").

C749 A Classic Art, by Boris de Schloezer; Translated from the French by Ezra Pound [II]. *Dial*, LXXXVI. 7 (July 1929) [597]–608.
Two passages from this translation, one captioned "Stravinsky and the Stage," the other "Renunciation," appear as part of a printed three-column broadside, *Clip-sheet from The Dial . . . June 30, 1929* ([New York, 1929]), distributed to the Press as publicity for the July issue.

C750 ✉ The Passport Nuisance. *Chicago Tribune*, Paris (9 Nov. 1929) 4.

C751 ✉ *Chicago Tribune*, Paris (18 Nov. 1929) 5.
To Wambly Bald, quoted in his column "La Vie de Bohème (as Lived on the Left Bank)." Signed: E.P.

C752 ✉ Mr. Pound Again. *Chicago Tribune*, Paris (19 Nov. 1929) 4.
On passports.

C753 ✉ [On passports]. *Chicago Tribune*, Paris (26 Nov. 1929) 4.

C754 ✉ Mr. Pound Approves. *Chicago Tribune*, Paris (7 Dec. 1929) 4.
Endorsing an editorial in the *Tribune* on naval parity for America.

C755 ✉ Concerning Hiler. *Chicago Tribune*, Paris (12 Dec. 1929) 4.
On Mr. Atlas' note on Hilaire Hiler in the *Tribune*.

1930

C756 Horace. *Criterion*, IX. 35 (Jan. 1930) 217–27.
Reprinted in *Arion*, Austin, Texas, IX. 2/3 (Summer/Autumn 1970) [178]–187.

C757 This Subsidy Business. *Poetry*, XXXV. 4 (Jan. 1930) 212–14.

C758 ✉ About Book Clubs. *Chicago Tribune*, Paris (13 Jan. 1930) 4.

C758a ✉ Married Women's Nationality. *Time & Tide*, London, XI. 5 (31 Jan. 1930) 140–1.
The first of two letters under this heading.

C759 ✉ *Chicago Tribune*, Paris (17 Feb. 1930) 2.
To Wambly Bald, quoted in his column. On the *Rime* of Guido Cavalcanti—B27.

C. CONTRIBUTIONS TO PERIODICALS

c760 ✉ *Morada*, Albuquerque, N.M., 3 ([Spring?] 1930) 90–91.

c761 ✉ Montparnasse Forever! *Chicago Tribune*, Paris (11 Mar. 1930) 5.

c762 ✉ Left vs. Right. *Chicago Tribune*, Paris (16 Mar. 1930) 5.
On Montparnasse and the two banks of the Seine.

c763 ✉ An Oz. from Lb. *Chicago Tribune*, Paris (22 Mar. 1930) 5.
Signed: E. P.

c764 CANTOS XXVIII, XXIX, XXX. *Hound & Horn*, Cambridge, Mass., III. 3
(Apr./June 1930) 358–[375].
With a note on the text of the Cantos, p. 358.

c765 ✉ And the Remainder. *Hound & Horn*, III. 3 (Apr./June 1930) 417–20.

c766 Epstein, Belgion, and Meaning. *Criterion*, IX. 36 (Apr. 1930) 470–5.

c767 Vita estera. *L'Indice*, Genoa, I. 6 (5 Apr. 1930) 7.
A note (in Italian), signed: P., on foreign periodicals.

c768 ✉ Pls. Pound This Thot Home. *Chicago Tribune*, Paris (16 Apr. 1930) 5.
Stating that he (Ezra Pound) is not an editor.

c768a Pound Paints Peccadilloes of Pedants in Money Murdered Marts of
Learning. *Chicago Tribune*, Paris (19 Apr. 1930)
Ezra Pound's own words are quoted extensively in this interview by Mary
Howell.

c769 ✉ Unindignant Denial. *Chicago Tribune*, Paris (19 Apr. 1930) 5.
On George Antheil and American opera.

c770 Appunti: Le mystère Cocteau. *L'Indice*, I. 8 (5 May 1930) [1].
(In Italian.)

c771 ✉ A Question to Mr. [Ambassador] Edge. *Chicago Tribune*, Paris (24 May
1930) 8.
On the Carnegie Peace Foundation.

c772 Honor and the United States Senate. *Poetry*, XXXVI. 3 (June 1930) 150–
2.

c773 ✉ Mr. Pound in Defense of Mr. Putnam. *New Republic*, LXIII. 809 (4 June
1930) 74–75.
On Samuel Putnam's translation of Rabelais.

c774 ✉ Newspapers, History, Etc. *Hound & Horn*, III. 4 (July/Sept. 1930) 574–
9.

c775 ✉ Brief von Ezra Pound. *Zeitschrift für Französischen und Englischen Unter-
richt*, Berlin, XXIX. 3 ([3rd quarter?] 1930) 229–30.
In English, making three corrections to F. Sefton Delmer's article "Ezra
Pound" in the preceding issue.

c776 ✉ Questions for Mr. X. *Chicago Tribune*, Paris (3 Aug. 1930) 4.
In part, about the Epstein monument for Oscar Wilde's grave, referring to
a letter written to the *Tribune*, signed: X, suggesting removal of the statue.

c777 ✉ An Open Offer. *Chicago Tribune*, Paris (8 Aug. 1930) 4.
Signed: E. P. On Charles MacArthur and Calvin Coolidge.

C. CONTRIBUTIONS TO PERIODICALS

c778 Storicamente Joyce (e censura). *L'Indice*, Genoa, I. 11 (Sept. 1930) 3.

c779 ✉ Ezra Speaks Sooth. *Chicago Tribune*, Paris (2 Sept. 1930) 4.
On passports.

c780 ✉ Congratulates South Carolina. *New York Herald*, Paris (15 Sept. 1930) 6.
On "having eliminated [Senator] Blease."

c781 ✉ Pound on [Senator] Blease. *Chicago Tribune*, Paris (16 Sept. 1930) 4.

c782 ✉ Criterionism. *Hound & Horn*, IV. 1 (Oct./Dec. 1930) 113–16.

c783 Appunti. I. Lettera al traduttore. *L'Indice*, I. 12 (Oct. 1930) [1].

c784 ✉ *New Masses*, VI. 5 (Oct. 1930) [3].
To Michael Gold, the Editor; quoted in his "Notes of the Month," p. [3],
with comment, pp. [3]–5.

c785 ✉ Marcus Graham [pseudonym of Robert Parsons]. *Chicago Tribune*, Paris
(15 Oct. 1930) 8.
Enclosing an article by S. A. de Witt on Graham and his *An Anthology of
Revolutionary Poetry*.

c786 ✉ Several Points of View. *Chicago Tribune*, Paris (24 Oct. 1930) 8.
On France.

c787 Small Magazines. *English Journal*, Chicago, Ill., (*College Edition*) XIX. 9
(Nov. 1930) 689–704.

c788 Appunti. II. Il mal francese [*i.e.* franxese]. *L'Indice*, I. 13 (Nov. 1930) [1].

c789 ✉ Says Mr. Pound. *Chicago Tribune*, Paris (1 Nov. 1930) 8.
On an article by Root on William Lyon Phelps's 100 best books.

c790 ✉ Mise au point. *Chicago Tribune*, Paris (14 Nov. 1930) 8.
(In English.) Signed: E. P. On William Lyon Phelps.

c791 ✉ Monticello and Tolerance. *Chicago Tribune*, Paris (19 Nov. 1930) 8.
Signed: E. P. On Thomas Jefferson.

c792 Credo. *Front*, The Hague, Holland, I. 1 (Dec. 1930) 11.

c793 Appunti. III. La parola. IV. D'accordo!! *L'Indice*, I. 14 (Dec. 1930) [1].

c794 Mike [Gold] and Other Phenomena. *Morada*, Gardone Sopra, Lago di Garda,
5 ([Dec.?] 1930) 43–47.
Under the heading: "Commentary."

c795 ✉ Strange Bedfellows. *Chicago Tribune*, Paris (7 Dec. 1930) 4.
Reprinting Article 211 of the U. S. penal code in full.

1931

c796 The First Year of "Pagany" and the Possiblity of Criteria. *Pagany*, Boston,
Mass., II. 1 (Jan./Mar. 1931) 104–11.

c797 After Election. *New Review*, Paris, I. 1 (Jan./Feb. 1931) [53]–55.
Notes.

c798 [Footnote, signed: E. P., to] The Inner Hermit [a review by Maxwell Bod-

C. CONTRIBUTIONS TO PERIODICALS

enheim of Margaret Anderson's *My Thirty Years' War*—B23]. *New Review*, I. 1 (Jan./Feb. 1931) 65.

C799 Zibaldone. *New Review*, I. 1 (Jan./Feb. 1931) 68.
Includes two notes signed: E. P.

c800 Appunti. IV [*bis*]. I "Ratés." *L'Indice*, II. 1 (10 Jan. 1931) 3.

c801 Appunti. V. *L'Indice*, II. 2 (25 Jan. 1931) [1].
Contents: "Mi piacerebbe"—"Vorrei leggere."

c802 Open Letter to Tretyakow, Kolchoznik. *Front*, I. 2 (Feb. 1931) 124–6.
Concerning "Report of S. Tretyakow, Kolchoznik" in the issue for Dec. 1930.

c803 [From a letter]. *Poetry*, XXXVII. 5 (Feb. 1931) 269.
Quoted in Louis Zukofsky's "Program: 'Objectivists' 1931," pp. 268–72. On Emanuel Carnevali.

c804 ✉ We Don't. *Chicago Tribune*, Paris (7 Feb. 1931) 8.
On the XVIIIth Amendment to the U.S. Constitution.

c805 ✉ Mr. Pound Is Studying. *Chicago Tribune*, Paris (10 Feb. 1931) 8.
Signed: E. P. On the XVIIIth Amendment.

c806 Appunti. VI. Non parlo d'esportazione. *L'Indice*, II. 3 (10 Feb. 1931) 3.

c807 ✉ Anent Art. *Chicago Tribune*, Paris (19 Feb. 1931) 8.
Signed: E. P. On modern art prices.

c808 ✉ Open Letter to Mr. Shadwell. *Chicago Tribune*, Paris (25 Feb. 1931) 8.
Signed: E. P. On a letter of Bertrand Shadwell.

c809 Appunti. VII. Importazione. VIII. Dialogo. IX. Venezia bella. *L'Indice*, II. 4 (25 Feb. 1931) 3, 4.
Section VII includes letter (in Italian) to G[ino]. S[aviotti]., signed: E. P.

c810 ✉ Murkn Libry. *Chicago Tribune*, Paris (4 Mar. 1931) 8.
Signed: E. P. On the American Library in Paris.

c811 Appunti. X. Tradizione; XI. Puntini. *L'Indice*, II. 5 (10 Mar. 1931) 4.
Section X is "Lettera aperta (a proposito di Petrarca)," beginning: "Caro Marchi," and signed: E. P.

c812 ✉ Ezra Replies to Harriet [Monroe]. *English Journal (High School Edition)*, XX. 4 (Apr. 1931) 340–1.

c813 Appunti. XII. Futurismo; XIII. Scultura (Lettera a Ernesto Thayaht). *L'Indice*, II. 7 (10 Apr. 1931) [1].

c814 Appunti. XIV. La bandiera gialla. *L'Indice*, II. 8 (25 Apr. 1931) [1].
Reprinted in *L'Indice: Almanacco critico delle lettere italiane. L'annata letteraria 1931–32* (Genova, 1932), as part of the Appendix, p. 118, under the heading: "Le letterature straniere e i loro riflessi in Italia: Francia."

c815 Our Contemporaries and Others. *New Review*, I. 2 (May/June/July 1931) [149]–152.
A quotation from Ezra Pound follows, p. [154].

c816 Definitions. *New Review*, I. 2 (May/June/July 1931) 159.

C. CONTRIBUTIONS TO PERIODICALS

Brief comments, with a note signed: E. P., on Norman Macleod's unwillingness to print these in *Front*.

c817 Tischreden. *New Review*, I. 2 (May/June/July 1931) 164, 165.
The first (including four lines of doggerel in French on Jean Cocteau), fourth, and seventh in this series of comments (in English) by the editors are signed: E. P.

c818 The Situation. *Poetry*, XXXVIII. 2 (May 1931) 95–97.

c819 ✉ Anent a Senator. *Saturday Review of Literature*, VII. 41 (2 May 1931) 805.
On copyright.

c820 Appunti. XV. Nunc dimittis. *L'Indice*, II. 9 (10 May 1931) [1].
An exchange of letters between Ezra Pound and Gino Saviotti.

c821 ✉ Penny Wise. *Chicago Tribune*, Paris (19 May 1931) 8.
On experimental magazines in America.

c822 ✉ In difesa del paesaggio: non deturpare. *Giornale di Genova*, Genoa (25 May 1931[?]).

c823 Appunti. XVI. Programma. *L'Indice*, II. 10 (25 May 1931) 3.

c824 Appunti. XVII. Traduzioni. *L'Indice*, II. 11 (10 June 1931) 2.
Under the heading: "Affari esteri."

c825 Appunti. XVIII. Sperimentale. *L'Indice*, II. 12 (5 June 1931) 2.
With an Italian translation by Ezra Pound of a poem by Parker Tyler, "Nome," from *5th Floor Window* for May 1931.

c826 ✉ Costa più della Divina Commedia. *Hound & Horn*, IV. 4 (July/Sept. 1931) 571–2.
(In English.)

c827 THREE CANTOS. *Pagany*, II. 3 (July/Sept. 1931) 43–53.
Contents: XXX [*i.e.* XXXI]—XXXII—XXXIII.

c828 ✉ To the Editor. *Criterion*, X. 41 (July 1931) 730.
On Prince D. S. Mirsky's review of John Gould Fletcher's *Europe's Two Frontiers* in the issue for April.

c829 Appunti. XIX. Traduzione. *L'Indice*, II. 13 (10 July 1931) 2.
Under the heading: "Affari esteri."

c830 ✉ American Book Censorship. *Saturday Review of Literature*, VII. 52 (18 July 1931) 978.

c831 Bruhl e i selvaggi. *L'Indice*, II. 14 (25 July 1931) 2.
Selections from Lévy-Bruhl, in Italian, with a note by Ezra Pound.

c832 Letter to S[amuel]. P[utnam]. re/ poem "As Browning would have said."
New Review, I. 3 (Aug./Sept./Oct. 1931) 62–63.
With unsigned "Additional note" by Putnam.

c833 Fungus, Twilight or Dry Rot. *New Review*, I. 3 (Aug./Sept./Oct. 1931) [112]–116.
Incorporates at the end miscellaneous comments captioned: "And yet again," "Ethica et politica," "Them critiks of hart [*i.e.* art]," "Meliora speramus

... ," "The press," "A distinguished American editor . . . ," and "The decline of Kipling."

c834 ✉ [Answers to questions concerning a proposed "prix littéraire de la Société des Nations"]. *Pologne Littéraire*, Warsaw, VI. 59/60 (15 Aug./15 Sept. 1931) [1].
Under the heading: "Ezra Pound (Rapallo)." With facsimile signature.

c835 ✉ Mr. Pound Again. *Saturday Review of Literature*, VIII. 6 (29 Aug. 1931) 92.
On an editorial note on Ezra Pound's letter in the issue for 18 July.

c836 Publishers, Pamphlets, and Other Things. *Contempo*, Chapel Hill, N.C., I. 9 (15 Sept. 1931) 1, 2.

c837 Miti dei primitivi. Pagine di Frobenius [with "Nota preliminare di E. P."]. *L'Indice*, II. 18 (25 Sept. 1931)

c838 Appunti. XX. Supplemento al mio Trattato d'armonia; XXI. Henry James. *L'Indice*, II. 19 (10 Oct. 1931) 2.
Under the heading: "Affari esteri."

c839 Machines [an introductory note to 15 photographs]. *New Review*, I. 4 (Winter 1931/1932) [291]–292.
The photographs are distributed through the issue.

c840 Terra italica. *New Review*, I. 4 (Winter 1931/1932) [386]–389.
(In English.)

c841 Anno nuovo (mirabilis?). *L'Indice*, II. 20/21 (25 Dec. 1931) 5.
Signed: E. P. Under the heading: "Affari esteri."

c842 ✉ *L'Ambrosiano*, Milan (29 Dec. 1931) 3.
(In Italian.) To P. M. Bardi, quoted in his column "Busta da Roma."

1932

c843 ✉ From Ezra Pound . . . *Contempo*, I. 15 (1 Jan. 1932) 1.
Under the heading: "Notes from Nowhere."

c844 The Depression Has Just Begun. *Contempo*, I. 16 (15 Jan. 1932) [1], 4.

c845 Critical Ethics for Commercial Weeklies. *Contempo*, I. 18 (15 Feb. 1932) [1].
Two letters, one to Gorham Munson, the other to Malcolm Cowley.

c846 ✉ A Questionnaire from Ezra Pound. *New York Sun*, New York (20 Feb. 1932) 22.
To the Editor of the column "The Bear Garden," on critical ethics. An editorial comment quotes "Mr. Pound's opinion on programs" from his article, "Small Magazines," in the *English Journal (College Edition)* for Nov. 1930—C787.

c847 ✉ Why the 1920s Went to Hades (Or 'As You Like It'). *New York Sun*, New York (5 Mar. 1932) 23.
To the Editor of "The Bear Garden."

c848 La merrdre. *Contempo*, I. 20 (15 Mar. 1932) [1].
(In English.)

c849 ✉ Ezraordinary! *New York Sun*, New York (26 Mar. 1932) 4.
To the Editor of "The Bear Garden."

c850 For Action. *English Journal (College Edition)*, XXI. 4 (Apr. 1932) 299–301.

c851 In Defense of Homosexuality, by Kay Boyle; Accompanied by a Letter
from Ezra Pound. *New Review*, II. 5 (Apr. 1932) [24]–25.
Dated: 9 Apr. 1928; presumably referring to this poem, submitted then to
Pound as Editor of *Exile*.

c852 ✉ Our English Number. *Poetry*, XL. 1 (Apr. 1932) 52.
On the issue for Feb. 1932.

c853 ✉ From Ezra Pound. *New York Sun*, New York (16 Apr. 1932) 18.
To the Editor of "The Bear Garden," chiefly on "[Henry S.] Canby and
Co."

c854 ✉ Q. E. D. and Q. E. F. The problem presented by Mr. P[ound]. in this
article is: Ought America Have an Intellectual Life? secondly: Ought such
life have an organism more complex than an amoeba? *New York Sun*, New
York (23 Apr. 1932) 18.
To the Editor of "The Bear Garden."

c854a "Pagany." *English Journal*, XXI. 5 (May 1932) 402.
On the periodical. Under the heading: "Round Table."

c855 ✉ Liberally Minded. *Chicago Tribune*, Paris (5 May 1932) 4.

c856 ✉ Honor Slayings. *Chicago Tribune*, Paris (8 May 1932) 4.

c857 ✉ Enquête. *Le Journal des Poètes*, Brussels, II. 23 (14 May 1932) [1].
Ezra Pound's reply (in French) to a questionnaire concerning poets and
war. Captioned: "d'Ezra Pound, Rapallo."

c858 ✉ That Messianic Urge. *New York Sun*, New York (4 June 1932) 12.
To the Editor of "The Bear Garden," on the literary situation in America.

c859 ✉ Pound to Rascoe. *New York Sun*, New York (11 June 1932) 36.
To the Editor of "The Bear Garden"; printed along with "[Burton] Rascoe's Riposte." Chiefly on Ernest Hemingway.

c860 ✉ Pound vs. Small. *Chicago Tribune*, Paris (15 June 1932) 4.
On an article by Alex Small in the issue for 6 June.

c861 Swelling of the Occiput. *New English Weekly*, London, I. 9 (16 June 1932)
205.

c862 ✉ Money and Prices. *New English Weekly*, I. 9 (16 June 1932) 219.

c863 ✉ Asking [Alex] Small Questions. *Chicago Tribune*, Paris (25 June 1932) 4.

c864 ✉ Pounding His Critics. *New York Sun*, New York (25 June 1932) 7.
To the Editor of "The Bear Garden."

c865 ✉ Money and Prices. *New English Weekly*, I. 11 (30 June 1932) 265.

c866 Harold Monro. *Criterion*, XI. 45 (July 1932) 581–92.

c867 ✉ Noo Yokkers. *Chicago Tribune*, Paris (6 July 1932) 4.
Signed: E. P.

C. CONTRIBUTIONS TO PERIODICALS

c868 ✉ *New English Weekly*, I. 12 (7 July 1932) 291–2.
Signed: E. P. On literary columnists. Under the heading: "Readers and Writers."

c869 ✉ Yours for Accuracy. *New York Sun*, New York (9 July 1932) 14.
To the Editor of "The Bear Garden," on letters to the Press, etc.

c869a ✉ Mr. Ezra Pound and the Press. *Time and Tide*, London, XIII. 31 (30 July 1932) 843.

c870 Appunto. *Il Mare*, Rapallo, XXV. 1223 (20 Aug. 1932) 3.
(Pages 3–4 of this issue are designated "Supplemento Letterario, I. 1." The special numbering continues through II. 16 (18 Mar. 1933). In the issue for 1 Apr. 1933, the Supplement becomes merely the "Pagina Letteraria" and there is no separate volume numbering.)

c871 Compositori Ungheresi a Rapallo. *Il Mare*, XXV. 1223 (20 Aug. 1932) 4.
Signed: William Atheling. An English translation of this article by R. Murray Schafer, "Hungarian Composers in Rapallo," was printed in *Ezra Pound and Music* ([1977])—A99—pp. 335–6.

c872 ✉ *New English Weekly*, I. 20 (1 Sept. 1932) 483.
Signed: E.P. Under the heading: "Readers and Writers."

c873 ✉ Objectivists. *Chicago Tribune*, Paris (2 Sept. 1932) 4.
On Louis Zukofsky and the *Objectivists Anthology*—B29.

c874 Appunti. *Il Mare*, XXV. 1225 (3 Sept. 1932) 3.
Signed: E.P.

c875 ✉ Invitation. *Chicago Tribune*, Paris (6 Sept. 1932) 4.
On the Literary Supplement of *Il Mare*.

c876 Appunti. *Il Mare*, XXV. 1227 (17 Sept. 1932) 3.
Signed: E. P.

c877 Critici e idioti. *Il Mare*, XXV. 1227 (17 Sept. 1932) 4.
Signed: E. P.

c878 ✉ Thoughts on Prizes. *Chicago Tribune*, Paris (27 Sept. 1932) 4.
On the *Yale Review*'s award of a prize to Arthur Salter.

c879 ✉ Social Credit. *New English Weekly*, I. 24 (29 Sept. 1932) 579.
Signed: E. P.

c880 Manifesto. *Poetry*, XLI. 1 (Oct. 1932) 40–43.
On *Poetry*.

c881 [A review of] *The Quattro Cento*, by Adrian Stokes. *Symposium*, Concord, N.H., III. 4 (Oct. 1932) 518–21.

c882 Nota in luogo d'Appunti. *Il Mare*, XXV. 1229 (1 Oct. 1932) 4.
Signed: E. P.

c883 By All Means Be Patriotic. *New English Weekly*, I. 25 (6 Oct. 1932) 589.

c884 ✉ Pounding Away. *Chicago Tribune*, Paris (12 Oct. 1932) 4.
On Herbert, Durant, and F. D. Roosevelt.

c885 Appunti. *Il Mare*, XXV. 1231 (15 Oct. 1932) 3.
Signed: E. P.

C. CONTRIBUTIONS TO PERIODICALS

c886 [Note, in Italian, signed: E. P., to "William Carlos Williams," by René Taupin, translated by Aurora Hughes]. *Il Mare*, XXV. 1231 (29 Oct. 1932) 4.

c887 ✉ Bureaucracy. *Chicago Tribune*, Paris (1 Nov. 1932) 4.
Signed: E. P. On the American government.

c888 Appunti. *Il Mare*, XXV. 1235 (12 Nov. 1932) 3.
The first part signed: E. P.; the second signed in full.

c889 ✉ Word from Rapallo. *Chicago Tribune*, Paris (13 Nov. 1932) 4.
On the Literary Supplement to *Il Mare*.

c890 ✉ Suppression of News. *Chicago Tribune*, Paris (20 Nov. 1932) 4.
Signed: E. P.

c891 Appunti. *Il Mare*, XXV. 1237 (26 Nov. 1932) 4.
Signed: E. P.

c892 P. M. Bardi. *Il Mare*, XXV. 1237 (26 Nov. 1932) 4.
Signed: E. P.

c892a ✉ Europe Rearms. *Chicago Tribune*, Paris (29 Nov. 1932)

c893 ✉ Isolation. *Chicago Tribune*, Paris (4 Dec. 1932) 3.
Signed: E. P.

c894 Nota . . . *Il Mare*, XXV. 1239 (10 Dec. 1932) 4.
A note to a passage in an article "Sexualité," by F. F. Cerio.

c895 Appunti. *Il Mare*, XXV. 1239 (10 Dec. 1932) 4.
Signed: E. P.

c895a News. *Il Mare*, XXV. 1239 (10 Dec. 1932) 4.
(In Italian.) Unsigned, but attributed to Ezra Pound in Niccolò Zapponi's *L'Italia di Ezra Pound* ([1976])—B119—p. 99.

c896 ✉ Munition Makers. *Chicago Tribune*, Paris (14 Dec. 1932) 4.

c897 ✉ The Carnegie Endowment. *Chicago Tribune*, Paris (15 Dec. 1932) 4.
Signed: E. P.

c898 Domanda. *Il Mare*, XXV. 1241 (24 Dec. 1932) 3.

c899 Si annuncia un libro di P. M. Bardi. *Il Mare*, XXV. 1241 (24 Dec. 1932) 3.
Signed: P.

c900 Libri. *Il Mare*, XXV. 1241 (24 Dec. 1932) 4.
Signed: E. P.

c901 Triste est la Steppe: A proposito del nuovo libro di McAlmon, annunciato da Crosby Editions. *Il Mare*, XXV. 1241 (24 Dec. 1932) 4.
Unsigned.

c902 Jas. T. Farrel [*sic*]. *Il Mare*, XXV. 1241 (24 Dec. 1932) 4.
Signed: p/.

c903 Orazio. *Il Mare*, XXV. 1241 (24 Dec. 1932) 4.
Signed: p/.

c904 [Note]. *Il Mare*, XXV. 1241 (24 Dec. 1932) 4.
Signed: p/.

C. CONTRIBUTIONS TO PERIODICALS

1933

c905 . . . Il libro americano: status rerum. *Almanacco Letterario* [*Bompiani*], Milan (1933) 264–7.

c906 ✉ Mr. Pound Replies to Mr. Tate. *Poetry*, XLI. 4 (Jan. 1933) 231–2.
On Allen Tate's review of *How to Read*—A33—and *Profile*—B28.

c907 Orientation and News Sense. *New English Weekly*, II. 12 (5 Jan. 1933) 273–4.

c908 [Note]. *Il Mare*, XXVI. 1243 (7 Jan. 1933) 3.
Signed: p/.

c909 Ave Roma. *Il Mare*, XXVI. 1243 (7 Jan. 1933) 3, 4.

c910 [Note]. *Il Mare*, XXVI. 1243 (7 Jan. 1933) 4.
Signed: p/.

c910a Francesco Orlando si compromette. *Il Mare*, XXVI. 1243 (7 Jan. 1933) 4.
Unsigned, but attributed to Ezra Pound in Niccolò Zapponi's *L'Italia di Ezra Pound* ([1976])—B119—p. 102.

c911 ✉ A Pound of Poetry. *New English Weekly*, II. 13 (12 Jan. 1933) 311.
Signed: E. P. On *Profile*—B28.

c912 ✉ Technocracy. *Chicago Tribune*, Paris (13 Jan. 1933) 4.
Signed: E. P.

c913 Leone Vivante. *Il Mare*, XXVI. 1245 (21 Jan. 1933) 3.
Signed: E. P.

c914 [Note]. *Il Mare*, XXVI. 1245 (21 Jan. 1933) 3.
Signed: p/.

c915 ✉ Any Objections? *Chicago Tribune*, Paris (27 Jan. 1933) 4.
Signed: E. P. On money.

c916 The European in America. *Poetry*, XLI. 5 (Feb. 1933) 273–5.

c917 ✉ Paging Mr. Lorimer. *Chicago Tribune*, Paris (2 Feb. 1933) 4.
On George Horace Lorimer and the *Saturday Evening Post*.

c918 ✉ Economics. *Chicago Tribune*, Paris (4 Feb. 1933) 4.
On money.

c919 Virgilio. *Il Mare*, XXVI. 1247 (4 Feb. 1933) 3.
Signed: p/.

c920 Appunto. *Il Mare*, XXVI. 1247 (4 Feb. 1933) 4.
Signed: E.P.

c921 Crosby Continental Editions. *New English Weekly*, II. 17 (9 Feb. 1933) 399–401.
In part, on Robert McAlmon.

c922 ✉ Mr. Pound to Mr. [Alex] Small. *Chicago Tribune*, Paris (12 Feb. 1933) 4.
Signed: E. P. On the problem of French security.

c923 ✉ Munition Makers. *Chicago Tribune*, Paris (16 Feb. 1933) 4.

c924 Riflessione nell' anno XI. *Il Mare*, XXVI. 1249 (18 Feb. 1933) 3.

C. CONTRIBUTIONS TO PERIODICALS

A note, signed: E. P., to a translation, by Edmondo Dodsworth, of "Vorticism"—D115.

c925 [Note on Zukofsky's *Objectivists Anthology*—B29—and *Profile*—B28]. *Contempo*, III. 6 (21 Feb. 1933) 7.

c926 Personalia. *New English Weekly*, II. 19 (23 Feb. 1933) 442–3.

c926a ✉ Rearmament. *Chicago Tribune*, Paris (27 Feb. 1933)

c927 ✉ Munitions Makers. *Chicago Tribune*, Paris (4 Mar. 1933) 4.

c928 ✉ Business Note. *Chicago Tribune*, Paris (13 Mar. 1933) 4.
Signed: E. P. On the League of Nations.

c928a ✉ England and America. *Chicago Tribune*, Paris (13 Mar. 1933)

c929 Écrevisse? *Il Mare*, XXVI. 1253 (18 Mar. 1933) 3–4.
Signed: E. P.

c930 ✉ "How to Read." *New English Weekly*, II. 23 (23 Mar. 1933) 551.
Signed: E. P.

c931 ✉ Ezra Pound Protests. *English Journal*, XXII. 4 (Apr. 1933) 318–19.
On an editorial in the Jan. issue on his *How to Read*—A33.

c932 CANTO XXXIV. *Poetry*, XLII. 1 (Apr. 1933) 1–10.

c933 [A review of] *The Secret International; The New and the Old Economics*, by Major C. H. Douglas; and *Mercanti di Cannoni*. *Symposium*, IV. 2 (Apr. 1933) 252–6.

c934 Baxigä. *Il Mare*, XXVI. 1255 (1 Apr. 1933) 2.

c935 ✉ More on Economics. *Chicago Tribune*, Paris (12 Apr. 1933) 4.
On Root's review of *ABC of Economics*—A34a.

c936 ✉ Who Profits? *Chicago Tribune*, Paris (20 Apr. 1933) 4.
Signed: E. P. Suggesting that J. R. Jarvie's *The Old Lady Unveiled* be reviewed in the *Tribune*.

c937 ✉ Mr. Pound's "A. B. C." *New English Weekly*, III. 1 (20 Apr. 1933) 24.
Signed: E. P.

c938 ✉ The Vickers Firm. *Chicago Tribune*, Paris (22 Apr. 1933) 4.
Signed: E. P.

c939 Past History. *English Journal (College Edition)*, XXII. 5 (May 1933) 349–58.
Chiefly on James Joyce. Reprinted in *College English*, Lincoln, Neb., XXII. 2 (Nov. 1960) 81–86.

c940 ✉ Reply to Xavier. *Chicago Tribune*, Paris (1 May 1933) 2.
Signed: E. P. In reply to a letter in the *Tribune* on economics, signed: Xavier.

c941 ✉ Useful Critter. *Time*, New York, XXI. 18 (1 May 1933) 2.
On *Time*'s review of *A Draft of XXX Cantos*—A31c, calling attention to *How to Read*—A33—and the two operas.

c942 ✉ Inflation. *Chicago Tribune*, Paris (2 May 1933) 4.
Signed: E. P.

C. CONTRIBUTIONS TO PERIODICALS

c943 ✉ More Economics. *Chicago Tribune*, Paris (7 May 1933) 4.
On F. D. Roosevelt's *Looking Forward*.

c944 ✉ Mr. Ezra Pound's "Cantos." *New English Weekly*, III. 4 (11 May 1933) 96.

c945 The New English Weekly. *Contempo*, III. 9 (15 May 1933) 2.

c946 ✉ A Letter from Ezra Pound. *Contemporaries*, Cambridge, Eng., I. 2 (Summer 1933) 92.
To John Drummond, one of the editors, signed: E. P., on his article on the Cantos.

c947 ✉ Comments on Major C. H. Douglas' Premises . . . Pro. *Economic Forum*, Concord, N.H., I. 3 (Summer 1933) [319]–321.

c948 ✉ Letter from Ezra Pound. *Observer*, Memphis, Tenn., I. 4 (Summer 1933) 2.
To G. Marion O'Donnell, an editor of the magazine, thanking him for the dedication of the issue for Apr. 1933 and for his review of the Cantos.

c949 ✉ "Eh Kaant Theunk." *Chicago Tribune*, Paris (19 June 1933) 2.
Signed: E. P. On Arthur Salter and the Economic Conference.

c950 Merit. *Spectator*, London, CL. 5478 (23 June 1933) 913.
A review of *The Collected Poems of Harold Monro*. Reprinted in *Agenda*, XVII. 3/4/XVIII. 1 (Autumn/Winter/Spring 1979/1980) 58–61.

c951 Murder by Capital. *Criterion*, XII. 49 (July 1933) 585–92.
On the effects of capitalism on art and letters.

c952 ✉ Slim Hope. *Chicago Tribune*, Paris (3 July 1933) 4.
On the Economic Conference.

c953 ✉ The Douglas Theory. *Chicago Tribune*, Paris (7 July 1933) 4.
Signed: E. P. On C. H. Douglas.

c953a Concerto Scriabino. *Il Mare*, Rapallo, XXVI. 1269 (8 July 1933) 2.
The second of two articles under this heading, the first, by Basil Bunting, entitled "Scriabine," the other, by Ezra Pound, entitled "Anti-Scriabine." An English translation of Pound's article by R. Murray Schafer, "Anti-Scriabin," was printed in *Ezra Pound and Music* ([1977])—A99—pp. 333–4.

c954 ✉ No Limit. *New English Weekly*, III. 14 (20 July 1933) 336.
Signed: E. P.

c955 La charogne. *Westminster Magazine*, Oglethorpe, Ga., XXII. 3 (Aug. 1933) 13–17.
(In English.)

c956 ✉ A Voice from Rapallo. *New Republic*, LXXV. 975 (9 Aug. 1933) 345.

c957 ✉ A Poet on Ignorance. *New York Herald*, Paris (16 Aug. 1933) 4.
On a letter of Herbert Fitch on Woergl.

c958 ✉ Economic Light from Parnassus. *New York Herald*, Paris (23 Aug. 1933) 4.
On the Woergl scheme.

c959 Points. *New Democracy*, New York, I. 1 (25 Aug. 1933) 4.

C. CONTRIBUTIONS TO PERIODICALS

On F. D. Roosevelt.

c960 ✉ A Writer with Encephalitis. *New York Herald*, Paris (26 Aug. 1933) 4.
On Emanuel Carnevali.

c961 ✉ The Retort Spirited. *New York Herald*, Paris (28 Aug. 1933) 4.
In reply to a letter by Herbert Fitch.

c962 ✉ Possibilities of Economics. *New York Herald*, Paris (31 Aug. 1933) 4.

c962a ✉ *Left Front*, Chicago, Ill., I. 2 (Sept./Oct. 1933) 16.

c963 *Cambridge Left*. *Poetry*, XLII. 6 (Sept. 1933) 353–5.
A review of the first issue of the periodical.

c964 ✉ Telling Them. *New York Herald*, Paris (4 Sept. 1933) 4.
Reminding readers that the Bank of England is a private corporation.

c965 Eccezionale programma di manifestazioni musicali a Rapallo. *Il Mare*, XXVI.
1279 (16 Sept. 1933) [1].
An English translation of this article by R. Murray Schafer, "Exceptional
Program of Musical Events in Rapallo," was printed in *Ezra Pound and
Music* ([1977])—A99—pp. 337–8.

c966 ✉ Wise Guys. *New York Herald*, Paris (18 Sept. 1933) 4.
On the threat of the New York Stock Exchange to leave New York.

c967 "Inverno musicale": Il pianista Münch. *Il Mare*, XXVI. 1280 (23 Sept.
1933) 2.
An English translation of this article by R. Murray Schafer, "The Pianist
Münch," was printed in *Ezra Pound and Music* ([1977])—A99—pp. 340–1.

c968 ✉ How to Avoid Inflation. *New York Herald*, Paris (25 Sept. 1933) 4.
Signed: E. P. On stamp-scrip and the theories of C. H. Douglas.

c969 CANTO THIRTY-EIGHT. *New English Weekly*, III. 24 (28 Sept. 1933)
564–5.

c970 ✉ Guns; Oh Yes? *New English Weekly*, III. 24 (28 Sept. 1933) 574.

c971 ✉ Taxing Writers. *Spectator*, CLI. 5492 (29 Sept. 1933) 407.

c972 "Inverno musicale": La violinista Olga Rudge [I]. *Il Mare*, XXVI. 1281
(30 Sept. 1933) [1].
An English translation of this article by R. Murray Schafer, "The Violinist
Olga Rudge," incorporating Ezra Pound's corrections (see C976), was printed
in *Ezra Pound and Music* ([1977])—A99—pp. 341–5.

c972a ✉ Is It War? *Time and Tide*, XIV. 39 (30 Sept. 1933) 1148–9.
On an editorial with this title in the issue for 17 Sept.

c973 ✉ To the Editor . . . *Criterion*, XIII. 50 (Oct. 1933) 128.
Ignorance of economics not excusable.

c974 ✉ Academic. *Chicago Tribune*, Paris (2 Oct. 1933) 2.
To the Book Page Editor, on Nicholas Murray Butler and the American
Academy.

c975 ✉ Treachery. *New English Weekly*, III. 25 (5 Oct. 1933) 598.
On economics.

C. CONTRIBUTIONS TO PERIODICALS

c976 ✉ *Il Mare*, XXVI. 1282 (7 Oct. 1933) 3.
Signed: E. P. Correcting errors in translating and printing the article of 30 Sept.—C972.

c977 Questions, with Simple Historical Reference. *New Democracy*, I. 4 (10 Oct. 1933) 4.

c978 ✉ Who or What? *New English Weekly*, III. 26 (12 Oct. 1933) 623.

c979 ✉ Raps from Rapallo. *Chicago Tribune*, Paris (17 Oct. 1933) 4.
Signed: E.P.

c980 "Writers!" (as Joe Gould says) "Ignite!" *New Democracy*, I. 5 (25 Oct. 1933) 6.

c981 Stamp Script. *New English Weekly*, IV. 2 (26 Oct. 1933) 31–32.
A review of *Stamp Script*, by Irving Fisher, assisted by H. L. Cohrssen and H. W. Fisher.

c982 "Abject and Utter Farce." *Harkness Hoot*, New Haven, Ct., IV. 2 (Nov. 1933) 6–14.
". . . on the present estate of our higher 'general' or 'cultural' education."

c983 The Master of Rapallo Speaks. *Outrider*, Cincinnati, O., I. 1 (1 Nov. 1933) 1.

c984 ✉ Ezra Arraigns 'Pinkies.' *Outrider*, I. 1 (1 Nov. 1933) 4.

c985 La violinista Olga Rudge [II]: Rudge-Antheil concerti a Parigi. *Il Mare*, XXVI. 1286 (4 Nov. 1933) 2.
Signed: E. P. An English translation of this article by R. Murray Schafer, "The Violinist Olga Rudge: Rudge-Antheil Concerts in Paris," was printed in *Ezra Pound and Music* ([1977])—A99—pp. 345–6.

c986 ✉ Woergl Stamp Scrip. *Chicago Tribune*, Paris (8 Nov. 1933) 4.

c987 ✉ "Selfless Service." *New English Weekly*, IV. 4 (9 Nov. 1933) 96.

c988 "Inverno musicale": Il secondo concerto: Martedì 14 novembre . . . *Il Mare*, XXVI. 1287 (11 Nov. 1933) 3.
Signed: E. P. An English translation of this article by R. Murray Schafer, "Second Concert: Tuesday 14th November . . . ," was printed in *Ezra Pound and Music* ([1977])—A99—pp. 347–8.

c989 ✉ Presenting Some Thoughts on Fascism. *New York World Telegram*, New York (14 Nov. 1933) 22.

c990 Commentary on Fisher. *New English Weekly*, IV. 5 (16 Nov. 1933) 103–4.
A review of *Inflation?* by Irving Fisher.

c991 Splendido esito del secondo concerto Inverno musicale. *Il Mare*, XXVI. 1288 (18 Nov. 1933) 3.
Unsigned, but the following article, signed: E. P., is printed under this same two-column spread. An English translation of this article by R. Murray Schafer, "Splendid Success of the Second Concert," was printed in *Ezra Pound and Music* ([1977])—A99—pp. 350–1.

c992 L'audizione Criscuolo. *Il Mare*, XXVI. 1288 (18 Nov. 1933) 3.
Signed: E. P. An English translation of this article by R. Murray Schafer,

"The Criscuolo Concert," was printed (as part of the preceding one) in *Ezra Pound and Music* ([1977])—A99–p. 351.

c993 Calda accoglienza ai musicisti Tigullini a Genova. *Il Mare*, XXVI. 1289 (25 Nov. 1933) 2.

An English translation of this article by R. Murray Schafer, "Warm Reception in Genoa for the Tigullian Musicians," was printed in *Ezra Pound and Music* ([1977])—A99—pp. 351-4.

c994 ✉ *New Democracy*, I. 7 (25 Nov. 1933) 6.

Signed: E. P. Under the heading: "The Bear Garden."

c994a ✉ *Along the North Wall* [of the Argus Book Shop], Chicago, Ill., 4 ([Dec.? 1933]) 83–84.

On first editions; addressed to the owner and editor, Ben Abramson.

c995 Ignite! Ignite! *Harvard Advocate*, Cambridge, Mass., CXX. 3 (Dec. 1933) 3-5.

On the (sad) state of affairs in the U.S.

c996 "Inverno musicale": Il terzo concerto si svolgerà Martedì 5 dicembre ... *Il Mare*, XXVI. 1290 (2 Dec. 1933) 3.

An English translation of this article by R. Murray Schafer, "'Inverno Musicale': The Third Concert ... ," was printed in *Ezra Pound and Music* ([1977])—A99—pp. 354-5.

c997 ✉ Nothing New. *New English Weekly*, IV. 9 (14 Dec. 1933) 215.

c997a [Reply to questionnaire on "la rencontre capitale de votre vie"]. *Minotaure*, Paris, I. 3/4 (15 Dec. 1933) 112.

In French, citing Yusuf Benamore and Guido Cavalcanti. Questionnaire circulated by André Breton and Paul Éluard.

c998 SENATE BANKING SUB-COMMITTEE (AS REPORTED IN THE PARIS HERALD, OCT. 28). *New Democracy*, I. 8 (15 Dec. 1933) 4.

Eighteen lines of doggerel, signed: B. Dias.

c999 Hel. . .up!!! *New Democracy*, I. 8 (15 Dec. 1933) 6.

c999a ✉ *New Democracy*, I. 8 (15 Dec. 1933) 6.

On an article by Paul Ernest Anderson, "Social Credit and Human Exploitation," in the issue for 25 Oct. Under the heading: "The Bear Garden."

c1000 ✉ "Clarté Latine." *New York Herald*, Paris (16 Dec. 1933) 4.

(In English.) Signed: E. P.

c1001 ✉ Logical Move. *New York Herald*, Paris (18 Dec. 1933) 4.

Signed: E. P.

c1002 ✉ "Active Anthology." *New English Weekly*, IV. 11 (28 Dec. 1933) 263.

1934

c1003 Mr. Housman at Little Bethel. *Criterion*, XIII. 51 (Jan. 1934) 216–24.

On *The Name and Nature of Poetry*, by A. E. Housman.

C. CONTRIBUTIONS TO PERIODICALS

c1004 Judas Had It. *Outrider*, I. 2 (Jan. 1934) 1, 3.

c1005 Current Hopes and Left-over Blind Spots. *New Democracy*, I. 9 (1 Jan. 1934) 4.

c1006 ✉ From the Sage of Rapallo. *New York Herald*, Paris (7 Jan. 1934) 6.

c1007 "Inverno musicale": Prossimi concerti. *Il Mare*, XXVII. 1296 (13 Jan. 1934) 2.
Signed: E. P.; with note signed: e. p. An English translation of this article by R. Murray Schafer, "Inverno Musicale: Future Concerts," was printed in *Ezra Pound and Music* ([1977])—A99—pp. 356–8.

c1008 ✉ The Case of Landor. *Observer*, London (14 Jan. 1934) 9.
On Palgrave's *Golden Treasury*, and its omission of Walter Savage Landor.

c1009 ✉ *New Democracy*, I. 10 (15 Jan. 1934) 6–7.
Two letters, the first signed: Ezra Pound; the second: E. P. Under the heading: "The Bear Garden."

c1010 C. H. Douglas, Etc. *Little Magazine*, New York, I. 2 (Feb./Mar. 1934) 16.

c1011 On the Divisions in Jewry. *Harkness Hoot*, IV. 3 (Feb. 1934) 51.

c1012 CANTO XXXVIII. *Harvard Advocate*, CXX. 4 (Feb. 1934) 24–26.
Reprinted from *New English Weekly* for 28 Sept. 1933—C969.

c1013 An Open Letter to John Gould Fletcher. *Poetry*, XLIII. 5 (Feb. 1934) 292.

c1014 VERY OLD TUNE. *New Democracy*, I. 11 (1 Feb. 1934) 2.
Seven lines of doggerel on Bernard Baruch, signed: E. P.

c1015 As to [O. M. W.] Sprague. *New Democracy*, I. 11 (1 Feb. 1934) 3–4.

c1016 To the Book Trade. *New Democracy*, I. 11 (1 Feb. 1934) 6.
Signed: E. P.

c1017 ✉ *New Democracy*, I. 11 (1 Feb. 1934) 7.
Signed: E. P. On the orthodox economist.

c1018 THE CHARGE OF THE BREAD BRIGADE. *New English Weekly*, IV. 16 (1 Feb. 1934) 364.
Signed: Alfie Venison (A.D. 1934). The first of the Alfred Venison poems; in words and metre imitative of Alfred Tennyson's "The Charge of the Light Brigade."

c1019 ✉ From Mr. Ezra Pound. *Harvard Crimson*, Cambridge, Mass. (2 Feb. 1934)

c1020 ✉ The Golden Treasury. *Observer*, London (4 Feb. 1934) 11.
On F. T. Palgrave.

c1021 ✉ THE NEO-COMMUNE. *New English Weekly*, IV. 18 (15 Feb. 1934) 432.
Signed: Alf Venison. Incorporated in a (prose) letter, headed: "Alf's Second Bit," written pseudonymously by A. R. Orage, the Editor.

c1022 Hunger Fighters. *New English Weekly*, IV. 19 (22 Feb. 1934) 451–2.
A review of *Hunger Fighters*, by Paul de Kruif.

c1023 ✉ DOLE THE BELL! BELL THE DOLE! *New English Weekly*, IV. 19 (22 Feb. 1934) 455.

Twenty lines of doggerel, signed: Alf Venison. Incorporated in a letter, headed: "Alf's Second [*i.e.* Third] Bit," written pseudonymously by A. R. Orage. Reprinted as "Alf's Third Bit."

c1024 Un magnifico libro di P. M. Bardi. *Il Mare*, XXVII. 1302 (24 Feb. 1934) 2.
On *Belvedere della architettura italiana d'oggi*.

c1025 NICKIE AND FRANKIE WEREN'T BROTHERS. *New Quarterly*, Rock Island, Ill., I. 1 (Spring 1934) 24.
Ten lines of doggerel on Lenin and F. D. Roosevelt, dated: 3 Feb. "High spots" from a "long letter received [from Ezra Pound] by the editors of *The Left*" are summarised in "Notes on Contributors," p. [25].

c1026 "THOU SHALT NOT," SAID MARTIN VAN BUREN. CANTO XXXVII. *Poetry*, XLIII. 6 (Mar. 1934) 297–305.
Reprinted as Canto XXXVII.

c1027 Commentary on W. C. Williams. *New Democracy*, I. 13 (1 Mar. 1934) 4.
On politics and economics; followed by "Spinach," consisting of quotations from periodicals, with comments.

c1028 ✉ ALF'S THIRD [*i.e.* FOURTH] BIT. *New English Weekly*, IV. 20 (1 Mar. 1934) 480.
An untitled poem of 19 lines, beginning: "Rudyard the dud yard," signed: Alf Venison; incorporated in a letter, written pseudonymously by A. R. Orage. Reprinted as "Alf's Fourth Bit."

c1029 "Inverno musicale": Importanza e significato della musica di William Young. *Il Mare*, XXVII. 1303 (3 Mar. 1934) [1].
An English translation of this article by R. Murray Schafer, "Meaning and Importance of William Young's Music," was printed in *Ezra Pound and Music* ([1977])—A99—pp. 358–60.

c1030 ✉ Money and Banks. *Chicago Tribune*, Paris (6 Mar. 1934) 5.

c1031 Mr. Eliot's Mare's Nest. *New English Weekly*, IV. 21 (8 Mar. 1934) 500.
A review, signed: E. P., of *After Strange Gods*, by T. S. Eliot.

c1032 ✉ ALF'S FOURTH [*i.e.* FIFTH] BIT. *New English Weekly*, IV. 21 (8 Mar. 1934) 504.
An untitled poem of 21 lines, beginning: "The pomps of butchery, financial power," signed: Alf Venison; incorporated in a letter, written pseudonymously by A. R. Orage. Reprinted as "Alf's Fifth Bit."

c1033 ✉ A Retrospect. *Chicago Tribune*, Paris (14 Mar. 1934) 5.
On economics.

c1034 ✉ ALF'S FIFTH [*i.e.* SIXTH] BIT. *New English Weekly*, IV. 22 (15 Mar. 1934) 528.
An untitled poem of 30 lines, beginning: "Let some new lying ass," signed: Alf Venison; incorporated in a letter, written pseudonymously by A. R. Orage. Reprinted as "Alf's Sixth Bit."

c1034a [Letter to Michael Gold]. *Daily Worker*, New York (17 Mar. 1934) 7.
Printed under the heading: "Ezra Pound Takes His Pen in Hand" in the "Change the World!" column of Sender Garlin, Gold's temporary succes-

sor as columnist. With Gold's reply, printed as "Mike Gold Lets Him Have It!"

C1035 ✉ A "Forbidden" Subject: Mr. Ezra Pound on Fascism and the British Press. *Morning Post*, London (20 Mar. 1934) 17.

C1036 ✉ Trusting the President. *Chicago Tribune*, Paris (22 Mar. 1934) 5. On F. D. Roosevelt.

C1037 ✉ ALF'S SIXTH [*i.e.* SEVENTH] BIT. *New English Weekly*, IV. 23 (22 Mar. 1934) 551.
An untitled poem of 20 lines, beginning: "Did I 'ear it 'arf in a doze," signed: Alf Venison; incorporated in a letter, written pseudonymously by A. R. Orage. Reprinted as "Alf's Seventh Bit."

C1038 Mr. Eliot's Quandaries. *New English Weekly*, IV. 24 (29 Mar. 1934) 558–9.
On *After Strange Gods*.

C1039 ✉ ALF'S SEVENTH [*i.e.* EIGHTH] BIT. *New English Weekly*, IV. 24 (29 Mar. 1934) 574.
An untitled poem of 35 lines, beginning: "Vex not thou the banker's mind," signed: A. Venison; incorporated in a letter, written pseudonymously by A. R. Orage. Reprinted as "Alf's Eighth Bit."

C1040 Declaration. *New Democracy*, II. 2/3 (30 Mar./15 Apr. 1934) 5.

C1041 Peace Pathology. *New Democracy*, II. 2/3 (30 Mar./15 Apr. 1934) 7.

C1042 DODDERING AND SLOW, MY COUNTRY. *New Democracy*, II. 2/3 (30 Mar./15 Apr. 1934) 8.
In 35 lines, "with apologies to Walt Whitman."

C1043 ✉ *New Democracy*, II. 2/3 (30 Mar./15 Apr. 1934) 10.
In reply to a letter of Andrew Cordian in the issue for 1 Feb.

C1044 ✉ E. P.'s Suspicions. *Chicago Tribune*, Paris (31 Mar. 1934) 4.
On economics.

C1045 ✉ *Hound & Horn*, VII. 3 (Apr./May 1934) [361].
Refusing to contribute to the Henry James issue.

C1046 Hell. *Criterion*, XIII. 52 (Apr. 1934) 382–96.
A review of *Dante's Inferno, Translated into English Triple Rhyme*, by Laurence Binyon.

C1047 [A review of] *Stones of Rimini*. [By] Adrian Stokes. *Criterion*, XIII. 52 (Apr. 1934) 495–7.

C1048 CANTO XXXVI. *Harkness Hoot*, IV. 4 (Apr. 1934) 26–29.
Reprinted in *Criterion*, London, XIV. 55 (Jan. 1935) 204–7. (The first 84 lines of this Canto are Ezra Pound's revised English version of Cavalcanti's canzone "Donna mi prega.")

C1049 EPITAPH. *Inland Review*, Ann Arbor, Mich., I. 1 (Apr. 1934) 14.
On Harriet Monroe.

C1050 Rimbaud. *New Act*, Millbrook, N. Y., 3 (Apr. 1934) 103–4.
On an article by Harold Rosenberg, "Sanity, Individuality and Poetry," in the issue for June 1933.

C. CONTRIBUTIONS TO PERIODICALS

C1051 ✉ Ezra's Easy Economics. *Chicago Tribune*, Paris (2 Apr. 1934) 2.
To the Book Page Editor, on R. McNair Wilson's *Promise to Pay*.

C1052 ✉ Italian Fascism: Sequel to Mr. Ezra Pound's Letter. *Morning Post*, London (2 Apr. 1934) 7.

C1053 ✉ Distinction. *Chicago Tribune*, Paris (3 Apr. 1934) 4.
Signed: E. P. On "Les Francistes" and "Les Franchistes."

C1054 ✉ Sapheads Assorted. *Chicago Tribune*, Paris (4 Apr. 1934) 4.
On economics.

C1055 ✉ The U. S. Social Credit Bill. *New English Weekly*, IV. 25 (5 Apr. 1934) 599–600.

C1056 ✉ ALF'S EIGHTH [*i.e.* NINTH] BIT. *New English Weekly*, IV. 25 (5 Apr. 1934) 600.
An untitled poem of 32 lines, beginning: "Listen, my children, and you shall hear," signed: Alf Venison; incorporated in a letter, written pseudonymously by A. R. Orage. Reprinted as "Alf's Ninth Bit."

C1057 Mussolini Defines State as "Spirit of the People": Fascism Analyzed by Ezra Pound, Noted American Writer. *Chicago Tribune*, Paris (9 Apr. 1934) 5.
"written for *The Tribune*."

C1058 ✉ ALF'S NINTH [*i.e.* TENTH] BIT. *New English Weekly*, IV. 26 (12 Apr. 1934) 623.
A 16-line poem, "Wind," signed: Alf Venison; incorporated in a letter, written pseudonymously by A. R. Orage. Reprinted as "Alf's Tenth Bit."

C1059 ✉ $0.87 for Sinclair. *Chicago Tribune*, Paris (16 Apr. 1934) 5.
Signed: E. P. On Upton Sinclair's campaign fund.

C1060 ✉ ALF'S TENTH [*i.e.* ELEVENTH] BIT. *New English Weekly*, V. 1 (19 Apr. 1934) 24.
A 24-line poem, "Sir Launcelot Has a Newspaper Now," signed: Alfred Venison; incorporated in a letter, written pseudonymously by A. R. Orage. Reprinted as "Alf's Eleventh Bit."

C1061 ✉ ALF'S ELEVENTH [*i.e.* TWELFTH] BIT. *New English Weekly*, V. 2 (26 Apr. 1934) 48.
A 21-line poem, "Ballad for the 'Times' Special Silver Number," signed: Alf Venison; incorporated in a letter, written pseudonymously by A. R. Orage. Reprinted as "Alf's Twelfth Bit."

C1062 ✉ Mr. T. S. Eliot's Quandaries. *New English Weekly*, V. 2 (26 Apr. 1934) 48.

C1063 Ignite. *Little Magazine*, I. 3 (May/June 1934) 26.

C1064 Address to the John Reed Club of Philadelphia. *Left Review*, Philadelphia, Pa., I. 3 ([May?] 1934) 4–5.

C1065 ✉ ALF'S LAST—AND AN OFFER. *New English Weekly*, V. 3 (3 May 1934) 71.
A 16-line poem, untitled, beginning: "I see by the morning papers," signed: A. V.; incorporated in a letter, written pseudonymously by A. R. Orage. Reprinted as "Another Bit—and an Offer."

C1066 La cantante Lonny Mayer. *Il Mare*, XXVII. 1312 (5 May 1934) [1].
An English translation of this article by R. Murray Schafer, "The Singer Lonny Mayer," was printed in *Ezra Pound and Music* ([1977])—A99—pp. 360–3. (Schafer points out that the program included two arias from Pound's opera "Cavalcanti," offered anonymously—one of the few occasions on which portions of the opera have been sung in public.)

C1067 ✉ Mr. Eliot's Looseness. *New English Weekly*, V. 4 (10 May 1934) 95–96.

C1068 Ahead. *New Democracy*, II. 5 (15 May 1934) 5.

C1069 ✉ Catholicism and Credit. *New English Weekly*, V. 5 (17 May 1934) 120.

C1070 What Price the Muses Now. *New English Weekly*, V. 6 (24 May 1934) 130–2.
A review of *The Use of Poetry and the Use of Criticism*, by T. S. Eliot.

C1071 ✉ From Italy. *New English Weekly*, V. 6 (24 May 1934) 143–4.
Chiefly on misrepresentation of conditions in Italy. A sentence concerning "Adolphe" [*i.e.* Adolf Hitler] was reprinted in *Agenda*, XVII. 3/4/XVIII. 1 (Autumn/Winter/Spring 1979/1980) 74.

C1072 ✉ Stamp Scrip. *New English Weekly*, V. 7 (31 May 1934) 167.

C1073 ✉ *New Quarterly*, I. 2 (Summer 1934) 24.
On economics.

C1074 ✉ *New Democracy*, II. 6 (1 June 1934) 11.
Signed: E. P. On the Social Credit bill.

C1075 ✉ Mr. Ezra Pound's Query: The Powers of the Crown. *Morning Post*, London (12 June 1934) 6.

C1076 SONG OF SIX HUNDRED M.P.'S. *New English Weekly*, V. 9 (14 June 1934) 205.
A 24-line poem, signed: A. Venison.

C1077 Mr. Roosevelt at the Crossroads (Tyburn). *New Democracy*, II. 7 (15 June 1934) 5.

C1078 ✉ [On Jean Barral]. *New Democracy*, II. 7 (15 June 1934) 11.
Under the heading: "Press Notes."

C1079 Murkn Magzeens. *New English Weekly*, V. 10 (21 June 1934) 235–6.
Signed: B. H. Dias. Reprinted, in part, anonymously, in *Blast*, New York, I. 5 (Oct./Nov. 1934) 1, under the heading: "Testimonials from England."

C1080 To the Young, If Any. *Little Magazine*, I. 4 (July/Aug. 1934) 1–3.

C1081 ✉ *Little Magazine*, I. 4 (July/Aug. 1934) 36.
An extract. Under the heading: "Reaction."

C1082 ✉ Individual and Statal Views: Mr. Ezra Pound's Views. *Plain Dealer*, Brighton, Eng., XIII (N.S.). 1 (July 1934), supplement, p.[3].

C1083 Ecclesiastical History (Or the work always falls on papa). *New English Weekly*, V. 12 (5 July 1934) 272–3.

C1084 Mr. Eliot's Solid Merit. *New English Weekly*, V. 13 (12 July 1934) 297–9.

C1084a ✉ Murkn Magzeens. *New English Weekly*, V. 13 (12 July 1934) 311.

C. CONTRIBUTIONS TO PERIODICALS

Signed: Your Reviewer.

C1085 ✉ The Future in America. *New English Weekly*, V. 13 (12 July 1934) 311.

C1086 OLE KATE. *New English Weekly*, V. 15 (26 July 1934) 348.
A 26-line poem, signed: A Venison.

C1087 Gaudier[-Brzeska]: A Postscript. *Esquire*, Chicago, Ill., II. 3 (Aug. 1934) 72–75.

C1088 THE BABY. *New English Weekly*, V. 16 (2 Aug. 1934) 380.
A 12-line poem, signed: A. Venison. Reprinted in *New Times* (15 June 1956) 7.

C1088a ✉ *G. K.'s Weekly*, London, XIX. 491 (9 Aug. 1934) 366.
Congratulations on printing Featherstone Hammond's articles (on economic matters).

C1089 A Banker's Elegy. *Time and Tide*, XV. 32 (11 Aug. 1934) 1009–10.
A review of *The Money Muddle*, by J. P. Warburg.

C1090 Volitionist Economics—Ratsnip for Professors of Economics, fer to See if They Understand ANYthing, or Have Merely Memorized What They Were Told. *Direction*, Peoria, Ill., I. 1 (Autumn 1934) 64.
A reprint of *Volitionist Economics* ([1934])—E2m. Reprinted also in *New Democracy*, III. 6 (15 Nov. 1934) 105, with title: "Mr. Pound Invites Correspondence on Volitionist Economics."

C1090a ✉ *Latin Quarter-ly*, New York, I. 3 ([Autumn 1934]) 177.
Asking questions.

C1091 ✉ A Poet's Questions for Economists: Mr. Ezra Pound's Posers. *Morning Post*, London (3 Sept. 1934) 12.
Incorporating part of *Volitionist Economics* ([1934])—E2m.

C1092 ✉ "Volitionist Economics." *Morning Post*, London (11 Sept. 1934) 5.
Quotes four items from *Volitionist Economics* ([1934])—E2m.

C1093 NATIONAL SONG (E. C.). *New English Weekly*, V. 22 (13 Sept. 1934) 421.
A 16-line poem, signed: A Venison.

C1094 Light. *New Democracy*, III. 2 (15 Sept. 1934) 30.

C1095 ✉ "Demurrage Money": Mr. Ezra Pound Explains. *Morning Post*, London (21 Sept. 1934) 9.

C1096 Teacher's Mission. *English Journal (College Edition)*, XXIII. 8 (Oct. 1934) 630–5.

C1097 ✉ Riposte from Rapallo. *Esquire*, II. 5 (Oct. 1934) 12.

C1098 ✉ The Firdausi Festival: Mr. Ezra Pound's Suggestion. *Morning Post*, London (1 Oct. 1934) 14.
Suggesting Basil Bunting instead of John Drinkwater to represent England.

C1099 "Opportunity." *New Democracy*, III. 3 (1 Oct. 1934) 48.

C1100 ✉ A Little Light Please. *New York Herald*, Paris (3 Oct. 1934) 4.

C. CONTRIBUTIONS TO PERIODICALS

CI101 Musica Tigulliana progettata "Inverno musicale." *Il Mare*, XXVII. 1334 (6 Oct. 1934) [1].
Reprinted as a broadside ([1934])—C2l. An English translation of the article by R. Murray Schafer, "Planned Tigullian Music: Inverno Musicale," was printed in *Ezra Pound and Music* ([1977])—A99—pp. 365–6.

CI102 ✉ Debt without Usury: Mr. Ezra Pound's Reply. *Morning Post*, London (9 Oct. 1934) 8.
In answer to "Mr. Biddulph's letter on Douglas Credit."

CI103 ✉ Items, Just Items. *New York Herald*, Paris (9 Oct. 1934) 4.
Signed: E. P.

CI104 ✉ Packages without Label. *New York Herald*, Paris (11 Oct. 1934) 4.
Signed: E. P.

CI105 ✉ Wonder Who Told Him. *New York Herald*, Paris (19 Oct. 1934) 4.
On Prof. George Warren.

CI106 ✉ More Light, Bert. *New York Herald*, Paris (23 Oct. 1934) 4.
In reply to Mr. Bert Pewee.

CI107 ✉ Scarcity Economics: Mr. Ezra Pound and the Duce. *Morning Post*, London (25 Oct. 1934) 15.

CI108 SAFE AND SOUND. *New English Weekly*, VI. 2 (25 Oct. 1934) 37–38.
A 28-line poem, signed: A. Venison. On Montagu Norman.

CI109 ✉ The Ignorant Ignorami. *New York Herald*, Paris (26 Oct. 1934) 4.

CI110 ✉ The Douglas Social Credit Scheme: Mr. Ezra Pound Explains. *Morning Post*, London (31 Oct. 1934) 5.

CI111 ✉ *New Democracy*, III. 5 (1 Nov. 1934) 87.
Signed: E. P. On economists.

CI112 ✉ Italian Fascism. *New English Weekly*, VI. 3 (1 Nov. 1934) 72.

CI113 ✉ Trees without Roots. *New York Herald*, Paris (1 Nov. 1934) 4.

CI114 CANTO XLI. *New English Weekly*, VI. 4 (8 Nov. 1934) 85–86.

CI115 Dust upon Hellas. *Time and Tide*, XV. 45 (10 Nov. 1934) 1429–30.
A review of *A History of Classical Greek Literature*, by T. A. Sinclair.

CI116 ✉ Right Use of Credit: Mr. Ezra Pound's Attack on Dogmas. *Morning Post*, London (13 Nov. 1934) 15.

CI117 Child's Guide to Economics 1934. *G.K.'s Weekly*, London, XX. 505 (15 Nov. 1934) 177–8.
Four paragraphs from this article were reprinted under the heading: "Free-Economy in the Press," in *Way Out*, San Antonio, Texas, for Jan. 1935.

CI118 ✉ He Pulled His Weight. *New English Weekly*, VI. 5 (15 Nov. 1934) 109.
On A. R. Orage, in the special Orage memorial issue; the first of 44 "Obituary Letters to the Editor."

CI119 ✉ Gold or Money? Mr. Ezra Pound's Poser. *Morning Post*, London (21 Nov. 1934) 15.

C. CONTRIBUTIONS TO PERIODICALS

C1120 A Problem of (Specifically) Style. *New English Weekly*, VI. 6 (22 Nov. 1934) 127–8.
Reprinted in *Harvard Advocate*, CXXII. 1 (Sept. 1935) 16–17.

C1121 ✉ Why Empires Decay: Mr. Ezra Pound on "Faulty Textbooks." *Morning Post*, London (28 Nov. 1934) 15.

C1122 The Acid Test. *Biosophical Review*, New York, IV. 2 (Winter 1934/1935) 22–30.
Incorporates *Volitionist Economics* ([1934])—E2m, pp. 29–30.

C1123 ✉ Gesell's "Natural Economic Order." *Morning Post*, London (6 Dec. 1934) 15.

C1124 Time Lag in the American Wilderness. *New English Weekly*, VI. 8 (6 Dec. 1934) 175.

C1125 ✉ The Work of A. R. Orage. *New English Weekly*, VI. 8 (6 Dec. 1934) 183.

C1126 ✉ "The Only True Function of the State." *Social Credit*, London, I. 18 (14 Dec. 1934) 243.
On a paragraph in the issue for 14 Sept.

C1127 Orage: Critic of Good Will. *New Democracy*, III. 8, part 2 (15 Dec. 1934) 152.

C1128 E. E. Cummings Alive. *New English Weekly*, VI. 10 (20 Dec. 1934) 210–11.

C1129 ✉ "The Next War." *Morning Post*, London (24 Dec. 1934) 7.

1935

C1130 ✉ 1934 in the Autumn. *Criterion*, XIV. 55 (Jan. 1935) 297–304.
Reprinted in the American edition of *Jefferson and/or Mussolini*—A41c—as "Letter Sent Autumn, 1934 . . . to Editor of the *Criterion*, London."

C1131 Reflexshuns on Iggurunce: Being a Seminar Session with Ole Ez to Which Only the Very Brightest Readers are Invited. *Esquire*, III. 1 (Jan. 1935) 55, 133.

C1132 ✉ Correspondence. *Poetry*, XLV. 4 (Jan. 1935) 234.
An extract, quoted in an editorial note, with an untitled poem, printed in 15 lines, beginning: "Hiram, my uncle, | My ole great uncle had a wooden leg." (Pound wrote to T. C. Wilson, 2 Feb., that "Zabel [the Editor] has printed the title as a first line, which is incorrect.")

C1133 To Hell With! *New Democracy*, III. 9 (1 Jan. 1935) 172.
On F. D. Roosevelt.

C1134 ✉ Ignored Aspects of History: Mr. Ezra Pound's Suggestions. *Morning Post*, London (2 Jan. 1935) 7.
On an *English* School of Economics.

C1135 American Notes. *New English Weekly*, VI. 12 (3 Jan. 1935) 251.
Signed: E. P.

C. CONTRIBUTIONS TO PERIODICALS

C1136 ✉ Monetary Reform: Mr. Ezra Pound and Credit. *Yorkshire Post*, Leeds (8 Jan. 1935) 6.

C1137 ✉ England's National Sport—According to Mr. Ezra Pound. *Morning Post*, London (9 Jan. 1935) 14.
The "chase of the jolly red herring."

C1138 American Notes. *New English Weekly*, VI. 13 (10 Jan. 1935) 270.
Signed: E. P.

C1139 Jean Cocteau Sociologist. *New English Weekly*, VI. 13 (10 Jan. 1935) 272–4.

C1140 ✉ From a Poet Planner. *Independent*, London, VI. 67 (12 Jan. 1935) 57.
On "liberty" based on financial liberty.

C1141 [A review, signed: E. P., of] *Health and Life*. By Edgard J. Saxon. *New Age*, LVI. 12 (17 Jan. 1935) 138.

C1142 American Notes. *New English Weekly*, VI. 14 (17 Jan. 1935) 290.
Signed: E. P.

C1143 ✉ Monetary Reform: Douglas System and Fixing Prices. *Yorkshire Post*, Leeds (17 Jan. 1935) 6.

C1144 American Notes. *New English Weekly*, VI. 15 (24 Jan. 1935) 310–11.
Signed: E. P.

C1145 ✉ "Befoozled." *Yorkshire Post*, Leeds (24 Jan. 1935) 6.

C1146 Leaving out Economics (Gesell as Reading Matter). *New English Weekly*, VI. 16 (31 Jan. 1935) 331–3.

C1147 Mug's Game? *Esquire*, III. 2 (Feb. 1935) 35, 148.

C1148 Such Language. *G. K.'s Weekly*, XX. 517 (7 Feb. 1935) 373–4.

C1149 American Notes. *New English Weekly*, VI. 17 (7 Feb. 1935) 349.
Signed: E. P.

C1150 ✉ Ezra Pound on Political Policy. *New Age*, LVI. 16 (14 Feb. 1935) 184.

C1151 Banking Beneficence and. . . . *New Age*, LVI. 16 (14 Feb. 1935) 184–5.

C1152 ✉ Landlords and Increment. *New Age*, LVI. 16 (14 Feb. 1935) 186.

C1153 American Notes. *New English Weekly*, VI. 18 (14 Feb. 1935) 369.
Signed: E. P.

C1154 V. Beonio-Brocchieri (An Introduction). *New English Weekly*, VI. 18 (14 Feb. 1935) 373–4.

C1155 To the Historical Society of America. *New Democracy*, III. 12 (15 Feb. 1935) 211.

C1156 The Root of Evil. *G.K.'s Weekly*, XX. 519 (21 Feb. 1935) 404–5.

C1157 American Notes. That Gold Clause. *New English Weekly*, VI. 20 (28 Feb. 1935) 409–10.
Signed: E. P.

C1158 Debabelization and Ogden. *New English Weekly*, VI. 20 (28 Feb. 1935) 410–11.

C. CONTRIBUTIONS TO PERIODICALS

C1159 ✉ Mussolini's Rome. *New English Weekly*, VI. 20 (28 Feb. 1935) 424.

C1160 Foreword [to the American Section]. *Westminster*, Oglethorpe, Ga., XXIV. 1 (Spring/Summer 1935) 21–22.
"An Anthology of modern English and American poetry, collected by T. C. Wilson, John Drummond, and Ezra Pound." Cover-title for the issue: "Poems by 126 outstanding modern English and American poets." This number issued with *Bozart*, IX. 1 as *Bozart-Westminster*. (Pound's *Volitionist Economics* ([1934])—E2m—is reprinted, boxed, p. [4].)

C1161 ✉ From Ezra Pound. *Mosaic*, New York, [I. 2] (Spring 1935) [38].
Signed: Ez P'o. "This is most of Mr. Pound's reply to Samuel Putnam's 'Ezra Pound, Cracker Barrell Revolutionist' in Mosaic Vol. I, No. 1."

C1162 ✉ Open Letter from Ezra Pound. *Rocking Horse*, Madison, Wisc., II. 3 (Spring 1935) 27–29.
Offering programs.

C1163 [Translation of a paragraph by Mussolini]. *Herald-Telegram*, Chippewa Falls, Wisc. (5 Mar. 1935)
Apparently an enclosure to a letter to the Editor from Homer L. Pound, printed first in Italian, then in English, with note: "Translation of the above by Ezra Pound."

C1164 American Notes. *New English Weekly*, VI. 21 (7 Mar. 1935) 429–30.
Signed: E. P.

C1165 ✉ G. K. Chesterton's Style and [H. G.] Wells's. *New English Weekly*, VI. 21 (7 Mar. 1935) 444.

C1166 ✉ Local Currency: Mr. Ezra Pound's Question to Sir A. Verdon-Roe. *Morning Post*, London (9 Mar. 1935) 4.

C1167 American Notes. *New English Weekly*, VI. 22 (14 Mar. 1935) 449.
Signed: E. P.

C1168 Waiting. *New Democracy*, IV. 2 (15 Mar. 1935) 28.

C1169 EPISCOPAL FERVOUR. *New English Weekly*, VI. 23 (21 Mar. 1935) 467.
A 19-line poem, signed: A. Venison.

C1170 American Notes. (General Motors). *New English Weekly*, VI. 23 (21 Mar. 1935) 469–70.
Signed: E. P.

C1171 Ez Sez: Being Some Pithy Promulgations ... *Santa Fe New Mexican*, Santa Fe, N.M. (26 Mar. 1935) 4.

C1172 American Notes. *New English Weekly*, VI. 24 (28 Mar. 1935) 490.
Signed: E. P.

C1173 Tibor Serly, Composer. *New English Weekly*, VI. 24 (28 Mar. 1935) 495.
Signed: Ezra Pound (Formerly "William Atheling," the "New Age" music critic.)

C1174 ✉ The Church and Society. *New English Weekly*, VI. 24 (28 Mar. 1935) 504.
On T. S. Eliot.

C. CONTRIBUTIONS TO PERIODICALS

C1175 Ez Says: Being Some Pithy Promulgations ... Re Durno's Remarks on Evaporated Myths. *Santa Fe New Mexican*, Santa Fe, N.M. (28 Mar. 1935) 4. Incorporates a doggerel poem, printed in 19 lines, headed: "'All the unemployed will have WORK for 25 years.'—Sec. Perkins." The poem was reprinted under this same heading in *New Democracy*, New York, IV. 4 (15 Apr. 1935) 68. A five-line quotation from the article was reprinted with the complete poem as "Ezra Pound Says ... WORK??? ..." in *Attack!*, London, 29 ([Apr.?] 1935) [4], followed by a reproduction of paper money issued by the Union Lumbering Co., Chippewa Falls, Wisc., signed: A. E. Pound, Secretary, with descriptive text drawn in part from the caption printed in *Social Credit* ([1935])—A40.

C1176 In the Wounds (Memoriam A. R. Orage). *Criterion*, XIV. 56 (Apr. 1935) 391–407.

C1177 American Notes. *New English Weekly*, VI. 25 (4 Apr. 1935) 509–10. Signed: E. P.

C1178 Gold's in His Heaven, All's (Nearly) Right with the World! (With Apologies to Our Super-Optimistic Daily Press for the Captions). *Social Credit*, II. 8 (5 Apr. 1935) 122.
Selections from various papers, unsigned, but made probably by Ezra Pound.

C1179 American Notes. *New English Weekly*, VI. 26 (11 Apr. 1935) 529–30. Signed: E. P.

C1180 Towards Orthology. *New English Weekly*, VI. 26 (11 Apr. 1935) 534.

C1181 Hidden Govt. *New Democracy*, IV.4 (15 Apr. 1935) 67.

C1182 ✉ Senator Long and Father Coughlin: Mr. Ezra Pound's Estimate. *Morning Post*, London (17 Apr. 1935) 14.

C1183 American Notes. Time Lag. *New English Weekly*, VII. 1 (18 Apr. 1935) 5–6.
Signed: E. P.

C1184 ✉ "Bank Money or State Money?" Mr. Pound Replies [to Sir Alliott Verdon-Roe]. *Morning Post*, London (22 Apr. 1935) 7.

C1185 American Notes. *New English Weekly*, VII. 2 (25 Apr. 1935) 25. Signed: E. P.

C1186 A Matter of Modesty. *Esquire*, III. 5 (May 1935) 31.

C1186a ✉ *Open Road*, Mountain View, N.J., XXX. 2 (May 1935) [2].
Under the heading: "The Voltaire Tempest."

C1187 Private Worlds. *New English Weekly*, VII. 3 (2 May 1935) 48–49.
Private Worlds, by Phyllis Bottome, "used as take-off." A brief passage was reprinted in *Agenda*, XVII. 3/4/XVIII. 1 (Autumn/Winter/Spring 1979/1980) 74.

C1188 ✉ Music and Money. *New English Weekly*, VII. 3 (2 May 1935) 60.

C1189 ✉ English Pronunciation. *New English Weekly*, VII. 3 (2 May 1935) 60.
Signed: Alfred Venison.

C. CONTRIBUTIONS TO PERIODICALS

C1189a ✉ "Taxation Will Die." *Middlesex County Times*, Ealing, LXXII. 4551 (4 May 1935) 14.
On F. J. Gould's letter printed under this title.

C1190 American Notes. *New English Weekly*, VII. 4 (9 May 1935) 65.
Signed: E. P. Incorporates reprint of editorial, "The Huey Long Menace," from a March issue of the *Santa Fe New Mexican*.

C1191 [Letter to Sir Norman Angell]. *Time and Tide*, XVI. 19 (11 May 1935) 685.
A typed letter, dated: 13 April, anno XIII, reproduced in facsimile. In a note to the Editor, sending the letter, Norman Angell explains that it was addressed to him at the Bank of England, which he has never entered. Intended presumably for Montagu Norman, then Governor of the Bank. Reproduced also as plate facing p. 298 in *After All, the Autobiography of Norman Angell* (London, Hamish Hamilton [1951]) and (New York, Farrar, Straus and Young, Inc. [1951]).

C1192 [*Entry deleted.*]

C1193 An "American" So-Called "Writers" Congress. *New Democracy*, IV. 6 (15 May 1935) 100.
Reprinted as "So-called 'Writers' Congress."

C1194 ✉ The Case of Jacques Romain. *Morning Post*, London (16 May 1935) 16.
Requesting investigation of his imprisonment at Port au Prince, Haiti.

C1195 "Amici del Tigullio": Olga Rudge e Gerhart Münch a Firenze e Chiavari. *Il Mare*, XXVIII. 1366 (18 May 1935) 2.
Signed: E. P. An English translation of this article by R. Murray Schafer, "Olga Rudge and Gerhart Münch in Florence and Chiavari," was printed in *Ezra Pound and Music* ([1977])—A99—pp. 368–70.

C1196 Ez Sez. *Santa Fe New Mexican*, Santa Fe, N.M. (20 May 1935) 4.

C1197 American Notes. *New English Weekly*, VII. 6 (23 May 1935) 105.
Signed: E. P.

C1198 The Italian Score. *New English Weekly*, VII. 6 (23 May 1935) 107.

C1199 Ez Sez. *Santa Fe New Mexican*, Santa Fe, N.M. (24 May 1935) 4.

C1200 Ez Sez. *Santa Fe New Mexican*, Santa Fe, N.M. (25 May 1935) 4.

C1201 Ez Sez. *Santa Fe New Mexican*, Santa Fe, N.M. (28 May 1935) 4.

C1202 Ez Sez. *Santa Fe New Mexican*, Santa Fe, N.M. (29 May 1935) 4.

C1203 Child's Guide to Economics. *G. K.'s Weekly*, XXI. 533 (30 May 1935) 181–2.
Twenty-four paragraphs from this article were reprinted in the *Hailey Times*, Hailey, Idaho (1 Aug. 1935) 2.

C1204 ✉ The Biennale. *New English Weekly*, VII. 7 (30 May 1935) 140.
Signed: E. P.

C1205 ✉ Message to Oxford. *Programme*, Oxford, Eng., 6 (31 May 1935) [3].

C. CONTRIBUTIONS TO PERIODICALS

C1206 Hickory [*i.e.* Andrew Jackson]—Old and New. *Esquire*, III. 6 (June 1935) 40, 156.

A lost portrait of Ezra Pound made "just after the war" by Wyndham Lewis is reproduced, p. 22, with descriptive caption by Pound.

C1207 A Bill. *New Democracy*, IV. 7 (1 June 1935) 122.

C1208 Ez Sez. *Santa Fe New Mexican*, Santa Fe, N.M. (1 June 1935) 3.
Signed: Ole Ez. P.

C1209 ✉ Cash and Calamity. *Reynolds's Illustrated News*, London (2 June 1935) 8.

C1210 Ez Sez. *Santa Fe New Mexican*, Santa Fe, N.M. (3 June 1935) 4.

C1211 American Notes. *New English Weekly*, VII. 8 (6 June 1935) 145–6.
Signed: E. P.

C1212 John Buchan's "Cromwell." *New English Weekly*, VII. 8 (6 June 1935) 149.
Signed: E. P. On *Oliver Cromwell*, by John Buchan. Reprinted as "Cromwell."

C1213 American Notes. *New English Weekly*, VII. 9 (13 June 1935) 165.
Signed: E. P.

C1214 American Notes. *New English Weekly*, VII. 10 (20 June 1935) 185.
Signed: E. P.

C1215 Toward Orthology: Sargent [*sic*] Florence. *New English Weekly*, VII. 10 (20 June 1935) 191–2.

A review of *Economics and Human Behaviour*, by P. Sargant Florence, and *The Standardization of Error*, by V. Stefansson.

C1216 American Notes. *New English Weekly*, VII. 11 (27 June 1935) 205.
Signed: E. P.

C1217 ✉ Reducing Wheat Acreage. *New English Weekly*, VII. 11 (27 June 1935) 220.
Signed: Alf Venison.

C1218 Peace in the Market. *Kingwood Review*, Salem, Oregon, II. 19 (July/Aug. 1935) 27.

On economics and American education. Reprinted in *New Democracy*, New York, VI. 3 (May 1936) 59.

C1219 ✉ More about Money. *National Citizen*, London, XVI. 7 (July 1935) 104.

C1220 A Little Personal Color. *New Democracy*, IV. 9 (1 July 1935) 157–8.
Signed: E. P.

C1221 American Notes. *New English Weekly*, VII. 12 (4 July 1935) 225–6.
Signed: E. P.

C1222 Ezra Pound Shouts the Money Money Money Chorus. *Attack!*, London, 30 ([after 10 July] 1935) [2].
Signed: E. P.

C1223 American Notes. *New English Weekly*, VII. 13 (11 July 1935) 245–6.
Signed: E. P.

C1224 Throttling Music. *New English Weekly*, VII. 13 (11 July 1935) 247–8.

C. CONTRIBUTIONS TO PERIODICALS

Signed: William Atheling (E. P.)

C1225 ✉ The Causes of War: "Why Do Pacifists Evade Them?" *Morning Post*, London (12 July 1935) 15.

C1226 ✉ La nuova economia di Ezra Pound. *L'Avvenire d'Italia*, Bologna (16 July 1935)
On the review by Lina Caico of *ABC of Economics*—A34—in the issue for 11 May.

C1227 American Notes. *New English Weekly*, VII. 14 (18 July 1935) 265.
Signed: E. P.

C1228 American Notes. *New English Weekly*, VII. 15 (25 July 1935) 285.
Signed: E. P.

C1229 History and Ignorance. *New English Weekly*, VII. 15 (25 July 1935) 287-8.

C1230 ✉ Reducing Wheat Acreage. *New English Weekly*, VII. 15 (25 July 1935) 298.

C1231 ✉ Economics. *National Citizen*, London, XVI. 8 (Aug. 1935) 124.

C1232 American Notes. *New English Weekly*, VII. 16 (1 Aug. 1935) 305.
Signed: E. P.

C1233 ✉ World Congress of Writers. *New English Weekly*, VII. 16 (1 Aug. 1935) 319.

C1234 Ez Sez: Cutting's Mind Was Best in the Senate. *Santa Fe New Mexican*, Santa Fe, N.M. (3 Aug. 1935) 4.

C1235 Ez Sez. *Santa Fe New Mexican*, Santa Fe, N.M. (5 Aug. 1935) 4.

C1236 Ez. Sez. *Santa Fe New Mexican*, Santa Fe, N.M. (8 Aug. 1935) 4.

C1237 ✉ Italy and Abyssinia. *Morning Post*, London (10 Aug. 1935) 8.

C1238 Ez Sez. *Santa Fe New Mexican*, Santa Fe, N.M. (13 Aug. 1935) 4.

C1239 Ez Sez. *Santa Fe New Mexican*, Santa Fe, N.M. (14 Aug. 1935) 4.

C1240 Ez Sez. *Santa Fe New Mexican*, Santa Fe, N.M. (16 Aug. 1935) 4.

C1241 Ez Sez. *Santa Fe New Mexican*, Santa Fe, N.M. (17 Aug. 1935) 4.

C1242 ✉ "Time to Reform the League": Failure to Tackle Money Problems. *Morning Post*, London (22 Aug. 1935) 9.
On the League of Nations.

C1243 American Notes. *New English Weekly*, VII. 17 (5 Sept. 1935) 325.
Signed: E. P.

C1244 100 o/o Money. *New English Weekly*, VII. 17 (5 Sept. 1935) 326-7.
A review of *100 o/o Money*, by Irving Fisher.

C1245 American Notes. "As for Huey [Long] . . ." *New English Weekly*, VII. 18 (12 Sept. 1935) 345.
Signed: E. P.

C1246 ✉ Sources of Empire Decay: A Plea for Social Credit. *Morning Post*, London (13 Sept. 1935) 9.

C. CONTRIBUTIONS TO PERIODICALS

C1247 American Notes. *New English Weekly*, VII. 19 (19 Sept. 1935) 365–6.
Signed: E. P.

C1247a ✉ The Nature of Money. *Spectator*, CLV. 5595 (20 Sept. 1935) 431.

C1248 Grist . . . . *Kingwood Review*, II. 20 (22 Sept. 1935) 19.
Eight short paragraphs on various subjects, chiefly economic.

C1249 American Notes. *New English Weekly*, VII. 20 (26 Sept. 1935) 385.
Signed: E. P.

C1250 The March of Man (Goose Step). *New English Weekly*, VII. 20 (26 Sept. 1935) 386.
A review of *The March of Man*, published by the Encyclopaedia Britannica Co.

C1251 ✉ Germany Now. *New English Weekly*, VII. 20 (26 Sept. 1935) 399.

C1252 The Individual in His Milieu. A Study of Relations and Gesell. *Criterion*, XV. 58 (Oct. 1935) 30–45.

C1253 ✉ A Word from Mr. Pound. *Poetry*, XLVII. 1 (Oct. 1935) 55.
In response to Horace Gregory's review article, "The A.B.C. of Ezra Pound," in the issue for Aug.

C1254 Ez Sez. *Santa Fe New Mexican*, Santa Fe, N.M. (4 Oct. 1935) 4.

C1255 American Notes. *New English Weekly*, VII. 22 (10 Oct. 1935) 425.
Signed: E. P.

C1256 The Episcopal Spirit. *New English Weekly*, VII. 22 (10 Oct. 1935) 428.
Signed: E. P. On the current *Criterion*.

C1257 . . . The Movement of Literature. *New Democracy*, V. 4 (15 Oct. 1935) 62–63.
At head of title: "Writers must know the economic facts of modern life to write *l'histoire morale contemporaine*. Title on cover: "Literature and the New Economics."

C1258 American Notes. *New English Weekly*, VIII. 1 (17 Oct. 1935) 5.
Signed: E. P.

C1259 Again the Rev. Coughlin. *New English Weekly*, VIII. 2 (24 Oct. 1935) 26.

C1260 GLORY AND YET AGAIN GLORY. *New English Weekly*, VIII. 2 (24 Oct. 1935) 28.
Signed: Ez. P. A 20-line poem on the Lords of England.

C1261 "Vu," No. 380, and Subsequent Issues. *New Age*, LVII. 27 (31 Oct. 1935) 218–19.
A review of this French periodical, with particular reference to articles by Francis Delaisi.

C1262 American Notes. *New English Weekly*, VIII. 3 (31 Oct. 1935) 45.
Signed: E. P.

C1263 ✉ Ezra Pound Asks Questions. *Current Controversy*, New York, I. 2 (Nov. 1935) 2–3.
On the policy of the magazine.

C. CONTRIBUTIONS TO PERIODICALS

C1264 A Thing of Beauty. *Esquire*, IV. 5 (Nov. 1935) 49, 195–7.

C1265 ✉ A Matter of Interest. *Reynolds's Illustrated News*, London, 4444 (3 Nov. 1935) 8.
On war and debt.

C1266 American Notes. *New English Weekly*, VIII. 4 (7 Nov. 1935) 65–66.
Signed: E. P.

C1267 American Notes. *New English Weekly*, VIII. 5 (14 Nov. 1935) 85–86.
Signed: E. P.

C1268 The Case against Geneva. *New English Weekly*, VIII. 5 (14 Nov. 1935) 88–89.

C1269 Alberta and the British Press. *Kingwood Review*, II. 21 (15 Nov. 1935) 10.

C1270 Hands Off Alberta. *New Democracy*, V. 6 (15 Nov. 1935) 99–100.

C1271 ✉ *New Democracy*, V. 6 (15 Nov. 1935) 106.
Signed: E. P. On "gross ignorance" in economics departments of colleges and universities.

C1272 American Notes. *New English Weekly*, VIII. 6 (21 Nov. 1935) 105.
Signed: E. P.

C1273 American Notes. "Press Release No. 1." *New English Weekly*, VIII. 7 (28 Nov. 1935) 125–6.
Signed: E. P.

C1274 ✉ Mr. Hargrave's "Summer Time Ends." *New English Weekly*, VIII. 7 (28 Nov. 1935) 139.

C1275 Who Gets It? *New Democracy*, V. 7 (1 Dec. 1935) 120–2.

C1276 Jean Barral with Us. *New English Weekly*, VIII. 8 (5 Dec. 1935) 146–7.

C1277 American Notes. *New English Weekly*, VIII. 10 (19 Dec. 1935) 185.
Signed: E. P.

C1278 Organicly [*sic*] speaking. *New English Weekly*, VIII. 11 (26 Dec. 1935) 211–12.
A brief passage (on his politics) was reprinted in *Agenda*, XVII. 3/4/XVIII. 1 (Autumn/Winter/Spring 1979/1980) 74.

C1279 Twelve Years and Twelve Years. "A Keystone of Europe." *British-Italian Bulletin*, London, I. 8 (27 Dec. 1935) 1.
The *British-Italian Bulletin* was issued as a supplement to *L'Italia Nostra*, a newspaper for Italian-speaking residents of Great Britain.

1936

C1280 CANTO XLVI. *New Directions in Prose and Poetry*, Norfolk, Ct., [1] (1936) [25–29].
This first issue of the annual was published 16 Nov. 1936. 513 copies were printed, of which 204 were bound in boards, 303 in wrappers, and six copies in cloth were for presentation.

C. CONTRIBUTIONS TO PERIODICALS

C1281 Moneta fascista. *La Vita Italiana*, Rome, XXIV. 274 (Jan./June 1936) [33]–37.

C1282 Money versus Music. *Delphian Quarterly*, Chicago, Ill., XIX. 1 (Jan. 1936) [2]–6, 52.

C1283 How to Save Business. *Esquire*, V. 1 (Jan. 1936) 35, 195–6.

C1284 American Notes. *New English Weekly*, VIII. 12 (2 Jan. 1936) 225–6. Signed: E. P.

C1285 American Notes. *New English Weekly*, VIII. 13 (9 Jan. 1936) 245–6. Signed: E. P.

C1286 A World Liability. *British-Italian Bulletin*, II. 2 (10 Jan. 1936) 3.

C1287 American Notes. *New English Weekly*, VIII. 14 (16 Jan. 1936) 265. Signed: E. P.

C1288 Confucius' Formula Up-to-date. *British-Italian Bulletin*, II. 3 (18 Jan. 1936) 4.

C1289 American Notes. *New English Weekly*, VIII. 15 (23 Jan. 1936) 285. Signed: E. P. A paragraph from this article was reprinted as the first of three "Tributes to the Gesell System in the New English Weekly, Social Credit Paper of London, England," in *Way Out*, San Antonio, Texas, VI. 4 (Apr. 1936) 3.

C1290 No Tame Robots in Fascist Italy. The Intellectual Frontier. *British-Italian Bulletin*, II. 4 (25 Jan. 1936) 2.

C1291 ✉ Our Polygot [*sic*] Rulers. *Saturday Review*, London, CLXI. 4190 (25 Jan. 1936) 119.

C1292 American Notes. *New English Weekly*, VIII. 16 (30 Jan. 1936) 305.

C1293 CANTO [XLV]—"WITH USURA." *Prosperity*, London, IV. 3 (Feb. 1936) 44.

C1294 Italy's Frame-up. *British-Italian Bulletin*, II. 5 (1 Feb. 1936) 2.

C1295 Loeb Report (A Refresher). *New English Weekly*, VIII. 17 (6 Feb. 1936) 326–7.

C1296 American Notes. *New English Weekly*, VIII. 18 (13 Feb. 1936) 345–6. Signed: E. P.

C1297 American Notes. Troubles. *New English Weekly*, VIII. 19 (20 Feb. 1936) 365–6. Signed: E. P.

C1298 Jacques Duboin and the Ligue du droit au travail. *New English Weekly*, VIII. 19 (20 Feb. 1936) 368–9. A review of the first two volumes of the "Collection Ligue du droit au travail," Duboin's *En route vers l'abondance.*.

C1299 ✉ Literary Note. *New English Weekly*, VIII. 19 (20 Feb. 1936) 380.

C1300 Why I Live in Sunny Rapallo. A Matter of Degrees. *British-Italian Bulletin*, II. 9 (29 Feb. 1936) 3.

C1301 CANTO XLVI. *New Democracy*, VI. 1 (Mar. 1936) 14–16. Under the heading: "New Directions, Edited by James Laughlin IV." Reprinted in *New Directions in Prose and Poetry* (1936)—C1280

C. CONTRIBUTIONS TO PERIODICALS

C1302 American Notes. *New English Weekly*, VIII. 21 (5 Mar. 1936) 405.
Signed: E. P.

C1303 American Notes. *New English Weekly*, VIII. 22 (12 Mar. 1936) 425–6.
Signed: E. P.

C1304 For a Decent Europe. *British-Italian Bulletin*, II. 11 (14 Mar. 1936) 3.

C1305 Studi Tigulliani. *Il Mare*, XXIX. 1409 (14 Mar. 1936) [1].
Unsigned. On Antonio Vivaldi. Reprinted as *Studi Tigulliani* ([1936])—
E2n. An English translation of this article by R. Murray Schafer, "Tigullian
Studies," was printed in *Ezra Pound and Music* ([1977])—A99—pp. 384–7.

C1306 Ezra Pound, Silvershirt. *New Masses*, XVIII. 12 (17 Mar. 1936) 15–16.
A letter written to Robert C. Summerville of the Silver Shirt Legion of
America, Inc., dated: 7 May 1934; with Summerville's reply, dated: 23 May
1934.

C1307 The Church of Rome. *Social Credit*, IV. 6 (20 Mar. 1936) 45.

C1308 For a Measure. *British-Italian Bulletin*, II. 12 (21 Mar. 1936) 4.

C1309 American Notes. *New English Weekly*, VIII. 24 (26 Mar. 1936) 465.
Signed: E. P.

C1310 The Treasure of a State. *British-Italian Bulletin*, II. 13 (28 Mar. 1936) 3, 4.

C1311 L'arte di Sant'Elia a Rapallo. *Il Mare*, XXIX. 1411 (28 Mar. 1936) [1].
On the architect's drawings for the Casa Littoria to be built by Rapallo.

C1312 American Notes. *New English Weekly*, VIII. 25 (2 Apr. 1936) 489–90.
Signed: E. P.

C1313 The Return of the Native. I. *New English Weekly*, VIII. 25 (2 Apr. 1936)
493–4.
On *Economic Democracy*, by C. H. Douglas. The first of four articles.

C1314 ✉ The Church of Rome. *Social Credit*, IV. 8 (3 Apr. 1936) 63.
Correcting two errors in the article of 20 Mar.—C1307.

C1315 Great Comfort of Latin Mind: The Italian Bank Act. *British-Italian Bulletin*, II. 14 (4 Apr. 1936) 4.

C1316 The Return of the Native [II]. *New English Weekly*, VIII. 26 (9 Apr. 1936)
510.

C1317 Organic Democracy. *British-Italian Bulletin*, II. 15 (11 Apr. 1936) 2.

C1318 Studi Tigulliani. *Il Mare*, XXIX. 1413 (11 Apr. 1936) [1].
Remarks by Ezra Pound at the "ora di studio" devoted to Vivaldi. An
English translation by R. Murray Schafer, "Tigullian Studies," was printed
in *Ezra Pound and Music* ([1977])—A99—pp. 387–9.

C1319 ✉ Irresponsible Government. *Social Credit*, IV. 10 (17 Apr. 1936) 79.
On the English Government.

C1320 The Fascist Ideal. *British-Italian Bulletin*, II. 16 (18 Apr. 1936) 2.

C1321 ✉ A "New Age" Anniversary. *New Age*, VIII. 25 (23 Apr. 1936) 200.
Noting the sixth anniversary of the censoring of the issue for 17 Apr. 1930,
which was forced to appear with two pages blank.

C. CONTRIBUTIONS TO PERIODICALS

C1322 A Rising Civilisation. *British-Italian Bulletin*, II. 17 (25 Apr. 1936) 3.

C1323 Studi Tigulliani. *Il Mare*, XXIX. 1415 (25 Apr. 1936) [1].
A talk at the "seconda ora di studio" in the "gran sala municipale" at Rapallo. An English translation by R. Murray Schafer, "Tigullian Studies," was printed in *Ezra Pound and Music* ([1977])—A99—pp. 390–2.

C1324 More on "Economic Democracy." *New English Weekly*, IX. 3 (30 Apr. 1936) 51–52.
A continuation of C1313 and 1316.

C1325 ✉ The Chinese Written Character. *New English Weekly*, IX. 3 (30 Apr. 1936) 60.

C1326 ✉ *New Democracy*, VI. 3 (May 1936) 48.
Incorporated in an editorial note, "A Great Poet Leads—Will You Follow?," asking support for the periodical.

C1327 New Italy's Challenge. *British-Italian Bulletin*, II. 18 (2 May 1936) 3.

C1328 Rapallo centro di cultura. *Il Mare*, XXIX. 1416 (2 May 1936) [1].
Signed: E. P.

C1329 Un grave lutto di [Alfonso] Marconi. *Il Mare*, XXIX. 1416 (2 May 1936) [1].
With obituary note.

C1330 Last Words on Economic Democracy. *New English Weekly*, IX. 4 (7 May 1936) 69–70.
The last of four articles, of which the others are C1313, 1316, and 1324. Reprinted, in part, as "Without a Distorting Lens."

C1331 ✉ The Limits of Education. *New English Weekly*, IX. 4 (7 May 1936) 79–80.

C1332 Lazy Minds. *British-Italian Bulletin*, II. 19 (9 May 1936) 2.

C1333 ✉ The Truth about Italy. *Saturday Review*, London, CLXI. 4205 (9 May 1936) 598.

C1334 ✉ Anti-Semitism. *New English Weekly*, IX. 5 (14 May 1936) 99–100.
The second of three letters printed under this heading.

C1335 British Labour's Great Blunder: The Fascist Bogey. *British-Italian Bulletin*, II. 20 (16 May 1936) 4.

C1336 A Civilising Force on the Move: The Bank Reform. *British-Italian Bulletin*, II. 21 (23 May 1936) 3.

C1337 Waiting on M. Blum. *British-Italian Bulletin*, II. 22 (30 May 1936) 3.

C1338 Building an Empire. *British-Italian Bulletin*, II. 23 (5 [i.e. 6] June 1936) 3.

C1339 Man v. Merchandise: Fascism in Action. *British-Italian Bulletin*, II. 24 (13 June 1936) 3.

C1340 ✉ The Prospects of Social Credit. *New English Weekly*, IX. 10 (18 June 1936) 199.
The third of three letters printed under this heading.

C. CONTRIBUTIONS TO PERIODICALS

c1341 Un compianto amico: Gilbert [K.] Chesterton. *Il Mare*, XXIX. 1423 (20 June 1936) [1].
Signed: E. P. An obituary note.

c1342 Amici dell'Italia: John Celli. *Il Mare*, XXIX. 1423 (20 June 1936) [1].
Signed: E. P. With a short note in English inviting foreigners to correspond with the Union of Friends of Italy.

c1343 Just Price Error: Degrees of Honesty. *British-Italian Bulletin*, II. 26 (27 June 1936) 3.

c1344 Possiblities of Civilization: What the Small Town Can Do. *Delphian Quarterly*, XIX. 3 (July 1936) 15–17, 44.

c1345 ✉ *New Democracy*, VI. 5 (July 1936) 105.
On an article on Social Credit by Ben Blake in the *New Masses* for 26 May.

c1346 Atrophy of the Leninists. I. *New English Weekly*, IX. 12 (2 July 1936) 227–8.
The first of four instalments. Excerpts from the series were reprinted with title "Lenin" in *Agenda*, XVII. 3/4/XVIII. 1 (Autumn/Winter/Spring 1979/1980) 208–9.

c1347 ✉ The World We Are Trying to Live In. *New English Weekly*, IX. 12 (2 July 1936) 238.

c1348 Why Italy Needs No Loan: No Use for Usury. *British-Italian Bulletin*, II. 27 (4 July 1936) 4.

c1349 Atrophy of the Leninists. II. *New English Weekly*, IX. 13 (9 July 1936) 249–50.

c1350 Atrophy of the Leninists . . . III. *New English Weekly*, IX. 14 (16 July 1936) 272–3.

c1351 I violini di Marconi. *Il Mare*, XXIX. 1427 (18 July 1936) [1].
Signed: E. P. On violins owned by Alfonso Marconi at Rapallo. An English translation of this article by R. Murray Schafer, "Marconi's Violins," was printed in *Ezra Pound and Music* ([1977])—A99—pp. 392–3.

c1352 Mediaeval Music and Yves Tinayre. *Listener*, London, XVI. 393 (22 July 1936) 187–8.

c1353 Atrophy of the Leninists . . . IV. *New English Weekly*, IX. 15 (23 July 1936) 289–90.

c1354 Replying to Larrañaga. On Stamp Scrip. *New English Weekly*, IX. 16 (30 July 1936) 315–16.

c1355 Lucrum tuum damnum publicum est. *Poetry*, XLVIII. 5 (Aug. 1936) 273–5.
(In English.) Includes Ezra Pound's offer of a prize of five dollars "(that is to say, one commensurate with the earning capacity of America's four best poets) for the best translation of a Greek epigram on the subject of usury and/or usurers. The prize to be known as the Rockefeller Nickel."

c1356 To-day and To-morrow. *British-Italian Bulletin*, II. 28 (8 Aug. 1936) [1].

C. CONTRIBUTIONS TO PERIODICALS

c1357 Ezra Pound Looks at U.S.: Volitionist Economics, Labor and the U.S.A. *Connecticut American*, Bridgeport, New Haven, Ct., II. 3 (8 Aug. 1936) [1].

c1358 Built for Stability. *British-Italian Bulletin*, II. 30 (22 Aug. 1936) 3.

c1359 The Language of Money. Extracts from an Unpublished Manuscript . . . *Fig Tree*, London, I. 2 (Sept. 1936) 157–62.
Reprinted, in part, as "Sincerity."

c1360 Readers of the *B. I. B.* Listen!! *British-Italian Bulletin*, II. 32 (5 Sept. 1936) 3.
An appeal for support for the periodical. Repeated, II. 33 (12 Sept. 1936) [1].

c1361 Responsibility. *British-Italian Bulletin*, II. 32 (5 Sept. 1936) 3.

c1362 Cheapness in the Derogatory Sense. *New English Weekly*, IX. 23 (17 Sept. 1936) 369.
A review of *Inside Europe*, by John Gunther.

c1363 In Detail. *British-Italian Bulletin*, II. 34 (19 Sept. 1936) [1].

c1364 A Social Creditor Serves Notice. *Fascist Quarterly*, London, II. 4 (Oct. 1936) 492–9.

c1365 ⊠ The Printing Press Was Invented. *Poetry*, XLIX. 1 (Oct. 1936) 55.

c1366 Bulletin [I]. *New English Weekly*, IX. 25 (1 Oct. 1936) 405–6.

c1367 ⊠ The Conviction for Seditious Libel. *New English Weekly*, IX. 25 (1 Oct. 1936) 420.

c1368 Bulletin [II]. *New English Weekly*, IX. 26 (8 Oct. 1936) 425–6.

c1369 On Devaluations. *British-Italian Bulletin*, II. 37 (10 Oct. 1936) [1].

c1370 ⊠ "La Lingua Italiana." *British-Italian Bulletin*, II. 37 (10 Oct. 1936) 3. (In English.)

c1371 Mostly Quartets. *Listener*, XVI. 405 (14 Oct. 1936) 743–4.
Reprinted in *Living Age*, New York, CCCLI. 4444 (Jan. 1937) [445]–447.

c1372 Race. *New English Weekly*, X. 1 (15 Oct. 1936) 12–13.

c1373 ⊠ Note in Time. *New English Weekly*, X. 1 (15 Oct. 1936) 19.

c1374 A Good Surgeon Does Not Always Amputate. *British-Italian Bulletin*, II. 39 (24 Oct. 1936) [1].
Unsigned.

c1375 The Coward Surrealists. *Contemporary Poetry and Prose*, London, 7 (Nov. 1936) 136.

c1376 ⊠ Sweden's Middle Way. *New English Weekly*, X. 4 (5 Nov. 1936) 80.

c1377 ⊠ A Pertinent Point. *Social Credit*, V. 14 (13 Nov. 1936) 111.
On an article by Pertinax in the *Daily Telegraph*, London, for 16 Oct., on the election of the Governor of the Bank of France.

c1378 Landon, or the Loser. *New English Weekly*, X. 6 (19 Nov. 1936) 105–6.

c1379 Vale. *Poetry*, XLIX. 3 (Dec. 1936) 137–8.
An obituary tribute to Harriet Monroe.

c1380 Music and Brains. *Listener*, XVI. 412 (2 Dec. 1936) 1068.

C. CONTRIBUTIONS TO PERIODICALS

c1381 Inaction Française. *New English Weekly*, X. 8 (3 Dec. 1936) 148–9.

c1382 ✉ Orthology. *New English Weekly*, X. 8 (3 Dec. 1936) 159–60.

c1383 ✉ Gen. Gough's "Tough Job": Foreigners and the 5th Army. From Mr. Ezra Pound, the Poet. *Daily Telegraph*, London (3 Dec. 1936) 16.
Enclosing a statement signed: An American [*i.e.* Pound].

c1383a ✉ War and Pacifism. *Listener*, XVI. 414 (16 Dec. 1936) 1157.
One of two letters printed under this heading in the "Points from Letters" section.

c1384 Bravo, Roosevelt! *New English Weekly*, X. 10 (17 Dec. 1936) 187.

c1385 The Dam' Nigger and the Banana Tree. *New English Weekly*, X. 11 (24 Dec. 1936) 207–8.

c1386 PEACE RACKET, WAR RACKET. *New English Weekly*, X. 12 (31 Dec. 1936) 237.
A 35-line poem, signed: Alf Venison.

1937

c1387 Demarcations. *British Union Quarterly*, London, I. 1 (Jan./Apr. 1937) 35–40.
Two sentences were reprinted in *Agenda*, XVII. 3/4/XVIII. 1 (Autumn/Winter/Spring 1979/1980) 75.

c1388 Music in Ca' Rezzonico. *Delphian Quarterly*, XX. 1 (Jan. 1937) 2–4, 11.

c1389 Ligurian View of a Venetian Festival. *Music & Letters*, London, XVIII. 1 (Jan. 1937) [36]–41.

c1390 "Amici del Tigullio": L'arte di Luigi Franchetti: Il concerto di Mercoledì 3 Febbraio. *Il Mare*, XXX. 1455 (30 Jan. 1937) [1].
An English translation of this article by R. Murray Schafer, "The Art of Luigi Franchetti . . . ," was printed in *Ezra Pound and Music* ([1977])—A99—pp. 418–19.

c1391 Woodward (W. E.) Historian [I]. *New English Weekly*, X. 17 (4 Feb. 1937) 329–30.
A review of *A New American History*, by W. E. Woodward. Reprinted, with c1392, as "W. E. Woodward, Historian."

c1392 Woodward (W. E.) Historian . . . II. *New English Weekly*, X. 18 (11 Feb. 1937) 349–50.

c1393 "Amici del Tigullio": Il nuovo Quartetto Ungherese nel gran salone municipale di Rapallo, Giovedì 18. *Il Mare*, XXX. 1457 (13 Feb. 1937) [1], 2.
An English translation of this article by R. Murray Schafer, "The New Hungarian Quartet," was printed in *Ezra Pound and Music* ([1977])—A99—pp. 420–2.

c1394 Abdication. *Globe*, Milwaukee, Wisc., I. 1 (Mar. 1937) 82–87.
On Edward VIII.

C. CONTRIBUTIONS TO PERIODICALS

C1395 ✉ Economists and the Public. *New English Weekly*, X. 21 (4 Mar. 1937) 420.

C1396 Amici del Tigullio: Il ritorno di Gerhart Münch. Concerti Rudge-Münch, 18 e 29 Marzo–1 Aprile. *Il Mare*, XXX. 1461 (13 Mar. 1937) 2.
An English translation of this article by R. Murray Schafer, "The Return of Gerhart Münch: Rudge-Münch Concerts . . . ," was printed in *Ezra Pound and Music* ([1977])—A99—pp. 422–4.

C1397 Method. *New English Weekly*, X. 23 (18 Mar. 1937) 446–7.

C1398 ✉ The Supreme Court. *New English Weekly*, X. 24 (25 Mar. 1937) 478.

C1399 "Amici del Tigullio": Concerti del 29 Marzo e del 1 Aprile . . . *Il Mare*, XXX. 1463 (27 Mar. 1937) 2.
Signed: E. P. An English translation of this article by R. Murray Schafer, "Concerts of March 29 and April 1 . . . ," was printed in *Ezra Pound and Music* ([1977])—A99—pp. 424–5.

C1400 Intellectual Money. *British Union Quarterly*, I. 2 (Apr./June 1937) 24–34.
A brief passage was reprinted in *Agenda*, XVII. 3/4/XVIII. 1 (Autumn/Winter/Spring 1979/1980) 75.

C1401 CANTOS XLII–XLIV. *Criterion*, XVI. 64 (Apr. 1937) 405–23.

C1402 When Will School Books . . . . . . ? An Author's Ideas on "What's Wrong with Modern Education?" *Delphian Quarterly*, XX. 2 (Apr. 1937) 16–18, 24.
With reproduction, p. 16, of a portrait of Ezra Pound by Guido Tallone.

C1403 ✉ Defining Money. *New English Weekly*, X. 25 (1 Apr. 1937) 499.

C1404 ✉ Defining Money. *New English Weekly*, XI. 1 (15 Apr. 1937) 19.

C1405 Totalitarian Scholarship and the New Paideuma . . . Edited by Douglas Fox. *Germany and You*, Berlin, VII. 4/5 (25 Apr. 1937) 95–96, 123–4.

C1406 Verso un'economia ortologica. *Rassegna Monetaria*, Rome, XXXIV. 5/6 (May/June 1937) [389]–398.
Fifty offprints of this article were prepared for the author. These have special title-page: . . . *Verso un'economia ortologica. Estratto dalla Rassegna Monetaria . . . Roma, Rassegna Monetaria* [*1937*]; they collate, 12 pp., measure 25 × 18 cm., and were issued, wire-stitched, in blue-grey paper wrappers printed in black. An English version of the article, "translated by Editorial," was printed with title "Towards an Economic Orthology" in *British Union Quarterly*, I. 4 (Oct./Dec. 1937) 12–22.

C1407 Europe-MCMXXXVI: Reflections Written on the Eve of a New Era. *Globe*, I. 2 (May 1937) [106]–110.
Six paragraphs from this article, with facsimile of Ezra Pound's signature, appear on p. [6] of an unpaged pamphlet issued to publicise the periodical: *Globe, intimate journal of travel · romance · adventure · world interest: a preview of a truly international magazine* ([St. Paul, Minn., 1936]).

C1408 Revolution by Radio. *Globe*, I. 3 (June 1937) 95–97.

C1409 Systems of Compensation, by Odon Por. Translated [with notes] by Ezra Pound. *British Union Quarterly*, I. 3 (July/Sept. 1937) 31–48.

C. CONTRIBUTIONS TO PERIODICALS

C1410 L'economia ortologica. Il problema centrale. *Rassegna Monetaria*, XXXIV. 7/8 (July/Aug. 1937) [705]–715.

Fifty offprints of this article were prepared for the author. These have special title-page: . . . *L'economia ortologica: Il problema centrale. Estratto dalla Rassegna Monetaria . . . Roma, Rassegna Monetaria* [*1937*]; they collate, 13 pp., 1 blank leaf, measure 25·1 × 17·5 cm., and were issued, wire-stitched, in blue-grey paper wrappers printed in black.

C1411 D'Artagnan Twenty Years After. *Criterion*, XVI. 65 (July 1937) 606–17.

C1412 Cross-Words an Abomination. A Letter from Ezra Pound . . . *Delphian Quarterly*, XX. 3 (July 1937) 42–43.

C1413 Net Result. *Globe*, I. 4 (July 1937) 101–4.

C1414 Immediate Need of Confucius. *Aryan Path*, Bombay, India, VIII. 8 (Aug. 1937) [354]–358.

C1415 Deflation Benefit. *Globe*, I. 5 (Aug. 1937) 66–71.

C1416 Economia ortologica. Le basi etiche. *Rassegna Monetaria*, XXXIV. 9/10 (Sept./Oct. 1937) [1101]–1106.

Fifty offprints of this article were prepared for the author. These have special title-page: . . . *Economia ortologica. Le basi etiche. Estratto dalla Rassegna Monetaria . . . Roma, Rassegna Monetaria* [*1937*]; they collate, 8 pp., measure 25 × 17·5 cm., and were issued, wire-stitched, in blue-grey paper wrappers printed in black.

C1417 For Practical Purposes. *Dynamic America*, New York, V. 2 (Sept. 1937) 21.

C1418 ✉ To the Editor . . . *Criterion*, XVII. 66 (Oct. 1937) 119.

On a misquotation of Pound in Henry S. Swabey's article "The English Church and Money" in the July issue. (In the letter following, Swabey makes the same correction.)

C1419 Interview with Mrs. Unterguggenberger. *Globe*, II. 1 (Oct. 1937) 70–74.

Under the heading: "Globes Intimate Letters."

C1419a ✉ Ezra Pound. *New Verse*, London, 26/27 (Nov. 1937) 28.

An excerpt, printed as one of "Sixteen Comments on [W. H.] Auden."

C1420 Social Credit Asses. *Action*, London, 92 (18 Nov. 1937) 9.

C1421 ✉ Extension of Factual Knowledge. *New English Weekly*, XII. 6 (18 Nov. 1937) 118.

C1422 The Jefferson-Adams Correspondence. *North American Review*, New York, CCXLIV. 2 (Winter 1937/1938) 314–24.

A condensed version of "The Jefferson-Adams Letters as a Shrine and a Monument." The complete article was printed in *Impact* (1960)—A78— and, with some slight changes, in *Modern Age*, Chicago, Ill., IV. 2 (Spring 1960) 136–44. See Matthew Little's "Corrections to Gallup's *Pound* and Some History of Pound's Essays on the Jefferson-Adams Letters," in *Papers of the Bibliographical Society of America*, New York, LXXIV. 3 (3d Quarter 1980) 270–2.

C1423 ✉ Poetry. *New English Weekly*, XII. 8 (2 Dec. 1937) 158.

C1424 Vita musicale Tigulliana. *Il Mare*, XXX. 1499 (4 Dec. 1937) [1].
An English translation of this article by R. Murray Schafer, "Tigullian
Musical Life," was printed in *Ezra Pound and Music* ([1977])—A99—pp.
426–7.

C1425 The Free Dumb of the Press. *Action*, 95 (9 Dec. 1937) 7.

C1426 Thought Resistance. *Action*, 96 (16 Dec. 1937) 12.

C1427 Why Parliament's Gone to Hell. *Action*, 98 (30 Dec. 1937) 7.

C1428 Peaceways. *New English Weekly*, XII. 12 (30 Dec. 1937) 227–8.

C1429 ✉ Poetry and "Obscurity." *New English Weekly*, XII. 12 (30 Dec. 1937)
238.

1938

C1430 The Revolution Betrayed. *British Union Quarterly*, II. 1 (Jan./Mar. 1938)
36–48.

C1431 For a New Paideuma. *Criterion*, XVII. 67 (Jan. 1938) 205–13.

C1432 M. POM-POM. *Townsman*, London, I. 1 (Jan. 1938) 3.
"Caf' Conc' song" in 11 lines, nine in French, two in English.

C1433 Vou Club [Introduction]. *Townsman*, I. 1 (Jan. 1938) 4.
Preface to a selection of poems (translated from the Japanese) contributed
to the periodical *Vou*, Tokyo.

C1434 Janequin, Francesco da Milano. *Townsman*, I. 1 (Jan. 1938) 18.
An introductory note to a chorus by Clement Janequin, reduced for the
lute as "La canzone de li ucelli," by Francesco da Milano (1500), transcribed and abbreviated for the violin by Gerhart Münch. (The music, in
facsimile of Münch's manuscript, follows, pp. 19–20.)

C1435 Condensare. *Townsman*, I. 1 (Jan. 1938) 24.
A three-line note, in English, signed: E. P. Repeated in I. 2 (Apr. 1938) 18.

C1436 Stagione Musicale del Tigullio, 21 Genn.—dal 2 al 5 Febb. *Il Mare*, XXXI.
1503 (1 Jan. 1938) [1].
Signed: E. P. Reprinted as a broadside ([1938])—E2 0. An English translation of this article by R. Murray Schafer, "Tigullian Musical Season: January
21—From February 2nd to 5th," was printed in *Ezra Pound and Music*
([1977])—A99—pp. 428–9.

C1437 Stagione musicale del Tigullio: I concerti di Febbraio: Renata Borgatti
pianista. *Il Mare*, XXXI. 1504 (8 Jan. 1938) [1].
Reprinted in *Musica a Rapallo* ([1938])—E2p. An English translation by
R. Murray Schafer, "February Concerts—The Pianist Renata Borgatti,"
was printed in *Ezra Pound and Music* ([1977])—A99—pp. 429–31.

C1438 Galleria degli Ospiti. *Il Mare*, XXXI. 1504 (8 Jan. 1938) 2.
Signed: P.

C1439 Stagione musicale del Tigullio: Il nuovo quartetto Ungherese nella Gran

C. CONTRIBUTIONS TO PERIODICALS

sala del municipio di Rapallo, Venerdì, 21 gennaio . . . *Il Mare*, XXXI. 1505 (15 Jan. 1938) [1].

An English translation of this article by R. Murray Schafer, "Tigullian Musical Studies: The New Hungarian Quartet . . . ," was printed in *Ezra Pound and Music* ([1977])—A99—pp. 431–2.

C1440 Stagione musicale del Tigullio. I concerti di Febbraio: Il successo di ieri sera. *Il Mare*, XXXI. 1506 (22 Jan. 1938) [1], 2.

An English translation of this article by R. Murray Schafer, "Tigullian Musical Season: The February Concerts: Last Night's Success," was printed in *Ezra Pound and Music* ([1977])—A99—pp. 432–3.

C1441 Responsibility? Shucks! *Globe*, II. 4 (Feb./Mar. 1938) 108–11.

C1442 ✉ Friends of Spain. *New English Weekly*, XII. 21 (3 Mar. 1938) 419.

C1443 Bury the Corpse! *Action*, 109 (19 Mar. 1938) 10.

C1444 A Cultural Level (Or should we say Possibilities of Cultural Eminence?) *British Union Quarterly*, II. 2 (Apr./June 1938) 37–42.

C1445 Notes on Micro Photography. *Globe*, II. 5 (Apr./May 1938) 29.

C1446 Significato di Leo Frobenius. *Broletto*, Como, III. 28 (Apr. 1938) 32–35. Under the heading: "Servizio di comunicazioni."

C1447 Reorganize Your Dead Universities. *Delphian Quarterly*, XXI. 2 (Apr. 1938) 20–22, 28.

C1448 "Heaulmière" from the Opera Villon by Ezra Pound. *Townsman*, I. 2 (Apr. 1938) 12–18.

Four and a half pages of music with text, in reproduction of Olga Rudge's manuscript, followed by an essay entitled: "Villon and Comment." Reprinted, without the essay, in *New Directions in Prose and Poetry*, Norfolk, Ct., [3] (1938), [168–72]. (This third issue of the annual was published 5 October 1938; 823 copies were printed.)

C1449 Rothschild Arrested. *Action*, 111 (2 Apr. 1938) 13.

C1450 Britain, Who Are Your Allies? *Action*, 112 (9 Apr. 1938) 5.

C1451 [*Entry deleted.*]

C1452 "Them There Frawgs." *Action*, 114 (23 Apr. 1938) 5.
On the political situation in France.

C1453 ✉ Il problema del critico. *Meridiano di Roma*, Rome, III. 17 (24 Apr. 1938) 9.
Signed: E. P. On an article in the paper by C. Di Marzio in answer to a review by Ariele in *L'Illustrazione Italiana* of "La Figlia di Jorio."

C1454 ✉ *Courier* [of the Friends of the Library of the University of Chicago], Chicago, Ill., 10 (May 1938) [13].
On Harriet Monroe and *Poetry*.

C1455 Sense *v.* Sadism—Or Vice Versa. *Action*, 117 (14 May 1938) 13.

C1456 ✉ The War Danger. *New English Weekly*, XIII. 8 (2 June 1938) 159.

C1457 Infamy of Taxes. *Action*, 120 (4 June 1938) 13.

C. CONTRIBUTIONS TO PERIODICALS

c1458 A Place for English Writers: Definition of "Usurer." *Action*, 122 (18 June 1938) 13.

c1459 Symposium—I. Consegna. *Purpose*, London, X. 3 (July/Sept. 1938) 164–8.
"intellectual agenda for the present year." Reprinted, in part, as "Marx."

c1460 Mang Tsze (The Ethics of Mencius). *Criterion*, XVII. 69 (July 1938) 603–25.

c1461 Inexcusable Darkness. *Delphian Quarterly*, XXI. 3 (July 1938) 14–17.
With reproduction of "death" mask by Nancy Cox McCormack, p. 14, and portrait by Wyndham Lewis, p. 16. Reprinted, in part, as "A Dull Subject."

c1462 Muzik, as Mistaught. *Townsman*, I. 3 (July 1938) 8–9.
Signed: E. P.

c1463 ✉ *Townsman*, I. 3 (July 1938) 15.
An extract. On "stage stuff."

c1464 ["... a brace of axioms for all poetry"]. *Townsman*, I. 3 (July 1938) 16.
Signed: E. P.

c1465 Willam [*sic*] Carlos Williams on the Passaic River. *Townsman*, I. 3 (July 1938) 30.
A note, signed: E. P., on *Life along the Passaic River*.

c1466 ✉ Fascist Finance. *New English Weekly*, XIII. 13 (7 July 1938) 251.

c1467 Musicians. *Action*, 126 (16 July 1938) 13.

c1468 The Just Price or Why Mosley? *Action*, 130 (13 Aug. 1938) 9.

c1469 Echi della stagione lirica: Anita de Alba è possibiltà per Rapallo. *Il Mare*, XXXI. 1535 (13 Aug. 1938) [1].
An English translation of this article by R. Murray Schafer, "Anita de Alba—and Possibilities for Rapallo," was printed in *Ezra Pound and Music* ([1977])—A99—pp. 441–2.

c1470 Suggesting a Kindergarten for British M.P.s. *Action*, 131 (20 Aug. 1938) 13.

c1471 The Liberal: Request for an Effective Burial of Him. *Action*, 132 (27 Aug. 1938) 13.

c1472 Another Chance. *Poetry*, LII. 6 (Sept. 1938) 344–7.

c1473 Italian Charter of Labour. *Action*, 135 (17 Sept. 1938) 4.

c1474 Purgatory. *New English Weekly*, XIII. 25 (29 Sept. 1938) 373.
A review of *Dante's "Purgatory,"* translated by Laurence Binyon. Reprinted in *Agenda*, XVII. 3/4/XVIII. 1 (Autumn/Winter/Spring 1979/1980) 62–64.

c1475 The State Should Move like a Dance. *British Union Quarterly*, II. 4 (Oct./Dec. 1938) 43–51.

c1476 ✉ Opportunity (Problematic). *British Union Quarterly*, II. 4 (Oct./Dec. 1938) 80–81.

c1477 Binyon: Salutiamo una traduzione pregevolissima della Divina Commedia. *Broletto*, III. 34 (Oct. 1938) 14–15.

C. CONTRIBUTIONS TO PERIODICALS

Under the heading: "Servizio di comunicazioni."

c1478 A Money Is. *Delphian Quarterly*, XXI. 4 (Oct. 1938) [45]–47.

c1478a ✉ Pound on Education. *Hika*, Gambier, O., V. 1 (Oct. 1938) 11.

c1479 Musicians; God Help 'Em. *Townsman*, I. 4 (Oct. 1938) 8–9.

c1480 ✉ Author Criticises Review. Exception Taken to Use of Words "Paradox" and "Worship." *Midland Daily Telegraph*, Coventry (5 Oct. 1938)
To the reviewer.

c1481 ✉ Pity. *Action*, 139 (15 Oct. 1938) 16.
Signed: E. P.

c1482 ✉ Patriotism. *New English Weekly*, XIV. 2 (20 Oct. 1938) 32.

c1483 Union! *Action*, 140 (22 Oct. 1938) 8.

c1484 United States of Europe? *Globe*, III. 1 (Nov./Dec. 1938) 42–44.

c1485 Who Profits? *New English Weekly*, XIV. 4 (3 Nov. 1938) 54–56.

c1486 Orientamenti. *Broletto*, III. 36 (Dec. 1938) 20–21.

c1487 The First Page. And a Mission for England. *Action*, 147 (10 Dec. 1938)
8.

c1488 ✉ Chinese Literature. *New English Weekly*, XIV. 10 (15 Dec. 1938) 163.

1939

c1489 Banks Are a Blessing. *British Union Quarterly*, III. 1 (Jan./Apr. 1939) 47–
53.

c1490 René Crevel. *Criterion*, XVIII. 71 (Jan. 1939) 225–35.

c1490a ✉ Correspondence. *Examiner*, Bethlehem, Ct., II. 1 (Winter [*i.e.* Jan.]
1939) 112.
On Charles Maurras.

c1491 ✉ Mr. Pound Replies. *Musical Times*, London, 1151 (Jan. 1939) 57–58.
To the article by "Feste" on Pound's treatment of music in *Guide to Kulchur*—A45a—in the issue for Nov. 1938.

c1492 ABU SALAMMAMM—A SONG OF EMPIRE. *Townsman*, II. 5 (Jan. 1939)
4–5.
Printed in 33 lines. "Written March, 1914. Published in 'Poetry,' August,
1914 [—C154]. Unfortunately only a few copies managed to get into England at that date."—*Editorial note (by Ronald Duncan).*

c1493 SLICE OF LIFE (FABLE). *Townsman*, II. 5 (Jan. 1939) 5.
Printed in 16 lines. Reprinted in *Agenda*, XVII. 3/4/XVIII. 1 (Autumn/
Winter/Spring 1979/1980) 65.

c1494 This [T. E.] Hulme Business. *Townsman*, II. 5 (Jan. 1939) 15.
Signed: E. P.

c1495 ✉ Money and Irving Fisher. *New English Weekly*, XIV. 12/13 (5 Jan.
1939) 195.

C. CONTRIBUTIONS TO PERIODICALS

C1496 Does the Government of England Control the B. B. C.? *Action*, 150 (7 Jan. 1939) 3.

C1497 ✉ Money and Warren [*i.e.* Irving] Fisher. *New English Weekly*, XIV. 17 (2 Feb. 1939) 259–60.

C1498 ✉ [George Holden] Tinkham Suggested for President. *Boston Herald*, Boston, Mass. (7 Feb. 1939) 10.

C1499 Concerti Mozartiani a Rapallo, in Marzo. *Il Mare*, XXXII. 1561 (11 Feb. 1939) [1].
Unsigned, but almost certainly by Ezra Pound (who organised these concerts). Reprinted in *Sedici sonate di Mozart* ... ([1939])—E2q. An English translation of this article by R. Murray Schafer, "Mozart Concerts in March in Rapallo," was printed in *Ezra Pound and Music* ([1977])—A99—pp. 448–9.

C1500 Are Universities Valid? *New English Weekly*, XIV. 19 (16 Feb. 1939) 281–2.

C1501 ✉ USURY. *New English Weekly*, XIV. 19 (16 Feb. 1939) 292.
A poem of 13 lines responding to Ronald Duncan's "Poem" in the issue for 2 Feb.

C1502 Ezra Pound Asks: 'Was the Ideal Liberty?' *Action*, 160 (18 Mar. 1939) 12.

C1503 ✉ Value. *New English Weekly*, XIV. 24 (23 Mar. 1939) 371–2.

C1504 The "Criterion" Passes. *British Union Quarterly*, III. 2 (Apr./June 1939) 60–72.
"Notes on the Solitudes and Depressions of my esteemed and distinguished contemporary, Mr. Thos. Stearns Eliot." A paragraph was reprinted in *Agenda*, XVII. 3/4/XVIII. 1 (Autumn/Winter/Spring 1979/1980) 75.

C1505 Communications. Introductory Text-Book ... [Followed by Four Brief Essays: I. Money; II. The Nazi Movement in Germany; III. Vocabulaire: But Will They Come When You Call Them?; IV. Bibliography (of Books as yet Unwritten but Wanted)]. *Townsman*, II. 6 (Apr. 1939) 12–13.

C1505a ✉ *Thursday*, Olivet College, Olivet, Mich. (6 Apr. 1939)
A letter to the Editors of this student publication, reproduced from typewritten copy. Reprinted in *American Literature*, XLIV. 3 (Nov. 1972) 467–9—C1940.

C1506 Gold Brokers. *Action*, 163 (8 Apr. 1939) 12.

C1507 L'ultimo "libro" di Ezra Pound. *Il Mare*, XXXII. 1569 (8 Apr. 1939) [1].
A note, followed by Italian translation of *Introductory Text Book* ([1939])—E2r.

C1508 ✉ Value. *New English Weekly*, XIV. 27 (13 Apr. 1939) 419.

C1509 Ezra Pound on Gold, War, and National Money. *Capitol Daily*, Washington, D. C., V. 89 (9 May 1939) [1], 4–5.
Reprinted as "Gold, War, and National Money" in *Mood*, St. Louis, Mo., 24 (Fall 1950) 3–10 (see C1726).

C. CONTRIBUTIONS TO PERIODICALS

c1510 Condutture avvelenate . . . *Meridiano di Roma*, IV. 19 (14 May 1939) 9.

c1511 Introductory Text-Book ⟨In Four Chapters⟩. *Furioso*, New Haven, Ct., I. 1 (Summer 1939) 28.

A reprint of *Introductory Text Book* ([1939])—E2r. Reprinted also, with brief notes in Japanese, in *Vou*, Tokyo, Japan, 30 (Oct. 1940) 21–22; and in other periodicals.

c1512 The Cabinet of a Dream, and Congress Should Go on the Air. *Greenwich Time*, Greenwich, Ct. (13 July 1939) 4.

Printed on the editorial page, under the heading: "The Forum."

c1513 ✉ Value. *New English Weekly*, XV. 14 (20 July 1939) 228.

c1514 Ford Madox (Hueffer) Ford; Obit. *Nineteenth Century and After*, London, CXXVI. 750 (Aug. 1939) 178–81.

Reprinted in *Furioso*, I. 3 (Spring 1940) 1–3, and, as part of an "Homage to Ford Madox Ford 1875–1939," in *New Directions*, 7 (1942) 479–83 (see C1623).

c1515 Statues of Gods. *Townsman*, II. 7 (Aug. 1939) 14.

c1516 . . . Mr. Chris Hollis in Need of a Guide! *Action*, 182 (19 Aug. 1939) 11.

c1517 Senza veleno. *Meridiano di Roma*, IV. 34 (27 Aug. 1939) [1].

c1518 ✉ The Ethical Issue. *New English Weekly*, XV. 23 (21 Sept. 1939) 307.

c1519 Un modo di comunicare. *Meridiano di Roma*, IV. 38 (24 Sept. 1939) [1].

c1520 ✉ On the Degrees of Honesty in Various Occidental Religions. *Aryan Path*, X. 10 (Oct. 1939) [510]–514.

c1521 ✉ Rettifica. *Meridano di Roma*, IV. 41 (15 Oct. 1939) [12].

Correcting a typographical error in his "Un modo di comunicare"—C1519.

c1522 Il giudizio di uno straniero. *AntiEuropa*, Rome, X. 11/12 (Nov./Dec. 1939) 718.

A section of this issue of the magazine is titled: "AntiLei," and Ezra Pound's contribution concerns the use in Italian of the form "Lei."

c1523 Religio. *Townsman*, II. 8 (Nov. 1939) 4–5.

A sub-section is titled: "Ecclesia."

c1524 ✉ Una lettera di Ezra Pound. *Prospettive*, Rome, III. 9 (15 Nov. 1939) [22].

In English. To Curzio Malaparte, the Editor.

c1525 Risveglio Vivaldiano. *Il Mare*, XXXII. 1602 (25 Nov. 1939) 3.

An English translation of this article by R. Murray Schafer, "The Vivaldi Revival," was printed in *Ezra Pound and Music* ([1977])—A99—pp. 450–1.

c1526 Vocale o verbale. *Meridiano di Roma*, IV. 47 (26 Nov. 1939) 3.

An English translation of this article by R. Murray Schafer, "Vocal or Verbal," was printed in *Ezra Pound and Music* ([1977])—A99—pp. 451–5.

c1527 Study of Noh Continues in West. Pound Outlines New Approach to Drama Using New Media. *Japan Times & Mail*, Tokyo (10 Dec. 1939) [8].

"Specially written for The Japan Times."

C. CONTRIBUTIONS TO PERIODICALS

1940

C1528 FIVE POEMS. *Furioso*, I. 2 (New Year Issue 1940) 5.
Contents: More—On the Elevation of Jackie—Parisian Winter (1923)—
The Draughty House ("ventus horribilem")—Spiaggia 1937.

C1529 ⊠ Fascism and Bolshevism. *Action*, 200 (4 Jan. 1940) 7.

C1530 A Letter form Rapallo: Annual Music Week Proposed to Introduce Each
Year Insufficiently Known Composer. *Japan Times & Mail*, Tokyo (7 & 8
Jan. 1940) [8].
"Special to The Japan Times."

C1531 Ancora pericolo. *Meridiano di Roma*, V. 1 (7 Jan. 1940) [1]–2.
Under the heading: "Lettere dall'America."

C1532 "No sacrificate ad uno spirito che non vi appartiene." *Meridiano di Roma*,
V. 4 (28 Jan. 1940) [1].

C1533 ⊠ Communication . . . *Hika*, Gambier, O., VI. 4 (Feb. 1940) 14.
With reprint of *Introductory Text Book* ([1939])—E2r.

C1534 The Inedible [*i.e.* gold]. *Townsman*, III. 10 (Feb. 1940) 2.

C1535 Cinema-movimento. *Meridiano di Roma*, V. 5 (4 Feb. 1940)

C1535a ⊠ Ezra Pound e i surrealisti. *Prospettive*, IV. 2 (15 Feb. 1940) 11.
Two letters, one in English, the other in Italian. To Curzio Malaparte, the
Editor.

C1535b Un polemista. *Libro e Moschetto*, Milan, XIV. 18 (24 Feb. 1940) 5.

C1536 Ezra Pound Asks Scholars Here to Solve Issues: Japanese Intellectuals
Can Discuss Them with Calm without Political Influence. *Japan Times &
Mail*, Tokyo (3 & 4 Mar. 1940) 6, 7.
Reprinted as "From Rappalo [*sic*]: An Ezra Pound Letter" in *Japan Times
Weekly*, V. 11 (14 Mar. 1940) 410–11.

C1537 The Inedible [*i.e.* gold]: Russia Has It. *America*, New York, LXII. 22 (9
Mar. 1940) 593–4.
Differs in content from C1534. Quoted extensively in *Social Justice*, London
(25 Mar. 1940) 14, under title: "You Can't Eat Gold, but Russia Has It."

C1538 ⊠ *Action*, 210 (14 Mar. 1940) 7.

C1539 [*Entry deleted.*]

C1540 ⊠ The Rights of Man. *New English Weekly*, XVI. 22 (21 Mar. 1940) 335.

C1540a Fuori i nomi. *Libro e Moschetto*, Milan, XIV. 22 (23 Mar. 1940) 2.

C1541 Gli Ebrei e questa guerra. *Meridiano di Roma*, V. 12 (24 Mar. 1940) [1]–2.
A summary in English, "The Jews and This War," was printed in *News
from Germany*, Starnberg, Bavaria, 10 (May 1940) 15–16.

C1541a ⊠ From Rappallo. *Hika*, VI. 6 (Apr. 1940) 5.

C1542 Economia ortologica. Di alcune intuizioni. *Rassegna Monetaria*, XXXVII.
4 (Apr. 1940) [278]–281.

C1543 ⊠ Creation of Credit. *Action*, 213 (4 Apr. 1940) 7.

C. CONTRIBUTIONS TO PERIODICALS

C1544 ☒ Is It about Gold? *New English Weekly*, XVI. 24 (4 Apr. 1940) 359.

C1545 ☒ War Finance. *New English Weekly*, XVI. 25 (11 Apr. 1940) 376.

C1546 ☒ Nego. *Giornale di Genova*, Genoa (13 Apr. 1940) 3.

C1547 ☒ Chinese Pronunciation—Spring Fashion. *Time and Tide*, XXI. 15 (13 Apr. 1940) 390.

C1548 Antifascisti. *Meridiano di Roma*, V. 15 (14 Apr. 1940) [1].

C1549 ☒ Una lettera di Ezra Pound. *Prospettive*, IV. 4 (15 Apr. 1940) 19.
For the most part in Italian. To Curzio Malaparte, the Editor.

C1550 From Rappalo [*sic*]: An Ezra Pound Letter. *Japan Times Weekly*, V. 16 (18 Apr. 1940) 590–1.

C1550a Paralleli storici. *Libro e Moschetto*, Milan, XIV. 26 (20 Apr. 1940) [1].

C1551 ☒ Comment on Lord Lothian. *Time and Tide*, XXI. 19 (11 May 1940) 507.

C1552 Faust, i protocolli ed il principio satanico. *Meridiano di Roma*, V. 19 (12 May 1940) [1].

C1553 Tri-Lingual System Proposed for World Communications: Noted Scholar of Noh Suggests Bilingual or Trilingual Edition of Hundred Best Books on Japanese Literature. *Japan Times & Mail*, Tokyo (17 May 1940)
"Special to The Japan Times."

C1554 ☒ German Romanticism. *New English Weekly*, XVII. 6 (30 May 1940) 76.

C1555 Classicismo e nemici del classicismo in America. *Maestrale*, Rome, I. 1 (June 1940) 46–48.

C1556 Ammassi. *Townsman*, III. 11 (June 1940) [11].
(In English.) Signed: E. P.

C1557 Deus est amor. *Townsman*, III. 11 (June 1940) [14].
(In English.)

C1558 Utopia. *Townsman*, III. 11 (June 1940) [15].
A one-line epigram, signed: E. P.

C1559 Snobismi e sindacati. *Meridiano di Roma*, V. 22 (2 June 1940) [1].

C1560 ☒ Request for More Light. *New English Weekly*, XVII. 7 (6 June 1940) 87–88.

C1561 From Rappalo [*sic*]: An Ezra Pound Letter. Why There Is a War in Europe. *Japan Times Weekly*, VI. 7 (13 June 1940) 244–5.

C1562 Da far capire agli Americani. *Meridiano di Roma*, V. 26 (30 June 1940) [1]–2.

C1563 The American System, Why Not Revive It? *Delphian Quarterly*, XXIII. 3 (July 1940) [17]–18.
Includes *Introductory Text Book* ([1939])—E2r.

C1564 Valuta, lavoro e decadenze. *Meridiano di Roma*, V. 27 (7 July 1940) [1].

C1565 Letter from Rapallo: ... In War Appear Responsibilities. *Japan Times & Mail*, Tokyo (21 & 22 July 1940) 8,(?).

C. CONTRIBUTIONS TO PERIODICALS

"Special to The Japan Times."

C1566 Perchè certe nebbie esistono ancora. *Meridiano di Roma*, V. 29 (28 [*i.e.* 21] July 1940) [1]–2.
Reprinted as "Nebbie."

C1567 Money: Will Experts Please Define It? *America*, LXIII. 16 (27 July 1940) 429–30.

C1568 Il sistema dei vampiri. *Meridiano di Roma*, V. 31 (4 Aug. 1940) [1]–2.

C1568a Letter from Rapallo. *Japan Times & Mail*, Tokyo (12 Aug. 1940) 8.
Reprinted as "From Rappalo [*sic*]: An Ezra Pound Letter" in *Japan Times Weekly*, VI. 17 (22 Aug. 1940) 604–5.

C1569 Opinioni da rivedere. *Meridiano di Roma*, V. 33 (18 Aug. 1940) [1].

C1570 Rapallo Letter. *Japan Times & Mail*, Tokyo (26 Aug. 1940) 8.
Includes text of *Introductory Text-Book* ([1939])—E21. Reprinted as "From Rappalo [*sic*]: An Ezra Pound Letter" in *Japan Times Weekly*, VII. 1 (5 Sept. 1940) 21–22, 24.

C1571 Sul serio. *Meridiano di Roma*, V. 35 (1 Sept. 1940) [1]–2.

C1572 [*Entry deleted.*]

C1573 Letter from Rapallo. *Japan Times & Mail*, Tokyo (1 & 2 Sept. 1940)
Reprinted as "From Rappalo [*sic*]: An Ezra Pound Letter," in *Japan Times Weekly*, VII. 2 (12 Sept. 1940) 54, 62.

C1574 I classici dell'avvenire. *Meridiano di Roma*, V. 37 (15 Sept. 1940) [1]–2.

C1575 Letter from Rapallo. *Japan Times & Mail*, Tokyo (29 Sept. 1940) 8.
"Special to The Japan Times." Reprinted in *Japan Times Weekly*, VII. 6 (10 Oct. 1940) 204.

C1576 Giappone. *Meridiano di Roma*, V. 39 (29 Sept. 1940) 9.

C1577 Di una nuova economia. *Meridiano di Roma*, V. 41 (13 Oct. 1940) [1].

C1578 Libero scambio. *Meridiano di Roma*, V. 42 (20 Oct. 1940) [1].

C1579 ⊠ Ammassi. *Townsman*, III. 12 (Nov. 1940) 26.
An extract, continuing the subject of the earlier article with this title—C1556.

C1580 In favore dei "due latini." *Meridiano di Roma*, V. 44 (3 Nov. 1940) 5.

C1581 Usura e società anonime. *Meridiano di Roma*, V. 47 (24 Nov. 1940) [1].

C1581a ... "Culture as (unusually) Usual" ... *Town & Country*, New York, XCV. 4219 (Dec. 1940) 78, 116.
At head of title: "Music by Ezra Pound. Titled:"

C1582 Di un sistema economico. *Meridiano di Roma*, V. 48 (1 Dec. 1940) [1]–2.
This and the preceding issue, containing Ezra Pound's list of 18 points submitted to "a personage of the Italian Government [*i.e.* Benito Mussolini]" on 30 Jan. 1933, were excluded from the U.S. mails because of Pound's contributions. See prefatory note to *Oro e Lavoro* ([1944])—A52a.

C1583 ⊠ I Bramini e l'usura. *Meridiano di Roma*, V. 49 (8 Dec. 1940) [12].
On C1581.

C. CONTRIBUTIONS TO PERIODICALS

C1584 Profili Americani. *Meridiano di Roma*, V. 52 (29 Dec. 1940) [1]–2.

1941

C1585 Augment of the Novel. *New Directions in Prose & Poetry*, 6 (1941) 705–13.
This sixth volume of the annual was published November 1941. 1500 copies were printed. Ezra Pound's contribution was reprinted in *Agenda*, VII. 3/XVIII. 1 (Autumn/Winter 1969/1970) 49–56.

C1586 Anglo-Israele. *Meridiano di Roma*, VI. 2 (12 Jan. 1941) [1].

C1587 ⊠ Dei due latini e di altre cose. *Meridiano di Roma*, VI. 3 (19 Jan. 1941) [12].

C1588 La moneta. *Meridiano di Roma*, VI. 6 (9 Feb. 1941) [1].

C1589 Libertà e dovere. *Meridiano di Roma*, VI. 8 (23 Feb. 1941) [1]–2.

C1590 The Central Problem. *Townsman*, IV. 13 (Mar. 1941) 13–17.
"This essay is contained in Mr. Pound's unpublished book, 'Money and Morals,' edited by the Rev. Henry Swabey." In part, a condensed English version of "L'economia ortologica: Il problema centrale," in *Rassegna Monetaria* (July/Aug. 1937)—C1410.

C1591 ⊠ Una lettera di Ezra Pound. *Prospettive*, V. 14/15 (15 Mar. 1941) 26. (In Italian.) To Curzio Malaparte, the Editor.

C1592 Tetti rossi. *Meridiano di Roma*, VI. 11 (16 Mar. 1941) [1].

C1593 Delle traduzioni. *Meridiano di Roma*, VI. 12 (23 Mar. 1941) [12].

C1594 Le fonti d'informazione del Signor Roosevelt. *Meridiano di Roma*, VI. 13 (30 Mar. 1941) [1].
Reprinted in *Il Lavoro Fascista*, Rome, Livorno (1 Apr. 1941).

C1595 Usura e coscienza. *Meridiano di Roma*, VI. 15 (13 Apr. 1941) [1].

C1596 Triplice infamia. *Meridiano di Roma*, VI. 16 (20 Apr. 1941) 2.

C1597 Confucio filosofo statale. *Meridiano di Roma*, VI. 19 (11 May 1941) [1]–2.

C1598 Impedimenti alla critica. *Vedetta Mediterranea*, 9 (19 May 1941)
Reprinted as "Ostacoli alla critica" in *Studi Americani*, Rome, 4 (1958).

C1599 Ancora Jefferson. *Meridiano di Roma*, VI. 21 (25 May 1941) [1].

C1600 Narrare. *Lettere d'Oggi*, Rome, III. 5/6 (June/July 1941) 61–62.

C1600a Saturno Montanari. *Meridiano di Roma*, VI. 23 (9 June 1941) 1.
Signed: Nemo. Attributed to Ezra Pound in Niccolò Zapponi's *L'Italia di Ezra Pound* ([1976])—B119—p. 123.

C1601 Vivaldi e Siena. *Meridiano di Roma*, VI. 24 (15 June 1941) 4.
An English translation of this article by R. Murray Schafer, "Vivaldi and Siena," was printed in *Ezra Pound and Music* ([1977])—A99—pp. 459–63.

C1602 Verso l'ortologia. *Meridiano di Roma*, VI. 25 (22 June 1941) [1].

C1603 Interesse al cento per cento. *Meridiano di Roma*, VI. 27 (6 July 1941) [1].

C1604 ⊠ Interesse al cento per cento. *Meridiano di Roma*, VI. 28 (13 July 1941)

C. CONTRIBUTIONS TO PERIODICALS

An extract, correcting a misprint in the article—C1603.

C1605 Monopoli. *Meridiano di Roma*, VI. 33 (17 Aug. 1941)
Signed: Nemo.

C1606 Jus italicum. *Meridiano di Roma*, VI. 34 (24 Aug. 1941) [1].
(In Italian.)

C1607 ✉ Ubicumque lingua romana ibi Roma. *Meridiano di Roma*, VI. 34 (24 Aug. 1941) [8].
(In Italian.)

C1608 Il problema delle tasse. *Meridiano di Roma*, VI. 35 (31 Aug. 1941) [1].

C1609 "Says Ez" [a letter to William Carlos Williams]. *Decision*, New York, II. 3 (Sept. 1941) 23–24.
Printed at the end of "Ezra Pound: Lord Ga-Ga," by Williams, pp. 16–23.

C1610 Il grano. *Meridiano di Roma*, VI. 36 (7 Sept. 1941) [1].

C1611 Critica e criteri. *Meridiano di Roma*, VI. 38 (21 Sept. 1941) [1].

C1612 Arachidi. *Meridiano di Roma*, VI. 40 (5 Oct. 1941) [1].

C1613 L'Ebreo, patologia incarnata. *Meridiano di Roma*, VI. 41 (12 Oct. 1941) [1].
The second section, captioned: "Bolscevismo e usura," was reprinted (with a slight change in the opening sentence) as "Considerazioni sull'usura" in *La Cultura nel Mondo*, Rome, I. 9/10 (Sept./Oct. 1958) 396.

C1614 ✉ Corsivo. *Meridiano di Roma*, VI. 41 (12 Oct. 1941) [8].
Signed: E. P.

C1615 ✉ *Meridiano di Roma*, VI. 42 (19 Oct. 1941)
(In Italian.)

C1616 Studio integrale. *Meridiano di Roma*, VI. 43 (26 Oct. 1941) 3.
A translation of *The Great Digest* of Confucius, Chapter I, by Ezra Pound and Alberto Luchini. Reprinted, with the Chinese text, in *Confucio. Ta S'eu. Dai Gaku. Studio integrale* (1942)—B46—pp. [3]–8.

C1617 Ta Hio. *Meridiano di Roma*, VI. 46 (16 Nov. 1941) 7.
On Confucius.

C1618 ✉ Da segnalare. *Meridiano di Roma*, VI. 46 (16 Nov. 1941) [8].
Signed: E. P. On the *Rivista Bancaria*.

C1619 Oro. *Meridiano di Roma*, VI. 47 (23 Nov. 1941) [1].
With reference to the Funk-Riccardi meeting.

C1620 Sul discorso di Hitler. *Meridiano di Roma*, VI. 48 (30 Nov. 1941) [1].

C1621 Architettura. *Meridiano di Roma*, VI. 50 (14 Dec. 1941) [8].

C1622 ✉ A proposito di precisione. *Meridiano di Roma*, VI. 52 (28 Dec. 1941) [8].
Pointing out that one should refer to the United States of *North* America

1942

C1623 Homage to Ford Madox Ford 1875–1939. *New Directions*, Norfolk, Ct., 7 (1942) 479–83.

C. CONTRIBUTIONS TO PERIODICALS

One of a group of tributes printed under this heading, pp. [441]–491. (This seventh volume of the annual was published November 1942. 1500 copies were printed.) A reprint of C1514.

C1624 [*Entry deleted.*]

C1625 CANTO PROCEEDING (72 CIRCA). *Vice Versa*, New York, I. 3/4/5 (Jan. 1942) 1–2.
Forty-one lines. Reprinted, with some changes, in *Drafts & Fragments of Cantos CX-CXVII* ([1969])—A91—as a fragment unassigned.

C1626 Mondiale. *Meridiano di Roma*, VII. 3 (18 Jan. 1942) [1].

C1627 ✉ A proposito dell'alfabeto nipponico. *Meridiano di Roma*, VII. 5 (1 Feb. 1942) [8].

C1628 Wallace. *Meridiano di Roma*, VII. 8 (22 Feb. 1942) [1]–2.
(In Italian.)

C1629 Pace decisiva. *Meridiano di Roma*, VII. 11 (15 Mar. 1942) [1].

C1630 Pubblicità dannata. *Meridiano di Roma*, VII. 13 (29 Mar. 1942) [1].

C1631 ✉ Per una biblioteca fascista. *Meridiano di Roma*, VII. 14 (5 Apr. 1942) [8].

C1632 La guerra degli usurai. *Meridiano di Roma*, VII. 18 (3 May 1942) [1].
The second and third sections are captioned, respectively: "Forze 'naturali' e lo sforzo umano nell'economia," and "Usura contro umanità."

C1633 Idee fondamentali. *Meridiano di Roma*, VII. 19 (10 May 1942) [1].

C1634 Ob pecuniae scarsitatem. *Meridiano di Roma*, VII. 23 (7 June 1942) [1]–2.
(In Italian.)

C1635 [Excerpts from letters to Allanah Harper]. *Partisan Review*, New York, IX. 4 (July/Aug. 1942) 316–17.
Quoted in an article by Allanah Harper, "A Magazine [*i.e. Échanges*] and Some People in Paris."

C1636 Moneta prescrittibile. *Meridiano di Roma*, VII. 27 (5 July 1942) [1].

C1637 La cambiale. *Meridiano di Roma*, VII. 31 (2 Aug. 1942) [1]–2.
Reprinted in *La Cultura nel Mondo*, Rome, I. 1 (Jan. 1958) 9–12.

C1638 Breviora. *Meridiano di Roma*, VII. 35 (30 Aug. 1942) [1].

C1639 Utopia. *Meridiano di Roma*, VII. 37 (13 Sept. 1942) [1].
(In Italian.)

C1640 Credito sociale. *Meridiano di Roma*, VII. 39 (27 Sept. 1942) [1].
The second section is captioned: "Distinguiamo."

C1641 Appunti . . . *Meridiano di Roma*, VII. 43 (25 Oct. 1942) [8].
Contents: Memoriale—Ed inoltre—Numisma.

C1642 Nella pelle di pantera. *Meridiano di Roma*, VII. 44 (1 Nov. 1942) [1]–2.

C1643 ✉ Erratum. *Meridiano di Roma*, VII. 44 (1 Nov. 1942) [8].
Correcting a misprint in his "Appunti"—C1641.

C1644 La seconda ondata. *Meridiano di Roma*, VII. 45 (8 Nov. 1942) [1].

C. CONTRIBUTIONS TO PERIODICALS

c1645 Rosanov e Cruet. *Meridiano di Roma*, VII. 50 (13 Dec. 1942) [1]–2.

c1646 Idee e libri per la vittoria dell'Asse. *Meridiano di Roma*, VII. 51 (20 Dec. 1942) [1].

c1647 ✉ Roma e gli stranieri. *Meridiano di Roma*, VII. 52 (27 Dec. 1942) [8]. With, at the end, a note on his "Rosanov e Cruet"—c1645.

1943

c1648 Dalle parole alla strage. *Meridiano di Roma*, VIII. 2 (10 Jan. 1943) [1].

c1649 ✉ Roma, gli studi e gli stranieri. *Meridiano di Roma*, VIII. 2 (10 Jan. 1943) [8]. Signed: E. P.

c1650 Seconda censura. *Meridiano di Roma*, VIII. 6 (7 Feb. 1943) [1]–2.

c1651 Problemi da risolvere. *Meridiano di Roma*, VIII. 7 (14 Feb. 1943) [1]. *Contents:* (1) Il problema ebraico—(2) Questione della burocrazia—(3) Propaganda.

c1652 Arretrati e snobisti. *Meridiano di Roma*, VIII. 10 (7 Mar. 1943) [1].

c1653 Problemi economici . . . *Meridiano di Roma*, VIII. 14 (4 Apr. 1943) [1]–2. Reprinted also as "Risparmio."

c1654 Amor di patria. *Meridiano di Roma*, VIII. 16 (18 Apr. 1943) [1].

c1655 Scrittori e zavorra. *Meridiano di Roma*, VIII. 18 (2 May 1943) [1]. Under the heading: "Letteratura americana."

c1656 L'usura e i debiti. *Meridiano di Roma*, VIII. 18 (2 May 1943) [8]. Signed: E. P.

c1657 ✉ Dell'importazione dei libri. *Meridiano di Roma*, VIII. 19 (9 May 1943) [8].

c1658 Terminologia. *Meridiano di Roma*, VIII. 20 (16 May 1943) [8].

c1659 Sulla propaganda. *Meridiano di Roma*, VIII. 23 (6 June 1943) [1].

c1660 Lentamente: sugli studi classici. *Meridiano di Roma*, VIII. 37 (12 Sept. 1943) [1].

c1661 ✉ *Il Lavoro*, Genoa (19 Oct. 1943) (In Italian.) On war, usury, and international bankers.

c1662 La guerra. *Il Popolo di Alessandria*, Alessandria ([ca. 9?] Nov. 1943) Signed: Ez. P. Reprinted as a letter to the Editor in *Il Lavoro*, Genoa (9 Nov. 1943) [1].

1944

c1663 Il fattore economico. Perno. *La Provincia Lavoratrice*, Vercelli (6 Jan. 1944) [1].

c1664 ✉ Da Rapallo. *La Fiamma Repubblicana*, (16 Jan. 1944)

C. CONTRIBUTIONS TO PERIODICALS

c1664a Una nazione che non vuole indebitarsi fa rabbia agli usurai. *Il Popolo di Alessandria*, Alessandria (10 Feb. 1944) [1].
Unsigned; but see E2u.

c1665 Pagamenti. *Il Popolo di Alessandria*, Alessandria (13 Feb. 1944) [1].
Signed: Ez. P.

c1665a La guerra. *Il Popolo di Alessandria*, Alessandria (13 Feb. 1944) 2.
Signed: Ez. P.

c1665b Il tesoro di una nazione non è il danaro ma l'onestà. *Il Popolo di Alessandria*, Alessandria (17 Feb. 1944) 2.
This one sentence, signed: Ez. Pound.

c1666 Il perno. *Il Popolo di Alessandria*, Alessandria (13 Feb. 1944)
Signed: Ez. P.

c1667 Il fattore economico. Il nemico. *La Provincia Lavoratrice*, Vercelli (24 Feb. 1944) [1].

c1668 Un vantaggio dell'essere Repubblica. *Il Popolo di Alessandria*, Alessandria (27 Feb. 1944) 2.
In the same issue, p. [1], is printed, under the heading: "Fiamma sul Tigullio," the (first) manifesto of the "Scrittori del Tigullio," signed by Ezra Pound and four Italian writers, the names arranged alphabetically. At least a part of the manifesto was written by Pound. (It was printed also in broadside form, on a leaf of unwatermarked wove paper measuring 28·3 × 27·7 cm., with text beginning: *GLI SCRITTORI DEL TIGULLIO salutano gli altri scrittori d'Italia,* | *dichiarando che:* | *[declaration in four sections]* | *GILBERTO GABURRI* | *EZRA POUND* | *EDGARDO ROSSARO* | *GIUSEPPE SOLDATO* | *MICHELE TANZI [Rapallo? 1944]*. A . . . *Secondo Manifesto del Tigullio,* dated: 23 Mar. 1945, is also signed by Pound, with G. B. Nassano, Rossaro, and Soldato, and with Pound's "Vivere in modo che le generazioni future abbiano a ringraziarti" quoted at upper right, but the text bears little evidence of his authorship.

c1669 Banchieri. *Il Popolo di Alessandria*, Alessandria (2 Mar. 1944) [1].
Signed: Ez. P.

c1670 La stampa. *Il Popolo di Alessandria*, Alessandria (2 Mar. 1944) [1].
Signed: Ez. P.

c1671 Giallo. *Il Popolo di Alessandria*, Alessandria (2 Mar. 1944) [1].
Quoting a passage from Anatole France, signed: E. P.

c1671a Liberali. *Il Popolo di Alessandria*, Alessandria (5 Mar. 1944) [1].
Unsigned, but marked as his on Ezra Pound's file copy (Yale).

c1672 È peccato ma . . . *Il Popolo di Alessandria*, Alessandria (9 Mar. 1944) [1].
Signed: Ez. P.

c1673 Etica. *Il Popolo di Alessandria*, Alessandria (12 Mar. 1944) [1].
Signed: Ez. P.

c1674 Razza o malattia. *Il Popolo di Alessandria*, Alessandria (12 Mar. 1944) [1].
Signed: Ez. P.

C. CONTRIBUTIONS TO PERIODICALS

C1675 "Una riforma." *Il Popolo di Alessandria*, Alessandria (16 Mar. 1944) [1].
Signed: Ez.P.

C1676 Commemorando Mazzini. *Il Popolo di Alessandria*, Alessandria (19 Mar.
1944) [1].
Signed: Ez. P.

C1677 Cosa? *Il Popolo di Alessandria*, Alessandria (23 Mar. 1944) [1].
Signed: Ez. P.

C1678 Educazione. *Il Popolo di Alessandria*, Alessandria (23 Mar. 1944) [1].
Signed: Ez. P.

C1679 Posizione. *Il Popolo di Alessandria*, Alessandria (26 Mar. 1944) [1].
Signed: Ez. P. Reprinted in *La Destra*, Rome, II. 11/12 (Nov./Dec. 1972)
119–20.

C1680 E. poi? *Il Popolo di Alessandria*, Alessandria (30 Mar. 1944) [1].
Signed: Ez. P.

C1681 Oro e lavoro. *Il Secolo XIX*, Genoa (6 Apr. 1944) [1].
Excerpts on "l'usurocrazia" reprinted from the first section of *Oro e Lavoro*
([1944])—A52a.

C1682 ✉ *La Marina Repubblicana*, Vicenza, I. 6 (16 Apr. 1944) [1].
An extract and a note are quoted under the heading: "Gli ignoranti" in a
column "Servizio di rotta," signed a. p. [*i.e.* Andrea Pais, the Editor].

C1682a E i massoni? *Il Popolo di Alessandria*, Alessandria (16 Apr. 1944) [1].
Signed: Ez. P.

C1683 Scopo o tecnica. *Il Popolo di Alessandria*, Alessandria (20 Apr. 1944) [1].
Signed: Ez. P. Reprinted in *La Destra*, II. 11/12 (Nov./Dec. 1972) 120.

C1684 Cambiamento di ditta. *Il Popolo di Alessandria*, Alessandria (20 Apr. 1944)
[2].
Signed: Ez. P.

C1685 Non insabbiarsi. *Il Popolo di Alessandria*, Alessandria (23 Apr. 1944) [1].
Signed: Ez. P. Reprinted in *La Destra*, II. 11/12 (Nov./Dec. 1972) 121.

C1686 Saggezze. *Il Popolo di Alessandria*, Alessandria (23 Apr. 1944) [1].
Three brief quotations, reprinted in *Ciung Iung. L'asse che non vacilla* (1945)—
A57.

C1687 I trenta libri. *Il Popolo di Alessandria*, Alessandria (27 Apr. 1944) [2].
Signed: E. Pound.

C1688 Del silenzio. *Il Popolo di Alessandria*, Alessandria (30 Apr. 1944) [1].
Signed: Ez. P. Reprinted in *La Destra*, II. 11/12 (Nov./Dec. 1972) 121.

C1689 ✉ Chiose di Pound. *Il Popolo di Alessandria*, Alessandria (11 May 1944)
[1].
To Gian Gaetano Cabella, the Editor.

C1690 Affari e moneta. *Il Popolo di Alessandria*, Alessandria (14 May 1944) [1].
Signed: Ez. P.

C1690a Mussolini e l'usurocrazia. *Il Popolo di Alessandria*, Alessandria (18 May
1944) [1].

C. CONTRIBUTIONS TO PERIODICALS

Signed: Ez. P.

C1690b Snobismo e credulità. *Il Popolo di Alessandria*, Alessandria (21 May 1944) [1].
Signed: Ez. P.

C1690c Ammassi. *Il Popolo di Alessandria*, Alessandria (21 May 1944) [1].
Signed: Ez. P.

C1690d Turbature avvelerate. *Il Popolo di Alessandria*, Alessandria (21 May 1944)
Signed: Ez. P.

C1691 "Mi rincresce . . ." *Il Popolo di Alessandria*, Alessandria (25 May 1944) [1].
Signed: Ez. P.

C1691a Aggiornare. *Il Popolo di Alessandria*, Alessandria (25 May 1944) [1].
Signed: Ez. P. Reprinted in *La Destra*, II. 11/12 (Nov./Dec. 1972) 121–2.

C1691b Scelta. *Il Popolo di Alessandria*, Alessandria (28 May 1944) 2.
Signed: Ez. P.

C1691c D'accordo. *Il Popolo di Alessandria*, Alessandria (8 June 1944)
Signed: Ez. P. Reprinted in *La Destra*, II. 11/12 (Nov./Dec. 1972) 122–3.

C1691d [Quotation from Confucius]. *Il Popolo di Alessandria*, Alessandria (15 June 1944)
Unsigned, but almost certainly contributed by Ezra Pound.

C1691e Idee di Pound. *Il Popolo di Alessandria*, Alessandria (22 June 1944) [2]
Signed: Ez. P. Printed under the heading: "Polemiche" and followed by
". . . e osservazioni a Pound," a letter to the Editor signed: G. Dozzo.

C1691f Umanistica. *Il Popolo di Alessandria*, Alessandria (2 July 1944) [1].
Signed: Ez. P.

C1692 Pound risponde. *Il Popolo di Alessandria*, Alessandria (2 July 1944) [2].
A reply to Dozzo (see C1691e), printed under the heading: Le nostre
polemiche.

C1692a 4 occhi valgono + di 2. *Il Popolo di Alessandria*, Alessandria (9 July 1944)
[2].
Signed: Ez. P. Further comments on Dozzo.

C1693 Apifenomeni. *Il Popolo di Alessandria*, Alessandria (10 Aug. 1944) [1].
Signed: Ez. P.

C1694 Gli opposti. *Il Popolo di Alessandria*, Alessandria (16 Nov. 1944) [1].
Signed: Ez. Pou.

C1694a Cosí scriveva Marcantonio. *Il Popolo di Alessandria*, Alessandria (21 Nov. 1944)
Signed: E. P. Reprinted in *La Destra*, II. 11/12 (Nov./Dec. 1972) 123–5.

C1695 Strategia. *Il Popolo di Alessandria*, Alessandria (23 Dec. 1944) 2.
Signed: Ez. P.

C1696 Confucio parla [I]. *Il Popolo di Alessandria*, Alessandria (23 Dec. 1944) 4.
[Maxims] No. 1–10. "Versione italiana di Ezra Pound." Reprinted, with
C1686, 1697, and 1698, in *Ciung Iung. L'asse che non vacilla* (1945)—A57—
and in *La Destra*, II. 11/12 (Nov./Dec. 1972) 125–8, 132.

C. CONTRIBUTIONS TO PERIODICALS

1945

C1696a Parla Confucio. *La Marina Repubblicana*, II. 1 (1 Jan. 1945) 5.
[Maxims] No. 1–26 printed with the omission of No. 6 as 1–25. Reprinted
in part from *Il Popolo di Alessandria* (23 Dec. 1944)—C1696. Reprinted in
Ciung Iung. *L'asse che non vacilla* (1945)—A57.

C1697 Confucio parla [II]. *Il Popolo di Alessandria*, Alessandria (2 Jan. 1945) 2.
[Maxims] No. 11–24. "Traduzione dal cinese di Ezra Pound."

C1697a Attendismo ⟨cioè una forma personale e diversa⟩. *Il Popolo di Alessandria*,
Alessandria (9 Jan. 1945) [1].
Ezra Pound's contribution to the paper's column, "Ta Pum . . . Ta Pum e
Ta Pum . . ." Reprinted in *La Destra*, II. 11/12 (Nov./Dec. 1972) 128–30.

C1697b PRESENZA DI F. T. MARINETTI. *La Marina Repubblicana*, II. 2 (15 Jan.
1945) 2.
Lines 9 through 35 of Canto LXXII, omitting line 18. With an introductory note by u[baldo]. d[egli]. u[berti]., who succeeded Andrea Pais as
Editor on 1 Jan. 1945.

C1698 Poundiana. *Il Popolo di Alessandria*, Alessandria (23 Jan. 1945) 2.
Includes "Le ultime 2 massime di Confucio. 25 & 26."

C1699 Oro e princisbecco. *Il Popolo di Alessandria*, Alessandria (23 Jan. 1945) 2.
Signed: E. P. Reprinted in *La Destra*, II. 11/12 (Nov./Dec. 1972) 132–4.

C1699a CANTO LXXIII: CAVALCANTI—CORRISPONDENZA REPUBBLICANA.
La Marina Repubblicana, II. 3 (1 Feb. 1945) 7.

C1699b Contro usura. *Il Popolo di Alessandria*, Alessandria (8 Feb. 1945)
Signed: Ez. P. Reprinted in *La Destra*, II. 11/12 (Nov./Dec. 1972) 134–5.

C1700 Assassino. *L'Idea Sociale*, Alessandria, I. 1 (5 Mar. 1945) [2].
Intended apparently to accompany a tribute in the next column to Alessandro Scaramelli, who was assassinated.

C1700a Qui Ezra Pound. *Il Popolo di Alessandria*, Alessandria (8 Mar. 1945)
Reprinted in *La Destra*, II. 11/12 (Nov./Dec. 1972) 135–6.

C1701 Appunti economici: Lavoro e capitale. *L'Idea Sociale*, Alessandria (26
Mar. 1945) [1].

C1702 L'armata difende il baluardo non il baluardo difende l'armata. *Il Popolo
di Alessandria*, Alessandria (29 Mar. 1945) 2.
Signed: Ez. P.

C1702a Pochi, ma chiarissimi . . . *Il Popolo di Alessandria*, Alessandria (5 Apr.
1945) [1].
Signed: Ez. P.

C1703 Appunti economici: Moneta e lavoro. *L'Idea Sociale*, Alessandria (9 Apr.
1945) [1].

C1703a Nazione e moneta. *Il Popolo di Alessandria*, Alessandria (19 Apr. 1945)
2.
Signed: Ez. P.

C. CONTRIBUTIONS TO PERIODICALS

c1703b Rappresentare. *L'Idea Sociale*, Alessandria (21 Apr. 1945) [1].

c1703c Appunti economici: Brani d'attualità. *L'Idea Sociale*, Alessandria (23 Apr. 1945) [1].

c1704 [Excerpts from Rome radio broadcasts]. *PM*, New York (25 Nov. 1945) [m 14].
Quoted in Charles Norman's "The Case For and Against Ezra Pound," pp. [m 12–m 14, m 16], m 17, which was reprinted, expanded, as *The Case of Ezra Pound* (1948)—B50.

1946

c1705 CANTO LXXXIV. *Quarterly Review of Literature*, Annandale-on-Hudson, N.Y., III. 2 (1946) [126]–129.

c1706 CANTO LXXVII. *Rocky Mountain Review*, Logan, Utah, X. 4 (Summer 1946) [179]–189.

c1707 FROM CANTO LXXX. *Poetry*, LXVIII. 6 (Sept. 1946) 310–21.

c1708 Confucius. The Unwobbling Pivot & The Great Digest, Translated by Ezra Pound ... *Pharos*, New Directions, Norfolk, Ct., 4 (Winter [1946/]1947) [1]–[53].
For description see A58a.

1947

c1709 CANTO LXXXIII. *Yale Poetry Review*, New Haven, Ct., 6 (1947) 3–8.
This is an "Ezra Pound Issue" of the magazine.

c1710 CANTO LXXVI. *Sewanee Review*, Sewanee, Tenn., LV. 1 (Jan./Mar. 1947) [56]–67.

c1711 ✉ *Cronos*, Columbus, O., I. 3 (Fall 1947) [25].
Five words, refusing to contribute.

c1712 Mencius, or The Economist. Translated from the Chinese by Ezra Pound. *New Iconograph*, New York, I. 1 (Fall 1947) 19–21.
Chapters I–IV of Book One: King Hwuy of Leans [*sic*] or King Benevolent of Woodbridge.

c1713 Madox Ford at Rapallo: A Conversation between Ford Madox Ford and Ezra Pound. *Western Review*, Logan, Utah, XII. 1 (Autumn 1947) [17]–18.
A conversation at the beginning of Aug. 1932, recorded and translated into Italian by Olga Rudge, here retranslated into English by Miss Rudge.

1948

c1714 [Marginal notes on] Philosopher at Bay, by Harold H. Watts. *Cronos*, II. 4 (Mar. 1948) [1]–17.
"Pound made several marginal notes on the manuscript, some of which

C. CONTRIBUTIONS TO PERIODICALS

we reproduce with the article in sans-serif type." Such notes appear on pp. 4, 11, 12, 15, and 16.

1949

C1715 TRANSLATIONS FROM CAVALCANTI ... *Quarterly Review of Literature*, V. 2 (1949), leaf preceding p. [103].
Sonnets 7 and 16, reprinted from *Guido Cavalcanti. Rime* (1932)—B27. Printed one on each side of a leaf of green paper, laid into the issue. Some copies were distributed separately by the editors.

C1716 Indiscretions. *Quarterly Review of Literature*, V. 2 (1949) [105]–135.
A reprint of *Indiscretions* (1923)—A23—with minor corrections by the author.

C1717 ✉ ENVOI. *Quarterly Review of Literature*, V. 2 (1949) 201.
An extract. A four-line stanza, dated: 1946; "to a ballade unwrit re a past age, i.e., Verlaine's."

C1718 Letters to a Young Poet. *Changing World*, London, 7 (Feb./Mar./Apr. 1949) 16–36.
Letters to Iris Barry, edited by D. D. Paige.

C1719 As Sextant. *Nine*, London, 1 (Autumn 1949) 7.
"... a postscript to [Guide to] Kulchur, found among Mr. Pound's papers."
A curriculum. Reprinted in *Guide to Kulchur* ([1952])—A45c & d—p. 352.
Reprinted also in *Current*, Provincetown, Mass., 15 (3 Oct. 1955) [1].

1950

C1720 The Analects [of Confucius]. Translated [with notes] by Ezra Pound [I]. *Hudson Review*, New York, III. 1 (Spring 1950) [8]–52.
Reprinted, with part II, below, as *Confucian Analects* ([1951])—A65a.

C1721 Letters ... Edited by D. D. Paige. *Hudson Review*, III. 1 (Spring 1950) [53]–65.
Contents: I. To T. S. Eliot concerning *The Waste Land* [including two letters to (the first with 27 lines of verse, "Sage Homme") and one from T. S. Eliot]—II. To W. H. D. Rouse concerning *The Odyssey* [including nine letters or parts of letters to Rouse]. Section I reprinted as "Letters on *The Waste Land*" in *Nine*, 4 (Summer 1950) 176–9, and in *Kavita*, XVI. 1 (Dec. 1950) 23–27.

C1722 "THAIS HABET NIGROS ..."—MARTIAL. *Imagi*, Allentown, Pa., V. 2 ([Spring?] 1950) [4].
A translation, signed: E. P., of an epigram. Reprinted as "Martial: Thais habet nigros," in *Edge*, Melbourne, Australia, 5 (May 1957) 34.

C1723 [Note in English on the influence of Tagore]. *Kavita*, Calcutta, XIV. 3 (Mar. 1950) 162.
In connexion with an article (in Bengali) on Ezra Pound, by Buddhadeva Bose.

C. CONTRIBUTIONS TO PERIODICALS

C1724 Introductory Text-Book. *Mood*, St. Louis, Mo., 23 (May 1950) [11].
A reprint of *Introductory Text Book* ([1939])—E2r.

C1725 The Analects [of Confucius]. Translated by Ezra Pound [II]. *Hudson Review*, III. 2 (Summer 1950) [237]–287.
Reprinted, with part I, above, as *Confucian Analects* ([1951])—A65a.

C1726 Containing Pound Items. *Mood*, 24 (Fall 1950) 3–16.
Contents: Ezra Pound on Gold, War and National Money—Écrire franchement ce qu'ils pensent [a translation of the letter of Remy de Gourmont quoted in French in C307]—Madox Ford at Rapallo: A Conversation between Ford Madox Ford and Ezra Pound (Translated [from the Italian] by Olga Rudge)—. . . A Draft Bill of Rights Adapted for the Needs of Great Britain—As Sextant.

C1727 ✉ *Four Pages*, Whitchurch, S. Wales, 12 (Sept. 1950) [3].
An extract; written in 1937. On the right to property and the right to produce.

C1728 Tre lettere al Dottor Rouse sul tradurre poesia, e una lettera a Joyce a proposito di una traduzione dell' "Odissea." *Letterature Moderne*, Milan, I. 2 (Sept. 1950) 220–2.
Edited by Luciano Anceschi. The letters are printed in English (the three to Rouse reprinted from *Hudson Review* for Spring 1950—C1721) and are followed (pp. 223–6) by a translation into Italian by Anceschi and D. D. Paige. Offprints of the article were prepared for the editors. These have title: *Ezra Pound. Tre lettere al Dottor Rouse sul tradurre poesia, e una lettera a Joyce, a proposito di una traduzione dell' "Odissea," a cura di Luciano Anceschi. Estratto dalla rivista Letterature Moderne . . . Settembre 1950. Milano, Malfasi Editore [1950]*; they collate: cover-title, 7 pp., measure 24·1 × 17 cm., and were issued, wire-stitched, in pale green paper wrappers printed in black.

C1729 Letters to a Young Poet . . . *Poetry*, LXXVI. 6 (Sept. 1950) 342–51.
Letters to Iris Barry (selection differing from that in *Changing World* for Feb./Mar./Apr. 1949—C1718), edited by D. D. Paige.

C1730 [FROM THE ORIGINAL FRENCH OF JAIME DE ANGULO]. *Kavita*, Calcutta, XVI. 1 (Dec. 1950) 3.
Reprinted, without indication of translator, in *Imagi*, V. 3 (1951) [17]; and in *Pavannes and Divagations*—A74.

C1730a Omaggio a Carlo Linati. *La Provincia*, Como (10 Dec. 1950) 4.
Includes a letter from Ezra Pound.

1951

C1731 GUIDES TO THE MONTANARI POEMS. *Imagi*, V. 3 (1951) 3, 5.
Translated anonymously by Ezra Pound. Italian and English on opposite pages. *Contents:* Autunno—Stagione di fiori—Pomeriggio di luglio—Notte dietro le persiane.

C1731a Slow Motion. *Four Pages*, II. 4 (Jan. 1951) [1].
Signed: T. Foster, U.S.A. Probably by Ezra Pound.

C. CONTRIBUTIONS TO PERIODICALS

c1731b [Letter to Cyril Clemens]. *Hobbies*, Chicago, Ill., LV. 12 (Feb. 1951) 138.
On G. B. Shaw, written *ca.* Feb. 1949. Quoted, with Shaw's comments, in an article by Clemens, "Notes on Bernard Shaw," pp. 137–8.

c1731c Browning's *The Inn Album*. *Explicator*, Lynchburg, Va., X. 3 (Dec. 1951) [7].
Signed: J. T. Foster.

1952

c1732 A Note. *Nine*, 9 (Summer/Autumn 1952) 358.
Signed: E. P. On categories of literature.

1953

c1733 Sovereignty [a note]. *European*, London, 1 (Mar. 1953) 51.

c1734 On Wyndham Lewis. *Shenandoah*, Lexington, Va., IV. 2/3 (Summer/Autumn 1953) [17].
Excerpts from articles in *Fortnightly Review* for 1 Sept. 1914—C158, *Exile* for Autumn 1928—C724, *Guide to Kulchur* ([1938])—A45, and a private letter.

c1735 Two Incidents. *Shenandoah*, IV. 2/3 (Summer/Autumn 1953) [112]–116.
Three letters to W. B. Yeats, written in 1931 and 1932.

c1736 ✉ Apologia: Letter from an Exile. *Listen*, Hessle, Yorks., I. [1] (Winter 1953/Spring 1954) 24.
Signed: E. P.

c1737 ON VALUES. *Nine*, 10 (Winter 1953/1954) 17.
Four lines of doggerel.

c1738 SOPHOKLES. WOMEN OF TRACHIS, A VERSION BY EZRA POUND. *Hudson Review*, VI. 4 (Winter [1953/]1954) [487]–523.

1954

c1738a [Message]. *Chinese World*, San Francisco (23 Sept. 1954)
One sentence: "Kung is to China as water to fishes."

c1739 British Tax System an Infamy. *New Times*, Melbourne, Australia (5 Nov. 1954)
A reprint of the section "On England" in *What Is Money For?* ([1939])—A46.

c1740 Una lettera dall'altro mondo: Ezra Pound legge "Il Mare." Ecco che cosa scrive ad un nostro collaboratore. *Il Mare*, XXXVI. 1741 (21 Nov. 1954) [1].
A letter (in Italian) to Pietro Berri.

c1741 CANTO 85. *Hudson Review*, VII. 4 (Winter [1954/] 1955) [487]–501.

C. CONTRIBUTIONS TO PERIODICALS

1955

C1742 Moscardino [by] Enrico Pea. Translated [from the Italian] by Ezra Pound. *New Directions*, 15 (1955) 86–131.
This 15th volume of the annual was published 15 Dec. 1955. 1200 copies were printed, bound in cloth. (An edition in paper wrappers was published simultaneously in New York by Meridian Books.)

C1743 CANTO 86–87. *Hudson Review*, VIII. 1 (Spring 1955) [13]–27.

C1744 What I Feel about Walt Whitman. *American Literature*, Concord, N.H., XXVII. 1 (Mar. 1955) [56]–61.
Incorporated in an article by Herbert Bergman, "Ezra Pound and Walt Whitman," pp. [56]–61. Printed from the manuscript in the Yale University Library. (Offprints of the article were prepared for Bergman. These have special title-page: *Ezra Pound and Walt Whitman by Herbert Bergman Reprinted from American Literature Vol. XXVII, No. 1, March 1955*; they collate, pp. [55]–61, measure 22·9 × 15·2 cm., and were issued stapled.)

C1745 On the Necessity of Preserving Language as a Means of Communication. *Comment*, New Haven, Ct., II. 6 (Apr. 1955) [17]–19.
Short passages selected by the editors from *ABC of Reading* (1934)—A35.

C1746 CANTO 88–89. *Hudson Review*, VIII. 2 (Summer 1955) [183]–204.

C1747 CANTO 90. *Meanjin*, Melbourne, Australia, XIV. 4 (Summer 1955) 488–91.

C1748 Observation. *Strike*, Washington, D.C. 1 (June 1955) 2.
Unsigned. Reprinted in *Paideuma*, III. 3 (Winter 1974[/1975]) [389].

C1749 Editorial. *Strike*, 1 (June 1955) 3.
Unsigned. Reprinted in *Paideuma*, III. 3 (Winter 1974[/1975]) [389].

C1750 [Note beginning "Most Publishers . . ."]. *Strike*, 2 (July 1955) 2.
Unsigned. Reprinted in *Paideuma*, III. 3 (Winter 1974[/1975]) [389].

C1751 [Prefatory note to "Amendatory Act . . ."]. *Strike*, 2 (July 1955) 2.
Unsigned. Reprinted, with "Amendatory Act," in *Paideuma*, III. 3 (Winter 1974[/1975]) [389].

C1752 Comment. *Strike*, 2 (July 1955) 2.
Unsigned. Reprinted in *Paideuma*, III. 3 (Winter 1974[/1975]) [389].

C1753 Editorial. *Strike*, 2 (July 1955) 3.
Unsigned. Reprinted in *Paideuma*, III. 3 (Winter 1974[/1975]) [389].

C1754 "Ci sarà un onorario legiero": Una curiosa lettera di Ezra Pound. *La Fiera Letteraria*, Rome, X. 30 (24 July 1955) 7.
A letter to Marino Moretti, 14 Jan. 1926. With facsimile of the original typed letter.

C1755 Manifesto for Mrs. Hobby's Successor. *Strike*, 3 (Aug. 1955) 1.
Unsigned. Reprinted in *Paideuma*, III. 3 (Winter 1974[/1975]) 390.

C1756 Comment on the Manifesto of the Vergilian Society . . . *Strike*, 3 (Aug. 1955) 2.

C. CONTRIBUTIONS TO PERIODICALS

Unsigned. Reprinted in *Paideuma*, III. 3 (Winter 1974[/1975]) 390.

C1757 [Note beginning: "We Nominate Ma Perkins . . ."]. *Strike*, 3 (Aug. 1955) 2.

Unsigned. Reprinted in *Paideuma*, III. 3 (Winter 1974[/1975]) 390.

C1758 Observation. *Strike*, 3 (Aug. 1955) 2.

Unsigned. Reprinted in *Paideuma*, III. 3 (Winter 1974[/1975]) 390.

C1759 Editorial. *Strike*, 3 (Aug. 1955) 3.

Unsigned. Reprinted in *Paideuma*, III. 3 (Winter 1974[/1975]) 390.

C1760 An Observation. *Strike*, 3 (Aug. 1955) 3.

On a quoted passage from Alexander Del Mar's preface to his *History of Monetary Systems*. Unsigned. Reprinted in *Paideuma*, III. 3 (Winter 1974 [/1975]) 390–1.

C1761 [Note beginning: "That the Communists . . ."]. *Strike*, 3 (Aug. 1955) 3.

Unsigned. Reprinted in *Paideuma*, III. 3 (Winter 1974[/1975]) 391.

C1761a The Douglas Analysis. *New Times*, Melbourne, Australia, XXI. 17 (26 Aug. 1955) 7.

An extract from *Social Credit* ([1935])—A40.

C1762 [Note on Cicero's *De Officiis*]. *Strike*, 4 (Sept. 1955) 2.

Unsigned. Reprinted in *Paideuma*, III. 3 (Winter 1974[/1975]) 391.

C1763 [Note beginning: "Employment for Empson . . ."]. *Strike*, 4 (Sept. 1955) 2.

Unsigned. Reprinted, in part, in *Paideuma*, III. 3 (Winter 1974 [/1975]) 392.

C1764 [Note beginning: "American educational system in bad way . . ."]. *Strike*, 4 (Sept. 1955) 2.

Signed: Michigan Correspondent. Reprinted in *Paideuma*, III. 3 (Winter 1974[/1975]) 392.

C1765 Editorial. *Strike*, 4 (Sept. 1955) 3.

Unsigned. Reprinted in *Paideuma*, III. 3 (Winter 1974[/1975]) 392.

C1766 [Note beginning: "Moving under a large amount of terminology . . ."]. *Strike*, 4 (Sept. 1955) 3.

Unsigned. Reprinted in *Paideuma*, III. 3 (Winter 1974[/1975]) 392.

C1767 [Note beginning: "Compliments to the lady . . ."]. *Strike*, 4 (Sept. 1955) 3.

Unsigned. Reprinted in *Paideuma*, III. 3 (Winter 1974[/1975]) 392.

C1768 Program [with footnote: "(not ours)"]. *Strike*, 4 (Sept. 1955) 3.

Unsigned. Reprinted in *Paideuma*, III. 3 (Winter 1974[/1975]) 392.

C1769 Piety, or an Earnest Prayer. *Strike*, 4 (Sept. 1955) 3.

Unsigned. Reprinted in *Paideuma*, III. 3 (Winter 1974[/1975]) 392.

C1770 Clarifications [first and second paragraphs]. *New Times*, XXI. 19 (23 Sept. 1955)

Unsigned. Repeated in *New Times* at intervals over a long period and reprinted in broadside form, in blue ink on glossy paper, measuring 11·4 × 8·1 cm., for distribution gratis.

C. CONTRIBUTIONS TO PERIODICALS

c1771 [Note on G. Vattuone's *L'uomo e la malattia mentale*]. *Strike*, 5 (Oct. 1955) 2.

Unsigned. Reprinted in *Paideuma*, III. 3 (Winter 1974[/1975]) 393.

c1772 [Note beginning: "And now Task Force . . ."]. *Strike*, 5 (Oct. 1955) 2.
Unsigned. Reprinted in *Paideuma*, III. 3 (Winter 1974[/1975]) 393.

c1773 For Services Rendered. *Strike*, 5 (Oct. 1955) 2.
Unsigned. Reprinted in *Paideuma*, III. 3 (Winter 1974[/1975]) 393.

c1774 Editorial. *Strike*, 5 (Oct. 1955) 3.
Unsigned. Reprinted in *Paideuma*, III. 3 (Winter 1974[/1975]) 393–4.

c1774a China and "Voice of America." *Strike*, 5 (Oct. 1955) 3.
A quotation from Mencius, followed by comment in three sentences, only the second of which ("Bolshevism started off as an attack on loan-capital and quickly shifted into an attack against the homestead.") was contributed by Ezra Pound. Reprinted in *Paideuma*, III. 3 (Winter 1974[/1975]) 393–4.

c1775 Vital Residue. *Strike*, 5 (Oct. 1955) 4.
Unsigned. Reprinted in *Paideuma*, III. 3 (Winter 1974[/1975]) 394.

c1776 [Note on "a novel called 'Liberty Street.'"]. *Strike*, 5 (Oct. 1955) 4.
Unsigned. Reprinted in *Paideuma*, III. 3 (Winter 1974[/1975]) 394.

c1776a New York Report. By John Foster. *New Times*, XXI. 21 (21 Oct. 1955) 6.

c1777 New York "Literary" Criticism as of Now. *Strike*, 6 (Nov. 1955) 2.
Unsigned. Reprinted in *Paideuma*, III. 3 (Winter 1974[/1975]) 394.

c1778 Travel Note. *Strike*, 6 (Nov. 1955) 2.
Unsigned. Reprinted in *Paideuma*, III. 3 (Winter 1974[/1975]) 395.

c1779 Observation. *Strike*, 6 (Nov. 1955) 2.
Unsigned. Reprinted in *Paideuma*, III. 3 (Winter 1974[/1975]) 395.

c1780 Editorial. *Strike*, 6 (Nov. 1955) 3.
Unsigned. Reprinted in *Paideuma*, III. 3 (Winter 1974[/1975]) 395.

c1781 [Note beginning: "Italian Librarian reports . . ."]. *Strike*, 6 (Nov. 1955) 3.
Unsigned. Reprinted in *Paideuma*, III. 3 (Winter 1974[/1975]) 395.

c1781a Comment from Tasmania. Men of Yalta. By Norville Brannon. *New Times*, XXI. 22 (4 Nov. 1955) 6.

c1781b Jefferson. *Current*, 19 (28 Nov. 1955) [1–2].
Brief excerpts from *Jefferson and/or Mussolini* ([1935])—A41.

c1782 [Note beginning: "However little we approve of Hitler's excitability . . ."]. *Strike*, 7 (Dec. 1955) 2.
Unsigned. Reprinted in *Paideuma*, III. 3 (Winter 1974[/1975]) 395.

c1783 [Note beginning: "Thought grows, administrative arrangements decay . . ."]. *Strike*, 7 (Dec. 1955) 2.
Unsigned. Reprinted in *Paideuma*, III. 3 (Winter 1974[/1975]) 395.

c1784 Urbanization. *Strike*, 7 (Dec. 1955) 2.
Unsigned. Reprinted in *Paideuma*, III. 3 (Winter 1974[/1975]) 395.

C. CONTRIBUTIONS TO PERIODICALS

C1785 Observation. *Strike*, 7 (Dec. 1955) 2.
Unsigned. Reprinted in *Paideuma*, III. 3 (Winter 1974[/1975]) 396.

C1786 Editorial. *Strike*, 7 (Dec. 1955) 3.
Unsigned. Reprinted in *Paideuma*, III. 3 (Winter 1974[/1975]) 396.

C1786a [Editor's footnote to] Ezra Pound, Economist: Justice the Final Goal. By
Renato Corsini. *New Times*, XXI. 25 (16 Dec. 1955) 7.
Translated, by Ezra Pound anonymously?, from *Il Secolo d'Italia* for 4 May
1955.

1956

C1787 23 Lettere e 9 Cartoline Inedite. *Nuova Corrente*, Genoa, 5/6 (Jan./June
1956) 123–154.
For the most part, in English (with Italian translations). To Carlo Izzo, for
whom offprints were prepared. These have title: *Carlo Izzo. Lettere inedite di
Ezra Pound. Estratto da "Nuova Corrente," 5–6, gennaio-giugno, 1956.*

C1788 [Note beginning: "Whether the Syndacalists [*sic*] have a moral aim or not
. . ."]. *Strike*, 8 (Jan. 1956) 2.
Unsigned. Reprinted in *Paideuma*, III. 3 (Winter 1974[/1975]) 396.

C1789 [Note beginning: "Of all things . . ."]. *Strike*, 8 (Jan. 1956) 2.
Unsigned. Reprinted in *Paideuma*, III. 3 (Winter 1974[/1975]) 396.

C1790 [Note beginning: "Nominations for an Honor Roll . . ."]. *Strike*, 8 (Jan.
1956) 2.
Unsigned. Reprinted in *Paideuma*, III. 3 (Winter 1974[/1975]) 396-7.

C1791 Editorial. *Strike*, 8 (Jan. 1956) 3.
Unsigned. Reprinted in Paideuma, III. 3 (Winter 1974[/1975]) 397.

C1792 [Note beginning: "Mr. Heilbronner . . ."]. *Strike*, 8 (Jan. 1956) 3.
Unsigned. Reprinted in *Paideuma*, III. 3 (Winter 1974[/1975]) 397.

C1793 [Note beginning: "The amendment to prevent presidents having a third
term . . ."]. *Strike*, 8 (Jan. 1956) 3.
Unsigned. Reprinted in *Paideuma*, III. 3 (Winter 1974[/1975]) 397.

C1794 [Note beginning: "Our enemies in Pakistan . . ."]. *Strike*, 8 (Jan. 1956) 4.
Unsigned. Reprinted in *Paideuma*, III. 3 (Winter 1974[/1975]) 397.

C1795 Utopia . . . *Strike*, 9 (Feb. 1956) 1.
Unsigned. Reprinted in *Paideuma*, III. 3 (Winter 1974[/1975]) 397.

C1796 Cleaners' Manifesto. *Strike*, 9 (Feb. 1956) 2.
Unsigned. Reprinted in *Paideuma*, III. 3 (Winter 1974[/1975]) 398.

C1797 Heart Throbs from New York. *Strike*, 9 (Feb. 1956) 2.
Unsigned. Reprinted in *Paideuma*, III. 3 (Winter 1974[/1975]) 398.

C1798 [Note beginning: "The late and meritorious H. L. Mencken . . ."]. *Strike*,
9 (Feb. 1956) 2.
Unsigned. Reprinted in *Paideuma*, III. 3 (Winter 1974[/1975]) 398.

C1799 [Note beginning: "'Power corrupts'"]. *Strike*, 9 (Feb. 1956) 2.

C. CONTRIBUTIONS TO PERIODICALS

Unsigned. Reprinted in *Paideuma*, III. 3 (Winter 1974[/1975]) 398.

c1800 Editorial. *Strike*, 9 (Feb. 1956) 3.
Unsigned. Reprinted in Paideuma, III. 3 (Winter 1974[/1975]) 398.

c1801 [Note beginning: "Our impression is that Mr. Poujade is a good guy
. . ."]. *Strike*, 9 (Feb. 1956) 3.
Unsigned. Reprinted in *Paideuma*, III. 3 (Winter 1974[/1975]) 398.

c1802 [Note beginning: "Republicans are over-estimating their opponents . . ."].
Strike, 9 (Feb. 1956) 3.
Unsigned. Reprinted in *Paideuma*, III. 3 (Winter 1974[/1975]) 398–9.

c1803 [Note beginning: "Opinion of our senior and oldest Hollywood reader
. . ."]. *Strike*, 9 (Feb. 1956) 4.
Unsigned. Reprinted in *Paideuma*, III. 3 (Winter 1974[/1975]) 399.

c1804 [Note beginning: "Remote control . . ."]. *Strike*, 9 (Feb. 1956) 4.
Unsigned. Reprinted in *Paideuma*, III. 3 (Winter 1974[/1975]) 399.

c1805 [Note beginning: "Cri d'alarme . . ."]. *Strike*, 9 (Feb. 1956) 4.
Unsigned. Reprinted in *Paideuma*, III. 3 (Winter 1974[/1975]) 399.

c1806 [Note beginning: "Either Baruch is responsible . . ."]. *Strike*, 9 (Feb. 1956)
4.
Unsigned. Reprinted in *Paideuma*, III. 3 (Winter 1974[/1975]) 399.

c1806a Our Common Heritage. *New Times*, XXII. 3 (11 Feb. 1956) 6.
Signed: John Vignon (Boston, U.S.A.)

c1806b French Blindness Harms Europe. Report from Paris. *New Times*, XXII.
4 (24 Feb. 1956) 6.
Unsigned.

c1807 CANTO 96. *Hudson Review*, IX. 1 (Spring 1956) 7–19.

c1808 [Note beginning: "Bird Watchers . . ."]. *Strike*, 10 (Mar. 1956) 3.
Unsigned. Reprinted in *Paideuma*, III. 3 (Winter 1974[/1975]) 399.

c1809 [Note beginning with quotation from Bret Harte]. *Strike*, 10 (Mar. 1956)
3.
Unsigned. Reprinted in *Paideuma*, III. 3 (Winter 1974[/1975]) 399–400.

c1810 The Subject. *Strike*, 10 (Mar. 1956) 4.
Unsigned. Reprinted in *Paideuma*, III. 3 (Winter 1974[/1975]) 400.

c1811 Red Peril. *Strike*, 10 (Mar. 1956) 4.
Unsigned. Reprinted in *Paideuma*, III. 3 (Winter 1974[/1975]) 400.

c1812 [Note beginning: "And it appears that Mr. Soekarno [*sic*] . . ."]. *Strike*, 10
(Mar. 1956) 4.
Unsigned. Reprinted in *Paideuma*, III. 3 (Winter 1974[/1975]) 400.

c1812a Observation. *New Times*, XXII. 5 (9 Mar. 1956) 4.
Unsigned.

c1812b Versailles and [World] War Two. *New Times*, XXII. 5 (9 Mar. 1956) 4.
Unsigned.

c1812c ✉ "Outrageous Rate." *Voice*, Belfast, II. 25 (24 Mar. 1956) 3.

C. CONTRIBUTIONS TO PERIODICALS

"Mr. Melvin Larkin writes . . ."

C1813 THE PINK. *Nine*, 11 (Apr. 1956) 28.
Four lines of doggerel, printed without title, but titled by first line (as above) on front cover.

C1813a Washington. *New Times*, XXII. 7 (6 Apr. 1956) 6.
Signed: Washington Correspondent. *Contents:* Yalta Paper—Filth in Legislature.

C1813b London. Douglas and Gesell. *New Times*, XXII. 7 (6 Apr. 1956) 6.
Signed: Melville Larkin.

C1813c Paris. U.N. and League of Nations. *New Times*, XXII. 7 (6 Apr. 1956) 6.
Signed: Paris Correspondent.

C1813d New York. Liars by Omission. *New Times*, XXII. 7 (6 Apr. 1956) 6.
Signed: F. W.

C1813e Perspectives. *New Times*, XXII. 7 (6 Apr. 1956) 7.
Contents: Dividends [signed: Diogenes]—Definition [from *The Great Digest* of Confucius, unsigned]—Racial Characteristics [signed: M. V.]—Breakdown of Blackout of History [unsigned]—Sound the Alarm [signed: Anon.]

C1813f "Total Morass." *Voice*, II. 26 (7 Apr. 1956) 4.
Signed: Herbert Briscoe. Summarised and quoted in part in *Paideuma*, III. 3 (Winter 1974[/1975]) 372.

C1814 [Extracts from letters]. *Spokesman-Review*, Salem, Oregon (15 Apr. 1956) 10–11.
To M. T. Cunningham, publisher of the Hailey, Idaho, *Times-News-Miner* weekly, 11 Nov. 1927; to the *Times-News Miner*, 31 Mar. [1928], concerning Senator Borah; to Mrs. M. T. (Lulu) Cunningham; to Mr. Cunningham, 21 June 1925. Quoted in "From a Tiny Town in Idaho Came . . . Ezra Pound . . . Idaho Neighbor Presents Some of Pound's Letters to Home Town . . .," by Carl E. Hayden.

C1814a London. *New Times*, XXII. 8 (20 Apr. 1956) 6.
Signed: London Correspondent. *Contents:* Law—Progress of Mind—Continental Survey.

C1814b Washington. *New Times*, XXII. 8 (20 Apr. 1956) 6.
Unsigned. *Contents:* Stirring in Europe—Southern Revival [including five lines of doggerel on Westbrook Pegler, "Mr. Pegler and the Federal Reserve"]—Roots of Bolshevism. (The second, third, and fourth of five items under this heading.)

C1814c Perspectives. Literature. *New Times*, XXII. 8 (20 Apr. 1956) 7.
Unsigned. (The second of four items under the heading: "Perspectives.")

C1814d New York. *New Times*, XXII. 9 (4 May 1956) 6.
Signed: New York Correspondent. *Contents:* Lone Voices—Details of Crime. (The first and second of three items under this heading.)

C1814e A New Note on Confucius. *New Times*, XXII. 9 (4 May 1956) 7.
A reprint of "Procedure," from *Confucian Analects* ([1956])—A65b—pp. 7–8.

C. CONTRIBUTIONS TO PERIODICALS

c1814f Perspectives. *New Times*, XXII. 9 (4 May 1956) 7.

Unsigned. *Contents:* Master-Plan? [first paragraph doubtful, but final paragraph certainly by Ezra Pound]—Advice—Comment on the News. (The final paragraph of "Master-Plan" is quoted in an article by William Fleming in *New Times*, XXII. 10 (18 May 1956) 7.) Pound's contributions are the first, third, and fourth of nine items printed under the heading: "Perspectives."

c1814g The Races of Mankind. *New Times*, XXII. 9 (4 May 1956) 12.

Unsigned.

c1814h The Tablet, N.Y. *Voice*, III. 1 (5 May 1956) 2.

Signed: V. B.

c1814i American Notes, by Herbert Briscoe. *Voice*, III. 1 (5 May 1956) 3.

Reprinted in *Paideuma*, III. 3 (Winter 1974[/1975]) 372–3.

c1814j New York. *New Times*, XXII. 10 (18 May 1956) 6.

Signed: New York Correspondent. *Contents:* Middle East Peace—Modern Education—Habeas Corpus—Brother Ashberg—Hitler and Feder. Basically by Ezra Pound, possibly with some editing or rephrasing. (The first, second, third, fifth, and sixth of six items printed under this heading.)

c1814k UNESCO's Power. *New Times*, XXII. 10 (18 May 1956) 6.

Signed: N[oel]. S[tock].(but definitely by Ezra Pound according to Stock).

c1814l Thought and Action. *New Times*, XXII. 10 (18 May 1956) 6.

Signed: T. G.

c1814m Perspectives. Production and Consumption. *New Times*, XXII. 10 (18 May 1956) 7.

Unsigned. A reprint of A. R. Lintell's statement from *Voice* for 25 Feb., with the addition of two paragraphs by Ezra Pound.

c1814n George Santayana's Letters, reviewed by H. Briscoe. *Voice*, III. 2 (19 May 1956) 3–4.

Summarised and quoted from, at length, in *Paideuma*, III. 3 (Winter 1974 [/1975]) 373–5.

c1814 o London. *New Times*, XXII. 11 (1 June 1956) 6.

Signed: London Correspondent. *Contents:* Christianity—The World of Books—From Our Mailbag—British Diplomacy.

c1814p Paris. French Thought. *New Times*, XXII. 11 (1 June 1956) 6.

Signed: Paris Correspondent.

c1814q New York. *New Times*, XXII. 11 (1 June 1956) 6.

Signed: N.Y. Correspondent. *Contents:* Education—Important Book—Monetary Issue. (The first, third, and fourth of four items under this heading.)

c1815 Perspectives. *New Times*, XXII. 11 (1 June 1956) 7–8.

Unsigned (with one exception). *Contents:* Every Man's Right—Laboratory versus Nonsense [by Ezra Pound only in part]—Government—Simple Truth [signed: M. L.]—Date Line.

C. CONTRIBUTIONS TO PERIODICALS

C1816 ✉ Basic Issues. *Voice*, III. 3 (2 June 1956) 2.
Signed: William Watson.

C1817 London. *New Times*, XXII. 12 (15 June 1956) 6.
Signed: M. L. *Contents:* Aristocracy—Races—Individual Liberty—Gentile Folly.

C1818 New York. *New Times*, XXII. 12 (15 June 1956) 6.
Signed: N.Y. Correspondent. *Contents:* Learn from Moscow?—Henry George—Sale of Debt.

C1819 Paris. French Sand Heap. *New Times*, XXII. 12 (15 June 1956) 6.
Signed: Paris Correspondent. Chiefly on Hubert Lagardelle's *Mission at Rome*.

C1820 Perspectives. *New Times*, XXII. 12 (15 June 1956) 7.
Unsigned. *Contents:* Exercise—Penology—Liberalism—Observation. (The first, third, fourth, and fifth of five items under this heading.)

C1820a Book Review: *Mission at Rome* [by Hubert Lagardelle] by W. Watson.
Voice, III. 4 (16 June 1956) 4.
Reprinted in *Paideuma*, III. 3 (Winter 1974[/1975]) 376–8. (Not same as C1819.)

C1820b New York. *New Times*, XXII. 13 (29 June 1956) 6.
Signed: John Foster. *Contents:* The Classics—Slavery—The Races—Drugs.

C1820c London. *New Times*, XXII. 13 (29 June 1956) 6.
Signed: J. T. *Contents:* The Enemy—Logic—Education.

C1820d Perspectives. *New Times*, XXII.13 (29 June 1956) 7.
Contents: The Hour Is Late [unsigned]—True Order [signed: T. McC.]—Query [unsigned]—American Blather [signed: B. G.]—Revelations [unsigned]—"To Paint" [unsigned].

C1820e Sturzo, Senator for Life in Demochristiania, His Level. *Voice*, III. 5 (30 June 1956) 2–3.
Signed: H. Briscoe. Summarised and quoted, in part, in *Paideuma*, III. 3 (Winter 1974[/1975]) 375.

C1820f New York. *New Times*, XXII. 14 (13 July 1956) 6.
Signed: John Foster. *Contents:* A Decent Life—Out of the Past—The Dregs.

C1820g London. *New Times*, XXII. 14 (13 July 1956) 6.
Signed: M. L. *Contents:* Simony—Reflection.

C1820h Rome. Courageous Stalin? *New Times*, XXII. 14 (13 July 1956) 6.
Signed: D. E. J.

C1820i Perspectives. *New Times*, XXII. 14 (13 July 1956) 7.
Contents: The Protocols—Truth!—St. Ambrose [all unsigned]—The Baruchracy [signed: M. L.]

C1820j "Decay of Mind." *Voice*, III. 6 (14 July 1956) 3.
Signed: A. Watson. Reprinted in *Academia Bulletin*, Washington, D.C., 2 ([Fall?] 1956) [3]. Summarised, and the opening and closing quoted, in *Paideuma*, III. 3 (Winter 1974[/1975]) 378.

C. CONTRIBUTIONS TO PERIODICALS

C1820k New York. *New Times*, XXII. 15 (27 July 1956) 6.
Signed: J. F. *Contents: Psychoanalysis—Henry James—Tobacco Dangerous—Price and Demand—Harriman the End.

C1820l A Fabian Hang-Over? *New Times*, XXII. 15 (27 July 1956) 7.
Signed: T. G. A review of Alex Comfort's *Authority and Delinquency in the Modern State*.

C1820m Perspectives. *New Times*, XXII. 15 (27 July 1956) 7.
Contents: Local Government [unsigned]—Quantity [signed: R. A. B.]—Mailbag [signed: J. T.]

C1820n Review: Calling Mr. Comfort. *Voice*, III. 7 (28 July 1956) 3.
A review of *Authority and Delinquency in the Modern State*, signed: W. Watson.

C1820 o New York. *New Times*, XXII. 16 (10 Aug. 1956) 6.
Signed: J. F. *Contents:* Banking—Bond Racket—"De-Segregation."

C1820p London. *New Times*, XXII. 16 (10 Aug. 1956) 6.
Unsigned.

C1820q ✉ "Collective Imbecility." *Voice*, III. 8 (11 Aug. 1956) 3.
Signed: J. D. (U.S.A.)

C1821 Zweck [*i.e.* "The aim of this organization . . ."]. *Academia Bulletin*, 2 ([Fall?] 1956) 1.
Unsigned. The entire issue of the periodical is reproduced in *Paideuma*, III. 3 (Winter 1974[/1975]) 385–8.

C1822 CANTO 97. *Hudson Review*, IX. 3 (Autumn 1956) [387]–398.
A note by Ezra Pound on the Canto appears on p. [322].

C1822a Mexico City. *New Times*, XXII. 13 (7 Sept. 1956) 6.
Signed: Jose Boler.

C1822b Square Dollar Series. *Voice*, III. 10 (8 Sept. 1956) 2.
Signed: W. Watson. Reprinted in *Paideuma*, III. 3 (Winter 1974[/1975]) 371.

C1822c An American Note. *Voice*, III. 10 (8 Sept. 1956) 2.
Signed: H. Briscoe. Two sentences quoted in *Paideuma*, III. 3 (Winter 1974 [/1975]) 375–6.

C1822d Painting. *Voice*, III. 10 (8 Sept. 1956) 2.
Signed: W. Watson. On Wyndham Lewis.

C1822e ✉ A Call to Fight Freudian Evil. *New Times*, XXII. 19 (21 Sept. 1956) 7.
From "An Overseas Correspondent."

C1823 FIVE FRENCH POEMS. *Edge*, Melbourne, Australia, 1 (Oct. 1956) [1–3].
Translations of five poems of which the texts were given in French in "A Study in French Poets" in *Little Review* for Feb. 1918—C327. *Contents:* Rimbaud: Comedy in Three Caresses; Cabaret Vert; Anadyomene—Laurent Tailhade: Rus—Rimbaud: Lice-Hunters. Reprinted as *Rimbaud* (1957)—B60. Reprinted also in *Listen*, III. 3/4 (Spring 1960) 22–25.

C. CONTRIBUTIONS TO PERIODICALS

c1824 Observations. *Edge*, 1 (Oct. 1956) [7].
Unsigned. (The second, fourth, fifth, and sixth of six items under this heading.)

c1825 Definitions. *Edge*, 1 (Oct. 1956) [18].
Unsigned.

c1826 Total War on "Contemplatio." *Edge*, 1 (Oct. 1956) [19–20].
A reprint of the introduction to *La Martinelli* (1956)—B56.

c1827 Beddoes: A Note. *Edge*, 1 (Oct. 1956) [28].
Signed: J. V.

c1827a Nile Water. *Voice*, III. 13 (20 Oct. 1956) 2.
Signed: Xavier Baylor.

c1827b ✉ "The Kahal System." *Voice*, III. 14 (3 Nov. 1956) [1].
"Mr. H. Briscoe writes from Boston." Reprinted in *Paideuma*, III. 3 (Winter 1974[/1975]) 376.

c1827c London. *New Times*, XXII. 24 (30 Nov. 1956) 6.
Signed: J. T.

c1827d New York. *New Times*, XXII. 24 (30 Nov. 1956) 6.
Unsigned.

1957

c1827e Press Lies. *Voice*, III. 19 (12 Jan. 1957) 2–3.
Unsigned. Summarised, with two brief quotations, in *Paideuma*, III. 3 (Winter 1974[/1975]) 371–2.

c1827f Pusillanimity. *Voice*, III. 19 (12 Jan. 1957) 3.
A single sentence, signed: A. Poet. Reprinted in *Paideuma*, III. 3 (Winter 1974[/1975]) 371.

c1827g Psychiatric Approach. *Voice*, III. 20 (26 Jan. 1957) 4.
Unsigned. On the "racket."

c1828 Greek Heritage. *Edge*, 3 (Feb. 1957) 12.
Signed: E. P. Reprinted in *Agenda*, XVII. 3/4/XVIII. 1 (Autumn/Winter/Spring 1979/1980) 75.

c1829 "Memoirs." *Edge*, 3 (Feb. 1957) 16.
Signed: E. P.

c1830 Hardy and James. *Edge*, 3 (Feb. 1957) 27.
Unsigned.

c1831 [Note on *American Colonial Documents to 1776* by Merrill Jensen]. *Edge*, 3 (Feb. 1957) 32.
Unsigned. Under the heading: "Notes."

c1831a New York. *New Times*, XXIII. 3 (8 Feb. 1957) 6.
Signed: J. B. *Contents:* The General Public ... —Eisenhower—Swedish Poets—Measurement—Progress in Baruchistan—Brooklyn Tablet.

c1831b London. *New Times*, XXIII. 3 (8 Feb. 1957) 6.

C. CONTRIBUTIONS TO PERIODICALS

Signed: K. R. O. *Contents:* [untitled]—Luigi Villari.

c1831c Questions. *New Times*, XXIII. 3 (8 Feb. 1957) 7.
Unsigned.

c1831d An American Re-Examines Douglas. *New Times*, XXIII. 4 (22 Feb. 1957) 5, 8.
Signed: George W. Gibson, New York City.

c1813e New York. *New Times*, XXIII. 4 (22 Feb. 1957) 6.
Signed: J. B. *Contents:* Money—Integrity. (The second and third of three items printed under this heading.)

c1832 "Rilke et le fascisme." *Edge*, 4 (Mar. 1957) 9.
(In English.) Signed: J. V.

c1833 In Captivity: Notebook of Thoughts in Ponza and La Maddalena. *Edge*, 4 (Mar. 1957) 10–26.
This unsigned translation from the original by Benito Mussolini was communicated by Ezra Pound and at least revised by him.

c1834 Heritage. *Edge*, 4 (Mar. 1957) 30.
Signed: H. B.

c1835 PAPILLON: FOR A SMALL BOOK UNREAD [*i.e. The Cultivation of Christmas Trees*, by T. S. Eliot]. *Edge*, 5 (May 1957) 12.
Signed: Anon.

c1836 Confucio. *Edge*, 5 (May 1957) 14.
Unsigned.

c1837 EX. *Edge*, 5 (May 1957) 27.
Signed: J. V. Four lines of doggerel on Anthony Eden and Henry Wallace.

c1838 CATULLUS ["THE DRAUGHTY HOUSE"]. *Edge*, 5 (May 1957) 34.
The first of two translations (the second reprinted from *Imagi*, 1950—C1722), signed: E. P. Reprinted, with changes, as "The Draughty House (Catullus)" in *European* for Jan. 1959—C1867. An earlier version was printed as "The Draughty House" in *Furioso* for New Year's 1940—C1528.

c1839 Guilds and Trade Unions. *Edge*, 5 (May 1957) 36.
Unsigned.

c1840 Square Dollar Series. *Edge*, 6 (June 1957) 28.
Signed: J. V.

c1841 [Note beginning: "Gathering the Limbs of Osiris . . ."]. *Edge*, 6 (June 1957) 30.
Unsigned.

c1842 APO Bulletin. *Edge*, 6 (June 1957) 30.
Unsigned.

c1843 All'Insegna del Pesce d'Oro. *Edge*, 6 (June 1957) 30.
Unsigned.

c1844 ✉ Mr. [T. S.] Eliot and Mr. Pound. *Times Literary Supplement*, London, 2891 (26 July 1957) 457.

C. CONTRIBUTIONS TO PERIODICALS

c1845 [Editorial note beginning: "A Curious Specimen . . ."]. *Edge*, 7 (Aug. 1957), p. [ii] of cover.
Unsigned.

c1846 Brancusi's Answers. *Edge*, 7 (Aug. 1957) 22.
"Ten sentences translated [by Ezra Pound] from Pesce d'Oro edition, 'Brancusi' [—D65], issued for the XIth Triennale di Milano [1957]."

c1847 [Note beginning: "A Great Light . . ."]. *Edge*, 7 (Aug. 1957) 28.
Unsigned. Under the heading: "Notes."

c1848 The Press. *Edge*, 7 (Aug. 1957) 29.
The first paragraph (14 lines), unsigned, is by Ezra Pound.

c1849 [Advertisement for] *In the American Grain*, by William Carlos Williams. *Edge*, 7 (Aug. 1957), p. [iv] of cover.
Unsigned.

c1850 [Editorial notes]. *Edge*, 8 (Oct. 1957), p. [ii] of cover.
Unsigned.

c1851 [Review of] *Leaves of Grass*, by Walt Whitman (Modern Library, U.S.) *Edge*, 8 (Oct. 1957) 26.
Signed: J. V.

c1852 [Note beginning: "What Are Called . . ."]. *Edge*, 8 (Oct. 1957) 28.
Signed: W. A. Under the heading: "Notes."

c1853 Diseases. *Edge*, 8 (Oct. 1957) 29.
Signed: N. B.

c1854 The Great Snare of Retrospect. *Edge*, 8 (Oct. 1957) 31.
Signed: J. V.

c1855 ✉ Writers Pound It Out. *Esquire*, XLVIII. 5 (Nov. 1957) 12.
Printed, with other correspondence concerning Ezra Pound, under this heading.

c1855a ✉ *Village Voice*, New York, III. 6 (4 Dec. 1957) 2.
A postcard to John Wilcox. Reproduced in facsimile.

c1856 ✉ Mr. Pound and His Friends. *Times Literary Supplement*, London, 2910 (6 Dec. 1957) 739.

1958

c1857 Alcune lettere . . . *Studi Americani*, Rome, 4 (1958) [421]–431.
Letters in Italian to Vittorio Bodini, edited by him with notes. Offprints of the article were prepared for Bodini.

c1857a ✉ Washington Bulletin. *Delta*, Montreal, Canada, 2 (Jan. 1958) 12.
An excerpt. On agenda and text books.

c1858 ✉ Mr. Pound Regrets. *Times Literary Supplement*, London, 2927 (4 Apr. 1958) 183.

c1859 [Letter to U.S. Attorney General Francis Biddle]. *Congressional Record—Appendix*, Washington, D.C. (29 Apr. 1958) A3896.

C. CONTRIBUTIONS TO PERIODICALS

Two paragraphs quoted in "The Medical, Legal, Literary and Political Status of Ezra Weston (Loomis) Pound. Extension of Remarks of Hon. Usher L. Burdick of North Dakota in the House of Representatives, Tuesday, April 29, 1958," pp. A3894–3901. (The letter is printed complete, with date 4 Aug. 1943, in *Carolina Quarterly*, Chapel Hill, N.C. (Winter 1959) 5–8.)

C1860 CANTO 99. *Virginia Quarterly Review*, Charlottesville, Va., XXXIV. 3 (Summer 1958) [339]–354.
Part of a letter from Ezra Pound about the Canto is printed under the heading: "The Green-Room," p. lxxiv.

C1861 Extracts from Pound's [Rome radio] broadcasts. *Washington Post and Times Herald*, Washington, D.C. (6 July 1958) E7.
Brief excerpts from broadcasts of 3 and 26 Feb., 2 and 8 Mar., 16 Apr., 26 May, 28 June, and 22 July 1942.

C1862 [Letters to John Theobald]. *Light Year*, Spring Valley, Calif. (Autumn 1958) [61–63, 69–71].
Two letters, 17 and 24 [?] Oct. 1957, are printed, with two letters to Pound from Theobald, and one to Pound from Miles Payne; under the title: Five Letters to and fro Ezra Pound," pp. [60–76].

C1863 CANTO 98. *L'Illustrazione Italiana*, Milan, LXXXV. 9 (Sept. 1958) 34–39.
In double columns, with Italian translation at left. With introductory note, in Italian, headed: "Sono felice d'esser tornato fra i miei . . . ," Brunnenburg, 22 July, p. 34. This note was reprinted as "Servizio di comunicazioni."

C1864 Letters from Ezra Pound. [Edited by] Patricia Hutchins. *Twentieth Century*, London, CLXIV. 980 (Oct. 1958) [355]–363.
Selections from letters to Patricia Hutchins, pp. 355, 356–7, 358, 359, and 363.

C1864a [Aphorism and statement]. *Dagens Nyheter*, Stockholm (5 Nov. 1958)
Reproduced in facsimile of the author's manuscript, with Swedish translations, as illustration for an interview with Pound by Giacomo Oreglia, "Möte med Ezra Pound." The interview is translated in Harry Meacham's *The Caged Panther*—B90—pp. 34–39, where the aphorism and statement are quoted, in Pound's English, p. 37.

C1865 CANTO C. *Yale Literary Magazine*, New Haven, Ct., CXXVI. 5 (Dec. 1958) 45–50.

1959

C1865a [Del Mar]. *Agenda*, London, 1 (Jan. 1959) [3].
The second of a series of anonymous "Items." Printed, under title "Del Mar," as by Ezra Pound in *Selected Prose* ([1973])—A93a—p. 322 (352 in A93b).

C1866 Of Misprision of Treason . . . *European*, XII. 5 (Jan. 1959) 282–3.

C1867 THREE POEMS. *European*, XII. 5 (Jan. 1959) 284.

C. CONTRIBUTIONS TO PERIODICALS

Contents: Old Zuk—The Draughty House (Catullus)—More.

C1868 ✉ How Now Red Horse? *Times Literary Supplement*, London, 2967 (9 Jan. 1959) 19.
In part, on Henry W. Longfellow.

C1869 ... Ezra Pound ai falsificatori. *Il Secolo d'Italia*, Rome (30 Jan. 1959) [1].
At head of title: Un articolo del maggiore poeta contemporaneo per il "Secolo d'Italia." On socialism.

C1870 CI DE LOS CANTARES. *European*, XII. 6 (Feb. 1959) 382–4.

C1871 CII DE LOS CANTARES. *Listen*, III. 2 (Spring 1959) [1]–3.

C1871a [Note on Danny Kaye]. *Agenda*, London, 3 (Mar. 1959) [1].

C1872 [Letter and inscription to Jaime García Terrés]. *Excelsior*, Mexico (29 Mar. 1959) [3].
Reproduced in facsimile, with Spanish translation below.

C1873 ✉ Poetry in a Brassbound World: A Challenge ... *Poetry Review*, I. 2 (Apr./June 1959) 115.
In the third person, to Thomas Moult, Chairman, Poetry Society. In acknowledgment of the dedication to him of an issue of the magazine.

C1873a ✉ Notre enquête: Ezra Pound est bref. *Le Journal des Poètes*, Brussels, XXIX. 4 (Apr. 1959) 1.

C1874 [Letter to Josef Stummvoll]. *Biblos*, Vienna, VIII. 2 ([Summer?] 1959) 75–78.
Dated 27 Apr. 1958. Printed, with German translation, pp. 78–83, and facsimile reproduction (as illustration, p. 79) of another letter, 28 July 1958, giving permission to print the earlier one, in Stummvoll's article, "Ezra Pound schreibt uns," pp. 74–83. With particular reference to a portrait of Pound by Sheri Martinelli.

C1875 [Note]. *Agenda*, 6 (July/Aug. 1959) [2].
Signed: E. P.

C1875a ✉ Ezra Pound: A Letter ... *Delta*, 8 (July 1959) 17.
Signed: E. P. An excerpt, congratulating Louis Dudek, the Editor, for his persistence, and commenting on editorial policies of little magazines in general.

C1876 ✉ Keynes Brainwashed Electorate with Economic Hogwash. *Richmond News Leader*, Richmond, Va. (14 July 1959) 12.
On an article by Chodorov, "State Control of Economy Cuts Freedom," in the issue for 13 June, concerning John Maynard Keynes and C. H. Douglas.

C1877 [Aphorisms]. *Ana Eccetera*, Genoa, 2 (30 Oct. 1959) 1.
Six in English (the first reprinted from *Dagens Nyheter* for 5 Nov. 1958— C1864a) and one in Italian. In the fascicule headed: "Servizio di comunicazione."

C1877a Ezra Pound Speaking ... Extracts from Pound's [Rome radio] Broadcasts. *Carolina Quarterly*, Chapel Hill, N.C., XII. 1 (Winter 1959 [/1960]) 9–12.

C. CONTRIBUTIONS TO PERIODICALS

Edited from the FCC transcripts by H. A. Sieber, who presumably supplied the titles. *Contents:* War or No War, Sooner or Later ["Those Parentheses"], 7 Dec. 1941—Wisdom from the Ancients ["On Resuming"], 29 Jan. 1942—Prospect of a 30 Years' War ["30 Years or a Hundred"], 3 Feb. 1942—For the American Heritage ["McArthur"], 26 Mar. 1942.

C1878 Ars vivendi. *Gadfly*, Cambridge, Mass., I. 2 (Dec. 1959) 10.
(Five lines of doggerel titled "Canzone alla rustica" are printed, p. 29, as one of the miscellaneous comments.) In English.

C1879 UN INEDITO POUNDIANO: A UN POETA CHE VOLEVA INDURMI A DIR BENE DI CERTI CATTIVI POETI, EMULI SUOI E MIEI. *L'Almanacco del Pesce d'Oro*, Milan, [1] ([Dec. 1959 for] 1960) 16.
An Italian translation by Ezra Pound of W. B. Yeats's four-line poem, "To a Poet, Who Would Have Me Praise Certain Bad Poets, Imitators of His and of Mine"; with a note in Italian about Yeats, dated Feb. 1959.

1960

C1880 Hommage à Ionesco. *Rhinozeros*, Munich, [1] (1960) [12–13].
(In English.)

C1881 [CONVERSATIONS IN COURTSHIP]. *Wort und Wahrheit*, Freiburg im Breisgau, XV. 1 (Jan. 1960) 45–49.
English text printed in double columns below German translation by Eva Hesse. Reprinted as "Conversations in Courtship" in *X, A Quarterly Review*, London, I. 4 (Oct. 1960) 253–7, and in *National Review*, New York, IX. 16 (22 Oct. 1960) 244–5. "Made from a literal rendering into Italian by Boris de Rachewiltz of an ancient Egyptian text, XXth dynasty, 1200–1169 B.C., or thereabouts." (*Note to reprint in National Review*)

C1882 VERSI PROSAICI. *Listen*, III. 3/4 (Spring 1960) 22.
Five lines. Continuing the series printed in *Versi Prosaici* ([1959])—A76.

C1882 Verse Is a Sword: Unpublished Letters. . . . Edited by Noel Stock. *X, A Quarterly Review*, London, I. 4 (Oct. 1960) 258–65.
Twelve letters to twelve correspondents, 1935–1940.

C1883a ✉ . . . Carta a C. J. C[ela]. *Los Papeles de Son Armadans*, Madrid, Palma de Mallorca, XIX. 57 *bis* (Dec. 1960) 70.
Dated 25 Apr. 1959, in English, with Spanish translation by A. K. following, pp. 71–72. (Fifty numbered copies of an offprint were prepared. These are in stiff buff paper wrappers, with title: *Ezra Pound. Carta a C.J. C. Madrid, Palma de Mallorca*, 1960 . They collate: cover-title, pp. 70–72, and measure 19·7 × 14 cm.)

1961

C1884 An Interview with Ezra Pound [by] D. G. Bridson. *New Directions in Prose and Poetry*, 17 (1961) 159–84.
Edited from actual recordings of Pound's words, and broadcast (with read-

ings) by the B.B.C. in July 1959. (This 17th volume of the annual was published 30 Nov. 1951. 8846 copies were printed. It was issued in paper wrappers.)

1962

C1885 FRAGMENT FROM CANTO 115. *Threshold*, Belfast, Ireland, 17 ([Spring? 1962]) 20.

Printed in 25 lines, only five of which appear (printed as six, two of them variant) in Canto CXV as collected in *Drafts & Fragments of Cantos CX–CXVII* ([1969])—A91. Six of the lines printed here (*i.e.* 16–18, 23–25) appear (in this order: 23, 16–18, 24–25) as "Canto 120," under by-line: The Fox (but copyrighted by Ezra Pound, 1969), in *Anonym*, Buffalo, N.Y., 4 ([Spring?] 1969) 1. The same six lines were reprinted in the same order, also as "Canto 120," as part of a New Directions advertisement in memory of Pound in the *New York Times Book Review* (26 Nov. 1972) 42, and in *The Cantos* (3d print., [New York] New Directions [1972])—A61f *note*—p. 803.

C1885a Two Early Letters of Ezra Pound [edited by] G. Thomas Tanselle. *American Literature*, XXXIV. 1 (Mar. 1962) 114–19.

Letters to Floyd Dell, written late Spring 1910 and 20 Jan. 1911. (Offprints of this article were prepared, with special title: *Two Early Letters of Ezra Pound . . . Reprinted from American Literature . . .* They collate: pp. [113]–119, and measure 22·8 × 15·5 cm.)

C1886 TWO CANTOS. *Paris Review*, Paris, 28 (Summer/Fall 1962) [13–16].
Contents: From Canto 115 [printed in 21 lines, of which all but four differ from those of C1885]—Canto 116.

C1887 A Prison-Letter. *Paris Review*, 28 (Summer/Fall 1962) [17].
"Note to Base Censor" (reproduced in facsimile of Ezra Pound's typescript) concerning *The Pisan Cantos*. (The first typed page of a draft of *The Pisan Cantos* is reproduced, p. [12].)

C1888 An Autobiographical Outline (Written for Louis Untermeyer). *Paris Review*, 28 (Summer/Fall 1962) [18]–21.
Dated, editorially, 1932, but actually written in 1930. Enrico Prampolini's sketch of Ezra Pound in Rapallo, 1934, is reproduced, p. [18].

C1889 Ezra Pound: An Interview [by Donald Hall]. *Paris Review*, 28 (Summer/Fall 1962) [22]–51.
Pound's actual words, recorded on tape and later edited by him, are quoted. Printed as the fifth in a series of interviews on "The Art of Poetry." Franco Gentilini's portrait of Pound is reproduced, p. [22], and Orfeo Tamburi's sketch of him, p. [35], along with three photographs.

C1890 FROM CANTO CXIII. *Poetry*, CI. 1/2 (Oct./Nov. 1962) 95–96.
Printed in 36 lines. (The first page of the corrected typescript of "Three Cantos, I," as printed in *Poetry* for June 1917—C260—is reproduced, p. [ix].)

C. CONTRIBUTIONS TO PERIODICALS

1963

C1891 Si c'est cela la trahison ... *Les Cahiers de L'Herne*, Paris, 3 ([Jan.?] 1963) 198–9.

The last two pages (24–25) of "A French Accent" in "*If This Be Treason......*" ([1948])—A59—translated by the author, printed in the section "Interférences" of this issue devoted to L.-F. Céline. Cover-title: *Louis-Ferdinand Céline: Des temoins, correspondance, inédits, interférences, essais, études, photographies, bibliographie.* (Of this issue, 100 special copies were also printed.)

C1892 A Letter by Ezra Pound. *Way Out*, Brookville, O., XIX. 1 (Jan. 1963) 19.

Signed: Ez. P. To an unidentified correspondent, 5 July 1957. Chiefly with reference to Frank Lloyd Wright.

C1893 On Writing and Writers [by Natalie C. Barney, translated from the French by Ezra Pound]. *Adam*, London, 299 (1962 [*i.e.* Spring? 1963]) 54–57.

This number of the periodical was reissued in book form in 1964 as *Selected Writings by Natalie Clifford Barney*—B77.

C1894 FROM CANTO CXI. *Agenda*, II. 11/12 (Mar./Apr. 1963) 1–2.

Printed in 43 lines. Reprinted, with revisions, and omission of 11 lines, as "Notes for Canto CXI."

C1895 Vi parla Ezra Pound: io so di non sapere nulla ... Intervista di Grazia Livi. *Epoca*, Milan, XIV. 652 (24 Mar. 1963) 90–93.

An English translation by Jean McClean, "Grazia Livi. Interview with Ezra Pound," was printed in *City Lights Journal*, San Francisco, Calif., 2 (1964) 37–46; another, by Natalie Harris, "The Poet Speaks: Interview by Grazia Livi," appeared in *Paideuma*, VIII. 2 (Fall 1979) [243]–247.

C1896 MINDSCAPES. *National Review*, New York, XV. 10 (10 Sept. 1963) 197.

A series of five untitled passages. Reprinted in *Agenda*, III. 3 (Dec./Jan. 1963/1964) 1–3, with title "Sections from New Cantos," and subtitles: "From CX" [parts I–II, each 13 lines]; "From CXII" [13 lines]; "Unassigned" ["Notes for Canto CXVII," 17 lines]; "From CXV" [*i.e.* 11 lines from Canto CIV, two lines unassigned, one line from "Notes for Canto CXVII," and four lines from Canto CXV].

1964

C1897 ✉ *Life*, New York, LVI. 16 (17 Apr. 1964) 27.

On the interview by Jordan Bonfante in the issue for 27 March.

C1898 FOUR TRANSLATIONS. *Agenda*, III. 5 (Sept. 1964) 1–3.

Contents: "L'ultima ora," from Montanari—"By the flat cup," from Horace—"Ask not ungainly," from Horace—"This monument will outlast," from Horace.

1965

C1899 ✉ *The Periodical*, Oxford, Eng., XXXVI. 288 (Spring 1965) 48.

A letter, 27 Aug. 1933, to the Editor of *The Oxford Book of Sixteenth Century*

C. CONTRIBUTIONS TO PERIODICALS

Verse [*i.e.* E. K. Chambers], printed from a carbon copy sent by Ezra Pound to the Oxford University Press with a note, which is also printed.

C1900 Documents on Imagism from the Papers of F. S. Flint [edited by] Christopher Middleton. *The Review*, Oxford, Eng., 15 (Apr. 1965) [35]–51.
In the course of this article, manuscript corrections by Ezra Pound on a typescript by Flint, "Les Imagistes: A Note and an Interview"—possibly a "trial run" for C73a—and manuscript notes by Pound are transcribed and letters from him to Flint are paraphrased. The notes are reproduced on page [i] of the cover and on pages [31–34].

C1901 ⊠ Pound's Bust. *Time*, New York, LXXXVI. 6 (6 Aug. 1965) 14.
With reference to an article on Gaudier-Brzeska in the issue for 23 July. (In the "Atlantic edition," the letter appears on page 8.)

C1902 [TWO CANTOS]. *Niagara Frontier Review*, Buffalo, N.Y., 1 (Fall 1965/Spring 1966) 29–36.
Contents: Canto CX—Canto 116.

C1903 FROM CANTO 115. *Agenda*, IV. 2 (Oct./Nov. 1965) 3.
Printed in 21 lines, not including four lines printed in C1896. (This number of the periodical is a "Special issue in honour of Ezra Pound's eightieth birthday.")

C1904 Selections from Ezra Pound's Letters to Robert Creeley, March 1950 to October 1951. *Agenda*, IV. 2 (Oct./Nov. 1965) 14–21.

C1905 AUS CANTO CXIV. *Text + Kritik*, Aachen, 10/11 (Oct. 1965) 48–50.
Canto CXIV, in English (omitting about 30 lines), printed along with a German translation by Eva Hesse.

C1906 Correspondance. *Les Cahiers de L'Herne*, Paris, 6 ([Nov.] 1965) 285–321.
This section of the first of two issues of the periodical devoted to Ezra Pound (of both of which 40 special copies were also issued) contains a letter to Gabrielle Buffet, 16 Feb. [1938], pp. 306–7, and one to Jean Cocteau, p. 308, both written in French; and letters to Vittorio Bodini, with notes by Bodini, pp. 317–21, all in French translation. (The notes include a French translation of Pound's "Impedimenti alla critica" from *Vedetta Mediterranea* for 19 May 1941—C1598.) The plates at the end of the issue include reproductions of a page of typescript of Mary de Rachewiltz's Italian translation of Canto XI, with Pound's corrections in Italian, and a page of proof of Canto 98, with his corrections in English.

C1907 For T. S. E[liot]. *Sewanee Review*, LXXIV. 1 (Winter [1965/]1966) [109].
Signed: E. P. An obituary tribute.

C1908 Tidings from Pound to Joyce. *Esquire*, LXIV. 6 (Dec. 1965) 152, 286, [288].
Dated 6 Sept. 1915, a letter congratulating Joyce on receiving a grant that Pound had helped him obtain. Part of an article, "Other People's Mail. A bundle of really first-class letters in various moods . . . ," pp. 149–52, 264, 266, 270, 272, 274, 276, 278, 280, 282, 284, 286, [288].

C. CONTRIBUTIONS TO PERIODICALS

1966

C1909 [Letters to W. Moelwyn Merchant]. *Les Cahiers de L'Herne*, 7 ([May 1966])
605–13.
Letters of 17 Sept., 1 and 7 Nov. 1957, and 25 Mar. 1958, with some notes
by Ezra Pound on Sir Edward Coke, are quoted in English, with French
translation below, in the course of an article, "Souvenirs d'Ezra Pound,"
by Merchant. (This is the second of two issues of the magazine devoted to
Ezra Pound. 40 special copies were also issued.)

C1910 Causerie écrite en français (1941). *Les Cahiers de L'Herne*, 7 ([May 1966])
693–5.
"Ces pages, publiées pour la première fois, ont été retrouvées dans les
archives de Pound à Brunnenburg."

C1911 [Letter in French to the Editor of *Le Figaro Littéraire*, Paris, 2 Oct. 1965].
Les Cahiers de L'Herne, 7 ([May 1966]), verso of third plate at end.
Reproduced in facsimile of Ezra Pound's handwritten original. (The letter
was not printed in *Le Figaro Littéraire*.)

C1912 Europe Calling—Pound Speaking. Ezra Pound Speaking. *International
Times*, London (31 Oct./13 Nov. 1966) [1]–2.
"On Continuity, July 6th 1942," edited from two consecutive Rome radio
broadcasts, 6 and 7 July, p. 2, preceded by short excerpts from other broadcasts, p. [1]. Reprinted in the issue for 27 Oct./9 Nov. 1967, pp. 4–5.

C1913 [Letter to James Joyce, 22 Nov. 1918]. *Tri-Quarterly*, Evanston, Ill., 8 (Winter
[1966/]1967) 176.
Part of an article, "Joyce Letters, Edited by Richard Ellmann," pp. 166–76.
Reprinted from *Letters of James Joyce* ([1966])—B85—vol. 2, pp. 423–4.

C1914 ... Una lettera inedita. *Nuovi Studi Gentiliani*, Rome, I. 3 (Dec. 1966) 7.
A letter, for the most part in English, to V[ittorio]. V[ettori]., Nov. 1959,
in facsimile.

1967

C1915 REDONDILLAS, OR SOMETHING OF THAT SORT. *Poetry Australia*, Sydney, Australia, 15 (Apr. 1967) 5–11.
Reprinted from page-proofs of *Canzoni* (1911)—A7—at the University of
Texas Library at Austin. Includes "Note on the Proper Names in the Redondillas," by Ezra Pound, p. 11. With a note by N[oel]. S[tock]., p. 4.

C1916 ... An Unpublished Letter by Ezra Pound [edited by David Farmer].
Texas Quarterly, Austin, X. 4 (Winter 1967[/1968]) 95–[104].
A typewritten letter to Samuel Putnam, 3 Feb. 1927, reproduced in facsimile, pp. [97–104], following an introductory note by the editor. The first
page of the letter is reproduced also as frontispiece for the issue, p. [6].

1968

C1917 [Letters to Thomas Hardy]. *Southern Review*, Baton Rouge, La., IV (N.S.).
1 (Jan. 1968) 97–103.

C. CONTRIBUTIONS TO PERIODICALS

Five letters, written between 20 Nov. 1920 and 28 Jan. 1925, printed in full in an article by Patricia Hutchins, "Ezra Pound and Thomas Hardy," pp. 90–104.

C1918 CANTO CXIV. *Stony Brook*, Stony Brook, L.I., N.Y., I. 1/2 (Fall 1968) 1–3.
This issue of the periodical also contains a reproduction of "How I Began"—C86—p. [i], and reprints "René Crevel"—C1490—pp. 154–9.

C1919 The "Lost" Manuscripts of T. S. Eliot, by Donald Gallup. *Times Literary Supplement*, London, 3480 (7 Nov. 1968) 1238–40.
In the course of this article describing the Eliot manuscripts given and sold to John Quinn and now in the Berg Collection of the New York Public Library, annotations by Ezra Pound on the original drafts of *The Waste Land* and other early poems of Eliot are summarised and/or quoted. On page 1239 is reproduced a page of typescript bearing the opening lines of Section II of *The Waste Land*, annotated by Eliot and Pound. The article, with the illustrations, was reprinted with corrections in the *Bulletin of the New York Public Library*, New York, LXXII. 10 (Dec. 1968) 641–52.

C1920 FROM CANTO CXIII. *New Yorker*, New York, XLIV. 41 (30 Nov. 1968) 64.
Ninety lines, omitting the first 36.

C1921 Words from Ezra Pound, [edited by] Jose Vasquez-Amaral. *Rutgers Review*, Rutgers, N.J., III (Winter 1968[/1969]) 40–43.
Selections from letters written to Vasquez-Amaral, 1952–1955, with reproduction of one page of a typed letter, p. 43.

1969

C1922 [Greeting in French to Ungaretti]. *Les Cahiers de L'Herne*, 11 (1969) 296.

C1923 Preface: *Discrete Series* by George Oppen. *Stony Brook*, 3/4 (Fall 1969) 21.
A reprint from B34. Reprinted also in *Paideuma*, X. 1 (Spring 1981) [13].

C1924 NOTES FOR CANTO CXI [AND NOTES FOR A LATER CANTO]. *Sumac*, Fremont, Mich., I. 2 (Winter 1969[/1970]) 5–7.
The "Notes for a Later Canto" are the final group printed in *Drafts & Fragments of Cantos CX–CXVII* ([1969])—A91—p. 32.

1970

C1925 . . . Letters to a Polish Scholar [edited by Stanisław Helsztyński]. *Kwartalnik Neofilologiczny*, Warsaw, XVII. 3 ([Mar.?] 1970) [299]–323.
Forty-three letters and cards to Stanisław Wiktor Jankowski, 15 June [1954] to 31 Jan. 1958, chiefly concerning his translation of Richard of Saint Victor's *Benjamin Minor* (1960)—B68; and four letters to Stefanie Jankowska, his sister, 14 Aug. to [11 Sept. 1953].

C1926 PIGEONS. *Sunday Times Weekly Review*, London (26 Apr. 1970) 36.

C. CONTRIBUTIONS TO PERIODICALS

A poem by Ugo Fasolo, translated by Ezra Pound; with a note by Cyril Connolly. Reprinted in *Atlantic*, CCXXVI. 5 (Nov. 1970) [94].

C1927 NOTES, PARTS OF WHICH HAVE BEEN USED IN LATER DRAFTS [OF THE CANTOS]. *Agenda*, VIII. 3/4 (Autumn/Winter 1970/1971) 3–4.
Sixty-seven lines. (This number of the magazine is a "Special Issue in Honour of Ezra Pound's Eighty-Fifth Birthday." It contains photographs and articles, especially on *Drafts & Fragments of Cantos CX–CXVII* ([1969])—A91.

C1928 [Letters to Lewis Leary]. *St. Andrews Review*, Laurinberg, N.C., I. 1 (Fall/Winter 1970/1971) 4, 6–7, 8–9.
In an article, "Pound-Wise, Penny Foolish: Correspondence on Getting together a Volume of Criticism [by] Lewis Leary," pp. 4–9, a postcard and one letter (of 4 or 5 Nov. 1953) from Ezra Pound to Leary are reproduced, and some eight other letters or parts of letters, 1953–1957, are printed. The complete article was reprinted "with considerable additions" in *Paideuma*, I. 2 (Winter 1972[/1973]) [153]–159.

C1929 A Letter [to Sadakichi Hartmann] from Ezra Pound ... 18 Aug. 1924. *Sadakichi Hartmann Newsletter*, Riverside, Calif., I. 4 (Winter 1970[/1971]) 2.
Printed, boxed, in connexion with an article, "The Ezra Pound Correspondence: Letters to a Member of the Lost Legion [edited by Harry Lawton]," pp. .[1]–3. Other letters from Pound to Hartmann are summarised and Pound's letter to the Editor of the *Transatlantic Review* [*i.e.* Ford Madox Ford] about Hartmann's *Confucius* is reprinted, p. 2, from the issue for Sept. 1924—C667

1971

C1930 Freedom de facto. *Agenda*, IX. 2/3 (Spring/Summer 1971) 23–25.
An essay "written *c.* 1940–41, but not published until now."

C1931 A New Letter by Ezra Pound about T. S. Eliot [edited by] Donald E. Herdeck. *Massachusetts Review*, Amherst, Mass., XII. 2 (Spring 1971) 287–92.
The typed letter, to Clarence Stratton, 1 Aug. 1923, is reproduced in facsimile, pp. [288–9]; it concerns Bel Esprit (see E2e, f) and Pound's plan to get Eliot out of Lloyds Bank.

C1932 ✉ *BOC Serien*, Staffanstorp, Sweden, 9 (15 Aug. 1971) 3.
A letter, in English, to Bo Cavefors, Ezra Pound's Swedish publisher, 12 Aug. 1960, reproduced in facsimile, in this number of the advertising brochure issued by the firm.

C1933 PRAYER FOR A DEAD BROTHER. *Antigonish Review*, Antigonish, N.S., 8 (Winter [1971/] 1972) 27.
An elegy for the brother of Sheri Martinelli, who shot himself on 23 Sept. 1954.

C. CONTRIBUTIONS TO PERIODICALS

1972

C1934 [Letters to Vianney M. Devlin, O. F. M.]. *Greyfriar: Siena [College] Studies in Literature*, Loudonville, N. Y., XIII (1972) 42, 44.

In an article, "In memoriam—E.P. [by] Vianney M. Devlin, O.F.M.," a postcard and a letter from Ezra Pound to Father Devlin are printed, pp. 42 and 44, respectively, and on the latter page appears Pound's definition of "Usury."

C1935 . . . Ching Ming: A New Paideuma. *Paideuma*, Orono, Me., I. 1 (Spring/Summer 1972), p. [ii] of cover.

Ideogram at head of title. Signed: E. P. Excerpts from *Guide to Kulchur* ([1938])—A45—pp. 57, 58, and from Ezra Pound's translation of *Confucius. [Ta Hsio:] The Great Digest* . . . (1947)—A58—pp. 29, 31, 33. Reprinted in all subsequent issues.

C1936 Letters to Viola Baxter Jordan, Edited with Commentary by Donald Gallup. *Paideuma*, I. 1 (Spring/Summer 1972) [107]–111.

Two letters, 12 and 24 Oct. 1907, with brief explanatory notes by Ezra Pound for "Malrin" and "To R[obert]. B[rowning]."

C1937 [Letter and note to Charles Martell]. *Bulletin of the Friends of the Owen D. Young Library*, St. Lawrence University, Canton, N.Y., II. 1 (June 1972) 3.

The letter, 22 June 1957, and the later note are printed in an article by Martell, "Uncle Ez and the Kid from Canton," pp. 2–8.

C1938 La collaborazione al "Popolo di Alessandria" di Ezra Pound. *La Destra*, Rome, II. 11/12 (Nov./Dec. 1972) [117]–137.

Contents: Storia e cronaca da ricordare—Posizione—Scopo o tecnica—Non insabbiarsi—Del silenzio—Aggiornare—D'accordo—Cosi' scriveva Marcantonio—Confucio parla [1–24]—. . . Attendismo ⟨cioè una forma personale e diversa⟩ —Poundiana—Le ultime 2 massime di Confucio [25–26]—Oro e princisbecco—Contro usura—Qui Ezra Pound. With "Premessa," signed: G[ianfranco]. D[e]. T[urris]., pp. [117]–118, and footnotes, pp. 136–7.

C1939 Appunti inediti per i "Cantos." *La Destra*, II. 11/12 (Nov./Dec. 1972) [146]–149.

Two pages of manuscript notes, in English and Latin, reproduced in facsimile, pp. [146], [148], with transcriptions opposite, pp. 147, 149.

C1940 Ezra Pound, Educator: Two Uncollected Pound Letters [edited by] Maurice Hungiville. *American Literature*, XLIV. 3 (Nov. 1972) 462–9.

A letter from Ezra Pound to President Joseph Brewer of Olivet College, Olivet, Mich., 1 July [1938], is printed, and a letter from Pound to the editors is reprinted from a mimeographed student publication, *Thursday* for 6 Apr. 1939—C1505a. (Offprints of this article were prepared, with special title: *Ezra Pound, Educator: Two Uncollected Pound Letters . . . Reprinted from American Literature* . . . They collate: pp. [461]–469, and measure 22·8 × 15·3 cm.) For a corrected version of the first letter see C1985.

C1941 Copy of "Note from E. P. to Chak," "March 1949." *Indian Journal of American Studies*, Hyderabad, India, II. 2 (Dec. 1972) 14.

C. CONTRIBUTIONS TO PERIODICALS

Printed at the end of an article, "A Note on Ezra Pound," by Amiya Chakravarty, pp. [12]–14. The "Note" concerns Pound's debt to Rabindranath Tagore. (The entire issue of the periodical is devoted to Pound.)

C1942 [Letters to Rabindranath Tagore]. *Indian Journal of American Studies*, II. 2 (Dec. 1972) [55–56].
Two letters, 28 Apr. [1929] and [Dec. 1912], are printed, the earlier preceded and the later followed by a plate reproducing the complete letter. In an article, "Ezra Pound and Rabindranath Thakur," which follows, pp. [57]–69, Deba P. Patnaik quotes parts of these letters and of letters from Tagore to Pound.

1973

C1943 . . . Letters to an Editor of His Anthology [edited by Stanisław Helsztyński]. *Kwartalnik Neofilologiczny*, XX. 1 ([Jan.?] 1973) [59]–65.
Eight letters to Eaghor G. Kostetzky, 15 July 1957 to 1959, chiefly concerning the Ukrainian translation of *Selected Works* (1960)—D240.

C1944 Note to Harry Crosby's "Torchbearer" (1931). *Alcheringa*, New York, 5 (Spring/Summer 1973) 92–93.
A reprint of Ezra Pound's "Notes" to Harry Crosby's *Torchbearer* (1931)—B25.

C1945 Three Unpublished Letters by Ezra Pound [edited by] Carlo Izzo. *Italian Quarterly*, Riverside, Calif., XVI. 64 (Spring 1973) 117–18.
Notes by Izzo, pp. 117–18, accompanying photographic reproductions of letters written to him: 2 Oct. [1956], on plate facing p. 118; 6 Nov. [1956], on its verso; and 10 Jan. 1958, on plate facing p. 3. (This is a special issue of the periodical "on Ezra Pound and Italy.")

C1946 Ezra Pound's Pennsylvania, by Carl Gatter & Noel Stock. *Poetry Australia*, 46 ([Spring?] 1973) 5–36.
In the course of this article "Ezra on the Strike"—C o—is reprinted, pp. 14–15, and various other Pound items are printed for the first time: 11 lines from three poems in the manuscript "Hilda's Book"; excerpts from letters and one complete letter to Mary Moore (of Trenton), pp. 23–25, including 12 lines from poems sent to her in 1907; and letters to the Gatters, pp. 30, 31–32. Reprinted with additions and revisions as *Ezra Pound's Pennsylvania* (1976)—B116.

C1947 Ezra Pound's Letters to Olivet [College, edited by] Maurice Hungiville. *Texas Quarterly*, Austin, XVI. 2 (Summer 1973) 77–87.
Transcriptions, reproduced from typewritten copy, of six letters, five of them addressed to Joseph Brewer, President. For corrected version see C1985.

C1948 "Damnation Bureaucrats . . ." [with accompanying letter to Judge Beals, 8 May [1930]]. *Hyperion*, Berkeley, Calif., III. 3 (Fall 1973) [4–6].
Ezra Pound's manuscript is reproduced, pp. [5–6], with transcription, p. [4].

C. CONTRIBUTIONS TO PERIODICALS

C1949 A Schema for XXX Cantos. *Paideuma*, II. 2 (Fall 1973) [201].
Written "on the back of an undatable form . . .". Transcribed with annotations by Hugh Kenner.

C1950 [Letters to Benito Mussolini]. *Storia Contemporanea*, Bologna, IV. 3 (Sept. 1973) 455, 456, 457, 458.
In Italian, dated 22 Dec. 1936, 12 Feb. 1940, and 10 May 1943, with a note to his private secretary, 13 May 1943. Quoted in an article, "Ezra Pound e il fascismo," by Niccolò Zapponi, pp. 423–74, which also includes an Italian translation of a passage from *Social Credit: An Impact* (1935)—A40, pp. 433–5. (Offprints were prepared: *Niccolò Zapponi. Ezra Pound e il fascismo. Estratto da "Storia contemporanea", anno IV, 1973, n. 3. Società Editrice Il Mulino, Bologna.* They collate: cover-title, pp. 423–479, 1 leaf, and measure 21·1 × 14·8 cm.)

C1951 [Letters to John Price]. *Paideuma*, II. 3 (Winter 1973[/1974]) 428–47.
In an article, "Ezra Pound, John Price, and *The Exile*," by Barry S. Alpert, 14 letters and a note from Pound to Price, 1925–1927, are quoted.

1974

C1952 [Notes on, and translation of, a poem by Li Po]. *Paideuma*, III. 1 (Spring 1974) [55]–59.
In an article, "E. P. Translating a Li Po Poem," by David Gordon, Pound's notes and his translation of a poem by Li Po (from an anthology by Chüan Tung-hua, Shanghai, 1935, p. 85) are reproduced.

C1953 [Note sent to Naresh Guha]. *Paideuma*, III. 1 (Spring 1974) 68.
The note is reproduced at the end of a descriptive statement, "E. P. and Naresh Guha," by Deba P. Patnaik, p. [67].

C1954 Transcript of a Shortwave Broadcast from Italy . . . on April 23, 1942 ["MacLeish"]. *Swarthmore College Bulletin*, Swarthmore, Pa. (Oct. 1974) 7.
Printed as a boxed illustration for Julien Cornell's article, "The Last Years of Ezra Pound," pp. 4–7.

C1955 Ezra Pound's Reply to an "Old-World" Letter [edited by] F. G. Atkinson. *American Literature*, XLVI. 3 (Nov. 1974) [357]–359.
A letter written, Oct. 1912, to Sir Arthur T. Quiller-Couch in response to his request for permission to include two lyrics by Pound in *The Oxford Book of Victorian Verse* ([1912]).

C1956 Addition to "As Sextant." *Paideuma*, III. 3 (Winter 1974[/1975]) 306.

C1957 [Letters to Prafulla Das]. *Paideuma*, III. 3 (Winter 1974[/1975]) 314, 315, 316, 317.
Quoted in an article, "Only the Quality of the Affection Endures," by Deba P. Patnaik, pp. [313]–318.

1975

C1958 Yoro (Name of the Waterfall in Mino), by Motokiyō. *Paideuma*, VI. 1 (Spring 1975) [349]–353.

C. CONTRIBUTIONS TO PERIODICALS

Ezra Pound's editing of Fenollosa's rough draft translation from the note-books. With explanatory introduction, "Ezra Pound: Editor of Nō," pp. [345]–347, and conclusion, p. 353, by Richard Taylor.

1976

C1959 . . . Letters to William Butler Yeats, edited with Comments by C. F. Terrell. *Antæus*, Tangier, London, New York, 21/22 (Spring/Summer 1976) 34–49.
Nine letters addressed to Yeats, 1914–[1932], and five to Mrs. Yeats, [1938]–1958.

C1960 Pound to Vasquez Amaral: Two Letters. *Point of Contact*, New York, 2 (Mar./Apr. 1976) [68].
Text reproduced from typewritten copy. The second letter is reprinted from *Rutgers Review* for Winter 1968[/1969]—C1917—where it had appeared with the omission of 24 words.

C1961 Letters to Natalie Barney. Edited with Commentary by Richard Sieburth. *Paideuma*, V. 2 (Fall 1976) [279]–295.
Ten letters and notes, 1919–1954, with brief excerpts from others.

C1962 [Letters to Henry Swabey]. *Paideuma*, V. 2 (Fall 1976) [329]–337.
Paraphrased and brief excerpts quoted in an article, "A Page without which . . . ," by Henry Swabey. At the end of the article, pp. 336–7, Ezra Pound's "E P Guide to Italy," prepared for Swabey, is printed.

C1963 NEWLY DISCOVERED POEMS OF EZRA POUND. *Atlantic Monthly*, Boston, Mass., CCXXXVIII. 3 (Sept. 1976) 48–50.
Contents: From Chebar [probably written between 1912 and 1915, submitted to Harriet Monroe for publication in *Poetry* but not printed there]—To Hulme (T. E.) and Fitzgerald (a certain) [set in type for *Canzoni* but deleted in proof]—Envoi: A mon bien aimé—Untitled Poem [*ca.* 1908, beginning: "Thoughts moving | in her eyes," from the San Trovaso notebook]. With a note by James Laughlin.

C1964 EZRA POUND. *Poetry*, CXXIX. 2 (Nov. 1976) 63–74.
Contents: Leviora (I Against Form; II Hic jacet)—Statement of Being—For the Triumph of the Arts: Jacques Chardinel of the Albigenses—Frag-menti—Fragment to W. C. W[illiams].'s Romance—In That Country—I Wait—Fragment ("I have felt the lithe wind | blowing")

C1965 A Letter to Jay Hubbell. *Paideuma*, V. 3 (Winter 1976[/1977]) [417–18].
The letter, postmarked 20 Oct. 1935, is reproduced, p. [418], along with its envelope, p. [417]; with an introductory note by Lewis Leary.

1977

C1966 BLUE DUN. *Fly Fisherman*, Dorset, Vt., VIII. 3 (Spring 1977) 28.
A reprint of lines 33–52 of Canto LI. The source of these lines is Charles Bowlker's *Art of Angling* (London, Proctor & Jones, 1829).

C. CONTRIBUTIONS TO PERIODICALS

C1967 A Manifesto. *Paideuma*, VI. 1 (Spring 1977) 114.

A reprint of the broadside ([1953])—E2ua—signed by ten individuals and, according to a note, "E P: Maker of Connections," by Margaret Bates (one of the signers), p. [115], written by Ezra Pound himself.

C1968 Two Unpublished Pound Letters: Pound's Aid to Dreiser [edited] by Louis Oldani. *Library Chronicle*, University of Pennsylvania, Philadelphia, Pa., XLII. 1 (Summer 1977) 67–70.

Letters to Harold Hersy in connexion with the protest against the suppression of Theodore Dreiser's *The "Genius"* (see C237). (Offprints of the article were prepared, with special title: *Offprint ... Two Unpublished Pound Letters ...* They collate: cover-title, pp. 67–70, and measure 22·9 × 15·3 cm.)

C1969 Ezra Pound's "Four Steps." Introduction by D. G. Bridson. *Southern Review*, XIII. 4 (Autumn 1977) 862–71.

The "Introduction," pp. 862–9, chiefly concerns the recordings Bridson made for the B.B.C., 8 and 9 Dec. 1956, of Ezra Pound reading his poems and 9 Dec. of Pound reading "a statement ['to be made impromptu ... purely for the record ...'] regarding what he called the 'four steps' which had brought him into conflict with the American authorities," and includes a note from Pound to Bridson, [Apr. 1958], concerning the "Four Steps." The statement was broadcast on the B.B.C. Home Service, 22 Apr. 1958, and again on the Third Programme, 7 May 1958. Reprinted in *Agenda*, XVII. 3/4/XVIII. 1 (Autumn/Winter/Spring 1979/1980) 131–41.

1979

C1970 CANTO 115. *Agenda*, XVII. 3/4/XVIII. 1 (Autumn/Winter/Spring 1979/1980) 3–4.

Printed in 52 lines, the first 24 of which are reprinted from *Threshold* (1962)—C1885. With a note by Mary de Rachewiltz concerning another version of the Canto with a variant line. (This is the "Twenty-first Anniversary Ezra Pound Special Issue" of the periodical.)

C1971 Some Letters to William Cookson 1956–1970. *Agenda*, XVII. 3/4/XVIII. 1 (Autumn/Winter/Spring 1979/1980) [6–47].

Thirty-five letters, page two of another letter, and a card, 1956–1970, are reproduced, with a note by Cookson about the letters, p. 5.

C1972 Four Uncollected Literary Essays. *Agenda*, XVII. 3/4/XVIII. 1 (Autumn/Winter/Spring 1979/1980) 48–64.

Contents: Lytton Strachey on Left Over Celebrity [actually reprinted from *Instigations* ([1920])—A18]—Arthur Symons—Merit—Purgatory.

C1973 Gists from Uncollected Prose, Chosen by William Cookson. *Agenda*, XVII. 3/4/XVIII. 1 (Autumn/Winter/Spring 1979/1980) 71–75.

Brief excerpts from C105, 127, 182, 321, 399, 483, 485, 487, 505, 511, 618, 1071, 1187, 1278, 1387, 1400, 1504, and 1828.

C1974 [Excerpts from the Rome radio broadcasts, and from letters]. *Agenda*, XVII. 3/4/XVIII. 1 (Autumn/Winter/Spring 1979/1980) 157–86.

C. CONTRIBUTIONS TO PERIODICALS

Quoted in an article, "Fragments of an Atmosphere," by Mary de Rachewiltz.

C1975 [Letter to Romano Bilenchi]. *Paideuma*, VIII. 3 (Winter 1979[/1980]) 430.
In Italian, dated 21 June [1942?]. Reproduced in connexion with an article, "Rapallo, 1941," by Bilenchi, translated, with notes and an introduction, by David Anderson, pp. [431]–442.

C1976 [Two letters to Adriano Ungaro, two to Cornelio di Marzio, and one to Odon Por]. *Paideuma*, VIII. 3 (Winter 1979[/1980]) 455–7.
Quoted, the first two in English, the others translated from the Italian by Tim Redman, in his article, "The Repatriation of Pound, 1939–1942: A View from the Archives," pp. [447]–457.

C1977 Letters to John Buchan, 1934–1935. Edited by S. Namjoshi. *Paideuma*, VIII. 3 (Winter 1979[/1980]) [461]–483.
Buchan's replies are quoted, pp. 480–3.

1980

C1978 Letters to Elizabeth Winslow. Edited with Commentary by James H. Thompson. *Paideuma*, IX. 2 (Fall 1980) [340]–356.
An inscription by Ezra Pound is reproduced, p. [340].

1981

C1979 Ezra Pound & Louis Zukofsky: Letters 1928–1930, edited by Barry Ahearn. *Montemora*, New York, 8 (1981) 149–83.
Ten letters to Zukofsky, Aug. 1928 to Dec. 1930, with nine letters from him to Pound. The Pound letters of 24/25 and 27 Nov. 1930 include stanzas for Pound's "song," "Yiddisher Charlestown Band" ["Yittischer Charleston"], printed in *An "Objectivists" Anthology, Edited by Louis Zukofsky*—B29—pp. [44]–45.

C1980 On Giving It Up (vide Mr Eliot, portrayed by the adolescent) . . . ⟨1934⟩. *Montemora*, 8 (1981) 184–6.

C1981 Paul Morand. Aurora. *Antæus*, 40/41 (Spring 1981) 145–59.
A chapter of *Tendres Stocks* (1921), translated from the French by Ezra Pound in 1922.

C1982 . . . FROM AN UNPUBLISHED DRAFT OF CANTO LXXXIV. *Sulfur*, Pasadena, Calif., 1 ([Summer] 1981) [4]–10.
A section of the Canto not published in *The Pisan Cantos* ([1948])—A60—printed in 121 lines, with reproduction of the final page of Ezra Pound's typescript. An introductory note by Matthew Jennett quotes also two lines present in another typescript of the Canto but not included in the published book.

C1983 FROM SYRIA: the worksheets, proofs, and text, edited with an introduction by Robin Skelton. *Malahat Review*, Victoria, B.C., 59 (July 1981) 60–[92].

363

This number of the periodical was actually issued Sept. 1981. The Pound contribution was printed separately as *From Syria* (1981)—A106, where a fuller description is given.

C1984 The Interview [of Vanni Ronsisvalle and Pier Paolo Pasolini with Ezra Pound in 1968]. *Paideuma*, X. 2 (Fall 1981) 333–42.

An English translation of Pasolini's questions, along with Pound's answers (in English) from "An Hour with Ezra Pound," a documentary filmed by R.A.I. Televisione Italiana. Printed as part of an article, "Breaking the Silence: The Interview of Vanni Ronsisvalle and Pier Paolo ,Pasolini with Ezra Pound in 1968," by David Anderson, pp. [331]–345. Excerpts from Pound's text (composed specifically for the interview) appear in Vittorugo Contino's *Ezra Pound in Italy* ([1970])—B100.

C1985 Letters from Ezra Pound to Joseph Brewer. Edited with Commentary by Brita Lindberg-Seyersted. *Paideuma*, X. 2 (Fall 1981) [369]–382.

A corrected version of letters printed in C1940 and 1947. A letter of 11 Sept. [1939], printed in *Impact* (1960)—A78—p. 277, is also included.

C1986 TRANSLATIONS FROM THE PROVENÇAL AND THE ITALIAN ... with an Introduction by James Laughlin. *Antæus*, 44 (Winter [1981/] 1982) [16]–33.

". . . assembled and edited by Charlotte Ward, who also did extensive research to identify the foreign-language texts from which Pound worked." (*Introduction*, "Pound and the Troubadours," *by* James Laughlin). The introduction quotes, in English translation, three lines from Canto LXXIII, and excerpts from a postcard from Pound to Dorothy Pound and two postcards from Mrs. Pound to her parents, 1919. *Contents:* Arnaut Daniel. [Poem V:] Lanquan vei fueill e flors e frug ("When I see leaf and flower and fruit"), *ca.* 1911, and second version, *ca.* 1917—[Poem VI:] Er vei vermeils, vertz, blaus, blancs, groucs ("Now I see red, gold, green, blue, white"), *ca.* 1911, and second version, *ca.* 1917—Amors e jois e liocs e tems ("Joy, Amor and the time and the place"), 30 Mar. 1911, and second version, *ca.* 1917—Jaufré Rudel. Amor de lonh ["Lan quand li iorn son lonc en mai"] ("When the days be long in May"), *ca.* 1905—Francesco Petrarch. Quel vago impallider ("That pallorous desire which thy sweet laughter"), *cà.* 1905–1908—Guido Cavalcanti (attributed). Guarda ben dico, guarda, ben ti guarda ("Guard thee well guard thee well I say"), *ca.* 1920. (The Arnaut Daniel versions differ from those printed in *The Translations* ([1953])—A66.)

C1987 Pound's *Personae*: from Manuscript to Print, by C. G. Petter. *Studies in Bibliography*, Charlottesville, Va., 35 ([Dec. 1981, for] 1982) [111]–132.

In this article on drafts and proofs relating to *Personae* ([1909])—A3—in the University of Victoria Library, corrections, annotations, and deletions by Pound on various proofs for the book are quoted. (A detailed catalogue of the material, citing variants, is given, pp. 124–32.) Reproduced on plate 1 is a corrected proof for the title-page; on plate 2, an early manuscript plan for the book; on plate 3, an early typed draft of "From Syria," with title "The Song of Piere Bremon Lo Tort, That he sent to his lady in

C. CONTRIBUTIONS TO PERIODICALS

Provence he being in Syria a crusader"; on plate 4, proofs of two pages of the "Notes," showing deletions; and on plate 5, corrected proofs of the dedication page. A postcard from Pound to Elkin Mathews, 31 Jan. 1908, is printed, p. 132.

C1988 QUEEN VICTORIA POEM. *Library Chronicle of the University of Texas at Austin*, Austin, Texas, New Series 17 (1981 [*i.e.* Feb. 1982]) 33–[34].

Eighteen lines, unfinished; written in 1905 on the end-papers of Swinburne's *Laus Veneris and Other Poems and Ballads*. The manuscript is reproduced (p. [34]) and the poem transcribed (p. 33) in an article by Michael J. King, "An ABC of E.P.'s Library," pp. [30]–45. The article includes brief examples of Pound's annotations and passages marked by him in other volumes from his library now at the University of Texas at Austin.

C1989 [Comments on "Medallion" in a letter to Eva Hesse, 28 Jan. 1953]. *Paideuma*, X. 3 (Winter 1981 [/1982]) 584.

Identifying "Luini" as referring to Raymonde Collignon. Nine lines of Ezra Pound's typed letter are reproduced in facsimile as the conclusion of a note by Eva Hesse, "Raymonde Collignon . . .," pp. [583]–584. (Through a printing error the reproduction was not actually included in the article as published. A corrected cancel leaf, with the article complete, was issued, with an explanatory note by the editor, 26 Jan. 1982.)

D. TRANSLATIONS
INTO FOREIGN LANGUAGES OF
BOOKS, POEMS, AND ESSAYS
BY EZRA POUND

Items are arranged alphabetically by language and, within language groups, chronologically under the respective headings: "Books," "Anthologies," and "Periodicals." Titles of poems and volumes of poetry are printed in small capital letters. An item not seen is marked by an asterisk.

D. TRANSLATIONS

ARABIC
BOOK:

D1*[ASH'ĀR AL-HUBB 'INDA QUDAMĀ AL-MIṢRIYĪN. Bayrūt? 1969]. 71 pp. illus. 17 cm. A translation of *Love Poems of Ancient Egypt.*

ANTHOLOGIES:

D2 [KHAMSŪN QAṢĪDAH MIN AL-SHI'R AL-AMRĪKĪ AL-MU'ĀṢIR . . . Bayrūt, Dār al-Yaqẓah al-'Arabīyah, 1963]. 1 blank leaf, 4 leaves, 11–216, [4] pp. 24.3 cm. Contains a translation, by Tawfīq Ṣāyigh, from Canto LXXXI, pp. 83–84.

D2a*[SELECTED POEMS, by Badre Shaker Al-Sayyab. Baghdad, *ca.* 1965?]. Contains a translation, by Al-Sayyab, of "The River-Merchant's Wife: A Letter," pp. 14–16.

PERIODICALS:

D3*[COMMISSION]. *Hasool el Arba'a,* Baghdad, 1 (Sept. 1954). Translated by Buland al Haidari and Desmond Stewart.

D3a THE RIVER MERCHANT'S WIFE. *Pound Newsletter,* Berkeley, Calif., 8 (Oct. 1955) 21. Translated by Buland al Haidari. (Reprinted in D240, p. 340.)

D3b* CANTO I. *Shi'r,* Beirut, 1 (1957) 73–81. Translated anonymously, possibly by Yousuf Al-Khal.

D3c* EZRA POUND. *Shi'r,* 29 (1964) 75–83. Translations, by Yousuf Al-Khal, of "La Fraisne," "The Tree," "Threnos," "A Girl," "And Thus in Nineveh," "The Eyes," and "A Virginal."

D3d* [POEMS]. *Shi'r,* 44 (1970). Translations, by Suheil Bashru'i, printed in the course of his article, "A Return to Ezra Pound and His Impact on Modern Poetry," pp. 69–81.

D3e [POEMS]. *Paideuma,* Orono, Me., VI. 3 (Winter 1977[/1978]) 407–10. Translations, by Mohammed Shaheen, of "Villonaud for This Yule," "The Return," and "The Gipsy," printed following his article, "Pound in Arabic," pp. [399]–406.

BENGALI
BOOK:

D4 . . . NIRBACHITA KABITA (THE SELECTED POEMS . . .)[Calcutta? Rupa & Co. [1974]. 37, [1] pp., 3 leaves, 187, [1] pp., 2 leaves. 22.5 cm. Rs. 30.00. English and Bengali on opposite pages. Translations, by Sushil Kumar Das Gupta, of "The Tree," "A Pact," "The Return," "The House of Splendour," "The Garret," "The Spring," "A Virginal," "Salutation," "The Rest," "A Song of the Degrees," "Apparuit," "Dance Figure," "Sestina: Alta-

369

D. TRANSLATIONS

forte," "Portrait d'une femme," "'Blandula, tenulla, vagula,'" "Erat hora," "The Garden," "Coda," "Δώρια," "The White Stag," "Tenzone," "Ité," "Arides," "Alba," "The Lake Isle," "The Tea Shop," "The Encounter," "'Ιμέρρω," "The Tomb of Akr Çaar," "The Coming of War: Actaeon," "Les Millwin," "Villanelle: The Psychological Hour," "April," "Ballad of the Goodly Fere," *Hugh Selwyn Mauberley*, Part 1, [VIII], "Envoi," "Chansson doil mot," "A War Song," "A Ballad of the Mulberry Road," "Four Poems of Departure," "The River Merchant's Wife: A Letter," "The River Song," "The Beautiful Toilet," "Lament of the Frontier Guard," "The Jewel Stairs' Grievance," "Pierrots" (Laforgue), "Cabaret vert" and "Comedy in Three Caresses" (Rimbaud), "Her Monument: The Image Cut Thereon" (Leopardi), "Autunno" (Montanari), "'Ask not ungainly'" (Horace), "To Formianus' Young Lady Friend, After Valerius Catullus," "Roma" (Rutilius), "Inscriptio fontis" (Andrea Navagero), "Certain Poems of Kabir," and Canto XIII.

PERIODICALS:

D5 [POEMS]. *Kavita*, Calcutta, XVI. 1 (Dec. 1950) 29–33. English and Bengali on opposite pages. Translations, by Buddhadeva Bose, of "An Immorality," "Ballad for Gloom," and "Portrait d'une femme."

D6 [POEMS]. *Kavita*, XIX. 3 (Mar. 1955) 192–6. Translations, by Bishnu Dey, of "Francesca," "Horae beatae inscriptio" ["Und Drang, IX"], "The Altar" ["Und Drang, X"], "In a Station of the Metro," "Ts'ai Chi'h," "Tenzone," "The Garret," "Ité," "Liu Ch'e," "Alba," "Δώρια," "The Picture," "*To Καλὸν*," and "An Immorality."

CZECH

BOOK:

D7 ... POEZIJA ... Zagreb, Izdavačko Knjižarsko Poduzeče Mladosí, 1967. 80 pp. 17 cm. (Biblioteka Orion). English and Czech on opposite pages. Translations, by Antun Šoljan, of "The Return," "The Garret," "The Garden," "Albâtre," "A Pact," "Further Instructions." "'Ione, Dead the Long Year,'" "Provincia deserta," "The River-Merchant's Wife: A Letter," "Monumentum aere, etc.," "Fratres minores," "Near Perigord," "Villanelle: The Psychological Hour," from *Hugh Selwyn Mauberley*, "Envoi," Canto XLV, and from Canto LXXXI.

ANTHOLOGY:

D7a AMERIČTÍ BÁSNÍCI. Svoboda, Nakladatelství v Praze [1946]. 286 pp., 1 leaf. 20 cm. 60 Kcs. Contains translations, by Arnošt Vaneček, of "And Thus in Nineveh," "A Girl," "The Garret," and "N. Y.," pp. 178–82.

PERIODICAL:

D7b CANTOS A JINÉ BÁSNĚ. *Světová Literatura*, Praha, II. 12 (1967) 209–25. Translations, by Kamil Bednar, of Cantos II and III, and by Jana Zábrany,

D. TRANSLATIONS

of "The Return," "The Rest," "Albâtre," *Hugh Selwyn Mauberley*, Part 1, XIII, "Further Instructions," "Alba," "Dum capitolium scandet," "Black Slippers: Bellotti," "Papyrus," "L'art, 1910," "Simulacra," "The Social Order," "The Lake Isle," "Monumentum aere, etc.," "Villanelle: The Psychological Hour," "Moeurs contemporaines," *Hugh Selwyn Mauberley*, Part 1, [IX], Cantos XXXVIII, XLV, and from Canto LXXXI.

DANISH

BOOKS:

D8 ... MASKER. Redigeret af Torben Brostrøm ... Fredensborg, Arena Lyrikkreds, 1959. 50 pp., 1 leaf. 22.8 cm. Kr. 9.75. 300 copies. Translations, by Jørgen Sonne, of Cantos II and III, from Canto XII, Canto XIII, from Cantos XXI, XXV, XXIX, XC, and XCIII, and by Ivan Malinovski, of Canto XLV, and from Canto LXXXI.

D9 ... ABC for laesere ... Fredensborg, Arena, 1960. 1 blank leaf, 5 leaves, 13–191, [1] pp. 21.2 cm. 1200 copies. A translation, by Jørgen Sonne, of *ABC of Reading*.

D9a ... DIGTE OG CANTOS ... [København] Gyldendal [1968]. 153, [1] pp., 1 blank leaf. 21 cm. Kr. 36. Translations, by Jørgen Sonne, of "Sestina: Altaforte," "Paracelsus in Excelsis," "A Girl," "The Needle," "Dance Figure," "Ité," "The Study in Aesthetics," "The Bath Tub," "The Temperaments," "Liu Ch'e," "In a Station of the Metro," "Papyrus," "Tame Cat," "L'art, 1910," "The Lake Isle," "Post mortem conspectu," "Song of the Bowmen of Shu," "The River-Merchant's Wife: A Letter," "Near Perigord, III," "Moeurs contemporaines, I, IV," *Homage to Sextus Propertius*, IV, VI, IX, *Hugh Selwyn Mauberley*, Part 1, I-V, Cantos II, III, from Cantos VII and IX, Cantos XII-XIV, XVI, from Cantos XXV, XXVII, XXIX, XXXV, and XLIV, Cantos XLVI, XLVII, XLIX, from Cantos LI, LXV, LXXIX-LXXXI, LXXXIII, XC, XCIII, and CVI.

DUTCH

BOOK:

D9b ... 15 CANTOS ... Amsterdam, De Bezige Bij, Athenaeum-Polak & Van Gennep, 1970. 153 pp., 1 leaf. 21.6 cm. Fl. 14.50. (Issued both clothbound and in paper wrappers.) English and Dutch on opposite pages. Translations, by H. C. ten Berge, of Cantos I, III, VI, VIII, XIII-XV, XX, XXXIX, XLIX, LXXXII, XC, and from Canto CXV, and by Rein Bloem, of Cantos II and IV.

PERIODICAL:

D9c [POEMS]. *De Gids*, Utrecht, CXIII. 8/9 (Aug./Sept. 1950) 171–4. Translations, by Koos Schuur, of "Dance Figure," "Lament of the Frontier Guard," and "The Alchemist," printed in connexion with his article, "Amerikaanse Dichters van de Twintigste Eeuw," pp. 160–7.

D. TRANSLATIONS
ENGLISH

[Translations into English of Ezra Pound's writings in French and Italian are entered under the original works in the appropriate section, A, B, or C.]

FINNISH

BOOKS:

D10 Kung-futse. Ta Hyyö, suur öpetus ... [no place, 1956?]. 1 blank leaf, 2 leaves, 2–16 numbered leaves. 18cm. Printed on rectos only. Reproduced from typewritten copy. A translation, by A. E. Marand, of Ezra Pound's version of "The Great Digest" of Confucius.

D10a ... Lukemisen aakkoset ... Helsingissä, Kustannusosakeyhtiö Otava [1967]. 227 pp. 19 cm. 7:—M. (Delfiinikirjat). A translation, by Hannu Launonen and Lassi Saastamoinen, of *ABC of Reading*.

D10b* PERSONAE ... Helsingissä, Kustannusosakeyhtiö Otava [1976]. 160 pp. 32:—M. A translation, by Tuomas Anhava, of *Personae* (1926).

ANTHOLOGY:

D11 Aale Tynni. TUHAT LAULUJEN VUOTTA: VALIKOIMA LÄNSIMAISTA LY-RIIKKAA ... [Helsingissä?] Osakeyhtiö Werner Söderström [1957]. xxiii, 866, [1] pp. 20.5 cm. English and Finnish on opposite pages. Contains translations, by Tuomas Anhava, of "The Tomb at Akr Çaar," "The Coming of [War:] Actaeon," "'Ione, Dead the Long Year,'" and Canto XLIX, pp. 746–55.

PERIODICALS:

D11a RUNOILIJA PUHUU. *Parnasso*, Helsinki, X. 1 (Feb. 1966) 1–6. Translations, by Tuomas Anhava, of "And Thus in Nineveh," "Tenzone," "The Condolence," "Salutation," "Salutation the Second," "Commission," "A Pact," "The Rest," "Further Instructions," "Ité," and "The Study in Aesthetics."

D11b ... KUNNIANOSOITUS SEXTUS PROPERTIUKSELLE. *Parnasso*, XIX. 3 (Apr. 1976) 159–73. A translation, by Tuomas Anhava, of *Homage to Sextus Propertius*.

FRENCH

BOOKS:

D12 ... CANTOS ET POÈMES CHOISIS ... Paris, Pierre Jean Oswald [1958]. 1 blank leaf, 3 leaves, [9]–77 pp., 1 leaf. double front. (ports.), 1 fold. facsim. 18.9 cm. 600 fr. (Collection "L'Aube dissout les monstres," 4). Also 100 copies listing Vanni Scheiwiller, Milan, as joint publisher on title-page and page [i] of wrappers, and 40 numbered copies on japon. English and French

D. TRANSLATIONS

on opposite pages. Translations, by René Laubiès, of *Hugh Selwyn Mauberley*, Part 2, IV, Canto VII, XII, XIII, from Canto XVI (in French only), Cantos XXVII and LXXXI, including also "Dans un omnibus de Londres" in Ezra Pound's original French. The translation of the Cantos was made "avec l'approbation et les corrections d'E. Pound lui-même." The folded facsimile is of a page of the typescript of the translation of Canto LXXXI, corrected in manuscript by Pound.

D12a ... LES CANTOS PISANS ... [Paris] Éditions de L'Herne [1965]. 1 blank leaf, 177 pp., 2 leaves. 22.5 cm. 3000 copies (100 *h.c.*), 30 fr. A translation, by Denis Roche, of *The Pisan Cantos*.

D12b ... ABC de la lecture ... [Paris] Éditions de L'Herne [1966]. 1 blank leaf, 3 leaves, [9]–250 pp., 1 leaf. 22.5 cm. 32 fr. A translation, by Denis Roche, of *ABC of Reading*.

D12c ... Comment lire ... [Paris] Éditions de L'Herne [1966]. 1 blank leaf, 2 leaves, 1 blank leaf, 9–61 pp., 1 leaf. 22.5 cm. 13 fr. 1000 copies (100 *h.c.*) A translation, by Victor Llona, of *How to Read*.

D12d ... Esprit des littératures romanes ... Paris, Christian Bourgois [1966]. 1 blank leaf, 2 leaves, 7–361, [1] pp., 3 leaves. 20 cm. 20 fr. A translation, by Pierre Alien, of *The Spirit of Romance*.

D12e ... CANTO CX ... [Paris, Éditions L'Herne; Lausanne, L'Age d'Homme] Collection Prodromos dirigée par Ioan Cusa [1967]. 1 blank leaf, 11 leaves, incl. plate (port.) 31 cm. 224 copies (plus 26 lettered copies not for sale on Bellegarde). (Collection Prodromos, 1). English and French on opposite pages. Translated by Pierre Alien. (The plate reproduces a sculptured head of Ezra Pound by Arno Breker.)

D12f ... Le travail et l'usure, trois essais ... [Lausanne] Éditions L'Age d'Homme [1968]. 1 blank leaf, 2 leaves, 7–111 pp., 2 leaves. 19.5 cm. 16.50 fr. (La Merveilleuse Collection). 1500 copies (plus 17 on Johannot paper). Translations, by Patrice de Nivard, of *Oro e Lavoro*, *L'America*, *Roosevelt e le cause della guerra presente*, and *Introduzione alla natura economica degli S. U. A.*

D12g Pound/Joyce ... [Paris] Mercure de France, 1970. 1 blank leaf, 2 leaves, 7–350 pp., 1 leaf, 1 blank leaf. 24 cm. 36 fr. Also 50 copies on vélin (plus 10 *h.c.*). Translated by Philippe Lavergne.

D12h CANTOS PISANS: CANTO LXXVII, CANTO LXXIX, CANTO LXXXI, CANTO [L]XXXIII ... [Bruxelles, Les Jeunesses Poétiques, 1970]. [40] pp. 27.5 cm. 30 fr. (La Collection de L'Arc). Translated by Denis Roche. Reprinted from D12a to accompany a recording, "réalisation: Yves Bacal avec Robert Lemaire."

D12i ... CANTO PISAN LXXVI. Huit eaux-fortes originales de Zao Wou-ki. [Paris] Pierre Belfond, 1972. 2 blank leaves, 33, [1] pp., 3 leaves, 2 blank leaves, incl. col. front., 7 col. plates. 51 cm. Issued unbound in cloth-board portfolio, 53.7 cm. 150 copies on Arches, 50 with an extra set of the engravings, plus 30 copies *h.c.* with a set on japon, of which 24 have the "décomposition" of a colored plate on Arches. Translated by Denis Roche. Reprinted from D12a.

D. TRANSLATIONS

D12j ... Le caractère écrit chinois matériau poétique ... [Paris] L'Herne [1972]. 1 blank leaf, 2 leaves, 7–55, [1] pp., 2 leaves, 2 blank leaves. 21 cm. (Les livres noirs). A translation, by Ghislain Sartoris, of *The Chinese Written Character as a Medium for Poetry*.

D12k ... EZRA POUND: une étude de Laurette Veza, avec un choix de poèmes, une bibliographie, des illustrations. [Paris] Éditions Seghers [1973]. 1 blank leaf, 3 leaves, 9–158 pp., 1 leaf, incl. plates, ports. 16 cm. (Poètes d'aujourd'hui, 210). Contains translations, by Jeannie Chauveau, of "In a Station of the Metro"; by Ludmila Savitzky, of "Albâtre"; by Veza, of "Liu Ch'e," "Come My Cantilations," and *Hugh Selwyn Mauberley*, Part 1, I; by René Laubiès, of "Dans un omnibus de Londres," *Hugh Selwyn Mauberley*, Part 2, IV, and Canto XII; by Maurice Le Breton, of "Portrait d'une femme"; by Michel Beaujour, of Canto I; by Pierre Alien, of Canto XLV; and by Denis Roche, of Cantos LXXIX and LXXXI.

D12l René Crevel. Les pieds dans le plat, préface de Ezra Pound. [Paris] Jean-Jacques Pauvert, 1974. 1 blank leaf, 3 leaves, 9–316 pp., 2 leaves. 21 cm. Contains "preface" by Pound, pp. 9–[21], a translation, by Pierre Alien, of "René Crevel"—C1490.

D12m ... Au cœur du travail poétique ... [Paris] L'Herne [1980]. 1 blank leaf, 3 leaves, [9]–452 pp., 1 leaf, 1 blank leaf. 22.1 cm. Translations, by François Sauzey, of "A Retrospect," "The Serious Artist," "The Teacher's Mission," "This Constant Preaching to the Mob," "Date Line," "The Tradition," from "Troubadours: Their Sorts and Conditions," "Arnaut Daniel, Razo" [with original Provençal and Pound's English versions followed by Sauzey's French prose translation]; "Cavalcanti," "Hell," "The Renaissance," "Irony, Laforgue, and Some Satire," "The Hard and the Soft in French Poetry," "Remy de Gourmont," "The Later Yeats," reviews of Robert Frost's *A Boy's Will*—C77—and *North of Boston*—C164, "D. H. Lawrence," "*Dubliners* and Mr. James Joyce," "Joyce" (from *Instigations*) and "Paris Letter. May, 1922. *Ulysses*," "Dr. Williams' Position," "T. S. Eliot," "Wyndham Lewis"—C146, and "Tarr"—C335, "Vers libre and Arnold Dolmetsch," and "Brancusi."

ANTHOLOGIES:

D12n ... LES CINQ CONTINENTS, anthologie mondiale de poésie contemporaine, par Ivan Goll. Paris, La Renaissance du Livre, 1922. 310 pp., 1 blank leaf. 19.1 cm. 12 fr. (Collection Littéraire et Artistique Internationale). Also 15 numbered copies on Lafuma. Contains translations, by Ludmila Savitzky, of "The Garret," and by Francis Treat, of "N. Y.," pp. 32–33.

D13 ANTHOLOGIE DE LA NOUVELLE POÉSIE AMÉRICAINE, par Eugène Jolas. Paris, Kra [1928]. 1 blank leaf, 3 leaves, 266 pp., 1 leaf. 19.5 cm. 25 fr. Also 100 copies on vélin. Contains translations, by Jolas, of "A Girl" and "The Coming of War: Actaeon," pp. [179]–180.

D14 Maurice Le Breton. ANTHOLOGIE DE LA POÉSIE AMÉRICAINE CONTEMPORAINE. Paris, Les Éditions Denoël [1948]. 1 blank leaf, 3 leaves, 9–346

D. TRANSLATIONS

pp., 1 leaf. 19.5 cm. 350 fr. English and French on opposite pages. Contains a translation, by Le Breton, of "Portrait d'une femme," pp. 166–67.

D14a Biennales internationales de poésie: Un demi-siècle de poésie, tome II. Dilbeek, Belgium, La Maison du Poète [1954]. 1 blank leaf, 2 leaves, 7–318 pp., 1 blank leaf. 21 cm. 150 fr. Contains translations, by Alain Bosquet, of "Further Instructions" and "Ortus," pp. 227–9.

D15 John Brown. Panorama de la littérature contemporaine aux États-Unis: introduction, illustrations, documents. [Paris, Gallimard, 1954]. 1 blank leaf, 3 leaves, 9–653, [1] pp., 1 blank leaf. plates. 19.3 cm. English and French on opposite pages (for poems only). Contains translations, by Jeannie Chauveau, of "L'art, 1910," "In a Station of the Metro," *Hugh Selwyn Mauberley*, Part 1, I, and from Canto LXXXI; by Maurice Le Breton, of "Portrait d'une femme"; by John Brown, from Canto XI and of Canto XLV, pp. 490–7; and by Jeannie Chauveau, of "Date Line" [sections I and II, omitting the last four paragraphs], pp. 578–81.

D15a Michel Butor. Répertoire: études et conférences, 1948–1959 . . . [Paris] Les Éditions de Minuit [1960]. 1 blank leaf, 2 leaves, [7]–274 pp., 2 leaves, 1 blank leaf. 21.5 cm. 15 fr. Also 40 copies on rag paper, plus 7 *h.c.* The essay "La tentative poétique d'Ezra Pound," pp. [234]–249, contains translations, by Butor, of excerpts from the Cantos.

D15b Louise Bogan. Réflexions sur la poésie américaine. Paris, Seghers, 1965. 1 blank leaf, 3 leaves, 9–248 pp., 4 leaves. 17 cm. 4.90 fr. (Collection Vent d'Ouest, 8). Contains translations, by Laurette Veza, of "Liu Ch'e," "Come My Cantilations," and *Hugh Selwyn Mauberley*, Part 1, I-II, pp. 90–95.

D15c Jean Pierre Attal. L'image "métaphysique" et autres essais. [Paris] NRF Gallimard [1969]. 1 blank leaf, [9]–460 pp., 5 leaves, 1 blank leaf. 19.7 cm. 30 fr. (Le Chemin). Contains "Ezra Pound. *Homage to Sextus Propertius.* Traduction et commentaire," pp. [217]–325, the English text above and the French translation, by Attal, below; with Latin text, edited and translated into French prose by D. Paganelli opposite, pp. [217]–307; the commentary follows, pp. [308]–325.

D15d Denis Roche. 3 POURRISSEMENTS POÉTIQUES: POUND CANTO 100; CUMMINGS EXTRAIT DE &; OLSON LES MARTINS-PÊCHEURS. [Paris] L'Envers/L'Herne [1972]. 35 leaves, 1 blank leaf. 14.4 cm. Also 25 copies on Hollande, 15.5 cm. English and French on opposite pages. Contains Roche's translation of Canto C, leaves 7–18.

PERIODICALS:

D16 QUELQUES POÈMES D'EZRA POUND. *Les Feuilles Libres: Lettres et Arts*, Paris, II. 10 (Aug. 1920) 396–7. Translations, by Ludmila Savitzky, of "Albâtre," "Ortus," "The Temperaments," "The Garret," and "Causa."

D17 [MOEURS CONTEMPORAINES, I-VIII]. *391*, Paris, 15 (10 July 1921): *Le Pilhaou-Thibaou*, [4]. Translated by "Christian," *i. e.* Georges Herbiet. The translations of I-III were reprinted in *Ça Ira*, Anvers, 16 (Nov. 1921).

D18 Post-scriptum à une version anglaise de "La Physique de l'amour." *Mercure*

D. TRANSLATIONS

de France, Paris, CL. 558 (15 Sept. 1921) 668–81. A translation, by V. M. Llona, of the essay later published as the "Translator's Postscript" to Remy de Gourmont's *The Natural Philosophy of Love* ([1922])—A22a.

D19 [TWO POEMS FROM CATHAY]. *Planètes*, Paris, 1 (1954) [36]–38]. Translations, by Alain Bosquet, of "The River-Merchant's Wife: A Letter" and "Lament of the Frontier Guard."

D19a NEW-YORK. *Le Journal des Poètes*, Dilbeek, Brussels, XXIV. 6 (June 1954) 8. Translated by Claire Goll.

D20 FROM CANTO LXXV. *Pound Newsletter*, Berkeley, Calif., 3 (July 1954) 4–5. Translated by René Laubiès.

D20a UN POÈME INÉDIT. *Arts*, Paris, 543 (23/29 Nov. 1955) [1]. An anonymous translation of about 38 lines from Canto LXXXI.

D21 ... CANTO 12 ... *Les Lettres et les Arts*, Paris, 1 (Apr./May 1956) 31–35. Translated by René Laubiès, "avec l'approbation et les corrections d'E. Pound lui-même."

D22 POÈMES. *Profils*, Paris, 16 (Summer 1956) [40]–55. English and French on opposite pages. Translations, by Alain Bosquet, of "De Aegypto," "Alba," "Ité," "Taking Leave of a Friend," *Homage to Sextus Propertius*, VII, *Hugh Selwyn Mauberly*, Part 1, III, Cantos III, XLV, and from Canto LXXXI. (*Profils* is the French edition of *Perspectives U. S. A.*)

D23 CANTO LXIX. *Parler*, Grenoble, III. 9 (Autumn 1959) 14–17. Translated by René Laubiès.

D23a I VECCHI [*sic*]. *Phantomas*, Brussels, VII. 15/16 (Jan. 1960) 98. A translation, by Pierre Zékéli, of "I Vechii."

D23b CANTO IV. *Tel Quel*, Paris, 6 (Summer 1961) [21]–24. Translated by D. Alexandre and P. Sanavio.

D23c L'art de la poésie, extraits. *Tel Quel*, 11 (Autumn 1962) [11]–16. A translation, by Denis Roche, of "Credo" and two extracts from *How to Read*.

D23d Si c'est cela la trahison. Céline. *Les Cahiers de L'Herne*, Paris, 3 ([Jan.?] 1963) 198–9. A translation, by Ezra Pound himself, of the latter half of his Rome radio broadcast talk, "A French Accent (11 May 1942)."

D23e Ezra Pound, 80 ans: la jeunesse de l'invective. *Arts* (27 Oct./2 Nov. 1965) 14, 15. Part of the Bridson interview with Pound, printed in advance of its appearance in *Les Cahiers de L'Herne*, 6—D23j.

D23f POÈMES. *Les Cahiers de L'Herne*, 6 ([Nov. 1965]) [15]–20. Translations, by Elisabeth Janvier, of "Albâtre," "Ortus," "The Temperaments," "The Garret," "Causa," "La Fraisne," "A Girl," "The Tree," "Threnos," "Francesca," "In a Station of the Metro," "April," and "N. Y." (This issue of the periodical is the first of two devoted entirely to Ezra Pound. There were also 60 copies on special paper with four original lithographs.)

D23g LES CANTOS. *Les Cahiers de L'Herne*, 6 ([Nov. 1965]) [21]–31. English and French on opposite pages. Translations, by Michel Beaujour, of Canto I, and by Michel Butor, of Canto XC. (The translation of Canto LXXIX, by Denis Roche, pp. 31–41, is reprinted from D12a.)

D. TRANSLATIONS

D23h Textes. *Les Cahiers de L'Herne*, 6 ([Nov. 1965]) [43]–108. Translations, by Michel Beaujour, of "Rimbaud"; by Pierre Alien, of "René Crevel," "National Culture, A Manifesto," "Possibilities of Civilization: What the Small Town Can Do," and "The Enemy Is Ignorance"; "James Joyce et Pécuchet" (in Ezra Pound's French); translations, by Victor Llona (corrected by Pound), of *How to Read*; by Christine Laure, of "Vorticism"; and anonymously, of "Orientamenti"—C1486—and "Integrity of the Word."

D23i Déclaration d'Ezra Pound à son retour en Italie. *Les Cahiers de L'Herne*, 6 ([Nov. 1965]) 187. A translation, by Pierre Alien, of Pound's introductory note (in Italian) to "Canto 98" in *L'Illustrazione Italiana* for Sept. 1958—C1863, reprinted as "Servizio di comunicazioni."

D23j Interviews. *Les Cahiers de L'Herne*, 6 ([Nov. 1965]) [189]–224. Translations, by Pierre Alien, of "An Interview with Ezra Pound [by] D. G. Bridson"—C1884; by Daniel Mauroc, of "Ezra Pound: An Interview [by Donald Hall]"—C1889; and anonymously, of "Vi parla Ezra Pound: Io so di non sapere nulla; intervista di Grazia Livi"—C1894a.

D23k Correspondance. *Les Cahiers de L'Herne*, 6 ([Nov. 1965]) [283]–321. Translations, by Denise Alexandre, of letters to Harriet Monroe, 18 Aug. [1912]; T. E. Lawrence, 20 Apr. [1920]; T. S. Eliot, [24 Dec. 1921, *i.e.* 24 Jan. 1922]; William Carlos Williams, 18 Mar. [1921]; Simon Guggenheim, 24 Feb. [1925]; James Joyce, June (?) 1920 and 19 Nov. [1926]—all from *The Letters*; by Marc Hanrez, of a letter to Louis Untermeyer, 1930; letters (in Ezra Pound's French) to Gabrielle Buffet, 16 Feb. [n.y.], and Jean Cocteau [n.d.]; translations, by Michel Beaujour, of extracts from letters to Robert Creeley; and by Pierre Alien, of letters to Vittorio Bodini, 26 Mar., 7, 27, and 30 May [1941], and of "Impedimenti alla critica"—C1598.

D23l LES CANTOS. *Les Cahiers de L'Herne*, 7 ([May 1966]) [343]–365. English and French on opposite pages (for Cantos II, XIV, XV, and XLV). Translations, by Denis Alexandre, of Canto IV; by Michel Beaujour, of Canto II; and by Pierre Alien, of Cantos XIV, XV, and XLV.

D23m Correspondance. *Les Cahiers de L'Herne*, 7 ([May 1966]) [425]–434. Translations, by Pierre Alien, of three letters to W. H. D. Rouse, Feb., Apr., and 23 May 1935; a letter to René Taupin, [1928], in Ezra Pound's French; and a translation, by Denis Alexandre, of a letter to Katue Kitasono, 15 Nov. [n.y.].

D23n [Letters to James Joyce]. *Les Cahiers de L'Herne*, 7 ([May 1966]) 497–501. Translations, by Pierre Alien, of letters of 6/12 Sept. 1915 and 10 June 1919, with notes by Forrest Read.

D23 o HOMAGE TO SEXTUS PROPERTIUS. *Les Cahiers de L'Herne*, 7 ([May 1966]) [521]–545. Ezra Pound's English text and French translation by Jean-Pierre Attal, printed in double columns, with Latin text, edited and translated into French prose, by D. Paganelli, also in double columns, opposite.

D23p [Letters to W. Moelwyn Merchant]. *Les Cahiers de L'Herne*, 7 ([May 1966]) 605–13. Letters of 17 Sept., 1 and 7 Nov. 1957, and 25 Mar. 1958, with some notes by Ezra Pound, as well as his "[Sir Edward] Coke on Prin-

D. TRANSLATIONS

ciples," are quoted, with anonymous French translations below, in an article, "Souvenirs d'Ezra Pound," by Merchant.

D23q George Antheil. *Les Cahiers de L'Herne*, 7 ([May 1966]) 617–25. A translation, by Michel Beaujour, of "Antheil, 1924–1926"—C686.

D23r Horace. *Les Cahiers de L'Herne*, 7 ([May 1966]) 626–32. A translation, by Michel Beaujour, of "Horace"—C756.

D23s The Exile ... *Les Cahiers de L'Herne*, 7 ([May 1966]) 633–9. Translations, by Pierre Alien, of Ezra Pound's editorial comments from No. 1—C689— and No. 3—C707, along with "Desideria"—C708—and "Interaction"— C709.

D23t A quoi sert l'argent? ... (Extraits). *Les Cahiers de L'Herne*, 7 ([May 1966]) 683–5. A translation, by Pierre Alien, of extracts from *What Is Money For?*

D23u Causeries prononcées à la radio de Rome. *Les Cahiers de L'Herne*, 7 ([May 1966]) 686–92. Translations, by Marc Hanrez, of the Rome radio broadcasts "E. E. Cummings/examind" and "A French Accent," with "Causerie écrite en français (1941)"—see C1909.

D23v Lettre envoyée par l'intermédiaire de la Légation Suisse, Août 1943. *Les Cahiers de L'Herne*, 7 ([May 1966]) 696–7. A translation, by Pierre Alien, of Ezra Pound's letter to U. S. Attorney General Francis Biddle.

D23w ... Une leçon de littérature. *La Quinzaine Littéraire*, Paris, 15 (1/15 Nov. 1966) 12–13. A translation, by Denis Roche, of selections from *ABC of Reading*.

D23x ... CANTOS CX. *La Quinzaine Littéraire*, 30 (15/31 June 1967) 11. A translation, by Pierre Alien, of Canto CX.

D23y UN INÉDIT D'EZRA POUND: (CANTO PISANS LXXIV). *Combat*, Paris (18 July 1967) 13. A translation, by Denis Roche, of Canto LXXIV.

D23z CANTO III. *Qui Lit*, Paris, 152 (16/30 Nov. 1972) 11–12. Translated by Serge Fauchereau, as part of his article "Ezra Pound."

D23za CANTOS DYNASTIQUES. *Dirty*, Antony, Paris (1981) 41–50. Translations, by Pierre Rival, of Cantos LII and LXI.

GERMAN

BOOKS:

D24 Das Testament des Confucius: Die grosse Unterweisung oder das Erwachsenenstudium übertragen von Ezra Pound. [Karlsruhe] Fragmente [1953]. 1 blank leaf, 1 leaf, 5–37, [1] pp., 1 blank leaf. 17 cm. (Schriftenreihe der Fragmente, 1). 2000 copies. A translation, by Rainer M. Gerhardt, of Pound's *Confucius. The Great Digest*.

D25 ... Wie lesen ... [Karlsruhe, Verlag der Fragmente, 1953]. 47, [1] pp. 17 cm. DM. 1.90. (Schriftenreihe der Fragmente, 4). 1000 copies. A translation, by Rainer M. Gerhardt, of *How to Read*.

D26 ... Dichtung und Prosa. Mit einem Geleitwort von T. S. Eliot. Zürich, Im

D. TRANSLATIONS

Verlag der Arche [1953]. 155 pp. 19.5 cm. Fr. 9.90. English and German on opposite pages (for poems). Translations, by Eva Hesse, of "Cino," "De Aegypto," "Sestina: Altaforte," "Portrait d'une femme," "Δώρια," "The Return," "Commission," "Dance Figure," "Further Instructions," "The Temperaments," "Meditatio," "The Coming of War: Actaeon," "In a Station of the Metro," "'Ione, Dead the Long Year,'" "Ἵμεϱϱω," "Tame Cat," "L'art, 1910," "The River-Merchant's Wife: A Letter," "Phanopoeia," *Hugh Selwyn Mauberley*, Part 1, I-V, "Envoi (1919), and Part 2, Cantos II, IV, XLV, from Cantos LXXIV and LXXIX-LXXXI, "Date Line," "A Stray Document," and an excerpt from a letter to Harriet Monroe, Jan. 1915. (A paperbound edition of this book was published in Frankfurt-am-Main by Ullstein Bücher in 1956.)

D27 ... FISCH UND SCHATTEN UND ANDERE DICHTUNGEN. Zürich, Im Verlag der Arche [1954]. 63, [1] pp. 19.5 cm. Fr. 3.80. English and German on opposite pages. Translations, by Eva Hesse, of "La Fraisne," "Na Audiart," "Marvoil," "And Thus in Nineveh," "Night Litany," "On His Own Face in a Glass," "Horae beatae inscriptio," "April," "A Girl," "The Garret," "The Seafarer," "The Spring," "To Καλὸν," "Pagani's, November 8," "The Rest," "Ladies," "Passing," "Liu Ch'e," "Alba," "The Jewel Stairs' Grievance," "The Social Order," "Shop Girl," "The Lake Isle," "The Faun," "Fish and the Shadow," Canto XLVII, and an excerpt from *Women of Trachis*.

D28 ... DIE PISANER GESÄNGE: vollständige Ausgabe ... Zürich, Im Verlag der Arche [1956]. 247, [1] pp., incl. front. 19.5 cm. Fr. 13.25. English and German on opposite pages. A translation, by Eva Hesse, "in Kontakt mit dem Autor," of *The Pisan Cantos*. (Later editions have title: *Pisaner Cantos (Cantos LXXIV-LXXXIV)*. A new "Studienausgabe," with illustrations, was published in 1969.)

D29 ABC des Lesens ... Berlin und Frankfurt a/M, Suhrkamp Verlag [1957]. 135, [1] pp., 2 leaves. 18.3 cm. DM. 4.80. (Bibliothek Suhrkamp, 40). A translation, by Eva Hesse, of *ABC of Reading*, omitting Part II.

D30 ... "Motz el son "—Wort und Weise: Didaktik der Dichtung. Mit Photos. Zürich, Im Verlag der Arche [1957]. 138, [2] pp., incl. front. plates (ports., facsims.) 15.6 cm. Fr. 9.40. (Sammlung Horizont). Translations, by Eva Hesse, of *How to Read*, "A Retrospect," "The Serious Artist," "The Teacher's Mission," "The Tradition," "Vers libre and Arnold Dolmetsch," "Treatise on Harmony," "Vorticism" and other excerpts from *Gaudier-Brzeska* (1916), and a series of brief passages.

D31 ... DIE FRAUEN VON TRACHIS NACH SOPHOKLES. Hamburg, Rowohlt Verlag G.M.B.H. Hamburg Theater-Verlag [1958]. 1 leaf, 50 pp., 1 leaf. 29.2 cm. "... Als unverkäufliches Manuskript vervielfältigt." Page [i] of wrapper printed; text reproduced from typewritten copy. A translation, by Eva Hesse, of *Women of Trachis*. (For published edition see D35.)

D32 ... Über Zeitgenossen. Mit Photos. Zürich, Im Verlag der Arche [1959]. 155, [1] pp., incl. front. (port.) plates (incl. ports., facsims.) 15.5 cm. Fr. 9.80. Edited by Eva Hesse. Translations, by Alfred Kuoni, of "The Later

D. TRANSLATIONS

Yeats," "*Dubliners* and Mr. James Joyce," "Robert Frost," "Henri Gaudier-Brzeska," "T. S. Eliot," "Joyce," "Arnold Dolmetsch," "Wyndham Lewis," "Brancusi," "James Joyce et Pécuchet," "Dr. Williams' Position," "Harold Monro," "Prefatio aut cimicium tumulus," "Mr. Housman at Little Bethel," and "Mr. Eliot's Solid Merit." (A statement beginning "The chinese art of verbal sonority" in Ezra Pound's handwriting, is reproduced in facsimile on the dust-jacket and, incomplete, on the plate following p. 48. It is repeated on the jackets of D33 and 34.)

D33 ... PERSONAE · MASKEN. Der ausgewählten Werke erster Teil. Zürich, Im Verlag der Arche [1959]. 400 pp., incl. front. (port.) 19.5 cm. Fr. 22.80. English and German on opposite pages. Translations, by Eva Hesse, of the poems in *Personae* (1926), with a few omissions.

D34 ... Patria mia. Ein Bekenntnis. Zürich, Verlag Die Arche [1960]. 99, [1] pp., incl. front. (port.) 4 ports, on 2 leaves. 15.5 cm. Fr. 7.80. (Sammlung Horizont). A translation, by Hedda Soellner, of *Patria mia*, with "Cantico del sole" printed, in German translation, as a foreword. Edited by Eva Hesse.

D35 Sophokles. DIE FRAUEN VON TRACHIS: EINE VERSION VON EZRA POUND ... Zürich, Im Verlag der Arche [1960]. 72 pp., incl. front. (port.) 19.5 cm. Fr. 3.80. (Die kleinen Bücher der Arche, 319/320). A translation, by Eva Hesse, of *Women of Trachis*. (For first edition see D31.)

D35a Dante Leonelli [Köln, Galerie Der Spiegel, 1961]. 2 blank leaves, 8 leaves, 2 blank ieaves, incl. 2 col. plates, 38.2 cm. 200 copies, with a serigraph loosely laid in following each of the blank leaves at the end. A catalogue of an exhibition of Leonelli's work, with introduction by Bryan Robertson and text by Ezra Pound, "A Stray Document," in Eva Hesse's translation (reprinted from D26).

D35b Nō - vom Genius Japans. Ezra Pound. Ernest Fenollosa. Serge Eisenstein. Zürich, Im Verlag der Arche [1963]. 309,]3] pp. illus., 4 plates. 19.4 cm. Fr. 19.80. (Sammlung Nippon, 4). Edited by Eva Hesse. Translations, by Wieland Schmied, of *Noh*, and by W. L. Fischer, of *The Chinese Written Character*, with two essays by Eisenstein. Appendix I, "Nō-Spiele in den Cantos," pp. 292–3, quotes brief references in translation. Appendix II, "Anmerkungen zu den Nō-Spielen," pp. 294–306, includes notes by Ezra Pound, translated.

D35c ... CANTOS I-XXX: vollständige Ausgabe. Der ausgewählten Werke zweiter Teil ... Zürich, Im Verlag der Arche [1964]. 340 pp., incl. front. (port.) 19.4 cm. Fr. 19.80. English and German on opposite pages. Translated by Eva Hesse.

D35d ... CANTOS 1916–1962: eine Auswahl ... München, Deutscher Taschenbuch Verlag, 1964. 213, [1] pp., 1 leaf, [8] pp. 18 cm. (Sonderreihe, D T V 29). English and German on opposite pages. Translations, by Eva Hesse, of Cantos I, II, VII, XIII-XV, XVII, XX, XXVII, XXX, XXXIX, XLV, XLVII, XLIX, LXXIV, LXXIX, LXXXI, LXXXII, XC, CII, CVI, and the fragmentary Cantos CXV and CXVI. (The last two appear here for the first time in book form in either language.)

D. TRANSLATIONS

D35e ... DER REVOLUTION INS LESEBUCH. Zürich, Im Verlag der Arche [1969]. 70, [2] pp. 19 cm. A selection, made and translated by Eva Hesse, of brief passages from the Cantos and *Personae* (1926).

D35f Ezra Pound · James Joyce: die Geschichte ihrer Beziehung in Briefen und Dokumenten, herausgegeben und kommentiert von Forrest Read. Zürich, Im Verlag der Arche [1972]. 479, [1] pp., incl. front. (facism.) 14 ports. on 4 plates. 19.5 cm. Fr. 37.80. Edited by Eva Hesse. A translation, by Hiltrud Marschall, of *Pound/Joyce*.

D35g ... LETZTE TEXTE (CANTOS CX-CXX) ENTWÜRFE & FRAGMENTE: vollständige Ausgabe mit Texterläuterungen ... Zürich, Im Verlag der Arche [1975]. 104 pp. 19.6 cm. English and German on opposite pages. A translation, by Eva Hesse, of *Drafts & Fragments of Cantos CX-CXVII* and Canto CXX.

D35h ... Das chinesische Schriftzeichen als poetisches Medium. Starnberg, J. Keller, 1972. 51 pp. illus. 22 cm. (Kunst und Umwelt, II). A translation, by Eugen Gomringer, of *The Chinese Written Character as a Medium for Poetry*.

ANTHOLOGIES:

D36 DIE NEUE WELT: eine Anthologie jüngster Amerikanischer Lyrik. Herausgegeben und übersetzt von Claire Goll. Berlin, S. Fischer Verlag, 1921. 1 blank leaf, 2 leaves, 7–102, [2] pp. 21.7 cm. Contains translations, by Claire Goll, of "A Girl" and "The Garret," pp. 54–55.

D37 DIE LYRA DES ORPHEUS: Lyrik der Völker in deutscher Nachdichtung. Wien, Paul Zsolnay Verlag, 1952. 984, [1] pp., 1 leaf. 20.5 cm. Edited by Felix Braun. Contains a translation, by Heinz Politzer, of "Night Litany," pp. 760–1.

D37a DIE PISANER GESÄNGE. Eine Sendung von Rainer M. Gerhardt. Manuskript ... Frankfurt/Main, Hessischer Rundfunk "Abendstudio," März 1952. cover-title, 2–37 pp., 1 leaf. 29 cm. Script for broadcast, including selections translated by Gerhardt from Cantos LXXIV, LXXXIII, and LXXXIV, as well as from Cantos XIII and XLV, *How to Read*, and *Confucius. The Great Digest*.

D38 ENGLISCH HORN: Anthologie angelsächsischer Lyrik von den Anfängen bis zur Gegenwart ... [Köln-Berlin] Phaidon [1953]. 262, [6] pp. 22.6 cm. Contains a translation, by Georg von der Vring, of "The Ballad of the Goodly Fere," pp. 215–16.

D39 Hans Hennecke. GEDICHTE VON SHAKESPEARE BIS EZRA POUND ... Wiesbaden, Limes Verlag [1955]. 352 pp. 21 cm. English and German on opposite pages. Contains translations, by Hennecke, of "[Und Drang, VIII:] The Flame," "Pan Is Dead," "Francesca," "$\Delta\omega\varrho\iota\alpha$," "Erat hora," "Paracelsus in excelsis," "Shop Girl," and "The Garden," pp. 302–11.

D40* GEDICHTE AUS NER NEUEN WELT: Amerikanische Lyrik seit 1910. Eingeleitet und übertragen von Kurt Heinrich Hansen. München, R. Piper &

D. TRANSLATIONS

Co. Verlag, 1956. Contains translations, by Hansen, of "The Lake Isle," "Meditatio," "Image from D'Orleans," and Canto XVII.

D40a Wie sie schreiben. Acht Gespräche mit Autoren der Gegenwart. Herausgegeben und eingeleitet von Van Wyck Brooks. [München] Deutscher Taschenbuch Verlag [1969]. 255, [1] pp., 2 leaves. 18 cm. (DTV, 604). A translation, by Günther Steinbrinker, Hermann Stresau, Manfred Helling, and Ulf Miehe, of *Writers at Work, The Paris Review Interviews, Second Series*. Contains "Ezra Pound [by Donald Hall]," translated by Steinbrinker, pp. 15–44.

D40b AMERIKANISCHE LYRIK VOM 17. JAHRHUNDERT BIS ZUR GEGENWART ... Ausgewählt, herausgegeben und kommentiert von Franz Link; Übersetzungen von Annemarie und Franz Link. Stuttgart, Philip Reclam Jun. [1974]. 512 pp. 15 cm. (Universal-Bibliothek). English and German on opposite pages. Contains translations, by the Links, of "The Tree," "A Girl," "In a Station of the Metro," *Hugh Selwyn Mauberley*, Part 1, I-V, Cantos IV, XLV, and from Canto LXXXI, pp. [258]–281.

PERIODICALS:

D41 Der Nobel-Preis. *Der Querschnitt*, Berlin, IV. 1 (Spring 1924) 44–46. An anonymous translation of "Le prix Nobel" in the same issue, pp. 41–44.

D42 James Joyce's "Ulysses" ... *Der Querschnitt*, IV. 2/3 (Summer 1924) 137–41. Translated by B. Schiratzki. Reprinted in *Analle*, Wietmarschen, IV. 8 (Aug./Sept. 1980) 159, 164–5.

D42a NACHT-LITANEI. *Der Turm*, Vienna, II. 9/10 ([Summer?] 1947) 332. A translation, by Heinz Politzer, of "Night Litany."

D43 Mediaevalismus ... *Fragmente*, Freiburg im Breisgau, 1 (1951) 1–7. A translation, by Rainer M. Gerhardt, of "Mediaevalism."

D44 E. P. ODE POUR L'ÉLECTION DE SON SÉPULCHRE ... *Fragmente*, 1 (1951) 28–32. A translation, by Rainer M. Gerhardt, of *Hugh Selwyn Mauberley*, Part 1, I-V.

D45 E. P. ODE POUR L'ÉLECTION DE SON SÉPULCHRE ... *Imagi*, Allentown, Pa., V. 3 (1951) [10–11]. A translation, by Eva Hesse, of *Hugh Selwyn Mauberley*, Part 1, I-V.

D46 CANTO LXXXIV ... *Fragmente*, 2 (1952) 35–39. Translated by Rainer M. Gerhardt.

D47 [FRÜHE GEDICHTE]. *Wort und Wahrheit*, Freiburg im Breisgau, 11 (Nov. 1952) 814, 833–4. Translations, by Hans Hennecke, of "Paracelsus in excelsis," "Pan Is Dead," "[Und Drang, VIII:] The Flame," and "Δώρια."

D48 GEDICHTE. *Perspektiven*, Frankfurt a/M, 16 (Autumn 1956) [60]–77. English and German on opposite pages. Translations, by Eva Hesse, of "De Aegypto," "Alba," "Ité," "Taking Leave of a Friend," *Homage to Sextus Propertius*, Part 1, III, VII, Cantos III, XLV, and from Canto LXXXI. (*Perspektiven* is the German edition of *Perspectives U.S.A.*)

D48a Die rechte Art, Dichtung anzugehen. *Dichten und Trachten: Jahresschau des*

D. TRANSLATIONS

Suhrkamps Verlages, Berlin and Frankfurt a/M, IX (Spring 1957) 64–70. Passages from *ABC of Reading*, selected and translated by Eva Hesse (see D29).

D49 [POEMS]. *Das Schönste*, Munich, 2 (Feb. 1959) 27–28. Translations, by Eva Hesse, of "And Thus in Nineveh," *Hugh Selwyn Mauberley*, Part 2, "Medallion," "On His Own Face in a Glass," and "Francesca."

D50 SCHAUPLÄTZE EINER ALTÄGYPTISCHEN LIEBE. *Wort und Wahrheit*, XV. 1 (Jan. 1960) 45–49. A translation, by Eva Hesse, of "Conversations in Courtship," with English text in double columns at the foot of each page.

D50a Neun Nô-Spiele. *Theater Heute*, Hanover, IV. 1 (Jan. 1963), Heft 1, pp. i–xvi. This special supplement to the periodical includes translations, by Wieland Schmied, of the Pound-Fenollosa versions of "Hagoromo," "Nishikigi," "Kinuta," and "Kagekiyo," and of Pound's notes to those plays, pp. viii–xiv.

D50b . . . CANTO XIII. *Merkur*, Cologne, Berlin, 187 (Sept. 1963) 833–6. Translated, with notes, by Eva Hesse.

D50c CANTO XCI. *Akzente*, Frankfurt a/M, XII. 5 (Oct. 1965) [466]-469. An excerpt, translated by Eva Hesse.

D50d AUS CANTO CXIV. *Text + Kritik*, Aachen, 10/11 (Oct. 1965) 49–50. Translated by Eva Hesse.

D50e . . . LATE CANTOS: SPÄTE CANTOS. *Ensemble: Lyrik, Prosa, Essay*, Munich, 3 (1972) 8–21. English (with some, mostly minor, corrections) and German on opposite pages. Translations, by Eva Hesse, of Canto CX and from Canto CXII.

GREEK

BOOKS:

D51 [. . . KATAI METAPHRASOON APO TO AGGLIKO . . . Athēnai, Neo-Phalero, Typographia S. M. Tarousopoulou] 1950. 1 blank leaf, 3 leaves, 9–49 pp., 1 leaf. 25 cm. 12,500 dr. 400 copies. A translation, by Zesimos Lorenzatos, of *Cathay* (1915), as printed in *Personae* (1926).

D51a [. . . POIĒMATA . . . Athēnai, P. Bolaris, 1966]. 1 blank leaf, 2 leaves, 7–211 pp., 1 leaf, 1 blank leaf. 23.5 cm. Translations, by Ilias Kirzirakos, of roughly half the poems of *Personae* (1926), including *Hugh Selwyn Mauberley* and *Homage to Sextus Propertius*, plus Cantos XVII, XLV, and from Cantos LXXXI and XIII (3 lines).

D51b [. . . Ē katēhēssē tou ohlou. Pōs na diabazete. Anaskopēssē. Athēnai, Pandōra, 1970?]. 108 pp. Translations, by Kōstas Iordanidēs, of "This Constant Preaching to the Mob," *How to Read*, and "A Retrospect."

D51c* [RIPOSTES . . . Athēnai, 1972]. 25 pp. Translated by Demosthenes Koukounas.

D51d* [. . . LUSTRA. POIĒMATA . . . Athēnai, Prosperos, 1977]. 96 pp. A translation, by Tasos Korfis, of *Lustra*.

D. TRANSLATIONS

ANTHOLOGIES:

D52 [Steph. Tsatsoula. ANTHOLOGIA TES AMERIKANIKĒS POIĒSEŌS . . . Athēnai] 1958. 1 blank leaf, 1 leaf, [5]–110 pp., 1 leaf. illus. (ports.) 18 cm. Contains translations, by Tsatsoula, of *Hugh Selwyn Mauberley*, Part 1, "Envoi (1919)," "The Tree," "Apparuit," "A Virginal," "The River-Merchant's Wife: A Letter," "Ité," "[Und Drang, VIII:] The Flame," "Dance Figure," "Lament of the Frontier Guard," and "Taking Leave of a Friend," pp. 95–106.

D52a [Nikos Spanias. METHAPHRASEIS 1941–1971 . . . New York, Athens Printing] 1972. xix pp., 2 leaves, 64 pp. 22 cm. Contains translation, by Spanias, of "Lament of the Frontier Guard."

D52b* [POIĒMATA EZRA PAOUNT KAI VEITSEL LINTSEY. Athēnai, A. Karabia, 1972]. 149 pp. illus. 21 cm. Contains translations, by Nikos Sēmēriōtēs, of poems by Pound.

PERIODICALS:

D52c [EXILE'S LETTER]. *Tanea Grammata*, Athens (Dec. 1935) 671–3. Translated by George Seferis.

D53 [HUGH SELWYN MAUBERLEY, PART 1, I-V]. *Kypriaka Grammata*, Cyprus, X. 236 (Feb. 1955) 77–79. Translated by Andreas S. Ioánnēs.

D54 [POEMS]. *Kypriaka Grammata*, X. 242 (Aug. 1955) 348–9. Translations, by N. Spanias, of "Near Perigord, III," "Taking Leave of a Friend," "Francesca," and "Further Instructions."

HUNGARIAN

BOOK:

D54a . . . CANTÓK . . . Párizs, Magyar Mühely, 1975. 175, [1] pp. 21 cm. Translations, by László Kemenes Géfin, of Cantos I-IV, IX, X, XIII, XIV, XVI, XVII, XXI, XXX, XXXV, XXXVI, XXXIX, XLV, XLVII, XLIX, L, LIV, LXII, LXXIX, LXXXI, LXXXIII, LXXXIV, XC, XCIX, CXV, CXVI, and CXX.

ANTHOLOGY:

D54b ÉSZAK-AMERIKAI KÖLTŐK ANTOLÓGIÁJA [Budapest] Kozmosz Könyvek, 1966. 539 pp., 2 leaves. 16.8 cm. 25— ft. Contains translations, by Amy Károlyi, of "A Virginal," "The Garden," "Coda," "In a Station of the Metro," and "Alba"; by Géza Képes, of "The Lake Isle," and "Ballad of the Goodly Fere"; by György Somlyo, of Canto XLV; and by Sándor Weöres, from Canto LXXXI, pp. 234–43.

ICELANDIC

BOOK:

D54x* KVEDI . . . Reykjavík, Almenna Bókafélagi [1969?]. 107 pp. Kr. 220.— Translations, by Kristinn Björnsson, of selected poems.

D. TRANSLATIONS
ITALIAN

BOOKS:

D55 ... Jefferson e Mussolini. Venezia, Casa Editrice delle Edizioni Popolari, 1944. 1 blank leaf, 2 leaves, [7]–110 pp., 1 leaf. 21.5 cm. L. 15. (Studi politici ed economici, 2). A rewriting by Ezra Pound in Italian of his *Jefferson and/or Mussolini* (1935). For fuller description see A56.

D56 L'ALLELUJA: POESIE DI ENNIO CONTINI E LA PRIMA DECADE DEI CANTOS DI EZRA POUND ... Mazara, Società Editrice Siciliana [1952]. 131 pp., 2 leaves. 22.5 cm. L. 1000. (Collana di poesia "L'Usignolo," 7). Contains translations, by Mary de Rachewiltz, "in collaborazione personale con l'autore," of Cantos I-IX, and from Canto X (lines 1–55), pp. 89–128.

D57 ... Secondo biglietto da visita. [Roma] Atlante [1953]. 1 blank leaf, 6 leaves, 15–91 pp., 2 leaves, incl. front. (port.), illus. 10.3 cm. (Biblioteca minima, 5). 350 numbered and 24 lettered copies. Ten passages, selected and translated by John Drummond, from *Guide to Kulchur*, preceded by part of "Mediaevalism" and followed by "As Sextant." The illustrations are a facsimile of part of a letter from Ezra Pound, 1933, and a drawing of him by Wyndham Lewis.

D58 CANTI PISANI ... con testo a fronte. Traduzione, introduzione e note di Alfredo Rizzardi. [Parma] Guanda [1953]. xlii, 253, [5] pp. 23.5 cm. L. 1600. (Collezione Fenice, 22). English and Italian on opposite pages. A translation, by Rizzardi, of *The Pisan Cantos*.

D59 ... TRE CANTOS ... Milano, All'Insegna del Pesce d'Oro [1954]. 51, [1] pp., 1 leaf, 1 blank leaf. 12.1 cm. L. 400. (Pagine di letterature straniere antiche e moderne, 1). 1000 copies (500 with wrapper printed in blue, 500 in sepia). English and Italian on opposite pages. Translations, by Mary de Rachewiltz, "in collaborazione personale con l'autore," of Cantos XIII, XX, and XXVII.

D60 Ernest Fenollosa. Ezra Pound. Introduzione ai Nô, con un dramma in un atto di Motokiyo: Kagekiyo. Milano, All'Insegna del Pesce d'Oro [1954]. 43 pp., 1 leaf, incl. col. front. 10 cm. L. 300. (Serie oltremare, 6). 2000 copies, plus not more than 6 special copies on japon. Translations, by Mary de Rachewiltz, of Pound's "Introduction" to *'Noh' or Accomplishment*, and the play "Kagekiyo" from *Certain Noble Plays of Japan*. Reprinted with corrections in 1956 and 1958 (for which later edition see D73). The play alone, in Mary de Rachewiltz's translation, was reprinted in 1956 in Leo Magnino's *Teatro giapponese*—D91—pp. [72]–78.

D61 Iconografia italiana di Ezra Pound, a cura di Vanni Scheiwiller; con una piccola Antologia Poundiana. Milano, All'Insegna del Pesce d'Oro [1955]. 22 pp., 23 leaves, incl. col. front., illus., ports., facsims. 10 cm. L. 400. (Serie illustrata, 50). Contains translations, by Salvatore Quasimodo, of "Vana" and "Motif"; by Giuseppe Ungaretti, of "Song" ("Love thou thy dream"); by Piero Jahier, of "The Garret"; by Vittorio Sereni, of "The

Study in Aesthetics," "In a Station of the Metro," "Coitus," "Shop Girl," "Villanelle: The Psychological Hour," and "Impressions of François-Marie Arouet (de Voltaire)"; by Attilio Bertolucci, of "The Gypsy"; by Eugenio Montale, of *Hugh Selwyn Mauberley*, Part 1, V; and by Mary de Rachewiltz, of "Venetian Night Litany." Includes reproductions of original manuscripts of "Venetian Night Litany," "Piaza [*sic*] San Marco," a page of typescript of Canto LXXIV, the title-page and a page of a typescript of *Section: Rock-Drill*, and a number of drawings, paintings, and photographs of Pound.

D62 ... ANTOLOGIA. Roma [Arti Grafiche Agostini] 1956. 1 blank leaf, 2 leaves, 7–33 pp., 1 leaf. 20 cm. 100 copies (with two special copies in a black outer wrapper). "Estratto da 'Stagione,' Roma, Anno II, n. 7 (1955)." See D148 for contents, except that Manning's "Korè" is omitted in this reprint.

D63 ... Saggi letterari. A cura e con introduzione di T. S. Eliot. [Milano] Garzanti [1957]. 1 blank leaf, 3 leaves, 11–585, [1] pp., 1 leaf. 22 cm. L. 3500. (Saggi). A translation, by Nemi d'Agostino, of *Literary Essays*.

D64 NISHIKIGI, a cura di Ernest Fenollosa ed Ezra Pound. Introduzione ai Nô di W. B. Yeats. Milano, All'Insegna del Pesce d'Oro [1957]. 44, [2] pp., 1 blank leaf. col. front. 10 cm. L. 300. (Serie oltremare, 12). 4000 copies. Translations, by Mary de Rachewiltz, of Yeats's "Introduction" to *Certain Noble Plays of Japan* (1916)—A12, and of the play "Nishikigi" contained in that volume.

D65 ... Brancusi. Milano, All'Insegna del Pesce d'Oro [1957]. 15, [4] pp., 1 leaf, 28 pp., 1 blank leaf, 6 leaves, incl. front., illus., facsim. 9.9 cm. (Serie illustrata, 57). 1000 copies. A translation, by Mary de Rachewiltz, of "Brancusi"—C627; with "Réponses de Brancusi ... à Irène Codreane" (in French).

D66 ... Gaudier-Brzeska, con un manifesto vorticista. Milano, All'Insegna del Pesce d'Oro [1957]. 27, [1] pp., 1 leaf, 28 pp., 5 leaves, 1 blank leaf, 1 leaf, incl. front. (port.), illus. 10 cm. L. 400. (Serie illustrata, 58). 500 copies (numbered in continuation of the edition in English). A translation, by Mary de Rachewiltz, of ... *Gaudier-Brzeska* ([1957])—A73.

D67 ... Henri Gaudier-Brzeska, con un manifesto vorticista ... Galleria Apollinaire Milano [Milano, All'Insegna del Pesce d'Oro, 1957]. [20] pp., incl. 12 numb. illus. 12.2 cm. 500 copies printed for the exhibition of Gaudier-Brzeska's work at the Galleria Apollinaire, Dec. 1957. A translation, by Mary de Rachewiltz, of extracts from "Gaudier: A Postscript" and "Vortex. [By] Pound" (omitting the last two paragraphs). A new edition (60 copies) was published ([Milano, All'Insegna del Pesce d'Oro, 1958]) for the Gaudier-Brzeska exhibition at the Sala delle Esposizioni, Merano, Jan. 1958.

D68 Sofocle—Pound. LE TRACHINIE ... Firenze, Centro Internazionale del Libro [1958]. 1 blank leaf, 1 leaf, 79, [1] pp. 20.7 cm. L. 1000. A translation, by Margherita Guidacci, of *Women of Trachis*.

D69 ... CANTOS 91, 96: BRANI ... [Genova] Ana Eccetera [1958]. cover-title, 1 leaf, 5 pp. 21.8 cm. Not for sale. 500 copies. Excerpts, translated by Enzo

D. TRANSLATIONS

Siciliano. (A translation of "Ité" is included as note 2, p. 1.) "Numero speciale in occasione del ritorno in Italia di Ezra Pound."

D70 ... Patria mia: discussione sulle arti, il loro uso e il loro futuro in America ... Firenze, Edizione del Centro Internazionale del Libro [1958]. 1 blank leaf, 1 leaf, 5–132 pp., 2 leaves. 20.5 cm. L. 1000. Also numbered signed copies, specially bound. L. 3000. A translation by Margherita Guidacci, of *Patria mia*, and "The Case of Ezra Pound ... ," from the *Congressional Record* for 27 Jan. 1958.

D71 ... A Lume Spento 1908–1958, a cura di Vanni Scheiwiller. Milano, All'Insegna del Pesce d'Oro [1958]. 1 blank leaf, 63 pp., 1 leaf, 1 blank leaf, incl. front. (port.), illus. (incl. ports., facsims.) 10 cm. L. 500. (Serie illustrata, 64). 2000 copies. Contains translations, by Salvatore Quasimodo, of "Vana" and "Motif"; by Margherita Guidacci, of "The Tree," "Invern," and "Prometheus"; by Giuseppe Ungaretti, of "Song" ("Love thou thy dream"); by Mary de Rachewiltz, of "Venetian Night Litany" and from Canto LXXVI; by Carlo Izzo, of "Statement of Being"; and by Marco Londonio, of "Nel biancheggiar." (For fuller description see B64.)

D72 ... CANTO 98 ... Milano, All'Insegna del Pesce d'Oro [1958]. 1 blank leaf, 2 leaves, 7–30 pp., 1 leaf, incl. front. 12 cm. L. 500. (Serie letteraria). 1000 copies. Translated by Mary de Rachewiltz. Contains also "Servizio di comunicazioni," dated 22 July 1958, by Ezra Pound, pp. 7–9. (For fuller description see B65.)

D73 Ernest Fenollosa. Ezra Pound. Introduzione ai Nô, con un dramma in un atto di Motokiyo: Kagekiyo. Milano, All'Insegna del Pesce d'Oro [1958]. 1 blank leaf, 1 leaf, 5–46, [2] pp. 10 cm. L. 300. (Serie oltremare, 6). 5000 copies. "Terza edizione." Contains "Un intervallo di 40 anni," dated Nov. 1958, by Ezra Pound, p. 45, not in the earlier editions.

D74 ... Lo spirito romanzo. [Firenze] Vallecchi [1959]. 1 blank leaf, 2 leaves, 7–349 pp., 1 leaf. 20 cm. L. 1800. (Collana Cederna). A translation, by Sergio Baldi, of *The Spirit of Romance* ([1952]).

D75 ... H. S. MAUBERLEY ... con tre disegni inediti di Jean Cocteau. Milano, All'Insegna del Pesce d'Oro, 1959. 1 blank leaf, 3 leaves, [9]–57 pp., 1 leaf. 2 plates. 20.6 cm. (Fascicoli del Verri, 4). L. 800. 1000 copies. English and Italian on opposite pages. A translation, by Giovanni Giudici, of *Hugh Selwyn Mauberley*.

D76 ... CATAI ... Milano, All'Insegna del Pesce d'Oro [1959]. 1 blank leaf, 2 leaves, [7]–49, [1] pp., 1 leaf, 2 blank leaves. front., plates, incl. facsims. 13.7 cm. L. 1000. (Strenna del Pesce d'Oro, 1960). 1000 copies. A translation, by Mary de Rachewiltz, of *Cathay* (1915) as printed in *Personae* (1926), plus "Baijo's Poem in the Koshigen" (added from the Pound-Fenollosa notebooks), p. 43, and a note by Pound concerning it, p. 45.

D77 Ernest Fenollosa. L'ideogramma cinese come mezzo di poesia, una ars poetica. Introduzione e note di Ezra Pound. Milano, All'Insegna del Pesce d'Oro, 1960. 1 blank leaf, 2 leaves, 7–65 pp., 1 leaf, 2 blank leaves. 18.2 cm. L. 1000. (Serie ideografica, a cura di Ezra Pound, 1). 1000 copies. A

D. TRANSLATIONS

translation, by Mary de Rachewiltz, of *The Chinese Written Character as a Medium for Poetry*. On the inside back flap is printed a note by Pound on the series, signed: E. P. 1960.

D78 ... LE POESIE SCELTE, con un saggio di T. S. Eliot. [Milano] Arnoldo Mondadori Editore [1960]. 187, [1] pp., 2 leaves. 19.5 cm. (I Poeti dello "Specchio"). L. 1500. English and Italian on opposite pages. Translations, by Alfredo Rizzardi, of *Selected Poems* ([1949]), and Cantos II, XVII, and XLIX. Three of these translations were reprinted, pp. 489–91, along with facsimile, p.[492], and text, p. 493, of a letter from Ezra Pound to Mondadori, 15 Apr. 1959, in *I Poeti dello "Specchio": Almanacco antologico a cura di Marco Forti* (Milano, Mondadori [1962]).

D79 ... CANTO 99 ... con un disegno inedito di Henri Gaudier-Brzeska. Milano, All'Insegna del Pesce d'Oro, 1960. 1 blank leaf, 29 pp., 1 leaf, incl. plate. 20.5 cm. L. 500. (Fascicoli del Verri, 5). 1000 copies. Translated by Mary de Rachewiltz.

D80 Alcuni nobili drammi del Giappone, da manoscritti di Ernest Fenollosa, scelti e finiti da Ezra Pound. Introduzione di W. B. Yeats. Milano, All'Insegna del Pesce d'Oro, 1961. 1 blank leaf, 2 leaves, 7–90 pp., 2 leaves, 1 blank leaf, incl. front., 1 illus. 18.2 cm. L. 1000. (Serie ideografica, a cura di Ezra Pound, 3). 2000 copies. A translation, by Mary de Rachewiltz, of *Certain Noble Plays of Japan*.

D81 I CANTOS ... VOLUME PRIMO. I PRIMI TRENTA CANTOS ... Milano, Lerici—Scheiwiller [1961]. 1 blank leaf, 329 pp., 3 leaves, 1 blank leaf, incl. illus. (ports., facsim.) 22 cm. in box 22.8 cm. L. 3000. (Poeti europei, 7). English and Italian on opposite pages. A translation, by Mary de Rachewiltz, of Cantos I-XXX, some of them as revised by the author. Preceded by a translation of Ezra Pound's letter to his father, 11 Apr. 1927, and a paragraph from *Guide to Kulchur*. A 15-page pamphlet, *I primi trenta Cantos di Ezra Pound: giudizi e testimonianze* ... (Milano, Lerici & Scheiwiller, 1961), a translation of *The Cantos of Ezra Pound, Some Testimonies* (New York, 1933), was issued with the volume.

D81a ... IL FIORE DEI CANTOS: 18 interpretazioni con un saggio introduttivo di Vittorio Vettori. Pisa, Giardini Editore, 1962. 63, [1] pp. 19.5 cm. L. 1000. (Biblioteca dell'Ussero, 14). Italian "interpretations" by Vettori of brief excerpts from Cantos I, V, XX, all of XLV, six selections from LXXIV, and short ones from LXXVI, LXXVIII, LXXXI, LXXXIII, and LXXXIV, pp. 39–61; with an essay "Pound in Italia," pp. 5–35.

D81b ... Confucio. L'ANTOLOGIA CLASSICA CINESE ... Milano, All'Insegna del Pesce d'Oro, 1964. 1 blank leaf, 3 leaves, 9–342 pp., 1 leaf. 18 cm. L. 2000. (Serie ideografica, a cura di Ezra Pound, 4). 1500 copies. A translation, by Carlo Scarfoglio, of *The Classic Anthology Defined by Confucius*.

D81c Il teatro giapponese Nō di Ernest Fenollosa e Ezra Pound ... [Firenze] Vallecchi Editore [1966]. 1 blank leaf, 3 leaves, 9–250 pp., 1 leaf. 4 plates (1 col.) 21.8 cm. L. 3000. (Collana Cederna). A translation, by Mary de

D. TRANSLATIONS

Rachewiltz, of *'Noh' or Accomplishment*, with the introduction by W. B. Yeats to *Certain Noble Plays of Japan*.

D81d . . . CANTO 90 . . . Milano, All'Insegna del Pesce d'Oro, 1966. 1 blank leaf, 2 leaves, [7]–27 pp., 1 leaf, 1 blank leaf. 15.5 cm. (Serie "Il Quadrato," 23). 1000 copies. English and Italian on opposite pages. Translated by Mary de Rachewiltz. Includes "Richardi Excerpta accurante Ezra Pound (1956)," brief excerpts, in Latin, selected by Pound from Richard of Saint Victor (see B57 and 68), pp. 25–27.

D81e FRANCESCA, RAGAZZA DI BOTTEGA E ALTRE POESIE . . . con due acqueforti di Bruno Cassinari. [Verona, 1968]. 2 blank leaves, 25 pp., 1 leaf, incl. 1 illus., 1 plate. 28.3 cm. in case 29 cm. 90 copies, of which 25 have a separate portfolio, 36 cm., containing an extra set of the two prints. (This has a special title-page: *Bruno Cassinari: Due acqueforti per Ezra Pound. Verona, Corubolo & Castiglioni, 1968*). Contains translations, by Alfredo Rizzardi (reprinted from D78) of "Francesca," "The Shop Girl," "N. Y.," "Apparuit," "The Garret," "Albâtre," "A Girl," "Dans un omnibus de Londres," *Hugh Selwyn Mauberley*, Part 2, I, IV, and "Medallion," and "'Ione, Dead the Long Year.'"

D81f Pound/Joyce . . . a cura di Forrest Read. [Milano] Rizzoli [1969]. 1 blank leaf, 2 leaves, 7–400, [1] pp., 3 leaves. 20.7 cm. L. 3000. Translated by Ruggero Bianchi.

D81g EZRA POUND TRADOTTO DA GIUSEPPE UNGARETTI. Milano, Strenna per gli amici [di Paolo Franci], 1969. 1 blank leaf, 2 leaves, [7]–19 pp., 2 leaves. 13.7 cm. Not for sale. 300 copies (distributed by Franci as a Christmas/New Year's greeting). Edited by Vanni Scheiwiller. English and Italian on opposite pages. Translations, by Ungaretti, of "Song" ("Love thou thy dream")—reprinted from D61 *et al.*—and from Cantos CX and CXV.

D81h . . . Opere scelte, a cura di Mary de Rachewiltz. Introduzione di Aldo Tagliaferri. [Milano] Arnoldo Mondadori Editore [1970]. 1 blank leaf, 4 leaves, [xiii]–xlii pp., 5 leaves, [9]–1466 pp., 1 leaf, 1 blank leaf. 17.5 cm. in box 17.8 cm. L. 6000. (I Meridiani). English and Italian on opposite pages (for poems only). Translations (many reprinted from earlier books), by Salvatore Quasimodo, of "Vana" and "Motif"; by Giuseppe Ungaretti, of "Song" ("Love thou thy dream"); by Carlo Izzo, of "Ballad for Gloom," "An Immorality," "Portrait d'une femme," and "The Return"; by Margherita Guidacci, of "The Tree"; by Mary de Rachewiltz, of "Threnos," "La Fraisne," "De Aegypto," "In Durance," "The White Stag," "Night Litany," "'Blandula, tenulla, vagula,'" "Meditatio," "Ancient Wisdom, Rather Cosmic," "Fratres minores," "Langue d'Oc: Alba," "Moeurs contemporaines, I, VII," "Cantico del sole," *Homage to Sextus Propertius*, VII, "The Seafarer," and *Cathay*; by Alfredo Rizzardi, of "Praise of Ysolt," "Sestina: Altaforte," "On His Own Face in a Glass," "Francesca," "N. Y.," "A Girl," "The Cloak," "Δώρια," "Apparuit," "Tenzone," "Commission," "A Pact," "April," "Ité," "Phyllidula," "The Patterns," "The Coming of War: Actaeon," "Ts'ai Chi'h," "Alba," "Heather," "'Ione, Dead the Long Year,'" "Ἱμέρρω," "The Lake Isle," "Epitaphs, I-II," "The Three Poets," "Dans un omnibus de Londres,"

389

D. TRANSLATIONS

and "Fish and the Shadow"; by Leone Traverso, of "Erat hora" and "The Tomb of Akr Çaar"; by Piero Jahier, of "The Garret"; by Carlo Linati, of "Albâtre"; by Virgilio Luciani, of "Dance Figure"; by Vittorio Sereni, of "The Study in Aesthetics," "In a Station of the Metro," "Coitus," "Shop Girl," "Villanelle: The Psychological Hour," and "Impressions of François-Marie Arouet (de Voltaire), III: To Madame Lullin"; by Attilio Bertolucci, of "The Gipsy"; by Mario Praz, of "Provincia deserta"; by Giovanni Giudici, of *Hugh Selwyn Mauberley*; by Mary de Rachewiltz, of *'Noh' or Accomplishment, The Chinese Written Character as a Medium for Poetry*, "Introduction" to *Sonnets and Ballate of Guido Cavalcanti*, "Vortex," "Henry Gaudier-Brzeska," and "Brancusi"; Confucius' *Ta Hsio*, in the original Italian by Pound and Alberto Luchini; *L'Asse che non vacilla*, in the original Italian by Pound; translations, by Carlo Scarfoglio, of selections from *The Classic Anthology*; by Sergio Baldi, of selections from *The Spirit of Romance*; by Nemi d'Agostino, of selections from *Literary Essays*, and of "Vers libre and Arnold Dolmetsch"; by Edmondo Dodsworth, of "Vorticism"; "Significato di Leo Frobenius," in the original Italian by Pound; translations, by Domenico de' Paoli, of "The Treatise on Harmony"; by Laura Caretti, of selections from *ABC of Reading*; "Lettera al traduttore" from *L'Indice* for Oct. 1930—C783—and "Traduzione" from *L'Indice* for 10 July 1931— C829—both in the original Italian by Pound; translations, by Margherita Guidacci, of *Patria mia*; by John Drummond, of selections from *Guide to Kulchur*, by Pound, of *Introductory Text Book*; "Ancora Jefferson," selections from *Carta da Visita*, and *Oro e Lavoro*, all in the original Italian by Pound.

D81i* OMAGGIO AD EZRA POUND: SETTE POEMI DI EZRA POUND e sette litografie di Luigi Boille con presentazione di Michel Tapié. Rapallo, Galleria Polymnia, 1971. 78 copies. Translations of seven poems, all reprinted from earlier books.

D81j ... ME FELICE, FELICE NOTTE ... con 5 acqueforti a colori di Antonietta Raphaël Mafai. Milano, Edizioni di Vanni Scheiwiller; Roma, L'Arco Edizioni d'Arte, 1972. 4 leaves, plus 5 mounted and matted col. plates (signed and numbered by the artist). 24.4 cm. in box 26 cm. 50 copies (at L. 120,000), plus 5 *h.c.* (at L. 150,000). English and Italian on opposite pages. A translation, by Mary de Rachewiltz, of *Homage to Sextus Propertius*, VII.

D81k ... Saggi letterari, a cura e con introduzione di T. S. Eliot. [Milano] Garzanti [1973]. 577, [1] pp., 1 leaf. 19 cm. L. 1800. (Saggi). A translation, by Nemi d'Agostino, of *Literary Essays*.

D81l ... LE NUVOLE DI PISA con un ritratto inedito di Giuseppe Viviani. Milano, [Vanni Scheiwiller, "all'insegna della Baïta van Gogh"], 1973. 1 blank leaf, 2 leaves, 7–33 pp., 1 leaf, incl. front. (port.), 2 plates. 7.3 cm. L. 500. (Also 1000 copies *h.c.* for the friends of Paolo Belforte, Livorno.) References to Pisa, selected and translated by Mary de Rachewiltz, from *The Pisan Cantos*.

D81m ... STESURE E FRAMMENTI DEI CANTOS CX-CXVII ... Milano, All'Insegna del Pesce d'Oro, 1973. 1 blank leaf, 2 leaves, [7]–71, [1] pp. 17.2 cm. L. 2000. (Acquario, 63). 2000 copies. English and Italian on opposite pages.

D. TRANSLATIONS

A translation, by Mary de Rachewiltz, of *Drafts & Fragments of Cantos CX-CXVII.*

D81n ... CANTOS SCELTI, a cura di Mary de Rachewiltz. [Milano] Arnoldo Mondadori Editore [1973]. 1 blank leaf, 6 leaves, [15]-289 pp., 3 leaves. 19.7 cm. L. 3800. (Lo Specchio). English and Italian on opposite pages. A translation, by Mary de Rachewiltz, of *Selected Cantos*, deleting Canto XVI, from Cantos LII and LXII, Cantos LXXXI, LXXXIV, from Canto LXXXVIII, Canto XCV, from Cantos CV, CVIII, and CIX; and adding Cantos XXVII, XLIII (complete), LXXVI, XC, XCVIII, XCIX (complete), from Canto CXV, and Canto CXVI.

D81o ... L'ABC del leggere. [Milano] Garzanti [1974]. 209 pp., 1 leaf. 21.8 cm. L. 4800. (Saggi). A translation, by Rodolfo Quadrelli, of *ABC of Reading.*

D81p CON USURA. [Milano, Tipografia A. Locatelli & F., 1974]. Broadside. 99 copies. Distributed by Dario Vermi as a Christmas greeting. An "interpretation," by Vittorio Vettori, of Canto XLV. Reprinted from D81a.

D81q Fausto Melotti. IL PESCE E L'OMBRA: 12 litografie con una poesia di Ezra Pound. Milano, 1975. 4 leaves, 12 plates. 80 numbered and 10 lettered copies. A translation, by Mary de Rachewiltz, of "Fish and the Shadow."

D81r François Villon. Il testamento e La ballata degli impiccati. Saggio introduttivo di Ezra Pound. Traduzione italiana a cura di Rina Sara Virgillito. [Milano] Rusconi [1976]. xxiii, 247, [1] pp. 22 cm. Contains "preface" by Pound, pp. v-xxiii, a translation, by Gilberto Forti, of "Montcorbier, alias Villon" from *The Spirit of Romance.*

D81s A che serve il danaro? ... [Napoli] Edizioni San Giorgio [1980]. 35, [1] pp. 16.7 cm. L. 1500. (Collezione Quaderni di Economia, I). A translation, by Olivia Rossetti Agresti, of *What Is Money For?*

D81t ... Lettere 1907-1958. Prefazione e cura di Aldo Tagliaferri. Milano, Feltrinelli Editore [1980]. 1 blank leaf, 2 leaves, 7-177 pp., 3 leaves. 22.2 cm. L. 8000. (I Fatti e le Idee: Saggi e Biografie, 468). Translations, by Girolamo Mancuso and Wilma Rodeghiero, of letters written to various correspondents in English and in French, in part from *The Letters*, and in part from other sources, with first publication, at least in book form, of many letters to Italian correspondents. For fuller description see A104.

D81u LECTURA DOMINICA ... La traduzione è di Mary d. R[achewiltz]. e l'acquaforte di Franca Ghitti ... Poiano, Franco Riva, 1980 [*i.e.* 1981]. 1 blank leaf, 6 leaves, 1 blank leaf, incl. 1 plate. 37.5 cm. in box 40 cm. L. 90,000. 100 copies printed by Riva "nelle domeniche dell'estate Mdccclxxx," issued in 1981. A translation, by Mary de Rachewiltz, of "The Seafarer." Reprinted from D81h.

D81v ... PROVE E FRAMMENTI DEI CANTI CX-CXVII. A cura di Carlo Alberto Corsi, con una nota introduttiva di Giovanni Raboni. [Milano] Guanda [1981]. 1 blank leaf, 2 leaves, 7-92 pp., 1 leaf, 1 blank leaf. 20 cm. L. 5500. (Quaderni della Fenice, 81). English and Italian on opposite pages. A translation, by Corsi and Michelangelo Coviello, of *Drafts & Fragments of Cantos CX-CXVII.*

D. TRANSLATIONS

D81w... IL LIBRO DI HILDA, a cura di Roberto Caterina e Alessandro Tesauro ... [Salerno, Roma, Edizioni] Ripostes [1981]. 1 blank leaf, 2 leaves, 7–54 pp., 1 leaf. 16.7 cm. L. 3500. ("Postea" Poeti, 2). 500 copies. English and Italian on opposite pages. A translation, by Caterina, of "Hilda's Book."

D81x... Jefferson e/o Mussolini ... Milano, Società Editrice Il Falco, 1981. 1 blank leaf, 3 leaves, 9–145 pp., 3 leaves. 21 cm. L. 6000. (Il Ponte, [7] 2000 copies. A translation, by Claudio Gattuso, of *Jefferson and/or Mussolini*.

ANTHOLOGIES:

D82 Carlo Linati. SCRITTORI ANGLO-AMERICANI D'OGGI. Milano, Corticelli Editore [1932]. 259 pp., 1 leaf. 20.5 cm. Contains translations, by Linati, of "Taking Leave of a Friend," "Phyllidula," "The Lake Isle," "Albâtre," "Dance Figure," and from *Homage to Sextus Propertius*, IV, pp. 101–5.

D83 Fascist Europe. Europa Fascista. An Anglo-Italian Symposium Edited by Erminio Turcotti ... Volume I. Milano, 1938. 1 blank leaf, 1 leaf, 5–157, [1] pp., 2 leaves, 1 blank leaf, [4] pp. 24.4 cm. L. 15. Contains "Ubicumque lingua romana," an Italian translation, by Erminio Turcotti?, pp. 47–52, of an essay of the same title printed in English, pp. 41–46. For fuller description see B43.

D84... Leone Traverso. POESIA MODERNA STRANIERA ... Roma, Edizioni di Prospettive [1942]. 2 blank leaves, 4 leaves, xiii-xix, 177 pp., 1 leaf. 19.4 cm. (Caratteri della letteratura moderna italiana straniera, 1). Contains translations, by Traverso, of "Erat hora," "The Coming of War: Actaeon," "The Tomb at Akr Çaar," and Canto XVII, pp. 147–52.

D85... Luigi Berti. L'IMAGISMO, CON UNA PICCOLA ANTOLOGIA. Padova, Cedam, 1944. 1 blank leaf, 2 leaves, [7]–120 pp., 1 leaf, 1 blank leaf. 19.6 cm. L. 350. (Guide di cultura contemporanea, 11). Contains translations, by Berti, of "De Aegypto," "Δώρια," "Motif," "A Girl," and "Provincia deserta," pp. [87]–91.

D86 POETI AMERICANI (1662–1945), a cura di Gabriele Baldini. Torino, Francesco De Silva, 1949. 1 blank leaf, 3 leaves, ix-xxxiii, 434 pp., 1 leaf, 1 blank leaf. 10 plates (ports.) 21.2 cm. (Maestri e compagni, 15). L. 1600. English and Italian on opposite pages. Contains translations, by Baldini, of "The Return"; by A. Guidi, of "The River-Merchant's Wife: A Letter"; and by Mario Praz, of "Provincia deserta," pp. 332–41.

D87 POESIA AMERICANA CONTEMPORANEA E POESIA NEGRA. Introduzione, versione e note di Carlo Izzo. [Parma] Guanda [1949]. xxxii, 596 pp. 23.4 cm. (Collana Fenice, 12). English and Italian on opposite pages. Contains translations, by Izzo, of "An Immorality," "Night Litany," "Portrait d'une femme," "Ballad for Gloom," "The Return," "The Coming of War: Actaeon," from Cantos II and III, and Canto XLV, pp. [228]–245.

D88* "ORFEO," antologia della lirica mondiale a cura di V. Errante e E. Mariano. Firenze, Sansoni, 1949. Contains translations of three Cantos.

D89 Alfredo Rizzardi. LIRICI AMERICANI. Caltanissetta—Roma, Edizioni Salvatore Sciascia [1955]. 1 blank leaf, 196 pp., 1 leaf. 20.1 cm. English and

D. TRANSLATIONS

Italian on opposite pages. Contains translations, by Rizzardi, of "Commission," "Heather," "'Ione, Dead the Long Year,'" *Hugh Selwyn Mauberley*, Part 1, I, II, and V, and Canto I, pp. [86]–99. (A second edition, "interamente rifatti," was published in 1966.)

D90 . . . POETI STRANIERI DEL '900, tradotti da poeti italiani; a cura di Vanni Scheiwiller. Milano, "All'Insegna del Pesce d'Oro" [1956]. 140, [1] pp., 2 leaves, incl. col. front., illus. 13.7 cm. L. 800. (Strenna del Pesce d'Oro, 1956). 2000 copies. Contains translations, by Giuseppe Ungaretti, of "Song" ("Love thou thy dream"); by Salvatore Quasimodo, of "Motif"; by Piero Jahier, of "The Garret"; by Vittorio Sereni, of "The Study in Aesthetics"; by Giovanni Giudici, of *Hugh Selwyn Mauberley*, Part 1, IV, and by Eugenio Montale, of Part 1, V, pp. 113–17.

D91 . . . Leo Magnino . . . Teatro giapponese. [Milano] Nuova Accademia Editrice [1956]. 289 pp., 1 leaf. plates. 21.7 cm. L. 3000. (Thesaurus Litterarum, Sezione 3a: "Teatro di tutto il mondo"). Contains translations, by Mary de Rachewiltz, of the Noh plays "Kagekiyo," pp. [72]–78, "Kinuta," pp. [82]–90, and "Shojo," pp. [94]–96, all from *'Noh' or Accomplishment*. (The other plays in the volume were translated directly from the Japanese by Magnino.) For earlier, separate publication of the translation of "Kagekiyo" see D60.

D92 Antologia della critica americana del novecento; a cura di Morton Dauwen Zabel. I . . . Roma, Edizioni di Storia e Letteratura, 1957. 1 blank leaf, 2 leaves, 7–346 pp., 1 leaf. 21.5 cm. ("Nuovo mondo"). A translation, by various hands, of Zabel's *Literary Opinion in America*, vol. 1, containing "Date Line," "A Stray Document," and *How to Read*, Part II, by Ezra Pound, pp. 321–46.

D93 POESIA STRANIERA DEL NOVECENTO, a cura di Attilio Bertolucci. [Milano] Garzanti [1958]. 1 blank leaf, 3 leaves, ix-xii, 875 pp., 1 leaf. plates (ports.) 22 cm. L. 6000. English and Italian on opposite pages. Contains translations, by A. Guidi, of "A Girl," "The River-Merchant's Wife: A Letter," *Hugh Selwyn Mauberley*, Part 1, I, and Canto XLV; by Bertolucci, of "The Gypsy"; and by Leone Traverso, of Canto XVII, pp. 448–71.

D94 Roberto Sanesi. POETI AMERICANI DA E. A. ROBINSON A W. S. MERWIN (1900–1956). Milano, Feltrinelli Editore [1958]. 1 blank leaf, 1028 pp., 1 leaf. 20.5 cm. L. 6000. English and Italian on opposite pages. Contains translations, by Sanesi, of "A Girl," "Dance Figure," "The Lake Isle," "Taking Leave of a Friend," *Hugh Selwyn Mauberley*, Part 1, I-V, and "Envoi (1919)," Canto I, from Cantos II and XX, Canto XLIX, from Canto LXXXI, and Canto XC, pp. 350–93.

D95 POETI DEL NOVECENTO: ITALIANI E STRANIERI. Antologia a cura di Elena Croce. [Torino] Einaudi [1960]. xxiv, 914 pp., 1 blank leaf, 1 leaf. 22.3 cm. English and Italian on opposite pages. Contains translations by various hands of "Salutation," "The Lake Isle," "The Gypsy," "Δώρια," Canto XLV, and "Francesca," pp. [554]–565.

D96 . . . IL NATALE: ANTOLOGIA DI POETI DEL '900; a cura di Mary de Ra-

D. TRANSLATIONS

chewiltz e Vanni Scheiwiller. Milano, All'Insegna del Pesce d'Oro, 1961. 1
blank leaf, 2 leaves, 7–135 pp., 1 leaf, 1 blank leaf. xii plates. 13.5 cm. L.
1000. (Strenna del Pesce d'Oro, 1962). 2000 copies. English and Italian on
opposite pages (for foreign poems). Contains translation, by Mary de Rachewiltz, of "A Prologue," pp. 82–89.

D96a Sergio Solmi. VERSIONI POETICHE DA CONTEMPORANEI. Milano,
All'Insegna del Pesce d'Oro, 1963. 1 blank leaf, 3 leaves, [9]–106 pp., 1
leaf. 17.9 cm. L. 1200. (Acquario, 15). 1000 copies. English and Italian on
opposite pages. Contains a translation, by Solmi, of "The Tomb at Akr
Çaar," pp. 78–81.

D96b PATERSON, di William Carlos Williams . . . Milano, Lerici Editori [1966].
xlix pp., 1 leaf, 523 pp., 3 leaves, 1 blank leaf, incl. illus. (ports.) 21.7 cm.
in box 22.5 cm. L. 4800. (Poeti europei, 24). English and Italian on opposite pages. Translated by Alfredo Rizzardi. Passages from letters of Ezra
Pound to William Carlos Williams (see B51 and 62) appear, pp. 307, 475–
7.

D96c Jorge Guillén. HOMENAJE. Milano, All'Insegna del Pesce d'Oro, 1967. 2
blank leaves, 5 leaves, 15–629, [1] pp., 1 leaf, 2 blank leaves. 20.8 cm. 450
copies, plus 50 de luxe. (In Italian.) Contains Guillen's translation of "Motif," p. 439.

D96d Fernando Ritter. Lo pseudocapitale, moderno strumento di dominio eco-
nomico-politico del mondo capitalistico, preceduto da un saggio su Ezra
Pound economista. Milano, All'Insegna del Pesce d'Oro, 1970. 1 blank
leaf, 3 leaves, 9–158, [2] pp. 21.5 cm. (La Primula Rossa, 9). 2000 copies.
Contains translation, by Mary de Rachewiltz, of Canto XLV, pp. [7–8].

D96e Vittorio Vettori. Ezra Pound e il senso dell'America. Roma, Ersi Editrice
[1975]. 1 blank leaf, 4 leaves, 11–272 pp., 1 blank leaf, 2 leaves, 1 blank
leaf. 23.9 cm. L. 5000. Contains reprint of "Il Fiore dei Cantos"—D81a—
pp. [135]–157. A following section, "Incontri e scontri (cronistoria del
'Fiore')," pp. [159]–166, prints letters to Vettori, 13 Dec. 1958, 10 Jan. 1959
(enclosing "G. Bottai" and "Ricordo di Bottai"), and 18 Jan. 1959.

D96f Rodolfo Quadrelli. COMMEDIA. Milano, All'Insegna del Pesce d'Oro, 1977.
1 blank leaf, 2 leaves, 7–78 pp., 1 leaf. 17 cm. L. 3000. ("Lunario" Fuori
Serie, 43). 1000 copies. Contains, as an appendix, pp. [49]–72, a translation, by Quadrelli, of *Hugh Selwyn Mauberley*.

D96g Alfred Rizzardi. Una ghirlanda per Ezra Pound. Urbino, Argalia Editore
[1981]. 3 leaves, iii–v pp., 1 leaf, 7–299 pp., 1 leaf. 20 cm. L. 9000. (Nuovi
Contesti). A collection of tributes to and essays on Ezra Pound, in Italian.
Contains translations, by Mary de Rachewiltz, of Canto XLVIII, and by
Rizzardi, of *Indiscretions*, pp. [223]–285.

PERIODICALS:

D97 [NEL BIANCHEGGIAR]. *La Bauta*, Venice (9 Aug. 1908). A translation, by
Marco Londonio, quoted at the end of his article, signed: m. l., "Celebrità

contemporanee: Miss Katherine Heyman." Reprinted by Ezra Pound in the "Notes on New Poems" in *Personae* (1909)—A3—p. 59.

D98* IL RITORNO. *Il Barco*, 13/16 ([*ca.* 1920–1921?]) 21. A translation, by Guido Hess, of "The Return."

D99 PROVINCIA DESERTA. *La Fiera Letteraria*, Rome, IV. 27 (1 July 1928) 3. Translated by Mario Praz.

D100 Alla scuola di Ezra Pound: Il manifesto degli "Imagistes." *La Fiera Letteraria*, V. 12 (24 Mar. 1929) 4. A translation, by Francesco Monotti, of "A Few Don'ts by an Imagiste."

D101 I più grandi poeti d'ogni secolo e d'ogni tempo. *L'Indice*, Genoa, I. 3 (20 Feb. 1930) 3. Translated, by Francesco Monotti, from *How to Read*.

D102 Come si deve leggere. *L'Indice*, I. 5 (20 Mar. 1930) [1]. Translated, by Francesco Monotti, from *How to Read*.

D103 Ciò che è essenziale nella letteratura. *Belvedere*, Milan, III. 1 (1931) 9–18. Translated and condensed, by Francesco Monotti, from *How to Read*.

D104 CINQUE POESIE . . . *L'Indice*, II. 15 (10 Aug. 1931) 3. Translations, by Emanuel Gazzo, of "Dans un omnibus de Londres," *Hugh Selwyn Mauberley*, Part 2, I, IV, "Francesca," and "Commission."

D105 CANTO OTTAVO . . . *L'Indice*, II. 17/18 (10 Nov. 1931) 5. A translation, by F. [*i.e.* Emanuel] Carnevali, of Canto VIII.

D106 Madox Ford a Rapallo. *Il Mare*, Rapallo, XXV. 1223 (20 Aug. 1932) 3, 4. A translation, by Olga Rudge, anonymously, of a conversation between Ezra Pound and Ford at Rapallo, set down by her in English.

D107 Poeti francesi [I]. *Il Mare*, XXV. 1225 (3 Sept. 1932) 3, 4. The first of 11 instalments of a translation, by Lina Caico, of "A Study of French Poets." With a brief prefatory note, unsigned, by Ezra Pound, p. 3.

D108 Poeti francesi [II]: Jules Laforgue (1860–'87). *Il Mare*, XXV. 1227 (17 Sept. 1932) 4.

D109 Poeti francesi [III]. *Il Mare*, XXV. 1231 (15 Oct. 1932) 4.

D110 Poeti francesi. 4. *Il Mare*, XXV. 1233 (29 Oct. 1932) 4.

D111 Poeti francesi. V. *Il Mare*, XXV. 1235 (12 Nov. 1932) 3, 4. With a brief note on the translation, signed: E. P.

D112 Poeti francesi [VI]. *Il Mare*, XXV. 1239 (10 Dec. 1932) 4.

D113 Poeti francesi [VII]. *Il Mare*, XXV. 1241 (24 Dec. 1932) 4.

D114 Poeti francesi [VIII]. *Il Mare*, XXV. 1243 (7 Jan. 1933) 4.

D115 Vorticismo [I]. *Il Mare*, XXVI. 1249 (18 Feb. 1933) 3. The first of four instalments of a translation, by Edmondo Dodsworth, of "Vorticism." With note, "Riflessione nell'anno XI," signed: E. P.

D116 Vorticismo, II. *Il Mare*. XXVI. 1251 (4 Mar. 1933) 3.

D117 Poeti francesi [IX]. Laurent Tailhade (1854–1919). *Il Mare*, XXVI. 1251 (4 Mar. 1933) 4.

D. TRANSLATIONS

D118 Vorticismo (seguito). *Il Mare*, XXVI. 1255 (1 Apr. 1933) 2.

D119 Vorticismo [IV]. *Il Mare*, XXVI. 1260 (6 May 1933) 2.

D120 Poeti francesi [X]. Moréas. *Il Mare*, XXVI. 1262 (20 May 1933) 2.

D121 Poeti francesi [XI]: Francis Jammes (nato 1868). *Il Mare*, XXVI. 1270 (15 July 1933) 2.

D122 [POEMS]. *Circoli*, Genoa, II. 6 (Nov./Dec. 1933) 66–77. English and Italian on opposite pages. Translations, by Giacomo Prampolini, of "Francesca," "A Girl," and "The Coming of War: Actaeon," and, by Mario Praz, of "Provincia deserta," the last reprinted from D99.

D123 Da "Chicago Daily Tribune" (edizione di Parigi) del 9 aprile ... *Quadrante*, Milan (Apr. 1934) 36. A translation, by Ubaldo degli Uberti, of "Mussolini Defines State as 'Spirit of the People'; Fascism Analyzed by Ezra Pound"—C1057. Reprinted in *Il Mare*, Rapallo, XXVII. 1318 (16 June 1934) [1].

D124 Menzogne straniere smentite da uno straniero. *Giornale di Genova*, Genoa (1 Apr. 1934) [1]. A letter to the Editor from Ubaldo degli Uberti, calling his attention to Ezra Pound's letter in the *Morning Post*, London, for 20 Mar.—C1035, quoting two paragraphs and citing proof of the points made.

D125* [OPENING OF CANTO XLI]. *Il Mondo d'Oggi* (Mar.? 1935). Translated by Ubaldo degli Uberti.

D126 [POEMS]. *Anteneo Veneto*, Venice, CXXVI. 5/6 (Nov./Dec. 1935) 243–6. Translations, by Carlo Izzo, of "Ballad for Gloom," "Night Litany," "The Return," and from Cantos II and III.

D127 La giornata di Jodindranath Mawhwor. *Broletto*, Como, II. 22 (Oct. 1937) 21–23. A translation, by N. Ruffini, of "Jodindranath Mawhwor's Occupation."

D128 [THREE POEMS]. *Circoli*, VI. 8 (Oct. 1937) 613–15. Translations, by Leone Traverso, of "Erat hora," "The Coming of War: Actaeon," and "The Tomb at Akr Çaar."

D129 UNA FANCIULLA. *Poeti d'Oggi*, Asti, I. 6 ([Winter?] 1937) 33. A translation, by Renzo Laurano, of "A Girl."

D130 ... CANTO XLV. *Broletto*, II. 27 (Mar. 1938) 19. A translation, by Carlo Izzo, printed at the end of his article, "'Nel mezzo del cammin ...,'" pp. 18–19. Under the heading: "Servizio di comunicazione."

D131 ... Due amici della verità. *Meridiano di Roma*, Rome, IV. 6 (5 Feb. 1939) 9. Translated by Ubaldo degli Uberti.

D132 Nazioni e scrittori. *Meridiano di Roma*, IV. 24 (18 June 1939) 5. Translated by L[ina]. C[aico].

D133 XVII DEI "CANTOS". ... *Prospettive*, Rome, IV. 4 (15 Apr. 1940) 7–8. A translation, by Leone Traverso, of Canto XVII.

D134 A che serve il danaro? *Meridiano di Roma*, VI. 30 (27 July 1941) [1], 6–7. A translation, by Olivia Rossetti Agresti, of *What Is Money For?*

D. TRANSLATIONS

D135 Henry James . . . I. *Lettere d'Oggi*, Rome, III. 8 (Sept. 1941) 24–31. Translated anonymously.

D136 Il dramma simbolico giapponese di E. Fenollosa e E. Pound. *Meridiano di Roma*, VII. 16 (19 Apr. 1942) 6. A translation, by Mary Rudge (later de Rachewiltz), of the "Introduction" to *'Noh' or Accomplishment*.

D137 UNA POESIA DI EZRA POUND . . . *Meridiano di Roma*, VII. 20 (17 May 1942) 6. A translation, by Virgilio Luciani, of "Dance Figure."

D138 IL 2° DEI CANTOS . . . *Prospettive*, VI. 32/33 (15 Aug./15 Sept. 1942) 11–14. A translation, by Luigi Berti, of Canto II.

D139 RITRATTO DI UNA DONNA. *La Fiera Letteraria*, IV. 11 (13 Mar. 1949) 1. A translation, by Romeo Lucchese, of "Portrait d'une femme."

D140 POESIE . . . *Ausonia*, Siena, 34 (May 1949) 3–4. Translations, by Virgilio Luciani, of "Dance Figure" and "Δώρια."

D141 [Letters]. *Letteratura Arte Contemporanea*, Florence, IV. 6 ([June?] 1950). In his article on *The Letters*, "Palinsesti del protoumanesimo poetico americano," Luciano Anceschi incorporates translations of Ezra Pound's letters to Iris Barry, [20] and 27 July 1916, Harriet Monroe, Jan. 1915, and T. S. Eliot, [24 Dec. 1921, *i.e.* Jan. 1922]. (Offprints of the article were prepared for Anceschi.)

D142 Tre lettere di Ezra Pound al Dottor Rouse sul tradurre poesia e una lettera a Joyce. *Letterature Moderne*, Milan, I. 2 (Sept. 1950) 223–6. Three letters to W. H. D. Rouse and one to James Joyce, translated by Luciano Anceschi and D. D. Paige, preceded by the original English text, pp. 220–2. (Offprints were prepared for the translators.)

D143 DAI CANTI PISANI. *La Fiera Letteraria*, V. 46 (19 Nov. 1950) 3. A translation, by Leone Traverso, of the "lynx chorus" from Canto LXXIX.

D144 POESIE . . . *La Fiera Letteraria*, VIII. 43 (25 Oct. 1953) 3. Translations, by Nemi d'Agostino, of *Hugh Selwyn Mauberley*, Part 1, II, IV-V, IX, "Envoi (1919)," and Part 2, IV, and V.

D145 LETTERA DELLA MOGLIE DEL MERCANTE FLUVIALE. *La Fiera Letteraria*, VIII. 43 (25 Oct. 1953) 4. A translation, by Nemi d'Agostino, of "The River-Merchant's Wife: A Letter."

D146 LETTERA DI UN ESILIATO. *Il Punto*, III. 1 (Spring 1954) 18–20. A translation, by Mary de Rachewiltz, of "Exile's Letter."

D147 FROM CANTO LXXI [AND LXXXIII]. *Pound Newsletter*, Berkeley, Calif., 5 (Jan. 1955) 9–10. Translated by Giovanni Cecchetti.

D148 ANTOLOGIA POUNDIANA. *Stagione: Lettere e Arti*, Rome, II. 7 ([July/Dec.] 1955) 4, 5, 6, 7, 8. Translations, by Salvatore Quasimodo, of "Vana" and "Motif"; by Margherita Guidacci, of "The Tree," "Invern," and "Prometheus"; by Giuseppe Ungaretti, of "Song" ("Love thou thy dream"); by Leone Traverso, of "Erat hora" and "The Tomb at Akr Çaar"; by Piero Jahier, of "The Garret"; by Vittorio Sereni, of "The Study in Aesthetics," "Shop Girl," and "In a Station of the Metro"; by Giacomo Prampolini, of

D. TRANSLATIONS

"The Coming of War: Actaeon"; by Attilio Bertolucci, of "The Gypsy"; by Giovanni Giudici, of *Hugh Selwyn Mauberley*, Part 1, IV, and, by Eugenio Montale, of Part 1, V; and by Maria Luisa Spaziani, of "Korè" (by Frederic Manning).

D149 HUGH JELWYN [*sic*] MAUBERLEY [PART 1], I, III, IV, V. *La Parrucca*, Milan, III. 6 (30 Sept. 1955) 83. Translated by Giorgio Manganelli.

D150 Dai "Literary Essays" ... *La Parrucca*, III. 6 (30 Sept. 1955) 86. Brief quotations, selected and translated by A. Giuliani.

D151 POESIE. *Prospetti*, Florence, 16 (1956) [110]–127. English and Italian on opposite pages. Translations, by Mary de Rachewiltz, of "De Aegypto," "Ité," "Alba," "Taking Leave of a Friend," *Homage to Sextus Propertius*, VII, *Hugh Selwyn Mauberley*, Part 1, III, Canto III, and from Canto LXXXI; and by Carlo Izzo, of Canto XLV. (Two offprints were prepared.) *Prospetti* is the Italian edition of *Perspectives U.S.A.*

D152 Due lettere su Dante. *Nuova Corrente*, Milan, 5/6 (Jan./June 1956) 58–63. Translations, by Luciano Anceschi, of two letters from Ezra Pound to Laurence Binyon, with a note, pp. 64–69.

D153 23 lettere e 9 cartoline inedite. *Nuova Corrente*, 5/6 (Jan./June 1956) 145–54. Translations, by Carlo Izzo, of the English portions of Ezra Pound's letters to him are included as notes to his article. For fuller description see B89 and C1787.

D154 [CONFUCIAN ODES]. *Nuova Antologia*, Rome, CCCCLXVI. 1863 (Mar. 1956) 411–20. At the end of his review of *The Classic Anthology Defined by Confucius*, Carlo Scarfoglio gives literal translations into Italian of Ezra Pound's English versions of poems numbered 112, 99, 102, 132, 127, 137, 72, 86, 91, 16, 18, 6, 153, 83, 118, 184, 185, 187, 209, and 288. (Offprints of the complete article, "L'Antologia classica cinese," pp. [409]–420, were prepared for Scarfoglio.)

D155 LA TOMBA AD AKAR CAAR [*sic*]. *La Posta Letteraria* [of the *Corriere dell'Adda e del Ticino*], Lodi, V. 19 (19 Oct. 1957) 1. A translation, by Sergio Solmi, of "The Tomb at Akr Çaar."

D156 Dalle lettere ... *Il Caffè*, Rome, VI (N.S.). 2 (Feb. 1958) 1–11. A translation, by Mary de Rachewiltz, of excerpts from *The Letters*, selected by Louis Dudek.

D157 [*Entry deleted.*]

D158 CANTO 98. *L'Illustrazione Italiana*, Milan, LXXXV. 9 (Sept. 1958) 35–39. Translated by Mary de Rachewiltz. Printed in double columns with English text at right.

D159 MR. NIXON. *Corriere d'Informazione*, Milan (4/5 Oct. 1958). A translation, by Giovanni Giudici, of *Hugh Selwyn Mauberley*, Part 1, IX.

D160 ODE POUR L'ÉLECTION DE SON SÉPULCHRE (MAUBERLEY). *L'Uomo Libero*, Milan, 3 (Mar. 1959). Translations, by Giancarlo Bonacina, of *Hugh Selwyn Mauberley*, Part 1, I-II, printed as part of his "Ezra Pound prima dei 'Cantos.'" (The other translations included are reprinted.)

D. TRANSLATIONS

D161 "L'immangiabile." *Le Arti*, Milan, X. 5/6 (May/June 1959) ii. A translation, by Mary de Rachewiltz, of "The Inedible"—C1534. (Translations, also by Mary de Rachewiltz, of three poems from *Cathay* are reprinted.) Reproduced is the first page of Mary de Rachewiltz's original typescript of her Italian translation of Canto XI, with manuscript corrections and suggestions by Ezra Pound, with text of the translation printed below.

D162 HUGH SELWYN MAUBERLEY. *Il Verri*, Milan, III. 3 (June 1959) 3–20. Translated by Giovanni Giudici.

D163 CANTO XIV. *Ana Eccetera*, 2 (10 Oct. 1959) 4–9. Translated by Enzo Siciliano. English and Italian on opposite pages. In fascicule headed: "Servizio di comunicazione."

D163a DUE VOLTE CROCIFISSO. *La Prima Fiamma*, Turin, IX. 4 (July/Aug. 1960) 1. An "interpretation," by Vittorio Vettori, of parts of Cantos LXXIV and LXXVIII.

D164 CANTO 99. *Il Verri*, IV. 5 (Oct. 1960). Translated by Mary de Rachewiltz.

D165 IO SENTII PIANGERE. *Corriere d'Informazione*, Milan (29/30 Oct. 1960) [2]. A translation, by Mary de Rachewiltz, of the first 24 lines of Canto XXX.

D166 VII CANTO . . . *Il Segnacolo*, Bologna, I. 6 (Nov./Dec. 1960) 25–29. A new version of her translation, prepared by Mary de Rachewiltz in collaboration with the author, for D81.

D167 ABC della lettura. *La Fiera Letteraria*, XVI. 41 (15 Oct. 1961) 1–2. An anonymous translation of part of Chapter I of *ABC of Reading*.

D167a SESTINA: ALTAFORTE . . . *La Vetta d'Italia*, Bolzano, V. 1 (10 Jan. 1964) 3. Translated anonymously, in connexion with an article, "Ezra Pound: l'ultimo dei grandi poeti."

D167b DUE POESIE . . . a cura di Massimo Cacciari. *Angelus Novus*, Venice, 1 (Nov. 1964) 92–95. Translations, by Cacciari, of "Dance Figure" and "To-Em-Mei's 'The Unmoving Cloud.'" English text printed at the foot of the page.

D167c CANTI . . . *L'Orologio*, Rome, II. 8/9 (July 1965) 18–19. "Interpretations," by Vittorio Vettori, of selections from the Cantos.

D167d CANTO XLIX. *Il Segnacolo*, Bologna, VI. 5 (Sept./Oct. 1965) 9–10. Translated by Mary de Rachewiltz.

D167e CANZONE. *Les Cahiers de L'Herne*, 7 ([May 1966]), recto of 3d plate at end. Reproduction of Ungaretti's manuscript of his translation of "Song" ("Love thou thy dream"), inscribed to Vanni Scheiwiller. See D61.

D167f CANTO 51 . . . *L'Approdo Letterario*, Turin, XIII. 38 (Apr./June 1967) 52–54. Translated by Mary de Rachewiltz, with an introductory note, p. 51. (Offprints were prepared.)

D167g DAL CANTO CX. DAL CANTO CXV. *Agenda*, London, VIII. 2 (Spring 1970) 98–99. Translations, by Giuseppe Ungaretti, from these two Cantos. Reprinted from D81g.

D. TRANSLATIONS

D167h CANTOS 90 E 116 ... *Almanacco dello Specchio*, Milan, 1 (1972) [87]–101. Translated by Mary de Rachewiltz. English and Italian on opposite pages.

D167i Per una cultura nazionale (manifesto). *La Destra*, Rome, II. 11/12 (Nov./ Dec. 1972) [107]–113. An anonymous translation of "Manifesto (1938)" from *Impact*. (This issue of the periodical is subtitled: "Omaggio a Pound.")

D167j Radio Roma (lettera all'Attorney General Biddle). *La Destra*, II. 11/12 (Nov./Dec. 1972) [114]–116. An anonymous translation of the letter to U.S. Attorney General Francis Biddle, 4 Aug. 1943.

D167k Lettere dal carcere. *La Destra*, II. 11/12 (Nov./Dec. 1972) 138–45. A facsimile of the letter to J[oseph] C[ornell], "Wednesday night," with translation opposite.

D167l ... NOTES FOR CANTO CXVII ET SEQ. *Paragone*, Florence, 274 (Dec. 1972) [3]–5. Translated by Mary de Rachewiltz. English text precedes Italian translation.

D167m Le conversazioni radiofoniche dell'autore dei "Cantos"—Parla Ezra Pound. *La Destra*, 3 (1976) [65]–114. Translations of Rome radio broadcasts: "Those Parentheses," "The Pattern," "Question of Motive," "Universality," "To Be Late," "With Phantoms," "As a Beginning," "The Fallen Gentleman," "Continuity," "Darkness," "To the Memory," "Materialism," and "Civilization."

JAPANESE

Starred entries supplied by Katue Kitasono, Sanehide Kodama, and Takeshi Onadera.

BOOKS:

D167x *Bungaku seishin no gensen ... Tokyo, Kinseido, 1933. 88 pp. 19.1 cm. A translation, by Tsunetaro Kinoshita, of *How to Read* and "James Joyce: At Last the Novel Appears."

D168 Sekai bungaku no yomikata ... Tokyo, Hobunkan, 1953. 1 leaf, 80, 14 pp., 1 leaf. 18.4 cm. ¥. 150. Translations, by Tamotsu Ueda, of *How to Read*, "Francesca," "A Girl," "The Picture," *Hugh Selwyn Mauberley*, Part 1, I, "To-Em-Mei's 'The Unmoving Cloud,'" "Tenzone," "The Garret," "April," "Further Instructions," "In a Station of the Metro," and "The Tea Shop."

D169 ... SHISHU ... [Tokyo] Arechi Shuppansha [1956]. 1 leaf, 109, 20 pp., 1 blank leaf, 1 leaf. 21.5 cm. ¥. 290. Translations, by Ryozo Iwasaki, of "Sestina: Altaforte," "Rome," "The Garden," "The Spring," "Dance Figure," "Gentildonna," "To Καλόν," "Ladies," "After Ch'u Yuan," "Fan-Piece, for Her Imperial Lord," "In a Station of the Metro," "Alba," "Papyrus," "To Formianus' Young Lady Friend," "The Lake Isle," "Epitaphs, I-II," "Homage to Quintus Septimius Florentis Christianus," "Moeurs contemporaines, VI. Stele," Cantos I and IV, and *Hugh Selwyn Mauberley*, with English text of the last, 20 pp. at end.

D. TRANSLATIONS

D169a ... SHISHU ... Tokyo, Kadokawa Shoten, 1976. 445 pp. 21.5 cm. ¥. 3800. Translations, by Toshikazu Niikura, of "The Garden," "The Spring," "Albâtre," "Surgit fama," "April," "Gentildonna," "The Rest," "To Κα-λòν," "Epitaph," "Arides," "The Bath Tub," "Amitiés," "To Dives," "Ladies," "Liu Ch'e," "Fan-Piece, for Her Imperial Lord," "In a Station of the Metro," "Heather," "Coitus," "The Encounter," "Black Slippers: Bellotti," "Society," "Papyrus," "'Ιμέρρω," "Shop Girl," "L'art, 1910," "Simulacra," "Women before a Shop," "The Social Order," "Epitaphs, I-II," "Ancient Wisdom, Rather Cosmic," "The Three Poets," *Hugh Selwyn Mauberley*, Part I, Cantos, I, II, IV, VIII, IX, XIII, XIV, XVI, XVII, XX, XXXI, XXXIX, XLIV, XLV, XLVII, XLIX, LII, LIII, LXXIV, LXXVI, LXXX-LXXXIV, "A Few Don'ts by an Imagist," "A Retrospect," "Vorticism," and W. B. Yeats's introduction to *Certain Noble Plays of Japan*.

D169b *Shigaku nyūmon ... Tokyo, Fuzambo, 1979. 396 pp. 17.3 cm. ¥. 950. A translation, by Junnosuke Sawasaki, of *ABC of Reading* and *How to Read*.

ANTHOLOGIES:

D169c *SATO HARUO ZENSHU ... Tokyo, Daiichi Shobo, 1925. Contains a translation, by Sato, of "An Immorality."

D169d *GENDAI EIBEI JOJO SHISEN ... Tokyo, Gendai Eigotsushinsha, 1930. Contains a translation, by Shichinosuke Anzai, of "Piccadilly."

D169e *GENDAI AMERIKA SHISHU ... Tokyo, Gendai Hyoronsha, 1931. Contains translations, by Kunizo Kishi, of "Piccadilly," "The Garden," and "N. Y."

D170 GENDAI SEKAI SHISEN ... [Tokyo] Mikasa Shobo [1955]. 480 pp., 3 leaves. 19.7 cm. (Gendai sekai bungaku zenshu, 27). Contains translations, by Minoru Osawa, of *Homage to Sextus Propertius*, XII, and "Pan Is Dead," pp. 317–21.

D171 *SEKAI SHIJIN ZENSHU: 6 ... [Tokyo] Kawade Shobo [1956]. 19.5 cm. Contains translations, by Ryozo Iwasaki, of "The Spring," "Dance Figure," "April," "To Καλòν," "Meditatio," "Ladies," "Phyllidula," "Fan-Piece for Her Imperial Lord," "Alba," "Papyrus," "Women before a Shop," "Epitaphs, I-II," "Moeurs contemporaines, VI: Stele," Canto I, and from *Hugh Selwyn Mauberley*.

D172 SEKAI MEISHISHU TAISEI: 11, AMERICA ... [Tokyo] Heibonsha [1959]. 1 leaf, 440 pp., 1 leaf. illus., 2 plates (ports.) 22.5 cm. Contains translations, by Ryozo Iwasaki, of "Francesca," "A Girl," "The Picture," "Albâtre," "A Pact," "April," "The New Cake of Soap," "The Bath Tub," "Meditatio," "Liu Ch'e," "'Ione, Dead the Long Year,'" "Shop Girl," "Women before a Shop," "The Tea Shop," "Ancient Wisdom, Rather Cosmic," Canto III, with 21 others reprinted from D169, pp. 254–77. A page of a corrected typescript of *Section: Rock-Drill* is reproduced, p. 268.

D172a *GENDAI EIBEISHI KENKYU ... Tokyo, Schichosha, 1962. Contains a translation, by Yuzuru Katagiri, of Canto XVII.

D. TRANSLATIONS

D172b *SEKAI BUNGAKU ZENSHU, 35 ... Tokyo, Shueisha, 1968. Contains a translation, by Hiroshi Izubuchi, of Canto LXXXI.

D172c *Eliot no kozai ... Tokyo, Arechi Shuppan, 1970. Contains a translation, by Masaru Otake, of "Prefatio aut cimicium tumulus."

D172d *SEKAI SHISHU ... Tokyo, Kodansha, 1972. Contains translations, by Toshikazu Niikura, of Cantos I and XLVII.

D172e *Dante ... Tokyo, Chikuma, 1973. Contains a translation, by Koji Toki, of "Dante."

D172f *Sekai hihyo taikei, 3 ... Tokyo, Chikuma, 1975. Contains a translation, by Koji Toki, of *How to Read.*

PERIODICALS:

D172g *[Introduction to "Awoi no Uye"]. *Yokyokukai* (Oct. 1916). An anonymous, rough translation, with substantial additions.

D173 *[A GIRL]. *Konnichi no Shi*, V (Apr. 1931). Translated by Naoe Inui.

D173a *[Horace]. *Sekidoku*, 1 (1933). Translated by Ryozo Iwasaki.

D174 *[Stark Realism]. *Shiho* (May 1935). Translated by Shin Abiru.

D175 [THREE POEMS]. *Vou*, Tokyo, 11 (Aug. 1936) 20. Translations, by Katue Kitasono, of "Ts'ai Chi'h," "Alba," and "Heather."

D176 ABC of Reading, [Chapter] I. *Vou*, 12 (Aug. [*i.e.* Sept.] 1936) 31–36. An abridged translation, by Shoko Ema.

D177 Mediaevalism ... [I]. *Vou*, 13 (Oct. 1936) 28–31. Translated by Katue Kitasono.

D178 Mediaevalisme [*sic.* II]. *Vou*, 14 (Nov./Dec. 1936) 32–34. Translated by Katue Kitasono.

D179 [FISH AND THE SHADOW]. *Vou*, 15 (1 Jan. 1937) 32. An incomplete translation by Katue Kitasono. Printed complete in *Vou*, 16 (1 Feb. 1937) 30.

D180 ITÉ. *Vou*, (1 Feb. 1937) 4. Translated by Katue Kitasono.

D181 *[Five Ways of Criticism]. *Shinryodo*, I. 4 (Aug. 1937). Translated by Ryozo Iwasaki.

D182 No, Diplomacy Can Not Do It. *Vou*, 21 (20 Jan. 1938) 1–4. Translated by Katue Kitasono.

D183 Vou Club [introduction]. *Vou*, 22 (20 Apr. 1938) 23. Translated by Katue Kitasono.

D184 *[Civilization]. *Shinryodo*, II. 10 ([Oct.? 1938?]). Translated by Ryozo Iwasaki.

D185 [SLICE OF LIFE (FABLE)]. *Vou*, 27 (Aug. 1939) 19. Translated by Katue Kitasono.

D186 [Statues of Gods]. *Vou*, 28 (Dec. 1939) 35. Translated by Katue Kitasono.

D187 [Reorganize Your Dead Universities]. *Vou*, 29 (June 1940) 19–20. Translated by Katue Kitasono.

D. TRANSLATIONS

D188 [Letter from Italy]. *Vou*, 30 (Oct. 1940) 21–22. Translated by Katue Kitasono.

D189 *[SEVEN POEMS]. *Vou*, 35 (1951). Translations, by Katue Kitasono, of "In a Station of the Metro," "Coitus," "Alba," "Ἱμέρρω," "The Encounter," "The Garret," and "Δώρια."

D190 *[A SONG OF THE DEGREES]. *Tsukue*, IV. 10 (1953). Translated by Katue Kitasono.

D191 *[TWO POEMS]. *Poetlore*, 4 (July 1954). Translations, by Minoru Osawa, of *Homage to Sextus Propertius*, XII, and "Pan Is Dead."

D192 [MIDDLE-AGED]. *Tsukue*, VI. 2 (1955). Translated by Katue Kitasono.

D192a *[THREE POEMS]. *Poetry*, 5 (1957). Translated, by Ryozo Iwasaki, of "A Pact," and Cantos XIII and LXXX.

D192b *[THREE POEMS]. *Poetry of Today*, 7 (1958). Translated by Kazuo Ando.

D193 [CANTO XX]. *Mugen*, Tokyo, 5 (Aug. 1960) 76–84. Translated by Ryozo Iwasaki.

D194 [Essays]. *Mugen*, 5 (Aug. 1960) 86–95. Translations, by Tamotsu Ueda, of part of *How to Read*, "A Prospect," and "A Few Don'ts by an Imagist."

D194a *[DOMPNA POIS DE ME NO'US CAL]. *Eibungaku Techo*, 6 (Spring 1962). Translated by Masao Okamoto.

D194b *[THE RETURN]. *Eibungaku Techo*, 7 (Fall 1962). Translated by Sanehide Kodama.

D194c *[CANTOS I-IV]. *Eigo Eibungaku Ronshu* (1965). Translated by Akira Yasukawa.

D194d [POEMS]. *Ao*, 7 (1968). Translations, by Makoto Takashima, of *Hugh Selwyn Mauberley*, Part 1; by Masao Nakagiri, of Canto XVI and "A Girl"; by Yasuo Fujitomi, of Canto XLIX, "April," "A Song of the Degrees," and "Dance Figure"; by Shozo Tokunaga, of "Portrait d'une femme" and "The Garden"; and by Tazuko Nagasaka, of "Sestina: Altaforte," pp. 3–19. (An "Ezra Pound Issue" of this periodical.)

D194e [Letter to René Taupin, Vienna, May 1928]. *Ao*, 7 (1968) 32–33. Translated (from the French) by Reiko Yokokura.

D194f *[CANTOS AND POEMS]. *Eureka*, IV. 13 (1972). Translations, by Hiroshi Izubuchi, Hiroshi Ebine, and Kenji Nakamura, of Canto LXXIX; by Junzaburo Nishiwaki, of Canto I; and by Masayoshi Yoshino, of "Portrait d'une femme," "A Virginal," "The Garret," "The Coming of War: Actaeon," "Near Perigord," and "Pagani's, November 8."

D194g *[Date Line]. *Eureka*, IV. 13 (1972). Translated by Bin Nakagawa.

D194h [CANTO LXXXIV]. *Nampo*, Tokyo, 1–5 (1974–1975), 11–16, 11–16, 11–16, 11–16, 11–16. Translated by Toshikazu Niikura.

D194i *[PISAN CANTOS]. *Nampo*, 6–7 (1976). Selections, translated by Toshikazu Niikura.

D194j *[*Ulysses*]. *Eureka* (Oct. 1977). Translated by Masaki Yoshino.

D. TRANSLATIONS

D194k *[CANTO LXXXII]. *Shin Bungaku Fukei*, 3 (1977). Translated by Atsuo Kurumisawa.

D194l *[CANTOS XLVII, XLVIII, LI, XCV]. *Bungaku ni Tsuite*, 6/7 (June 1978). Translated by Atsuo Kurumisawa.

D194m *[ELEVEN POEMS]. *Eureka* (June 1980). Translations, by Junnosuke Sawasaki, of "Na Audiart," "Portrait d'une femme," "A Girl," "A Virginal," "Salutation the Second," "Ité," "The Temperaments," "The Coming of War: Actaeon," "In a Station of the Metro," "The Tea Shop," and "Provincia deserta."

LITHUANIAN

ANTHOLOGY:

D194w BALSAI: iš pasaulinės poezijos, sudarė ir išvertė Tomas Venclova. [Southfield, Mich.] Ateitis, 1979. 200 pp. 21 cm. (Literatūros serija, 18). Contains a translation, by Venclova, of Canto I, pp. [46]–48.

NORWEGIAN

BOOK:

D194x ... DIKT I UTVALG ved Paal Brekke [Oslo] Den Norske Bokklubben [1971]. 95, [1] pp. 19.6 cm. Kr. 17. Translations, by Brekke, of "The Tree," "And Thus in Nineveh," "Praise of Ysolt," "Francesca," "The Altar," "Ballatetta," "In Durance," "Sestina: Altaforte," "N. Y.," "A Girl," "The Needle," "The Cloak," Portrait d'une femme," from "The Seafarer," "The River-Merchant's Wife: A Letter," "Surgit fama," "Dance Figure," "Ortus," "The Garden," "Salutation," "A Pact," "Salutation the Second," "Commission," "The Social Order, II," "The Tea Shop," "Black Slippers: Bellotti," "Ladies, IV," "Tame Cat," "The Bath Tub," "Meditatio," "Further Instructions," "The Encounter," "In a Station of the Metro," "Coda," "To Καλòν," "Fan-Piece, for Her Imperial Lord," "Alba," "Papyrus," "Ancient Wisdom, Rather Cosmic," "Epitaphs, I-II," "The Three Poets," "Shop Girl," "Provincia deserta," *Hugh Selwyn Mauberley*, Part 1, and Cantos I, II, XII, XIII, XLV, and from Canto LXXXI.

ANTHOLOGY:

D194y AMERIKANSK LYRIKK ... ved Paal Brekke. Oslo, Aschehoug, 1957. 150 pp., 2 leaves, 1 blank leaf. 22 cm. Contains translations, by Brekke, of "A Girl," "Praise of Ysolt," "Dance Figure," "Francesca," "The Cloak," "The Encounter," "The Garden," "In a Station of the Metro," "Coda," "A Pact," Canto XLV, and from Canto LXXXI, pp. 66–75.

PERIODICALS:

D195 *KOM, MINE SANGER. *Dagbladet*, Oslo (26 Aug. 1955). A translation, by Carl Frederik Prytz, of "Further Instructions." Reprinted in *Pound Newsletter*, 9 (Jan. 1956) 8, and in D240, p. 318.

D. TRANSLATIONS

D196 ... NATT-LITANI. *Samtiden*, Oslo, LXIV. 10 ([Oct.?] 1955) [629]–331 [*i.e.* 631]. A translation, by Carl Frederik Prytz, of "Night Litany."

ORIYA

BOOK:

D197 [... KABITA (... "SELECTED POEMS") Cuttack, Orissa, India, Prafulla Chandra Das, 1958]. [2] pp., 2 blank leaves (the first laid in before the frontispiece), [3–36] pp., 1 blank leaf, [37–118] pp., 1 leaf. col. front. (port.) 18.8 cm. Contains "Introduction," by T. S. Eliot (reproduced in facsimile, pp. [8–9], with Oriya translation, pp. [5–6]; reproduction of typed copy of a letter from Ezra Pound to Prafulla Chandra Das, 28 June 1957, p. [13], with translation into Oriya, p. [11]; and translations, by Gyanindra Verma, of Cantos I, XLIX, LIII, "Cino," "The White Stag," "The Tomb at Akr Çaar," "Tenzone," "The Garret," "Salutation," "A Pact," "Dance Figure," "Ité," "Salvationists," "Meditatio," "Alba," "Coda," "Coitus," "The Encounter," "The Tea Shop," "The Lake Isle," "Epitaphs, I-II," "Song of the Bowmen of Shu," "The Coming of War: Actaeon," "Langue d'Oc: Alba," "The Beautiful Toilet," "The River-Merchant's Wife: A Letter," "Exile's Letter," "Taking Leave of a Friend," "A Ballad of the Mulberry Road," "Villanelle: The Psychological Hour," *Hugh Selwyn Mauberley*, Part 1, IX, "Amitiés," and Canto XXXVIII.

ANTHOLOGY:

D198 [DURBADALA (... Walt Whitman's Leaves of Grass). Cuttack, Orissa, India, Prafulla Chandra Das, 1957]. [92] pp. front. (port.) 18.3 cm. Contains reproduction of typed copy of a letter from Ezra Pound to Prafulla Chandra Das, 16 Nov. 1956, incorporating "A Pact," p. [7], with translation of the complete letter into Oriya, p. [5].

POLISH

Starred entries supplied by Jerzy Niemojowski and Leszek Engelking.

BOOK

D199 ... MASKA I PIEŚŃ, ANTOLOGIA POEZJI ... Monachium [Editions "On the Mountain"] 1960. 47, [1] pp., incl. front. (port.) 20.3 cm. 300 copies, "published privately by Elisabeth Kottmeier and Eaghor G. Kostetzky," plus 50 special copies. Translations, by Jerzy Niemojowski, of "Night Litany," "Cino," "Δῶρια," "Leave-taking near Shoku," "The Garden," "Epitaph," "The Encounter," "Women before a Shop," "Fan-Piece for Her Imperial Lord," "Ts'ai Chi'h," "Ancient Wisdom, Rather Cosmic," "The Lake Isle," "Causa," "To Καλὸν," "Coda," "Moeurs contemporaines, I: Mr. Styrax," *Homage to Sextus Propertius*, XI, *Hugh Selwyn Mauberley*, Part 1, II, IV, Cantos III, XVIII, and XLV, from Canto LXXXI (lines 133–73), and Canto XC. (Selections from this volume were published a few weeks earlier in D240, pp. 319–35.)

D. TRANSLATIONS

ANTHOLOGIES:

D200 CZAS NIEPOKOJU. Antologia współczesnej poezji brytyjskiej i amerykańskiej. Wybrał i opracował Paweł Mayewski. Wstęp napisał Karl Shapiro. New York, Criterion Books, 1958. 1 blank leaf, xviii, 382 pp. 18.8 cm. $2.50. English and Polish on opposite pages. Contains translations by Jerzy Niemojowski, of "Ité," "Portrait d'une femme," and Canto I, pp. 106–13.

D200a *H. Poświatowska. ODA DO RĄK. Warsaw, "Czytelnik," 1966. Contains translations, by Poświatowska, of Canto XIII, "The Lake Isle," "Sestina: Altaforte," and "The Study in Aesthetics," pp. 76–82.

D200b *L. Elektorowicz. PRZEDMOWY DO CISZY. Krakow, Wydawnictwo Literackie, 1968. Contains a translation, by Elektorowicz, of "Night Litany," pp. 50–51.

D200c *H. Krzeczkowski, J. S. Sito, and J. Żuławski, eds. POECI JĘZYKA ANGIELSKIEGO. Vol. 3. Warsaw, PIW, 1975. Contains translations, by Jerzy Niemojowski, of "Near Perigord," and by J. A. Ihnatowicz, from Canto LXXXI, with other translations reprinted from D199, 200, 200a, and 200b, pp. 203–229.

D200d *Krzysztof Boczkowski. W NIEWOLI W ŚNIEGU W CIEPŁYM CZŁNIE DRWI. Wrocław, Ossolineum, 1981. Contains translations, by Boczkowski, of "Coda," "Epitaphs, I-II," "A Girl," "Meditatio," "A Pact," "Pagani's, November 8," "Shop Girl," and "The Temperaments," pp. 55–57.

PERIODICALS:

D201 POEZJA I GRAFIKA. EZRA POUND ... Orzeł Biały, London, XIII. 7 (14 Feb. 1953) 3. Translations, by Jerzy Niemojowski, of "Night Litany," "Ité," "Francesca," "Dance Figure," and "Cino." (The graphics are two reproductions of drawings by Zygmunt Turkiewicz, not illustrations to the poems.)

D202 [POEMS]. Pound Newsletter, Berkeley, Calif., 4 (Oct. 1954) 5–6. Translations, by Jerzy Niemojowski, of "Coda," "To Καλòν," "Fan-Piece for Her Imperial Lord," and Hugh Selwyn Mauberley, Part 1, IV.

D202a *NIEŚMIERTELNOŚĆ. Pod Wiatr, Warsaw?, 1 (1956) 2. A translation by A. Tchórzewski, of "An Immorality."

D203 *[A GIRL]. Współczesność, Warsaw, 6 (May 1957) 8. Translated by A. Tchórzewski.

D204 *[POEMS]. Współczesność, Warsaw, 10 (Dec. 1957) 1. Translations, by Jerzy Niemojowski, of "Ancora" and "The Lake Isle."

D204a *[VILLANELLE;: THE PSYCHOLOGICAL HOUR]. Poglądy, Katowice, 26 ([Dec.?] 1957) 2. Translated by J. Kaniewicz.

D204b *[FROM CANTO LXXXI]. Życie Literackie, Krakow, 38 ([Dec.?] 1957) 7. Translated by S. Czycz.

D204c WIERSZE Odgłosy, London, II. 50 (28 June 1958) 4. Translations, by Jerzy Niemojowski, of "Portrait d'une femme," "Tenzone," "The Garret," Homage to Sextus Propertius, XI, and Hugh Selwyn Mauberley, Part 1, IV.

D. TRANSLATIONS

D205 [DWIE PIEŚNI]. *Kontynenty-Nowy Merkuriusz*, London, I. 9 (Sept. 1959) 3. Translations, by Jerzy Niemojowski, of Canto XLV and from Canto LXXXI (lines 133–73).

D205a *[THE RETURN]. *Tygodnik Powszechny*, Krakow, 22 (1961) 5. Translated by J. Prokop.

D206 ... CIENIOM SEKSTUSA PROPERCJUSZA, VI. *Kontynenty-Nowy Merkuriusz*, II. 21/22 (Sept./Oct. 1960) 13. A translation, by Jerzy Niemojowski, of *Homage to Sextus Propertius*, VI.

D206a *[CANTO XIV]. *Tygodnik Powszechny*, 22 (1961) 5. Translated by J. Prokop.

D206b TRZY PIEŚNI. *Tematy*, New York, III. 9 (Winter [1963/] 1964) [137]–149. Translations, by Jerzy Niemojowski, of Cantos VII, XLVII, and LXXXI. (The translation of Canto LXXXI was reprinted, with extensive notes by Niemojowski, in *Oficyna Poetów*, London, XV. 2 (May 1980) 8–15.)

D206c POD PERIGORD. *Tematy*, IV. 13 (Winter [1964/] 1965) [27]–33. A translation, by Jerzy Niemojowski, of "Near Perigord."

D206d BALLADA O PIĘKNYM PRZYJACIELU. *Oficyna Poetów*, London, I. 3 (Nov. 1966) 3. A translation, by Zofii Bohdanowiczowa, of "Ballad of the Goodly Fere."

D206e HUGH SELWYN MAUBERLEY. *Tematy*, V. 17 (Spring 1966) [35]–49. Translated by Jerzy Niemojowski. (Reprinted, with extensive annotations by Niemojowski, in *Oficyna Poetów*, XIV. 1–2 (Feb.-May 1979) 3–12, 3–10.)

D206f Linia graniczna. *Tematy*, V. 18 (Summer 1966) [17]–21. A translation, by Bogusław Grodzícki, of a selection from *How to Read* and *ABC of Reading*.

D206g PIEŚŃ IV [& XIV]. *Tematy*, VIII. 29/30 (Spring/Summer 1969) [34]–40. Translations, by Jerzy Niemojowski, of Cantos IV and XIV.

D206h LUSTRA. *Poezja*, VI. 3 (Mar. 1970) 66–75. Translations, by Jerzy Niemojowski, of "The Garret," "Salutation," "Commission," "Surgit fama," "Dance Figure," "Ité," "Dum capitolium scandet," "*To Καλòν*" "The New Cake of Soap," "Salvationists," "The Temperaments," "To Dives," "The Seeing Eye," "Dompna pois de me no'us cal," "The Coming of War: Actaeon," "Alba," "Heather," "Coitus," "Society," and "Three Poets." (Four others are reprinted from D199.)

D206i *[POEMS]. *Literatura na Świecie*, Warsaw, 1 (Jan. 1972) 27–32. Translations, by Jerzy Niemojowski, of "Ancora," "Arides," "The Bath Tub," "The Faun," "Meditatio," "A Pact," "Salutation the Second," "The Social Order," "A Song of the Degrees," "Shop Girl," and "Tenzone." (One other is reprinted from D199.)

D206j [POEMS]. *Poezja*, 89 (Apr. 1973) 73–74. Translations, by Bohdana Drozdowski, of "The Beautiful Toilet," "Erat hora," and "A Virginal," and by Adriana Szymánska, of "The Lake Isle," and "Epitaphs, I-II."

D206k [POEMS]. *Twórczość*, Warsaw, XXIX. 4 (Apr. 1973) 5–8. Translations, by Jarsoław Marek Rymkiewicz, of "De Aegypto," "Fish and the Shadow," "Threnos," "Lament of the Frontier Guard," and "The Lake Isle."

D. TRANSLATIONS

D206l HAIKU-IMAGE. *Poezja*, 110 (Jan. 1975) 45–46. Translations, by Andrzej Szuba, of "In a Station of the Metro," "Alba," "Ts'ai Chi'h," "L'art, 1910," and "Fan-Piece, for Her Imperial Lord."

D206m *[POEMS]. *Kierunki*, Warsaw, 35 (1975) 8. Translations, by A. Bartkowicz, of "Alba," "Langue d'Oc: Alba," and "Taking Leave of a Friend."

D206n *[POEMS]. *Odra*, Breslau, 7/8 (July/Aug. 1975) 63–65. Translations, by Jerzy Niemojowski, of "After Ch'u Yuan," "Albâtre," "Further Instructions," "'Ιμέρρω," "Liu Ch'e," "The Rest," "Simulacra," and "The Tea Shop," and by P. Kajewski, of "Ortus."

D206 o [POEMS]. *Poezja*, 134 (Jan. 1977) 76–85. Translations, by Krzysztof Boczkowski, of "A Pact," and by Jan Marszałek, of *Homage to Sextus Propertius*, I and III. (Others are reprinted from D199, 206b, and 206g.)

D206p Uwagi Imagisty. *Poezja*, 134 (Jan. 1977) 86–[89]. Translations, by Krzysztof Boczkowski, of part of a letter from Ezra Pound to William Carlos Williams, 21 Oct. 1908, "Imagisme," by F. S. Flint, part of "A Retrospect," and "Vorticism."

D206q [WIERSZE]. *Literatura na Świecie*, III. 71 (Mar. 1977) 195–6. Translations, by Krzysztof Boczkowski, of "The Temperaments," "Meditatio," "Coda," "Shop Girl," "Epitaphs, I-II," and "Pagani's, November 8."

D206r *[POEMS]. *Magazyn Kulturalny*, Krakow, 4 (1978) 16. Translations, by L. Szwed, of "Meditatio," and "The Tree," and by A. Kaliszewski, of "A Pact."

D206s *[POEMS]. *Literatura na Świecie*, 4 (Apr. 1980) 286–303. Translations, by Leszek Engelking, of "After Ch'u Yuan," "Alba," "Ancient Wisdom, Rather Cosmic," "April," "Arides," "The Bath Tub," Canto CXX, "Cantus planus," "Causa," "Δώρια," "The Encounter," "Epitaphs, I-II," "Erat hora," "Fan-Piece, for Her Imperial Lord," "A Girl," "'Ιμέρρω," "In a Station of the Metro," "Ité", "L'art, 1910," "The Lake Isle," "Liu Ch'e," "Meditatio," "The New Cake of Soap," "N. Y.," "Ortus," "A Pact," "Papyrus," "The Patterns," "Phyllidula," "The Picture," "Shop Girl," "Tempora," "The Tea Shop," "The Three Poets," "To Dives," "Τό Καλὸν," and "Ts'ai Chi'h." (A corrected text for "Ancient Wisdom, Rather Cosmic" was printed in *Literatura na Świecie*, 8 (Aug. 1980).)

PORTUGUESE

BOOKS:

D207 ... CANTARES [São Paulo] Ministerio da Educação e Cultura, Serviço de Documentação [1960]. 1 blank leaf, 153 pp. front. (port.), plate. 23.5 cm. Not for sale. (Coleção "Letras e Artes"). English and Portuguese on opposite pages. Translations, by Augusto de Campos, Décio Pignatari, and Haroldo de Campos, of Cantos I-VII, XII, XIII, XX, XXX, XLV, XLIX, from Cantos LXXXIX-LXXXI, and Canto XC; with a brief quotation from a letter from Ezra Pound to the translators, 11 Apr. 1957, concerning the title, p. [5].

D. TRANSLATIONS

D207a ... ABC da literature ... São Paulo, Editôra Cultrix [1970]. 5 leaves, 9–218 pp., 1 leaf, 1 blank leaf. 19.6 cm. A translation, by Augusto de Campos and José Paulo Paes, of *ABC of Reading*.

D207b ... A arte da poesia, ensaios escolhidos ... São Paulo, Editôra Cultrix, Editôra da Universidade de São Paulo [1976]. 5 leaves, 9–164 pp., 1 leaf. 19.5 cm. Translations, by Heloysa de Lima Dantas and José Paes, of "A Retrospect," *How to Read*, "The Serious Artist," "The Teacher's Mission," "Date Line," "Troubadours—Their Sorts and Conditions," "Irony, Laforgue and Some Satire," "The Hard and the Soft in French Poetry," "*Ulysses*," and from *The Spirit of Romance*: "Camoens" and "Montcorbier, alias Villon."

PERIODICALS:

D208 [A GIRL]. *Diário Popular*, Lisbon (31 Mar. 1948). Translated by Tomaz Kim.

D209 *CANTOS. *Noigandres*, São Paulo, 1 (Nov. 1952). Translated by Augusto and Haroldo de Campos.

D210 CANTO XLV. *Pound Newsletter*, Berkeley, Calif., 3 (July 1954) 5–6. Translated by Augusto and Haroldo de Campos.

D211 CANTO XIII. *Forum*, São Paulo (Aug. 1955). Translated by Augusto and Haroldo de Campos. Reprinted in *Correio da Manhã* (7 June 1958) [9].

D212 [CANTO III]. *Pound Newsletter*, 8 (Oct. 1955) 29. Translated by Augusto and Haroldo de Campos.

D213 5 POEMAS. *O Debate*, Lisbon, VI. 265 (14 Apr. 1956) 6. Translations, by Carlos Alberto de Secca, of "Moeurs contemporaines, I-V."

D214 FIGURA DE DANÇA ... *O Debate*, VI. 265 (14 Apr. 1956) 7. A translation, by Gualter Póvoas, of "Dance Figure."

D214a CANTO XXX. *Jornal do Brasil. Suplemento Dominical*, Rio de Janeiro (24 Feb. 1957) 3. Translated by Augusto de Campos, Décio Pignatari, and Haroldo de Campos.

D215 CANTO XX. *Jornal do Brasil. Suplemento Dominical* (28 Apr. 1957) [1]. Translated by Augusto and Haroldo de Campos and Décio Pignatari.

D215a CINO. *Jornal do Brasil. Suplemento Dominical* (6 Jan. 1958) 7. Translated by Mário Faustino? Printed in connexion with his article, "Ezra Pound, I."

D215b CANTO 81/FRAGMENTO. *Correio da Manhã* (5 July 1958) [9]. Translated by Augusto and Haroldo de Campos and Décio Pignatari.

D215c [HOMAGE TO SEXTUS PROPERTIUS]. *Jornal do Brasil. Suplemento Dominical* (8 Oct. 1958). Translations, by Mário Faustino?, of Part 1, IX, Part 2, I, III, VI, and "Cantus planus"; printed as part of his "Ezra Pound, VII."

D216 [TRÉS POESIAS]. *Tempo Presente*, Lisbon, 2 (June 1959) 19–22. Translations, by Fernando Guedes, of "Commission," and by Goulart Nogueira, of "Revolt against the Crepuscular Spirit of Modern Poetry" and Canto XLV.

D. TRANSLATIONS

D216a HUGH SELWYN MAUBERLEY. *O Estado de São Paulo. Suplemento Literário*
(30 Oct. 1965) 3. Translated by Augusto de Campos.

ROMANIAN

Starred entries supplied by Peter Schneeman.

BOOK:

D216g ... CANTOS ŞI ALTE POEME ... Prefata de Vasile Nicolescu. Bucureşti,
Editura Univers, 1975. 339, [1] pp. 16.5 cm. Lei 18. Translations, by Ion
Caraion, of "Ballad for Gloom," *Personae* (1926) omitting 18 poems, Cantos I-III, from Canto IV, Cantos IX, XIII, from Canto XIV, Canto XVII,
from Cantos XX, XXV, XXX, and XXXVI, Cantos XXXVIII, XLV, XLVII,
XLIX, LI, from Cantos LIII and LXXIV, Cantos LXXVII, LXXVIII, and
from Cantos LXXX-LXXXIV, XCI, and XCIII.

ANTHOLOGIES:

D216h *Margareta Sterian, *ed.* AUD CÎNTÎND AMERICA: antologie de poezie
moderna americana ... Bucureşti, Editura Dacia, 1973. 260 pp. 24 cm.
Contains translations, by Margareta Sterian, of "A Pact," "A Girl," "Salutation," "In a Station of the Metro," "L'art, 1910," "The Garden," and
from Canto LXXXI, pp. 129–33.

D216i *Leon Levitchi and Tudor Dorin, *eds.* ANTOLOGIE DE POEZIE AMERI-
CANĂ DE LA ÎNCEPUTURI PÎNĂ AZI ... Vol. 2. Bucureşti, Editura Mi-
nerva, 1978. 337 pp. 16.5 cm. Contains translations, by Dorin, of "La
Fraisne," "A Virginal," "Dance Figure," "Meditatio," "The Three Poets,"
"River Song," and *Hugh Selwyn Mauberley*, Part 1, XII, pp. 68–77.

D216j Ion Caraion, *ed.* ANTOLOGIA POEZIEI AMERICANE ... Bucureşti, Editura Univers, 1979. 756 pp. 20.5 cm. Contains translations, by Vasile Nicolescu, of "A Girl," "In a Station of the Metro," from Canto LXXXI,
"The Picture," "Alba," and "Taking Leave of a Friend," with other translations by Caraion himself reprinted from D216g, pp. 199–208.

D216k LIRICĂ AMERICANĂ CONTEMPORANĂ ... Bucureşti, Editura Albatros,
1980. 269, [1] pp., 1 leaf. 14.1 cm. Lei 4.75. (Cele mai frumoase poezii,
182). Contains translations, by Virgil Teodorescu and Petronela Negoşanu, of Canto I, "La Fraisne," "Threnos," and "A Pact," pp. 26–35.

PERIODICALS:

D216m *[VILLANELLE: THE PSYCHOLOGICAL HOUR]. *Orizont*, XVI. 8 (Aug.
1965) 59. Translated by Petru Sfetca. Reprinted in *Familia*, IV. 1 (Jan. 1968)
19.

D216ma *[POEMS]. *Orizont*, XVI. 11 (Nov. 1965) 38–40. Translations, by A. E.
Bakonsky, of Canto XLIX, "Epitaphs, I-II," "April," and "The Garret."

D216mb *[POEMS]. *Ateneu*, III (Mar. 1966) 20. Translations, by Petru Sfetca, of
"Lament of the Frontier Guard," "The Return," "In a Station of the Metro,"

D. TRANSLATIONS

Hugh Selwyn Mauberley, Part 1, V; and by Modest Morariu, of "Ortus," "Causa," and "Francesca."

D216mc *[CANTO XVII]. *Orizont*, XVII. 5 (May 1966) 63–65. Translated by Nina Cionca.

D216md *[POEMS]. *Tribuna*, X. 23 (9 June 1966) 8. Translations, by Virgil Stanciu, of "Ortus" and "A Girl."

D216me *[A PACT]. *Astra*, I. 5 (Oct. 1966) 20. Translated by Victor Felea.

D216mf *[DANCE FIGURE]. *Cronica*, I. 44 (10 Dec. 1966) 11. Translated by E. Simion.

D216mg *[POEMS]. *Amfiteatru*, II. 17 (May 1967) 280. Translations, by Mircea Ivănescu, of "N. Y.," "Δώρια," "A Pact," and "On His Own Face in a Glass."

D216mh EZRA POUND. *Secolul 20*, Bucharest, [73] (June 1967) 30–31. Translations, by I. Dragomir, of "In a Station of the Metro," "Women before a Shop," and "Dans un omnibus de Londres."

D216mi *[CANTOS XLIX & LXXXI]. *Ateneu*, IV. 7 (July 1967) 12–13. Translations, by Mihail Sabin, of Canto XLIX, and by Vasile Nicolescu, from Canto LXXXI.

D216mj *[CINO]. *Cronica*, II. 41 (14 Oct. 1967) 11. Translated by E. Stefan.

D216mk *[POEMS]. *Ramuri*, V. 1 (15 Jan. 1968) 24. Translations, by Ion Caraion, of "Alba," "In a Station of the Metro," "Pagani's, November 8," and "The Beautiful Toilet."

D216ml *[N. Y.]. *Ateneu*, V. 5 (May 1968) 20. Translated by Ion Caraion.

D216mm EZRA POUND. *Secolul 20*, 103 (July 1969) 30–[33]. Translations, by Virgil Teodorescu, of "The Tree," "Francesca," "A Girl," "Ortus," "April," "The Garret," "Causa," and "The Temperaments"; and, by Petronela Negoșanu, of "Albâtre," "N. Y.," "A Pact," and "In a Station of the Metro."

D216mn . . . ARTA 1910. *Viaţa Românească*, XXII. 7 (July 1969) xvii. A translation, by Ion Caraion, of "L'art, 1910."

D216mo *[CANTO LXXXI]. *România Literară*, II. 31 (31 July 1969) 23. A translation, by Vasile Nicolescu, of a selection from Canto LXXXI.

D216mp *[A GIRL]. *Steaua*, XX. 10 (Oct. 1969) 65. Translated by Sylvia Otan.

D216mq *[LAMENT OF THE FRONTIER GUARD]. *Steaua*, XX. 12 (Dec. 1969) 131. Translated by Virgil Stanciu.

D216mr *[POEMS]. *România Literară*, II. 5 (29 Jan. 1970) 21. Translations, by Ion Caraion, of "On His Own Face in a Glass," "Francesca," "Pan Is Dead," "Rome," and "And Thus in Nineveh."

D216ms *[ALBA]. *Orizont*, XXI. 5 (May 1970) 67–68. Translated by Petre Stoica.

D216mt Ezra Pound. *Secolul 20*, 113, 5 (May 1970) 5–[17]. Translations, by Ada Savin, of a selection from Chapter 4 of *ABC of Reading*; and, by Andrei Brezlanu, of "A Retrospect" and fragments from "Hell" and "Date Line."

D. TRANSLATIONS

D216mu... BURUIANA. *Viaţa Românească*, XXIII. 10 (Oct. 1970) [xxvii]. A translation, by Ion Caraion, of "Heather."

D216mv *[CANTO XI]. *Steaua*, XXII. 4 (June 1971) 15. A selection from Canto XI, translated by A. Zărnescu.

D216mw EZRA POUND. *Secolul 20*, 124/131 (Oct./Dec. 1971) 109–[113]. A translation, by Mircea Ivănescu, of Canto II.

D216mx... Despre teatrul "Nô." *Secolul 20*, 137/138, 6/7 (June/July 1972) 57–[69]. Translations, by Mircea Ivănescu, of edited selections from '*Noh,' or Accomplishment*, from Pound's introduction and "Fenollosa on the Noh," and the Pound-Fenollosa version of "Nishikigi."

D216my [... 15 [*sic*] POEME]. *Secolul 20*, 140, 9 (Sept. [*i.e.* Nov.?] 1972) 4–[23]. Translations, by Vasile Nicolescu, of a selection from Canto LXXXI, "A Girl," "The Picture," "In a Station of the Metro," "Alba," and "Taking Leave of a Friend"; by Virgil Teodorescu and Petronela Negoşanu, of Canto I, "La Fraisne," "Threnos," "Causa," "A Girl," "Silet," and "The Return"; and by Mircea Ivănescu, of "Erat hora," "The Tree," "Exile's Letter," "Apparuit," and "Dance Figure."

D216n *[POEMS]. *România Literară*, V. 46 (9 Nov. 1972) 28. Translations, by Mircea Ivănescu, of Canto I, and "A Pact."

D216na *[POEMS]. *Luceafărul*, Paris, XV. 50 (9 Dec. 1972) 10. Translations, by Mircea Ivănescu, of "Portrait d'une femme," "Apparuit," "La Fraisne," and Cantos II, V, and XVII.

D216nb *[EZRA POUND]. *Luceafărul*, XVI. 43 (27 Oct. 1973) 10. Translations, by Cezar Baltag, of *Hugh Selwyn Mauberley*, Part 2, III, Canto XVII, selections from Cantos XXV, XXX, and XLVII, and "Brancusi."

D216nc *[POEMS]. *Steaua*, XXIV. 23 (Dec. 1973) 25. Translations, by A. Zărnescu, of "Albâtre," and "Come My Cantilations."

D216nd *[POEMS]. *Tomis*, VII. 23 (10 Dec. 1973) 25. Translations, by Nicolae-Ioan Bîtea, of "Francesca," and "A Pact."

D216ne *[A GIRL]. *Familia*, XII. 8 (Aug. 1976) 11. Translated by Alexandru and Mihai Andriţorin.

D216nf *[Confessions]. *Ateneu*, XV. 1 (Mar. 1978) 16. Excerpts from the *Paris Review* interviews of Henry Miller, Ernest Hemingway, and Ezra Pound, translated anonymously.

RUSSIAN

ANTHOLOGIES:

D216s Vernon Duke. POEZDKA KYDA-TO. [Munich] 1968. 58, [2] pp. 20.9 cm. Contains translations, by Duke, of "The Garden," "A Pact," "Salutation," "Arides," "Tame Cat," "Erat hora," "The Garret," "Meditatio," *Hugh Selwyn Mauberley*, Part 2, [V:] "Medallion," and "The Tree," pp. 48–52.

D216t [POETS OF EAST AND WEST, edited by Jacob Berger. London, Printed

D. TRANSLATIONS

by Multilingual Printing Services, 1973]. 92 pp., 2 blank leaves, 22 cm. Contains translations, by Berger, of "The Garden," "Sage homme," and two excerpts from other poems.

SERBO-CROATIAN

BOOKS:

D216u... POEZIJA ... Zagreb, Mladost, 1967. 80 pp. 17 cm. (Biblioteka Orion). English and Serbo-Croatian on opposite pages. Translations, by Antun Šoljan, of "The Return," "The Garret," "The Garden," "Albâtre," "A Pact," "Further Instructions," "'Ione, Dead the Long Year,'" "Provincia deserta," "The River-Merchant's Wife: A Letter," "Monumentum aere, etc.," "Fratres minores," "Near Perigord," "Villanelle: The Psychological Hour," *Hugh Selwyn Mauberley*, Part 1, I-V, and "Envoi (1919)," Canto XLV, and from Canto LXXXI.

D216v *CANTOS ... Split, Izdavčki Centar Mladih "Marko Marulić" [1968?]. 166 pp. A selection, translated by Tomislav Ladan.

D216w... Kako da čitamo ... [Novi Sad, Matica Srpska, 1974]. 240 pp., 2 leaves. 20 cm. (Biblioteka "Danas"). Translations, by Milovan Danojlič, of "A Retrospect," *ABC of Reading*, "The Serious Artist," "The Prose Tradition in Verse," "James Joyce et Pécuchet," "The Later Yeats," "A Treatise on Metre," "The Tradition," "Troubadours: Their Sorts and Conditions," and "Cavalcanti."

D216x... PESME... Beogradski, Izdavačko-Graficki Zavod [1975]. 269, [1] pp., 1 leaf, incl. illus., ports. 20.5 cm. (Biblioteka Vrhovi). Translations, by Milovan Danojlič, of "The Tree," "La Fraisne," "The Return," "The Coming of War: Actaeon," "Silet," "De Aegypto," "Night Litany," "Francesca," "Ballatetta," "Erat hora," "N. Y.," "Mr. Housman's Message," "The Patterns," "The Garret," "A Pact," "Commission," "Ité," "To Καλὸν," "Coda," "The Lake Isle," "Fratres minores," "The Three Poets," "Monumentum aere, etc.," "'Ione, Dead the Long Year,'" "In a Station of the Metro," "Image from D'Orleans," "The Gipsy," "Provincia deserta," "Cantico del sole," *Hugh Selwyn Mauberley*, Part 1, *Homage to Sextus Propertius*, Cantos I-IV, from Canto XII, Canto XIV, from Canto XXX, Cantos XXXI, XLV, from Canto XLVII, Canto XLIX, from Canto LIII, Cantos LXXIV, LXXVI, LXXXI, LXXXIV, from Cantos XCIX and CXV, and Canto CXVI.

ANTHOLOGY:

D216y ANTOLOGIJA SAVREMENE ENGELSKE POEZIJE (1900–1950), priredili Miodrag Pavlović i Svetozar Brkić. Beograd, Nolit, 1957. 337 pp., 1 leaf. 18.5 cm. (Biblioteka Orfej, 11). Contains translations, by Pavlović and Brkić, of "'Ione, Dead the Long Year,'" and "The Coming of War: Actaeon," pp. 147-8.

D. TRANSLATIONS

PERIODICAL:

D217 [POEMS]. *Pound Newsletter*, Berkeley, Calif., 9 (Jan. 1956) 7. Translations, by Jiří Doufácek, of "April," "Tame Cat," and "Coitus." Reprinted in D240, p. 336.

SLOVENE

BOOK:

D217a POUND [Ljubljana] Mladinska Knjiga [1973]. 167 pp., 2 leaves. 20.6 cm. (Lirika, 16). Din 45. Translations, by Veno Taufer, of "Sestina: Altaforte," "Paracelsus in excelsis," "Prayer for His Lady's Life," "Portrait d'une femme," "A Girl," "An Object," "The Cloak," "Sub mare," "The Picture," "Of Jacopo del Sellaio," "The Return," "The Garden," "Causa," "A Pact," "Dance Figure," "Gentildonna," "Further Instructions," "A Song of the Degrees," "Dum capitolium scandet," "A Study in Aesthetics," "Epitaphs, I-II," "The Bath Tub," "Meditatio," "Ladies," "Phyllidula," "The Patterns," "Coda," "The Coming of War: Actaeon," "Liu ch'e," "Fan-Piece for Her Imperial Lord," "Ts'ai chi'h," "In a Station of the Metro," "Alba," "The Encounter," "Papyrus," "'Ione, Dead the Long Year,'" "Tame Cat," "L'art, 1910," "Song of the Bowmen of Shu," "The River-Merchant's Wife: A Letter," "Poem by the Bridge of Ten-Shin," "The Jewel Stairs' Grievance," "Lament of the Frontier Guard," "Four Poems of Departure," "A Ballad of the Mulberry Road," "Near Perigord," *Hugh Selwyn Mauberley*, Cantos I-III, XIII, XIV, XVII, XLV, and from Canto LXXXI.

SPANISH

BOOKS:

D218 CINCO POESIAS ... Miami [Fla.], Pandanus Press [1952]. 2 blank leaves, 3 leaves, [1], 16, [1] pp., 2 blank leaves. 29.8 cm. 225 copies. Translations, by Margaret Bates and Violeta Gaudry Bancayan, of "Exile's Letter" and "Song of the Bowmen of Shu," and by E. L. Revol and A. J. Weiss, of Cantos I, XIII, and XLV.

D219 ... LOS CANTARES DE PISA ... México, Imprenta Universitaria, 1956. 1 blank leaf, 147 pp., 1 leaf. 20.6 cm. 1000 copies. A translation, by José Vásquez Amaral, of *The Pisan Cantos*.

D219a PERSONAE ... Versiones y paráfrasis de Guillermo Rousset Banda. [México] El Unicornio [1959]. 1 blank leaf, 19 leaves. 25 cm. 300 copies (20 h.c.). Translations and "paraphrases," by Rousset Banda, of "Prayer for His Lady's Life," "Marvoil," "Francesca," "The Altar," "Au jardin," "Quies," "The Needle," "Albâtre," "April," "*To Καλòν*," "Arides," "The Bath Tub," "The Temperaments," "Ladies," "Phyllidula," "The Patterns," "The Seeing Eye," "Alba," "The Encounter," "Tame Cat," "The Three Poets," "The Game of Chess," "Monumentum aere, etc.," "Post mortem conspectu," "Fratres minores," "Moeurs contemporaines, I: Mr. Styrax; II:

D. TRANSLATIONS

Clara," "Cantico del sole," *Homage to Sextus Propertius*, XII, and from Canto LXXXI; with an appendix of translations of selections from letters to Harriet Monroe, 1912–1913, 1915, and Margaret Anderson, 1917.

D220... LOS CANTOS PISANOS ... Madrid, Ediciones Rialp, 1960. 1 blank leaf, 4 leaves, 11–227 pp., 8 leaves. 14.9 cm. (Adonais, 178/179). 1000 copies, plus 120 on special paper. Translations, by Jesús Pardo, from Cantos II, III, V, VII, XIII, XVI, XIX, XX, XXIX, XXX, XXXIX, Canto XLV, from Cantos XLIX, LXXIV, LXXVI, LXXVIII-LXXXIV, and Canto XC.

D220a... ANTOLOGÍA POETICA: selección, traducción y prólogo de Carlos Viola Soto. Buenos Aires, Compañia General Fabril Editora [1963]. 1 blank leaf, 3 leaves, 9–165 pp., 1 leaf. front. (port.) 18.9 cm. $230. (Los Poetas, Colección dirigida por Aldo Pellegrini). Translations, by Viola Soto, of "The Tree," "Praise of Ysolt," "De Aegypto," "Marvoil," "Night Litany," "Sestina: Altaforte," "On His Own Face in a Glass," "Francesca," "Ballatetta," "Motif," "Erat hora," "The Tomb at Akr Çaar," "Portrait d'une femme," "N. Y.," "A Girl," "The Cloak," "Δώρια," "Apparuit," "The Return," "The Alchemist," "Tenzone," "The Condolence," "The Garret," "The Garden," "Salutation," "Albâtre," "Commission," "A Pact," "Dance Figure," "April," "Further Instructions," "Ité," "The Temperaments," "Phyllidula," "The Coming of War: Actaeon," "Ts'ai Chi'h," "In a Station of the Metro," "Alba," "The Faun," "Coitus," "The Encounter," "Society," "'Ione, Dead the Long Year,'" "'Ιμέρρω," "Shop Girl," "The Lake Isle," "Epitaphs, I-II," "Provincia deserta," "Song of the Bowmen of Shu," "The Beautiful Toilet," "The River-Merchant's Wife: A Letter," "Lament of the Frontier Guard," "Taking Leave of a Friend," from "Near Perigord," "Dans un omnibus de Londres," "Fish and the Shadow," *Hugh Selwyn Mauberley*, Part 1, I-VII, "Envoi (1919)," Part 2, I, III, [V], Cantos I, II, XVII, XLV, XLIX, and from Canto LXXIV.

D220b... LXXV CANTO PISANO. Málaga, Rafael León, 1964. 4 leaves, 24.1 cm. Not for sale. Printed on one side of a single sheet folded twice. English and Spanish on opposite pages, with music below. A translation, by León, of Canto LXXV.

D220c El ABC de la lectura ... [Buenos Aires] Ediciones de La Flor [1968]. 1 blank leaf, 3 leaves, 9–202 pp., 3 leaves. 20.1 cm. A translation, by Patricio Canto, of *ABC of Reading*.

D220d... Sobre Joyce. Edición y comentarios de Forrest Read ... [Barcelona] Barral Editores, 1971. 1 blank leaf, 3 leaves, 9–438 pp., 1 leaf. 19.5 cm. (Breve Biblioteca de Balance). A translation, by Mirko Lauer, of *Pound/Joyce*.

D220e... Ensayos literarios, selección y prólogo de T. S. Eliot. [Caracas] Monte Avila Editores [1971]. 1 blank leaf, 3 leaves, 9–419 pp., 2 leaves. 19.5 cm. (Colección Prisma). A translation, by Julia J. de Natino, of *Literary Essays*.

D220f *Patria mía ... Barcelona, Tusquets, 1971. 75 pp. (Cuadernos marginales, 23). Translated by Mirko Lauer.

D. TRANSLATIONS

D220g *HUGH SELWYN MAUBERLEY: VIDA Y CONTACTOS, poesías ... Lima, Jurídica [1972?]. 45 pp. Translated by Mercedes Ibáñez Rosazza.

D220h ... CATHAY [Barcelona] Tusquets [1972]. 42 pp., 3 leaves. 18.5 cm. (Cuadernos marginales, 25). Translated by Ricardo Silva-Santisteban.

D220i Introducción a Ezra Pound, antología general de textos ... Barcelona, Barral Editores, 1973. 200 pp., 4 leaves. 18.5 cm. (Ediciones de Bolsillo, 242). Ptas. 150. English and Spanish on opposite pages (for poems). Translations, by Carmen R. de Velasco and Jaime Ferrán, of "Threnos," "La Fraisne," "Francesca," "N. Y.," "A Girl," "The Garret," "Ortus," "Albâtre," "Causa," "April," Cantos I, II, XLV, XC, and CXIV; *How to Read*, "T. S. Eliot," from *What Is Money For?*; and a section of "Testimonios, homenajes, criticas," pp. [139]–183, including "Motif," translated by Jorge Guillén, p. 168, and Grazia Livi's interview with Ezra Pound, pp. 177–83.

D220j ... CANTARES COMPLETOS (I-CXX): introducción, anecdotario, cronología y versión directa de José Vásquez Amaral. [México] J[oaquín] M[ortiz, 1975]. 1 blank leaf, xxiv, 731, [1] pp., incl. front. (port.) 20 cm. in box 21 cm. (Los Nuevos Clásicos). Translations, by Vásquez Amaral, of Cantos I-CXX.

D220k Ezra Pound. Confucio. Las analectas. El gran compendio. El eje firme ... Barcelona, Las Ediciones Liberales, Editorial Labor [1975]. 207 pp. 19 cm. (Colección Maldoror, 31). Translations, by E. Hegewicz, of *The Analects*, *The Great Digest*, and *The Unwobbling Pivot*.

D220l ... Guia de la kultura ... [Madrid, Ediciones Felmar, 1976]. 1 blank leaf, 5 leaves, 13–371 pp., 5 leaves, 1 blank leaf, incl. front., facsims. (music). 21.8 cm. (La Fontana Mayor, 7). A translation, by José González Vallarino, of *Guide to Kulchur*.

D220m ... BREVE ANTOLOGÍA: selección, traducción y notas de Rafael Vargas. [México] Universidad Nacional Autónoma de México, Dirección General de Difusión Cultural, Departamento de Humanidades [1977?]. 34 pp., 1 leaf, incl. 1 illus. (port.) 21.2 cm. (Material de Lectura, Serie Poesia Moderna, 8). Translations, by Vargas, of "On His Own Face in a Glass," "Women before a Shop," "Society," "The Picture," "Night Litany," "In exitum cuiusdam," "Δώρια," "An Object," "De Aegypto," "A Girl," "The Cloak," "Satiemus," "And Thus in Nineveh," "Impressions of François-Marie Arouet (de Voltaire), III: To Madame Lullin," "Silet," "The Garret," "N. Y.," "Famam librosque cano," "Cino," "Coitus," "Ancient Wisdom, Rather Cosmic," "In a Station of the Metro," "Cantico del sole," and "Portrait d'une femme."

D220n *EZRA POUND: prólogo, selección y notas de Gerardo César Hurtado [San José, Costa Rica] Ministerio de Cultura, Juventud y Deportes, Departamento de Publicaciones, 1978. 494 pp. illus., plates. 19 cm. (Serie Pensamiento de América, 12). A selection, translated by César Hurtado.

D220 o ... Memoria de Gaudier-Brzeska ... [Barcelona] Antoni Bosch, Editor [1980]. 1 blank leaf, 4 leaves, [xi]-xvii, 181 pp., 1 leaf, 1 blank leaf. 9 illus.

D. TRANSLATIONS

on 4 plates. 18.4 cm. (Savón, 5). A translation, by Jesús Imirizaldu, of *Gaudier-Brzeska* ([1970])—A10f.

ANTHOLOGIES:

D221 LA POESÍA INGLESA. LOS CONTEMPORÁNEOS: selección, traducción y prólogo de M. Manent. [Barcelona] Ediciones Lauro, 1948. 502 pp., 1 leaf. 20.3 cm. Ptas. 75. English and Spanish on opposite pages. Contains translations, by Manent, of "A Virginal," "Dance Figure," and "Δώρια," pp. 110–13.

D222 ... ANTOLOGÍA DE LA POESÍA NORTEAMERICANA CONTEMPORÁNEA: selección, traducción y estudio preliminar de Eugenio Florit. Washington, D. C., Union Pan-americana [1955]. 1 blank leaf, 2 leaves, viii, 145, 145, 147–164 pp., 2 leaves, 1 blank leaf. 22.5 cm. (Pensamiento de America). English and Spanish on opposite pages (paged in separate sequences). Contains translations, by Florit, of "The Return," "Liu Ch'e," "Come My Cantilations," and Canto XVII, pp. 35–42.

D222a ANTOLOGÍA DE LA POESÍA NORTEAMERICANA: selección, versión y prólogo de Agustí Bartra. México, Universidad Nacional Autónoma de México, 1959. 1 blank leaf, 2 leaves, [7]–329 pp., 2 leaves, 1 blank leaf. 17 cm. (Nuestros Clásicos, 11). English and Spanish on opposite pages. Translations, by Bartra, of "In a Station of the Metro," "The Coming of War: Actaeon," "Ité," "Revolt against the Crepuscular Spirit of Modern Poetry," "Apparuit," and from Canto XVII, pp. [189]–201.

D222b Armando Uribe Arce. Pound [Santiago de Chile, Editorial Universitaria, 1963]. 1 blank leaf, 2 leaves, 7–143, [2] pp., 1 blank leaf. front. (port.) 19 cm. (El Espejo de Papel: Cuadernos del Centro de Investigaciones de Literatura Comparada, Universidad de Chile). Contains "Antología de sus poemas," pp. [101]–135, translations, by Uribe Arce, of "On His Own Face in a Glass," "Translations and Adaptations from Heine, IV," "The Altar," "The Picture," "Of Jacopo del Sellaio," "Meditatio," "Coda," "In a Station of the Metro," "Alba," "'Ione, Dead the Long Year,'" "Ἱμέρρω," "To Formianus' Young Lady Friend," "Separation on the River Kiang," "Taking Leave of a Friend," "Come My Cantilations," "Langue d'Oc: Alba," *Hugh Selwyn Mauberley*, Part 1, IV, "Above the Dock" and "Autumn," by T. E. Hulme, Canto XLV, *Homage to Sextus Propertius*, and "Cantus planus."

D222c *Edward Stresino. EZRA POUND, WILLIAM CARLOS WILLIAMS AND T. S. ELIOT: tres poetas de habla inglesa. Bogotá, Editora A.B.C., 1968. 127 pp. Contains poems of Pound, selected and translated by Stresino.

D222d POETAS NORTEAMERICANOS TRADUCIDOS POR POETAS VENEZOLANOS: una antología escogida por Jaime Tello. Caracas [Ministerio de Educación, Departamento de Publicaciones] 1976. 1 blank leaf, xv, 426 pp., 3 leaves. 22.5 cm. Contains translations, by Tello, of "A Girl," "The Return," "Dance Figure," and Canto XVII, pp. 164–71.

D222da LA FLORA EN LA POESÍA: mil y más poemas sobre las plantas. Selección, normas, prólogos, notas y traducciones de Victor Manuel Patiño ...

417

D. TRANSLATIONS

Tomo I.—Poetas ibéricos y panamericanos. Cali, Colombia, Imprenta Departamental, 1976. 1 blank leaf, 2 leaves, 7–929 pp., 2 leaves, 1 blank leaf. 24 cm. Contains translation, by Patiño (printed as footnote to the English text), of "The Tree," p. 148.

D222e SEIS POETAS DE LENGUA INGLESA ... Presentados y traducidos por Isabel Fraire. [México] SepSetentas 244 [1976]. 206 pp., 1 leaf. 17.5 cm. $10.MN. Contains translations, by Isabel Fraire, of "Erat hora," "Francesca," "Ballatetta," "The Garret," "In a Station of the Metro," "Albâtre," "Salutation," "A Virginal," "Plunge," "N. Y.," "Horae beatae inscriptio," "A Pact," "Meditatio," "The Bath Tub," "Fratres minores," "A Study in Aesthetics," "*To Καλὸν*," "Impressions of François-Marie Arouet (de Voltaire), I-III," "Commission," *Hugh Selwyn Mauberley*, Part 1, I-V, "Cantico del sole," "Salutation the Second," "Portrait d'une femme," and Cantos I-II; and by Salvador Elizondo, of "Tame Cat," and Canto XLV, pp. 20–46.

PERIODICALS:

D223 La isla de Paris. *Hermes*, Bilbao, IV. 65 (Nov. 1920) 663–75. An anonymous translation of "The Island of Paris: A Letter," from the *Dial*, New York, for Oct. 1920—C599.

D224 *NEW YORK. *El Universal*, Mexico ([*ca.* Apr. 1926]). A translation, by S. N., of "N. Y." Reprinted in *Pan-American Union Bulletin*, Washington, D. C., LX. 4 (Apr. 1926) 374.

D225 [TWO POEMS]. *Disco*, Buenos Aires, 9 (Mar. 1947) 18–23. Translations, by J. R. Wilcock?, of "The Tomb at Akr Çaar" and "Apparuit." English and Spanish on opposite pages.

D226 *CANTOS I, XIII, XLV. *Reunión*, Buenos Aires (Aug. 1949). Translated by E. L. Revol and A. J. Weiss.

D227 EL CORO DE LOS LINCES. *Universidad de México*, Mexico, VIII. 11 (July 1954) 5–6. A translation, by José Vásquez Amaral, of the lynx chorus from Canto LXXIX. Printed also in *Pound Newsletter*, 3 (July 1954) 3.

D228 EN PERIGORD. *Sur*, Buenos Aires, 242 (Sept./Oct. 1956) 24–30. A translation, by M. Teresa Maiorana and M. Clothilde Rezzano de Martini, of "Near Perigord."

D228a [POEMS]. *Indice*, Arroyomolinos, Cuba (Sept. 1958) 11. Translations, by Vicente Gaos, of "An Immorality," "Sestina: Altaforte," and Canto XLV.

D229 CUATRO POEMAS ... *Excelsior*, Mexico (29 Mar. 1959) [3]. Translations, by Jaime García Terrés, of "Song of the Bowmen of Shu," "Francesca," "Dum capitolium scandet," and "The Lake Isle."

D230 FIGURA DE DANZA ... *Caracola*, Málaga, 95 (Sept. 1960) 13. A translation, by José Ruiz Sánchez, of "Dance Figure."

D230a ✉ ... Carta a C. J. C[ela]. *Los Papeles de Son Armadans*, Madrid, Palma de Mallorca, XIX. 57 *bis* (Dec. 1960) 70–72. In English, with translation by A. K. following, pp. 71–72. (Offprints were prepared.)

D230b ... Varios "No." *El Pez y la Serpiente*, Managua, Nicaragua, 1 (Jan./Feb./

D. TRANSLATIONS

Mar. 1961) 129–34. A translation, by José Coronel Urtecho and Ernesto Cardenal, of "A Retrospect."

D230c POEMAS . . . *Cultura*, San Salvador, El Salvador, 21 (July/Sept. 1961) 13–21. Translations, by José Caronel Urtecho and Ernesto Cardenal, of "Francesca," "Albâtre," "Tame Cat," "Black Slippers: Bellotti," "Society," "Epitaphs, I-II," and Cantos XXXII and LVII.

D230d THE TOMB AT AKR ÇAAR [&] DANCE FIGURE. *Sur*, 274 (Jan./Feb. 1962) [26]–33. Spanish and English on opposite pages. Translated by Carlos Viola Soto.

D230e . . . MOTIVO. *Les Cahiers de L'Herne*, Paris, 6 ([Nov. 1965]) 240. A translation, by Jorge Guillén, of "Motif."

D230f TRADUCCIONES. *El Zaguan*, Mexico, [1] (28 Oct. 1975) 21–33. Original texts and Spanish translations on opposite pages. Translations, by Alberto Blanco, of "A Song of the Degrees," "Meditatio," and "Ité"; and by Alfonso René Gutiérrez, of "Ortus," "The Altar," and "Dans un omnibus de Londres."

D230g TRADUCCIONES. *El Zaguan*, 2 (28 Jan. 1976) 30–43. English and Spanish on opposite pages. Translations, by Manuel Ulacia, of "The Tea Shop" and "April"; by Alberto Blanco, of "Religio," "The Coming of War: Actaeon," and "The Garret"; by Maria Gertrudis Martínez de Hoyos and Luis Roberto Vera, of "Dance Figure," "Alba," "In a Station of the Metro," and "Albâtre"; and by Alfonso René Gutiérrez, of "The Lake Isle" and "Sub mare."

SWEDISH

BOOKS:

D231 . . . 25 DIKTER . . . Stockholm, A. Bonniers Förlag [1953]. 30, [2] pp. 17.3 cm. (Lilla Lyrikserien, 13). Translations, by Lars Forssell, of "And Thus in Nineveh," "Praise of Ysolt," "[Und Drang, XII:] Au jardin," "Provincia deserta," "Ladies [II]," "*To Kαλòν*" "The Temperaments," "Meditatio," "To Dives," "Ancient Wisdom, Rather Cosmic," "The Encounter," "Alba," "[Epitaphs, I:] Fu I; [II:] Li Po," "Fan-Piece, for Her Imperial Lord," "The Bath Tub," *Homage to Sextus Propertius*, X, XI, "Cantus planus," Cantos XIII, XVII, XXX, XLV, XLIX, and from LXXXI.

D232 . . . ABC för läsare . . . [Malmö-Lund] Bo Cavefors Bokförlag [1959]. 201, [1] pp., 1 blank leaf, incl. plate (port.) 15.5 cm. 18.50 kr. A translation, by Jan Olov Ullén, of *ABC of Reading*.

D233 . . . CANTOS I-XVII . . . [Malmö-Lund] Bo Cavefors Bokförlag [1959]. 103, [1] pp., incl. illus. (port.) 15.5 cm. 15.75 kr. Translated by Lars Forssell.

D234 . . . SÅNGER FRÅN PISA: CANTOS LXXIV-LXXXIV . . . Malmö-Lund, Bo Cavefors Bokförlag [1960]. 146 pp., 1 leaf. 15.4 cm. 17 kr. A translation, by Göran Sonnevi and Jan Olov Ullén, of *The Pisan Cantos*.

D235 . . . CANTOS XVIII-XXX . . . Malmö-Lund, Bo Cavefors Bokförlag [1961]. 91, [1] pp., 2 blank leaves. 15.5 cm. 14.25 kr. Translated by Mario Grut.

D. TRANSLATIONS

D236 Sofokles. Ezra Pound. KVINNORNA FRÅN TRACHIS ... Malmö-Lund, Bo Cavefors Bokförlag [1961]. 47, [1] pp. 19.5 cm. 9 kr. A translation, by Claes von Rettig, of *Women of Trachis*. (The photograph on the wrappers is of the production of the play at Millessgården, Stockholm, Summer 1960).

D236a E P HUGH SELWYN MAUBERLEY (LIV OCH MÖTEN) ... [Malmö-Lund] Bo Cavefors Bokförlag [1962]. 49, [3] pp. 22.3 cm. 25 kr. 750 copies. English and Swedish on opposite pages. A translation, by Bengt Höglund, of *Hugh Selwyn Mauberley*.

D236b ... Romansens själ ... [Malmö-Lund] Bo Cavefors Bokförlag [1965]. 363, [1] pp., 1 leaf, 1 blank leaf. 15.2 cm. 47 kr. A translation, by Hans Axel Holm, of *The Spirit of Romance*.

D236c ... CANTOS I-XXX, SÅNGER FRÅN PISA, HUGH SELWYN MAUBERLEY ... [Staffanstorp] Bo Cavefors Bokförlag [1969]. 303, [1] pp. 18.5 cm. 19 kr. (BOC Serien). Translations, by Lars Forssell, of *Cantos I-XVII*; by Mario Grut, of *Cantos XVIII-XXX*; by Göran Sonnevi and Jan Olov Ullén, of *The Pisan Cantos*; and by Bengt Höglund, of *Hugh Selwyn Mauberley*. (A collected edition of D233, 235, 234, and 236a.)

D236d ... 26 DIKTER ... [Lund] Bo Cavefors Bokförlag [1973]. 40 pp. 18.5 cm. (BOC Serien). A new edition of D231, adding Forssell's translation of Canto XC and, on p. [2], with title: "Till minne ... ," his rearrangement of lines translated from *Drafts & Fragments of Cantos CX-CXVII*, incorporating Canto CXX.

D236e THE XVII CANTO [Lund, 1973]. [4] pp. col. illus. 29.7 cm. Not for sale. 70 copies. Lars Forssell's translation reprinted from D236d, with Gladys Hynes's initial and heading (from *A Draft of Cantos 17-27*). Distributed by Bo Cavefors as a greeting for the New Year.

D236f ... 8 DIKTER ... [Lund] Bo Cavefors [1974]. 15 pp. 15 cm. Not for sale. 250 copies. Translations, by Elmer Diktonius, of "A Pact," "Ancient Wisdom, Rather Cosmic," "The Garret," "Plunge," "Salutation," "A Girl," "The Three Poets," and "Further Instructions." (Reprinted from D236j.)

D236g ... Litterära essäer, utgivna och introducerade av T. S. Eliot; efterskrift av Harry Järv. [Staffanstorp] Bo Cavefors Bokförlag [1975]. 2 blank leaves, 716 pp., incl. front., illus., ports. 20.5 cm. A translation, by Eva Andersson, Harald Bohrn, Eva Dillman, Kristina Eriksson, Harry Järv, Ingrid Molander, Åke Nylinder, Marianne Sandels, and Barbro Widegren, of *Literary Essays*.

D236h ... Om harmoni: musikessäer ... [Zürich] Bo Cavefors Bokförlag [1978]. 96 pp. 20.5 cm. A translation, by Jan Olov Ullén, of *Antheil and The Treatise on Harmony*.

D236i ... Gajd till kultyren ... [Staffanstorp] Cavefors [1981]. 303 pp., incl. front., facsims. (music). 20.5 cm. A translation, by Stewe Claeson and Åke Nylinder, of *Guide to Kulchur* ([1952]).

D. TRANSLATIONS

ANTHOLOGIES:

D236j *Elmer Diktonius. UNGT HAV, NY DIKT I ÖVERSÄTTNING. Helsingfors, Holger Schildts Förlag, 1923. Contains translations, by Diktonius, of "A Pact," "Ancient Wisdom, Rather Cosmic," "The Garret," "Plunge," "Salutation," "A Girl," "The Three Poets," and "Further Instructions." (Reprinted in D236f.)

D236ja MODERN AMERIKANSK LYRIK FRÅN WALT WHITMAN TILL VÅRA DAGAR, tolkad av Erik Blomberg. Stockholm, Albert Bonniers Förlag [1937]. 219 pp. 24 cm. 7:50 kr. Contains translations, by Blomberg, of "A Girl," "The Coming of War: Actaeon," and "Δώρια," pp. 132–5.

D237 Johannes Edfelt. TOLKNINGAR AV TYSK, ENGELSK OCH AMERIKANSK LYRIK. Stockholm, Albert Bonniers Förlag [1940]. 133 pp., 1 blank leaf. 23.8 cm. 5:50 kr. Contains translations, by Edfelt, of "Ballad of the Goodly Fere," "The Lake Isle," "Commission," and "Threnos," pp. 119–30.

D237a ENGELSKA DIKTER FRÅN MEDELTIDEN TILL VÅRA DAGAR, i urval och översättning av Erik Blomberg. Stockholm, Albert Bonniers Förlag [1942]. 149, [1] pp., 1 blank leaf. 18.7 cm. Contains translations, by Blomberg, of "The Coming of War: Actaeon," and "Δώρια," pp. 137–9.

D237b ENGELSK LYRIK: EN ANTOLOGI RELIGIÖS VERS, tolkad av Elis Erlandsson. [Osby, B. W. Erikson & C. Boktr., 1946]. 59 pp. 19 cm. 3 kr. Contains translations, by Erlandsson, of "To Our Lady of Vicarious Atonement" and "A Prologue," pp. 55–59.

D237c Johannes Edfelt. VOTIVTAVLOR TOLKNINGAR. Stockholm, Albert Bonniers Förlag [1967]. 85, [1] pp., 1 blank leaf. 19.5 cm. 19.50 kr. Contains translations, by Edfelt, of "'Ione, Dead the Long Year,'" "Pagani's, November 8," "Impressions of François-Marie Arouet (de Voltaire), III," "Moeurs contemporaines, III: Soirée, and VIII: Ritratto," pp. 65–69.

PERIODICALS:

D237d HUSTRU TILL EN FLODFARANDE KÖPMAN: ETT BREV. *Ord och Bild*, Stockholm, XLIX. 12 (Dec. 1940) 544. A translation, by Claes Hoogland, of "The River-Merchant's Wife: A Letter."

D237e TVÅ DIKTER. *Bokvännen*, Stockholm, V. 1 (Feb. 1950) 3. Translations, by Johannes Edfelt, of "The Tea Shop" and "Dum capitolium scandet."

D238 CANTO XC. *Bonniers Litterära Magasin*, Stockholm, XXV. 2 (Feb. 1956) 95–98. Translated by Lars Forssell.

TURKISH

BOOK:

D238x *CATHAY . . . Istanbul, De Yayinevi, 1963. 63 pp. 300 kr. Translated by Ülkü Tamer.

D. TRANSLATIONS

ANTHOLOGY:

D239 Özdemir Nutku ile Tarik Dursun K. ... ÇAĞDAŞ AMERIKAN ŞIIRLERI
... [Dinar] Şairler Yapraği, Yayinlari [1956]. 71, [1] pp. 19.8 cm. Contains
translations, by Nutku and Dursun K., of "Dance Figure" and "Δώρια,"
pp. 59–60.

UKRAINIAN

BOOK:

D240 [Selected Works, Vol. I: Poems, Essays, Cantos ... Munich, "On the
Mountain" Editions-in-Exile, 1960]. 343, [1], [22] pp., 1 leaf, incl. illus.,
ports., facsims. 21 cm. $2.75. 500 copies (50 numbered). Includes English
texts of some of the shorter poems translated. Translations, by Eaghor G.
Kostetzky, in collaboration with Elisabeth Kottmeier and Valentina Kar-
powa, of "The Tree," "Threnos," "Na Audiart," "De Aegypto," "And Thus
in Nineveh," "The White Stag," "Guido Invites You Thus," "Sestina: Al-
taforte," "On His Own Face in a Glass," "N. Y.," "A Girl," "The Seafarer,"
"Apparuit," "Pan Is Dead," "The Return," "Tenzone," "The Garret," "A
Pact," "To Whistler, American," "Dance Figure," "April," "A Song of the
Degrees," "Dum capitolium scandet," "Arides," "Meditatio," "Coda," "The
Coming of War: Actaeon," "Liu Ch'e," "In a Station of the Metro," "Alba,"
"Coitus," "The Encounter," "Papyrus," "L'art, 1910," "Epitaphs, I-II,"
"Ancient Wisdom, Rather Cosmic," "The Beautiful Toilet," "The Jewel
Stairs' Grievance," "Four Poems of Departure," "South-Folk in Cold
Country," "Sennin Poem by Kakuhaku," "Ballad of the Mulberry Road,"
"Fish and the Shadow," "Phanopoeia," *Hugh Selwyn Mauberley*, Part 1, V-
VI, IX, *Homage to Sextus Propertius*, from I and V, and VII, "A Retrospect"
(condensed), "Brancusi," Cantos I-IV, VI, VIII, from Canto IX, Cantos
XIII, XVII, from Canto XX, Canto XXI, from Cantos XXVII and XXIX,
Canto XXX, from Cantos XXXI, XXXIII, XXXV, and XXXIX, Canto
XLV, from Cantos LI-LIII, LVI, LIX, LXI, LXVII, LXXI, LXXIV, Canto
LXXV, from Cantos LXXVI-LXXXIX, Canto XC, from Cantos XCI-
XCVI, XCVIII-C, and Cantos CII and CIX; by Yar Slavutych, of "Δώρια,";
by Boghdan Boychuk, of "Ité" and "Ιμέρρω"; and by Ostap Tarnavsky,
of *Hugh Selwyn Mauberley*: "Envoi (1919)." With appendices: "I. Some
Specimens of E. P.'s Own Translations from Other Languages" [Guido
Cavalcanti's "Sonnet VII," "Planh for the Young English King," "Rome,"
"Arthur Rimbaud: Anadyomene," speech of Chorus from *Women of Trachis*,
selections from *Confucius. The Unwobbling Pivot*, and an ode from *The Classic
Anthology as Defined by Confucius*]; "II. A Letter of E. P. in '*L'Illustrazione
Italiana*,' settembre 1958" ["Servizio di comunicazioni," translated into
Ukrainian]; and "III. Several of E. P.'s Poems Translated by Different Poets
into Their Languages" [for those printed here for the first time, see entries
under individual languages]. Includes also reproductions of letters, in English, from Pound to Kostetzky, 10 Jan. 1958, pp. [16]–17, and 25 Nov.
1958, p. 35.

D. TRANSLATIONS

PERIODICALS:

D241 *[THREE POEMS]. *Ukraina i Svit*, Hannover, 8/9 (1953). Translations by V. Derzhavín, of "Satiemus," "Apparuit," and "Paracelsus in excelsis."

D242 *[ΔΩΡΙΑ]. *Ukraina i Svit*, 12/13 (1954). Translated by Yar Slavutych.

D243 *[DANCE FIGURE]. *Novi Poezii*, New York, 1 (1959). Translated by Uri Tarnavsky.

D244 CANTO XLV. *Ukraina i Svit*, 19/20 (1959) 30–31. Translated by Eaghor G. Kostetzky.

D245 *[THREE POEMS]. *Ukrains'ka Literaturna Gazeta*, Munich, 12 (Dec. 1959). Translations, by Boghdan Boychuk, of "Δώρια," "Ἱμέρρω," and "Ité."

YIDDISH

ANTHOLOGY:

D246 Michel Licht. MODERN AMERICAN POETRY (TRANSLATIONS). Buenos Aires, 1954. 76 pp., 2 leaves. 20.3 cm. Contains translations, by Licht, of "Albâtre," "A Girl," "A Pact," "The Garret," "The Garden," "Ité," and "N. Y.," pp. 49–55.

E. MISCELLANEA

E. MISCELLANEA

E1a The Polytechnic, 309 Regent Street, W. . . . Courses of Afternoon Lectures to Be Delivered during the Spring Term . . . The Development of Literature in Southern Europe, Ezra Pound, M. A. . . . [London] Pollock & Co., Printers, 81 Mortimer Street, W [1908].

12 pp. 16·5 × 11·5 cm. Wire-stitched.

Issued gratis probably in December 1908; number of copies unknown.

This announcement for the complete series of lectures includes a synopsis for Pound's course, p. 8, giving the dates as 18 Jan. to 22 Feb. 1909. Page 7 gives the correct beginning date as 21 Jan., and an inserted slip gives the correct dates as 21 Jan. to 25 Feb.

E1b The Polytechnic, Regent Street, W. . . . Short Introductory Course on The Development of the Literature of Southern Europe. By Ezra Pound, M. A. . . . [London, Pollock & Co., Printers, 1908]

[4] pp. 15 × 10 cm.

Issued gratis probably in December 1908; number of copies unknown.

Announcement for the six weekly lectures to be given 21 Jan. to 25 Feb. 1909, with "Synopsis of the Course," p. [3]. (Reprinted, in large part, in Charles Norman, *Ezra Pound*—B69—pp. 31–32.)

E1c The Polytechnic, Regent Street, W. . . . Course of Lectures on Mediaeval Literature. By Ezra Pound, M. A. . . . [London, Pollock & Co., Printers, 1909]

[4] pp. 15 × 10 cm.

Issued gratis probably in September 1909; number of copies unknown.

Announcement for 21 weekly lectures to be given 11 Oct. 1909 to 28 Mar. 1910, with "Synopsis of the Course," pp. [2–3]. (The final lecture was in fact cancelled because it fell on Bank Holiday Monday.) Summarised in Charles Norman, *Ezra Pound*—B69—p. 34.

E1d "Università Commerciale Luigi Bocconi" . . . An Historic Background for Economics . . . Ezra Pound . . . Milano, 15 Marzo 1933 . . .

Broadside. 11·8 × 14·8 cm. Printed in blue ink on medium-weight white card.

Distributed gratis in March 1933; number of copies unknown.

An invitation to Pound's course of 10 lectures, 21–31 Mar. 1933, listing, in English, a summary of the principal topics. (From these lectures, *ABC of Economics* (1933)—A34—was developed.)

E2a . . . A Song of the Virgin Mother in the Play "Los Pastores de Bellen [*sic*]" from the Spanish of Lope de Vega. [*Text in 28 lines*] Ezra Pound [*Calendar for 1910 on 12 leaves, pasted to a thirteenth leaf, which is pasted to the card.* Philadelphia, Pa., Printed for Homer L. Pound, 1909]

[2] pp. 27·9 × 10·4 cm.

E. MISCELLANEA

At head of title: Christmas Greetings Yours Sincerely Homer L. Pound [with, at top, an embossed sprig of holly in green and red] Greetings and text printed in black on cream-coloured, medium-weight card; the calendar, also in black but on white paper, measures 3·5 × 6 cm. The verso of the card is blank save for the imprint at the foot: "'Il Vesuvio' 764 S. 9th Street, Phila., Pa." The card has a hole punched at top centre to facilitate hanging. The only copy seen (Yale) is without the envelope in which other copies must have been mailed.

Printed probably in November 1909 and distributed gratis by Pound's father for Christmas 1909. Pound had written to his parents, *ca.* 18 Oct. 1909: "I enclose some of my proof [of *Exultations*]. The translation from Lope de Vega may be of use for your Xmas cards." The proof is dated by the printer: "12.10.09 [*i.e.* 12 Oct. 1909]. Besides the error in the spelling of "Bellen" in the sub-title, there are two misprints in the text: "see" for "sees" in line 23, and "Werewith" for "Wherewith" in line 24.

E2b With the Season's Greeting Yours sincerely Homer L. Pound [Philadelphia, Pa.? Christmas 1910?]

[3] pp. 16 × 14 cm.

Printed and distributed gratis probably for Christmas 1910; number of copies unknown.

Contains "Sandalphon," by Ezra Pound, pp. [2–3], with note: "From 'Exultations' of Ezra Pound," although the text is actually that of the poem as printed in the first issue of *A Quinzaine for This Yule* ([1908])—A2a—with the misprint "earth-hoard's" for "earth-horde's" in lines 4 and 41.

E2ba Ballata . . . [Philadelphia, Pa., Printed for Homer L. Pound by "Il Vesuvio," Christmas 1911]

Broadside. 13·9 × 20·2 cm.

Printed and distributed gratis for Christmas 1911; number of copies unknown. (It is probable that the only copy seen—at Brunnenburg, 1981—is a proof, the finished product intended to be folded and to bear on its verso printed greetings from Homer Pound.)

Consists of text of Cavalcanti's "Io vidi donne con la donna mia," in 10 lines, with Pound's translation, "Ladies I saw a passing where she passed," in parallel columns, the first with note in Italian, the second with note in English: "This ballata and the translation from Cavalcanti which may hereafter appear, are in reality the advance sheets of Mr. Pound's edition of 'The Sonnets and Ballate of Guido Cavalcanti.'"

E2bb [*Woodcut*] A Song of the Virgin Mother [*text in 34 lines*] From the Spanish of Lope de Vega. Translated by Ezra Pound. To wish you all Christmas Joy Emma Mary and Charles Clinch Bubb [Cleveland, O., 1917 or 1918?]

Broadside. 26 × 13 cm.

Distributed gratis for Christmas 1917 or 1918; number of copies unknown. For earlier separate printing see E2a.

E2c Preliminary Announcement of the College of Arts. [*First page of text, in 56 lines.* London, Printed at the Complete Press, 1914]

[4] pp. 26·8 × 21 cm.

428

E. MISCELLANEA

Issued gratis in late November 1914; number of copies unknown.

Reprinted from the *Egoist* for 1 Nov. 1914—C163. A proof (on four separate leaves) was received by Ezra Pound on 10 Nov. 1914 and sent to Harriet Monroe on the same day.

A proposal for an educational institution in London, to be staffed by, among others, Henri Gaudier-Brzeska in Sculpture, Wyndham Lewis and Edward Wadsworth in Painting, Arnold Dolmetsch and Katherine Ruth Heyman in Music, Pound himself and John Cournos in Letters, Alvin Langdon Coburn in Photography, and Mrs. Arnold Dolmetsch in the Dance. The plan came to nothing, presumably because of the First World War. (Reprinted, omitting the list of proposed faculty members, in *The Letters*—A64—pp. 41–43, *note* 2.)

E2d From B. W. Huebsch, Publisher, New York. 1. We are Indebted to The Egoist (London) for This Extraordinary Account, by Ezra Pound, of the Difficulties That Preceded the Publication of "Dubliners" in Great Britain ... A Curious History [*text, with six lines of publisher's comments*. New York, B. W. Huebsch, 1917]

Broadside. 38 × 18·5 cm.

Issued gratis 5 May 1917; 500 copies printed.

This promotional broadside is the first separate publication of "A Curious History," reprinted from the *Egoist* for 15 Jan. 1914—C124. The text consists of Pound's letter, incorporating two letters from James Joyce concerning the publication of his *Dubliners*.

E2e Bel Esprit. [*First page of text*] ⟨This Notice for private circulation only.⟩ [London, Printed by John Rodker, 1922]

[3] pp. 19 × 12·7 cm.

Printed and distributed gratis beginning March 1922; number of copies unknown.

An account by Ezra Pound of this philanthropic project (christened "Bel Esprit" by Natalie C. Barney) appeared in the *New Age* for 30 Mar. 1922—C638, and summaries of the scheme are included in Pound's letters of that month (see "carbon outline" quoted as footnote 1 to his letter to William Carlos Williams, 18 Mar. 1922, in *The Letters*—A64—pp. 172–3). Pound wrote to Jeanne Robert Foster (envelope postmarked 25 June 1922) that "These slips [were] printed at J[ohn]. Q[uinn].'s request and as nearly as possible in accord with his suggestions." The names of Richard Aldington and May Sinclair were introduced to give the project wider appeal, and although both had indicated their willingness to contribute, they seem to have had no part in drafting the appeal. The first year's funds were to be used for T. S. Eliot, to enable him to leave his position at Lloyd's Bank in London; when Eliot refused to accept the money, the funds were returned to the subscribers and the project was abandoned.

The text of the leaflet is reprinted in *The Letters*—A64—pp. 174–5, as footnote 1 to letter from Pound to Kate Buss, [?23] Mar. 1922.

E2f Bel Esprit. [*Quotation in French from* "The 'Tchoung-Young,' of Confucius"]

Form of letter used in reply to Secretary of the Persian Legation, in answer to his questions regarding qualification for membership in Bel Esprit, and adopted as a general answer to further queries. November, 1922. [*First page of text*. London, Printed by John Rodker, 1922]

2 leaves. 19 × 12·6 cm.

With printed signature on leaf 2: "for Bel Esprit, Ezra Pound. . . . "

The only copy located of this printed letter, designed for use in distributing the Bel Esprit leaflet described above, is in the Houghton Library, Harvard. A typed description of it, prepared presumably by the Gotham Book Mart, quotes John Rodker, whose copy this was, as stating that this is "the only proof copy that ever existed. Ezra Pound was dissatisfied with it and re-wrote it slightly." Pound's own copy of a galley proof, 27·5 × 12·5 cm., with printed text in the same state but with his manuscript corrections, is in the Lilly Library, Indiana University. No copy of a revised printing has been located. Because the Bel Esprit project was dissolved shortly after this leaflet was being prepared, it is almost certain that no copies were actually distributed.

E2g Under the Editorial Direction of Mr. Ezra Pound The Three Mountains Press is about to issue the following books: [*list of titles and authors in seven lines, followed by text descriptive of the series in 33 lines*] The Three Mountains Press 19 Rue d'Antin, Paris [1922]

Broadside. 27·9 × 12·5 cm.

Issued gratis late in 1922; number of copies unknown.

Drafted by Ezra Pound and issued to publicise the series of six volumes, published 1923–1924, later identified as "The Inquest" (see A23). In this prospectus, the sixth (final) volume is listed as "BLANK by Ernest M. Hemingway"; it was eventually published as *In Our Time* (1924).

A second state of the broadside, measuring 32·5 × 12·5 cm., issued later in 1922, has a device stamped at the top of the sheet and the following printed at the bottom: "**Or to Mr. F. B. Neumayer, Bookseller, 70, Charing Cross Road, London, W. C. 2."

E2h . . . An Immorality . . . Poem by Ezra Pound Decorations by Paul Nash [London] The Poetry Bookshop [1923]

Broadside. 2 col. illus. 43·3 × 19·3 cm. Issued at 4*d.* as "The New Broadside . . . No. 2," with numbers 1 and 3–6 of the series, not later than 13 Dec. 1923 (date of receipt of the British Library set).

This is the first separate edition of this poem. It is reprinted from *Ripostes* (1912)—A8.

E2ha [Announcement of the *Exile*. London, Printed for the Editor, 1927?]

Postcard, with printed frame for "½d. STAMP" on verso. 8·8 × 13·9 cm.

Distributed gratis probably early in 1927; number of copies unknown.

Announcing that the periodical "will appear three times per annum until I get bored with producing it." Listing price, contributors to the first issue ("Guy Hickok, John Rodker, E. W. [*sic*] Hemingway and | yours as circum-stances permit | EZRA POUND, editor."), and authorised agents in London, Paris, and New York. (Another printed postcard, titled: "Literary An-nouncement," announcing the review before its name had been chosen,

E. MISCELLANEA

was mailed from New York, 23 Dec. 1926, by the American agent, John M. Price. This card quotes Pound as describing the writing to appear in the magazine as "preferably magnificent or unspeakable.")

E2i Dawn Song [*text in 12 lines*. Philadelphia, Pa.? Printed for Homer L. Pound? after 1928?]
Broadside. 21 × 14·5 cm.
Probably printed not earlier than 1928; number of copies unknown.
The only copy located (at Brunnenburg, 1981) has Homer Pound's manuscript note on its verso: "Ezra Pounds [*sic*] first poem, that was printed in the Munsey Magazine, Dec. 1906."

E2j Mr. Housman's Message . . . [*Text in 15 lines*. Palo Alto, Calif., The Harvest Press, 1931]
[2] pp. 31·6 × 25·5 cm.
Distributed gratis in 1931; 25 copies printed. *Colophon (page* [2]): Twenty Five Copies Only Printed at the Harvest Press by J[ames]. D. H[art].
Presumably the first separate edition of the poem.

E2k Exhibition Hilaire Hiler October 26—November, 1933. Mellon Galleries, 27 South 18th Street, Philadelphia, C. Philip Boyer, Director [Philadelphia, Pa., 1933]
4 leaves. 21·5 × 14 cm.
Printed on the outside of a single sheet folded twice.
Distributed gratis October 1933; number of copies unknown.
Contains on the verso of the second leaf, headed "Ezra Pound—Rapallo, Italie," a tribute to Hilaire Hiler. (A list of "Paintings & Gouaches" appears on the recto of the third leaf.)

E2l Musica Tigulliana progettata "Inverno Musicale" [*text in two columns, with printed signature:*] E. Pound. Rapallo: Concerti nella Gran Sala del Municipio [Printed at the Office of Il Mare, 1934]
Broadside. 28·3 × 22·3 cm.
Distributed gratis October 1934; number of copies unknown.
An appeal for subscribers for the winter season, outlining six possible subscription concerts and two special concerts. Reprinted from *Il Mare* for 6 Oct. 1934—C1101.

E2m Volitionist economics [*text in 48 lines*] Answer to E. Pound Via Marsala, 15/ 5 [*sic*]. Rapallo. Italy. [Printed at the Office of Il Mare? 1934]
Broadside. 29 × 22·5 cm.
Printed in a single column at the left side of the sheet of paper (watermarked: ORIGINAL EXTRA STRONG | GLADIATOR), the right side being left blank for answers to the eight questions posed in the text. Distributed gratis by Pound beginning *ca.* 18 Aug. 1934; 100 copies printed. All copies located have the misprint ("15/5" for "12/5" in the address) corrected in ink by the author.
A second printing, distributed after the first had been exhausted, *ca.* 27 Oct. 1934, is identical with the first except that the misprint has been corrected in type, and the paper is watermarked simply: EXTRA STRONG.

E. MISCELLANEA

E2n Studi Tigulliani [*text in two columns*] Ore di Studio alle 21 di: Giovedì 2
Aprile Mercoledì 22 Aprile Mercoledì 13 Maggio [Rapallo, Arti Grafiche
Tigullio, 1936]
Broadside. 44 × 14·5 cm.
Distributed gratis March 1936; number of copies unknown.
Outlining a program of studies devoted to the work of Antonio Vivaldi
(1685–1743) and appealing for subscribers, who are referred to "E. Pound,
Albergo Rapallo. Tessera di riconoscimento quella dell'Istituto Fascista di
Cultura." Reprinted from *Il Mare* for 14 Mar. 1936—C1305.

E2 o Stagione Musicale del Tigullio 21 Gennaio dal 2 al 5 Febbraio [*text in two
columns, with printed signature:*] E. P. Tip del "Mare" – Rapallo [1938]
Broadside. 32 × 14·5 cm. Printed in blue ink.
Issued gratis January 1938; number of copies unknown.
A first section gives the program for the concert of 21 Jan., and a second
section outlines concerts and events for the first week of February. Reprinted from *Il Mare* for 1 Jan. 1938—C1436.

E2p Musica a Rapallo Musique á [*sic*] Rapallo Music in Rapallo [*illustration*] Arti
Grafiche Tigullio – Rapallo [1938]
[6] pp. illus. 26·5 × 16·5 cm. Printed in blue ink on both sides of a single
sheet folded vertically twice, with outside centre section as above and with
text on the inside.
Distributed gratis January 1938; number of copies unknown.
Page [1] of text headed: "I Concerti di Febbraio"; page [2] of text headed:
"Renata Borgatti pianista," with conclusion at foot of page [3], signed:
E. P. Programs for 1–5 Feb. appear above text on page [3]. Reprinted from
Il Mare for 8 Jan. 1938—C1437. (The list of programs appeared also as a
broadside, printed on yellow paper, 24·6 × 17·1 cm., headed: "Stagione
Musicale de Tigullio | I Concerti di Febbraio".)

E2pa [Announcement of *Broletto*'s new department "Communications Service."]
. . . Como, Tip. Edit Cesare Nani [1938]
Broadside. 28·6 × 21·8 cm.
Distributed gratis probably in 1938; number of copies unknown.
This notice, printed on *Broletto* stationery, invites exchange of copies "with
any publication to which one of the present notices comes" of foreign
books "selected largely because they have not received adequate attention
from the commercial press in their own countries, but in any case because
they are regarded as of special interest either as provocative or as possess-
ing permanent merit." Suggested and drafted, at least in part, by Ezra
Pound.

E2q Sedici Sonate di Mozart e Arie Cantate Rapallo Anno XVII Olga Rudge
Renata Borgatti Guido Guidi [*illustration.* Rapallo, Arti Grafiche Tigullio,
1939]
[4] pp. 2 illus. 26·5 × 16·5 cm. Printed in blue ink.
Distributed gratis February 1939; number of copies unknown.
Outlining concerts and giving programs for March, and soliciting sub-

scriptions. Subscribers are asked to apply to "E. Pound—Albergo 'Rapallo'." Reprinted from *Il Mare* for 11 Feb. 1939—C1499.

E2r Introductory Text Book E. P. [Rapallo, 1939]

[3] pp. 18·9 × 12·7 cm.

Printed privately in London by Bonner and Company Limited for gratis distribution by the author to his correspondents and friends, with first copies sent out in March 1939; 500 copies printed. (The type page on page [2] measures 14·8 × 8·4 cm. and the author's name on page [3] is set in capital and small-capital letters.)

Consists of quotations from John Adams, Thomas Jefferson, Abraham Lincoln, and the Constitution of the United States, p. [2], with "Note" by Ezra Pound, p. [3].

Reprinted in various periodicals in 1939 (see Section C) and in Stanley J. Kunitz and Howard Haycraft, *eds.*, *Twentieth Century Authors* (New York, 1942)—B47—pp. 1121–22, and, with *What Is Money For?* (London, Peter Russell, 1951), as Number 3 of "Money Pamphlets by £." It is included also, with facsimile reproduction of page [1], in the appendix to the revised edition of *Guide to Kulchur* ([1952])—A45c, d—pp. [353]–356, and was reprinted, without the final note, on the verso of an advertisement leaf issued in the late 1950s for the edition of *Confucius. The Unwobbling Pivot & The Great Digest* in the Square Dollar Series, at least some copies with a typed statement added along the lefthand side: "Lincoln was shot for understanding what Jeff wrote to Crawford in 1816" (see B36a *note*).

E2s Introductory Text Book E. P. [2nd ed. Rapallo, 1945]

[3] pp. 20·1 × 12·5 cm.

At Ezra Pound's request, the pamphlet was reprinted in Rapallo for Olga Rudge in December 1945 for distribution gratis. Although set from a copy of the first edition, different fonts of type and an inferior grade of paper were used. The type page on page [2] measures 16 × 9 cm., and the author's name on page [3] is set in capital and lower-case letters.

E2t [Posters. Rapallo, Arti Grafiche Tigullio? *ca.* 1944]

Broadsides. Each approximately 6·5–7·5 × 49 cm. Printed on green paper for posting by Ezra Pound on walls in Rapallo. Printed probably in 1944; number of copies unknown.

The texts are as follows:

E2t (1) COSI' VIVERE CHE I TUOI FIGLI E I | LORO DISCENDENTI TI RINGRAZINO

E2t (2) FORMANDO DI DISIO | NUOVA PERSONA [Cavalcanti]

E2t (3) La Purezza Funge Senza Termine, | in tempo e in spazio senza termine. [Confucius]

E2t (4) L'ARCIERE che manca il centro del bersaglio | cerca la causa dell' errore *dentro sè stesso* [Confucius]

E2t (5) *LUCRO* privato NON costituisce | la prosperità.

E2u [Poster. Rapallo, Arti Grafiche Tigullio? *ca.* 1944]

Broadside. 33 × 69·5 cm.

Printed probably in 1944; number of copies unknown.

E. MISCELLANEA

With text: Ai liberali domandiamo: perchè | gli usurai sono tutti liberali? | Una Nazione che non vuole | indebitarsi fa rabbia agli usurai! The third and fourth lines appear in *Oro e lavoro* (1944)—A52—p. 11.

E2ua [A Manifesto. Washington, D. C., W. James, *i.e.* Ezra Pound, 1953]
Broadside. 27·6 × 21·6 cm.
Distributed gratis in 1953; number of copies unknown.
Against "the punk of the universities". Written by Pound, but signed (in facsimile) by ten American university professors, including Clark Emery, Hugh Kenner, H. M. McLuhan, Margaret Bates, and Robert Stallman. See Margaret Bates, "E P: Maker of Connections," in *Paideuma*, VI. 1 (Spring 1977) 114–[115], where the manifesto is reproduced, p. 114.

E2v Papillon Quattuor Epigrammata 30 Ottobre 1957 [Milano, Vanni Scheiwiller, 1957]
4 leaves. illus. 16·5 × 13 cm. Printed on both sides of a single sheet of japon, folded twice. (The illustrations are reproductions of drawings by Henri Gaudier-Brzeska.)
Distributed gratis beginning 30 October 1957; 59 numbered copies privately printed for Pound's 72nd birthday. *Imprint on recto of fourth leaf:* ... Tipografia "Esperia" – Milano [*number written in*] "Edited by V[anni]. S[cheiwiller]." *Contents:* The Pink [*signed:* E. P.]—Catullus [Draughty House. *Unsigned*]—Martial: Thais habet nigros [*signed:* E. P.]—Papillon: For a small book unread [*i.e. The Cultivation of Christmas Trees*, by T. S. Eliot. *Signed:* Anon]

E2w 228ᵃ mostra Liselotte Höhs Pittura galleria d'arte Il Traghetto – 2 Campo S. Maria del Giglio Venezia 11 maggio 23 maggio 1969
cover-title, [4] pp., incl. illus. 21·2 × 15·5 cm. Wire-stitched.
Distributed gratis beginning 11 May 1969; number of copies unknown.
Contains comment in Italian on the artist, signed: Ezra Pound; followed by two lines, in Italian translation, of "Night Litany," signed and dated in facsimile of Pound's manuscript: "Venezia 4 maggio 1969"

E2x ... Night Litany to Venice [*text in 10 lines*] Sold in aid of the Venice in Peril Fund (The British Committee for the Preservation of Venice, 18 Carlton House Terrace, London, S. W. 1 [*ca.* 1971?]
Christmas card (with reproduction of Jacopo Tintoretto's "Presentation of the Virgin (detail)," Church of the Madonna dell'Orto, completely restored with British contributions (Italian Art & Archives Rescue Fund)) sold probably in 1971; number of copies unknown.

E2y From Simplicities [*text in 29 lines*] Ezra Pound [Boston] My Dukes [Printed by Joseph Wilmot for Bill Little, 1971]
Broadside. 33·2 × 28 cm.
Published May 1971 at $10.00; 1000 copies printed.
Reprinted from the *Exile* for Autumn 1928, not from "Simplicities," but paragraphs 19–22 and 31–34 of the following article, "Bureaucracy the Flail of Jehovah"—C720.

E2z Plaint ... [Clinton, N. Y., Printed on the Alexander Hamilton Press at Hamilton College by Mark Holmes Walpole, 1972] cover-title, 6 leaves. 22 × 13·7 cm. Heavy blue paper wrappers printed in black; sewn with white cord.

Published September 1972 for gratis distribution; 350 copies printed. *Colophon (recto of sixth leaf):* ... [*in pencil:*] 350 [*in type:*] numbered copies ... This is copy number [*number written in in pencil*]

A keepsake to mark the opening of the new library of Hamilton and Kirkland Colleges, 10 Sept. 1972. Reprinted from *Etruscan Gate*, by Dorothy Pound—B102—p.3. (The poem is an early, slightly variant version of "Planh: Of white thoughts he saw in a Forest," first printed in *Exultations* (1909)—A4.)

E2za The Rest [*text in 19 lines*] ... Ezra Pound October 30, 1885 November 1, 1972 [Berkeley, Calif.] ĀRIF Press [Printed by Wesley Tanner, 1972] Broadside. 11·5 × 24·6 cm.

Distributed gratis to friends of the Press, 2 November 1972, in memory of Ezra Pound; 400 copies printed (of which 10 were numbered and signed by the printer). Printed on medium-weight, buff paper.

E2zb ... Four Poems of Departure ... 1915 [London] Holborn, In officinâ Guidonis Londinensis, January 1973

[4] pp. 20·1 × 12·7 cm. White paper envelope printed in black.

Published January 1973; 200 copies printed. *Colophon (page* [4]*):* Officina Mauritiana ... Edition of 200 numbered copies of which 150 are for sale This is No [Page [1] printed in silver, black, and gold]

At head of title: In Memoriam Ezra Pound

Contents: The Gates of Go [the epigraph]—Taking Leave of a Friend—Separation on the River Kiang—Leave-Taking near Shoku. (A reprint of the epigraph and the first three of the "Four Poems of Departure" from *Cathay* (1915)—A9.)

E2zc ... "This Monument Will Outlast" ... [with note by] James Taylor. [Sydney, Australia?] Pluralist, 1973

vi, [2] pp., incl. mounted port. 28·5 × 22·5 cm. Blue paper wrappers (over cardboard), printed in black and blue; heavy dark blue end-paper; sewn.

Published in 1973; 110 copies printed. *Colophon (page* [viii]*):* One hundred and ten copies printed ... Twenty-six copies numbered I–XXVI and signed by the author [*i.e.* James Taylor] of which this is number [*number written in in ink on a row of dots, followed by signature in ink*]

Contents: "This Monument Will Outlast" from Horace (Odes, Book III, 30)—Note by Taylor—From *Homage to Sextus Propertius*, I, [lines] i–xxiv.

E2zd [Announcement of the establishment of the Center for the Study of Ezra Pound and His Contemporaries at Yale. New Haven, Beinecke Rare Book and Manuscript Library, 1973]

[4] pp. illus. 21·6 × 14 cm.

Published 30 October 1973 for distribution gratis; 750 copies printed.

Contains, as p. [2], facsimile reproduction of Pound's autograph letter to the Provost of Yale University, 4 Apr. 1966, relating to the Pound Center.

E2ze ... From Canto VIII [Vancouver, Canada, The Cobblestone Press Society, 1977]

E. MISCELLANEA

1 blank leaf, 5 leaves. 28 × 18·7 cm. (Rectos of first and fourth leaves printed in gold, black, grey, and maroon.) Heavy buff paper wrappers printed in black and gold; sewn.

Published May 1977; 100 copies printed. *Colophon (recto of fourth leaf):* ... Designed & hand-set by Giampa ... The Edition is limited to one hundred copies, all being numbered and signed by the typographer. ... Ten copies have been forwarded for distribution to Pound's family, and for lodgement in those libraries where his manuscripts are held. *Title on page* [i] *of wrappers:* The Letter of Sigismundo Malatesta to Giovanni de Medici.

E2zf The Child's Guide to Knowledge ... [no place, no date]

2 leaves. 26·4 × 18·5 cm.

Caption title. With 12-line prefatory note, printed in red, signed: W. B. Details of publication not known.

A reprint of "Religio, or The Child's Guide to Knowledge" from the *New Freewoman* for 15 Oct. 1913—C106a—and *Pavannes and Divisions* (1918)—A15.

E2zg An Immorality ... [*text in eight lines*] From the Corrected [*sic*] Early Poems ... [New York? Printed for Stuart Wright, 1980]

Broadside. 1 illus. 35·2 × 32·3 cm. Printed in black on green paper with drawing (by Robert Gwathmey) in green in left side of the sheet.

Privately printed 14 November 1980, not for sale; 20 copies printed. *Colophon:* Twenty copies ... privately printed ... on the occasion of the 80th birthday of ... Aaron Copland. ... For earlier separate printing see E2h.

E2zh [Impressions of François-Marie Arouet (de Voltaire), III: To Madame Lullin] Ediciones Dominicae [Poiano, Verona, Franco Riva, *ca.* 1980?]

2 leaves. 18·5 × 25·2 cm.

Distributed gratis apparently in 1980; number of copies unknown. Text appears, without title, on recto of second leaf.

E2zi The Coward Surrealists ... [London] Printed by an amateur [*i.e.* Eric Stevens] 1981

2 blank leaves, 2 leaves, 2 blank leaves. 25·3 × 16·2 cm. Yellow paper wrappers printed in black; sewn.

Published Spring 1981 at £ 3.00, through the bookshop of Eric & Joan Stevens; "Less than 100 [*i.e. ca.* 97] copies printed."

Reprinted from *Contemporary Poetry and Prose* for Nov. 1936—C1375.

E2.5 FOREIGN EDITION

E2.5a *Chinese:*

Comprehensive Study Guide to Seven Poems by Ezra Pound Annotated and Edited by The Literary Study Guides Association, Taipei [Student Review Magazine Press, 1979]. 1 blank leaf, 2 leaves, 120 pp., 1 blank leaf. 17·8 cm. Contains English text, with annotations in Chinese, of "A Virginal," "Portrait d'une femme," *Hugh Selwyn Mauberley*, Cantos I, LIII, LXII, and LXXIV.

E. MISCELLANEA

Arranged alphabetically by title. The notation "(P)" after the date of performance of a work indicates that a programme was printed.

E3a "Cavalcanti"

Ezra Pound's second opera, in three acts, with libretto arranged from poems of Cavalcanti and Sordello, was completed in a first draft during the summer of 1932. Plans were discussed for its broadcast, in whole or in part, in the Spring of 1933 by the B. B. C., but the performance did not take place. Some of the songs, especially the lyric "Tos temps serai," have been sung on various occasions by Raymonde Collignon, Lonny Mayer, and others. A short example of the music is included in Murray Schafer's "Ezra Pound and Music," in *Canadian Music Journal*, V. 4 (Summer 1961) 42.

E3b "Collis O Heliconii"

In his note concerning his opera "Villon" in *Townsman* for Apr. 1938—C1448, Ezra Pound refers to a musical composition with this title as "half done, and no small technical problem." This was to have been a third opera, based upon the poem of Catullus. It was never finished.

E3c "Fanfare, Violin and Tambourin"

Performed by Olga Rudge at the Salle Pleyel, Paris, 7 July 1924 (P), along with George Antheil's Two Sonatas for Violin and Piano and his String Quartet.

E3d "Fiddle Music, First Suite"

Performed by Olga Rudge at the Aeolian Hall, London, 10 May 1924 (P), along with music by George Antheil. Repeated by Miss Rudge at the Salle Pleyel, Paris, 7 July 1924 (P). Reproduced, in facsimile of Ezra Pound's manuscript, in *Transatlantic Review*, II. 2 (Aug. 1924) 220–1—C663.

E3e "Hommage à Froissart"

A violin sonata, with piano accompaniment, performed by Olga Rudge and Alfredo Casella at the Sala Sgambati, Rome, 6 May 1926 (P).

E3f "Sonate 'Ghuidonis' pour violon seul"

Performed by Olga Rudge at 52, avenue de la Motte-Picquet, Paris, 5 Dec. 1931 (P). Later amplified by Tibor Serly for a complete, full-string orchestra.

E3g "Sujet pour violon (resineux)"

Performed by Olga Rudge at the Salle du Conservatoire, Paris, 11 Dec. 1923 (P), along with George Antheil's Two Sonatas for Violin and Piano, the composer at the piano. Repeated by Miss Rudge at the Aeolian Hall, London, 10 May 1924 (P), along with music by George Antheil.

E3h "Le Testament"

Ezra Pound's principal musical composition, a one-act opera (referred to also as "Villon" and "The Testament of François Villon") was written in Paris during 1920, 1921, and 1922. The libretto is taken from the poems of Villon, with ballades and rondeaux providing material for the arias, sung in the original French. Brief spoken passages in English, partly translated

E. MISCELLANEA

from Villon, partly written by Pound, provide continuity. A summary of the action and an analysis of the music, including four short examples, are given in Murray Schafer's "Ezra Pound and Music" in *Canadian Music Journal*, V. 4 (Summer 1961) 35–41. Except for the song "Suivez, beautez," taken from the *Collection Yvette Guilbert* in the arrangement of Gustave Ferrari (see B3), and "Mère au Sauveur," from the *Hesternae Rosae* (see B5), the music is entirely by Pound.

Two songs from the opera, "Mort, j'appelle" and "Je renye amours," were included in the Rudge-Antheil concert at the Salle Pleyel, Paris, 7 July 1924 (P), performed by Yves Tinayre, tenor, and Olga Rudge, violin.

A concert (commonly referred to as the "première" of the opera), entitled "Paroles de Villon: Airs and Fragments from an Opera Le Testament," was given at the Salle Pleyel, Paris, 29 June 1926 (P), by Yves Tinayre, tenor, Robert Maitland, bass, Olga Rudge, violin, and Paul Tinayre, horn. For this concert, the Pounds in mid-June distributed a flier, measuring 21 × 13·3 cm., headed: "M. et Mme Ezra Pound vous invite à une audition privée Paroles de Villon . . . ," giving the programme "(probablement)," and ending: "admet [*space for number to be written in*] personnes On vous prie de présenter cette fiche Salle Pleyel. 29 Juin, 9h.15 du soir E.P." The French text of the selections included in the programme was printed as a stapled pamphlet, measuring 29 × 19·2 cm., collating [7] pp., with title: *Paroles de Villon Musique d'Ezra Pound . . . Salle Pleyel 28 Juin 1926* ([Paris], 1926]). Four songs from the opera were sung by Robert Maitland, accompanied by Olga Rudge on the violin, at the home of Mrs. Christian Gross, Paris, 12 July 1926 (P).

In connexion with preparations for the 1926 concerts, Ezra Pound had the two songs "Mort, j'appelle" and "Je renye amours" engraved in February of that year. One hundred plate proofs, bearing the page numbers "2–3" and "4–5," and the plate number "15032," and measuring 33·5 × 27 cm., were pulled. (One set is marked by Pound: "proofs. private circulation only.") These proofs are reproduced, much reduced, as pp. [2–5] of the following pamphlet printed apparently for the 1926 concerts:

E3h(1) Two Songs from Ezra Pound's Opera Le Testament. Paroles de Villon. 1—Ythier's Song: Mort, j'appelle. 2.—Le Galant: Je renye amours. As presented at the Salle Pleyel, Paris, July 7, 1924, by Yves Tinayre – tenor, Olga Rudge – violin. The violin accompaniment was written for the concert and makes no attempt to condense or to represent the orchestration intended for use in the opera. [Paris? 1926?] [5] pp., 1 blank leaf. 22·5 × 14 cm.

Printed June? 1926?; number of copies unknown.

The "Heaulmière," one of the principal arias of the opera, was included (sung by tenor singing falsetto) in the concert at the Salle Pleyel, 29 June 1926 (P). It was printed, in facsimile of Olga Rudge's manuscript, in *Townsman*, I. 2 (Apr. 1938) 12–16—C1448, and was reprinted in *New Directions in Prose and Poetry*, 3 (1938) [168–72]—C1448 n., and in *Guide to Kulchur* ([1953])—A45c, d—pp. 361–5.

A second, much more complete, performance of the opera, largely rear-

ranged for violin accompaniment, was given by the B.B.C., 26 and 27 Oct.
1931. For this production, Ezra Pound supplied dialogue in "hobo language." The libretto was reproduced from typewritten copy:

E3h(2) "The Testament of François Villon" a Melodrama by Ezra Pound.
    Words by François Villon. Music by Ezra Pound. [London, B.B.C.,
    1931]
        2 leaves, 2–12 numbered leaves. 32·5 × 20 cm. Punched and fastened
        at upper left.

A third performance of the opera, in a version edited by Murray Schafer,
using the same dialogue as in 1931, was broadcast, also by the B.B.C., in
June 1962, and was repeated in August.

The first American performance of the opera was presented by the Western Opera Theater (the touring and educational wing of the San Francisco
Opera) at the Zellerbach Auditorium of the University of California at
Berkeley, 13 Nov. 1971 (P). For this production, Pound's staging and cos-
tuming instructions and the complete, original score (except for the ac-
companiments to Nos. 9 and 11, which were missing and were supplied
by Murray Schafer for No. 9 and by Robert Hughes for No. 11) were
utilised. Fragments of Villon's text were made use of at points where Pound
indicated (but did not supply) dialogue in the original manuscript. The
libretto, with English translations of the songs by Peter Dale Scott, was
reproduced from typewritten copy on 14 pages, stapled at the top, measuring 28 × 21·6 cm. (For the Fantasy Records' recording of this production see E5g.)

The complete opera was performed as part of the Holland Festival in 1980.
(For the Philips recording of this production see E5h.) In 1965, the opera
was staged by Gian Carlo Menotti as a ballet, choreographed by John
Butler, presented as one of the "Rarità Musicali" of the Eighth Festival of
Two Worlds at the Teatro Caio Melisso, Spoleto, Italy, on 14, 16, and 17
July (P). A revised, reduced orchestration by Lee Hoiby and Stanley Hol-
lingsworth was used, with the singers in the orchestra pit.

E4 MUSICAL SETTINGS

E4a Three Songs of Ezra Pound for a Voice with Instrumental Accompaniment
    by Walter Morse Rummel (1911) I. Madrigale II. Au bal masqué III. Aria.
    With Piano . . . London, Augener Ltd. . . . [1911]
    33·8 × 25·5 cm.

The title as above remains unchanged for the first three songs (for the
fourth, see b below) with the appropriate title underlined in red. Each song
has individual collation (including above title) as follows:

E4a(1) I. Madrigale: 2 leaves, 3, [1] pp. *Imprint at foot of page 3:* [*plate no.*]
    14263 Augener's Music Printing Office.

E4a(2) II. Au bal masqué: 1 leaf, 5, [1] pp. *Imprint at foot of page 5:* [*plate
    no.*] 14264 Augener's Music Printing Office.

E4a(3) III. Aria: 2 leaves, 7, [1] pp. *Imprint at foot of page 7:* [*plate no.*] 14300
    Augener's Music Printing Office.

E. MISCELLANEA

The last page of each has the same list of other songs by Walter Morse Rummel.

All three songs published simultaneously 19 September 1911 at 2s. (each). "Madrigale" and "Aria" reprinted from *Canzoni* (1911)—A7; "Au bal masqué" printed here for the first time. The price of each song was later raised to 2s.6d., and at that price the songs were still being sold by the publisher in 1957.

E4b Songs of Ezra Pound for a Voice with Instrumental Accompaniment by Walter Morse Rummel I. Madrigale II. Au bal masqué III. Aria IV. The Return. With Piano . . . London, Augener Ltd.; Paris, Max Eschig; Boston, Boston Music Co. [1913]

1 leaf, 4 pp., 1 leaf. 33·8 × 25·5 cm.

Contains only "The Return," with that title underlined in red.

Published 4 January 1913 at 2s. *Imprint at foot of page 4:* [*plate no.*] 14539 Augener's Music Printing Office

The verso of the last leaf lists other songs by Walter Morse Rummel, including *3 Songs of Ezra Pound* (1911).

E4c . . . Salutation. Ezra Pound. Josef Holbrooke. [London] Curwen Edition [1922]

3 leaves, 3–7, [1] pp. 29·9 × 23·7 cm.

For voice, piano, oboe, and viola. Published 1922 at 2s. as No. 1 of the composer's "Opus 77 [Seven Socialist Songs]." *Imprint on page* [8]: London: J. Curwen & Sons Ltd., 24 Berners Street, W. 1 238/3/22

At head of title: 2261

E4d . . . The Garret. Ezra Pound. Josef Holbrooke. [London] Curwen Edition [1922]

3 leaves, 3–7, [1] pp. 29·9 × 23·7 cm.

For voice, piano, oboe, and viola. Published 1922 at 2s. as No. 2 of the composer's "Opus 77 [Seven Socialist Songs]." *Imprint on page* [8]: London: J. Curwen & Sons Ltd., 24 Berners Street, W. 1 239/3/22

At head of title: 2260

E4e The Tea-Shop Girl (Paxton's Edition, No 40,332) Song with clarinet obligato; Words by Ezra Pound; Music by Joseph [*sic*] Holbrooke. London, W. Paxton & C. Ltd. [1923]

5 pp., 1 leaf. 29·9 × 23·7 cm.

For voice, piano, and clarinet. Published 1923 at 2s. as No. 4 of the composer's "Opus 77 [Seven Socialist Songs]." *At foot of verso of last leaf:* A 329/7/22

A setting of "The Tea Shop."

E4f "Tame-Cat" (Paxton's Edition, No 40,333) Song with Clarinet Obligato; Words by Ezra Pound; Music by Joseph [*sic*] Holbrooke. London, W. Paxton & Co., Ltd. [1923]

5 pp., 1 leaf. 29·9 × 23·7 cm.

For voice, piano, and clarinet. Published 1923 at 2s. as No. 5 of the composer's "Opus 77 [Seven Socialist Songs]." *At foot of verso of last leaf:* A. 329/7/22

E. MISCELLANEA

E4g Sir Granville Bantock. South Folk in Cold Country. Words ... by Ezra
Pound ... London, Boosey, 1923.
1 leaf, 9, [1] pp. 25 cm.
For chorus. Published 28 June 1923 at 6*d.* as "Boosey's Modern Festival
Series of Choral Music, 303."

E4h Sir Granville Bantock. Song of the Bowmen of Shu. Words ... by Ezra
Pound ... London, Boosey, 1923.
1 leaf, 17, [1] pp. 25 cm.
For chorus. Published 28 June 1923 at 9*d.* as "Boosey's Modern Festival
Series of Choral Music, 301."

E4i Sir Granville Bantock. Lament of the Frontier Guard. Words ... by Ezra
Pound ... London, Boosey, 1923.
16 pp. 25 cm.
For chorus. Published 31 July 1923 at 9*d.* as "Boosey's Modern Festival
Series of Choral Music, 302."

E4j ... An Immorality, Three-part Chorus for Women's Voices with Soprano
Solo. From "Lustra" by Ezra Pound. Aaron Copland ... [Boston, Mass.]
E. C. Schirmer Music Co., 1926
15, [1] pp. 27·4 cm.
Caption title.
Published 27 September 1926 at 25¢. For earlier separate publication of
the poem, see E2h.

E4k Dance Figure. Poem by Ezra Pound. Music by John J. Becker. 1932.
58 leaves. 34 × 29·5 cm.
For orchestra. Negative photostat of autograph manuscript.
Copy at New York Public Library. Apparently not regularly published.

E4ka The Monstrous Flea ... by Tibor Serly ... Radio City, New York, Leeds
Music Corporation [1952]
5, [1] pp. 30·5 × 23 cm.
For low voice. Published 12 March 1952 at 60¢. in the series of Leeds
Concert Songs.
"Poetic translation from the Hungarian by Ezra Pound." Text transmitted
to Serly, with suggested title "The Buck Flea," in a letter, Oct. 1939 (see
The Letters, p. 326, *footnote*). The music is "Based on a Transylvanian Folk
Song."

E4kb An Immorality ... Words by Ezra Pound; Music by Lee Hoiby ... New
York, G. Schirmer [1956]
5, [1] pp. 30·5 × 22·7 cm.
For voice and piano. Published 1956 at 60¢.
For earlier separate publication of the poem see E2h.

E4l Ingvar Lidholm. Canto LXXXI av Ezra Pound för Blandad Kör a cappella.
[1961?]
pp. [41]–67. 27·3 × 17·5 cm.
Reproduced from holograph. Apparently not regularly published.

E. MISCELLANEA

"Svensk tolkning av Lars Forssell," pp. 42–43; title, p. 44; music, pp. 45–67.

E4m William Strickland. Three Songs . . . 2. Ione, Dead the Long Year (Ezra Pound) . . . New York, Galaxy Music Corporation [1961]
4 pp., 1 leaf. 30·3 × 23 cm.
For voice and piano. Published 26 April 1961 at 60¢.
Contains only the Pound setting. The other two songs (texts by James Joyce) were published separately.

E4n Tame Cat: poem by Ezra Pound; music by John Koch. New York, General Music Publishing Co., Inc. [1965]
3, [1] pp. 30·3 × 23 cm.
For voice and piano. Published 2 June 1965.
For earlier setting of the poem, see E4f.

E4 o The Tea Shop: Poem by Ezra Pound; Music by John Koch. New York, General Music Publishing Co., Inc. [1965]
5, [1] pp. 30·5 × 22·8 cm.
For voice and piano. Published 2 June 1965.

E4p An Immorality: Poem by Ezra Pound; Music by John Koch. New York, General Music Publishing Co., Inc. [1965]
3, [1] pp. 30·3 × 23 cm.
For voice and piano. Published 9 June 1965.

E4q Four Ladies [music by] David Diamond . . . New York, Southern Music Publishing Co.; Hamburg, Peer Musikverlag [1966].
7, [1] pp. 31 × 23 cm.
For voice and piano. Published 17 May 1966 at 65¢.
Contents: 1. Agathas—2. Young Lady—3. Lesbia illa—4. Passing. (A setting of "Ladies.")

E4r . . . [J. Robert] Carroll: Songs of the Heart (1. In Vain; 2. White Butterflies; 3. Return from Town) . . . New York, G. Schirmer, Inc. [1968]
11, [1] pp. 26·5 × 17·5 cm.
For three-part chorus of women's voices. Published 14 May 1968 at 30¢.
Contents: 1. In Vain [by Ezra Pound: "Vana," three quatrains from "Praise of Ysolt"]—2. White Butterflies [text by Isabel Kfoury]—3. The Return from Town [text by Edna St. Vincent Millay].

E4s Udo Kasemets. Octagonal octet and/or ode [A calceolaria (time/space) variation based on I Ching trigrams and hexagrams and (optional) words extracted from Ezra Pound's Confucian odes . . .] Don Mills, Ont., BMI Canada [1968]
cover-title, 21 numbered leaves, 8 leaves. 36cm. (Music of the 1960s and after).
For "8 performers using any aural/visual/choreographic media."

E4t De Aegypto, cantata [by] Otto E. Laske . . . Op. 3. [Boston, Mass.? 1968?]
36pp. 28 × 44 cm.
Reproduced from holograph. Apparently not regularly published.
For tenor, viola, harp, horn, and percussion. With text and explanation of

E. MISCELLANEA

signs used in the score, reproduced from typewritten copy, 4 leaves bound in at end.

E4u Hans Zender. Canto II, für Solo-Sopran, gemischten Chor, Orchester; nach "Canto XXXIX" von Ezra Pound. Klavierauszug von Georg Kröll. Berlin, Wiesbaden, Bote & Bock [1968]
1 leaf, 96 pp. 31 cm.
For solo soprano, mixed choir, and orchestra. Published 1968.

E4v Henrik Otto Donner (Ezra Pound) [Canto] XC. [Helsinki] Commissioned by the Finnish Radio [1970]
39, [1] pp. 31 cm.
For solo soprano, chorus, and orchestra. Published 1970.

E4w Hans-Joachim Hespos. Palimpsest. [München] Edition Modern [1970]
2 leaves, 29 pp. 34 × 47 cm.
For voice and percussion. Published 1970.
A setting for lines from Cantos VII, XIV, XV, and CXVI.

E4x ... [Sestina] Altaforte [music by] Allen Brings ... New York, Seesaw Music Corp., 1973.
16 pp. 31 cm.
Reproduced from holograph. Apparently not regularly published.
For quartet with piano accompaniment.

E4y Werner Heider. Commission ... Gedichte von Ezra Pound (1916) ... Frankfurt, London, New York, Henry Litolff's Verlag/C. F. Peters [1976]
36 pp. 26·5 × 33·5 cm.
"Study score," for baritone and chamber orchestra. Published 1976.
"Composition commissioned by the South German Broadcasting Company, Stuttgart. First performed in Stuttgart on 15. 12. 1972 ... "

E4z David Wooldridge. The Hieratic Head: Settings of five poems by Ezra Pound ... [Bridgewater, Ct., 1979?]
18 pp. 28 cm.
For unaccompanied voices. Published 1979?
Contents: from Canto LXXXI—Hugh Selwyn Mauberley, Part 1, I, VII, and "Envoi (1919)"—Canto XLV.

E4za The River-Merchant's Wife, for Soprano and Ensemble Op. 20 (1980) Lawrence Willingham Text from the Poem by Ezra Pound ... From Personae ... [New York, American Composers Alliance, 1980]
1 leaf, 39 pp., 1 blank leaf. 33·1 × 27·1 cm.
Reproduced from holograph. signed at end: "finished Aug. 1, 1980". Apparently not regularly published.

E5 RECORDINGS

E5a During his visit to the United States in 1939, Ezra Pound recorded for the Vocarium Series at Harvard on 17 May the following poems: Cantos XVII, XXX, XLV, LVIII; "Sestina: Altaforte" and "The Seafarer" (both read to the accompaniment of drums); Homage to Sextus Propertius, VI; "Cantico del sole"; and Hugh Selwyn Mauberley, Part 1, "Envoi (1919)" and Part 2,

E. MISCELLANEA

I. These recordings, except those of Cantos XXX and LVIII, were released as part of Cassette 1 in a series of six one-hour cassettes, "The Poet's Voice . . . Selected and Edited by Stratis Haviaras," issued by the Harvard University Press in Fall 1978 at $60.00.

E5b On 2, 11, and 17 July 1959 the B. B. C. broadcast a series of three "Ezra Pound: Readings and Recollections," produced and introduced by D.G. Bridson on the Third Programme. The broadcasts, which were taped, were themselves compiled from recordings made for the most part by Bridson in Washington, D. C., and in Italy at Brunnenburg. A transcription of selected portions of the recollections was printed as "An Interview with Ezra Pound [by] D. G. Bridson" in *New Directions in Prose and Poetry*, 17 (1961) 159–84—C1884. For use in preparing the broadcast the script was reproduced from typewritten copy:

E5b(1) As Broadcast. Ezra Pound: Readings and Recollections, 1. The Early Years. Produced and Introduced by D. G. Bridson. Third Programme: Transmission: Thursday, 2nd July, 9.–35—10.20 p.m. R. P. Ref. No.: TLO 89769 [London, B.B.C., 1959]
2 leaves, 2–17 numbered leaves. 33 × 20·5 cm. Punched and fastened at upper left.
Includes Pound's readings of *Hugh Selwyn Mauberley*, Part 1, I–IX, and Part 2, II; *Homage to Sextus Propertius*, VI and VIII; T. E. Hulme's "The Man in the Crow's Nest"; Max Beerbohm's epitaph for George Bernard Shaw; "Moeurs contemporaines," VII–VIII; and "Cantico del sole."

E5b(2) As Broadcast. Ezra Pound: Readings and Recollections, 2. The Cantos. Produced and Introduced by D. G. Bridson. Third Programme: Transmission: Saturday, 11th July, 10.00—10.45 p.m. R.P.Ref. No.: TLO 89770 [London, B.B.C., 1959]
2 leaves, 2–15 numbered leaves. 33 × 20·5 cm. Punched and fastened at upper left.
Includes Pound's readings of the opening passage of Canto I, and Cantos XIII, XLV, XLIX, and CI (the last read from manuscript).

E5b(3) As Broadcast. Ezra Pound: Readings and Recollections, 3. The Later Years. Produced and Introduced by D. G. Bridson. Third Programme: Transmission: Friday, 17th July, 10.10—10.55 p.m. R.P. Ref. No.: TLO 90737 [London, B. B. C., 1959]
2 leaves, 2–17 numbered leaves. 33 × 20·5 cm. Punched and fastened at upper left.
Includes Pound's readings of "To-Em-Mei's 'The Unmoving Cloud'"; from *The Classic Anthology as Defined by Confucius*, the following poems: Nos. 52, 57, 98, 105, 208, 219, 253, 193; "Conversations in Courtship" (read from manuscript); and Joel Chandler Harris's "De Tar-Baby Story."

E5c Ezra Pound Reading His Poetry [New York, Caedmon Publishers, 1960]
1 long-playing 33⅓ r.p.m. microgroove record (Caedmon TC 1122). Recorded in Washington, D. C., 1958. Published 1960 at $5.95.

E. MISCELLANEA

Contents: SIDE A: 1. *Hugh Selwyn Mauberley*—2. Cantico del sole—3. Moeurs contemporaines—SIDE B: 1. Canto I—2. Canto IV—3. Canto XXVI—4. Canto LXXXIV.

This recording has been reprinted several times, with reprint notes indicated on the sleeve (which carries a portrait of Pound by Dillon).

E5d Ezra Pound Reading His Poetry Volume 2 [New York, Caedmon Publishers, 1962]

1 long-playing 33 ⅓ r.p.m. microgroove record (Caedmon TC 1155). Recorded in Washington, D. C., 12, 13, and 26 June 1958.

Contents: SIDE ONE: Canto XLV—Canto LI—Canto LXXVI (second half)—The Gypsy—The Exile's Letter—SIDE TWO: Canto XCIX. The sleeve carries the same portrait of Pound by Dillon used for the first volume.

E5e . . . Ezra Pound Reading His Cantos III, XVI, XLIX, LXXXI, XCII, CVI, CXV [New York, Spoleto Recordings, 1969]

1 long-playing 12-inch 33⅓ r.p.m. microgroove record (SP 411M). Published 1969 at $5.95. Recorded at Spoleto, Italy, at the Festival of Two Worlds in 1967.

Contents: SIDE ONE: Canto III, XVI, XLIX, LXXXI—SIDE TWO: Canto LXXXI (a different reading, separated by one hour from the previous one), XCII, CVI, CXV (read from manuscript).

At head of title: The World's Great Poets Reading at the Festival of Two Worlds, Spoleto, Italy.

The sleeve carries a note, "Ezra Pound at Spoleto," by Hugh Kenner, and three photographs of Pound at Spoleto, one with Gian Carlo Menotti.

E5f Ezra Pound Reading His Translations of The Confucian Odes Presented by Arthur Luce Klein [New Rochelle, N. Y.] Spoken Arts [1970?]

1 long-playing 33⅓ r.p.m. microgroove record (Spoken Arts SA 1098 Stereo). Recorded in Italy in 1970?

Contents: SIDE ONE: Nos. 1, 6, 11, 18, 23, 69, 70 (Aliter), 76, 105, 109, 110, 113, 119, 126, 133, 185, 187, 195—SIDE TWO: Nos. 206, 214, 219, 253, 256, 265, 301.

The sleeve carries a note by Hugh Kenner.

E5g . . . Le Testament (Music by Ezra Pound; Text from the Poetry of Villon) . . . Robert Hughes conducting soloists of the Western Opera Theater . . . and the Associated Students of the University of California. Sung in Medieval French . . . Berkeley, Calif., Fantasy Records, 1972.

1 long-playing 12-inch microgroove record (Fantasy 12001). Recorded in the Berkeley studios of Fantasy Records on 18 and 19 November 1971. Published 1972.

Contents: SIDE 1: Nos. 1–9—SIDE 2: Nos. 10–15. The printed text of the songs was enclosed with the recording, a folder headed: *Ezra Pound Le Testament de Villon* ([Berkeley, Calif., Fantasy Records [1972]). It collates [4] pp., and measures 30·5 × 30·5 cm. The text is in the medieval French, with English translations by Peter Dale Scott, except for "No. 9. The Priest" (Williaume li Viniers' "Mère au sauveur") and "No. 11. The Priest" ("Suyvez beauté"), both in Pound's translations. The sleeve has a discussion of the

E. MISCELLANEA

opera, including a synopsis, by Robert Hughes. The painting of Pound on the sleeve is by Philip Carroll.

E5h Ezra Pound Le Testament de Villon ASKO-ensemble, ASKO-koor dirigent Reinbert de Leeuw [1980]

1 long-playing 12-inch microgroove record (Philips Stereo 9500 927). Published 1980.

Contents: SIDE A: [Nos.] 1–9—SIDE B: [Nos.] 10–15. The printed text of the songs was enclosed with the recording, a medium-weight leaflet, [2] pp., headed: Ezra Pound Le Testament de Villon (1980). It measures 30·5 × 30·5 cm. The text is in the medieval French, with Dutch translation. The sleeve has a note on the opera by Reinbert de Leeuw.

E5i . . . Fragmente aus den Cantos XVII, XXV, XXVI. St. Gallen, Erker Verlag . . . [1972]

1 long-playing, 7-inch, 45 r.p.m. microgroove record.

Published with *An Angle* ([1972])—A92a.

Contents: SIDE A: Cantos XVII, XXV—SIDE B: Canto XXVI.

E6 BOOKS CONTRACTED FOR BUT NOT PUBLISHED

E6a The Canzoni of Arnaut Daniel, translated by Ezra Pound, with original music by Walter Morse Rummel (1912–1918).

The Ralph Fletcher Seymour Company, Chicago, Ill., agreed in 1912 to publish Pound's "The Canzoni of Arnaut Daniel." A typescript seems to have been submitted early in 1913 to Seymour, who printed and mailed out a prospectus "to about 300 poetry readers . . . in the neighborhood of Chicago" for a book of 180 pages, 8 × 11 inches, in an edition of 300 copies at between $4 and $5, with ten copies on Japanese vellum at $15.00. Seymour advertised the book in the *New Freewoman*, in October, November, and December 1913, but eventually decided that there was too little evidence of interest at that time to warrant proceeding with the publication. In that same year the Seymour firm became incorporated as Seymour, Daughaday and Company and Daughaday "did not care for Pound's work." Pound's typescript had been returned to him before the Seymour-Daughaday partnership was dissolved in 1915.

By late 1917, Pound could express himself as "profoundly glad" that the book had not been published as planned in 1913. He revised his manuscript during December 1917 and January 1918, and reported to his father, 24 Jan. 1918, that he had sent it off by registered mail to Rev. Charles Clinch Bubb, Cleveland, Ohio. "Dare say he will print it in time, and send you a copy." (Bubb at this time was operating a private press on which he printed works by H. D. and Richard Aldington.) Unfortunately, the manuscript did not arrive in Cleveland. Pound at first suspected that it had been held up by American war censorship and imagined it being "decoded by some asst. sec. of the N. J. Y.M.C.A." When it still had not reached its destination on 1 September, Pound wrote John Quinn asking him to do what he could to trace it. Quinn tried and failed, and Pound eventually came to the conclusion that the ship carrying his manuscript must have

446

E. MISCELLANEA

been "submarined." He reported to his father, 3 Nov. 1918, that he had sent off "a condensed 'Arnaut Daniel'" to Cleveland, but Bubb apparently decided not to print that version. In any case, the book was not published.

E6b This Generation (1915–1917).

In December 1915, Ezra Pound began to collect some of his essays printed in periodicals over the past five years for a book at first titled "The Half Decade," and, finally, "This Generation." This would treat of art and literature in London and Paris in the twentieth century. A new publisher, John Marshall at 331 Fourth Avenue in New York, expressed interest in seeing the book. Terms were drawn up in March 1916, and Pound sent the manuscript off to him early in May. Meanwhile, John Quinn in New York had taken it upon himself to ask questions about Marshall's financial stability and advised Pound, too late, not to publish with him: "the chances are absolutely against his making a go of it from a business point of view." With Pound's approval, Quinn attempted on several occasions to see Marshall but without success, eventually discovering from Alfred Kreymborg that the publisher had gone off to Canada with his young bride, who had developed tuberculosis. On 11 September 1916, Pound wrote Quinn that if "This Generation" was gone with Marshall then it was lost for good, since no other copy of the manuscript existed.

Quinn proposed Alfred A. Knopf as a much more reliable American publisher for Pound's work. When Knopf agreed to issue an American edition of '*Noh*,' bringing it out promptly in January 1917, and contracted to publish an American edition of *Lustra*, Quinn approached him on the subject of the prose book, reporting to Pound, 13 Jan. 1917, that "he [*i.e.* Knopf] thinks he might be able to get the MS. of 'This Generation' from Marshall." Whether or not Knopf succeeded is unclear. In any case, *Pavannes and Divisions* (1918)—A15, eventually published by Knopf, was a book of much broader scope which both Pound and Quinn were quite content to accept in place of the ill-fated "This Generation."

E6c Massenet's Cendrillon: libretto translated by Ezra Pound.

Through Lady Cunard, Sir Thomas Beecham commissioned from Ezra Pound an English verse translation of Massenet's four-act opera "Cendrillon," for use at the Royal Opera House, Covent Garden, where he then conducted. Pound set about the translation on 27 September 1916, and by 12 October had finished a first typed copy. But on the 31st he reported to his parents that "Old Beecham is dead and [Eugene] Goossens has been conducting in place of T. B. so I have not yet finished the revising of the libretto." Pound did finish the commissioned work (reporting the fact to his father, 13 Dec. 1916) and was paid his fee of £40–£50 for it, but the opera was not done and the English libretto was not then needed. No copy of the translation is reported to exist in the Covent Garden archives in London or in the Ezra Pound Archive at Yale. (The statement in the program for the Eighth Festival of Two Worlds at Spoleto in 1965 that Pound " . . . ha curato la versione inglese della 'Cenerentola' di Rossini" resulted from a confusion of the two Cinderella operas.)

E. MISCELLANEA

E6d *Ouvert la Nuit* and *Tendres Stocks*, by Paul Morand; translated by Ezra Pound (1922).

On 22 May 1922, Ezra Pound and the London firm of Chapman and Dodd (later Chapman and Hall) entered into an agreement whereby Pound was to provide translations of Paul Morand's *Ouvert la Nuit* and *Tendres Stocks*, "suitable for publication in English." The first translation was to be submitted on or before 30 June 1922, the second six months later. Pound had already begun the first translation in 1921, and the *Dial* in its issue for September of that year had printed one section, "Turkish Night"—C629. Morand expressed himself to Pound (11 Apr. 1922) as "glad to have you as translator" and suggested English equivalents for the section-titles. In May, Pound submitted specimens of his translations from both books to Victor M. Llona, a professional translator, who judged them "an excellent piece of work," and agreed on 19 May to go over both translations for a fee of 400 francs. (He corrected at least "Roman Night" and "Six-Day Night" from *Ouvert la Nuit*, and "Clarissa" from *Tendres Stocks*, for the typescripts now in the Lilly Library at Indiana University have his manuscript annotations.)

Pound submitted the complete translation of *Ouvert la Nuit* on time (the typescripts of "Catalan Night," "The Turkish Night," "The Roman Night," "The Six-Day Night," "Hungarian Night," and "Borealis"—"La nuit nordique"—all have Chapman and Hall receipt stamps), and by 14 July had completed his translation of *Tendres Stocks* and of Marcel Proust's preface to that book.

Unfortunately, Guy Chapman found the translations "quite appalling." Knowing of only two English critics who had reviewed *Ouvert la Nuit*, J. Middleton Murry (in the *Nation*) and A. B. Walkley (in the *Times*), he at first wrote Murry asking whether he would be willing to give an opinion of the quality of Pound's translations. Murry was reluctant to accept the commission on the ground that Morand himself was quite competent enough in English to estimate the value of a translation of his own books. However he expressed himself as willing to do this "rather exacting work" for a fee of not less than five guineas. He added that the translations and copies of the two books would have to be sent to him in Montana, Switzerland, where he was then living. Chapman dared not trust the translations to the mail and so turned to A. B. Walkley for an evaluation of them. Walkley's opinion, rendered on 7 August (for a fee of ten pounds) was that Chapman and Hall could not, "with credit, or indeed without ridicule, publish this translation." He went on to detail the faults he had found:

> ... Mr. Pound ... is literal without tact; he fills in or waters down without taste, often without necessity; he misses, apparently unconsciously, the lilt or rather, the jerk of the author's phrase; he often dulls the edge of the author's sharp epithets. Further he perpetrates some absolute "howlers," showing that he does not even understand the author's meaning. There is frequent evidence of sheer carelessness. Lastly, his own style is American, and vulgar American; whereas

Morand, though brutal enough, provocative, even slangy, is never vulgar.

He enclosed a list of some twenty-two examples of infelicities, chosen chiefly from the first twenty-two pages of Pound's translation.

Walkley's report confirmed Chapman in his decision to reject the translations as not suitable for publication. Pound protested that the translations had been gone over with Morand himself and that any changes of idiom and condensation of phrase had been made with his approval. "If your critics don't yet know that there is a difference between the structure of sentences in English and french, and that conversations have to be translated into speakable phrases, they might do well to learn these primary lessons. (also you might deliver them from their somewhat suspicious anonymity.)" But protestations were of no avail, the contract was cancelled, and the only satisfaction Pound ever received was the payment of the twenty-five pounds due him. *Ouvert la Nuit* was eventually published by Chapman and Hall in a translation by Vyvyan Holland.

Nor did Pound have the satisfaction of learning the identity of Chapman's reader. On 25 August 1922, apparently having heard that Murry was the critic responsible for the damaging estimate, he fired off a vituperative blast to "J. M. Murray [*sic*] | 'writer of standing' | advisette to Chapman and Dodd | 25 Denmark St. | London, W. C. 1 | Angleterre," addressing him as "My Dear Little Llord [*sic*] Fauntleroy." Of course the letter was not forwarded. Pound's final statement on the affair was made in a letter to Frank Morley of Faber and Faber, 15 Jan. 1935, reporting that Chapman had broken the contract in 1922 and rejoicing that the firm had gone bankrupt a few years afterward. "I believe a translation of *Ouvert la Nuit*, nacherly inferior to mine, wuz pubd. and did badly . . . "

E6e Machine Art (1927–1928, 1931).

Pascal Covici, Publisher, Inc., Chicago, Ill., agreed by telegram, 21 Mar. 1927, to publish a book on modern machinery and spare parts for which Ezra Pound had been actively gathering photographs since the summer of 1925. The project had been begun as a planned article for *This Quarter*, Paris, and some of the material, possibly including "Tentative Propositions or Outline for Discussion" (printed in *Ezra Pound and the Visual Arts* ([1980])—A105—pp. 302–3), was submitted just before the death of Ernest Walsh, one of the editors, brought the periodical to an end. There was some expectation that Ethel Moorhead, the surviving editor, might use Pound's material in the issue of *This Quarter* that she planned to publish after Walsh's death. When that hope vanished, the manuscript and photographs were returned to Pound. He sent them on to Covici in Chicago and reported to his father, 29 July 1927, that "Covici . . . likes the Machine book very much . . . "

Covici did apparently like Pound's manuscript but felt that the illustrations were not sufficiently varied in design and construction. He was certain that he could procure far better ones. "If you will give your permission, I can have them done." Pound presumably agreed to this, but, in April 1928, Covici was "still hunting for decent illustrations for 'Machine Art.'" On 1

E. MISCELLANEA

June, Covici moved to New York, joining with Donald S. Friede to establish a new firm, Covici, Friede, at 79 West 45th Street. It was Friede who, on 9 October, gave Pound the bad news that Covici, Friede would have to turn down his book. Pound remonstrated, but to no avail. Covici himself explained apologetically, 13 Nov. 1928: "Your ANTHEIL and your EXILE numbers [published by Covici] have proved a total loss. When your MACHINE ART was taken up and opinions were asked from the leading bookstores as to its saleability the reports we received were very discouraging. ... Since we are a perfectly new firm we cannot afford to act contrary to the advice of our Financial Board." He went on to say that if Pound "should insist on some compensation for our holding your MACHINE ART as long as we did, it would have to come out of my pocket. Do as your conscience dictates." Apparently Pound's conscience kept him from claiming damages and he gave up any idea of publishing the book at that time.

The project was briefly revived a few years later when Pound supplied a two-page note, "Machines," for reproductions of fifteen photographs of modern machinery published in Samuel Putnam's *New Review*, Paris, for Winter 1931/1932, but the book itself never appeared. Some of the photographs Pound collected for it are in the Ezra Pound Archive at Yale.

E6f Guido Cavalcanti. Donna mi prega, translated by Ezra Pound. With a commentary by W. B. Yeats.

Ezra Pound reported to his father, 1 Sept. 1928, that the Cuala Press was, he thought, "about to start on 'Donna mi prega,'" in Pound's translation, with a commentary by W. B. Yeats. "By the time Unkl. Wm. Yeats has done his commentary it [*i.e.* the canzone] will have reentered the domain of the wholly incomprehensible and all will be well." Plans for publication were cancelled later in the Fall of 1928 because of Yeats's illness.

E6g The Probable Music of Beowulf, a Conjecture. With reproduction of the music (1928–1929).

In the *New Age* for 28 March 1918, Ezra Pound (as William Atheling) reviewed, under the title "The Gaelic," a concert of "Songs from the Hebrides" given by Marjory Kennedy-Fraser, her daughter Patuffa, and their associates. One particular song made an impression which was to remain with him for the next decade. This was the "Aillte," collected from old Calum Macmillan, last of the Sacred Singers. Pound commented in his review that "If anything can be, this is the sound of the Ossianic bards and Homer would have been sung in such manner." Trying to think of a text that the music could have accompanied, he found that two lines fitted "a bit of" the *Beowulf*, then the third line wouldn't fit. When he asked Marjory Kennedy-Fraser about this, she explained that that particular line of the music had simply been left out as "very uninteresting." And so Pound found support for his theory. He nursed his idea for more than ten years before circumstances combined to persuade him to set it down on paper.

In July 1928, his old friend Nancy Cunard had set herself up in a new role—as printer, at Réanville, using the press that she had just acquired from William Bird and rechristened the Hours Press. On the 29th she sent Pound a tentative, wishful, printed prospectus, announcing that her first two books (by George Moore and Alvaro Guevara) would be followed by "Other Plaquettes of Poetry by Ezra Pound ... T. S. Eliot ... [and] John Rodker ... " In her letter she explained that she hoped Pound would agree to not just one but two different publications, the poems " ... some 8–10 pages, large size" and "a book of 48 [pages] or so. In the style of Indiscretions, perfect, same format ... " Since she offered very generous terms— a 50–50 division of all proceeds once costs were recouped, Pound agreed that she could print a Canto and suggested for the prose book "The Probable Music of Beowulf."

Nancy Cunard was delighted at his willingness to collaborate and explained that she was in no hurry. By December, there was still no hurry, at least not for two more months, and she urged him on a postcard written on the 7th to " ... Make Beowulf as long as you will," explaining in a letter the next day that she wanted as much text as he would afford—up to 20 pages, "Make it as you please." Her enthusiasm had spurred him, on 8 December, into setting down a first draft of the *Beowulf* essay, planned to include reproduction of the music of the Kennedy-Fraser "Aillte" song, and presenting his ideas concerning the kind of accompaniment to which the bards had sung the *Beowulf*: "The accents must be gnarled, bitten, snarled, hurled out of the throat; it is not a soft song to sing from a cushion."

Early in 1929, Nancy Cunard ventured to announce both "A Canto" and "The Probable Music of Beowulf, a Conjecture," the "Beowulf," in an edition of 120 signed copies at 10s. 6d., to appear in May. But Pound ran into some difficulty in matching text with music. Unfortunately, time now became a factor, for Nancy Cunard was planning to be away from Réanville for several months and would close down her printing operations after May. On 5 February she reported to Pound that advance orders for the "Beowulf" had been received, and queried him on the 27th: "What *exactly* is the hitch ... ? in any case let us repair, fill, obviate or whatever verb-is-indicated it. ... I remember it as done but without the music(?) It should be in my hands by early April ... So don't fob me off ... " On 8 March, the need for expediting matters was even more urgent: "if I can't do Beowulf before I close in May perhaps I can't do it at all, which I should much regret. Am not cognisant of *actual* difficulty or hold-up in fitting text to music. I mean if it's a piece of the said work to be looked up, or copied (in Bib[liothèque] Nat[ionale] here (or Brit[ish] Mus[eum] in London) why can't Richard [Aldington] do it and send copy or whatever data, detail, etc is necessary to you? *Printing will stop in May*. I shan't do any more for some months, shall be gone." Whatever the hitch, Pound failed to resolve it in time and the book was not issued as promised in May. The closing-down of the press in June 1929 threatened for a time to become permanent, but on 12 December, Nancy Cunard wrote Pound that she had decided to begin again "immediately, and with vigour. Only the 'modern,' AND in Paris ... With help. ... Now, DO I GET THE CANTO? ... If I do, I'd much

E. MISCELLANEA

like to start with it in the NEW year ... I take it I can do something of yours, not the poor Beowulf I suppose?"

As it turned out, Miss Cunard got not one but thirty Cantos, and published them in August 1930; but the "poor Beowulf" never materialised. Only the eight typed pages of what must be the draft of 8 December 1928 exist in the Ezra Pound Archive at Yale, and it is doubtful that Pound ever carried the essay beyond that stage. The difficulty about fitting text and music for reproduction had by no means caused him to abandon his theory, for he repeated its basic proposition five years later in *ABC of Reading* (1934)—A35—pp 38–39.

E6h Collected Prose (1929, 1932, 1959).

In 1929, the Aquila Press in England agreed to publish Ezra Pound's Cavalcanti, his Collected Prose, and his translations of the Odes of Confucius. The story of the Cavalcanti edition is told in detail in the entry for the *Guido Cavalcanti Rime*—B27. Apparently the failure of the Aquila Press came before Pound had begun the proposed translations of the Confucian Odes (eventually published by the Harvard University Press in 1954—A69), but he did begin work at this time on the Collected Prose project, and after the Aquila Press failure, continued to work on the edition for publication by To, Publishers. Only a single volume of that edition appeared, as "Prolegomena 1–2," containing *How to Read* and Part 1 of *The Spirit of Romance* (Chapters I–IV, with a new short prefatory note and new footnotes dated 1929 and 1932, and a new Chapter V, "Psychology and Troubadours: A Divagation from Questions of Technique," reprinted from the *Quest*—C55). Later volumes of "Prolegomena" had been planned to include Part 2 of *The Spirit of Romance* and other prose work, but the publishers went out of business before the plans could be realised.

Extensive materials gathered by Pound for eight volumes of the Collected Prose are in the Ezra Pound Archive at Yale. They consist for the most part of tear-sheets from the various periodicals in which the essays had been printed, often very extensively corrected and frequently accompanied by linking, autobiographical comments. (One of these comments is printed in *Ezra Pound and the Visual Arts* ([1980])—A105—pp. 304–5.)

E6i Stravinsky, by Boris de Schloezer, translated by Ezra Pound (1931–1932). Ezra Pound's translation of de Schloezer's book on Igor Stravinsky had appeared in the *Dial* between October 1928 and July 1929. The *New Review*, Paris, edited by Samuel Putnam, planned to bring it out as one of their "New Review Editions," paperbound. It was advertised, to sell at 20 francs (4 s., $1.00), in the issues of the periodical for Aug./Sept./Oct. 1931 and Winter 1931/1932. In the latter issue, it was described as "ready soon," and the statement was made that de Schloezer had prepared especially for this edition a new chapter on Stravinsky's recent work. In January 1932, Samuel Putnam and his associate editor Peter Neagoë still hoped to get the book out "as speedily as possible," but the advance of 1500 francs that Putnam had promised to pay de Schloezer became a point of contention. Apparently de Schloezer refused to accept a reduced amount of 500 francs—

all the editors felt they could manage in a rather precarious financial situation—and the book was not published.

E6j National Culture (1938).

William Fitzgerald, Boston, Mass., began in 1938 a series of "Reactionary Pamphlets." The first of the series was his own *Art and Interference* (1938), which began: "Wanted at once—a national culture in good condition for purposes of protection against subversion of Marxist internationalists, Jews and such." Fitzgerald wrote to Pound on 4 March 1938, enclosing his pamphlet and asking for a contribution to the series "to help dynamite the deep-rooted conspiracy of (American) publishers against 'unorthodox' ideologies ... " Pound replied promptly on the 18th, making some suggestions, specifically a translation of the *Rassegna Monetaria* articles—C1406, 1410, and 1416—and trusting that his *Guide to Kulchur*, when published by Fabers in May [*sic*] would serve as a possible rallying point. But on thinking the matter over, he decided he could probably do something better for the series than offer a reprint of his Italian articles on money. Although he was just back at his desk after an attack of bronchitis and "possibly shd/ have waited till ... [I] was at higher voltage," he wrote and sent off to Fitzgerald the carbon of an essay, "National Culture: A Manifesto." Although Pound made it clear in his covering letter of 19 March that this was only a first draft, Fitzgerald liked the essay and expressed himself as willing to publish it. But he had already explained to Pound that he was operating on very limited funds and could pay no royalties. "If you are satisfied to forego remuneration, I'll try to get out your essay & distribute it like hell. & will play fair." Apparently Pound agreed, but Fitzgerald's financial problems put an end to the series before "National Culture" could appear. (The essay was included in *Impact* (1960)—A78—pp. 3–11.)

E6k One Man's Aim, edited by Noel Stock (1959).

A selection of 145 unpublished letters by Ezra Pound, along with other related documents, was accepted for publication in 1959 by Henry Regnery, Chicago, Ill. The book was actually announced, but Mrs. Pound, as Committee for her husband, decided that it should be withdrawn.

INDEX

Titles of books and pamphlets by Ezra Pound or with contributions by him are set in small capital letters (with the reference number for the principal descriptive entry, in each case, set in bold-face type). Titles of other separately published works are italicised. Titles of poems, essays, etc., not separately published, are set within quotation marks.

INDEX

INDEX

INDEX

Benington, Walter, A10
BENJAMIN MINOR (RICHARD OF SAINT
    VICTOR), B57, **68**
Benton, Thomas H., B54b, 56a
Beonio-Brocchieri, Vittorio, C1154
Beowulf, E6g
"Berceuse," B8
Berg Collection, New York Public Li-
    brary, C1919 *n.*
Bergamin, José, B41
Berger, Jacob, D216t
Bergman, Herbert, C1744
"Berlin," C724 *n.*
Berman, Louis, C637 *n.*
Bernart de Palazol, B5
Bernart de Ventadour (of Ventadorn), A5,
    66e; B5, 20
Bernouard, François, A31a, b; C626 *n.*
Berri, Pietro, C1740
Berthaud, B3
Berti, Luigi, A104; D85, 138
Bertolucci, Attilio, D61–62, 81h, 93, 148
Bertrand (Bertrans) de Born, A4–6, 11,
    20, 27, 30, 66e; B78; C132, 212; D4,
    240
"The Best in English," A105
De Bezige Bij, D9b
Bianchi, Ruggero, D81f
Bibi-la-Bibiste (Les Soeurs X.), C594
"Bibliography of Books and . . . Articles
    by Ezra Pound," B17
"Bibliography (of Books as yet Unwritten
    but Wanted)," C1505
Biblioteca del Castello, B71
Biblioteca dell'Ussero, B73, 99a; D82
Biblioteca di cultura politica, A51a, 53a
Biblioteca di Studi Americani, B89
Biblioteca minima, A76; D57
Biblioteca minima tempus, A50a
Biblioteka "Danas," D216w
Biblioteka Orfej, D216y
Biblioteka Orion, D7, 216u
Biblioteka Vrhovi, D216x
Bibliothek Suhrkamp, D29
Biblos, Vienna, C1874
Biddle, Francis, B69–70; C1859; D23v,
    167j
Biddulph, *Mr.,* C1102 *n.*
"The Biennale," A105; C1204
BIENNALES INTERNATIONALES DE
    PÓESIE, D**12n**
"Big Jew," A101

Bilenchi, Romano, C1974
"A Bill," C1207
Billings, B123c
Binyon, Laurence, A74; C195, 1046, 1474,
    1477; D152
"Biography: E. P.," A62b
Biosophical Review, New York, C1122
Bird, William, A23, 25 *n.,* 26; B21; E6g.
    See also Three Mountains Press
"Bird-Latin" (Arnaut Daniel), C43
"Bird Watchers . . . ," C1808
Bishop, W., & Sons, B118
Bîtea, Nicolae-Ioan, D216nd
"The bitter air" (Arnaut Daniel, IX), A18,
    20, 36, 66–67; C33
Björnsson, Kristinn, D54x
Black, Clementina, C537 *n.*
"The Black Crusade," C64, 66
"Black Slippers: Bellotti," A11, 27, 30;
    C208; D7b, 169a, 194x, 230c
Black Sun Books, A26
Black Sun Press, A32; B25
"Blackwood's," C276
Blake, Ben, C1345
Blanco, Alberto, D230f, g
"'Blandula, tenulla, vagula,'" A7, 11c, d,
    27, 30, 62, 97; D4, 81h
"Blast," A59, 101, 105
Blast, London, A59, 74; C148–9, 186a,
    194–5, 202
Blast, New York, C1079 *n.*
"A Blast from London," A15; C171
"Blazed," A98
Blease, Coleman L., C780–1
Bloch, Jean Richard, B41
Bloch, Regina Miriam, B1
Blomberg, Erik, D236ja, 237a
Blood Money (Seton), A34a *n.*
"Blue Dun," C1966
Blue Ridge Mountain Press, B53
Blues, Columbus, Miss., C739
Blunt, Wilfrid, C131
Bocconi, Luigi, Università Commerciale,
    A34a
Boczkowski, Krzysztof, D200d, 206 o–q
Bodenheim, Maxwell, B10; C310, 798
Bodini, Vittorio, A104; C1857, 1906 *n.*;
    D23k
Bodley Head, A10a; B104 *n.*
Bodley Press, B50
Bogan, Louise, D15b
Bohdanowiczowa, Zofii, D206d

465

INDEX

INDEX

Brendon, William, and Sons, A22b; B12, 45

"Brennbaum." *See* HUGH SELWYN MAUBERLEY, Part 1, Section [VIII]

Breton, André, C905a *n.*

Brett Young, Francis, C353

BREVE ANTOLOGÍA, D**220m**

Breve Biblioteca de Balance, D220d

"Breviora" (*Little Review*), B54; C406; (*Meridiano di Roma*), C1638

Brewer, Joseph, A78; B99; C1940, 1947, 1985

Brezlanu, Andrei, D216mt

Bridgehead Books, B72a

Bridges, Robert, C207

Bridson, D. G., B112; C1884, 1969; D23j, l; E5b

"Brief Concordance," A65a *n.*, b

"Brief Note," C380

"Brief von Ezra Pound," C775

"Briefly bursteth season brisk" (Arnaut Daniel, XI), A18, 20, 36, 66–67

"The Bright and Snappy," C300

Brimont, A. de, C261

Brings, Allen, E4x

Brinnin, John Malcolm, A19 *n.*, 61a *n.*

Briscoe, Herbert, *pseud.*, C1813f, 1814i, n, 1820e, 1822c, 1827b

"Britain, Who Are Your Allies?," C1450

British Broadcasting Corporation, C1496, 1884 *n.*; E3a, h, 5b

British Committee for the Preservation of Venice, E2x

"British Diplomacy," C1814 o

"The British Imperium," A101

British-Italian Bulletin, London, C1279, 1286, 1288, 1290, 1294, 1300, 1304, 1308, 1310, 1315, 1317, 1320, 1327, 1332, 1335–9, 1343, 1348, 1356, 1358, 1360–1, 1363, 1369–70, 1374

"British Labour's Great Blunder," C1335

"British Tax System an Infamy," C1739

British Union Quarterly, London, C1387, 1400, 1406 *n.*, 1409, 1430, 1444, 1475–6, 1489, 1504

British Weekly, C305

Brkić, Svetozar, D216y

Broadcasts, Rome Radio. *See* Radio Broadcasts, Rome

Brodzky, Horace, A18

Broletto, Como, A55; C1446, 1477, 1486; D127, 130; E2pa

Bronner, Milton, B99, 103

Brookhart, S. S., A78

"Brooklyn Tablet," C1831a

Brooks, Van Wyck, A78; B75, 99; D40a

Brostrøm, Torben, D8

"Brother Ashberg," C1814j

Brown, Bob, B26

Brown, Ernest, & Phillips, B18

Brown, John, D15

Brown, Robert Carlton, B26

Brown, Rose, B26

Browning, Robert, C832, 1731c, 1936

"Browning's *The Inn Album*," C1731c

Bruce Humphries, A33b *n.*; B29 *n.*

"Bruhl e i selvaggi," C831

Brunel, Antoine de, A5

"The 'Brunhild' of Frederic Manning," C11

Brustein, Robert, B94

"Brutus and Faustina." *See* DIALOGUES OF FONTENELLE, VIII

Bryher, B21

Bubb, Charles C., E2bb, 6a

Bubb, Emma M., E2bb

Buchan, John, C1212, 1977

"Buck Flea," A64; E4ka

THE BUCK FLEA (SERLY), E**4ka**

Bucktrout, Daisy, B2

Buffet, Gabrielle, C1906 *n.*; D23k

"Building an Empire," C1338

"Building, Ornamentation," A105; C398

"Buildings—I," A105; C389

"Built for Stability," C1358

"Bulletin," C1366, 1368

Bulletin of the Friends of the Owen D. Young Library, Canton, N.Y., C1937

Bulletin of the New York Public Library, New York, C1919 *n.*

Bulzoni Editore, B119

BUNGAKU NI TSUITE, D**1941**

BUNGAKU SEISHIN NO GENSEN, D**167x**

Bunno. *See* "Song of the Bowmen of Shu"

Bunting, Basil, A45, 78; B28–29, 32; C1098

Burdick, Usher L., C1859 *n.*

"Bureaucracy," C887

"Bureaucracy the Flail of Jehovah," A78, 93; E2y

"Burgos, a Dream City of Old Castile," B69; C4

Burn, James, B45

"Buruiana," D216mu

INDEX

INDEX

INDEX

INDEX

479

INDEX

486

INDEX

INDEX

INDEX

INDEX

INDEX

INDEX

INDEX

"M. Antonius Flamininus and John Keats," C7

"M. de Gourmont and the Problem of Beauty" (Manning), C439

"M. Pom-Pom," A27b–c, 74; C1432

McAlmon, Robert, A23 n.; B21, 26, 28, 29, 93; C693a, 711, 901

"McArthur," A101; C1877a

MacArthur, Charles, C777

McC., T., *pseud.*, C1820d

McCarthy, Mary, B75

McCartney, Eugene, A1, 3, 6, 20, 27, 30

McClelland and Stewart, A94

McCormack, Nancy Cox, C1461

MacDonagh, Thomas, C235

MacGibbon & Kee, B51 n., 62 n.

McGraw-Hill Book Co., B90

McGraw-Hill Paperbacks, B90 n.

"Machine Art," E6e

"Machines," A105; C839; E6e

Mackay, W. & J., & Co., B98, 112

MacKenzie, Donal, B26, 103

Mackinnon, Lilias, C368 n., 605 n.

MacLehose, R., and Co., A27c, 31d, 34a–b, 37c, 38, 43a, 45a–b, 47a, 60b, 66a–d, 67; B32, 52, 86

MacLeish, Archibald, A31c n., 38b; B28

"MacLeish," A101; B83, 117; C1954

Macleod, Joseph Gordon, B28

Macleod, Norman, B26

McLuhan, H. M., E2ua

Macmillan, Calum, E6g

Macmillan (and) Co., A13a; B9, 14, 42, 69, 110

Macmillan Press, B110

MacPherson, D., A78

"Madame, ye ben of beauté shryne" (Chaucer), B20

"Madox Ford a Rapallo," D106

"Madox Ford at Rapallo," A74; C1713, 1726; D106

"Madrigal" (Cavalcanti), A86; B4

MADRIGALE, A7; E 4a(1)

Maestrale, Rome, C1555

Maestri e compagni, D86

Maestrini, Franco, B70b

"Il Maestro," A5

"Maestro di tocar," A7

Maeterlinck. *See* "For a Play (Maeterlinck)"

Mafai, Antonietta R., D81j

Magazyn Kulturalny, D206r

"Un magnifico libro di P. M. Bardi," C1024

Magnino, Leo, D60, 91

Magyar Mühely, D54a

"Maiden and Virgin loyal" (Williaume li Viniers), B5

"Mailbag," C1820m

Mailer, Norman, B121

Mailla, B80

Maine, University of, A102

Maine, University of, Press, A102

"Mainly Stroesco," A99; C459

"Mainta ien ne mal razona" (Pierol), B5

Maiorana, M. Teresa, D228

La Maison du Poète, D14a

Maitland, Robert, E3h

Majno, Luigi, A38b

"Le major C.-H. Douglas et le situation en Angleterre," A84; C624

MAKE IT NEW, A36

"Make strong old dreams," A1; C10a n.

The Makers of Modern Literature, B54x

Malahat Review, Victoria, B.C., A106; C1983

Malaparte, Curzio, A104; B119; C1524, 1535a n., 1549, 1591

Malatesta, Sigismundo, E2ze

"Malatesta Cantos," C652

Malfasi, C1728 n.

Malinovski, Ivan, D8

Mallarmé, Stéphane, C601a

"Malrin," A1; C1936

"M'amour, m'amour," A91

THE MAN FROM NEW YORK (REID), B95

"The Man in the Crow's Nest" (Hulme), E5b(1)

"Man v. Merchandise: Fascism in Action," C1339

"Mana Aboda" (Hulme), A8, 20, 27b–c; C36

Manchester University Press, C628a n.

Mancuso, Girolamo, A103; D81t

"Mang Tze (The Ethics of Mencius)," A78, 93; C1460

Manganelli, Giorgio, D149

"Manifesto" (1932), C880; (1936), B99; (1938), D167i

A MANIFESTO (1953), C1967; E2ua

"Manifesto for Mrs. Hobby's Successor," C1755

Mann, Heinrich, B41

INDEX

INDEX

1116, 1119, 1121, 1123, 1129, 1134, 1137, 1166, 1182, 1184, 1194, 1225, 1242, 1246

Morrison and Gibb, A33a

Morrison's Chinese dictionary, B108

"Mort, j'appelle," E3h

"Morte gentil, rimedio d'cattivi" (Cavalcanti "Sonnet XXXIII"), A20, 66; B4, 27

Mortiz, Joaquín, D220j

Morton, Frank, C186a

Mosaic, New York, C1161

MOSCARDINO (PEA), A71; C1742

Mosher, Thomas Bird, A1

Mosley, Oswald, C1468

"Most Publishers . . . ," C1750

"Mostly Quartets," A99; C1371

Mostra delle edizioni Poundiane 1908–1958, A26

. . . MOSTRA DELLE EDIZIONI SCHEIWILLER 1925–1968, A79 *n.*; B39

Mostyn, Tom E., C443

"Motif," A1, 3; D61–62, 81h, 85, 90, 96c, 148, 220a, i, 230e

"Motivo," D230e

Motokiyo, A12–13; C138, 230, 1958; D60, 64, 73

"MOTZ EL SON"—WORT UND WEISE, D30

Moult, Thomas, C1873

"The Mourn of Life," B69, 99; C677

Moussorgsky, M. P., C434

"Moussorgsky, Rosing, Stroesco, Haley," A99; C434

Mouton & Co., B82

"The Movement of Literature," A78; C1257

"Moving under a large amount of terminology . . . ," C1766

Mozart, Wolfgang Amadeus, B2; C1499

"Mozart Concerts in March in Rapallo," A99; C1499 *n.*

Much Ado, St. Louis, Mo., C256 *n.*, 521, 523, 535, 556, 593, 603

Münch, Gerhart, A60a *n.*; C967, 1195, 1396, 1434

Mugen, D193–4

"Mug's Game?," C1147

Il Mulino, C1950 *n.*

Mullins, Eustace, B72

Muncie, Wendell, B83

"Munition Makers," C896, 923, 927

Munsey's Magazine, New York, C5

Munson, Gorham, C845

Murat, *Princess* Lucien, C629

"Murder by Capital," A78, 93; C951

"Murkn Libry," C810

"Murkn Magzeens" (Dias), B82; C1079; 1084a

Murphy, Franklin, B16

Murray, Douglas, C562

Murray Printing Co., A72b; B75

Murry, J. Middleton, C199a *n.*; E6d

"Music" (Atheling), A99; C311, 320, 326, 329, 331, 340–3, 349, 357, 359, 361, 365, 368, 376, 378, 384, 387, 396, 400, 409–10, 413, 423–4, 426, 429–30, 434–5, 442, 445, 450, 453, 457, 459, 463, 465, 469, 472, 493, 507, 510, 515, 520, 525, 530, 536, 538–9, 546, 552, 564, 575, 600, 604–5, 609–10, 613, 1581a *n.*

"Music and Brains," A99; C1380

Music & Letters, London, C1389

"Music and Money," A99; C1188

"Music in Ca' Rezzonico," A99; C1388

"The Music of Beowulf," B80

. . . THE MUSIC OF THE TROUBADOURS, B5 *n.*

MUSICA A RAPALLO, E2p

MUSICA TIGULLIANA PROGETTATA. "INVERNO MUSICALE," A99; C1101; E2l

"Musical Comedy" (T.J.V.), A99; C559

Musical Times, London, C1491

"Musicians," A99; C1467

"Musicians; God Help 'Em," A74, 99; B87; C1479

Mussolini, Benito, A41, 56; B117, 119; C693a, 1057, 1107, 1159, 1163, 1582 *n.*, 1690a, 1833, 1950

"Mussolini Defines State as 'Spirit of the People,'" C1057; D123

"Mussolini e l'usurocrazia," C1690a

"Mussolini's Rome," C1159

"The mutilated choir boys" (Heine). *See* "Translations from Heine, V"

"Muzik, as Mistaught," A99; B80; C1462

My Dukes, E2y

"My Lady's face is it they worship there" (Cavalcanti "Sonnet XXXV"), A20, 66; B4; C27

MY LIFETIME IN LETTERS (SINCLAIR), B67

INDEX

INDEX

"Paris Letter, February, 1921" (Germain), C617a

Paris Review, Paris, A81 *n*.; B75; C1886–9; D23j, 40a, 216nf

PARIS SALONS, CAFÉS, STUDIOS (HUD-DLESTON), B21ab

Paris *Tribune*. *See Chicago Tribune*, Paris

PARIS WAS OUR MISTRESS (PUTNAM), B48

"Parisian Literature," C626

"Parisian Winter (1923)," C1528

Parkes, H. B., B112

"Parla Confucio," C1696a

Parler, Grenoble, D23

Parnasso, Helsinki, D11a, b

"Paroles de Villon . . . ," E3h

La Parrucca, Milan, D149–50

Parsons, Robert, C785

"Part of Canto XX," C688

"Part of Canto XXIII," C705

"Part of Canto XXVII," C700

"Partenza di Venezia," A2

"Partial Explanation," A36; C717

Partisan Review, New York, C1635

Pasolini, Pier Paolo, B100; C1984

PASSAGES FROM THE LETTERS OF JOHN BUTLER YEATS, B15; C270, 319

"Passages from the Opening Address in a Long Poem," C260 *n*.

"Passante." *See* "Ladies, IV"

"Passing." *See* "Ladies, IV"

"The Passing of the Ang-Sax?," C696

"A Passport Collector," C657

"The Passport Nuisance" (*Chicago Tribune*), C648, 750; (*Nation*), B99; C697

"Passports and Hughes," C676

"Past History," A88; B98–99; C939

Pasternak, Boris, B75

"Pastiche: The Regional," A78; C470, 473, 475, 478, 480, 482–3, 485, 487–8, 490, 492, 494, 500–1, 505, 508–9, 511, 597a

"Pastoral," A98; C148

Pastorales Parisiennes (Cros), C622b

"Pastorella" (Marcabrun), A5

"Los Pastores de Belen" (Lope de Vega), A4, 6; E2a

PATERSON (WILLIAMS), D96b

PATERSON (BOOK THREE) (WIL-LIAMS), B51

PATERSON (BOOK FIVE) (WILLIAMS), B62

PATERSON, BOOKS I–V (WILLIAMS), B51 *n*., 62 *n*.

Patiño, Victor M., D222da

Patmore, Brigit, A11, 27; B104

Patnaik, Deba P., C1942, 1953, 1957

PATRIA MIA, A63, 93b, 105; C48–51, 56–60, 62–63; D34, 70, 81h, 220f

PATRIA MIA AND THE TREATISE ON HARMONY, A25 *n*., 63b

"Patriotism," C1482

"Patriotism" (Gourmont), C617 *n*.

"The Pattern," A96, 101; D167m

"The Patterns," A11a, c–d, 27, 30; B11; C210; D81h, 206s, 216x, 217a, 219a

Patterson, Ernest Minor, A78

"Paul Castiaux," C118

Pauthier, M. G., C740a *n*.

Pauvert, Jean-Jacques, D12l

"Pavannes," C256 *n*.

PAVANNES AND DIVAGATIONS, A74

PAVANNES AND DIVISIONS, A15; E6b

Pavlova, Anna, C570

"Pavlova" (T.J.V.), A99; C570

Pavlović, Miodrag, D216y

"Pax Saturni," A27d, 64, 98; C76

Paxton, W., & Co., E4e–f

Payne, Miles, C1862 *n*.

Pea, Enrico, A71, 104; C1742

"Peace," A78, 93; C721

"Peace in the Market," C1218

"Peace Pathology," A78; C1041

"Peace Racket, War Racket" (Venison), A39 *n*.; C1386

"Peaceways," C1428

"Peals of Iron," C115

Pearce, T. M., B122

Pearlman, Daniel D., B96

Pearson, Norman Holmes, B56a, 123

Peer Musikverlag, E4q

Pegler, Westbrook, C1814b

Peire Bremon, A3, 106; C1983, 1987

Peire Vidal, A4–5, 11c–d, 20, 27, 30

Peitieu, Guilhem de. *See* "Langue d'Oc, II"

Péladan, Joséphin, C3

Pelican Books, B85 *n*.

Pelican Books, B85 *n*.

Penguin Books, B85 *n*.

Pennsylvania, University of, C505 *n*., 1965; Press, B37

Pennsylvania State University Press, B109

"Penny Wise," C821

INDEX

INDEX

INDEX

INDEX

INDEX

INDEX

INDEX

INDEX